PEARSON ALWAYS LEARNING

William Stallings

Wireless Communication & Networks

With contributions from Gary Rogers

Custom Edition

Taken from:
Wireless Communications & Networks, Second Edition
by William Stallings

Mobile Communications, Second Edition
by Jochen Schiller

Cover Image: Courtesy of BrandX Pictures.

Taken from:

Wireless Communications & Networks, Second Edition
by William Stallings

Published by Prentice Hall
Upper Saddle River, New Jersey 07458

Mobile Communications, Second Edition
by Jochen Schiller

Published by Addison-Wesley
Edinburgh Gate, Harlow, Essex CM20 2JE, England

Pearson Learning Solutions, 501 Boylston Street, Suite 900, Boston, MA 02116
A Pearson Education Company
www.pearsoned.com

Printed in the United States of America

1 2 3 4 5 6 7 8 9 10 V0CR 17 16 15 14 13 12

000200010271284067

RG

PEARSON

ISBN 10: 1-256-50832-2
ISBN 13: 978-1-256-50832-8

To my dearest life partner
and love, Linda
—Gary Rogers

CONTENTS

PREFACE

OBJECTIVES

Wireless technology has become the most exciting area in telecommunications and networking. The rapid growth of mobile telephone use, various satellite services, and now the wireless Internet and wireless LANs are generating tremendous changes in telecommunications and networking. This book explores the key topics in the field in the following general categories:

- **Technology and architecture:** There is a small collection of ingredients that serves to characterize and differentiate wireless communication and networking, including frequency band, signal encoding technique, error correction technique, and network architecture.
- **Network type:** This book covers the important types of wireless networks, including satellite, cellular, fixed wireless access, and wireless LANs.
- **Design approaches:** The book examines alternative design choices and assesses their relative merits.
- **Applications:** A number of key technologies and applications have been developed on top of wireless infrastructures, especially mobile IP and wireless Web access.

Throughout, there is an emphasis on both technology and on standards. The book provides a comprehensive guide to understanding specific wireless standards, such as those promulgated by ITU and IEEE 802, as well as standards developed by other organizations. This emphasis reflects the importance of such standards in defining the available products and future research directions in this field.

INTENDED AUDIENCE

This book is intended for a broad range of readers who will benefit from an understanding of wireless communications and networks, and the associated technologies. This includes students and professionals in the fields of data processing and data communications, designers and implementers, and data communication and networking customers and managers. For the professional interested in this field, the book serves as a basic reference volume and is suitable for self-study.

As a textbook, it is suitable for an advanced undergraduate or graduate course. It covers the material in the CS332 Wireless and Mobile Computing advanced course of the joint ACM/IEEE Computing Curricula 2001. The chapters and parts of the book are sufficiently modular to provide a great deal of flexibility in the design of courses.

PLAN OF THE BOOK

The book treats a number of advanced topics and provides a brief survey of the required elementary topics. For the reader with little or no background in data communications, Part One and the appendices cover a number of basic topics. The book is divided into four parts:

- Technical Background
- Wireless Communication Technology

- Wireless Networking
- Wireless LANs

In addition, the book includes an extensive glossary, a list of frequently used acronyms, and a bibliography. Each chapter includes problems, suggestions for further reading, and a list of relevant Web sites. Each chapter also includes, for review, a list of key words and a number of review questions.

INTERNET SERVICES FOR INSTRUCTORS AND STUDENTS

There is a Web site for this book that provides support for students and instructors. The site includes links to other relevant sites, transparency masters of figures and tables from the book in PDF (Adobe Acrobat) format, PowerPoint slides, and sign-up information for the book's Internet mailing list. The Web page is at WilliamStallings.com/Wireless/Wireless2e.html; see Section 1.8 for more information. An Internet mailing list has been set up so that instructors using this book can exchange information, suggestions, and questions with each other and with the author. As soon as typos or other errors are discovered, an errata list for this book will be available at WilliamStallings.com. I also maintain the Computer Science Student Resource Site at WilliamStallings.com/StudentSupport.html.

WHAT'S NEW IN THE SECOND EDITION

In the three years since the first edition of this book was published, the field has seen continued innovations and improvements. In this new edition, I try to capture these changes while maintaining a broad and comprehensive coverage of the entire field. To begin the process of revision, the first edition of this book was extensively reviewed by a number of professors who teach the subject. The result is that, in many places, the narrative has been clarified and tightened, and illustrations have been improved. Also, a number of new "field-tested" problems have been added.

Beyond these refinements to improve pedagogy and user friendliness, the technical content of the book has been updated throughout, to reflect the ongoing changes in this exciting field. Every chapter has been revised. Highlights include the following:

- **Minimum shift keying:** MSK is a form of modulation that is found in some mobile communications systems. This material is now covered.
- **CDMA2000:** The first 3G (third generation) wireless system to be deployed commercially is known as CDMA2000 1xEV-DO. A discussion of this important standard is included.
- **WiMAX and IEEE 802.16a:** Work on wireless local loop has evolved, including the introduction of the WiMAX specification to provide interoperability specifications for 802.16. Chapter 11 includes new material on 802.16, including the recent 802.16a standard.
- **Orthogonal frequency division multiplexing:** The popularity of OFDM is increasing and is used in a variety of local and wide area wireless standards. The material on OFDM has been updated and expanded.
- **Wi-Fi and IEEE 802.11:** The coverage of 802.11a and 802.11b has been expanded significantly, and treatment of 802.11g had been added.
- **Data scrambling:** Scrambling is a technique often used to improve signal quality. An overview of data scrambling is provided in Chapter 14.

- **Wi-Fi protected access:** WPA has replaced Wireless Equivalent Privacy (WEP) as the specification for providing security in wireless LANs. Chapter 14 provides coverage of WPA.
- **IEEE 802.15 and personal area networks:** The initial 802.15.1 standard provides an official specification for Bluetooth, which was covered in the first edition as well as this edition. This edition also covers two new standards: the 802.15.3 high-speed wireless PAN standard and the 802.15.4 low-speed wireless PAN standard.
- **Trellis-coded modulation:** TCM is a technique that provides for efficient use of bandlimited channels; it is described in Chapter 15.

In addition, throughout the book, virtually every topic has been updated to reflect the developments in standards and technology that have occurred since the publication of the first edition.

ACKNOWLEDGMENTS

This new edition has benefited from review by a number of people, who gave generously of their time and expertise. The following people reviewed all or a large part of the manuscript: Dr. Albert Cheng (University of Houston-University Park), Dale W. Callahan (University of Alabama, Birmingham), Ravi Sankar (University of South Florida, Tampa), Pei Zheng (Arcadia University, Pennsylvania), and Anne Cox (Austin Community College, Texas).

Thanks also to the many people who provided detailed technical reviews of a single chapter: Lars Poulsen, Howard Eisenhauer, D. E. Jennings, Paul Robichaux, John Adams, Jerry Huang, Andreas Kasenides, Munira Ahmed, Hossein Izadpanah, Aaron King, Benoit d'Udekem, Marco Casole, Kevin Peterson, Dinesh Lal Pradhan, and Cathal Mc Daid.

Finally, I would like to thank the many people responsible for the publication of the book, all of whom did their usual excellent job. This includes the staff at Prentice Hall, particularly my editors Alan Apt and Toni Holm; their assistant Patrick Lindner: production manager Rose Kernan; and supplements manager Sarah Parker. Also, Jake Warde of Warde Publishers managed the reviews; and Patricia M. Daly did the copy editing.

CHAPTER 1

INTRODUCTION

This book is a survey of the technology of wireless communications and networks. Many factors, including increased competition and the introduction of digital technology, have led to unprecedented growth in the wireless market. In this chapter, we discuss some of the key factors driving this new telecommunications revolution.

This book, and the accompanying Web site, covers a lot of material. Following the general discussion, this chapter gives the reader an overview of the book.

1.1 WIRELESS COMES OF AGE

Guglielmo Marconi invented the wireless telegraph in 1896.[1] In 1901, he sent telegraphic signals across the Atlantic Ocean from Cornwall to St. John's Newfoundland; a distance of about 3200 km. His invention allowed two parties to communicate by sending each other alphanumeric characters encoded in an analog signal. Over the last century, advances in wireless technologies have led to the radio, the television, the mobile telephone, and communications satellites. All types of information can now be sent to almost every corner of the world. Recently, a great deal of attention has been focused on satellite communications, wireless networking, and cellular technology.

Communications satellites were first launched in the 1960s. Those first satellites could only handle 240 voice circuits. Today, satellites carry about one-third of the voice traffic and all of the television signals between countries [EVAN98]. Modern satellites typically introduce a quarter-second propagation delay to the signals they handle. Newer satellites in lower orbits, with less inherent signal delay, have been deployed to provide data services such as Internet access.

Wireless networking is allowing businesses to develop WANs, MANs, and LANs without a cable plant. The IEEE has developed 802.11 as a standard for wireless LANs. The Bluetooth industry consortium is also working to provide a seamless wireless networking technology.

The cellular or mobile telephone is the modern equivalent of Marconi's wireless telegraph, offering two-party, two-way communication. The first-generation wireless phones used analog technology. These devices were heavy and coverage was patchy, but they successfully demonstrated the inherent convenience of mobile communications. The current generation of wireless devices is built using digital technology. Digital networks carry much more traffic and provide better reception and security than analog networks. In addition, digital technology has made possible value-added services such as caller identification. Newer wireless devices connect to the Internet using frequency ranges that support higher information rates.

The impact of wireless communications has been and will continue to be profound. Very few inventions have been able to "shrink" the world in such a manner. The standards that define how wireless communication devices interact are quickly

[1]The actual invention of radio communications more properly should be attributed to Nikola Tesla, who gave a public demonstration in 1893. Marconi's patents were overturned in favor of Tesla in 1943 [ENGE00].

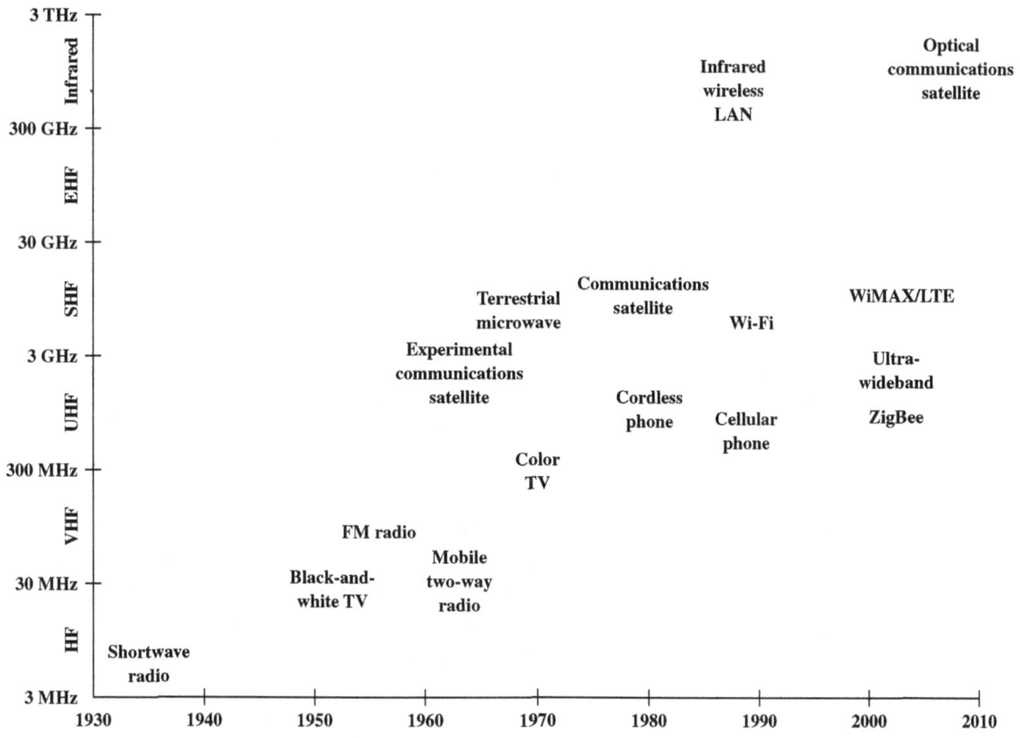

Figure 1.1 Some Milestones in Wireless Communications

converging and soon will allow the creation of a global wireless network that will deliver a wide variety of services.

Figure 1.1 highlights some of the key milestones in the development of wireless communications.[2] Wireless technologies have gradually migrated to higher frequencies. As will be seen in later chapters, higher frequencies enable the support of greater data rates and throughput.

1.2 THE CELLULAR REVOLUTION

The cellular revolution is apparent in the growth of the mobile phone market alone. In 1990, the number of users was approximately 11 million [ECON99]. Today, that number is in the billions. According to the ITU (International Telecommunications Union),[3] the number of mobile phones worldwide outnumbered

[2]Note the use of a log scale for the *y*-axis. A basic review of log scales is in the math refresher document at the Computer Science Student Resource Site at **WilliamStallings.com/StudentSupport.html.**

[3]A description of ITU and other standards-making bodies is contained in a supporting document at this book's Web site.

fixed-line phones for the first time in 2002. By 2011, this number exceeded 4 billion![4] And 61.5 million of those users are in the U.S. alone.[5] The newer generation devices, with access to the Internet and built-in digital cameras, add to this momentum. There are a number of reasons for the increasing dominance of mobile phones. Mobile phones are convenient; they move with people. In addition, by their nature, they are location aware. A mobile phone communicates with regional base stations that are at fixed locations.

Also, a cultural revolution is transpiring. Millions of people throughout the world are now expecting to access the Web at any time and almost anyplace. Mobile phones such as the iPhone allow this to happen quickly and inexpensively. And, they are not using these smartphones for just voice; they are accessing more advanced services. For example, 67.1% of U.S mobile subscribers used text messaging, with over a third of users (35.3%) using a mobile browser. Subscribers who used downloaded applications amounted to 33.4% of the smartphone audience.[6] Rising generations as young as six are using Web resources easily and seamlessly, thus establishing a new and higher set of expectations relating to information access and use.

Technical innovations have contributed to the success of mobile phones. The handsets have become smaller and lighter, battery life has increased, and digital technology has improved reception and allowed better use of a finite spectrum. As with many types of digital equipment, the costs associated with mobile telephones have been decreasing. In areas where competition flourishes, prices have dropped dramatically since 1996. You can now, for example, purchase advanced mobile phones, typically called smartphones, for as little as one penny![7]

In many geographic areas, mobile telephones are the only economical way to provide phone service to the population. Operators can erect base stations quickly and inexpensively when compared with digging up ground to lay copper in harsh terrain.

Mobile telephones are only the tip of the cellular revolution. Increasingly, new types of wireless devices are being introduced. These new devices have access to the Internet. They include personal organizers and telephones, but now they have Web access, instant messaging, e-mail, and other services available on the Internet. Wireless devices in automobiles allow users to download maps and directions on demand. Soon, the devices may be able to call for help when an accident has occurred or perhaps notify the user of the lowest-priced fuel in the immediate area. Other conveniences will be available as well. For example, refrigerators may one day be able to order groceries over the Internet to replace consumed items.

The first rush to wireless was for voice. Now, the attention is on data. A big part of this market is the "wireless" Internet. Wireless users use the Internet differently than fixed users. Wireless devices have limited displays and input capabilities compared with typical fixed devices such as the PC. Transactions and messaging will be the rule instead of lengthy browsing sessions. Because wireless devices are location aware, information can be tailored to the geographic location of the user. Information will be able to find users, instead of users searching for information.

---

[4]www.gsmworld.com

[5]http://thenextweb.com/google/2011/01/07/android-users-now-outnumber-iphone-users-in-u-s/

[6]http://thenextweb.com/google/2011/01/07/android-users-now-outnumber-iphone-users-in-u-s/

[7]www.att.com/wireless

1.3 THE GLOBAL CELLULAR NETWORK

Today there is no single cellular network. Devices support one or two of a myriad of technologies and generally work only within the confines of a single operator's network. To move beyond this model, more work must be done to define and implement standards.

The ITU is working to develop a family of standards for the next-generation wireless devices. The new standards will use higher frequencies to increase capacity. The new standards will also help overcome the incompatibilities introduced as the different first- and second-generation networks were developed and deployed over the last decade.

The dominant first-generation digital wireless network in North America was the Advanced Mobile Phone System (AMPS). This network offers a data service using the Cellular Digital Packet Data (CDPD) overlay network, which provides a 19.2-kbps data rate. The CPDP uses idle periods on regular voice channels to provide the data service.

The key second-generation wireless systems are the Global System for Mobile Communications (GSM), Personal Communications Service (PCS) IS-136, and PCS IS-95. The PCS standard IS-136 uses time division multiple access (TDMA) while IS-95 uses code division multiple access (CDMA). The GSM and PCS IS-136 use dedicated channels at 9.6 kbps to deliver the data service.

The ITU also developed International Mobile Telecommunications-2000 (IMT-2000). This family of standards paved the way toward a seamless global network. And now major carriers such as AT&T and Verizon have superceded that by deploying 4G services, providing much higher data rates. 4G is the fourth generation of cellular wireless standards. It is a successor to the 3G and 2G families of standards. In 2009, the ITU-R organization specified the IMT-Advanced (International Mobile Telecommunications Advanced) requirements for 4G standards, setting peak speed requirements for 4G service at 100 Mbit/s for high mobility communication (such as from trains and cars) and 1 Gbit/s for low mobility communication (such as pedestrians and stationary users).

In addition to defining frequency usage, encoding techniques, and transmission, standards also need to define how mobile devices will interact with the Internet. Several standards bodies and industry consortiums are working to that end. For example, the Wireless Application Protocol (WAP) Forum has developed a common protocol that allows devices with limited display and input capabilities to access the Internet.

1.4 BROADBAND

The Internet is increasingly a multimedia experience. Graphics, video, and audio abound on the pages of the World Wide Web. Business communications are following the same trend. For example, e-mail frequently includes large multimedia attachments. In order to participate fully, wireless networks require the same high data rates as their fixed counterparts. The higher data rates are obtainable with broadband wireless technology.

Broadband wireless service shares the same advantages of all wireless services: convenience and reduced cost. Operators can deploy the service faster than a fixed service and without the cost of a cable plant. The service is also mobile and can be deployed almost anywhere.

There are many initiatives developing broadband wireless standards around many different applications. The standards cover everything from the wireless LAN to the small wireless home network. Data rates vary from 2 Mbps to well over 100 Mbps. Many of these technologies are available now and many more will become available in the next several years. We will discuss these in some length throughout this text.

Wireless LANs (WLANs) provide network services where it is difficult or too expensive to deploy a fixed infrastructure. The primary WLAN standard is IEEE 802.11, which provides for data rates as high as 54 Mbps.

A potential problem with 802.11 is compatibility with Bluetooth. Bluetooth is a wireless networking specification that defines wireless communications between devices such as laptops, PDAs, and mobile phones. Bluetooth and some versions of 802.11 use the same frequency band. The technologies would most likely interfere with each other if deployed in the same device.

1.5 FUTURE TRENDS

Much of the development effort in new wireless technology makes use of portions of the frequency spectrum that do not, in many countries, require licensing. In the United States, two such frequency bands are Industrial, Scientific, and Medical (ISM) band near 2.4 GHz and the newly allocated unlicensed radio band, the Unlicensed National Information Infrastructure (UNII) band. UNII was created by the FCC (Federal Communications Commission) to allow manufacturers to develop high-speed wireless networks. In order to find enough bandwidth to satisfy needs, the band was established at 5 GHz, making it incompatible with 2.4-GHz equipment. The free, unlicensed portions of the radio spectrum enable manufacturers to avoid billions of dollars in licensing fees. Newer devices use this frequency or even both! For example, the latest 802.11n standard uses both frequencies.[8]

For years, these radio frequencies were neglected, the lonely domain of cordless phones and microwave ovens. In recent years however, spurred by consumer demand and active standards bodies, considerable research and development is underway. The first significant fruit of this activity was **Wi-Fi** (Wireless Fidelity), the very popular wireless LAN technology based on the IEEE 802.11 standards. In essence, Wi-Fi refers to 802.11-compatible products that have been certified as interoperable by the Wi-Fi Alliance, a body specifically set up for this certification process. Today, in every continent, one in ten people around the world use Wi-Fi at home, at work, in countless ways. Wi-Fi adoption continues to grow, and common goals still bind together more than 400 Wi-Fi Alliance member companies from dozens of countries.[9] Wi-Fi covers not only office-based LANs, but also home-based

[8]www.ieee.org/80211

[9]http://www.wi-fi.org/organization.php

LANs and publicly available *hot spots*, which are areas around a central antenna in which people can wirelessly share information or connect to the Internet with a properly equipped laptop. And these hotspots have become so commonplace, you can find listings of the thousands of these in the U.S. at numerous websites such as WiFi Freespot.[10] Wi-Fi is examined in some detail in Chapter 14.

Wi-Fi is just the first major step in utilizing these bands. Four other innovative technologies are working their way through the research, development, and standardization efforts: WiMAX, Long Term Evolution (LTE), Mobile-Fi, ZigBee, and Ultrawideband. We survey these technologies briefly later.

WiMAX is similar to Wi-Fi. Both create hot spots, but while Wi-Fi can cover several hundred meters, WiMAX has a range of 40 to 50 km. Thus, WiMAX provides a wireless alternative to cable, DSL, and T1/E1 for last-mile broadband access. It will also be used as complimentary technology to connect 802.11 hot spots to the Internet. Initial deployments of WiMAX are in fixed locations, but a mobile version is under development. WiMAX is an interoperability specification based on IEEE 802.16 and is discussed in more detail in Chapter 11.

LTE is a set of enhancements to the Universal Mobile Telecommunications System (UMTS) which was introduced in 3rd Generation Partnership Project (3GPP) Release 8. Much of 3GPP Release 8 focuses on adopting 4G mobile communication technology, including an all-IP flat networking architecture. On August 18, 2009, the European Commission announced it will invest a total of €18 million into researching the deployment of LTE and the certified 4G system LTE Advanced.[11] And Verizon, the second largest U.S. carrier, is deploying LTE nationally and is expected to have it available by 2010 in all major U.S. markets with Canada soon thereafter.[12]

While it is commonly seen as a cell phone or common carrier development, LTE is also endorsed by public safety agencies in the US as the preferred technology for the new 700 MHz public-safety radio band.[13]

Mobile-Fi is similar to the mobile version of WiMAX in terms of technology. The objective with Mobile-Fi is to provide Internet access to mobile users at data rates even higher than those available in today's home broadband links. In this context, mobile truly means mobile, not just movable. Thus, a Mobile-Fi user could enjoy broadband Internet access while traveling in a moving car or train.

ZigBee functions at a relatively low data rate over relatively short distances, compared to Wi-Fi. The objective is to develop products that are very low cost, with low power consumption and low data rate. ZigBee technology enables the coordination of communication among thousands of tiny sensors, which can be scattered throughout offices, farms, or factories, picking up bits of information about temperature, chemicals, water, or motion. They're designed to use little energy because they'll be left in place for 5 or 10 years and their batteries need to last. ZigBee devices communicate efficiently, passing data over radio waves from one to the other

---

[10]http://www.wififreespot.com/

[11]European Commission pumps €18 million into LTE research | Wireless News. Betanews. http://www.betanews.com/article/European-Commission-pumps-a18-million-into-LTE-research/1250618141

[12]www.verizon.com/LTE

[13]NPSTC Votes To Endorse LTE Technology for Broadband Network. *National Public Safety Telecommunications Council*

like a bucket brigade. At the end of the line the data can be dropped into a computer for analysis or picked up by another wireless technology like Wi-Fi or WiMAX.

Ultrawideband serves a very different purpose than the other technologies mentioned in this section. Ultrawideband enables the movement of massive files at high data rates over short distances. For example, in the home, Ultrawideband would allow the user to transfer hours of video from a PC to a TV without any messy cords. On the road, a passenger who has a laptop in the trunk receiving data over Mobile-Fi could use Ultrawideband to pull that information up to a handheld computer in the front seat. UWB has been a proposed technology for use in personal area networks and appeared in the IEEE 802.15.3a draft PAN standard. However, after several years of deadlock, the IEEE 802.15.3a task group was dissolved in 2006. The work was completed by the WiMedia Alliance and the USB Implementer Forum. Slow progress in UWB standards development, high cost of initial implementations and performance significantly lower than initially expected are some of the reasons for the limited success of UWB in consumer products, which caused several UWB vendors to cease operations during 2008 and 2009.[14,15]

1.6 THE TROUBLE WITH WIRELESS

Wireless is convenient and often less expensive to deploy than fixed services, but wireless is not perfect. There are limitations, political and technical difficulties that may ultimately prevent wireless technologies from reaching their full potential. Two issues are incompatible standards and device limitations.

As mentioned previously, in North America there are two standards for digital cellular service. Internationally, there is at least one more. A device using PCS IS-136 will not work in an area where the deployed technology is PCS IS-95. And, the two largest U.S. vendors, AT&T and Verizon, use very different networking technologies, TDMA and CDMA. Also mentioned previously is the inability to use Bluetooth and 802.11 in the same device. These are just several examples of problems that arise when industrywide standards do not exist. The lack of an industrywide standard holds the technologies back from delivering one of the true ideals of wireless: ubiquitous access to data. This is likely to continue however due to the competitive nature of U.S. firms and the lack of Federal forceful intervention as is implemented in a more standards-centric European market.

Device limitations also restrict the free flow of data. The small display on a mobile telephone is inadequate for displaying more than a few lines of text. Initially, this proved to be a problem with many users. However, over time, most users have gotten used to this environment and Web browsing on these smaller screens is now ubiquitous. Also, newer devices such as the iPad/iPad2 and similar tablet computers have screens smaller than a typical laptop or desktop and yet users seem satisfied with this size. These tablet sizes range form 7 inches to 10 inches and above, still smaller than a typical laptop size of around 15–17 inches.[16] It used to be said that no

[14]http://standards.ieee.org/about/sasb/nescom/projects/802-15-3a.pdf
[15]http://www.ieee802.org/15/pub/TG3a.html
[16]www.apple.com/iPad

one wireless device will be able to meet every need. However, tablets such as the iPad or Samsumg's Galaxy are proving this assumption to be incorrect. Users can and do perform a wide range of functions with these devices. Wireless will continue to proliferate and become commonplace in society because it is increasingly quicker, inexpensive and meets a wide variety of modern information needs.

1.7 OUTLINE OF THE BOOK

The objective of this book is to provide a comprehensive technical survey of wireless communications fundamentals, wireless networks, and wireless applications. The book is organized into four parts (Figure 1.2). The reader who is already familiar with data communications and networking technology can safely skip or just skim Part One. Part Two discusses underlying principles common to all of the material covered

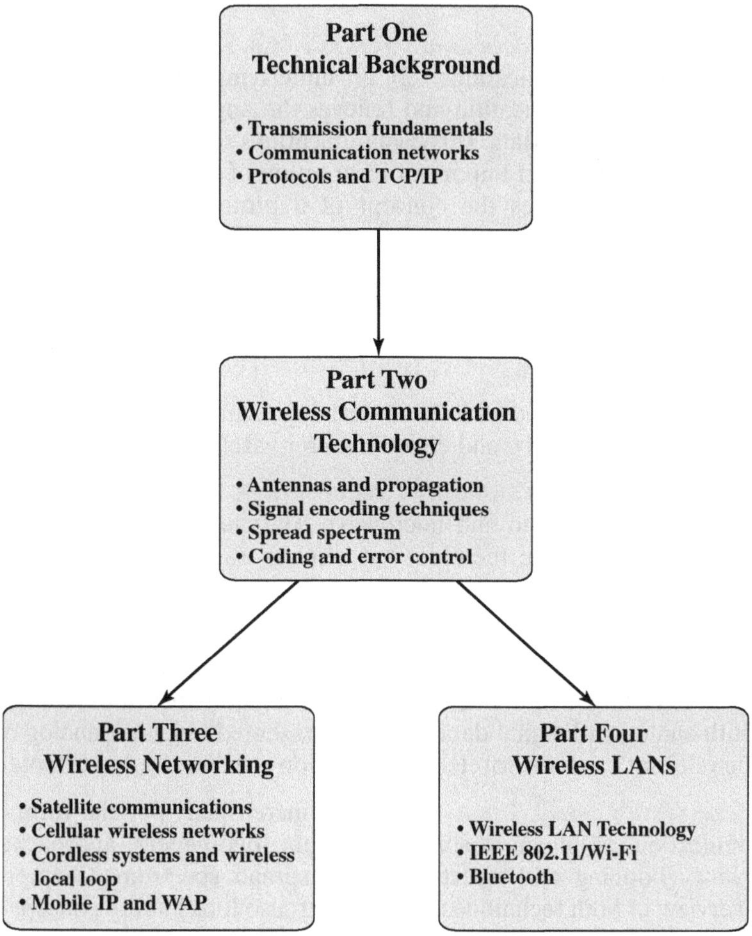

Figure 1.2 Wireless Topics

in the remainder of the book and should be read next. Parts Three and Four are independent and may be covered in either order. Within Part Three, all of the chapters are more or less independent and can be read in any order depending on your level of interest. The same is true of Chapters 14 and 15 in Part Five.

Part One: Technical Background

Part One provides a preview and context for the remainder of the book, covering basic topics in data communications as well as TCP/IP. Part One, together with the appendices at the end of the book, is intended to make the book as self-contained as possible.

Chapter 2: Wireless Transmission Chapter 2 introduces basic wireless communications concepts including propagation effects, the various wireless technologies, and their impact.

Chapter 3: Communication Networks This chapter provides an overview and comparison of basic communication network technologies, including circuit switching, packet switching, and ATM.

Chapter 4: Protocols and the TCP/IP Suite Data network communication and distributed applications rely on underlying communications software that is independent of application and relieves the application of much of the burden of reliably exchanging data. This communications software is organized into a protocol architecture, the most important incarnation of which is the TCP/IP protocol suite. Chapter 4 introduces the concept of a protocol architecture and provides an overview of TCP/IP. Another architecture, the Open Systems Interconnection (OSI) reference model, is briefly described. Finally, the concept of internetworking and the use of TCP/IP to achieve internetworking are discussed.

Part Two: Wireless Communication Technology

This part is concerned with the underlying technology of wireless transmission and the encoding of analog and digital data for wireless transmission.

Chapter 5: Antennas and Propagation Chapter 5 examines the fundamental principles of radio and microwave. The chapter discusses relevant aspects of antenna performance, then looks at wireless transmission modes, and finally examines the key issue of fading.

Chapter 6: Signal Encoding Techniques Data come in both analog (continuous) and digital (discrete) form. For transmission, input data must be encoded as an electrical signal that is tailored to the characteristics of the transmission medium. Both analog and digital data can be represented by either analog or digital signals; the relevant cases for wireless transmission are discussed in Chapter 6.

Chapter 7: Spread Spectrum An increasingly popular form of wireless communications is known as spread spectrum. Two general approaches are used: frequency hopping and direct sequence spread spectrum. Chapter 7 provides an overview of both techniques. The chapter also looks at the concept of code division multiple access (CDMA), which is an application of spread spectrum to provide multiple access.

Chapter 8: Coding and Error Control Wireless communications systems are highly prone to error, and virtually all wireless transmission schemes include techniques for forward error correction (FEC) by adding redundancy to the transmitted data so that bit errors can be corrected at the receiver. Chapter 8 examines FEC in detail. In addition, Chapter 8 looks at the use of redundancy for error detection, which is also found in many wireless schemes. Finally, error detection is often combined with automatic repeat request (ARQ) techniques that enable a transmitter to retransmit blocks of data in which the receiver has detected an error.

Part Three: Wireless Networking

This part examines the major types of wireless networks. These include satellite-based networks, cellular networks, cordless systems, fixed wireless access schemes, and the use of mobile IP and the Wireless Application Protocol (WAP) to provide Internet and Web access.

Chapter 9: Satellite Communications This chapter covers the basic principles of satellite communications, the various orbital platforms being utilized, their propagation effects, and their uses by government, industry, and the public.

Chapter 10: Cellular Wireless Networks Chapter 10 begins with a discussion of the important design issues related to cellular wireless networks. Next, the chapter covers the traditional mobile telephony service, now known as first-generation analog. Chapter 10 then examines second-generation digital cellular networks, looking at the two principal approaches: time division multiple access (TDMA) and code division multiple access (CDMA). Finally, an overview of third-generation networks is provided.

Chapter 11: Cordless Systems and Wireless Local Loop Chapter 11 looks at two technologies that bring wireless access into the residence and office: cordless systems and wireless local loop (WLL). Cordless systems have evolved from the simple single-user cordless telephones used within the home to accommodate multiple users over much larger ranges. Sometimes called radio in the loop (RITL) or fixed wireless access (FWA), WLL is a system that connects subscribers to the public switched telephone network (PSTN) using radio signals as a substitute for copper for all or part of the connection between the subscriber and the switch. Chapter 11 looks at the design issues related to WLL and then examines the IEEE 802.16 standard.

Chapter 12: Mobile IP and Wireless Access Protocol Chapter 12 examines the modifications to IP to accommodate wireless access to the Internet. The chapter then examines the Wireless Application Protocol (WAP). WAP provides mobile users of wireless phones and other wireless terminals, such as pagers and personal digital assistants (PDAs), access to telephony and information services, including the Internet and the Web.

Part Four: Wireless LANs

In recent years, a whole new class of local area networks have arrived to provide an alternative to LANs based on twisted pair, coaxial cable, and optical fiber—wireless LANs. The key advantages of the wireless LAN are that it eliminates the wiring cost, which is often the most costly component of a LAN, and that it accommodates mobile workstations. This part examines underlying wireless LAN technology and then examines two standardized approaches to local wireless networking.

Chapter 13: Wireless LAN Technology Wireless LANs use one of three transmission techniques: spread spectrum, narrowband microwave, and infrared. Chapter 13 provides an overview of LANs and wireless LAN technology and applications.

Chapter 14: Wi-Fi and the IEEE 802.11 Wireless LAN Standard The most significant set of standards defining wireless LANs are those defined by the IEEE 802.11 committee. Chapter 14 examines this set of standards in depth.

Chapter 15: Bluetooth and IEEE 802.15 Bluetooth is an open specification for wireless communication and networking among PCs, mobile phones, and other wireless devices. Bluetooth is one of the fastest growing technology standards ever. It is intended for use within a local area. Chapter 15 examines this specification in depth.

1.8 INTERNET AND WEB RESOURCES

There are a number of resources available on the Internet and the Web to support this book and to help one keep up with developments in this field.

Web Sites for This Book

A special Web page has been set up for this book at **WilliamStallings.com/Wireless/Wireless2e.html.** The site includes the following:

- **Useful Web sites:** There are links to other relevant Web sites, including the sites listed in this section and throughout this book.
- **Errata sheet:** An errata list for this book will be maintained and updated as needed. Please e-mail any errors that you spot to me. Errata sheets for my other books are at **WilliamStallings.com.**
- **Documents:** Includes a number of documents that expand on the treatment in the book. Topics include standards organizations and the TCP/IP checksum.
- **Figures:** All of the figures in this book in PDF (Adobe Acrobat) format.
- **Tables:** All of the tables in this book in PDF format.
- **Slides:** A set of PowerPoint slides, organized by chapter.
- **Internet mailing list:** The site includes sign-up information for the book's Internet mailing list.
- **Wireless courses:** There are links to home pages for courses based on this book; these pages may be useful to other instructors in providing ideas about how to structure their course.

I also maintain the Computer Science Student Resource Site, at **WilliamStallings.com/StudentSupport.html;** the purpose of this site is to provide documents, information, and useful links for computer science students and professionals. Links are organized into four categories:

- **Math:** Includes a basic math refresher, a queuing analysis primer, a number system primer, and links to numerous math sites
- **How-to:** Advice and guidance for solving homework problems, writing technical reports, and preparing technical presentations
- **Research resources:** Links to important collections of papers, technical reports, and bibliographies
- **Miscellaneous:** A variety of useful documents and links

Other Web Sites

There are numerous Web sites that provide information related to the topics of this book. In subsequent chapters, pointers to specific Web sites can be found in the "Recommended Reading and Web Sites" section. Because the addresses for Web sites tend to change frequently, I have not included these in the book. For all of the Web sites listed in the book, the appropriate link can be found at this book's Web site.

The following Web sites are of general interest related to wireless communications:

- **Vendors:** Links to thousands of hardware and software vendors who currently have WWW sites, as well as a list of thousands of computer and networking companies in a Phone Directory
- **Wireless Developer Network:** News, tutorials, and discussions on wireless topics
- **Wireless.com:** An amazing list of links to all aspects or wireless communications, networking, and standards

USENET Newsgroups

A number of USENET newsgroups are devoted to some aspect of data communications or networking. As with virtually all USENET groups, there is a high noise-to-signal ratio, but it is worth experimenting to see if any meet your needs. The most relevant are

- **comp.std.wireless:** General discussion of wireless standards for wide area and local area networks. This is a moderated group, which keeps the discussion focused.
- **comp.dcom.*:** There are a number of data communications related newsgroups that begin with "comp.dcom."

PART ONE

Technical Background

CHAPTER 2

WIRELESS TRANSMISSION

This book focuses on higher layer aspects of mobile communications, the computer science element rather than on the radio and transmission aspects, the electrical engineering part. This chapter introduces only those fundamental aspects of wireless transmission which are necessary to understand the problems of higher layers and the complexity needed to handle transmission impairments. Wherever appropriate, the reader is referred to literature giving a deeper insight into the topic. To avoid too many details blurring the overall picture, this chapter sometimes simplifies the real-world characteristics of wireless transmission. Readers who are more interested in the details of wireless transmission, calculation of propagation characteristics etc. are referred to Pahlavan (2002) or Stallings (2002).

While transmission over different wires typically does not cause interference,[1] this is an important topic in wireless transmission. The frequencies used for transmission are all regulated. The first section gives a general overview of these frequencies. The following sections recall some basic facts about signals, antennas, and signal propagation. The varying propagation characteristics create particular complications for radio transmission, frequently causing transmission errors. Multiplexing is a major design topic in this context, because the medium is always shared. Multiplexing schemes have to ensure low interference between different senders.

Modulation is needed to transmit digital data via certain frequencies. A separate section of this chapter presents standard modulation schemes that will reoccur together with wireless communication systems. The next section discusses spread spectrum, a special transmission technique that is more robust against errors. A short introduction to cellular systems concludes this chapter.

2.1 FREQUENCIES FOR RADIO TRANSMISSION

Radio transmission can take place using many different frequency bands. Each frequency band exhibits certain advantages and disadvantages. Figure 2.1 gives a rough overview of the frequency spectrum that can be used for data transmission. The figure shows frequencies starting at 300 Hz and going up to over 300 THz.

Directly coupled to the frequency is the wavelength λ via the equation:

$$\lambda = c/f,$$

where $c \cong 3 \cdot 10^8$ m/s (the speed of light in vacuum) and f the frequency. For traditional wired networks, frequencies of up to several hundred kHz are used for distances up to some km with twisted pair copper wires, while frequencies of several hundred MHz are used with coaxial cable (new coding schemes work with several hundred MHz even with twisted pair copper wires over distances of some 100 m). Fiber optics are used for frequency ranges of several hundred THz, but here one typically refers to the wavelength which is, e.g., 1500 nm, 1350 nm etc. (infra red).

Radio transmission starts at several kHz, the **very low frequency (VLF)** range. These are very long waves. Waves in the **low frequency (LF)** range are used

[1]However, if the transmitted frequencies are too high for a certain wire crosstalk takes place. This is a common problem, e.g., for DSL or Powerline installations, especially if many wires are bundled.

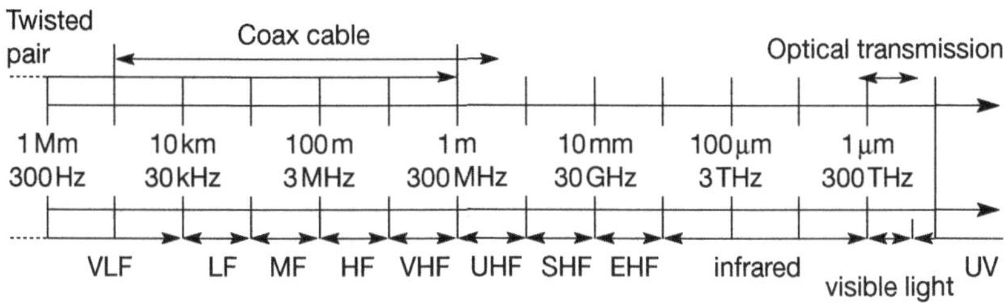

Figure 2.1 Frequency Spectrum

by submarines, because they can penetrate water and can follow the earth's surface. The **medium frequency (MF)** and **high frequency (HF)** ranges are typical for transmission of hundreds of radio stations either as amplitude modulation **(AM)** between 520 kHz and 1605.5 kHz, as short wave **(SW)** between 5.9 MHz and 26.1 MHz, or as frequency modulation **(FM)** between 87.5 MHz and 108 MHz. The frequencies limiting these ranges are typically fixed by national regulation and vary from country to country. Short waves are typically used for (amateur) radio transmission around the world, enabled by reflection at the ionosphere. Transmit power is up to 500 kW—which is quite high compared to the 1 W of a mobile phone.

As we move to higher frequencies, the TV stations follow. Conventional analog TV is transmitted in ranges of 174–230 MHz and 470–790 MHz using the very high frequency **(VHF)** and ultra high frequency **(UHF)** bands. In this range, digital audio broadcasting (DAB) takes place as well (223–230 MHz and 1452–1472 MHz) and digital TV uses frequencies 470–697 MHz in North America, reusing some of the old frequencies for analog TV. UHF is also used for mobile phones with analog technology (450–465 MHz), the digital GSM (890–960 MHz, 1710–1880 MHz), digital cordless telephones following the DECT standard (1880–1900 MHz), or at 2.4 and 5.8. 3G cellular systems follow the UMTS standard (1900–1980 MHz, 2020–2025 MHz, 2110–2190 MHz) and many more. And LTE and Wi-Max are fighting it out in the 4G arena. VHF and especially UHF allow for small antennas and relatively reliable connections for mobile telephony.

Super high frequencies (SHF) are typically used for directed microwave links (approx. 2–40 GHz) and fixed satellite services in the C-band (4 and 6 GHz), Ku-band (11 and 14 GHz), or Ka-band (19 and 29 GHz). Some systems are planned in the **extremely high frequency** (EHF) range which comes close to infra red. All radio frequencies are regulated to avoid interference, with each country regulating its own airspace. In the U.S, for example, the Federal Communications Commission regulates this. Also, a number of forums and standards bodies work on standards for frequency allocation, including:

- *International Telecommunication Union* (ITU)
- *European Conference of Postal and Telecommunications Administrations* (CEPT)
- *European Telecommunications Standards Institute* (ETSI)
- *International Special Committee on Radio Interference* (Comité international spécial des perturbations radioélectriques—CISPR)

These standards bodies have assigned frequency bands in three types of allocation:

- No one may transmit: frequencies *reserved for radio astronomy* to avoid interference at *radio telescopes*
- Anyone may transmit, as long as they respect certain transmission power and other limits: *open spectrum* bands such as the unlicensed *ISM bands* and the unlicensed *ultra-wideband* band, and the somewhat more regulated *amateur radio frequency allocations.* Often users use a "listen before talk" *contention based protocol.*
- Only the licensed user of that band may transmit: the licensing body may give the same frequency to several users as a form of *frequency reuse* if they cannot interfere because their *coverage map* areas never overlap.

High-demand sections of the electromagnetic spectrum may sometimes be allocated through *auctions.*

The next step into higher frequencies involves optical transmission, which is not only used for fiber optical links but also for wireless communications. **Infra red (IR)** transmission is used for directed links, e.g., to connect different buildings via laser links. The most widespread IR technology, infra red data association (IrDA), uses wavelengths of approximately 850–900 nm to connect laptops, PDAs etc. Finally, visible light has been used for wireless transmission for thousands of years. While light is not very reliable due to interference, it is nevertheless useful due to built-in human receivers.

2.1.1 Regulations

As the examples in the previous section have shown, radio frequencies are scarce resources. Many national (economic) interests make it hard to find common, worldwide regulations. The International Telecommunications Union (ITU) located in Geneva is responsible for worldwide coordination of telecommunication activities (wired and wireless). ITU is a sub-organization of the UN. The ITU Radiocommunication sector (ITU-R) handles standardization in the wireless sector, so it also handles frequency planning (formerly known as Consultative Committee for International Radiocommunication, CCIR).

To have at least some success in worldwide coordination and to reflect national interests, the ITU-R has split the world into three regions: **Region 1** covers Europe, the Middle East, countries of the former Soviet Union, and Africa. **Region 2** includes Greenland and North and South America, and **region 3** comprises the Far East, Australia, and New Zealand. Within these regions, national agencies are responsible for further regulations, e.g., the Federal Communications Commission (FCC) and the NTIA in the US. Several nations have a common agency such as European Conference for Posts and Telecommunications (CEPT) in Europe. While CEPT is still responsible for the general planning, many tasks have been transferred to other agencies (confusing anybody following the regulation process). For example, the European Telecommunications Standards Institute (ETSI) is responsible for standardization and consists of national standardization bodies, public providers, manufacturers, user groups, and research institutes.

IEEE To achieve at least some harmonization, the ITU-R holds the World Radio Conference (WRC) to periodically discuss and decide frequency allocations for all three regions. This is obviously a difficult task as many regions or countries may have already installed a huge base of a certain technology and will be reluctant to change frequencies just for the sake of harmonization. Harmonization is, however, needed as soon as satellite communication is used. Satellites, especially low earth-orbiting satellites do not 'respect' national regulations, but should operate world-wide. While it is difficult to prevent other nations from setting up a satellite system it is much simpler to ban the necessary devices or the infrastructure needed for operation. Satellite systems should operate on frequencies available worldwide to support global usage with a single device.

Table 2.1 gives some examples for frequencies used for (analog and digital) mobile phones, cordless telephones, wireless LANs, and other radio frequency (RF) systems for countries in the three regions representing the major economic powers.

While older analog **mobile phone** systems like NMT or its derivatives at 450 MHz are still available, Europe is heavily dominated by the fully digital GSM at 900 MHz and 1800 MHz (also known as DCS1800, Digital Cellular System). In contrast to Europe, the US FCC allowed several cellular technologies in the same frequency bands around 850 MHz. Starting from the analog advanced mobile phone system (AMPS), this led to the co-existence of several solutions, such as dual mode mobile phones supporting digital time division multiple access (TDMA) service and analog AMPS according to the standard IS-54. AMPS was discontinued in the US in 2008. All digital TDMA phones according to IS-136 (also known as Digital Advanced Mobile Phone Service) and digital code division multiple access (CDMA) phones according to IS-95 have been developed. In addition, the US did not adopt a common mobile phone system, but waited for market forces to decide. This led to many islands of different systems and, consequently, as in Europe, full coverage is not available in the US. The long discussions about the pros and cons of TDMA and CDMA also promoted the worldwide success of GSM. GSM is available in over 219 countries and used by more than 5 billion people (GSM World, 2002). A user can roam with the same mobile phone from Zimbabwe, via Uzbekistan, Sweden, Singapore, USA, Tunisia, Russia, Canada, Italy, Greece, Germany, China, and Belgium to Austria.

Carriers world-wide are adopting LTE also known as 4G. At the present time the LTE implemented is not true LTE as specified in the ITU-R IMT-Advanced (International Mobile Telecommunications Advanced) requirements for 4G standards. LTE supports bandwidth from 1.4 MHz to 20 MHz.

Wimax is another system which is used world-wide. It is based on the IEEE 802.16 standard. It operates at 2.3 GHz in the US and Korea, 2.5 both in the US and abroad, 3.5 GHz, 3.65 GHz and 5.8 GHz in the US.

Another system, the personal digital cellular (**PDC**), formerly known as Japanese digital cellular (JDC) was established in Japan. Quite often mobile phones covering many standards have been announced. New frequency bands, e.g., for the universal mobile telecommunications system (**UMTS**) or the freedom of mobile multi-media access (**FOMA**) are located at 1920–1980 MHz and 2110–2170/2190 MHz.

Many different **cordless telephone** standards exist around the world. However, this is not as problematic as the diversity of mobile phone standards. Some older analog systems such as cordless telephone (**CT1+**) are still in use, but digital technology has been introduced for cordless telephones as well. Examples include **CT2**, the first digital cordless telephone introduced in the UK, digital enhanced

Table 2.1 Example Systems and Their Frequency Allocations (All Values in MHz)

	Europe	US	Japan
Mobile phones	**NMT** 453–457 463–467	**AMPS, TDMA, CDMA** 824–849 869–894	**PDC** 810–826 940–956 1429–1465 1477–1513
	GSM 890–915 935–960 1710–1785 1805–1880	**GSM, TDMA, CDMA** 1850–1910 1930–1990	
	UMTS (FDD)/ W-CDMA 1920–1980 2110–2190		**FOMA/ W-CDMA** 1920–1980 2110–2170
	UMTS (TDD) 1900–1920 2020–2025		
Cordless telephones	**CT1+** 885–887 930–932	**PACS** 1850–1910 1930–1990	**PHS** 1895–1918
	CT2 864–868	**PACS-UB** 1910–1930	**JCT** 254–380
	DECT 1880–1900		
Wireless LANs	**IEEE 802.11** 2400–2483	**IEEE 802.11** 902–928 2400–2483	**IEEE 802.11** 2400–2497
	HiperLAN2, IEEE 802.11a 5150–5350 5470–5725	**HiperLAN2, IEEE 802.11a** 5150–5350 5725–5825	**HiperLAN2, IEEE 802.11a** 5150–5250
Others	**RF-Control** 27, 128, 418, 433, 868	**RF-Control** 315, 915	**RF-Control** 426, 868
	Satellite (e.g., Iridium, Globalstar) 1610–1626, 2483–2500		

cordless telecommunications (**DECT**) as a European standard, personal access communications system (PACS) and PACS-Unlicensed Band (**PACS-UB**) in the US, as well as personal handyphone system (PHS) as replacement for the analog Japanese cordless telephone (**JCT**) in Japan. Mobile phones covering, e.g., DECT and GSM are available but they have not been a commercial success.

Finally, the area of **WLAN** standards is of special interest for wireless, mobile computer communication on a campus or in buildings. Here the computer industry developed products within the license-free **ISM** band, of which the most attractive is located at 2.4 GHz and is available for license-free operation almost everywhere around the world (with national differences limiting frequencies, transmit power etc.). The most widespread standard in this area is **IEEE 802.11b**. The wireless LAN standards **HiperLAN2** and **IEEE 802.11a** operate in the 5 GHz range, but depending on the region on different frequencies with different restrictions.

Many more frequencies have been assigned for trunk radio (e.g., trans-European trunked radio (TETRA), 380–400 MHz, 410–430 MHz, 450–470 MHz—depending on national regulations), paging services, terrestrial flight telephone system (TFTS), 1670–1675 MHz and 1800–1805 MHz, satellite services (Iridium: 1610–1626 MHz, Globalstar: 1610–1626 MHz and 2483–2500 MHz) etc. Higher frequencies are of special interest for high bit-rate transmission, although these frequencies face severe shadowing by many obstacles. License-free bands at 17.2, 24 and even 61 GHz are under consideration for commercial use. Additionally, a lot of license-free wireless communication takes place at lower frequencies. Garage openers, car locks, wireless headsets, radio frequency identifications (RFID) etc. operate on, e.g., 433 or 868 MHz.

2.2 SIGNALS

Signals are the physical representation of data. Users of a communication system can only exchange data through the transmission of signals. Layer 1 of the ISO/OSI basic reference model is responsible for the conversion of data, i.e., bits, into signals and vice versa (Halsall, 1996), (Stallings, 1997 and 2002).

Signals are functions of time and location. Signal parameters represent the data values. The most interesting types of signals for radio transmission are **periodic signals**, especially **sine waves** as carriers. (The process of mapping of data onto a carrier is explained in section 2.6.) The general function of a sine wave is:

$$g(t) = A_t \sin(2\,\pi\, f_t\, t + \varphi_t)$$

Signal parameters are the **amplitude** A, the **frequency** f, and the **phase shift** φ. The amplitude as a factor of the function g may also change over time, thus A_t, (see section 2.6.1). The frequency f expresses the periodicity of the signal with the period $T = 1/f$. (In equations, ω is frequently used instead of $2\pi f$.) The frequency f may also change over time, thus f_t, (see section 2.6.2). Finally, the phase shift determines the shift of the signal relative to the same signal without a shift. An example for shifting a function is shown in Figure 2.2. This shows a sine function without a phase shift and the same function, i.e., same amplitude and frequency, with a phase shift φ. Section 2.6.3 shows how shifting the phase can be used to represent data.

Sine waves are of special interest, as it is possible to construct every periodic signal g by using only sine and cosine functions according to a fundamental equation of **Fourier**:

$$g(t) = \frac{1}{2}c + \sum_{n=1}^{\infty} a_n \sin(2\pi nft) + \sum_{n=1}^{\infty} b_n \cos(2\pi nft)$$

In this equation the parameter c determines the **Direct Current (DC)** component of the signal, the coefficients a_n and b_n are the amplitudes of the nth sine and

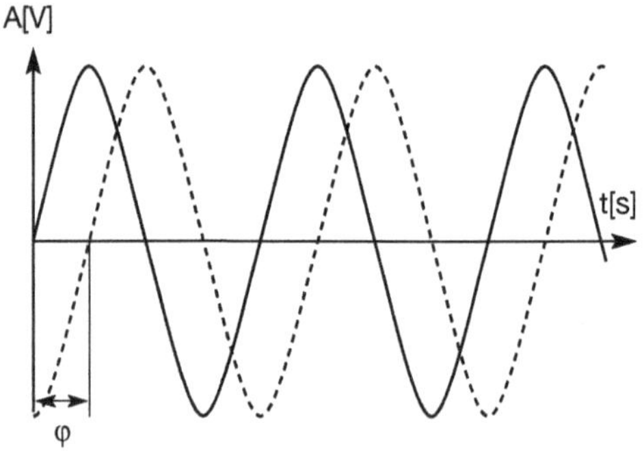

Figure 2.2 Time Domain Representation of a Signal

cosine function. The equation shows that an infinite number of sine and cosine functions is needed to construct arbitrary periodic functions. However, the frequencies of these functions (the so-called **harmonics**) increase with a growing parameter n and are a multiple of the **fundamental frequency** f. The bandwidth of any medium, air, cable, transmitter etc. is limited, and there is an upper limit for the frequencies. In reality therefore, it is enough to consider a limited number of sine and cosine functions to construct periodic functions—all real transmitting systems exhibit these bandwidth limits and can never transmit arbitrary periodic functions. It is sufficient for us to know that we can think of transmitted signals as composed of one or many sine functions. The following illustrations always represent the example of one sine function, i.e., the case of a single frequency.

A typical way to represent signals is the time domain (see Figure 2.2). Here the amplitude A of a signal is shown versus time (time is mostly measured in seconds s, amplitudes can be measured in, e.g., volt V). This is also the typical representation known from an oscilloscope. A phase shift can also be shown in this representation.

Representations in the time domain are problematic if a signal consists of many different frequencies (as the Fourier equation indicates). In this case, a better representation of a signal is the **frequency domain** (see Figure 2.3). Here the amplitude of a certain frequency part of the signal is shown versus the frequency. Figure 2.3 only shows one peak and the signal consists only of a single frequency part (i.e., it is a

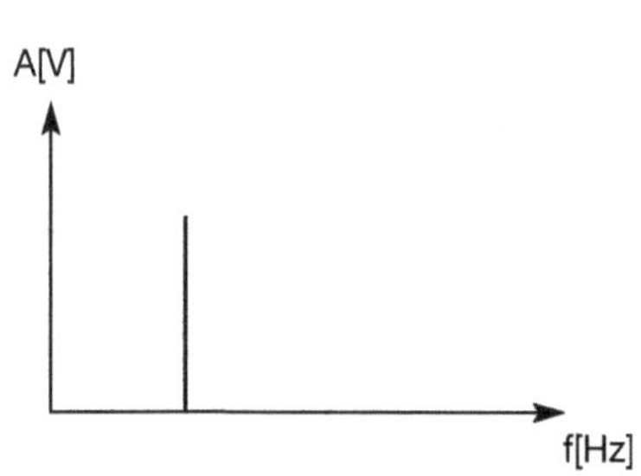

Figure 2.3 Frequency Domain Representation of a Signal

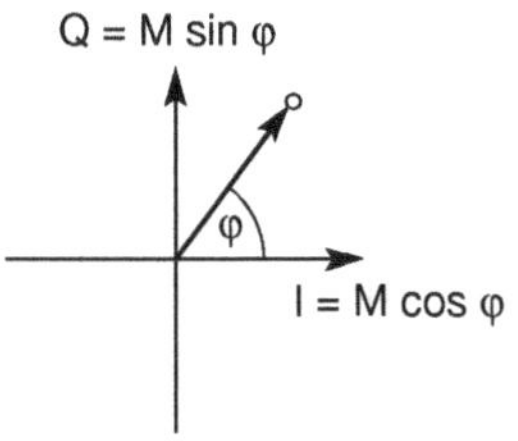

Figure 2.4 Phase Domain Representation of a Signal

single sine function). Arbitrary periodic functions would have many peaks, known as the frequency spectrum of a signal. A tool to display frequencies is a spectrum analyzer. Fourier transformations are a mathematical tool for translating from the time domain into the frequency domain and vice versa (using the inverse Fourier transformation).

A third way to represent signals is the **phase domain** shown in Figure 2.4. This representation, also called phase state or signal constellation diagram, shows the amplitude M of a signal and its phase φ in polar coordinates. (The length of the vector represents the amplitude, the angle the phase shift.) The x-axis represents a phase of 0 and is also called **In-Phase (I).** A phase shift of 90° or $\pi/2$ would be a point on the y-axis, called **Quadrature (Q).**

2.3 ANTENNAS

As the name wireless already indicates, this communication mode involves 'getting rid' of wires and transmitting signals through space without guidance. We do not need any 'medium' (such as an ether) for the transport of electromagnetic waves. Somehow, we have to couple the energy from the transmitter to the outside world and, in reverse, from the outside world to the receiver. This is exactly what **antennas** do. Antennas couple electromagnetic energy to and from space to and from a wire or coaxial cable (or any other appropriate conductor).

A theoretical reference antenna is the **isotropic radiator**, a point in space radiating equal power in all directions, i.e., all points with equal power are located on a sphere with the antenna as its center. The **radiation pattern** is symmetric in all directions (see Figure 2.5, a two dimensional cross-section of the real three-dimensional pattern).

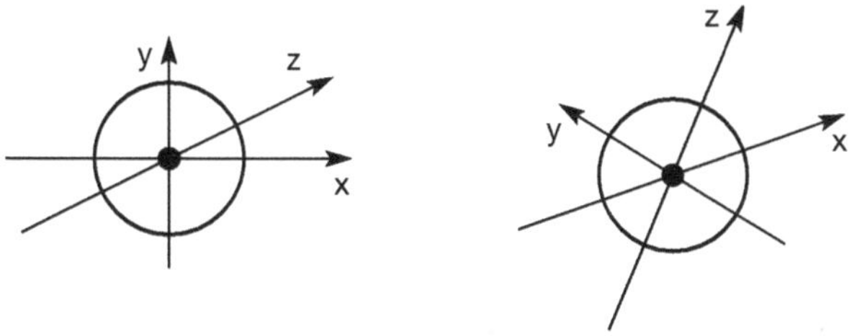

Figure 2.5 Radiation Pattern of an Isotropic Radiator

However, such an antenna does not exist in reality. Real antennas all exhibit **directive effects**, i.e., the intensity of radiation is not the same in all directions from the antenna. The simplest real antenna is a thin, center-fed **dipole**, also called Hertzian dipole, as shown in Figure 2.6 (right-hand side). The dipole consists of two collinear conductors of equal length, separated by a small feeding gap. The length of the dipole is not arbitrary, but, for example, half the wavelength λ of the signal to transmit results in a very efficient radiation of the energy. If mounted on the roof of a car, the length of $\lambda/4$ is efficient. This is also known as Marconi antenna.

A $\lambda/2$ dipole has a uniform or **omni-directional** radiation pattern in one plane and a figure eight pattern in the other two planes as shown in Figure 2.7. This type of antenna can only overcome environmental challenges by boosting the power level of the signal. Challenges could be mountains, valleys, buildings etc.

If an antenna is positioned, e.g., in a valley or between buildings, an omni-directional radiation pattern is not very useful. In this case, **directional antennas** with certain fixed preferential transmission and reception directions can be used. Figure 2.8 shows the radiation pattern of a directional antenna with the main lobe in the direction of the x-axis. A special example of directional antennas is constituted by satellite dishes.

Directed antennas are typically applied in cellular systems as presented in section 2.8. Several directed antennas can be combined on a single pole to construct a **sectorized antenna**. A cell can be sectorized into, for example, three or six sectors,

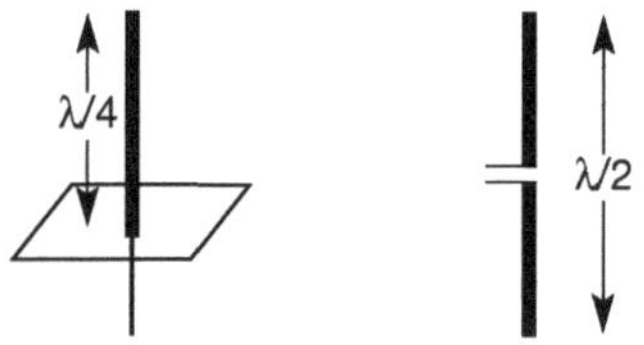

Figure 2.6 Simple Antennas

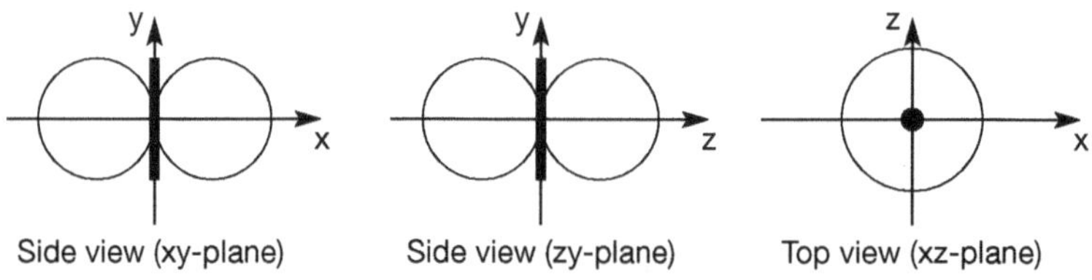

Figure 2.7 Radiation Pattern of a Simple Dipole

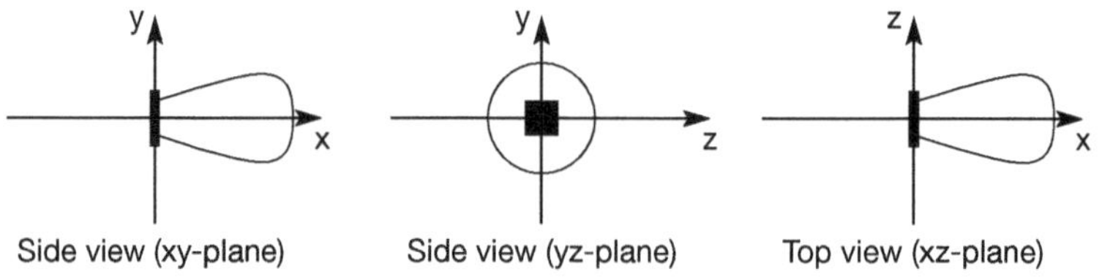

Figure 2.8 Radiation Pattern of a Directed Antenna

thus enabling frequency reuse as explained in section 2.8. Figure 2.9 shows the radiation patterns of these sectorized antennas.

Two or more antennas can also be combined to improve reception by counteracting the negative effects of multi-path propagation (see section 2.4.3). These antennas, also called **multi-element antenna arrays**, allow different diversity schemes. One such scheme is **switched diversity** or **selection diversity**, where the receiver always uses the antenna element with the largest output. **Diversity combining** constitutes a combination of the power of all signals to produce gain. The phase is first corrected (cophasing) to avoid cancellation. As shown in Figure 2.10, different schemes are possible. On the left, two $\lambda/4$ antennas are combined with a distance of $\lambda/2$ between them on top of a ground plane. On the right, three standard $\lambda/2$ dipoles are combined with a distance of $\lambda/2$ between them. Spacing could also be in multiples of $\lambda/2$.

A more advanced solution is provided by **smart antennas** which combine multiple antenna elements (also called antenna array) with signal processing to optimize the radiation/reception pattern in response to the signal environment. These antennas can adapt to changes in reception power, transmission conditions and many signal propagation effects as discussed in the following section. Antenna arrays can also be used for beam forming. This would be an extreme case of a directed antenna which can follow a single user thus using space division multiplexing (see section 2.5.1). It would not just be base stations that could follow users with an individual beam. Wireless devices, too, could direct their electromagnetic radiation, e.g., away from the human body towards a base station. This would help in reducing the absorbed radiation. Today's handset antennas are omni-directional as the integration of smart antennas into mobiles is difficult and has not yet been realized.

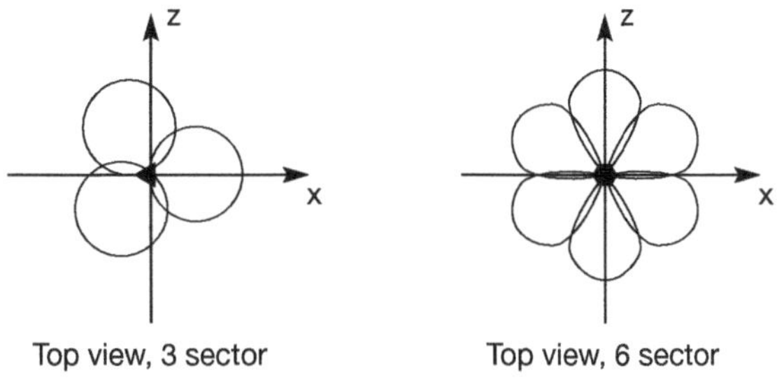

Figure 2.9 Radiation Patterns of Sectorized Antennas

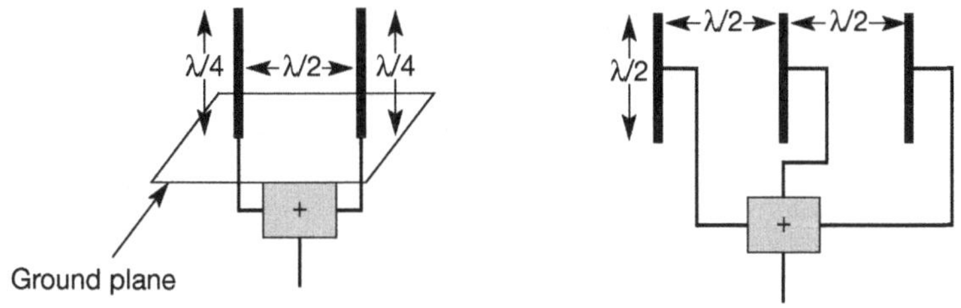

Figure 2.10 Diversity Antenna Systems

2.4 SIGNAL PROPAGATION

Like wired networks, wireless communication networks also have senders and receivers of signals. However, in connection with signal propagation, these two networks exhibit considerable differences. In wireless networks, the signal has no wire to determine the direction of propagation, whereas signals in wired networks only travel along the wire (which can be twisted pair copper wires, a coax cable, but also a fiber etc.). As long as the wire is not interrupted or damaged, it typically exhibits the same characteristics at each point. One can precisely determine the behavior of a signal travelling along this wire, e.g., received power depending on the length. For wireless transmission, this predictable behavior is only valid in a vacuum, i.e., without matter between the sender and the receiver. The situation would be as follows (Figure 2.11):

- **Transmission range**: Within a certain radius of the sender transmission is possible, i.e., a receiver receives the signals with an error rate low enough to be able to communicate and can also act as sender.
- **Detection range**: Within a second radius, detection of the transmission is possible, i.e., the transmitted power is large enough to differ from background noise. However, the error rate is too high to establish communication.
- **Interference range**: Within a third even larger radius, the sender may interfere with other transmission by adding to the background noise. A receiver will not be able to detect the signals, but the signals may disturb other signals.

This simple and ideal scheme led to the notion of **cells** around a transmitter (as briefly discussed in section 2.8). However, real life does not happen in a vacuum; radio transmission has to contend with our atmosphere, mountains, buildings, moving senders and receivers etc. In reality, the three circles referred to above will be bizarrely-shaped polygons with their shape being time and frequency dependent.

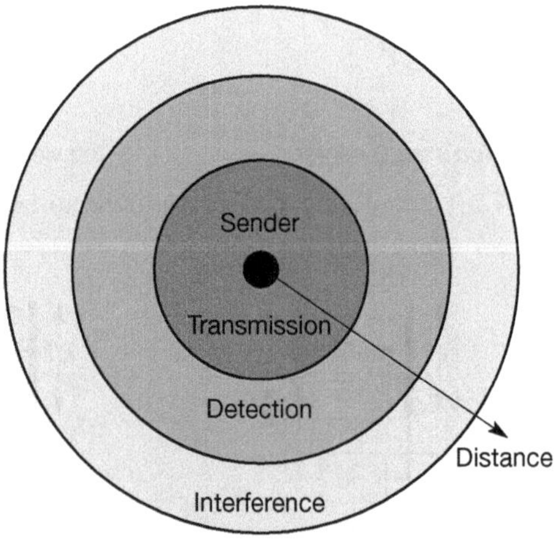

Figure 2.11 Ranges for Transmission, Detection, and Interference of Signals

The following paragraphs discuss some problems arising in this context, thereby showing the differences between wireless and wired transmission.

2.4.1 Path Loss of Radio Signals

In free space radio signals propagate as light does (independently of their frequency), i.e., they follow a straight line (besides gravitational effects). If such a straight line exists between a sender and a receiver it is called **line-of-sight (LOS)**. Even if no matter exists between the sender and the receiver (i.e., if there is a vacuum), the signal still experiences the **free space loss**. The received power P_r is proportional to $1/d^2$ with d being the distance between sender and receiver (**inverse square law**). The reason for this phenomenon is quite simple. Think of the sender being a point in space. The sender now emits a signal with certain energy. This signal travels away from the sender at the speed of light as a wave with a spherical shape. If there is no obstacle, the sphere continuously grows with the sending energy equally distributed over the sphere's surface. This surface area s grows with the increasing distance d from the center according to the equation $s = 4\pi\, d^2$.

Even without any matter between sender and receiver, additional parameters are important. The received power also depends on the wavelength and the gain of receiver and transmitter antennas. As soon as there is any matter between sender and receiver, the situation becomes more complex. Most radio transmission takes place through the atmosphere—signals travel through air, rain, snow, fog, dust particles, smog etc. While the **path loss** or **attenuation** does not cause too much trouble for short distances, e.g., for LANs, the atmosphere heavily influences transmission over long distances, e.g., satellite transmission. Even mobile phone systems are influenced by weather conditions such as heavy rain. Rain can absorb much of the radiated energy of the antenna (this effect is used in a microwave oven to cook), so communication links may break down as soon as the rain sets in.

Depending on the frequency, radio waves can also penetrate objects. Generally the lower the frequency, the better the penetration. Long waves can be transmitted through the oceans to a submarine while high frequencies can be blocked by a tree. The higher the frequency, the more the behavior of the radio waves resembles that of light—a phenomenon which is clear if one considers the spectrum shown in Figure 2.1.

Radio waves can exhibit three fundamental propagation behaviors depending on their frequency:

- **Ground wave** (<2 MHz): Waves with low frequencies follow the earth's surface and can propagate long distances. These waves are used for, e.g., submarine communication or AM radio.
- **Sky wave** (2–30 MHz): Many international broadcasts and amateur radio use these short waves that are reflected[2] at the ionosphere. This way the waves can bounce back and forth between the ionosphere and the earth's surface, travelling around the world.

[2]Compared to, e.g., the surface of a building, the ionosphere is not really a hard reflecting surface. In the case of sky waves the 'reflection' is caused by refraction.

- **Line-of-sight** (>30 MHz): Mobile phone systems, satellite systems, cordless telephones etc. use even higher frequencies. The emitted waves follow a (more or less) straight line of sight. This enables direct communication with satellites (no reflection at the ionosphere) or microwave links on the ground. However, an additional consideration for ground-based communication is that the waves are bent by the atmosphere due to refraction (see next section).

Almost all communication systems presented in this book work with frequencies above 100 MHz so, we are almost exclusively concerned with LOS communication. But why do mobile phones work even without an LOS?

2.4.2 Additional Signal Propagation Effects

As discussed in the previous section, signal propagation in free space almost follows a straight line, like light. But in real life, we rarely have a line-of-sight between the sender and receiver of radio signals. Mobile phones are typically used in big cities with skyscrapers, on mountains, inside buildings, while driving through an alley, etc. Here several effects occur in addition to the attenuation caused by the distance between sender and receiver, which are again very much frequency dependent.

An extreme form of attenuation is **blocking** or **shadowing** of radio signals due to large obstacles (see Figure 2.12, left side). The higher the frequency of a signal, the more it behaves like light. Even small obstacles like a simple wall, a truck on the street, or trees in an alley may block the signal. Another effect is the **reflection** of signals as shown in the middle of Figure 2.12. If an object is large compared to the wavelength of the signal, e.g., huge buildings, mountains, or the surface of the earth, the signal is reflected. The reflected signal is not as strong as the original, as objects can absorb some of the signal's power. Reflection helps transmitting signals as soon as no LOS exists. This is the standard case for radio transmission in cities or mountain areas. Signals transmitted from a sender may bounce off the walls of buildings several times before they reach the receiver. The more often the signal is reflected, the weaker it becomes. Finally, the right side of Figure 2.12 shows the effect of **refraction**. This effect occurs because the velocity of the electromagnetic waves depends on the density of the medium through which it travels. Only in vacuum does it equal c. As the figure shows, waves that travel into a denser medium are bent towards the medium. This is the reason for LOS radio waves being bent towards the earth: the density of the atmosphere is higher closer to the ground.

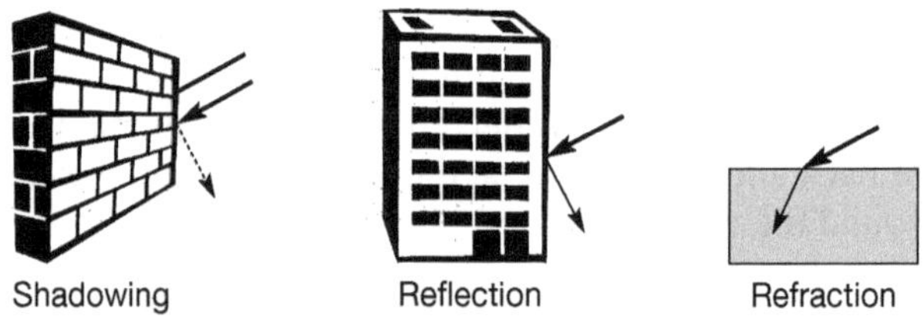

Figure 2.12 Blocking (Shadowing), Reflection and Refraction of Waves

Figure 2.13 Scattering and Diffraction of Waves

While shadowing and reflection are caused by objects much larger than the wavelength of the signals (and demonstrate the typical 'particle' behavior of radio signals), the following two effects exhibit the 'wave' character of radio signals. If the size of an obstacle is in the order of the wavelength or less, then waves can be **scattered** (see Figure 2.13, left side). An incoming signal is scattered into several weaker outgoing signals. In school experiments, this is typically demonstrated with laser light and a very small opening or obstacle, but here we have to take into consideration that the typical wavelength of radio transmission for, e.g., GSM or AMPS is in the order of some 10 cm. Thus, many objects in the environment can cause these scattering effects. Another effect is **diffraction** of waves. As shown on the right side of Figure 2.13, this effect is very similar to scattering. Radio waves will be deflected at an edge and propagate in different directions. The result of scattering and diffraction is patterns with varying signal strengths depending on the location of the receiver.

Effects like attenuation, scattering, diffraction, and refraction all happen simultaneously and are frequency and time dependent. It is very difficult to predict the precise strength of signals at a certain point in space. How do mobile phone operators plan the coverage of their antennas, the location of the antennas, the direction of the beams etc.? Two or three dimensional maps are used with a resolution down to several meters. With the help of, e.g., ray tracing or radiosity techniques similar to rendering 3D graphics, the signal quality can roughly be calculated in advance. Additionally, operators perform a lot of measurements during and after installation of antennas to fill gaps in the coverage.

2.4.3 Multi-Path Propagation

Together with the direct transmission from a sender to a receiver, the propagation effects mentioned in the previous section lead to one of the most severe radio channel impairments, called **multi-path propagation**. Figure 2.14 shows a sender on the left and one possible receiver on the right. Radio waves emitted by the sender can either travel along a straight line, or they may be reflected at a large building, or scattered at smaller obstacles. This simplified figure only shows three possible paths for the signal. In reality, many more paths are possible. Due to the finite speed of light, signals travelling along different paths with different lengths arrive at the receiver at different times. This effect (caused by multi-path propagation) is called **delay spread**: the original signal is spread due to different delays of parts of the signal. This delay spread is a typical effect of radio transmission, because no wire

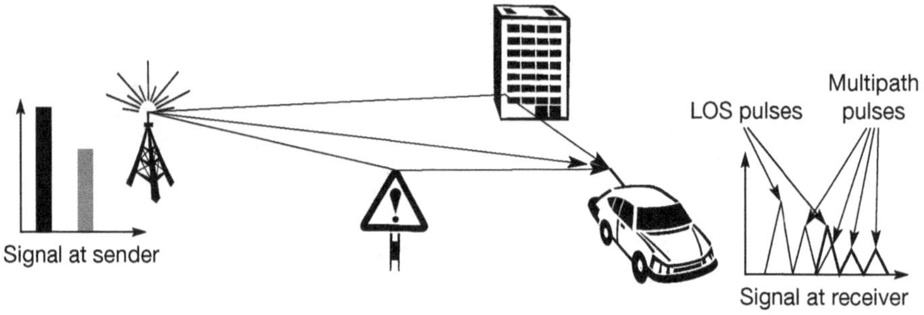

Figure 2.14 Multi-Path Propagation and Intersymbol Interference

guides the waves along a single path as in the case of wired networks (however, a similar effect, dispersion, is known for high bit-rate optical transmission over multimode fiber, see Halsall, 1996, or Stallings, 1997). Notice that this effect has nothing to do with possible movements of the sender or receiver. Typical values for delay spread are approximately 3 μs in cities; up to 12 μs can be observed. GSM, for example, can tolerate up to 16 μs of delay spread, i.e., almost a 5 km path difference.

What are the **effects** of this delay spread on the signals representing the data? The first effect is that a short impulse will be smeared out into a broader impulse, or rather into several weaker impulses. In Figure 2.14 only three possible paths are shown and, thus, the impulse at the sender will result in three smaller impulses at the receiver. For a real situation with hundreds of different paths, this implies that a single impulse will result in many weaker impulses at the receiver. Each path has a different attenuation and, the received pulses have different power. Some of the received pulses will be too weak even to be detected (i.e., they will appear as noise).

Now consider the second impulse shown in Figure 2.14. On the sender side, both impulses are separated. At the receiver, both impulses interfere, i.e., they overlap in time. Now consider that each impulse should represent a symbol, and that one or several symbols could represent a bit. The energy intended for one symbol now spills over to the adjacent symbol, an effect which is called **intersymbol interference (ISI)**. The higher the symbol rate to be transmitted, the worse the effects of ISI will be, as the original symbols are moved closer and closer to each other. ISI limits the bandwidth of a radio channel with multi-path propagation (which is the standard case). Due to this interference, the signals of different symbols can cancel each other out leading to misinterpretations at the receiver and causing transmission errors.

In this case, knowing the channel characteristics can be a great help. If the receiver knows the delays of the different paths (or at least the main paths the signal takes), it can compensate for the distortion caused by the channel. The sender may first transmit a **training sequence** known by the receiver. The receiver then compares the received signal to the original training sequence and programs an **equalizer** that compensates for the distortion (Wesel, 1998), (Pahlavan, 2002), (Stallings, 2002).

While ISI and delay spread already occur in the case of fixed radio transmitters and receivers, the situation is even worse if receivers, or senders, or both, move. Then the channel characteristics change over time, and the paths a signal can travel

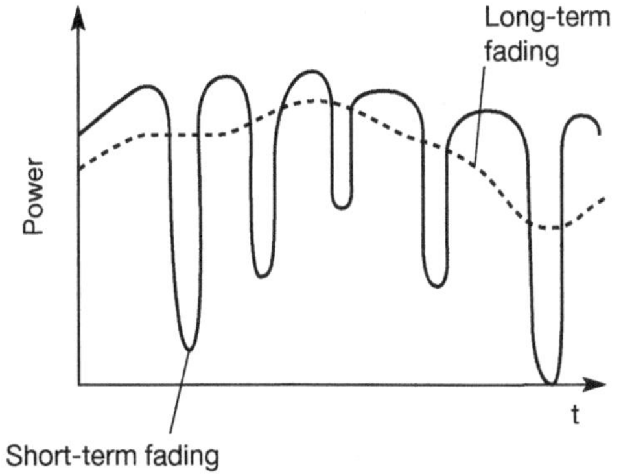

Figure 2.15 Short-Term and Long-Term Fading

along vary. This effect is well known (and audible) with radios while driving. The power of the received signal changes considerably over time. These quick changes in the received power are also called **short-term fading**. Depending on the different paths the signals take, these signals may have a different phase and cancel each other as shown in Figure 2.15. The receiver now has to try to constantly adapt to the varying channel characteristics, e.g., by changing the parameters of the equalizer. However, if these changes are too fast, such as driving on a highway through a city, the receiver cannot adapt fast enough and the error rate of transmission increases dramatically.

An additional effect shown in Figure 2.15 is the **long-term fading** of the received signal. This long-term fading, shown here as the average power over time, is caused by, for example, varying distance to the sender or more remote obstacles. Typically, senders can compensate for long-term fading by increasing/decreasing sending power so that the received signal always stays within certain limits.

There are many more effects influencing radio transmission which will not be discussed in detail—for example, the **Doppler shift** caused by a moving sender or receiver. While this effect is audible for acoustic waves already at low speed, it is also a topic for radio transmission from or to fast moving transceivers. One example of such a transceiver could be a satellite—there Doppler shift causes random frequency shifts. The interested reader is referred to Anderson (1995), (Pahlavan, 2002), and (Stallings, 2002) for more information about the characteristics of wireless communication channels. For the present it will suffice to know that multi-path propagation limits the maximum bandwidth due to ISI and that moving transceivers cause additional problems due to varying channel characteristics.

2.5 MULTIPLEXING

Multiplexing is not only a fundamental mechanism in communication systems but also in everyday life. Multiplexing describes how several users can share a medium with minimum or no interference. One example is highways with several lanes. Many users (car drivers) use the same medium (the highways) with hopefully no interference (i.e., accidents). This is possible due to the provision of several lanes (space division multiplexing) separating the traffic. In addition, different cars use the same medium (i.e., the same lane) at different points in time (time division multiplexing).

While this simple example illustrates our everyday use of multiplexing, the following examples will deal with the use of multiplexing in wireless communications.

2.5.1 Space Division Multiplexing

For wireless communication, multiplexing can be carried out in four dimensions: **space**, **time**, **frequency**, and **code**. In this field, the task of multiplexing is to assign space, time, frequency, and code to each communication channel with a minimum of interference and a maximum of medium utilization. The term communication channel here only refers to an association of sender(s) and receiver(s) who want to exchange data.

Figure 2.16 shows six channels k_i and introduces a three dimensional coordinate system. This system shows the dimensions of code c, time t and frequency f. For this first type of multiplexing, **space division multiplexing (SDM)**, the (three dimensional) space s_i is also shown. Here space is represented via circles indicating the interference range as introduced in Figure 2.11. How is the separation of the different channels achieved? The channels k_1 to k_3 can be mapped onto the three 'spaces'

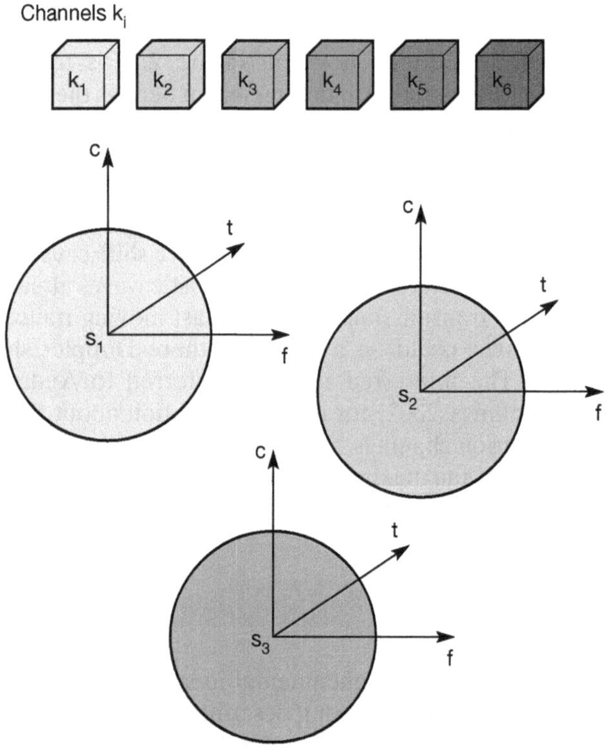

Figure 2.16 Space Division Multiplexing (SDM)

s_1 to s_3 which clearly separate the channels and prevent the interference ranges from overlapping. The space between the interference ranges is sometimes called **guard space**. Such a guard space is needed in all four multiplexing schemes presented.

For the remaining channels (k_4 to k_6) three additional spaces would be needed. In our highway example this would imply that each driver had his or her own lane. Although this procedure clearly represents a waste of space, this is exactly the principle used by the old analog telephone system: each subscriber is given a separate pair of copper wires to the local exchange. In wireless transmission, SDM implies a separate sender for each communication channel with a wide enough distance between senders. This multiplexing scheme is used, for example, at FM radio stations where the transmission range is limited to a certain region—many radio stations around the world can use the same frequency without interference. Using SDM, obvious problems arise if two or more channels were established within the same space, for example, if several radio stations want to broadcast in the same city. Then, one of the following multiplexing schemes must be used (frequency, time, or code division multiplexing).

2.5.2 Frequency Division Multiplexing

Frequency division multiplexing (FDM) describes schemes to subdivide the frequency dimension into several non-overlapping frequency bands as shown in Figure 2.17. Each channel k_i is now allotted its own frequency band as indicated. Senders using a certain frequency band can use this band continuously. Again, **guard spaces** are needed to avoid frequency band overlapping (also called **adjacent channel interference**). This scheme is used for radio stations within the same region, where each radio station has its own frequency. This very simple multiplexing scheme does not need complex coordination between sender and receiver: the receiver only has to tune in to the specific sender.

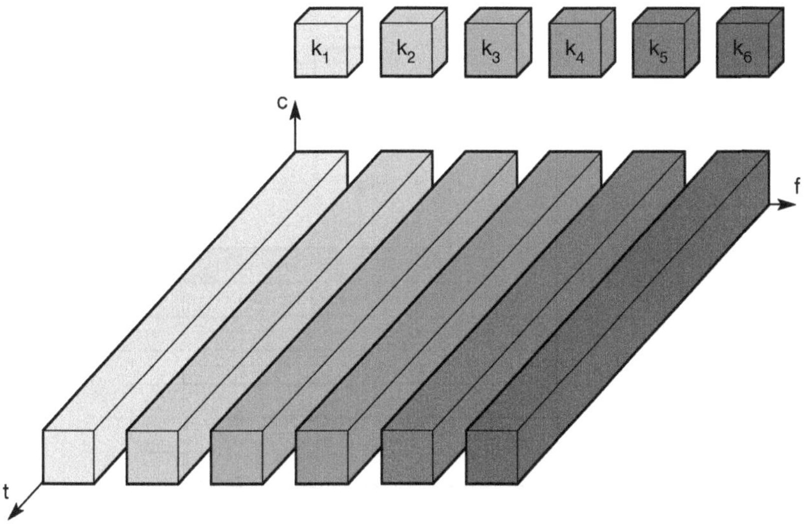

Figure 2.17 Frequency Division Multiplexing (FDM)

However, this scheme also has disadvantages. While radio stations broadcast 24 hours a day, mobile communication typically takes place for only a few minutes at a time. Assigning a separate frequency for each possible communication scenario would be a tremendous waste of (scarce) frequency resources. Additionally, the fixed assignment of a frequency to a sender makes the scheme very inflexible and limits the number of senders.

2.5.3 Time Division Multiplexing

A more flexible multiplexing scheme for typical mobile communications is **time division multiplexing (TDM)**. Here a channel k_i is given the whole bandwidth for a certain amount of time, i.e., all senders use the same frequency but at different points in time (see Figure 2.18). Again, **guard spaces**, which now represent time gaps, have to separate the different periods when the senders use the medium. In our highway example, this would refer to the gap between two cars. If two transmissions overlap in time, this is called co-channel interference. (In the highway example, interference between two cars results in an accident.) To avoid this type of interference, precise synchronization between different senders is necessary. This is clearly a disadvantage, as all senders need precise clocks or, alternatively, a way has to be found to distribute a synchronization signal to all senders. For a receiver tuning in to a sender this does not just involve adjusting the frequency, but involves listening at exactly the right point in time. However, this scheme is quite flexible as one can assign more sending time to senders with a heavy load and less to those with a light load.

Frequency and time division multiplexing can be combined, i.e., a channel k_i can use a certain frequency band for a certain amount of time as shown in Figure 2.19. Now guard spaces are needed both in the time and in the frequency dimension. This scheme is more robust against frequency selective interference, i.e., interference in a certain small frequency band. A channel may use this band only for

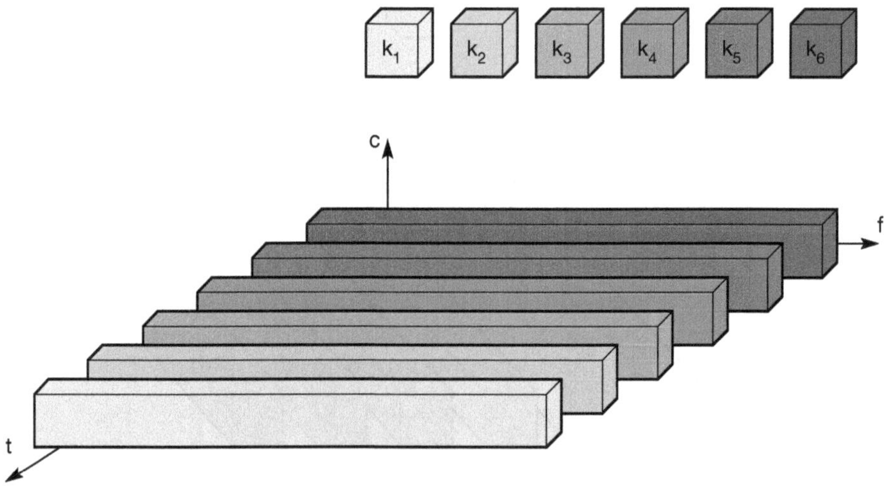

Figure 2.18 Time Division Multiplexing (TDM)

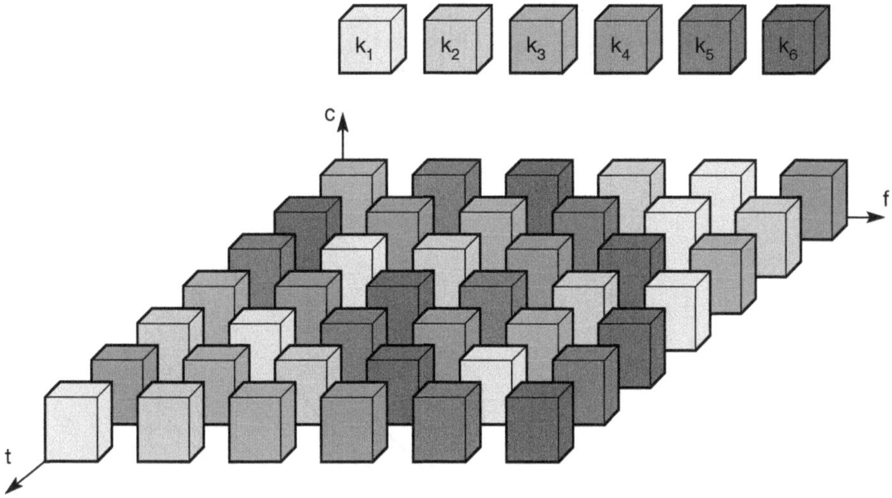

Figure 2.19 Frequency and Time Division Multiplexing Combined

a short period of time. Additionally, this scheme provides some (weak) protection against tapping, as in this case the sequence of frequencies a sender uses has to be known to listen in to a channel. The mobile phone standard GSM uses this combination of frequency and time division multiplexing for transmission between a mobile phone and a so-called base station.

A disadvantage of this scheme is again the necessary coordination between different senders. One has to control the sequence of frequencies and the time of changing to another frequency. Two senders will interfere as soon as they select the same frequency at the same time. However, if the frequency change (also called frequency hopping) is fast enough, the periods of interference may be so small that, depending on the coding of data into signals, a receiver can still recover the original data. (This technique is discussed in section 2.7.2.)

2.5.4 Code Division Multiplexing

While SDM and FDM are well known from the early days of radio transmission and TDM is used in connection with many applications, **code division multiplexing (CDM)** is a relatively new scheme in commercial communication systems. First used in military applications due to its inherent security features (together with spread spectrum techniques, see section 2.7), it now features in many civil wireless transmission scenarios thanks to the availability of cheap processing power. Figure 2.20 shows how all channels k_i use the same frequency at the same time for transmission. Separation is now achieved by assigning each channel its own 'code'; **guard spaces** are realized by using codes with the necessary 'distance' in code space, e.g., **orthogonal codes**. The technical realization of CDM is discussed in section 2.7 together with the medium access mechanisms. An excellent book dealing with all aspects of CDM is Viterbi (1995).

The typical everyday example of CDM is a party with many participants from different countries around the world who establish communication channels, i.e.,

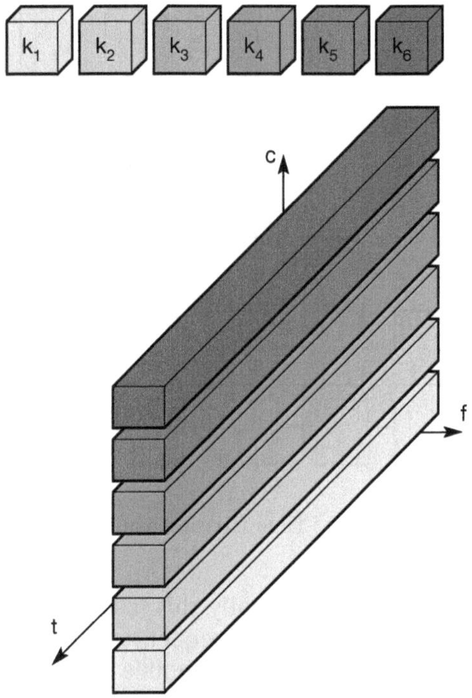

Figure 2.20 Code Division Multiplexing (CDM)

they talk to each other, using the same frequency range (approx. 300–6000 Hz depending on a person's voice) at the same time. If everybody speaks the same language, SDM is needed to be able to communicate (i.e., standing in groups, talking with limited transmit power). But as soon as another code, i.e., another language, is used, one can tune in to this language and clearly separate communication in this language from all the other languages. (The other languages appear as background noise.) This explains why CDM has built-in security: if the language is unknown, the signals can still be received, but they are useless. By using a secret code (or language), a secure channel can be established in a 'hostile' environment. (At parties this may cause some confusion.) Guard spaces are also of importance in this illustrative example. Using, e.g., Swedish and Norwegian does not really work; the languages are too close. But Swedish and Finnish are 'orthogonal' enough to separate the communication channels.

The main advantage of CDM for wireless transmission is that it gives good protection against interference and tapping. Different codes have to be assigned, but code space is huge compared to the frequency space. Assigning individual codes to each sender does not usually cause problems. The main disadvantage of this scheme is the relatively high complexity of the receiver. A receiver has to know the code and must separate the channel with user data from the background noise composed of other signals and environmental noise. Additionally, a receiver must be precisely synchronized with the transmitter to apply the decoding correctly. The voice example also gives a hint to another problem of CDM receivers. All signals should reach a receiver with almost equal strength, otherwise some signals could drain others. If some people close to a receiver talk very loudly the language does not matter. The receiver cannot listen to any other person. To apply CDM, precise power control is required.

2.6 MODULATION

Section 2.2 introduced the basic function of a sine wave which already indicates the three basic modulation schemes (typically, the cosine function is used for explanation):

$$g(t) = A_t \cos(2\pi f_t t + \varphi_t)$$

This function has three parameters: amplitude A_t, frequency f_t, and phase φ_t which may be varied in accordance with data or another modulating signal. For **digital modulation**, which is the main topic in this section, digital data (0 and 1) is translated into an analog signal (baseband signal). Digital modulation is required if digital data has to be transmitted over a medium that only allows for analog transmission. One example for wired networks is the old analog telephone system—to connect a computer to this system a modem is needed. The modem then performs the translation of digital data into analog signals and vice versa. Digital transmission is used, for example, in wired local area networks or within a computer (Halsall, 1996), (Stallings, 1997). The three basic methods for this translation are **amplitude shift keying (ASK)**, **frequency shift keying (FSK)**, and **phase shift keying (PSK)**. These are discussed in more detail in the following sections.

Apart from the translation of digital data into analog signals, wireless transmission requires an additional modulation, an **analog modulation** that shifts the center frequency of the baseband signal generated by the digital modulation up to the radio carrier. For example, digital modulation translates a 1 Mbit/s bit-stream into a baseband signal with a bandwidth of 1 MHz. There are several reasons why this baseband signal cannot be directly transmitted in a wireless system:

- **Antennas**: As shown in section 2.3, an antenna must be the order of magnitude of the signal's wavelength in size to be effective. For the 1 MHz signal in the example this would result in an antenna some hundred meters high, which is obviously not very practical for handheld devices. With 1 GHz, antennas a few centimeters in length can be used.
- **Frequency division multiplexing**: Using only baseband transmission, FDM could not be applied. Analog modulation shifts the baseband signals to different carrier frequencies as required in section 2.5.2. The higher the carrier frequency, the more bandwidth that is available for many baseband signals.
- **Medium characteristics**: Path-loss, penetration of obstacles, reflection, scattering, and diffraction—all the effects discussed in section 2.4 depend heavily on the wavelength of the signal. Depending on the application, the right carrier frequency with the desired characteristics has to be chosen: long waves for

submarines, short waves for handheld devices, very short waves for directed microwave transmission etc.

As for digital modulation, three different basic schemes are known for analog modulation: **amplitude modulation (AM)**, **frequency modulation (FM)**, and **phase modulation (PM)**. The reader is referred to Halsall (1996) and Stallings (2002) for more details about these analog modulation schemes.

Figure 2.21 shows a (simplified) block diagram of a radio transmitter for digital data. The first step is the digital modulation of data into the analog baseband signal according to one of the schemes presented in the following sections. The analog modulation then shifts the center frequency of the analog signal up to the radio carrier. This signal is then transmitted via the antenna.

The receiver (see Figure 2.22) receives the analog radio signal via its antenna and demodulates the signal into the analog baseband signal with the help of the known carrier. This would be all that is needed for an analog radio tuned in to a radio station. (The analog baseband signal would constitute the music.) For digital data, another step is needed. Bits or frames have to be detected, i.e., the receiver must synchronize with the sender. How synchronization is achieved depends on the digital modulation scheme. After synchronization, the receiver has to decide if the signal represents a digital 1 or a 0, reconstructing the original data.

The digital modulation schemes presented in the following sections differ in many issues, such as **spectral efficiency** (i.e., how efficiently the modulation scheme utilizes the available frequency spectrum), **power efficiency** (i.e., how much power is needed to transfer bits—which is very important for portable devices that are battery dependent), and **robustness** to multi-path propagation, noise, and interference (Wesel, 1998).

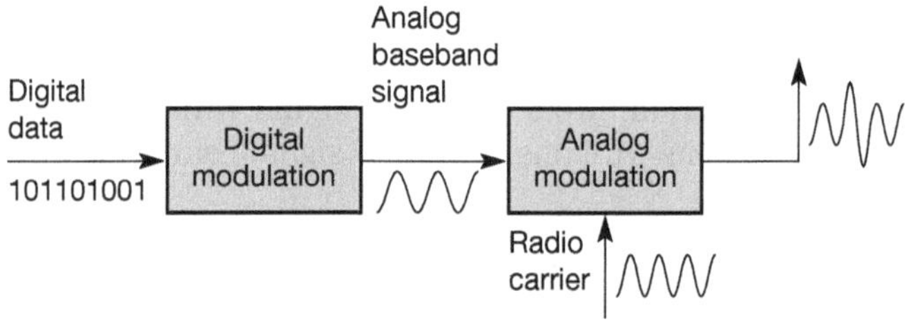

Figure 2.21 Modulation in a Transmitter

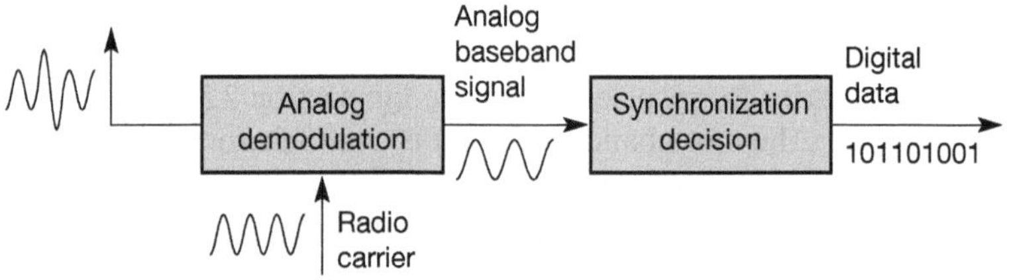

Figure 2.22 Demodulation and Data Reconstruction in a Receiver

2.6.1 Amplitude Shift Keying

Figure 2.23 illustrates **amplitude shift keying (ASK)**, the most simple digital modulation scheme. The two binary values, 1 and 0, are represented by two different amplitudes. In the example, one of the amplitudes is 0 (representing the binary 0). This simple scheme only requires low bandwidth, but is very susceptible to interference. Effects like multi-path propagation, noise, or path loss heavily influence the amplitude. In a wireless environment, a constant amplitude cannot be guaranteed, so ASK is typically not used for wireless radio transmission. However, the wired transmission scheme with the highest performance, namely optical transmission, uses ASK. Here, a light pulse may represent a 1, while the absence of light represents a 0. The carrier frequency in optical systems is some hundred THz. ASK can also be applied to wireless infra red transmission, using a directed beam or diffuse light.

2.6.2 Frequency Shift Keying

A modulation scheme often used for wireless transmission is **frequency shift keying (FSK)** (see Figure 2.24). The simplest form of FSK, also called **binary FSK (BFSK)**, assigns one frequency f_1 to the binary 1 and another frequency f_2 to the binary 0. A very simple way to implement FSK is to switch between two oscillators, one with the frequency f_1 and the other with f_2, depending on the input. To avoid sudden changes in phase, special frequency modulators with **continuous phase modulation (CPM)**

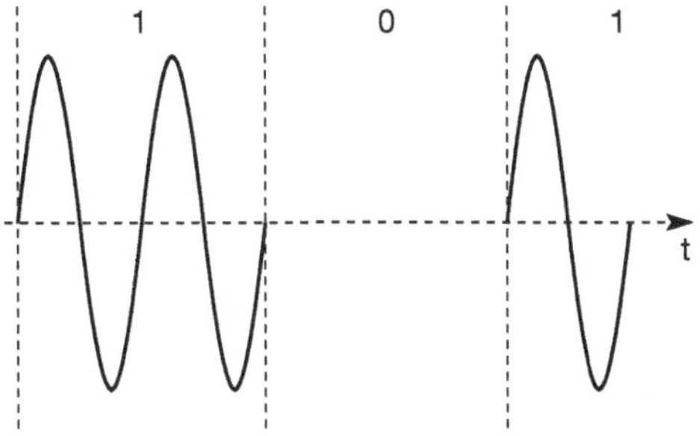

Figure 2.23 Amplitude Shift Keying (ASK)

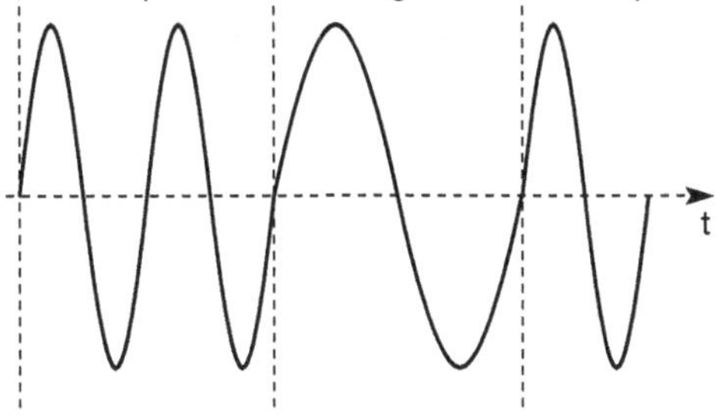

Figure 2.24 Frequency Shift Keying (FSK)

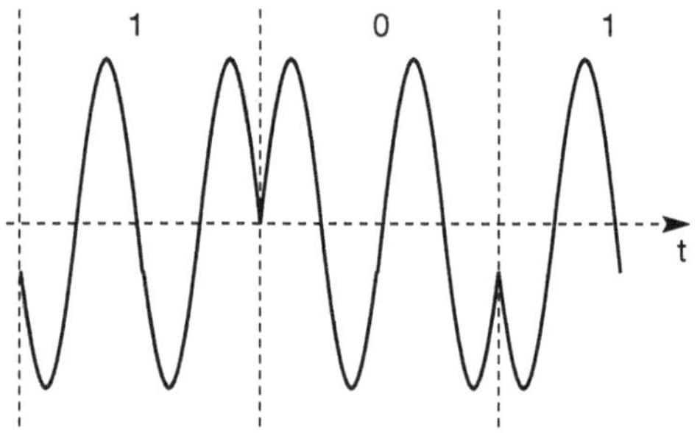

Figure 2.25 Phase Shift Keying (PSK)

can be used. Sudden changes in phase cause high frequencies, which is an undesired side-effect.

A simple way to implement demodulation is by using two bandpass filters, one for f_1 the other for f_2. A comparator can then compare the signal levels of the filter outputs to decide which of them is stronger. FSK needs a larger bandwidth compared to ASK but is much less susceptible to errors.

2.6.3 Phase Shift Keying

Finally, **phase shift keying (PSK)** uses shifts in the phase of a signal to represent data. Figure 2.25 shows a phase shift of 180° or π as the 0 follows the 1 (the same happens as the 1 follows the 0). This simple scheme, shifting the phase by 180° each time the value of data changes, is also called **binary PSK (BPSK)**. A simple implementation of a BPSK modulator could multiply a frequency f with +1 if the binary data is 1 and with –1 if the binary data is 0.

To receive the signal correctly, the receiver must synchronize in frequency and phase with the transmitter. This can be done using a **phase lock loop (PLL)**. Compared to FSK, PSK is more resistant to interference, but receiver and transmitter are also more complex.

2.6.4 Advanced Frequency Shift Keying

A famous FSK scheme used in many wireless systems is **minimum shift keying (MSK)**. MSK is basically BFSK without abrupt phase changes, i.e., it belongs to CPM schemes. Figure 2.26 shows an example for the implementation of MSK. In a first step, data bits are separated into even and odd bits, the duration of each bit being doubled. The scheme also uses two frequencies: f_1, the lower frequency, and f_2, the higher frequency, with $f_2 = 2f_1$.

According to the following scheme, the lower or higher frequency is chosen (either inverted or non-inverted) to generate the MSK signal:

- if the even and the odd bit are both 0, then the higher frequency f_2 is inverted (i.e., f_2 is used with a phase shift of 180°);
- if the even bit is 1, the odd bit 0, then the lower frequency f_1 is inverted. This is the case, e.g., in the fifth to seventh columns of Figure 2.26,

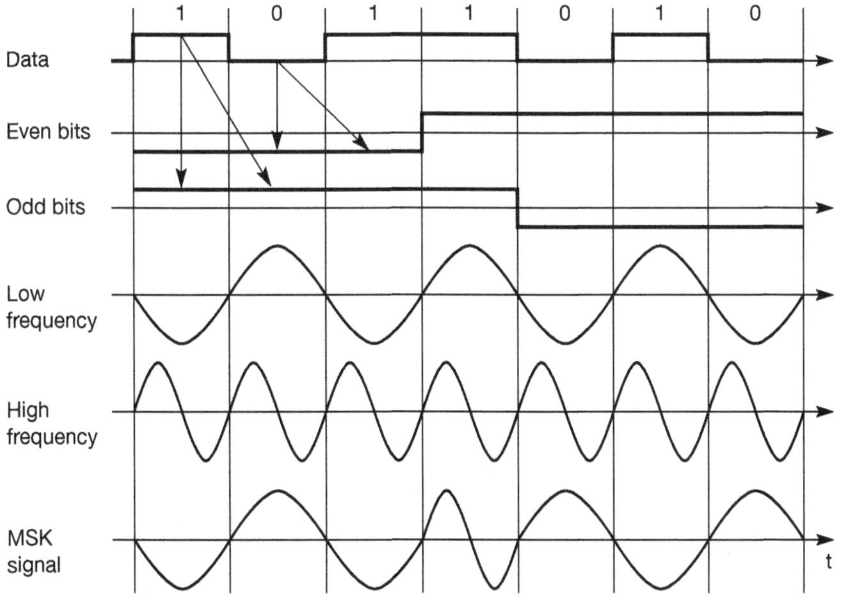

Figure 2.26 Minimum Shift Keying (MSK)

- if the even bit is 0 and the odd bit is 1, as in columns 1 to 3, f_1 is taken without changing the phase,
- if both bits are 1 then the original f_2 is taken.

A high frequency is always chosen if even and odd bits are equal. The signal is inverted if the odd bit equals 0. This scheme avoids all phase shifts in the resulting MSK signal.

Adding a so-called Gaussian lowpass filter to the MSK scheme results in **Gaussian MSK (GMSK)**, which is the digital modulation scheme for many European wireless standards. The filter reduces the large spectrum needed by MSK.

2.6.5 Advanced Phase Shift Keying

The simple PSK scheme can be improved in many ways. The basic BPSK scheme only uses one possible phase shift of 180°. The left side of Figure 2.27 shows BPSK in the phase domain (which is typically the better representation compared to the time domain in Figure 2.25). The right side of Figure 2.27 shows **quadrature PSK (QPSK)**, one of the most common PSK schemes (sometimes also called quaternary PSK). Here, higher bit rates can be achieved for the same bandwidth by coding two bits into one phase shift. Alternatively, one can reduce the bandwidth and still achieve the same bit rates as for BPSK.

QPSK (and other PSK schemes) can be realized in two variants. The phase shift can always be relative to a **reference signal** (with the same frequency). If this scheme is used, a phase shift of 0 means that the signal is in phase with the reference signal. A QPSK signal will then exhibit a phase shift of 45° for the data 11, 135° for

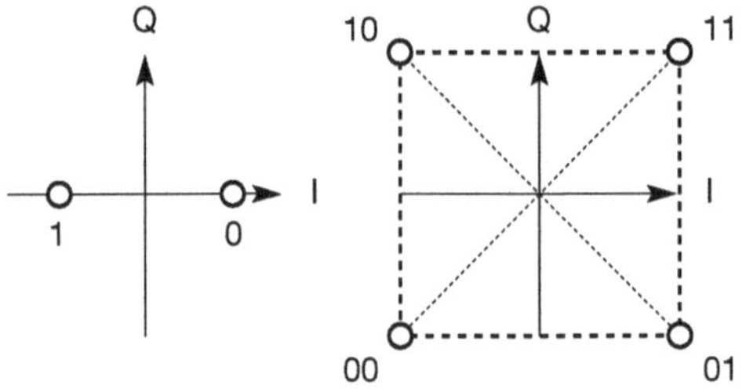

Figure 2.27 BPSK and QPSK in the Phase Domain

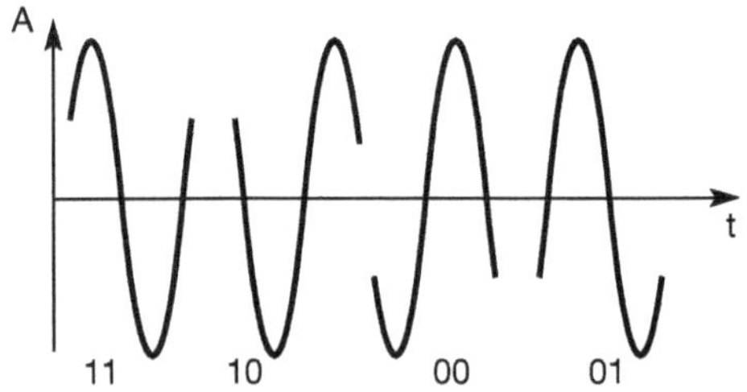

Figure 2.28 QPSK in the Time Domain

10, 225° for 00, and 315° for 01—with all phase shifts being relative to the reference signal. The transmitter 'selects' parts of the signal as shown in Figure 2.28 and concatenates them. To reconstruct data, the receiver has to compare the incoming signal with the reference signal. One problem of this scheme involves producing a reference signal at the receiver. Transmitter and receiver have to be synchronized very often, e.g., by using special synchronization patterns before user data arrives or via a pilot frequency as reference.

One way to avoid this problem is to use **differential QPSK (DQPSK)**. Here the phase shift is not relative to a reference signal but to the phase of the previous two bits. In this case, the receiver does not need the reference signal but only compares two signals to reconstruct data. DQPSK is used in US wireless technologies IS-136 and PACS and in Japanese PHS.

One could now think of extending the scheme to more and more angles for shifting the phase. For instance, one can think of coding 3 bits per phase shift using 8 angles. Additionally, the PSK scheme could be combined with ASK as is done for example in **quadrature amplitude modulation (QAM)** for standard 9,600 bit/s modems (left side of Figure 2.29). Here, three different amplitudes and 12 angles are combined coding 4 bits per phase/amplitude change. Problems occur for wireless communication in case of noise or ISI. The more 'points' used in the phase domain, the harder it is to separate them. DQPSK has been proven as one of the most efficient schemes under these considerations (Wesel, 1998).

A more advanced scheme is a hierarchical modulation as used in the digital TV standard DVB-T. The right side of Figure 2.29 shows a 64 QAM that contains a

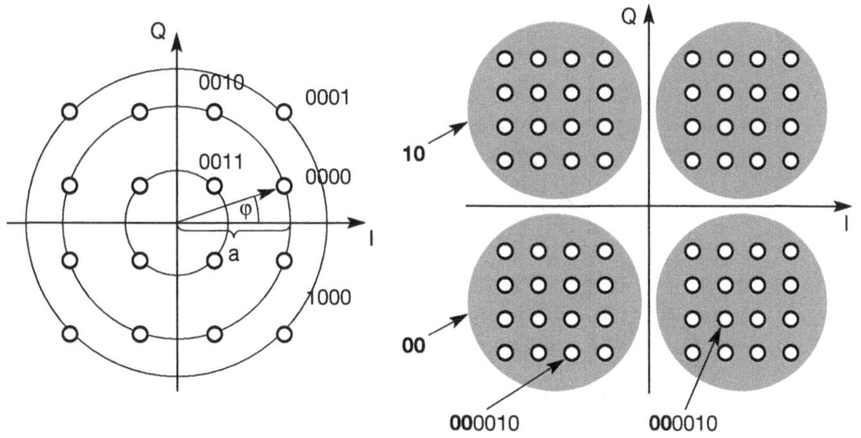

Figure 2.29 16 Quadrature Amplitude Modulation and Hierarchical 64 QAM

QPSK modulation. A 64 QAM can code 6 bit per symbol. Here the two most significant bits are used for the QPSK signal embedded in the QAM signal. If the reception of the signal is good the entire QAM constellation can be resolved. Under poor reception conditions, e.g., with moving receivers, only the QPSK portion can be resolved. A high priority data stream in DVB-T is coded with QPSK using the two most significant bits. The remaining 4 bits represent low priority data. For TV this could mean that the standard resolution data stream is coded with high priority, the high resolution information with low priority. If the signal is distorted, at least the standard TV resolution can be received.

2.6.6 Multi-Carrier Modulation

Special modulation schemes that stand somewhat apart from the others are **multi-carrier modulation (MCM)**, **orthogonal frequency division multiplexing (OFDM)** or **coded OFDM (COFDM)** that are used in the context of digital radio system DAB and the WLAN standards IEEE 802.11a/g/n and HiperLAN2. The main attraction of MCM is its good ISI mitigation property. As explained in section 2.4.3, higher bit rates are more vulnerable to ISI. MCM splits the high bit rate stream into many lower bit rate streams (see Figure 2.30), each stream being sent using an independent carrier frequency. If, for example, n symbols/s have to be transmitted, each subcarrier transmits n/c symbols/s with c being the number of subcarriers. One symbol could, for example represent 2 bit as in QPSK. DAB, for example, uses between 192 and 1,536 of these subcarriers. The physical layer of HiperLAN2 and IEEE 802.11a uses 48 subcarriers for data.

Figure 2.31 shows the superposition of orthogonal frequencies. The maximum of one subcarrier frequency appears exactly at a frequency where all other subcarriers equal zero.

Using this scheme, frequency selective fading only influences some subcarriers, and not the whole signal—an additional benefit of MCM. Typically, MCM transmits symbols with guard spaces between single symbols or groups of symbols. This helps the receiver to handle multi-path propagation. OFDM is a special method of

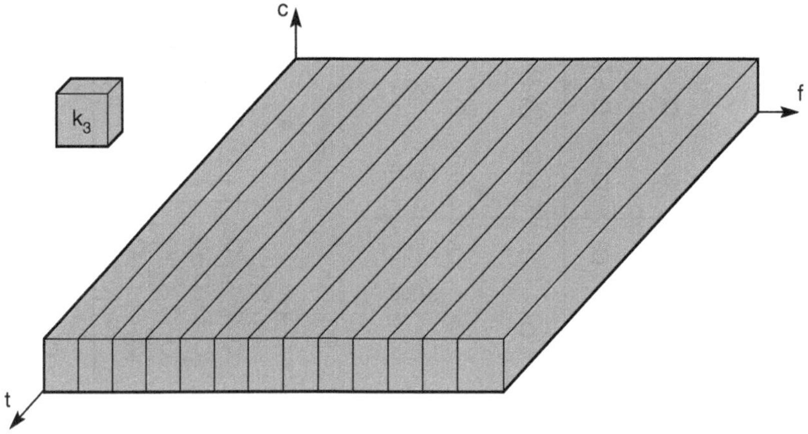

Figure 2.30 Parallel Data Transmission on Several Subcarriers with Lower Rate

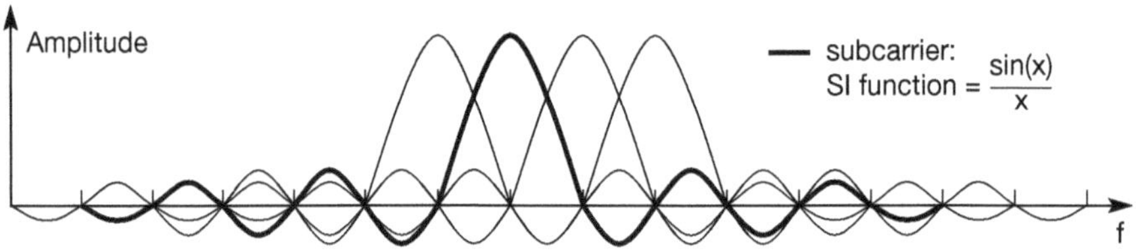

Figure 2.31 Superposition of Orthogonal Frequencies

implementing MCM using orthogonal carriers. Computationally, this is a very efficient algorithm based on fast Fourier transform (FFT) for modulation/demodulation. If additional error-control coding across the symbols in different subcarriers is applied, the system is referred to as COFDM. More details about the implementation of MCM, OFDM, and COFDM can be found in Wesel (1998), Pahlavan (2002), and ETSI (1997).

2.7 SPREAD SPECTRUM

As the name implies, **spread spectrum** techniques involve spreading the bandwidth needed to transmit data—which does not make sense at first sight. Spreading the bandwidth has several advantages. The main advantage is the resistance to **narrowband interference**. In Figure 2.32, diagram i) shows an idealized narrowband signal from a sender of user data (here power density dP/df versus frequency f). The sender now spreads the signal in step ii), i.e., converts the narrowband signal into a broadband signal. The energy needed to transmit the signal (the area shown in the diagram) is the same, but it is now spread over a larger frequency range. The power level of the spread signal can be much lower than that of the original narrowband signal without losing data. Depending on the generation and reception of the spread signal, the power level of the user signal can even be as low as the background noise.

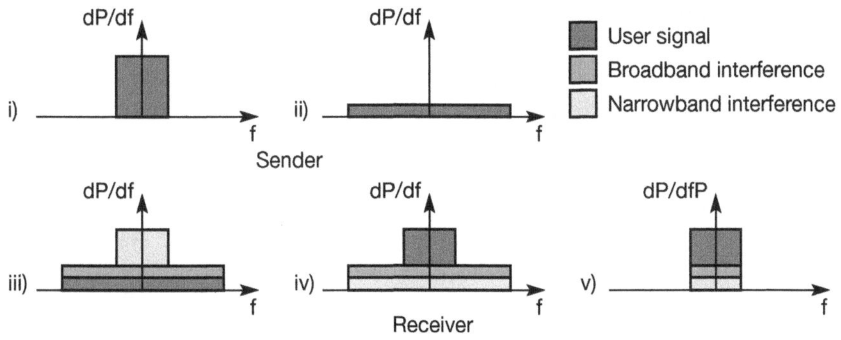

Figure 2.32 Spread Spectrum: Spreading and Despreading

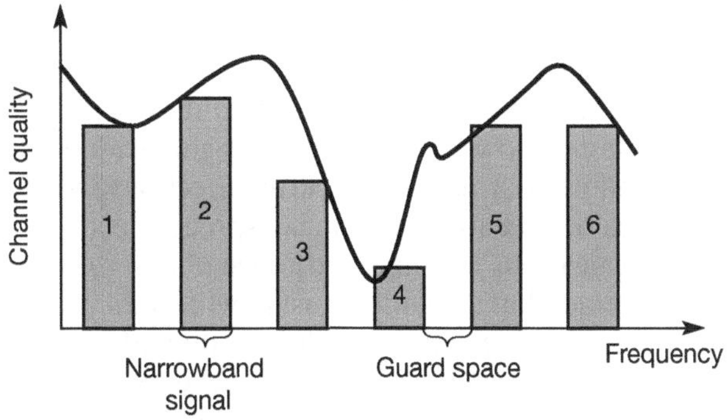

Figure 2.33 Narrowband Interference without Spread Spectrum

This makes it difficult to distinguish the user signal from the background noise and thus hard to detect.

During transmission, narrowband and broadband interference add to the signal in step iii). The sum of interference and user signal is received. The receiver now knows how to despread the signal, converting the spread user signal into a narrowband signal again, while spreading the narrowband interference and leaving the broadband interference. In step v) the receiver applies a bandpass filter to cut off frequencies left and right of the narrowband signal. Finally, the receiver can reconstruct the original data because the power level of the user signal is high enough, i.e., the signal is much stronger than the remaining interference. The following sections show how spreading can be performed.

Just as spread spectrum helps to deal with narrowband interference for a single channel, it can be used for several channels. Consider the situation shown in Figure 2.33. Six different channels use FDM for multiplexing, which means that each channel has its own narrow frequency band for transmission. Between each frequency band a guard space is needed to avoid adjacent channel interference. As mentioned in section 2.5.2, this method requires careful frequency planning. Additionally, Figure 2.33 depicts a certain channel quality. This is frequency dependent and is a measure for interference at this frequency. Channel quality also changes over time—the diagram only shows a snapshot at one moment. Depending on receiver characteristics, channels 1, 2, 5, and 6 could be received while the quality of channels 3 and 4 is too bad to reconstruct transmitted data. Narrowband interference destroys the transmission of channels 3 and 4. This illustration only represents a snapshot and the situation could be completely different at the next moment. All in all, communication may be very difficult using such narrowband signals.

How can spread spectrum help in such a situation? As already shown, spread spectrum can increase resistance to narrowband interference. The same technique is now applied to all narrowband signals. As shown in Figure 2.34, all narrowband signals are now spread into broadband signals using the same frequency range. No more frequency planning is needed (under these simplified assumptions), and all senders use the same frequency band. But how can receivers recover their signal?

To separate different channels, CDM is now used instead of FDM. This application shows the tight coupling of CDM and spread spectrum. Spreading of a narrowband signal is achieved using a special code as shown in sections 2.7.1 and 2.7.2. Each channel is allotted its own code, which the receivers have to apply to recover the signal. Without knowing the code, the signal cannot be recovered and behaves like background noise. This is the security effect of spread spectrum if a secret code is used for spreading. Features that make spread spectrum and CDM very attractive for military applications are the coexistence of several signals without coordination (apart from the fact that the codes must have certain properties), robustness against narrowband interference, relative high security, and a characteristic like background noise. Only the appropriate (secret) codes have to be exchanged.

Apart from military uses, the combination of spread spectrum and CDM is becoming more and more attractive for everyday applications. As mentioned before, frequencies are a scarce resource around the world, particularly license-free bands. Spread spectrum now allows an overlay of new transmission technology at exactly the same frequency at which current narrowband systems are already operating. This is used by US mobile phone systems. While the frequency band around 850 MHz had already been in use for TDM and FDM systems (AMPS and IS-54), the introduction of a system using CDM (IS-95) was still possible.

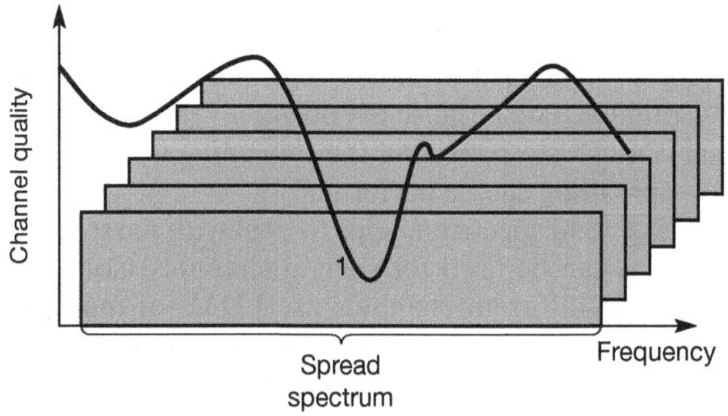

Figure 2.34 Spread Spectrum to Avoid Narrowband Interference

Spread spectrum technologies also exhibit drawbacks. One disadvantage is the increased complexity of receivers that have to despread a signal. Today despreading can be performed up to high data rates thanks to digital signal processing. Another problem is the large frequency band that is needed due to the spreading of the signal. Although spread signals appear more like noise, they still raise the background noise level and may interfere with other transmissions if no special precautions are taken.

Spreading the spectrum can be achieved in two different ways as shown in the following two sections.

2.7.1 Direct Sequence Spread Spectrum

Direct sequence spread spectrum (DSSS) systems take a user bit stream and perform an (XOR) with a so-called **chipping sequence** as shown in Figure 2.35. The example shows that the result is either the sequence 0110101 (if the user bit equals 0) or its complement 1001010 (if the user bit equals 1). While each user bit has a duration t_b, the chipping sequence consists of smaller pulses, called **chips**, with a duration t_c. If the chipping sequence is generated properly it appears as random noise: this sequence is also sometimes called **pseudo-noise** sequence. The **spreading factor** $s = t_b/t_c$ determines the bandwidth of the resulting signal. If the original signal needs a bandwidth w, the resulting signal needs s·w after spreading. While the spreading factor of the very simple example is only 7 (and the chipping sequence 0110101 is not very random), civil applications use spreading factors between 10 and 100, and military applications use factors of up to 10,000. Wireless LANs complying with the standard IEEE 802.11 use, for example, the sequence 10110111000, a so-called Barker code, if implemented using DSSS. Barker codes exhibit a good robustness against interference and insensitivity to multi-path propagation. Other known Barker codes are 11, 110, 1110, 11101, 1110010, and 1111100110101 (Stallings, 2002).

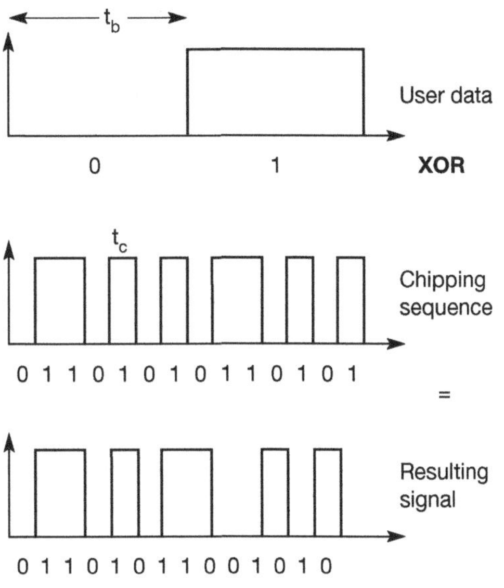

Figure 2.35 Spreading with DSSS

Up to now only the spreading has been explained. However, transmitters and receivers using DSSS need additional components as shown in the simplified block diagrams in Figure 2.36 and Figure 2.37. The first step in a DSSS transmitter, Figure 2.36, is the spreading of the user data with the chipping sequence (**digital modulation**). The spread signal is then modulated with a radio carrier as explained in section 2.6 (**radio modulation**). Assume for example a user signal with a bandwidth of 1 MHz. Spreading with the above 11-chip Barker code would result in a signal with 11 MHz bandwidth. The radio carrier then shifts this signal to the carrier frequency (e.g., 2.4 GHz in the ISM band). This signal is then transmitted.

The DSSS receiver is more complex than the transmitter. The receiver only has to perform the inverse functions of the two transmitter modulation steps. However, noise and multi-path propagation require additional mechanisms to reconstruct the original data. The first step in the receiver involves demodulating the received signal. This is achieved using the same carrier as the transmitter reversing the modulation and results in a signal with approximately the same bandwidth as the original spread spectrum signal. Additional filtering can be applied to generate this signal.

While demodulation is well known from ordinary radio receivers, the next steps constitute a real challenge for DSSS receivers, contributing to the complexity of the system. The receiver has to know the original chipping sequence, i.e., the receiver basically generates the same pseudo random sequence as the transmitter. Sequences at the sender and receiver have to be precisely synchronized because the receiver calculates the product of a chip with the incoming signal. This comprises another XOR operation, together with a medium access mechanism that relies on this scheme. During a bit period, which also has to be derived via synchronization, an **integrator** adds all these products. Calculating the products of chips and signal,

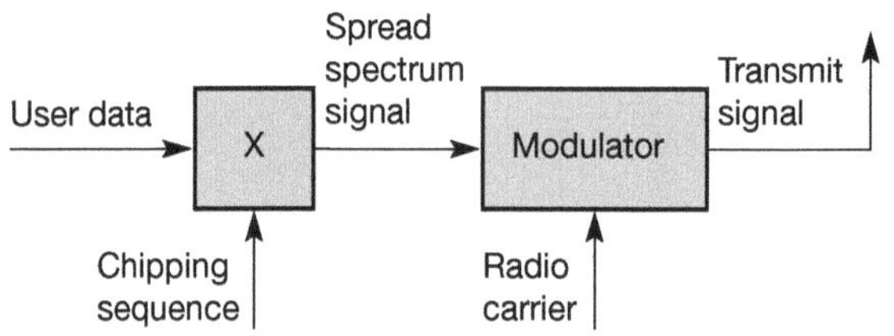

Figure 2.36 DSSS Transmitter

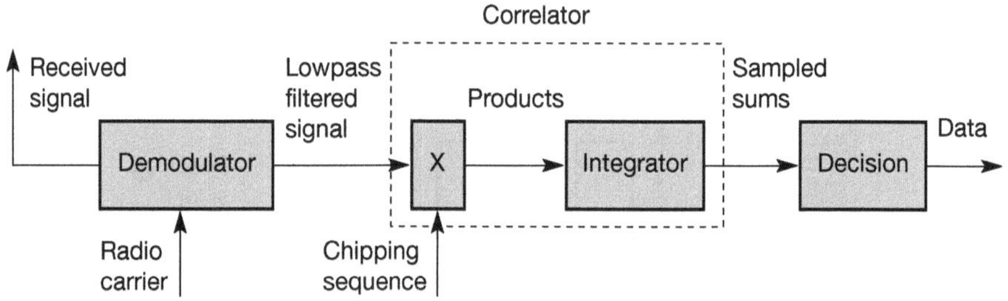

Figure 2.37 DSSS Receiver

and adding the products in an integrator is also called correlation, the device a **correlator**. Finally, in each bit period a **decision unit** samples the sums generated by the integrator and decides if this sum represents a binary 1 or a 0.

If transmitter and receiver are perfectly synchronized and the signal is not too distorted by noise or multi-path propagation, DSSS works perfectly well according to the simple scheme shown. Sending the user data 01 and applying the 11-chip Barker code 10110111000 results in the spread 'signal' 1011011100001001000111. On the receiver side, this 'signal' is XORed bit-wise after demodulation with the same Barker code as chipping sequence. This results in the sum of products equal to 0 for the first bit and to 11 for the second bit. The decision unit can now map the first sum (=0) to a binary 0, the second sum (=11) to a binary 1—this constitutes the original user data.

In real life, however, the situation is somewhat more complex. Assume that the demodulated signal shows some distortion, e.g., 1010010100001101000111. The sum of products for the first bit would be 2, 10 for the second bit. Still, the decision unit can map, e.g., sums less than 4 to a binary 0 and sums larger than 7 to a binary 1. However, it is important to stay synchronized with the transmitter of a signal. But what happens in case of multi-path propagation? Then several paths with different delays exist between a transmitter and a receiver. Additionally, the different paths may have different path losses. In this case, using so-called rake receivers provides a possible solution. A **rake receiver** uses n correlators for the n strongest paths. Each correlator is synchronized to the transmitter plus the delay on that specific path. As soon as the receiver detects a new path which is stronger than the currently weakest path, it assigns this new path to the correlator with the weakest path. The output of the correlators is then combined and fed into the decision unit. Rake receivers can even take advantage of the multi-path propagation by combining the different paths in a constructive way (Viterbi, 1995).

2.7.2 Frequency Hopping Spread Spectrum

For **frequency hopping spread spectrum (FHSS)** systems, the total available bandwidth is split into many channels of smaller bandwidth plus guard spaces between the channels. Transmitter and receiver stay on one of these channels for a certain time and then hop to another channel. This system implements FDM and TDM. The pattern of channel usage is called the **hopping sequence**; the time spent on a channel with a certain frequency is called the **dwell time**. FHSS comes in two variants, slow and fast hopping (see Figure 2.38).

In **slow hopping**, the transmitter uses one frequency for several bit periods.[3] Figure 2.38 shows five user bits with a bit period t_b. Performing slow hopping, the transmitter uses the frequency f_2 for transmitting the first three bits during the dwell time t_d. Then, the transmitter hops to the next frequency f_3. Slow hopping systems are typically cheaper and have relaxed tolerances, but they are not as immune to narrowband interference as fast hopping systems. Slow frequency hopping is an option for GSM.

For **fast hopping** systems, the transmitter changes the frequency several times during the transmission of a single bit. In the example of Figure 2.38, the transmitter

[3]Another definition refers to the number of hops per signal element instead of bits.

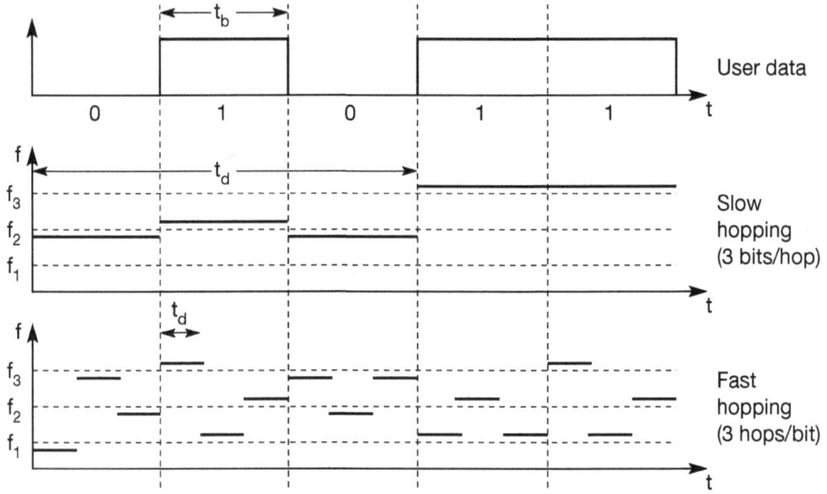

Figure 2.38 Slow and Fast Frequency Hopping

hops three times during a bit period. Fast hopping systems are more complex to implement because the transmitter and receiver have to stay synchronized within smaller tolerances to perform hopping at more or less the same points in time. However, these systems are much better at overcoming the effects of narrowband interference and frequency selective fading as they only stick to one frequency for a very short time.

Another example of an FHSS system is Bluetooth. Bluetooth performs 1,600 hops per second and uses 79 hop carriers equally spaced with 1 MHz in the 2.4 GHz ISM band.

Figures 2.39 and 2.40 show simplified block diagrams of FHSS transmitters and receivers respectively. The first step in an FHSS transmitter is the modulation of user data according to one of the digital-to-analog modulation schemes, e.g., FSK or BPSK, as discussed in section 2.6. This results in a narrowband signal, if FSK is used with a frequency f_0 for a binary 0 and f_1 for a binary 1. In the next step, frequency hopping is performed, based on a hopping sequence. The hopping sequence is fed into a frequency synthesizer generating the carrier frequencies f_i. A second modulation uses the modulated narrowband signal and the carrier frequency to generate a new spread signal with frequency of f_i+f_0 for a 0 and f_i+f_1 for a 1 respectively. If different FHSS transmitters use hopping sequences that never overlap, i.e., if two transmitters never use the same frequency f_i at the same time, then these two transmissions do not interfere. This requires the coordination of all transmitters and their hopping sequences. As for DSSS systems, pseudo-random hopping sequences can also be used without coordination. These sequences only have to fulfill certain properties to keep interference minimal.[4] Two or more transmitters may choose the same frequency for a hop, but dwell time is short for fast hopping systems, so interference is minimal.

[4]These sequences should have a low cross-correlation.

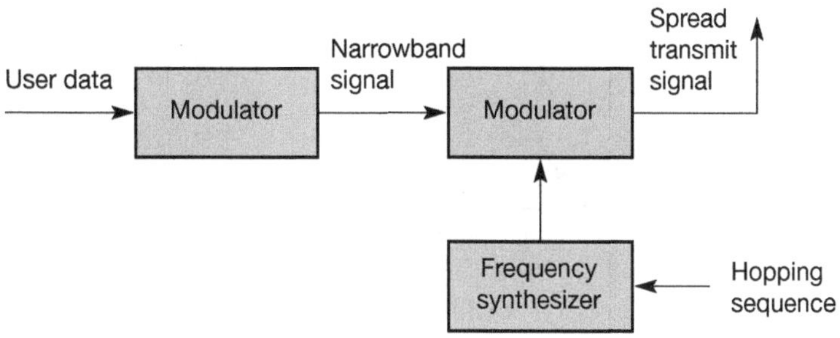

Figure 2.39 FHSS Transmitter

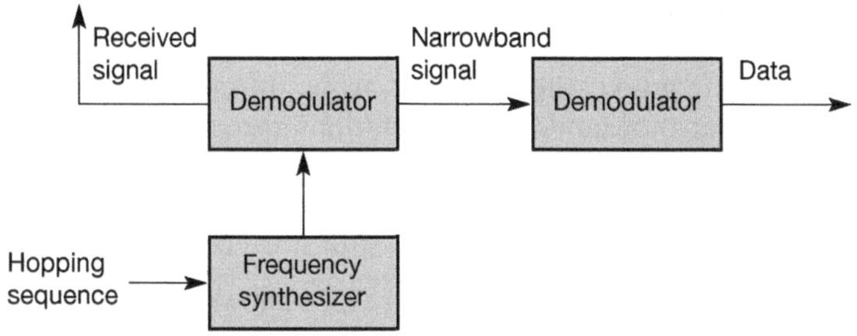

Figure 2.40 FHSS Receiver

The receiver of an FHSS system has to know the hopping sequence and must stay synchronized. It then performs the inverse operations of the modulation to reconstruct user data. Several filters are also needed (these are not shown in the simplified diagram in Figure 2.40).

Compared to DSSS, spreading is simpler using FHSS systems. FHSS systems only use a portion of the total band at any time, while DSSS systems always use the total bandwidth available. DSSS systems on the other hand are more resistant to fading and multi-path effects. DSSS signals are much harder to detect—without knowing the spreading code, detection is virtually impossible. If each sender has its own pseudo-random number sequence for spreading the signal (DSSS or FHSS), the system implements CDM. More details about spread spectrum applications and their theoretical background can be found in Viterbi (1995), Peterson (1995), Ojanperä (1998), and Dixon (1994).

2.8 CELLULAR SYSTEMS

Cellular systems for mobile communications implement SDM. Each transmitter, typically called a **base station**, covers a certain area, a **cell**. Cell radii can vary from tens of meters in buildings, and hundreds of meters in cities, up to tens of kilometers in the countryside. The shapes of cells are never perfect circles or hexagons (as shown in Figure 2.41), but depend on the environment (buildings, mountains, valleys etc.), on weather conditions, and sometimes even on system load. Typical systems using this approach are mobile telecommunication systems, where a mobile station

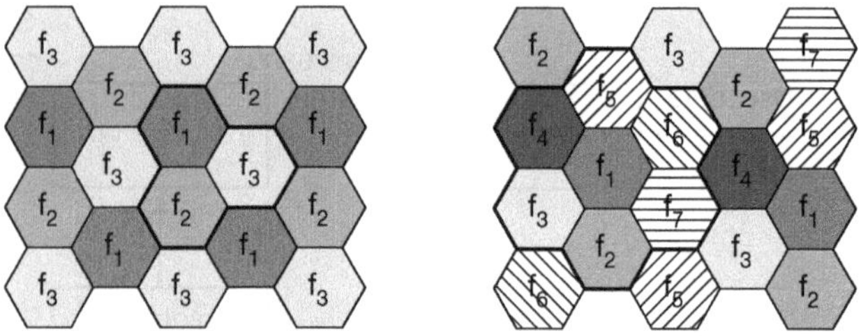

Figure 2.41 Cellular System with Three and Seven Cell Clusters

within the cell around a base station communicates with this base station and vice versa.

In this context, the question arises as to why mobile network providers install several thousands of base stations throughout a country (which is quite expensive) and do not use powerful transmitters with huge cells like, e.g., radio stations, use.

Advantages of cellular systems with small cells are the following:

- **Higher capacity**: Implementing SDM allows frequency reuse. If one transmitter is far away from another, i.e., outside the interference range, it can reuse the same frequencies. As most mobile phone systems assign frequencies to certain users (or certain hopping patterns), this frequency is blocked for other users. But frequencies are a scarce resource, and the number of concurrent users per cell is very limited. Huge cells do not allow for more users. On the contrary, they are limited to less possible users per km^2. This is also the reason for using very small cells in cities where many more people use mobile phones.
- **Less transmission power**: While power aspects are not a big problem for base stations, they are indeed problematic for mobile stations. A receiver far away from a base station would need much more transmit power than the current few Watts. But energy is a serious problem for mobile handheld devices.
- **Local interference only**: Having long distances between sender and receiver results in even more interference problems. With small cells, mobile stations and base stations only have to deal with 'local' interference.
- **Robustness**: Cellular systems are decentralized and so, more robust against the failure of single components. If one antenna fails, this only influences communication within a small area.

Small cells also have some **disadvantages**:

- **Infrastructure needed**: Cellular systems need a complex infrastructure to connect all base stations. This includes many antennas, switches for call forwarding, location registers to find a mobile station etc, which makes the whole system quite expensive.
- **Handover needed**: The mobile station has to perform a handover when changing from one cell to another. Depending on the cell size and the speed of movement, this can happen quite often.

- **Frequency planning**: To avoid interference between transmitters using the same frequencies, frequencies have to be distributed carefully. On the one hand, interference should be avoided; on the other, only a limited number of frequencies is available.

To avoid interference, different transmitters within each other's interference range use FDM. If FDM is combined with TDM (see Figure 2.19), the hopping pattern has to be coordinated. The general goal is never to use the same frequency at the same time within the interference range (if CDM is not applied). Two possible models to create cell patterns with minimal interference are shown in Figure 2.41. Cells are combined in **clusters**—on the left side three cells form a cluster, on the right side seven cells form a cluster. All cells within a cluster use disjointed sets of frequencies. On the left side, one cell in the cluster uses set f_1, another cell f_2, and the third cell f_3. In real-life transmission, the pattern will look somewhat different. The hexagonal pattern is chosen as a simple way of illustrating the model. This pattern also shows the repetition of the same frequency sets. The transmission power of a sender has to be limited to avoid interference with the next cell using the same frequencies.

To reduce interference even further (and under certain traffic conditions, i.e., number of users per km^2) **sectorized antennas** can be used. Figure 2.42 shows the use of three sectors per cell in a cluster with three cells. Typically, it makes sense to use sectorized antennas instead of omni-directional antennas for larger cell radii.

The fixed assignment of frequencies to cell clusters and cells respectively, is not very efficient if traffic load varies. For instance, in the case of a heavy load in one cell and a light load in a neighboring cell, it could make sense to 'borrow' frequencies. Cells with more traffic are dynamically allotted more frequencies. This scheme is known as **borrowing channel allocation (BCA)**, while the first fixed scheme is called **fixed channel allocation (FCA)**. FCA is used in the GSM system as it is much simpler to use, but it requires careful traffic analysis before installation.

A **dynamic channel allocation (DCA)** scheme has been implemented in DECT. In this scheme, frequencies can only be borrowed, but it is also possible to freely assign frequencies to cells. With dynamic assignment of frequencies to cells, the danger of interference with cells using the same frequency exists. The 'borrowed' frequency can be blocked in the surrounding cells.

Cellular systems using CDM instead of FDM do not need such elaborate channel allocation schemes and complex frequency planning. Here, users are separated through the code they use, not through the frequency. Cell planning faces

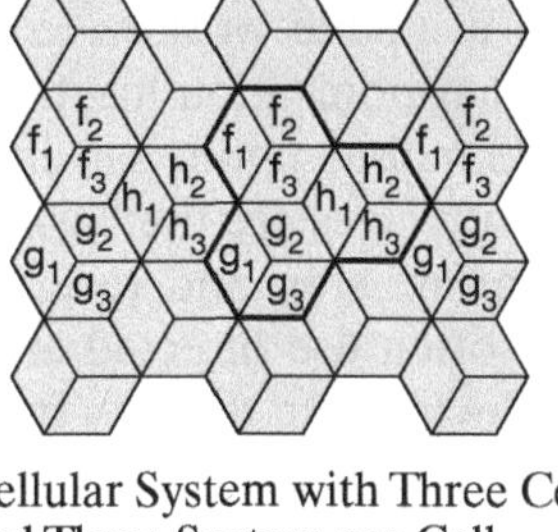

Figure 2.42 Cellular System with Three Cell Clusters and Three Sectors per Cell

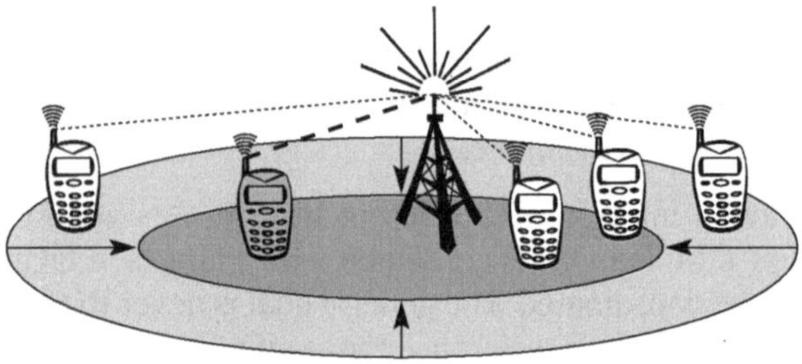

Figure 2.43 Cell Breathing Depending on the Current Load

another problem—the cell size depends on the current load. Accordingly, **CDM cells** are commonly said to '**breathe**'. While a cell can cover a larger area under a light load, it shrinks if the load increases. The reason for this is the growing noise level if more users are in a cell. (Remember, if you do not know the code, other signals appear as noise, i.e., more and more people join the party.) The higher the noise, the higher the path loss and the higher the transmission errors. Finally, mobile stations further away from the base station drop out of the cell. (This is similar to trying to talk to someone far away at a crowded party.) Figure 2.43 illustrates this phenomenon with a user transmitting a high bit rate stream within a CDM cell. This additional user lets the cell shrink with the result that two users drop out of the cell. In a real-life scenario this additional user could request a video stream (high bit rate) while the others use standard voice communication (low bit rate).

2.9 SUMMARY

This chapter introduced the basics of wireless communications, leaving out most formulae found in books dedicated to wireless transmission and the effects of radio propagation. However, the examples, mechanisms, and problems discussed will hopefully give the reader a good idea as to why wireless communication is fundamentally different from wired communication and why protocols and applications on higher layers have to follow different principles to take the missing wire into account.

A topic of worldwide importance is the regulation and harmonization of frequencies used for radio transmission. The chapter showed many different systems using either different or the same frequencies. Hopefully, the future will bring more frequencies which are available worldwide to avoid more expensive multi-mode devices. At least some harmonization has taken and continues to take place in the area of WLANs and 3G mobile phone systems.

As electromagnetic waves are the basis for wireless communication, antennas are needed for the transmission and reception of waves. While base stations of mobile phone systems often use directed antennas, omni-directional antennas are the choice for mobile devices. On the way from sender to receiver, many things can happen to electromagnetic waves. The standard effects, such as shadowing, fading, reflection, diffraction, and scattering have been presented. All these effects lead to one of the biggest problems in wireless communication: multi-path propagation. Multi-path propagation limits the bandwidth of a channel due to intersymbol interference, i.e., one symbol is 'smeared' into another symbol due to delay spread.

As we only have one 'medium' for wireless transmission, several multiplexing schemes can be applied to raise overall capacity. The standard schemes are SDM, FDM, TDM, and CDM. To achieve FDM, data has to be 'translated' into a signal with a certain carrier frequency. Therefore, two modulation steps can be applied. Digital modulation encodes data into a baseband signal, whereas analog modulation then shifts the centre frequency of the signal up to the radio carrier. Some advanced schemes have been presented that can code many bits into a single phase shift, raising the efficiency.

With the help of spread spectrum technology, several features can be implemented. One is (at least some) security—without knowing the spreading code, the signal appears as noise. Spread spectrum lays the basis for special medium access schemes using the code space. Spread spectrum also makes a transmission more robust against narrowband interference, as the signal is spread over a larger bandwidth so the narrowband interference only influences a small fraction of the signal.

Finally, this chapter has presented the concept of cellular systems. Cellular systems implement SDM to raise the overall capacity of mobile phone systems. While these systems require detailed planning (i.e., matching the cell size with the traffic expected), it presents one of the basic solutions for using the scarce frequency resources efficiently.

2.10 REVIEW EXERCISES

2.1 Frequency regulations may differ between countries. Check out the regulations valid for your country (within Europe the European Radio Office may be able to help you, www.ero.dk, for the US try the FCC, www.fcc.gov, for Japan ARIB, www.arib.or.jp).

2.2 Why can waves with a very low frequency follow the earth's surface? Why are they not used for data transmission in computer networks?

2.3 Why does the ITU-R only regulate 'lower' frequencies (up to some hundred GHz) and not higher frequencies (in the THz range)?

2.4 What are the two different approaches in regulation regarding mobile phone systems in Europe and the US? What are the consequences?

2.5 Why is the international availability of the same ISM bands important?

2.6 Is it possible to transmit a digital signal, e.g., coded as square wave as used inside a computer, using radio transmission without any loss? Why?

2.7 Is a directional antenna useful for mobile phones? Why? How can the gain of an antenna be improved?

2.8 What are the main problems of signal propagation? Why do radio waves not always follow a straight line? Why is reflection both useful and harmful?

2.9 Name several methods for ISI mitigation. How does ISI depend on the carrier frequency, symbol rate, and movement of sender/receiver? What are the influences of ISI on TDM schemes?

2.10 What are the means to mitigate narrowband interference? What is the complexity of the different solutions?

2.11 Why, typically, is digital modulation not enough for radio transmission? What are general goals for digital modulation? What are typical schemes?

2.12 Think of a phase diagram and the points representing bit patterns for a PSK scheme (see Figure 2.29). How can a receiver decide which bit pattern was originally sent when a received 'point' lies somewhere in between other points in the diagram? Why is it difficult to code more and more bits per phase shift?

2.13 What are the main benefits of a spread spectrum system? How can spreading be achieved? What replaces the guard space in Figure 2.33 when compared to Figure 2.34? How can DSSS systems benefit from multi-path propagation?

2.14 What are the main reasons for using cellular systems? How is SDM typically realized and combined with FDM? How does DCA influence the frequencies available in other cells?

2.15 What limits the number of simultaneous users in a TDM/FDM system compared to a CDM system? What happens to the transmission quality of connections if the load gets higher in a cell, i.e., how does an additional user influence the other users in the cell?

2.11 REFERENCES

Anderson, J.B., Rappaport, T.S., Yoshida, S. (1995) 'Propagation measurements and models for wireless communications channels,' *IEEE Communications Magazine,* 33, (1).

Dixon, R. (1994) *Spread spectrum systems with commercial applications.* John Wiley.

ETSI (1997) *Digital Audio Broadcasting (DAB) to mobile, portable, and fixed receivers,* European Telecommunications Standards Institute, ETS 300 401.

GSM World (2002), GSM Association, http://www.gsmworld.com/.

Halsall, F. (1996) *Data communications, computer networks and open systems.* Addison-Wesley Longman.

Ojanperä, T., Prasad, R. (1998) *Wideband CDMA for Third Generation Mobile Communications.* Artech House.

Pahlavan, K., Krishnamurthy, P. (2002) *Principles of Wireless Networks.* Prentice Hall.

Peterson, R., Ziemer, R., Borth, D. (1995) *Introduction to spread spectrum communications.* Prentice Hall.

Stallings, W. (1997) *Data and computer communications.* Prentice Hall.

Stallings, W. (2002) *Wireless Communications and Networking.* Prentice Hall.

Viterbi, A. (1995) *CDMA: Principles of spread spectrum communication.* Addison-Wesley Longman.

Wesel, E. (1998) *Wireless multimedia communications: networking video, voice, and data.* Addison-Wesley Longman.

CHAPTER 3

COMMUNICATION NETWORKS

This chapter provides an overview of various approaches to communication networking. The chapter begins with a survey of different type of networks based on geographic extent. Then circuit switching, packet switching, and ATM (asynchronous transfer mode) networks are examined.

3.1 LANs, MANs, AND WANs

Local area networks (LANs), metropolitan area networks (MANs), and wide area networks (WANs) are all examples of communications networks. Figure 3.1 illustrates these categories, plus some special cases. By way of contrast, the typical range of parameters for a multiple-processor computer is also depicted.

Wide Area Networks

WANs cover a large geographical area, may require the crossing of public right-of-ways, and may rely at least in part on circuits provided by a common carrier. Typically, a WAN consists of a number of interconnected switching nodes. A transmission from any one device is routed through these internal nodes to the specified destination device.

Traditionally, WANs have provided only relatively modest capacity to subscribers. For many years, for data attachment, either to a data network or to a telephone network by means of a modem, data rates of 64,000 bps or less have been

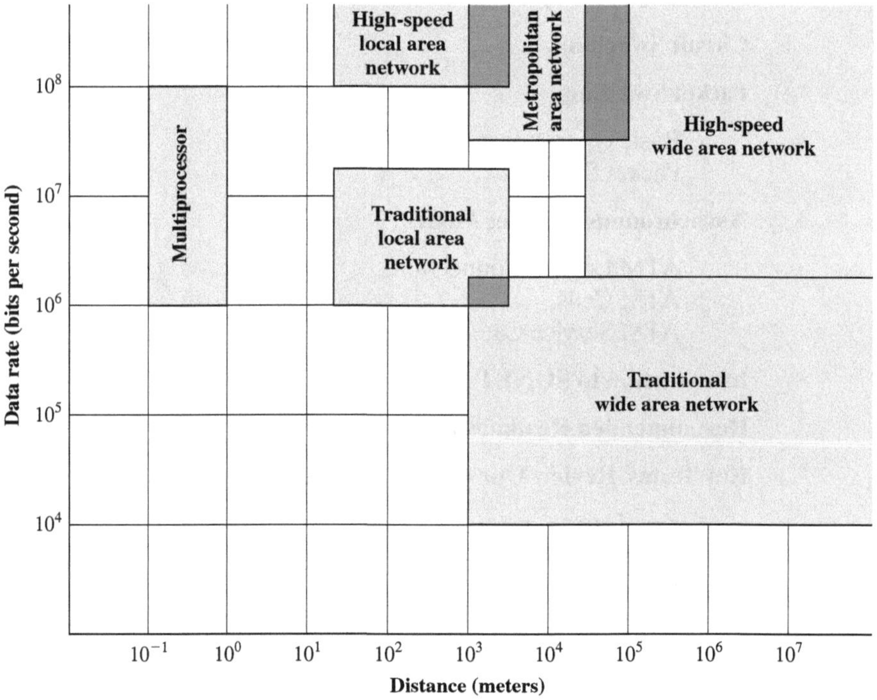

Figure 3.1 Comparison of Multiprocessor Systems, LANs, MANs, and WANs

common. Business subscribers have been able to obtain higher rates, with a service known as T1, which operates at 1.544 Mbps, being common. Currently, businesses frequently acquire rates at a T3 service level, thus being provided bandwidth exceeding 43 Mbps at a reasonable cost of $3–4K/month. A T-3 line is basically about the same as 672 regular voice grade telephone lines, which is wide enough to transmit full motion, real-time video, and very large databases over a network.[1]

The continuing development of practical optical fiber facilities has led to the standardization of much higher data rates for WANs, and these services are becoming more widely available. These high-speed WANs provide user connections in the 10s and 100s of Mbps, using a transmission technique known asynchronous transfer mode (ATM). In fact, fiber optic technologies have overtaken copper-based to the point that most if not all ultra-fast network links are now fiber-based. An example might be transoceanic lines. Why? This table shows the speeds that can be obtained via fiber optics:[2]

Optical Carrier:

OC-1	51.48Mbps
OC-3	155.52Mbps
OC-12	622.08Mbps
OC-48	2.4Gbps
OC-192	9.6Gbps
OC-256	13.1Gbps
OC-768	40Gbps

Local Area Networks

As with WANs, a LAN is a communications network that interconnects a variety of devices and provides a means for information exchange among those devices. There are several key distinctions between LANs and WANs:

1. The scope of the LAN is small, typically a single building or a cluster of buildings. This difference in geographic scope leads to different technical solutions.
2. It is usually the case that the LAN is owned by the same organization that owns the attached devices. For WANs, this is less often the case, or at least a significant fraction of the network assets are not owned. This has two implications. First, care must be taken in the choice of LAN, since there may be a substantial capital investment (compared with dial-up or leased charges for WANs) for both purchase and maintenance. Second, the network management responsibility for a LAN falls solely on the user.
3. The internal data rates of LANs are typically much greater than those of WANs.

A simple example of a LAN that highlights some of its characteristics is shown in Figure 3.2. All of the devices are attached to a shared transmission medium. A transmission from any one device can be received by all other devices attached to the same network.

[1]http://www.infobahn.com/research-information.htm

[2]http://www.lageman.com/bandwidth.htm

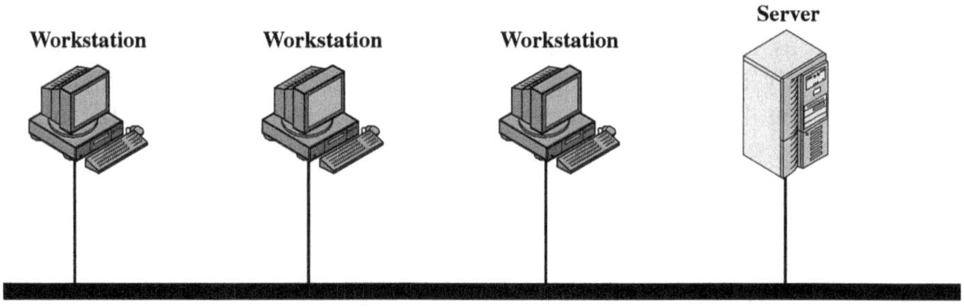

Figure 3.2 A Simple Local Area Network

Traditional LANs have provided data rates in a range from about 1 to 20 Mbps. These data rates, though substantial, have become increasingly inadequate with the proliferation of devices, the growth in multimedia applications, and the increased use of the client/server architecture. As a result, much of the effort in LAN development has been in the development of high-speed LANs, with data rates of 100 Mbps to 10 Gbps. Even higher speeds are being reached in the laboratory.

As of mid-2011, it is common to see LANs at speeds from 10Gbps to 40Gbps to even as fast as 100Gbps over short distances over fiber optics. After 10 Gigabit Ethernet, 100Gbps was the obvious next step. However, transmitting at 100Gbps over fiber has several challenges. Why? Due to simple physics, laser pulses that carry information through fiber become so short that they have a hard time maintaining their shape as they travel. The IEEE therefore kept open the option to make a smaller step towards 40Gbps instead of its customary tenfold boost in speeds.

Currently, there are a large set of 100GBASE-* standards, but many of them use four parallel data paths to reach 40 or 100Gbps and/or only work over short distances. Work is still ongoing to create the one 100GBASE standard to rule them all.[3] This is expected to occur sometime in 2012–2013.

Metropolitan Area Networks

As the name suggests, a MAN occupies a middle ground between LANs and WANs. Interest in MANs has come about as a result of a recognition that the traditional point-to-point and switched network techniques used in WANs may be inadequate for the growing needs of organizations. While ATM promises to meet a wide range of high-speed needs, there is a requirement now for both private and public networks that provide high capacity at low costs over a large area. The high-speed shared-medium approach of the LAN standards provides a number of benefits that can be realized on a metropolitan scale. As Figure 3.1 indicates, MANs cover greater distances at higher data rates than LANs, although there is some overlap in geographical coverage.

MAN is basically a hybrid of both LAN and WAN technologies. Some legacy technologies used for MAN are ATM, FDDI, DQDB and SMDS. These older technologies are in the process of being displaced by Gigabit Ethernet and 10 Gigabit

[3]http://www.wired.com/epicenter/2011/07/speed-matters/3/

Ethernet. At the physical level, MAN links between LANs have been built on fiber optical cables or using wireless technologies such as microwave or radio.

The Metropolitan Area Network (MAN) protocols are mostly at the data link level (layer 2 in the *OSI model*), which are defined by IEEE, ITU-T, etc.

The primary market for MANs is the customer that has high-capacity needs in a metropolitan area. A MAN is intended to provide the required capacity at lower cost and greater efficiency than obtaining an equivalent service from the local telephone company.

3.2 SWITCHING TECHNIQUES

For transmission of data beyond a local area, communication is typically achieved by transmitting data from source to destination through a network of intermediate switching nodes; this switched network design is sometimes used to implement LANs and MANs as well. The switching nodes are not concerned with the content of the data; rather their purpose is to provide a switching facility that will move the data from node to node until they reach their destination. The end devices that wish to communicate may be referred to as stations. The stations may be computers, terminals, telephones, or other communicating devices. We will refer to the switching devices whose purpose is to provide communication as *nodes*. The nodes are connected to each other in some topology by transmission links. Each station attaches to a node, and the collection of nodes is referred to as a *communication network*.

Figure 3.3 illustrates a simple network. Signals entering the network from a station are routed to the destination by being switched from node to node. For example, information from station A intended for station F is sent to node 4. It may then be routed via nodes 5 and 6 or nodes 7 and 6 to the destination. Several observations are in order:

1. Some nodes connect only to other nodes (e.g., 5 and 7). Their sole task is the internal (to the network) switching of information. Other nodes have one or more stations attached as well; in addition to their switching functions, such nodes accept information from and deliver information to the attached stations.
2. Node-station links are generally dedicated point-to-point links. Node-node links are usually multiplexed links, using either frequency division multiplexing (FDM) or some form of time division multiplexing (TDM).
3. Usually, the network is not fully connected; that is, there is not a direct link between every possible pair of nodes. However, it is always desirable to have more than one possible path through the network for each pair of stations. This enhances the reliability of the network.

Two quite different technologies are used in wide area switched networks: circuit switching and packet switching. These two technologies differ in the way the nodes switch information from one link to another on the way from source to destination. In the remainder of this chapter, we look at the details of both of these technologies and then look at an important special case of packet switching known as cell relay, or ATM.

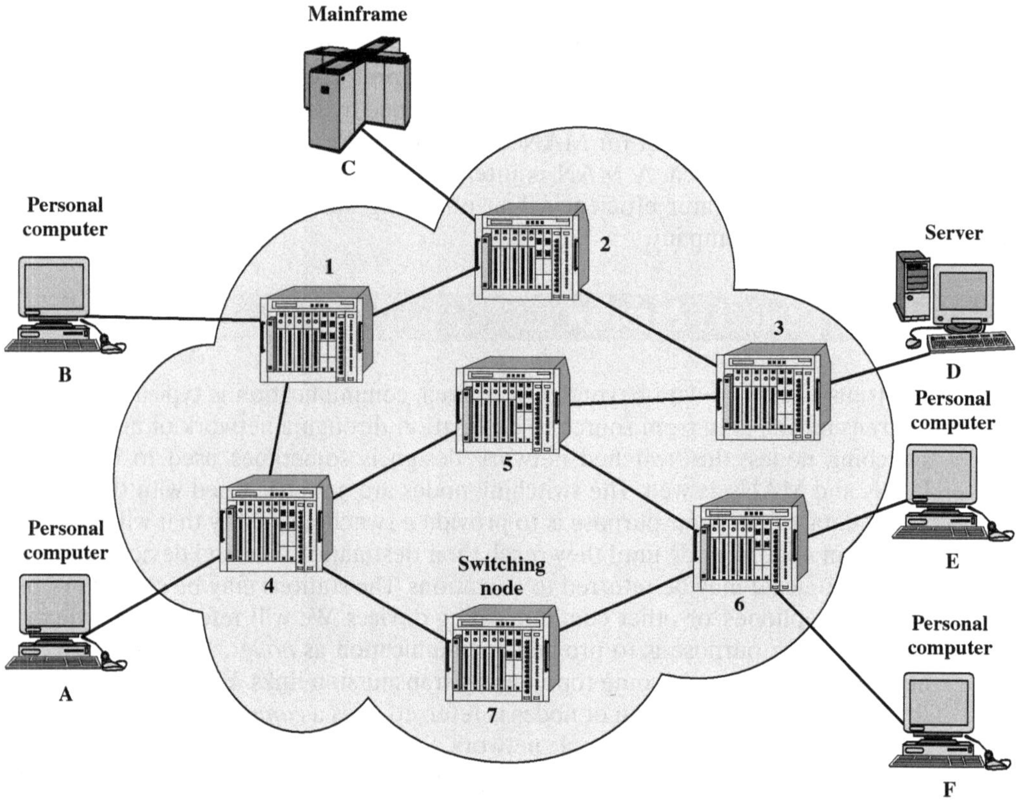

Figure 3.3 Simple Switching Network

3.3 CIRCUIT SWITCHING

Circuit switching has been the dominant technology for both voice and data communications. Communication via circuit switching implies that there is a dedicated communication path between two stations. That path is a connected sequence of links between network nodes. On each physical link, a channel is dedicated to the connection. The most common example of circuit switching is the telephone network.

Communication via circuit switching involves three phases, which can be explained with reference to Figure 3.3.

1. **Circuit establishment.** Before any signals can be transmitted, an end-to-end (station-to-station) circuit must be established. For example, station A sends a request to node 4 requesting a connection to station E. Typically, the link from A to 4 is a dedicated line, so that part of the connection already exists. Node 4 must find the next leg in a route leading to E. Based on routing information and measures of availability and perhaps cost, node 4 selects the link to node 5,

allocates a free channel (using frequency division multiplexing, FDM, or time division multiplexing, TDM) on that link, and sends a message requesting connection to E. So far, a dedicated path has been established from A through 4 to 5. Because a number of stations may attach to 4, it must be able to establish internal paths from multiple stations to multiple nodes. How this is done is discussed later in this section. The remainder of the process proceeds similarly. Node 5 dedicates a channel to node 6 and internally ties that channel to the channel from node 4. Node 6 completes the connection to E. In completing the connection, a test is made to determine if E is busy or is prepared to accept the connection.

2. **Information transfer.** Information can now be transmitted from A through the network to E. The transmission may be analog voice, digitized voice, or binary data, depending on the nature of the network. As the carriers evolve to fully integrated digital networks, the use of digital (binary) transmission for both voice and data is becoming the dominant method. The path is A-4 link, internal switching through 4, 4-5 channel, internal switching through 5, 5-6 channel, internal switching through 6, 6-E link. Generally, the connection is full duplex, and signals may be transmitted in both directions simultaneously.
3. **Circuit disconnect.** After some period of information transfer, the connection is terminated, usually by the action of one of the two stations. Signals must be propagated to nodes 4, 5, and 6 to deallocate the dedicated resources.

Note that the connection path is established before data transmission begins. Thus, channel capacity must be reserved between each pair of nodes in the path and each node must have available internal switching capacity to handle the requested connection. The switches must have the intelligence to make these allocations and to devise a route through the network.

Circuit switching can be rather inefficient. Channel capacity is dedicated for the duration of a connection, even if no data are being transferred. For a voice connection, utilization may be rather high, but it still does not approach 100%. For a terminal-to-computer connection, the capacity may be idle during most of the time of the connection. In terms of performance, there is a delay prior to signal transfer for call establishment. However, once the circuit is established, the network is effectively transparent to the users. Information is transmitted at a fixed data rate with no delay other than the propagation delay through the transmission links. The delay at each node is negligible.

Circuit switching was developed to handle voice traffic but is now also used for data traffic. The best-known example of a circuit-switching network is the public telephone network (Figure 3.4). This is actually a collection of national networks interconnected to form the international service. Although originally designed and implemented to service analog telephone subscribers, it handles substantial data traffic via modem and is well on its way to being converted to a digital network. Another well-known application of circuit switching is the private branch exchange (PBX), used to interconnect telephones within a building or office. Circuit switching is also used in private networks. Typically, such a network is set up by a corporation or other large organization to interconnect its various sites. Such a network usually

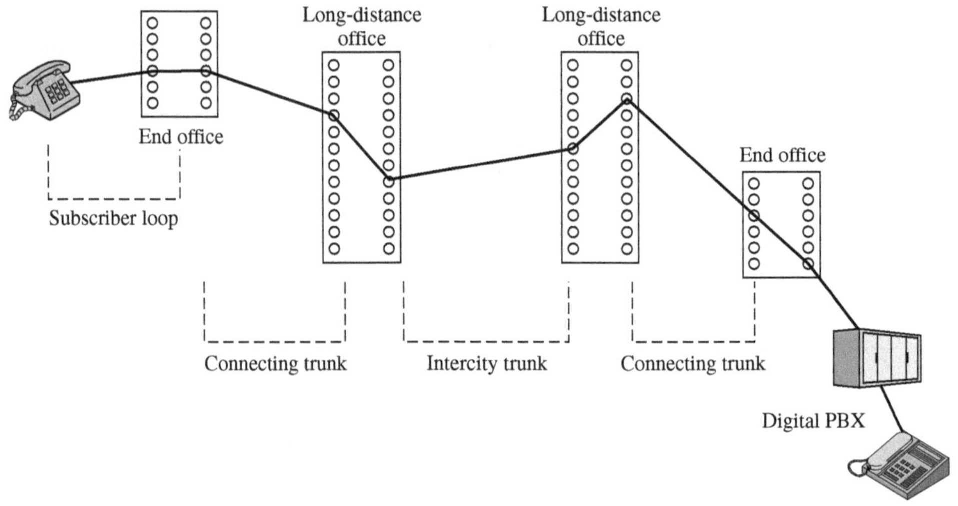

Figure 3.4 Example Connection Over a Public Circuit-Switching Network

consists of PBX systems at each site interconnected by dedicated, leased lines obtained from one of the carriers, such as AT&T. A final common example of the application of circuit switching is the data switch. The data switch is similar to the PBX but is designed to interconnect digital data processing devices, such as terminals and computers.

A public telecommunications network can be described using four generic architectural components:

- **Subscribers:** The devices that attach to the network. It is still the case that most subscriber devices to public telecommunications networks are telephones, but the percentage of data traffic increases year by year.
- **Subscriber line:** The link between the subscriber and the network, also referred to as the local loop. Almost all subscriber line connections use twisted pair wire. The length of a subscriber line is typically in a range from a few kilometers to a few tens of kilometers. The subscriber line is also known as a **subscriber loop**, or a **local loop**.
- **Exchanges:** The switching centers in the network. A switching center that directly supports subscribers is known as an end office. Typically, an end office will support many thousands of subscribers in a localized area. There are over 19,000 end offices in the United States, so it is clearly impractical for each end office to have a direct link to each of the other end offices; this would require on the order of 2×10^8 links. Rather, intermediate switching nodes are used.
- **Trunks:** The branches between exchanges. Trunks carry multiple voice-frequency circuits using either FDM or synchronous TDM. Earlier, these were referred to as carrier systems.

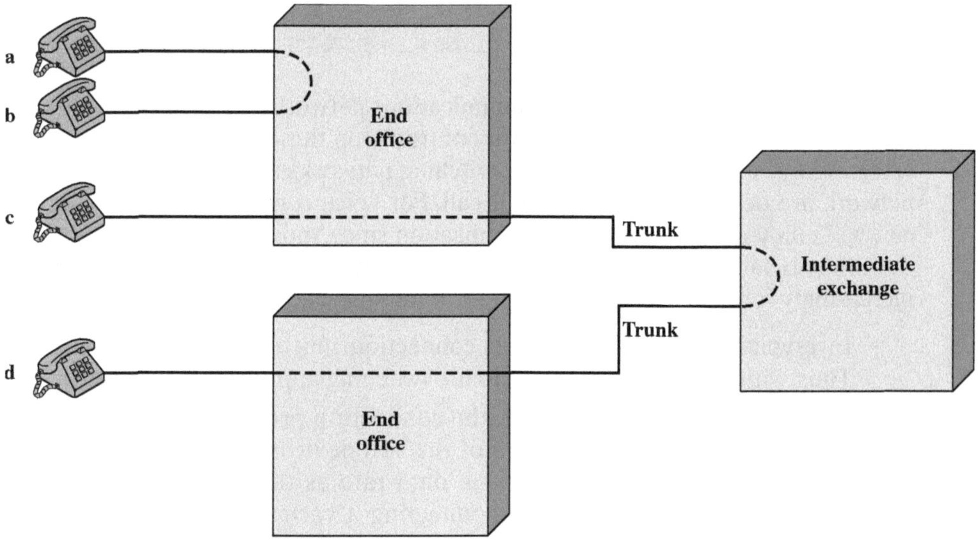

Figure 3.5 Circuit Establishment

Subscribers connect directly to an end office, which switches traffic between subscribers and between a subscriber and other exchanges. The other exchanges are responsible for routing and switching traffic between end offices. This distinction is shown in Figure 3.5. To connect two subscribers attached to the same end office, a circuit is set up between them in the same fashion as described before. If two subscribers connect to different end offices, a circuit between them consists of a chain of circuits through one or more intermediate offices. In the figure, a connection is established between lines a and b by simply setting up the connection through the end office. The connection between c and d is more complex. In c's end office, a connection is established between line c and one channel on a TDM trunk to the intermediate switch. In the intermediate switch, that channel is connected to a channel on a TDM trunk to d's end office. In that end office, the channel is connected to line d.

Circuit-switching technology has been driven by its use to carry voice traffic. One of the key requirements for voice traffic is that there must be virtually no transmission delay and certainly no variation in delay. A constant signal transmission rate must be maintained, because transmission and reception occur at the same signal rate. These requirements are necessary to allow normal human conversation. Further, the quality of the received signal must be sufficiently high to provide, at a minimum, intelligibility.

Circuit switching achieved its widespread, dominant position because it is well suited to the analog transmission of voice signals. In today's digital world, its inefficiencies are more apparent. However, despite the inefficiency, circuit switching is and will remain an attractive choice for both local area and wide area networking. One of its key strengths is that it is transparent. Once a circuit is established, it appears like a direct connection to the two attached stations; no special networking logic is needed at the station.

3.4 PACKET SWITCHING

Long-haul circuit-switching telecommunications networks were originally designed to handle voice traffic, and the majority of traffic on these networks continues to be voice. A key characteristic of circuit-switching networks is that resources within the network are dedicated to a particular call. For voice connections, the resulting circuit will enjoy a high percentage of utilization since, most of the time, one party or the other is talking. However, as the circuit-switching network began to be used increasingly for data connections, two shortcomings became apparent:

- In a typical terminal-to-host data connection, much of the time the line is idle. Thus, with data connections, a circuit-switching approach is inefficient.
- In a circuit-switching network, the connection provides for transmission at a constant data rate. Thus each of the two devices that are connected must transmit and receive at the same data rate as the other, which limits the utility of the network in interconnecting a variety of host computers and terminals.

To understand how packet switching addresses these problems, let us briefly summarize packet-switching operation. Data are transmitted in blocks, called packets. A typical upper bound on packet length is 1000 octets (bytes). If a source has a longer message to send, the message is broken up into a series of packets (Figure 3.6). Each packet consists of a portion of the data (or all of the data for a short message) that a station wants to transmit, plus a packet header that contains control information. The control information, at a minimum, includes the information that the network requires in order to be able to route the packet through the network and deliver it to the intended destination. At each node en route, the packet is received, stored briefly, and passed on to the next node.

Figure 3.7 illustrates the basic operation. A transmitting computer or other device sends a message as a sequence of packets (a). Each packet includes control

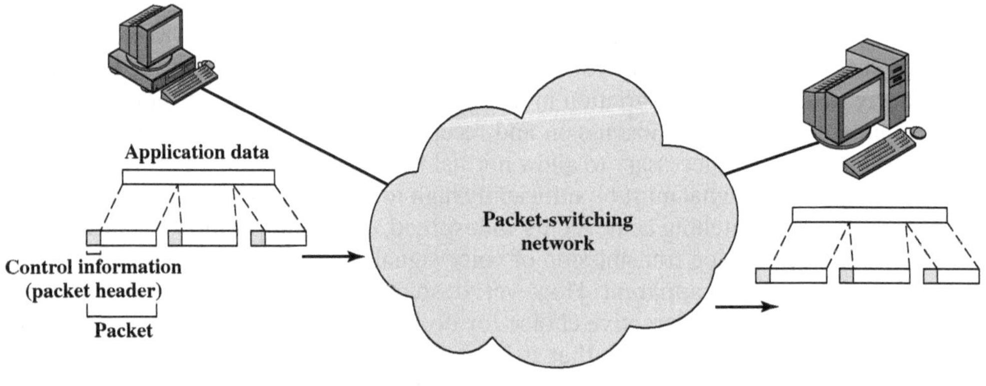

Figure 3.6 The Use of Packets

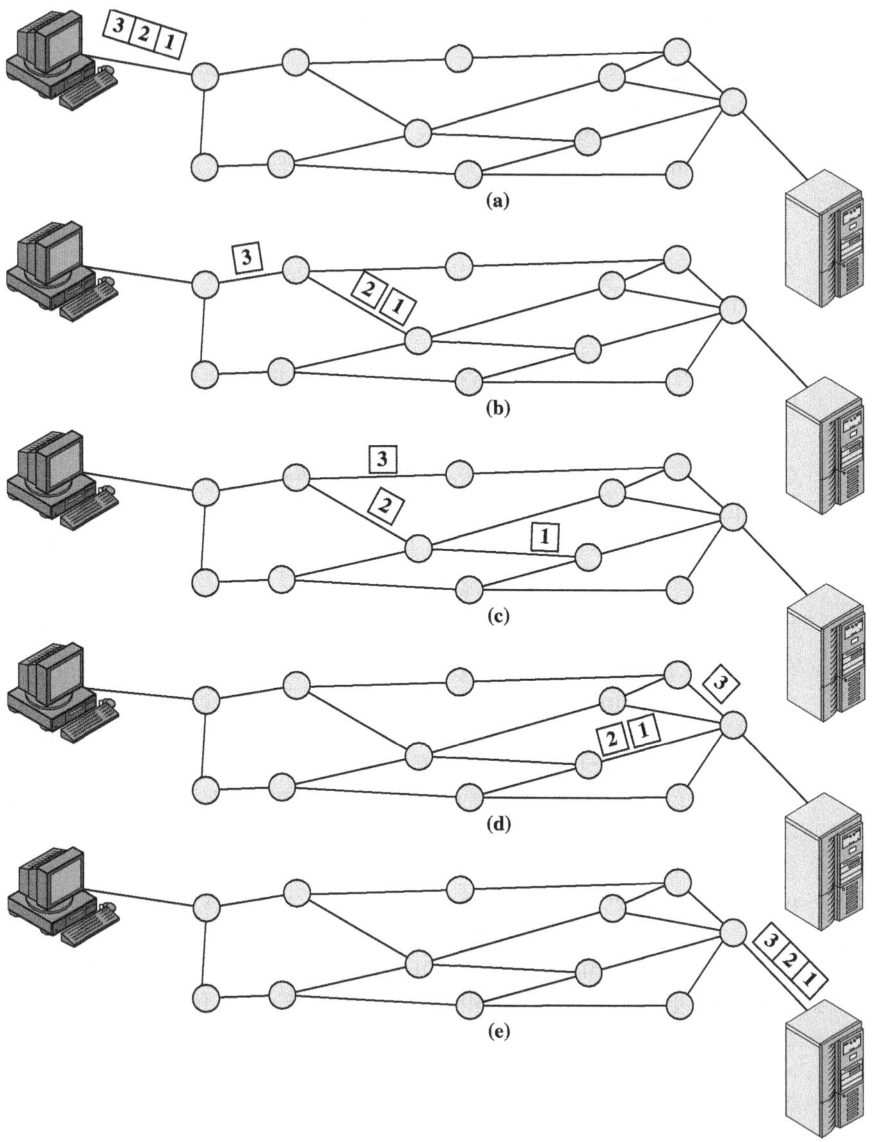

Figure 3.7 Packet Switching: Datagram Approach

information indicating the destination station (computer, terminal, etc.). The packets are initially sent to the node to which the sending station attaches. As each packet arrives at this node, it stores the packet briefly, determines the next leg of the route, and queues the packet to go out on that link. Each packet is transmitted to the next node (b) when the link is available. All of the packets eventually work their way through the network and are delivered to the intended destination.

The packet-switching approach has a number of advantages over circuit switching:

- Line efficiency is greater, since a single node-to-node link can be dynamically shared by many packets over time. The packets are queued up and transmitted as rapidly as possible over the link. By contrast, with circuit switching, time on a node-to-node link is preallocated using synchronous time division multiplexing. Much of the time, such a link may be idle because a portion of its time is dedicated to a connection that is idle.
- A packet-switching network can carry out data-rate conversion. Two stations of different data rates can exchange packets, since each connects to its node at its proper data rate.
- When traffic becomes heavy on a circuit-switching network, some calls are blocked; that is, the network refuses to accept additional connection requests until the load on the network decreases. On a packet-switching network, packets are still accepted, but delivery delay increases.
- Priorities can be used. Thus, if a node has a number of packets queued for transmission, it can transmit the higher-priority packets first. These packets will therefore experience less delay than lower-priority packets.

Packet switching also has disadvantages relative to circuit switching:

- Each time a packet passes through a packet-switching node it incurs a delay not present in circuit switching. At a minimum, it incurs a transmission delay equal to the length of the packet in bits divided by the incoming channel rate in bits per second; this is the time it takes to absorb the packet into an internal buffer. In addition, there may be a variable delay due to processing and queuing in the node.
- Because the packets between a given source and destination may vary in length, may take different routes, and may be subject to varying delay in the switches they encounter, the overall packet delay can vary substantially. This phenomenon, called jitter, may not be desirable for some applications (for example, in real-time applications, including telephone voice and real-time video).
- To route packets through the network, overhead information, including the address of the destination, and often sequencing information must be added to each packet, which reduces the communication capacity available for carrying user data. This is not needed in circuit switching once the circuit is set up.
- More processing is involved in the transfer of information using packet switching than in circuit switching at each node. In the case of circuit switching, there is virtually no processing at each switch once the circuit is set up.

Basic Operation

A station has a message to send through a packet-switching network that is of greater length than the maximum packet size. It therefore breaks the message into packets and sends these packets, one at a time, to the network. A question arises as to how the network will handle this stream of packets as it attempts to route them through the network and deliver them to the intended destination. Two approaches are used in contemporary networks: datagram and virtual circuit.

In the **datagram** approach, each packet is treated independently, with no reference to packets that have gone before. This approach is illustrated in Figure 3.7. Each node chooses the next node on a packet's path, taking into account information received from neighboring nodes on traffic, line failures, and so on. So the packets, each with the same destination address, do not all follow the same route (c), and they may arrive out of sequence at the exit point (d). In this example, the exit node restores the packets to their original order before delivering them to the destination (e). In some datagram networks, it is up to the destination rather than the exit node to do the reordering. Also, it is possible for a packet to be destroyed in the network. For example, if a packet-switching node crashes momentarily, all of its queued packets may be lost. Again, it is up to either the exit node or the destination to detect the loss of a packet and decide how to recover it. In this technique, each packet, treated independently, is referred to as a datagram.

In the **virtual circuit** approach, a preplanned route is established before any packets are sent. Once the route is established, all the packets between a pair of communicating parties follow this same route through the network. This is illustrated in Figure 3.8. Because the route is fixed for the duration of the logical connection, it is somewhat similar to a circuit in a circuit-switching network and is referred to as a virtual circuit. Each packet contains a virtual circuit identifier as well as data. Each node on the preestablished route knows where to direct such packets; no routing decisions are required. At any time, each station can have more than one virtual circuit to any other station and can have virtual circuits to more than one station.

So the main characteristic of the virtual circuit technique is that a route between stations is set up prior to data transfer. Note that this does not mean that this is a dedicated path, as in circuit switching. A packet is still buffered at each node and queued for output over a line. The difference from the datagram approach is that, with virtual circuits, the node need not make a routing decision for each packet. It is made only once for all packets using that virtual circuit.

If two stations wish to exchange data over an extended period of time, there are certain advantages to virtual circuits. First, the network may provide services related to the virtual circuit, including sequencing and error control. Sequencing refers to the fact that, because all packets follow the same route, they arrive in the original order. Error control is a service that assures not only that packets arrive in proper sequence, but also that all packets arrive correctly. For example, if a packet in a sequence from node 4 to node 6 fails to arrive at node 6, or arrives with an error, node 6 can request a retransmission of that packet from node 4 (Figure 3.3). Another advantage is that packets should transit the network more rapidly with a virtual circuit; it is not necessary to make a routing decision for each packet at each node.

One advantage of the datagram approach is that the call setup phase is avoided. Thus, if a station wishes to send only one or a few packets, datagram delivery will be quicker. Another advantage of the datagram service is that, because it is more primitive, it is more flexible. For example, if congestion devel-

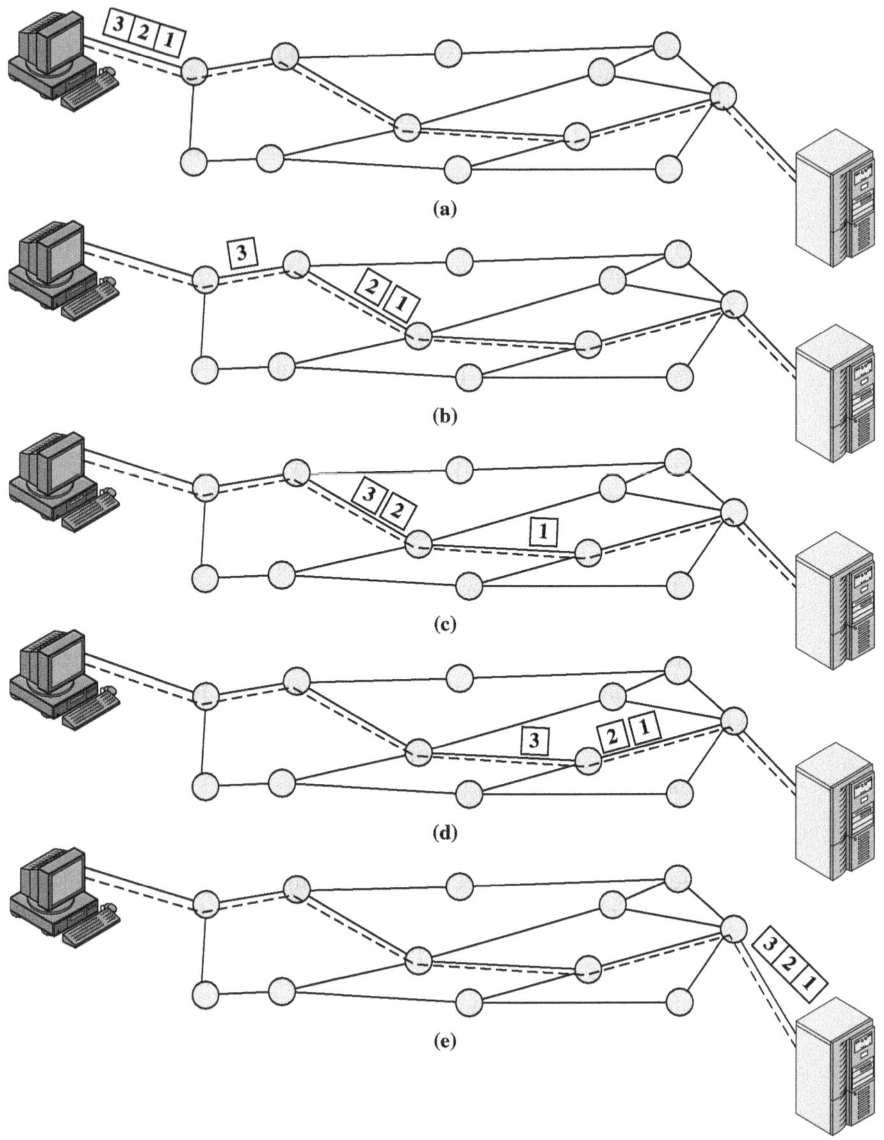

Figure 3.8 Packet Switching: Virtual-Circuit Approach

ops in one part of the network, incoming datagrams can be routed away from the congestion. With the use of virtual circuits, packets follow a predefined route, and thus it is more difficult for the network to adapt to congestion. A third advantage is that datagram delivery is inherently more reliable. With the use of virtual circuits, if a node fails, all virtual circuits that pass through that node are lost. With datagram delivery, if a node fails, subsequent packets may find an alternate route that bypasses that node.

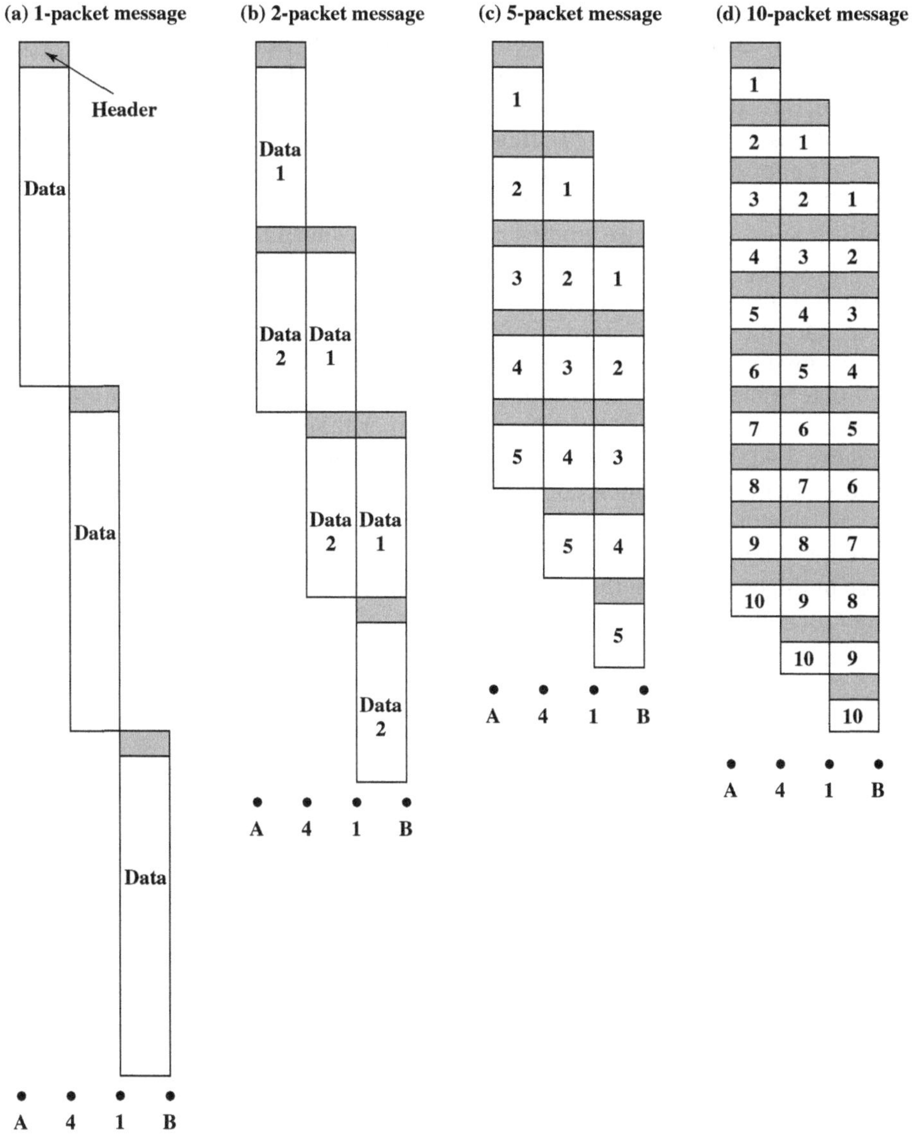

Figure 3.9 Effect of Packet Size on Transmission Time

Packet Size

There is a significant relationship between packet size and transmission time, as shown in Figure 3.9. In this example, it is assumed that there is a virtual circuit from station A through nodes 4 and 1 to station B (Figure 3.3). The message to be sent comprises 40 octets, and each packet contains 3 octets of control information, which is placed at the beginning of each packet and is referred to as a header. If the entire message is sent as a single packet of 43 octets (3 octets of header plus 40 octets of data), then the packet is first transmitted from station A to node 4 (Figure 3.9a). When the entire packet is received, it can then be transmitted from 4 to 1. When the entire packet is received at node 1, it is then transferred to station B. Ignoring switching time, total transmission time is 129 octet-times (43 octets × 3 packet transmissions).

Suppose now that we break the message up into two packets, each containing 20 octets of the message and, of course, 3 octets each of header, or control information. In this case, node 4 can begin transmitting the first packet as soon as it has arrived from A, without waiting for the second packet. Because of this overlap in transmission, the total transmission time drops to 92 octet-times. By breaking the message up into five packets, each intermediate node can begin transmission even sooner and the savings in time is greater, with a total of 77 octet-times for transmission. However, this process of using more and smaller packets eventually results in increased, rather than reduced, delay as illustrated in Figure 3.9d. This is because each packet contains a fixed amount of header, and more packets mean more of these headers. Furthermore, the example does not show the processing and queuing delays at each node. These delays are also greater when more packets are handled for a single message. However, we shall see in the next section that an extremely small packet size (53 octets) can result in an efficient network design.

3.5 ASYNCHRONOUS TRANSFER MODE

Asynchronous transfer mode (ATM), also known as cell relay, is in some ways similar to packet switching. Like packet switching, ATM involves the transfer of data in discrete chunks. Also, like packet switching, ATM allows multiple logical connections to be multiplexed over a single physical interface. In the case of ATM, the information flow on each logical connection is organized into fixed-size packets, called cells.

ATM is a streamlined protocol with minimal error and flow control capabilities. This reduces the overhead of processing ATM cells and reduces the number of overhead bits required with each cell, thus enabling ATM to operate at high data rates. Further, the use of fixed-size cells simplifies the processing required at each ATM node, again supporting the use of ATM at high data rates.

ATM Logical Connections

Logical connections in ATM are referred to as virtual channel connections (VCCs). A VCC is analogous to a virtual circuit in a packet-switching network; it is the basic unit of switching in an ATM network. A VCC is set up between two end users through the network, and a variable-rate, full-duplex flow of fixed-size cells is exchanged over the connection. VCCs are also used for user-network exchange (control signaling) and network-network exchange (network management and routing).

For ATM, a second sublayer of processing has been introduced that deals with the concept of virtual path (Figure 3.10). A virtual path connection (VPC) is a

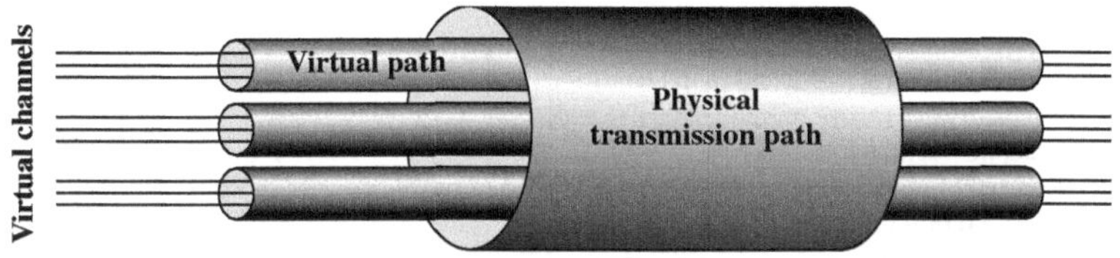

Figure 3.10 ATM Connection Relationships

bundle of VCCs that have the same endpoints. Thus all of the cells flowing over all of the VCCs in a single VPC are switched together.

The virtual path concept was developed in response to a trend in high-speed networking in which the control cost of the network is becoming an increasingly higher proportion of the overall network cost. The virtual path technique helps contain the control cost by grouping connections sharing common paths through the network into a single unit. Network management actions can then be applied to a small number of groups of connections instead of a large number of individual connections.

ATM Cells

ATM uses fixed-size cells, consisting of a 5-octet header and a 48-octet information field. There are several advantages to the use of small, fixed-size cells. First, the use of small cells may reduce queuing delay for a high-priority cell, because it waits less if it arrives slightly behind a lower-priority cell that has gained access to a resource (e.g., the transmitter). Second, it appears that fixed-size cells can be switched more efficiently, which is important for the very high data rates of ATM. With fixed-size cells, it is easier to implement the switching mechanism in hardware.

Header Format Figure 3.11a shows the header format at the user-network interface. Figure 3.11b shows the cell header format internal to the network. Internal to the network, the Generic Flow Control field, which performs end-to-end functions, is not retained. Instead, the Virtual Path Identifier field is expanded from 8 to 12 bits. This allows support for an expanded number of VPCs internal to the network, to include those supporting subscribers and those required for network management.

The **Generic Flow Control** (GFC) field can be used for control of cell flow at the local user-network interface. The details of its application are for further study. The field could be used to assist the customer in controlling the flow of traffic for different qualities of service. One candidate for the use of this field is a multiple-priority level indicator to control the flow of information in a service-dependent manner. In any case, the GFC mechanism is used to alleviate short-term overload conditions in the network.

The **Virtual Path Identifier** (VPI) field constitutes a routing field for the network. It is 8 bits at the user-network interface and 12 bits at the network-network interface, allowing for more virtual paths to be supported within the network. The **Virtual Channel Identifier** (VCI) field is used for routing to and from the end user. Thus, it functions much as a service access point.

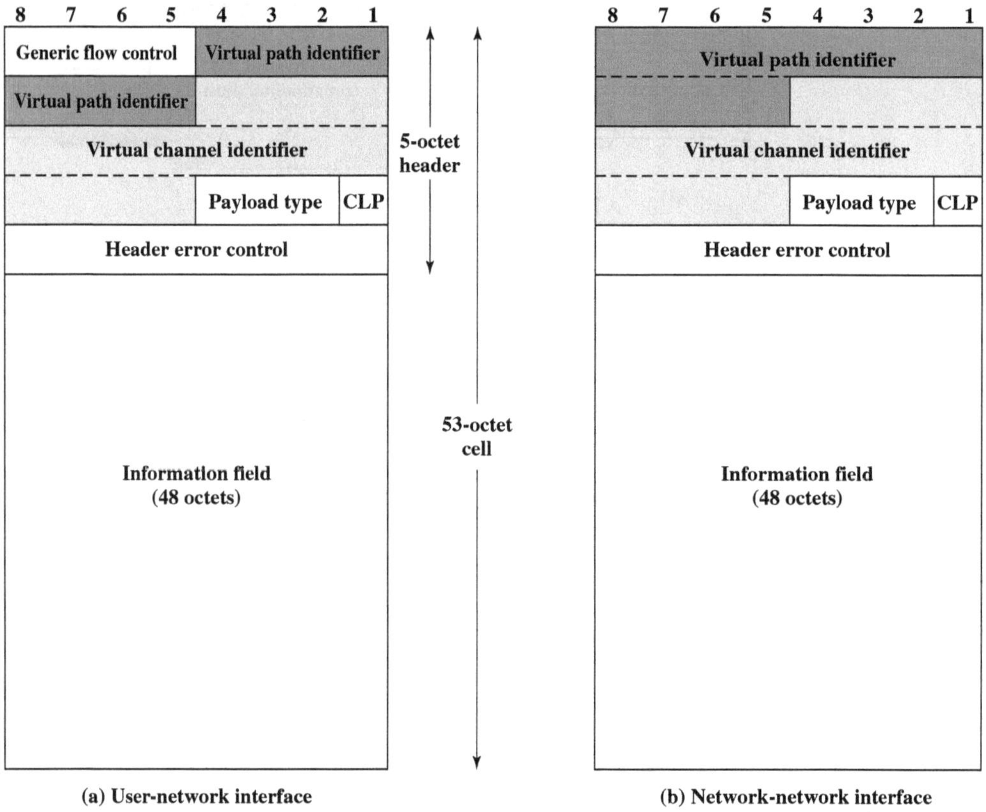

Figure 3.11 ATM Cell Format

The **Payload Type** (PT) field indicates the type of information in the information field. Table 3.1 shows the interpretation of the PT bits. A value of 0 in the first bit indicates user information (that is, information from the next higher layer). In this case, the second bit indicates whether congestion has been experienced; the third bit, known as the service data unit (SDU)[4] type bit, is a one-bit field that can be used to discriminate two types of ATM SDUs associated with a connection. The term *SDU* refers to the 48-octet payload of the cell. A value of 1 in the first bit of the payload type field indicates that this cell carries network management or maintenance information. This indication allows the insertion of network-management cells onto a user's VCC without impacting the user's data. Thus, the PT field can provide inband control information.

The **Cell Loss Priority** (CLP) field is used to provide guidance to the network in the event of congestion. A value of 0 indicates a cell of relatively higher priority, which should not be discarded unless no other alternative is available. A value

[4]This is the term used in ATM Forum documents. In ITU-T documents, this bit is referred to as the ATM-user-to-ATM-user (AAU) indication bit. The meaning is the same.

Table 3.1 Payload Type (PT) Field Coding

PT Coding	Interpretation		
000	User data cell,	congestion not experienced,	SDU-type = 0
001	User data cell,	congestion not experienced,	SDU-type = 1
010	User data cell,	congestion experienced,	SDU-type = 0
011	User data cell,	congestion experienced,	SDU-type = 1
100	OAM segment associated cell		
101	OAM end-to-end associated cell		
110	Resource management cell		
111	Reserved for future function		

SDU = Service Data Unit
OAM = Operations, Administration, and Maintenance

of 1 indicates that this cell is subject to discard within the network. The user might employ this field so that extra information may be inserted into the network, with a CLP of 1, and delivered to the destination if the network is not congested. The network may set this field to 1 for any data cell that is in violation of a agreement between the user and the network concerning traffic parameters. In this case, the switch that does the setting realizes that the cell exceeds the agreed traffic parameters but that the switch is capable of handling the cell. At a later point in the network, if congestion is encountered, this cell has been marked for discard in preference to cells that fall within agreed traffic limits.

The **Header Error Control** (HEC) field is an 8-bit error code that can be used to correct single-bit errors in the header and to detect double-bit errors. In the case of most existing protocols, the data that serve as input to the error code calculation are in general much longer than the size of the resulting error code. This allows for error detection. In the case of ATM, the input to the calculation is only 32 bits, compared with 8 bits for the code. The fact that the input is relatively short allows the code to be used not only for error detection but also, in some cases, for actual error correction. This is because there is sufficient redundancy in the code to recover from certain error patterns.

The error protection function provides both recovery from single-bit header errors and a low probability of the delivery of cells with errored headers under bursty error conditions. The error characteristics of fiber-based transmission systems appear to be a mix of single-bit errors and relatively large burst errors. For some transmission systems, the error correction capability, which is more time consuming, might not be invoked.

ATM Service Categories

An ATM network is designed to be able to transfer many different types of traffic simultaneously, including real-time flows such as voice, video, and bursty TCP flows. Although each such traffic flow is handled as a stream of 53-octet cells traveling through a virtual channel, the way in which each data flow is handled within the network depends on the characteristics of the traffic flow and the QoS requirements of the application. For example, real-time video traffic must be delivered within minimum variation in delay.

In this subsection, we summarize ATM service categories, which are used by an end system to identify the type of service required. The following service categories have been defined by the ATM Forum:

- **Real-time service**
  — Constant bit rate (CBR)
  — Real-time variable bit rate (rt-VBR)
- **Non-real-time service**
  —Non-real-time variable bit rate (nrt-VBR)
  —Available bit rate (ABR)
  —Unspecified bit rate (UBR)
  —Guaranteed frame rate (GFR)

Real-Time Services The most important distinction among applications concerns the amount of delay and the variability of delay, referred to as jitter, that the application can tolerate. Real-time applications typically involve a flow of information to a user that is intended to reproduce that flow at a source. For example, a user expects a flow of audio or video information to be presented in a continuous, smooth fashion. A lack of continuity or excessive loss results in significant loss of quality. Applications that involve interaction between people have tight constraints on delay. Typically, any delay above a few hundred milliseconds becomes noticeable and annoying. Accordingly, the demands in the ATM network for switching and delivery of real-time data are high.

The **constant bit rate (CBR)** service is perhaps the simplest service to define. It is used by applications that require a fixed data rate that is continuously available during the connection lifetime and a relatively tight upper bound on transfer delay. CBR is commonly used for uncompressed audio and video information. Examples of CBR applications include

- Videoconferencing
- Interactive audio (e.g., telephony)
- Audio/video distribution (e.g., television, distance learning, pay-per-view)
- Audio/video retrieval (e.g., video-on-demand, audio library)

The **real-time variable bit rate (rt-VBR)** category is intended for time-sensitive applications; that is, those requiring tightly constrained delay and delay variation. The principal difference between applications appropriate for rt-VBR and those appropriate for CBR is that rt-VBR applications transmit at a rate that varies with time. Equivalently, an rt-VBR source can be characterized as somewhat bursty. For example, the standard approach to video compression results in a sequence of image frames of varying sizes. Because real-time video requires a uniform frame transmission rate, the actual data rate varies.

The rt-VBR service allows the network more flexibility than CBR. The network is able to statistically multiplex a number of connections over the same dedicated capacity and still provide the required service to each connection.

Non-Real-Time Services Non-real-time services are intended for applications that have bursty traffic characteristics and do not have tight constraints on delay and delay variation. Accordingly, the network has greater flexibility in handling such traffic flows and can make greater use of statistical multiplexing to increase network efficiency.

For some non-real-time applications, it is possible to characterize the expected traffic flow so that the network can provide substantially improved quality of service (QoS) in the areas of loss and delay. Such applications can use the **non-real-time variable bit rate (nrt-VBR)** service. With this service, the end system specifies a peak cell rate, a sustainable or average cell rate, and a measure of how bursty or clumped the cells may be. With this information, the network can allocate resources to provide relatively low delay and minimal cell loss.

The nrt-VBR service can be used for data transfers that have critical response-time requirements. Examples include airline reservations, banking transactions, and process monitoring.

At any given time, a certain amount of the capacity of an ATM network is consumed in carrying CBR and the two types of VBR traffic. Additional capacity is available for one or both of the following reasons: (1) Not all of the total resources have been committed to CBR and VBR traffic, and (2) the bursty nature of VBR traffic means that at some times less than the committed capacity is being used. All of this unused capacity could be made available for the **unspecified bit rate (UBR)** service. This service is suitable for applications that can tolerate variable delays and some cell losses, which is typically true of TCP-based traffic. With UBR, cells are forwarded on a first-in-first-out (FIFO) basis using the capacity not consumed by other services; both delays and variable losses are possible. No initial commitment is made to a UBR source and no feedback concerning congestion is provided; this is referred to as a **best-effort service**. Examples of UBR applications include

- Text/data/image transfer, messaging, distribution, retrieval
- Remote terminal (e.g., telecommuting)

Bursty applications that use a reliable end-to-end protocol such as TCP can detect congestion in a network by means of increased round-trip delays and packet discarding. However, TCP has no mechanism for causing the resources within the network to be shared fairly among many TCP connections. Further, TCP does not minimize congestion as efficiently as is possible using explicit information from congested nodes within the network.

To improve the service provided to bursty sources that would otherwise use UBR, the **available bit rate (ABR)** service has been defined. An application using ABR specifies a peak cell rate (PCR) that it will use and a minimum cell rate (MCR) that it requires. The network allocates resources so that all ABR applications receive at least their MCR capacity. Any unused capacity is then shared in a fair and controlled fashion among all ABR sources. The ABR mechanism uses explicit feedback to sources to assure that capacity is fairly allocated. Any capacity not used by ABR sources remains available for UBR traffic.

An example of an application using ABR is LAN interconnection. In this case, the end systems attached to the ATM network are routers.

The most recent addition to the set of ATM service categories is **Guaranteed Frame Rate (GFR)**, which is designed specifically to support IP backbone subnetworks. GFR provides better service than UBR for frame-based traffic, including IP and Ethernet. A major goal of GFR is to optimize the handling of frame-based traffic that passes from a LAN through a router onto an ATM backbone network. Such ATM networks are increasingly being used in large enterprise, carrier, and Internet service provider networks to consolidate and extend IP services over the wide area. While ABR is also an ATM service meant to provide a greater measure of guaranteed packet performance over ATM backbones, ABR is relatively difficult to implement between routers over an ATM network. With the increased emphasis on using ATM to support IP-based traffic, especially traffic that originates on Ethernet LANs, GFR may offer the most attractive alternative for providing ATM service.

3.6 INTRODUCTION TO SONET

Before SONET, the first generations of fiber optic systems in the public telephone network used proprietary architectures, equipment, line codes, multiplexing formats, and maintenance procedures. The users of this equipment—Regional Bell Operating Companies and inter-exchange carriers (IXCs) in the U.S., Canada, Korea, Taiwan, and Hong Kong—wanted standards so they could mix and match equipment from different suppliers. This was obviously a mish-mash of ideas, implementations, designs and so on and was difficult to implement and maintain, much less interoperable. So, it was realized that there needed to be a standard connecting one fiber system to another. This standard is called SONET for Synchronous Optical NETwork.

SONET (Synchronous Optical NETwork) is relatively recent telecommunications standard for optical telecommunications transport. It was created by the Exchange Carriers Standards Association (ECSA) for the American National Standards Institute (ANSI). ANSI establishes industry standards in the U.S. for a wide range of telecommunications and other industries. SONET was developed to be a standard for at least several decades, but, of course as quickly as technology advances, this is probably naïve.

SONET provides significant advantages over older telecommunications technologies. These advantages include:[5]

1. A significant reduction in equipment requirements
2. Network reliability is increased dramatically primarily since fiber optics is much more reliable than copper-based technologies.
3. Overload space is included to accompany the data. This is so you can discern faults in data integrity quickly, thus reducing costs.

[5]http://www.tek.com/Measurement/App_Notes/SONET/intro.pdf

4. A unique and effective synchronous multiplexing format designed for carrying lower level digital signals (such as DS1, DS3) and a synchronous structure which greatly simplifies the interface to digital switches, digital cross-connect switches, and add-drop multiplexers.
5. Interoperability attributes which enable products from different vendors to be connected.
6. The careful definition of an adaptable architecture easily capable of accommodating future applications, with a variety of transmission rates.

SONET defines an effective and efficient technology for carrying many signals of different capacities through a synchronous, flexible, optical network. This is accomplished via the use of a byte-interleaved multiplexing scheme. Byte-interleaving greatly simplifies multiplexing, and provides effective end-to-end management of the network.

The first aspect in the SONET multiplexing process involves the generation of the lowest level or base signal. In SONET, this base signal is referred to as Synchronous Transport Signal level-1, or simply STS-1, which operates at 51.84 Mb/s. Higher-level signals are integer multiples of STS-1, creating the family of STS-N signals in Table 3.2. An STS-N signal is composed of N byte-interleaved STS-1 signals. This table also includes the optical counterpart for each STS-N signal, designated OC-N (Optical Carrier level-N).

Synchronous and Non-synchronous line rates and the relationships between each are shown in Tables 3.2 and 3.3.

Table 3.2 SONET Hierarchy

Signal	Bit Rate	Capacity
STS-1, OC-1	51.840 Mb/s	28 DS1s or 1 DS3
STS-3, OC-3	155.520 Mb/s	84 DS1s or 3 DS3s
STS-12, OC-12	622.080 Mb/s	336 DS1s or 12 DS3s
STS-48, OC-48	2488.320 Mb/s	1344 DS1s or 48 DS3s
STS-192, OC-192	9953.280 Mb/s	5376 DS1s or 192 DS3s
STS-768, OC-768	39813.12 Mb/s	21504 DS1s or 768 DS3s

STS = Synchronous Transport Signal
OC = Optical Carrier

Table 3.3 Non-Synchronous Hierarchy

Signal	Bit Rate	Channels
DS0	64 kb/s	1 DS0
DS1	1.544 Mb/s	24 DS0s
DS2	6.312 Mb/s	96 DS0s
DS3	44.736 Mb/s	28 DS1s

3.7 RECOMMENDED READINGS AND WEB SITES

As befits its age, circuit switching has inspired a voluminous literature. Two good books on the subject are [BELL00] and [FREE04]. The literature on packet switching is also enormous. Books with good treatments of this subject include [SPOH02] and [BERT92]. [MCDY99] and [BLAC99] provide good coverage of ATM.

[STAL04] covers all of the topics in this chapter in greater detail.

BELL00 Bellamy, J. *Digital Telephony.* New York: Wiley, 2000.

BERT92 Bertsekas, D., and Gallager, R. *Data Networks.* Englewood Cliffs, NJ: Prentice Hall, 1992.

BLAC99 Black, U. *ATM Volume I: Foundation for Broadband Networks.* Upper Saddle River, NJ: Prentice Hall, 1992.

FREE04 Freeman, R. *Telecommunication System Engineering.* New York: Wiley, 2004.

MCDY99 McDysan, D., and Spohn, D. *ATM: Theory and Application.* New York: McGraw-Hill, 1999.

SPOH02 Spohn, D. *Data Network Design.* New York: McGraw-Hill, 2002.

STAL04 Stallings, W. *Data and Computer Communications, Seventh Edition.* Upper Saddle River: NJ: Prentice Hall, 2004.

Recommended Web Sites:

- **ATM Hot Links:** Good collection of white papers and links
- **ATM Forum Web Site:** Contains technical specifications and white papers
- **Cell Relay Retreat:** Contains archives of the cell-relay mailing list, links to numerous ATM-related documents, and links to many ATM-related Web sites

3.8 KEY TERMS, REVIEW QUESTIONS, AND PROBLEMS

Key Terms

asynchronous transfer mode (ATM)	header	packet switching
cell	local area network (LAN)	subscriber loop
cell relay	local loop	virtual channel
circuit switching	metropolitan area network (MAN)	virtual circuit
datagram	packet	virtual path
		wide area network (WAN)

Review Questions

3.1 Differentiate between WANs and LANs.

3.2 Why is it useful to have more than one possible path through a network for each pair of stations?

3.3 What is the principal application that has driven the design of circuit-switching networks?

3.4 Distinguish between static and alternate routing in a circuit-switching network.

3.5 What is a semipermanent connection?

3.6 What data rates are offered for ISDN primary access?

3.7 Explain the difference between datagram and virtual circuit operation.

3.8 What are some of the limitations of using a circuit-switching network for data transmission?

3.9 What is the difference between a virtual channel and a virtual path?

Problems

3.1 Define the following parameters for a switching network:

N = number of hops between two given end systems
L = message length in bits
B = data rate, in bits per second (bps), on all links
P = fixed packet size, in bits
H = overhead (header) bits per packet
S = call setup time (circuit switching or virtual circuit) in seconds
D = propagation delay per hop in seconds

a. For $N = 4, L = 3200, B = 9600, P = 1024, H = 16, S = 0.2, D = 0.001$, compute the end-to-end delay for circuit switching, virtual circuit packet switching, and datagram packet switching. Assume that there are no acknowledgments. Ignore processing delay at the nodes.

b. Derive general expressions for the three techniques of part (a), taken two at a time (three expressions in all), showing the conditions under which the delays are equal.

3.2 What value of P, as a function of N, L, and H, results in minimum end-to-end delay on a datagram network? Assume that L is much larger than P, and D is zero.

3.3 Consider a simple telephone network consisting of two end offices and one intermediate switch with a 1-MHz full-duplex trunk between each end office and the intermediate switch. The average telephone is used to make four calls per 8-hour workday, with a mean call duration of six minutes. Ten percent of the calls are long distance. What is the maximum number of telephones an end office can support?

3.4 Explain the flaw in the following reasoning: Packet switching requires control and address bits to be added to each packet. This introduces considerable overhead in packet switching. In circuit switching, a transparent circuit is established. No extra bits are needed. Therefore, there is no overhead in circuit switching, and, because there is no overhead in circuit switching, line utilization must be more efficient than in packet switching.

3.5 Assuming no malfunction in any of the stations or nodes of a network, is it possible for a packet to be delivered to the wrong destination?

3.6 Consider a packet-switching network of N nodes, connected by the following topologies:

a. Star: One central node with no attached station; all other nodes attach to the central node.

b. Loop: Each node connects to two other nodes to form a closed loop.

c. Fully connected: Each node is directly connected to all other nodes.

For each case, give the average number of hops between stations.

3.7 One key design decision for ATM was whether to use fixed- or variable-length cells. Let us consider this decision from the point of view of efficiency. We can define transmission efficiency as

$$N = \frac{\text{Number of information octets}}{\text{Number of information octets} + \text{Number of overhead octets}}$$

a. Consider the use of fixed length packets. In this case the overhead consists of the header octets. Define

L = Data field size of the cell in octets
H = Header size of the cell in octets
X = Number of information octets to be transmitted as a single message

Derive an expression for N. *Hint:* The expression will need to use the operator $\lceil \bullet \rceil$, where $\lceil Y \rceil =$ the smallest integer greater than or equal to Y.

b. If cells have variable length, then overhead is determined by the header, plus the flags to delimit the cells or an additional length field in the header. Let Hv = additional overhead octets required to enable the use of variable-length cells. Derive an expression for N in terms of X, H, and Hv.

c. Let $L = 48$, $H = 5$, and $Hv = 2$. Plot N versus message size for fixed and variable-length cells. Comment on the results.

3.8 Another key design decision for ATM is the size of the data field for fixed-size cells. Let us consider this decision from the point of view of efficiency and delay.

a. Assume that an extended transmission takes place, so that all cells are completely filled. Derive an expression for the efficiency N as a function of H and L.

b. Packetization delay is the delay introduced into a transmission stream by the need to buffer bits until an entire packet is filled before transmission. Derive an expression for this delay as a function of L and the data rate R of the source.

c. Common data rates for voice coding are 32 kbps and 64 kbps. Plot packetization delay as a function of L for these two data rates; use a left-hand y-axis with a maximum value of 2 ms. On the same graph, plot transmission efficiency as a function of L; use a right-hand y-axis with a maximum value of 100%. Comment on the results.

3.9 Consider compressed video transmission in an ATM network. Suppose standard ATM cells must be transmitted through 5 switches. The data rate is 43 Mbps.

a. What is the transmission time for one cell through one switch?

b. Each switch may be transmitting a cell from other traffic all of which we assume to have lower (non-preemptive for the cell) priority. If the switch is busy transmitting a cell, our cell has to wait until the other cell completes transmission. If the switch is free, our cell is transmitted immediately. What is the maximum time from when a typical video cell arrives at the first switch (and possibly waits) until it is finished being transmitted by the fifth and last one? Assume that you can ignore propagation time, switching time, and everything else but the transmission time and the time spent waiting for another cell to clear a switch.

c. Now suppose we know that each switch is utilized 60% of the time with the other low-priority traffic. By this we mean that with probability 0.6 when we look at a switch it is busy. Suppose that if there is a cell being transmitted by a switch, the average delay spent waiting for a cell to finish transmission is one-half a cell transmission time. What is the average time from the input of the first switch to clearing the fifth?

d. However, the measure of most interest is not delay but jitter, which is the variability in the delay. Use parts (b) and (c) to calculate the maximum and average variability, respectively, in the delay.

In all cases assume that the various random events are independent of one another; for example, we ignore the burstiness typical of such traffic.

CHAPTER 4

PROTOCOLS AND THE TCP/IP SUITE

We begin this chapter by introducing the concept of a layered protocol architecture. We then examine the most important such architecture, the TCP/IP protocol suite. TCP/IP is an Internet-based concept and is the framework for developing a complete range of computer communications standards. Virtually all computer vendors now provide support for this architecture. Another well-known architecture is the Open Systems Interconnection (OSI) reference model. OSI is a standardized architecture that is often used to describe communications functions but that is now rarely implemented.

Following a discussion of protocol architectures, the important concept of internetworking is examined. Inevitably, an organization will require the use of more than one communication network. Some means of interconnecting these networks is required, and this raises issues that relate to the protocol architecture.

4.1 THE NEED FOR A PROTOCOL ARCHITECTURE

When computers, terminals, and/or other data processing devices exchange data, the procedures involved can be quite complex. Consider, for example, the transfer of a file between two computers. There must be a data path between the two computers, either directly or via a communication network. But more is needed. Typical tasks to be performed include the following:

1. The source system must either activate the direct data communication path or inform the communication network of the identity of the desired destination system.
2. The source system must ascertain that the destination system is prepared to receive data.
3. The file transfer application on the source system must ascertain that the file management program on the destination system is prepared to accept and store the file for this particular user.
4. If the file formats used on the two systems are incompatible, one or the other system must perform a format translation function.

It is clear that there must be a high degree of cooperation between the two computer systems. Instead of implementing the logic for this as a single module, the task is broken up into subtasks, each of which is implemented separately. In a protocol architecture, the modules are arranged in a vertical stack. Each layer in the stack performs a related subset of the functions required to communicate with another system. It relies on the next lower layer to perform more primitive functions and to conceal the details of those functions. It provides services to the next higher layer. Ideally, layers should be defined so that changes in one layer do not require changes in other layers.

Of course, it takes two to communicate, so the same set of layered functions must exist in two systems. Communication is achieved by having the corresponding, or *peer*, layers in two systems communicate. The peer layers communicate by means of formatted blocks of data that obey a set of rules or conventions known as a *protocol*. The key features of a protocol are as follows:

- **Syntax:** Concerns the format of the data blocks
- **Semantics:** Includes control information for coordination and error handling
- **Timing:** Includes speed matching and sequencing

4.2 THE TCP/IP PROTOCOL ARCHITECTURE

The TCP/IP protocol architecture is a result of protocol research and development conducted on the experimental packet-switched network, ARPANET, funded by the Defense Advanced Research Projects Agency (DARPA), and is generally referred to as the TCP/IP protocol suite. This protocol suite consists of a large collection of protocols that have been issued as Internet standards by the Internet Architecture Board (IAB).

The TCP/IP Layers

In general terms, communications can be said to involve three agents: applications, computers, and networks. Examples of applications include file transfer and electronic mail. The applications that we are concerned with here are distributed applications that involve the exchange of data between two computer systems. These applications, and others, execute on computers that can often support multiple simultaneous applications. Computers are connected to networks, and the data to be exchanged are transferred by the network from one computer to another. Thus, the transfer of data from one application to another involves first getting the data to the computer in which the application resides and then getting the data to the intended application within the computer.

With these concepts in mind, it appears natural to organize the communication task into five relatively independent layers:

- Physical layer
- Network access layer
- Internet layer
- Host-to-host, or transport layer
- Application layer

The **physical layer** covers the physical interface between a data transmission device (e.g., workstation, computer) and a transmission medium or network. This layer is concerned with specifying the characteristics of the transmission medium, the nature of the signals, the data rate, and related matters.

The **network access layer** is concerned with the exchange of data between an end system (server, workstation, etc.) and the network to which it is attached. The sending computer must provide the network with the address of the destination computer, so that the network may route the data to the appropriate destination. The sending computer may wish to invoke certain services, such as priority, that might be provided by the network. The specific software used at this layer depends on the type of network to be used; different standards have been developed for circuit switching, packet switching (e.g., ATM), LANs (e.g., Ethernet), and others. Thus it makes sense to separate those functions having to do with network access into a separate layer. By doing this, the remainder of the communications software, above the network access layer, need not be concerned about the specifics of the network to be used. The same higher-layer software should function properly regardless of the particular network to which the computer is attached.

The network access layer is concerned with access to and routing data across a network for two end systems attached to the same network. In those cases where two devices are attached to different networks, procedures are needed to allow data to traverse multiple interconnected networks. This is the function of the **internet layer**. The Internet Protocol (IP) is used at this layer to provide the routing function across multiple networks. This protocol is implemented not only in the end systems but also in routers. A router is a processor that connects two networks and whose primary function is to relay data from one network to the other on its route from the source to the destination end system.

Regardless of the nature of the applications that are exchanging data, there is usually a requirement that data be exchanged reliably. That is, we would like to be assured that all of the data arrive at the destination application and that the data arrive in the same order in which they were sent. As we shall see, the mechanisms for providing reliability are essentially independent of the nature of the applications. Thus, it makes sense to collect those mechanisms in a common layer shared by all applications; this is referred to as the **host-to-host layer**, or **transport layer**. The Transmission Control Protocol (TCP) is the most commonly used protocol to provide this functionality.

Finally, the **application layer** contains the logic needed to support the various user applications. For each different type of application, such as file transfer, a separate module is needed that is peculiar to that application.

Operation of TCP and IP

Figure 4.1 indicates how these protocols are configured for communications. To make clear that the total communications facility may consist of multiple networks, the constituent networks are usually referred to as *subnetworks*. Some sort of network access protocol, such as the Ethernet logic, is used to connect a computer to a subnetwork. This protocol enables the host to send data across the subnetwork to another host or, in the case of a host on another subnetwork, to a router. IP is implemented in all of the end systems and the routers. It acts as a relay to move a block of data from one host, through one or more routers, to another host. TCP is implemented only in the end systems; it keeps track of the blocks of data to assure that all are delivered reliably to the appropriate application.

For successful communication, every entity in the overall system must have a unique address. Actually, two levels of addressing are needed. Each host on a subnetwork must have a unique global internet address; this allows the data to be delivered to the proper host. Each process with a host must have an address that is unique within the host; this allows the host-to-host protocol (TCP) to deliver data to the proper process. These latter addresses are known as **ports**.

Let us trace a simple operation. Suppose that a process, associated with port 1 at host A, wishes to send a message to another process, associated with port 3 at host B.

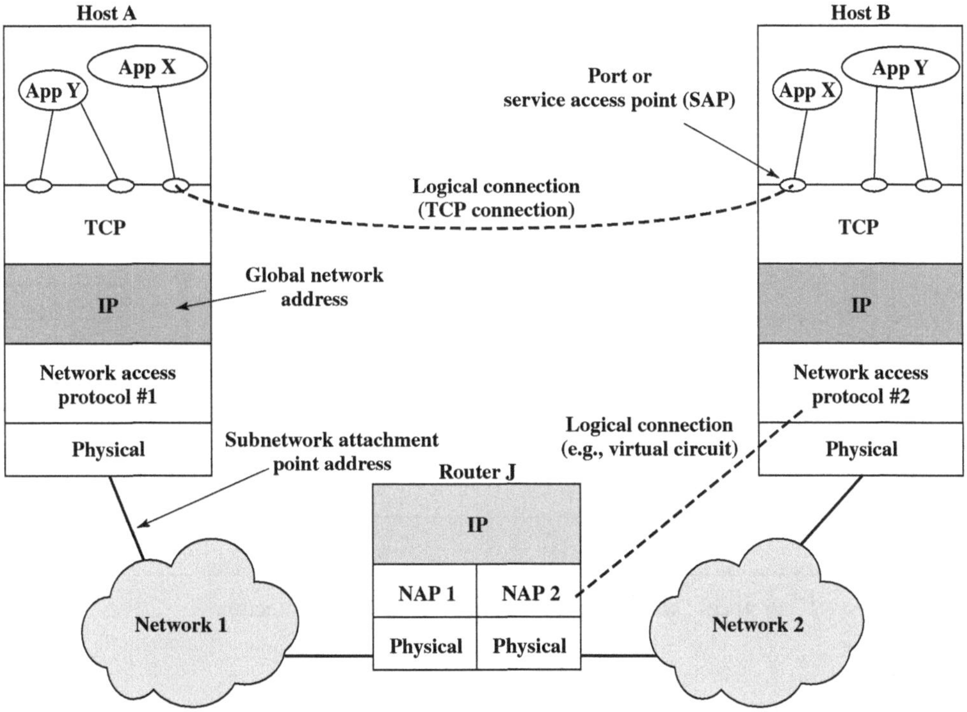

Figure 4.1 TCP/IP Concepts

The process at A hands the message down to TCP with instructions to send it to host B, port 3. TCP hands the message down to IP with instructions to send it to host B. Note that IP need not be told the identity of the destination port. All it needs to know is that the data are intended for host B. Next, IP hands the message down to the network access layer (e.g., Ethernet logic) with instructions to send it to router J (the first hop on the way to B).

To control this operation, control information as well as user data must be transmitted, as suggested in Figure 4.2. Let us say that the sending process generates a block of data and passes this to TCP. TCP may break this block into smaller pieces to make it more manageable. To each of these pieces, TCP appends control information known as the TCP header, forming a *TCP segment*. The control information is to be used by the peer TCP protocol entity at host B. Examples of items in this header include

- **Destination port:** When the TCP entity at B receives the segment, it must know to whom the data are to be delivered.
- **Sequence number:** TCP numbers the segments that it sends to a particular destination port sequentially, so that if they arrive out of order, the TCP entity at B can reorder them.
- **Checksum:** The sending TCP includes a code that is a function of the contents of the remainder of the segment. The receiving TCP performs the same calculation and compares the result with the incoming code. A discrepancy results if there has been some error in transmission.

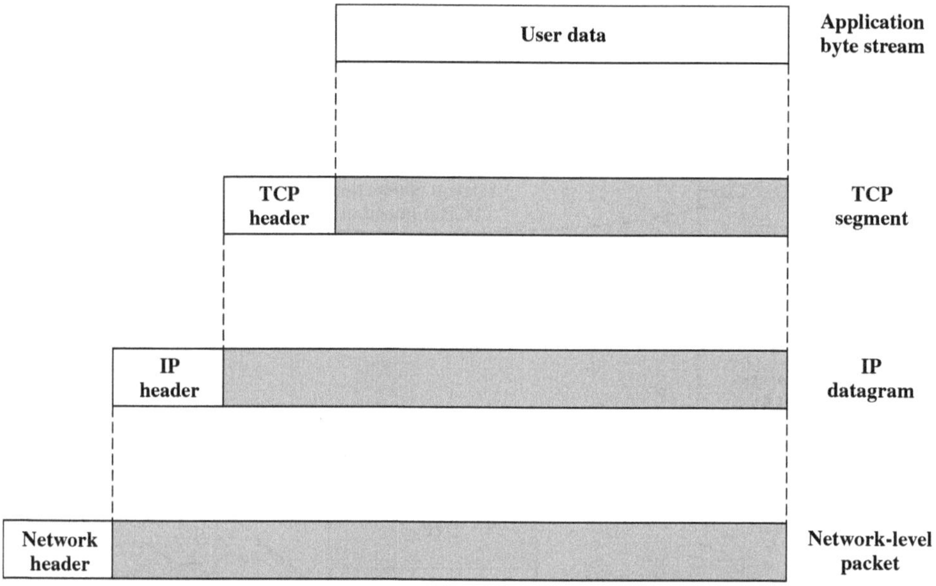

Figure 4.2 Protocol Data Units (PDUs) in the TCP/IP Architecture

Next, TCP hands each segment over to IP, with instructions to transmit it to B. These segments must be transmitted across one or more subnetworks and relayed through one or more intermediate routers. This operation, too, requires the use of control information. Thus IP appends a header of control information to each segment to form an *IP datagram*. An example of an item stored in the IP header is the destination host address (in this example, B).

Finally, each IP datagram is presented to the network access layer for transmission across the first subnetwork in its journey to the destination. The network access layer appends its own header, creating a packet, or frame. The packet is transmitted across the subnetwork to router J. The packet header contains the information that the subnetwork needs to transfer the data across the subnetwork. Examples of items that may be contained in this header include

- **Destination subnetwork address:** The subnetwork must know to which attached device the packet is to be delivered.
- **Facilities requests:** The network access protocol might request the use of certain subnetwork facilities, such as priority.

At router J, the packet header is stripped off and the IP header examined. On the basis of the destination address information in the IP header, the IP module in the router directs the datagram out across subnetwork 2 to B. To do this, the datagram is again augmented with a network access header.

When the data are received at B, the reverse process occurs. At each layer, the corresponding header is removed, and the remainder is passed on to the next higher layer, until the original user data are delivered to the destination process.

As an aside, the generic name for a block of data exchanged at any protocol level is referred to as a **protocol data unit** (PDU). Thus, a TCP segment is a TCP PDU.

TCP/IP Applications

A number of applications have been standardized to operate on top of TCP. We mention three of the most common here.

The **Simple Mail Transfer Protocol (SMTP)** provides a basic electronic mail facility. It provides a mechanism for transferring messages among separate hosts. Features of SMTP include mailing lists, return receipts, and forwarding. The SMTP protocol does not specify the way in which messages are to be created; some local editing or native electronic mail facility is required. Once a message is created, SMTP accepts the message and makes use of TCP to send it to an SMTP module on another host. The target SMTP module will make use of a local electronic mail package to store the incoming message in a user's mailbox.

The **File Transfer Protocol (FTP)** is used to send files from one system to another under user command. Both text and binary files are accommodated, and the protocol provides features for controlling user access. When a user wishes to engage in file transfer, FTP sets up a TCP connection to the target system for the exchange of control messages. This connection allows user ID and password to be transmitted and allows the user to specify the file and file actions desired. Once a file transfer is approved, a second TCP connection is set up for the data transfer. The file is transferred over the data connection, without the overhead of any headers or control information at the application level. When the transfer is complete, the control connection is used to signal the completion and to accept new file transfer commands.

TELNET provides a remote logon capability, which enables a user at a terminal or personal computer to logon to a remote computer and function as if directly connected to that computer. The protocol was designed to work with simple scroll-mode terminals. TELNET is actually implemented in two modules: User TELNET interacts with the terminal I/O module to communicate with a local terminal. It converts the characteristics of real terminals to the network standard and vice versa. Server TELNET interacts with an application, acting as a surrogate terminal handler so that remote terminals appear as local to the application. Terminal traffic between User and Server TELNET is carried on a TCP connection.

4.3 THE OSI MODEL

The Open Systems Interconnection (OSI) reference model was developed by the International Organization for Standardization (ISO)[1] as a model for a computer protocol architecture and as a framework for developing protocol standards. The OSI model consists of seven layers:

- Application
- Presentation

[1]ISO is not an acronym (in which case it would be IOS), but a word, derived from the Greek *isos*, meaning *equal*.

- Session
- Transport
- Network
- Data link
- Physical

Figure 4.3 illustrates the OSI model and provides a brief definition of the functions performed at each layer. The intent of the OSI model is that protocols be developed to perform the functions of each layer.

The designers of OSI assumed that this model and the protocols developed within this model would come to dominate computer communications, eventually replacing proprietary protocol implementations and rival multivendor models such

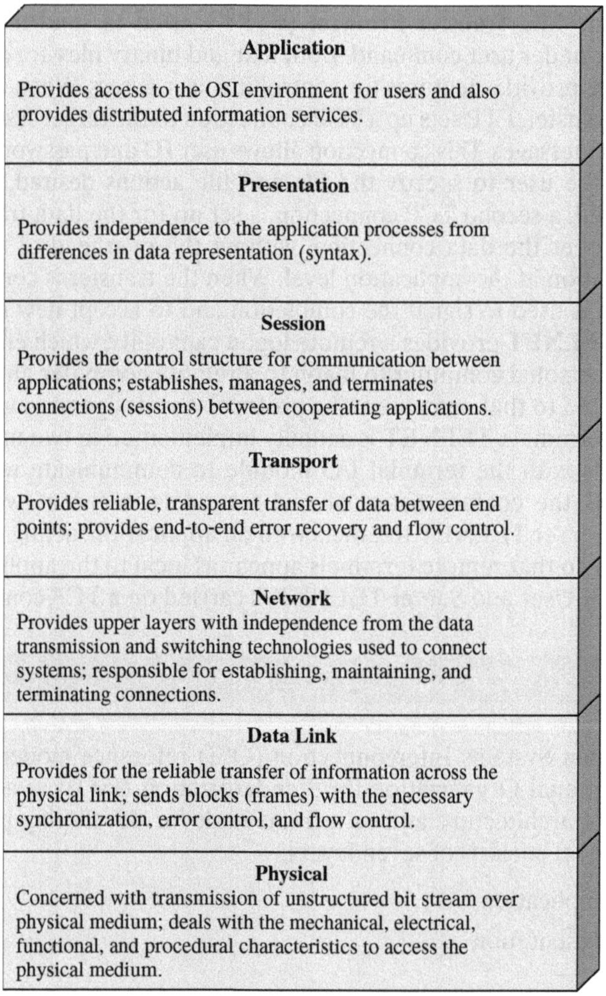

Figure 4.3 The OSI Layers

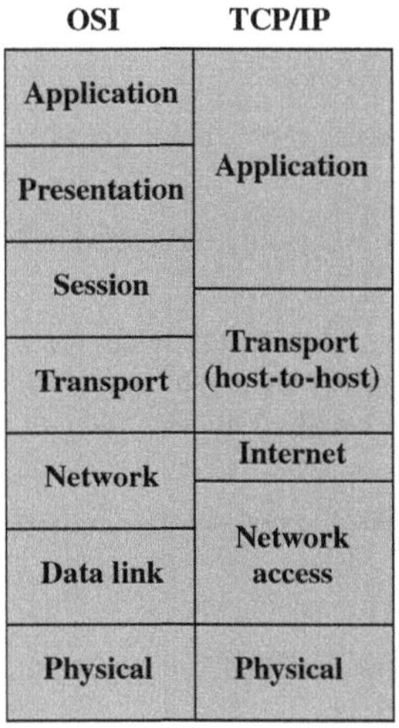

Figure 4.4 A Comparison of the OSI and TCP/IP Protocol Architectures

as TCP/IP. This has not happened. Although many useful protocols have been developed in the context of OSI, the overall seven-layer model has not flourished. Instead, the TCP/IP architecture has come to dominate. There are a number of reasons for this outcome. Perhaps the most important is that the key TCP/IP protocols were mature and well tested at a time when similar OSI protocols were in the development stage. When businesses began to recognize the need for interoperability across networks, only TCP/IP was available and ready to go. Another reason is that the OSI model is unnecessarily complex, with seven layers to accomplish what TCP/IP does with fewer layers.

Figure 4.4 illustrates the layers of the TCP/IP and OSI architectures, showing roughly the correspondence in functionality between the two.

4.4 INTERNETWORKING

In most cases, a LAN or WAN is not an isolated entity. An organization may have more than one type of LAN at a given site to satisfy a spectrum of needs. An organization may have multiple LANs of the same type at a given site to accommodate performance or security requirements. And an organization may have LANs at various sites and need them to be interconnected via WANs for central control of distributed information exchange.

Table 4.1 lists some commonly used terms relating to the interconnection of networks, or internetworking. An interconnected set of networks, from a user's point of view, may appear simply as a larger network. However, if each of the constituent networks retains its identity, and special mechanisms are needed for communicating across multiple networks, then the entire configuration is often referred to as an **internet**. The most important example of an internet is referred to simply as the Internet. As the Internet has evolved from its modest beginnings as a research-oriented packet-

Table 4.1 Internetworking Terms

Communication Network

A facility that provides a data transfer service among devices attached to the network.

Internet

A collection of communication networks interconnected by bridges and/or routers.

Intranet

An internet used by a single organization that provides the key Internet applications, especially the World Wide Web. An intranet operates within the organization for internal purposes and can exist as an isolated, self-contained internet, or may have links to the Internet.

End System (ES)

A device attached to one of the networks of an internet that is used to support end-user applications or services.

Intermediate System (IS)

A device used to connect two networks and permit communication between end systems attached to different networks.

Bridge

An IS used to connect two LANs that use similar LAN protocols. The bridge acts as an address filter, picking up packets from one LAN that are intended for a destination on another LAN and passing those packets on. The bridge does not modify the contents of the packets and does not add anything to the packet. The bridge operates at layer 2 of the OSI model.

Router

An IS used to connect two networks that may or may not be similar. The router employs an internet protocol present in each router and each end system of the network. The router operates at layer 3 of the OSI model.

switching network, it has served as the basis for the development of internetworking technology and as the model for private internets within organizations. These latter are also referred to as **intranets**.

Each constituent subnetwork in an internet supports communication among the devices attached to that subnetwork; these devices are referred to as **end systems** (ESs). In addition, subnetworks are connected by devices referred to in the ISO documents as **intermediate systems** (ISs). ISs provide a communications path and perform the necessary relaying and routing functions so that data can be exchanged between devices attached to different subnetworks in the internet.

Two types of ISs of particular interest are bridges and routers. The differences between them have to do with the types of protocols used for the internetworking logic. In essence, a **bridge** operates at layer 2 of the OSI seven-layer architecture and acts as a relay of frames between like networks. A **router** operates at layer 3 of the OSI architecture and routes packets between potentially different networks. Both the bridge and the router assume that the same upper-layer protocols are in use.

The roles and functions of routers were introduced in the context of IP earlier in this chapter. However, because of the importance of routers in the overall networking scheme, it is worth providing additional comment in this section.

Routers

Internetworking among dissimilar subnetworks is achieved by using routers to interconnect the subnetworks. Essential functions that the router must perform include the following:

1. Provide a link between networks.
2. Provide for the routing and delivery of data between processes on end systems attached to different networks.
3. Provide these functions in such a way as not to require modifications of the networking architecture of any of the attached subnetworks.

The third point implies that the router must accommodate a number of differences among networks, such as the following:

- **Addressing schemes:** The networks may use different schemes for assigning addresses to devices. For example, an IEEE 802 LAN uses 48-bit binary addresses for each attached device; an ATM network typically uses 15-digit decimal addresses (encoded as 4 bits per digit for a 60-bit address). Some form of global network addressing must be provided, as well as a directory service.
- **Maximum packet sizes:** Packets from one network may have to be broken into smaller pieces to be transmitted on another network, a process known as **segmentation** or **fragmentation**. For example, Ethernet imposes a maximum packet size of 1500 bytes; a maximum packet size of 1000 bytes is common on X.25 packet-switching networks. A packet that is transmitted on an Ethernet system and picked up by a router for retransmission on an X.25 network may have to be fragmented into two smaller ones.

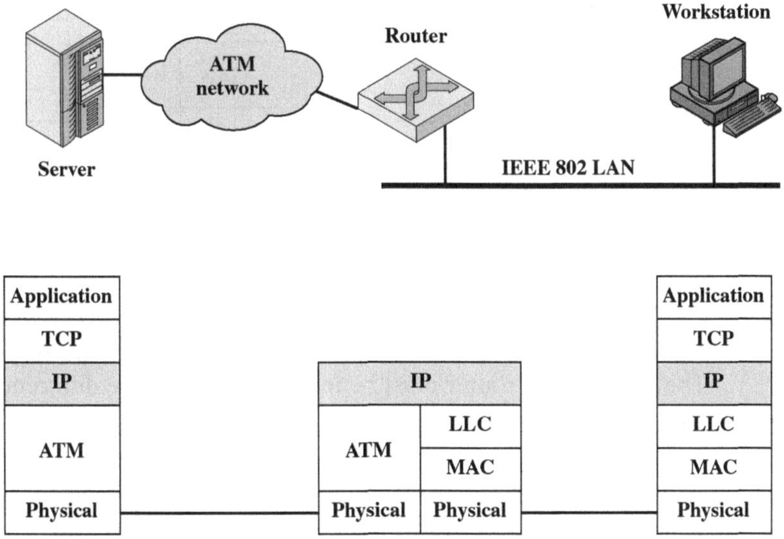

Figure 4.5 Configuration for TCP/IP Example

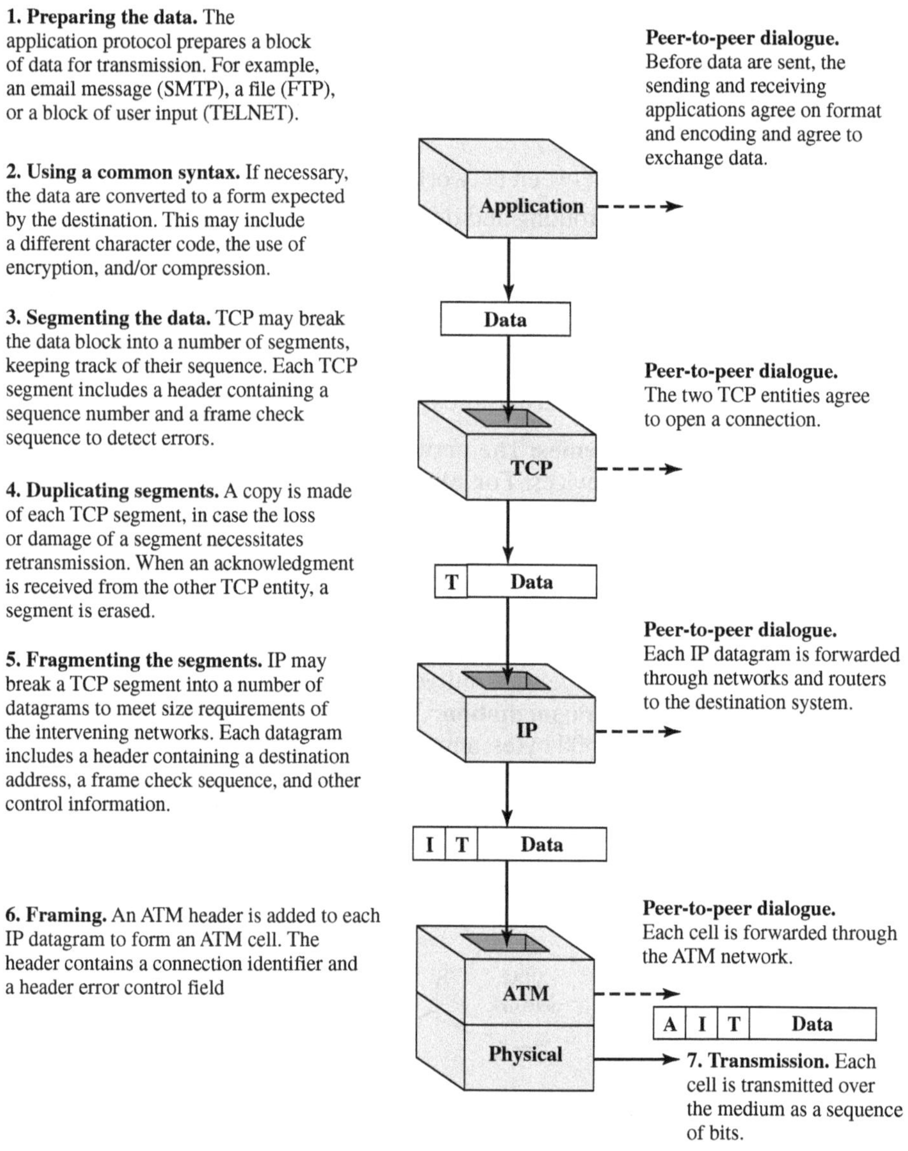

Figure 4.6 Operation of TCP/IP: Action at Sender

- **Interfaces**: The hardware and software interfaces to various networks differ. The concept of a router must be independent of these differences.
- **Reliability:** Various network services may provide anything from a reliable end-to-end virtual circuit to an unreliable service. The operation of the routers should not depend on an assumption of network reliability.

The preceding requirements are best satisfied by an internetworking protocol, such as IP, that is implemented in all end systems and routers.

Internetworking Example

Figure 4.5 depicts a configuration that we will use to illustrate the interactions among protocols for internetworking. In this case, we focus on a server attached to an ATM WAN and a workstation attached to an IEEE 802 LAN, with a router connecting the two networks.[2] The router will provide a link between the server and the workstation that enables these end systems to ignore the details of the intervening networks.

Figures 4.6 through 4.8 outline typical steps in the transfer of a block of data, such as a file or a Web page, from the server, through an internet, and ultimately to an application in the workstation. In this example, the message passes through just one router. Before data can be transmitted, the application and transport layers in the server establish, with the corresponding layer in the workstation, the applicable ground rules for a communication session. These include character code to be used, error-checking method, and the like. The protocol at each layer is used for this purpose and then is used in the transmission of the message.

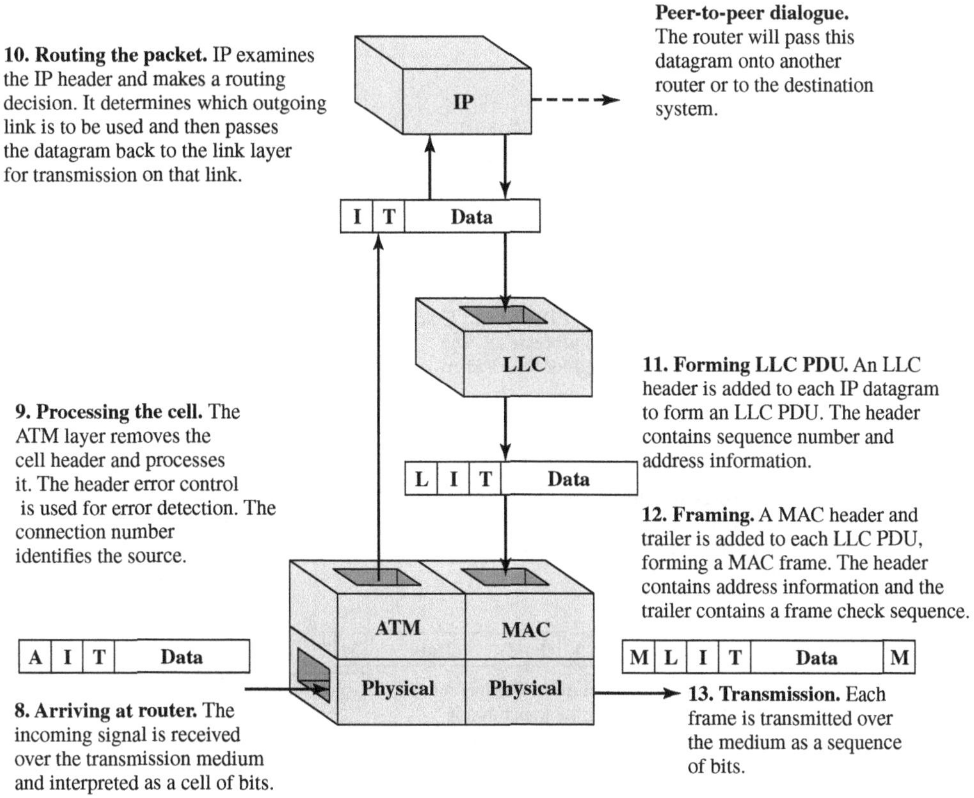

Figure 4.7 Operation of TCP/IP: Action at Router

[2]Section 14.1 describes the IEEE 802 protocol architecture. For now, you need to know that the architecture consists of a physical layer; a medium access control (MAC) layer concerned with addressing and error control, and a logical link control (LLC) layer, concerned with logical connections and identifying the user of LLC.

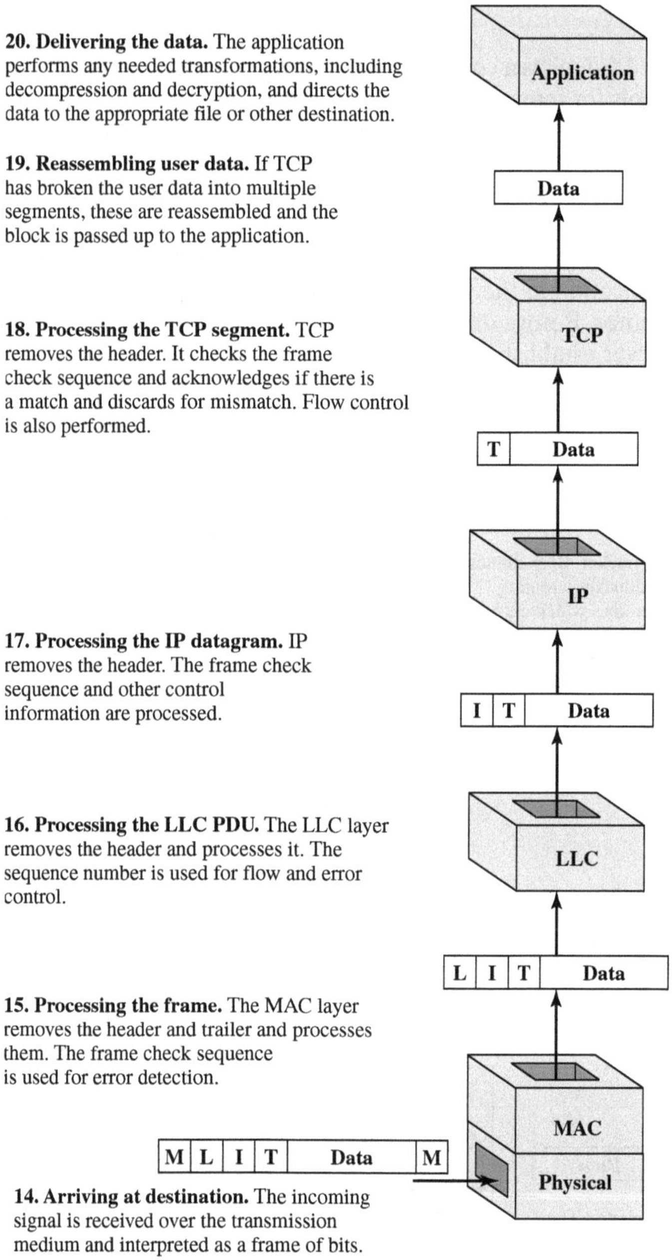

Figure 4.8 Operation of TCP/IP: Action at Receiver

4.5 RECOMMENDED READINGS AND WEB SITES

[STAL04] provides a detailed description of the TCP/IP model and of the standards at each layer of the model. A very useful reference work on TCP/IP is [RODR02], which covers the spectrum of TCP/IP-related protocols in a technically concise but thorough fashion.

RODR02 Rodriguez, A., et al. *TCP/IP Tutorial and Technical Overview*. Upper Saddle River: NJ: Prentice Hall, 2002.

STAL04 Stallings, W. *Computer Networking with Internet Protocols and Technology*. Upper Saddle River, NJ: Prentice Hall, 2004.

Recommended Web Sites:

- **Networking Links:** Excellent collection of links related to TCP/IP
- **IPv6:** Information about IPv6 and related topics

4.6 KEY TERMS, REVIEW QUESTIONS, AND PROBLEMS

Key Terms

application layer	internetworking	service access point (SAP)
checksum	network layer	Transmission Control Protocol (TCP)
frame check sequence (FCS)	physical layer	transport layer
header	port	User Datagram Protocol (UDP)
internet	protocol	
Internet Protocol (IP)	protocol architecture	
intranet	protocol data unit (PDU)	
IPv6	router	

Review Questions

4.1 What is the major function of the network access layer?

4.2 What tasks are performed by the transport layer?

4.3 What is a protocol?

4.4 What is a protocol data unit (PDU)?

4.5 What is a protocol architecture?

4.6 What is TCP/IP?

4.7 What are some advantages to layering as seen in the TCP/IP architecture?

4.8 What is a router?

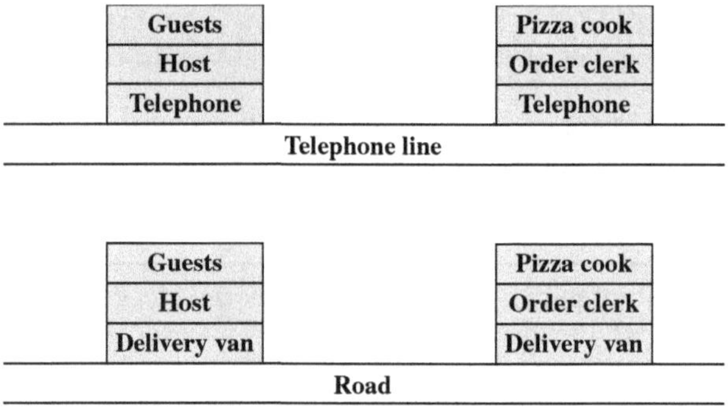

Figure 4.9 Architecture for Problem 4.1

Problems

4.1 Using the layer models in Figure 4.9, describe the ordering and delivery of a pizza, indicating the interactions at each level.

4.2 a. The French and Chinese prime ministers need to come to an agreement by telephone, but neither speaks the other's language. Further, neither has on hand a translator that can translate to the language of the other. However, both prime ministers have English translators on their staffs. Draw a diagram similar to Figure 4.9 to depict the situation, and describe the interaction and each level.

b. Now suppose that the Chinese prime minister's translator can translate only into Japanese and that the French prime minister has a German translator available. A translator between German and Japanese is available in Germany. Draw a new diagram that reflects this arrangement and describe the hypothetical phone conversation.

4.3 List the major disadvantages with the layered approach to protocols.

4.4 Two blue armies are each poised on opposite hills preparing to attack a single red army in the valley. The red army can defeat either of the blue armies separately but will fail to defeat both blue armies if they attack simultaneously. The blue armies communicate via an unreliable communications system (a foot soldier). The commander with one of the blue armies would like to attack at noon. His problem is this: If he sends a message to the other blue army, ordering the attack, he cannot be sure it will get through. He could ask for acknowledgment, but that might not get through. Is there a protocol that the two blue armies can use to avoid defeat?

4.5 A broadcast network is one in which a transmission from any one attached station is received by all other attached stations over a shared medium. Examples are a bus-topology local area network, such as Ethernet, and a wireless radio network. Discuss the need or lack of need for a network layer (OSI layer 3) in a broadcast network.

4.6 Among the principles used by ISO to define the OSI layers were

- The number of layers should be small enough to avoid unwieldy design and implementation but large enough so that separate layers handle functions that are different in process or technology.
- Layer boundaries should be chosen to minimize the number and size of interactions across boundaries.

Based on these principles, design an architecture with eight layers and make a case for it. Design one with six layers and make a case for that.

4.7 In Figure 4.2, exactly one protocol data unit (PDU) in layer N is encapsulated in a PDU at layer $(N - 1)$. It is also possible to break one N-level PDU into multiple $(N - 1)$-level PDUs (segmentation) or to group multiple N-level PDUs into one $(N - 1)$-level PDU (blocking).

a. In the case of segmentation, is it necessary that each $(N - 1)$-level segment contain a copy of the N-level header?
b. In the case of blocking, is it necessary that each N-level PDU retain its own header, or can the data be consolidated into a single N-level PDU with a single N-level header?

4.8 A TCP segment consisting of 1500 bits of data and 160 bits of header is sent to the IP layer, which appends another 160 bits of header. This is then transmitted through two networks, each of which uses a 24-bit packet header. The destination network has a maximum packet size of 800 bits. How many bits, including headers, are delivered to the network layer protocol at the destination?

4.9 Why is UDP needed? Why can't a user program directly access IP?

4.10 IP, TCP, and UDP all discard a packet that arrives with a checksum error and do not attempt to notify the source. Why?

4.11 Why does the TCP header have a header length field while the UDP header does not?

APPENDIX 4A INTERNET PROTOCOL

Within the TCP/IP protocol suite, perhaps the most important protocol is the Internet Protocol (IP). The version that has been used for decades is known as IPv4. Recently, a new version, IPv6, has been standardized, although it is not yet widely deployed.

IPv4

Figure 4.10a shows the IPv4 header format, which is a minimum of 20 octets, or 160 bits. The fields are as follows:

- **Version (4 bits):** Indicates version number, to allow evolution of the protocol; the value is 4.
- **Internet Header Length (IHL) (4 bits):** Length of header in 32-bit words. The minimum value is five, for a minimum header length of 20 octets.
- **DS/ECN (8 bits):** Prior to the introduction of differentiated services, this field was referred to as the **Type of Service** field and specified reliability, precedence, delay, and throughput parameters. This interpretation has now been superseded. The first 6 bits of the TOS field are now referred to as the DS (differentiated services) field. The DS field supports a quality-of-service (QoS) capability for the Internet. The remaining 2 bits are reserved for an ECN (explicit congestion notification) field, which provides congestion control functionality for the Internet.
- **Total Length (16 bits):** Total IP packet length, in octets.
- **Identification (16 bits):** A sequence number that, together with the source address, destination address, and user protocol, is intended to identify a packet uniquely. Thus, the identifier should be unique for the packet's source address, destination address, and user protocol for the time during which the packet will remain in the internet.
- **Flags (3 bits):** Only two of the bits are currently defined. When a packet is fragmented, the More bit indicates whether this is the last fragment in the original packet. The Don't Fragment bit prohibits fragmentation when set. This bit may be useful if it is known that the destination does not have the capability to reassemble fragments. However, if this bit is set, the packet will be discarded if it exceeds the maximum size of an en route subnetwork. Therefore, if the bit is set, it may be advisable to use source routing to avoid subnetworks with small maximum packet size.

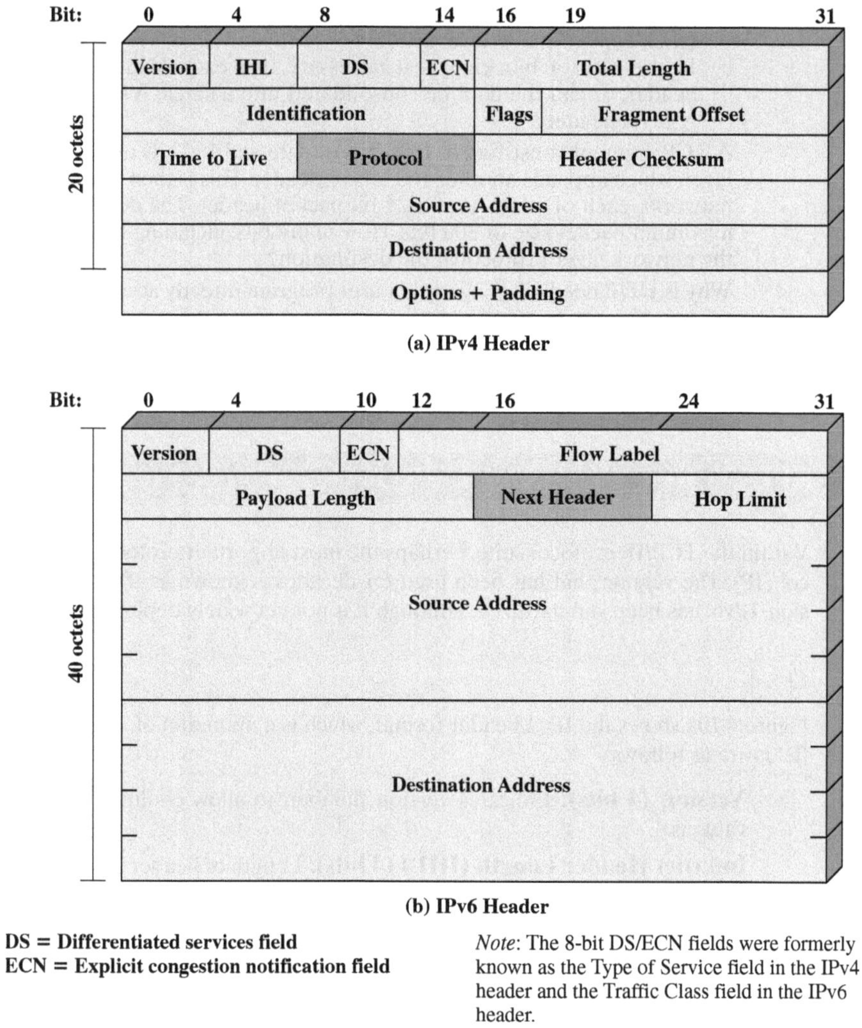

Figure 4.10 IP Headers

- **Fragment Offset (13 bits):** Indicates where in the original packet this fragment belongs, measured in 64-bit units. This implies that fragments other than the last fragment must contain a data field that is a multiple of 64 bits in length.
- **Time to Live (8 bits):** Specifies how long, in seconds, a packet is allowed to remain in the internet. Every router that processes a packet must decrease the TTL by at least one, so the TTL is somewhat similar to a hop count.
- **Protocol (8 bits):** Indicates the next higher level protocol, which is to receive the data field at the destination; thus, this field identifies the type of the next header in the packet after the IP header.
- **Header Checksum (16 bits):** An error-detecting code applied to the header only. Because some header fields may change during transit (e.g., time to live, segmentation-related fields), this is reverified and recomputed at each router. The checksum field is

the 16-bit ones complement addition of all 16-bit words in the header. For purposes of computation, the checksum field is itself initialized to a value of zero.[3]

- **Source Address (32 bits):** Coded to allow a variable allocation of bits to specify the network and the end system attached to the specified network, as discussed subsequently.
- **Destination Address (32 bits):** Same characteristics as source address.
- **Options (variable):** Encodes the options requested by the sending user; these may include security label, source routing, record routing, and timestamping.
- **Padding (variable):** Used to ensure that the packet header is a multiple of 32 bits in length.

The source and destination address fields in the IP header each contain a 32-bit global internet address, generally consisting of a network identifier and a host identifier. The address is coded to allow a variable allocation of bits to specify network and host, as depicted in Figure 4.11. This encoding provides flexibility in assigning addresses to hosts and allows a mix of network sizes on an internet. The three principal network classes are best suited to the following conditions:

- **Class A:** Few networks, each with many hosts
- **Class B:** Medium number of networks, each with a medium number of hosts
- **Class C:** Many networks, each with a few hosts

In a particular environment, it may be best to use addresses all from one class. For example, a corporate internetwork that consist of a large number of departmental local area networks may need to use Class C addresses exclusively. However, the format of the addresses is such that it is possible to mix all three classes of addresses on the same internetwork; this is what

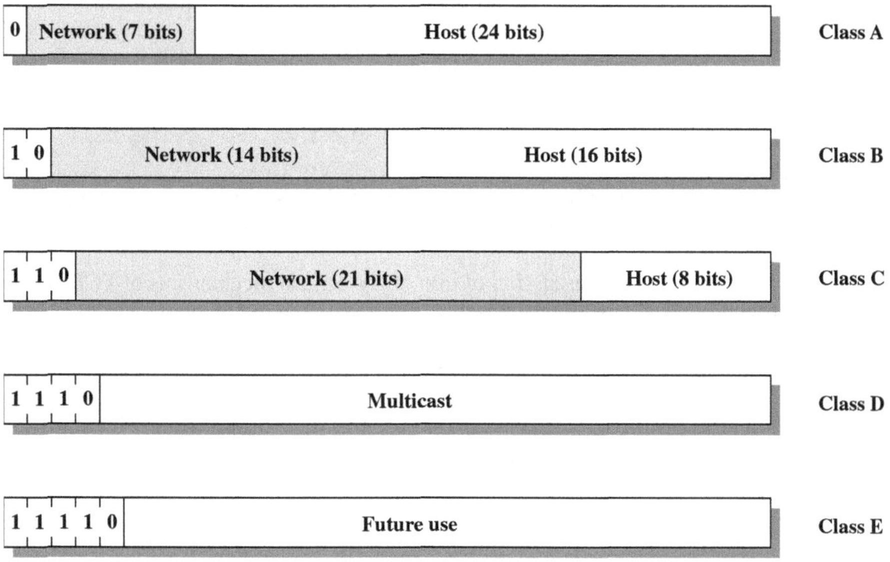

Figure 4.11 IP Address Formats

[3]A discussion of this checksum is contained in a supporting document at this book's Web site.

is done in the case of the Internet itself. A mixture of classes is appropriate for an internetwork consisting of a few large networks, many small networks, plus some medium-sized networks.

IP addresses are usually written in what is called *dotted decimal notation*, with a decimal number representing each of the octets of the 32-bit address. For example, the IP address 11000000 11100100 00010001 00111001 is written as 192.228.17.57.

Note that all Class A network addresses begin with a binary 0. Network addresses with a first octet of 0 (binary 00000000) and 127 (binary 01111111) are reserved, so there are 126 potential Class A network numbers, which have a first dotted decimal number in the range 1 to 126. Class B network addresses begin with a binary 10, so that the range of the first decimal number in a Class B address is 128 to 191(binary 10000000 to 10111111). The second octet is also part of the Class B address, so that there are $2^{14} = 16,384$ Class B addresses. For Class C addresses, the first decimal number ranges from 192 to 223 (11000000 to 11011111). The total number of Class C addresses is $2^{21} = 2,097,152$.

IPv6

In 1995, the Internet Engineering Task Force (IETF), which develops protocol standards for the Internet, issued a specification for a next-generation IP, known then as IPng (RFC 1752). This specification led to the development of a standard known as IPv6 (RFC 2460). IPv6 provides a number of functional enhancements over the existing IP (known as IPv4), designed to accommodate the higher speeds of today's networks and the mix of data streams, including graphic and video, that are becoming more prevalent. But the driving force behind the development of the new protocol was the need for more addresses. IPv4 uses a 32-bit address to specify a source or destination. With the explosive growth of the Internet and of private networks attached to the Internet, this address length became insufficient to accommodate all systems needing addresses. As Figure 4.10b shows, IPv6 includes 128-bit source and destination address fields. Ultimately, all installations using TCP/IP are expected to migrate from the current IP to IPv6, but this process will take many years, if not decades.

APPENDIX 4B TRANSMISSION CONTROL PROTOCOL

For most applications that make use of the TCP/IP protocol suite, the application relies on TCP to assure reliable delivery of data; TCP in turn relies on IP to handle addressing and routing chores.

We begin with a discussion of one of the central mechanisms of TCP: flow control. The functionality of TCP is then summarized by discussing the elements in the TCP header.

TCP Flow Control

As with most protocols that provide flow control, TCP uses a form of sliding-window mechanism. It differs from the mechanism used in many other protocols, such as LLC, HDLC, and X.25, in that it decouples acknowledgment of received data units from the granting of permission to send additional data units.

The flow control mechanism used by TCP is known as a credit allocation scheme. For the credit scheme, each individual octet of data that is transmitted is considered to have a sequence number. In addition to data, each transmitted segment includes in its header three fields related to flow control: the sequence number (*SN*) of the first data byte in the segment, acknowledgment number (*AN*), and window (*W*). When a transport entity sends a segment, it includes the sequence number of the first octet in the segment data field. A transport entity acknowledges an incoming segment with a return segment that includes $(AN = i, W = j)$, with the following interpretation:

- All octets through sequence number $SN = i - 1$ are acknowledged; the next expected octet has sequence number i.
- Permission is granted to send an additional window of $W = j$ octets of data; that is, the j octets corresponding to sequence numbers i through $i + j - 1$.

Figure 4.12 illustrates the mechanism. For simplicity, we show data flow in one direction only and assume that 200 octets of data are sent in each segment. Initially, through the connection establishment process, the sending and receiving sequence numbers are synchronized and A is granted an initial credit allocation of 1400 octets, beginning with octet number 1001. After sending 600 octets in three segments, A has shrunk its window to a size of 800 octets (numbers 1601 through 2400). Following receipt of these segments, B acknowledges receipt of all octets through 1601 and issues a credit of 1000 octets. This means that A can send octets 1601 through 2600 (5 segments). However, by the time that B's message has arrived at A, A has already sent two segments, containing octets 1601 through 2000 (which was permissible under the initial allocation). Thus, A's remaining credit at this point is only 400 octets (2 segments). As the exchange proceeds, A advances the trailing edge of its window each time that it transmits and advances the leading edge only when it is granted credit.

The credit allocation mechanism is quite flexible. For example, consider that the last message issued by B was $(AN = i, W = j)$ and that the last octet of data received by B was octet number $i - 1$. Then

- To increase credit to an amount $k(k > j)$ when no additional data have arrived, B issues $(AN = i, W = k)$.
- To acknowledge an incoming segment containing m octets of data $(m < j)$ without granting additional credit, B issues $(AN = i + m, W = j - m)$.

TCP Segment Format

TCP uses only a single type of protocol data unit, called a TCP segment. The header is shown in Figure 4.13a. Because one header must serve to perform all protocol mechanisms, it is rather large, with a minimum length of 20 octets. The fields are as follows:

- **Source Port (16 bits):** Source TCP user.
- **Destination Port (16 bits):** Destination TCP user.
- **Sequence Number (32 bits):** Sequence number of the first data octet in this segment except when the SYN flag is set. If SYN is set, this field contains the initial sequence number (ISN) and the first data octet in this segment has sequence number ISN + 1.
- **Acknowledgment Number (32 bits):** A piggybacked acknowledgment. Contains the sequence number of the next data octet that the TCP entity expects to receive.
- **Header Length (4 bits):** Number of 32-bit words in the header.
- **Reserved (6 bits):** Reserved for future use.
- **Flags (6 bits):** For each flag, if set to 1, the meaning is

  CWR: congestion window reduced

  ECE: ECN-Echo; the CWR and ECE bits, defined in RFC 3168, are used for the explicit congestion notification function

  URG: urgent pointer field significant

  ACK: acknowledgment field significant

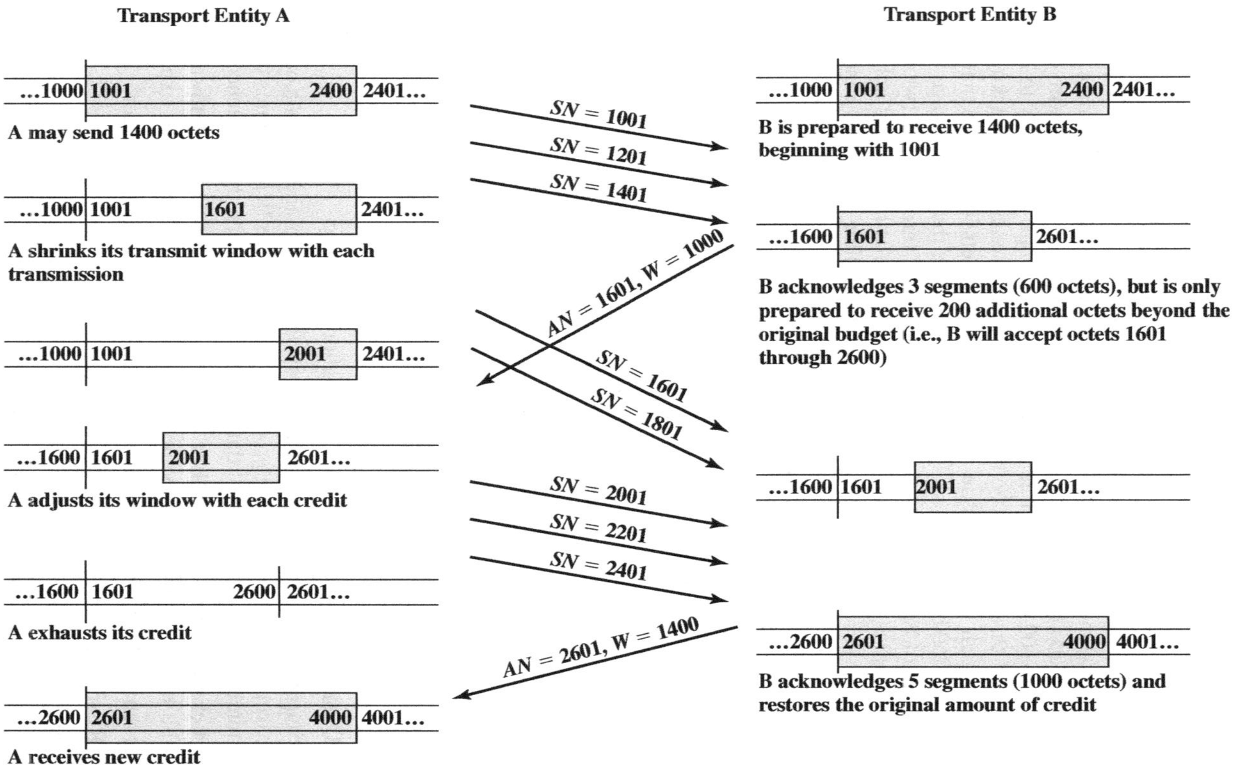

Figure 4.12 Example of TCP Credit Allocation Mechanism

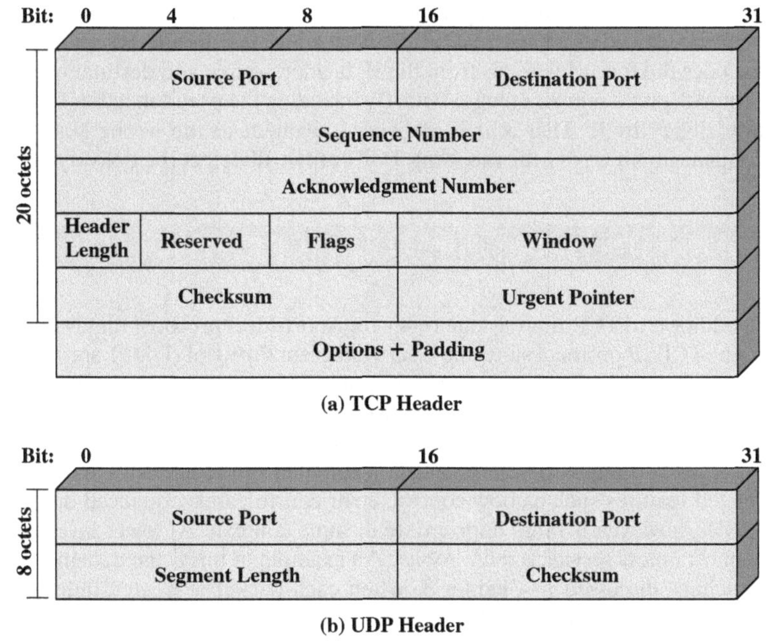

Figure 4.13 TCP and UDP Headers

PSH: push function

RST: reset the connection

SYN: synchronize the sequence numbers

FIN: no more data from sender

- **Window (16 bits):** Flow control credit allocation, in octets. Contains the number of data octets, beginning with the sequence number indicated in the acknowledgment field that the sender is willing to accept.
- **Checksum (16 bits):** The ones complement of the ones complement sum modulo of all the 16-bit words in the segment plus a pseudoheader, described subsequently.[4]
- **Urgent Pointer (16 bits):** This value, when added to the segment sequence number, contains the sequence number of the last octet in a sequence of urgent data. This allows the receiver to know how much urgent data are coming.
- **Options (Variable):** An example is the option that specifies the maximum segment size that will be accepted.

The *sequence number* and *acknowledgment number* are bound to octets rather than to entire segments. For example, if a segment contains sequence number 1001 and includes 600 octets of data, the sequence number refers to the first octet in the data field; the next segment in logical order will have sequence number 1601. Thus, TCP is logically stream oriented: It accepts a stream of octets from the user, groups them into segments as it sees fit, and numbers each octet in the stream.

[4]A discussion of this checksum is contained in a supporting document at this book's Web site.

The *checksum* field applies to the entire segment plus a pseudoheader prefixed to the header at the time of calculation (at both transmission and reception). The pseudoheader includes the following fields from the IP header: source and destination internet address and protocol, plus a segment length field. By including the pseudoheader, TCP protects itself from misdelivery by IP. That is, if IP delivers a segment to the wrong host, even if the segment contains no bit errors, the receiving TCP entity will detect the delivery error.

APPENDIX 4C USER DATAGRAM PROTOCOL

In addition to TCP, there is one other transport-level protocol that is in common use as part of the TCP/IP protocol suite: the User Datagram Protocol (UDP), specified in RFC 768. UDP provides a connectionless service for application-level procedures. Thus, UDP is basically an unreliable service; delivery and duplicate protection are not guaranteed. However, this does reduce the overhead of the protocol and may be adequate in many cases.

The strengths of the connection-oriented approach are clear. It allows connection-related features such as flow control, error control, and sequenced delivery. Connectionless service, however, is more appropriate in some contexts. At lower layers (internet, network), connectionless service is more robust. An example of this is the datagram approach to packet switching, discussed in Chapter 3. When each packet is treated independently and routed independently, the impact of congestion or loss in the network is less than if there is a predefined route or connection over which all packets travel.

In addition, a connectionless service represents a "least common denominator" of service to be expected at higher layers. Further, even at transport and above there is justification for a connectionless service. There are instances in which the overhead of connection establishment and maintenance is unjustified or even counterproductive. Examples include the following:

- **Inward data collection:** Involves the periodic active or passive sampling of data sources, such as sensors, and automatic self-test reports from security equipment or network components. In a real-time monitoring situation, the loss of an occasional data unit would not cause distress, because the next report should arrive shortly.
- **Outward data dissemination:** Includes broadcast messages to network users, the announcement of a new node or the change of address of a service, and the distribution of real-time clock values.
- **Request-response:** Applications in which a transaction service is provided by a common server to a number of distributed transport service users, and for which a single request-response sequence is typical. Use of the service is regulated at the application level, and lower-level connections are often unnecessary and cumbersome.
- **Real-time applications:** Such as voice and telemetry, involving a degree of redundancy and/or a real-time transmission requirement. These must not have connection-oriented functions such as retransmission.

Thus, there is a place at the transport level for both a connection-oriented and a connectionless type of service.

UDP sits on top of IP. Because it is connectionless, UDP has very little to do. Essentially, it adds a port addressing capability to IP. This is best seen by examining the UDP header, shown in Figure 4.13b. The header includes a source port and destination port. The length field contains the length of the entire UDP segment, including header and data. The checksum is the same algorithm used for TCP and IP. For UDP, the checksum applies to the entire UDP segment plus a pseudoheader prefixed to the UDP header at the time of calculation and is the same pseudoheader used for TCP. If an error is detected, the segment is discarded and no further action is taken.

The checksum field in UDP is optional. If it is not used, it is set to zero. However, it should be pointed out that the IP checksum applies only to the IP header and not to the data field, which in this case consists of the UDP header and the user data. Thus, if no checksum calculation is performed by UDP, then no check is made on the user data.

PART TWO

Wireless Communication Technology

CHAPTER 5

ANTENNAS AND PROPAGATION

This chapter provides some fundamental background for wireless transmission. We begin with an overview of antennas and then look at signal propagation.

5.1 ANTENNAS

An antenna can be defined as an electrical conductor or system of conductors used either for radiating electromagnetic energy or for collecting electromagnetic energy. For transmission of a signal, radio-frequency electrical energy from the transmitter is converted into electromagnetic energy by the antenna and radiated into the surrounding environment (atmosphere, space, water). For reception of a signal, electromagnetic energy impinging on the antenna is converted into radio-frequency electrical energy and fed into the receiver.

In two-way communication, the same antenna can be and often is used for both transmission and reception. This is possible because any antenna transfers energy from the surrounding environment to its input receiver terminals with the same efficiency that it transfers energy from the output transmitter terminals into the surrounding environment, assuming that the same frequency is used in both directions. Put another way, antenna characteristics are essentially the same whether an antenna is sending or receiving electromagnetic energy.

Radiation Patterns

An antenna will radiate power in all directions but, typically, does not perform equally well in all directions. A common way to characterize the performance of an antenna is the radiation pattern, which is a graphical representation of the radiation properties of an antenna as a function of space coordinates. The simplest pattern is produced by an idealized antenna known as the isotropic antenna. An **isotropic antenna** is a point in space that radiates power in all directions equally. The actual radiation pattern for the isotropic antenna is a sphere with the antenna at the center. However, radiation patterns are almost always depicted as a two-dimensional cross section of the three-dimensional pattern. The pattern for the isotropic antenna is shown in Figure 5.1a. The distance from the antenna to each point on the radiation pattern is proportional to the power radiated from the antenna in that direction. Figure 5.1b shows the radiation pattern of another idealized antenna. This is a directional antenna in which the preferred direction of radiation is along one axis.

The actual size of a radiation pattern is arbitrary. What is important is the relative distance from the antenna position in each direction. The relative distance determines the relative power. To determine the relative power in a given direction, a line is drawn from the antenna position at the appropriate angle, and the point of intercept with the radiation pattern is determined. Figure 5.1 shows a comparison of two transmission angles, A and B, drawn on the two radiation patterns. The isotropic antenna produces an omnidirectional radiation pattern of equal strength in all directions, so the A and B vectors are of equal length. For the antenna pattern of Figure 5.1b, the B vector is longer than the A vector, indicating that more power is radiated in the B direction than in the A direction, and the relative lengths of the two vectors are proportional to the amount of power radiated in the two directions.

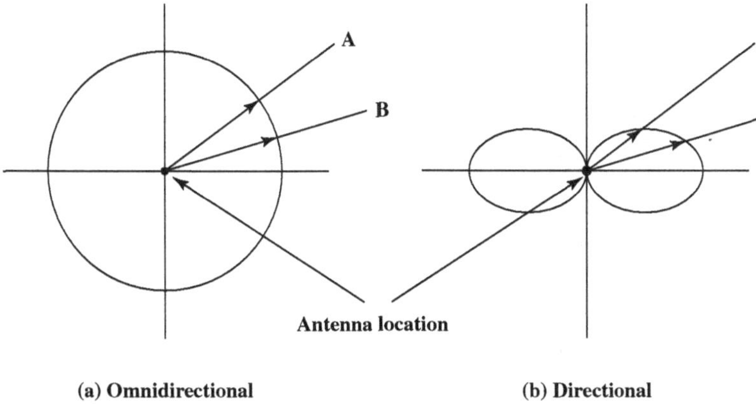

Figure 5.1 Idealized Radiation Patterns

The radiation pattern provides a convenient means of determining the **beam width** of an antenna, which is a common measure of the directivity of an antenna. The beam width, also referred to as the half-power beam width, is the angle within which the power radiated by the antenna is at least half of what it is in the most preferred direction.

When an antenna is used for reception, the radiation pattern becomes a **reception pattern**. The longest section of the pattern indicates the best direction for reception.

Antenna Types

Dipoles Two of the simplest and most basic antennas are the half-wave dipole, or Hertz, antenna (Figure 5.2a) and the quarter-wave vertical, or Marconi[1], antenna (Figure 5.2b). The half-wave dipole consists of two straight collinear conductors of equal length, separated by a small gap. The length of the antenna is one-half the

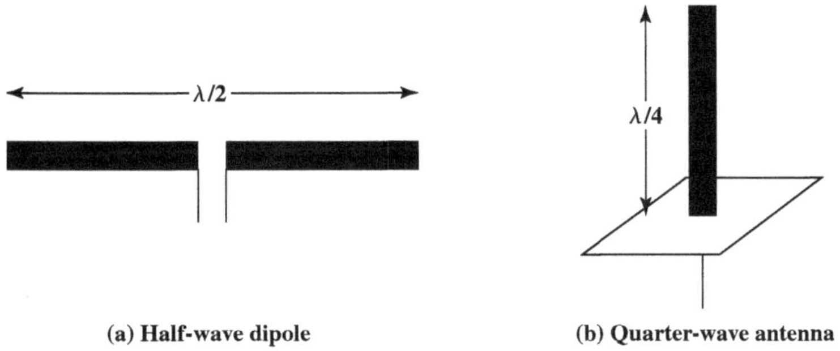

Figure 5.2 Simple Antennas

[1]http://nobelprize.org/nobel_prizes/physics/laureates/1909/marconi-bio.html. Guglielmo Marconi, holder of the Nobel Prize for Physics, is called the "Father of Modern Radio" for transmitting the first wireless signals in 1901.

wavelength of the signal that can be transmitted most efficiently. A vertical quarter-wave antenna is the type commonly used for automobile radios and portable radios.

A half-wave dipole has a uniform or omnidirectional radiation pattern in one dimension and a figure eight pattern in the other two dimensions (Figure 5.3a). More complex antenna configurations can be used to produce a directional beam. A typical directional radiation pattern is shown in Figure 5.3b. In this case the main strength of the antenna is in the x-direction.

Parabolic Reflective Antenna An important type of antenna is the **parabolic reflective antenna**, which is used in terrestrial microwave and satellite applications. A parabola is the locus of all points equidistant from a fixed line and a fixed point not on the line. The fixed point is called the *focus* and the fixed line is called the *directrix* (Figure 5.4a). If a parabola is revolved about its axis, the surface generated is called a *paraboloid*. A cross section through the paraboloid parallel to its axis forms a parabola and a cross section perpendicular to the axis forms a circle. Such surfaces are used in automobile headlights, optical and radio telescopes, and microwave antennas because of the following property: If a source of electromagnetic energy (or sound) is placed at the focus of the paraboloid, and if the paraboloid is a reflecting surface, then the wave will bounce back in lines parallel to the axis of the paraboloid; Figure 5.4b shows this effect in cross section. In theory, this effect creates a parallel beam without dispersion. In practice, there will be some dispersion, because the source of energy must occupy more than one point. The converse is also true. If incoming waves are parallel to the axis of the reflecting paraboloid, the resulting signal will be concentrated at the focus.

Figure 5.4c shows a typical radiation pattern for the parabolic reflective antenna, and Table 5.1 lists beam widths for antennas of various sizes at a frequency

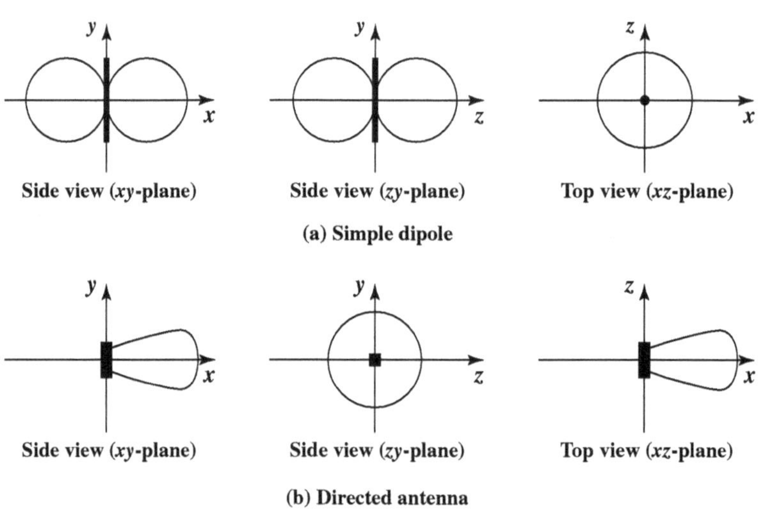

Figure 5.3 Radiation Patterns in Three Dimensions [SCHI00]

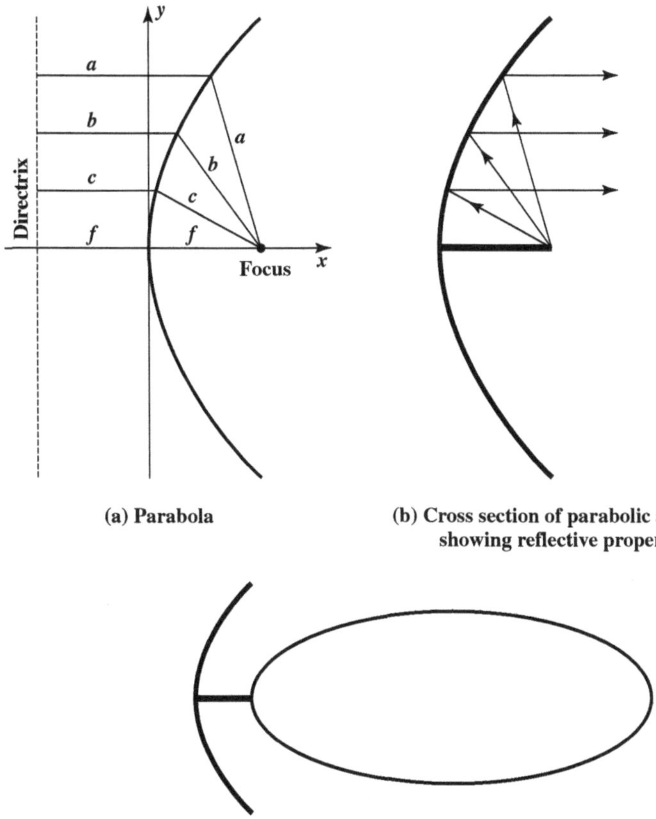

(a) Parabola

(b) Cross section of parabolic antenna showing reflective property

(c) Cross section of parabolic antenna showing radiation pattern

Figure 5.4 Parabolic Reflective Antenna

Table 5.1 Antenna Beam Widths for Various Diameter Parabolic Reflective Antennas at f = 12 GHz [FREE97]

Antenna Diameter (m)	Beam Width (degrees)
0.5	3.5
0.75	2.33
1.0	1.75
1.5	1.166
2.0	0.875
2.5	0.7
5.0	0.35

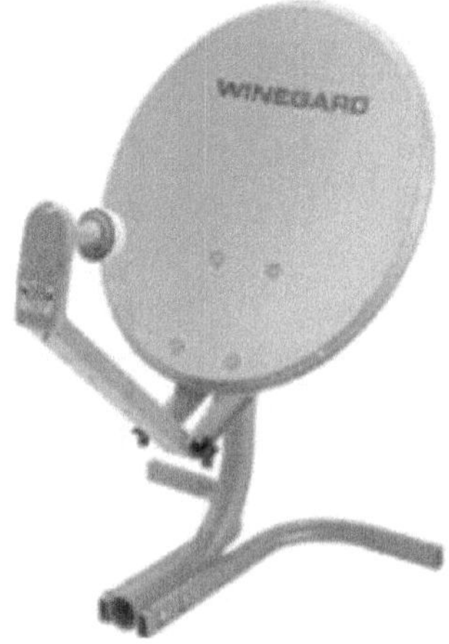

Figure 5.5 A Typical Parabolic Dish

of 12 GHz. Note that the larger the diameter of the antenna, the more tightly directional is the beam. Figure 5.5 shows a typical parabolic antenna used for communications with satellites.[2]

Antenna Gain

Antenna gain is a measure of the directionality of an antenna. Antenna gain is defined as the power output, in a particular direction, compared to that produced in any direction by a perfect omnidirectional antenna (isotropic antenna). For example, if an antenna has a gain of 3 dB, that antenna improves upon the isotropic antenna in that direction by 3 dB, or a factor of 2. The increased power radiated in a given direction is at the expense of other directions. In effect, increased power is radiated in one direction by reducing the power radiated in other directions. It is important to note that antenna gain does not refer to obtaining more output power than input power but rather to directionality.

A concept related to that of antenna gain is the **effective area** of an antenna. The effective area of an antenna is related to the physical size of the antenna and to its shape. The relationship between antenna gain and effective area is

$$G = \frac{4\pi A_e}{\lambda^2} = \frac{4\pi f^2 A_e}{c^2} \tag{5.1}$$

[2]http://www.google.com/products/catalog?hl=en&q=satellite+dish&bav=on.2,or.r_gc.r_pw.&biw=1680&bih=834&wrapid=tlif131231209446010&um=1&ie=UTF-8&tbm=shop&cid=8199734353453891856&sa=X&ei=IUs4TqC0LtSXtwe5v9CZAw&ved=0CI0BEPICMAE#

Table 5.2 Antenna Gains and Effective Areas [COUC01]

Type of Antenna	Effective Area A_e (m^2)	Power Gain (relative to isotropic)
Isotropic	$\lambda^2/4\pi$	1
Infinitesimal dipole or loop	$1.5\lambda^2/4\pi$	1.5
Half-wave dipole	$1.64\lambda^2/4\pi$	1.64
Horn, mouth area A	$0.81A$	$10A/\lambda^2$
Parabolic, face area A	$0.56A$	$7A/\lambda^2$
Turnstile (two crossed, perpendicular dipoles)	$1.15\lambda^2/4\pi$	1.15

where

G = antenna gain
A_e = effective area
f = carrier frequency
c = speed of light ($\approx 3 \times 10^8$ m/s)
λ = carrier wavelength

Table 5.2 shows the antenna gain and effective area of some typical antenna shapes.

Example 5.1 For a parabolic reflective antenna with a diameter of 2 m, operating at 12 GHz, what is the effective area and the antenna gain? We have an area of $A = \pi r^2 = \pi$ and an effective area of $A_e = 0.56\pi$. The wavelength is $\lambda = c/f = (3 \times 10^8)/(12 \times 10^9) = 0.025$ m. Then

$$G = (7A)/\lambda^2 = (7 \times \pi)/(0.025)^2 = 35{,}186$$
$$G_{\pi B} = 45.46 \text{ dB}$$

5.2 PROPAGATION MODES

A signal radiated from an antenna travels along one of three routes: ground wave, sky wave, or line of sight (LOS). Table 5.3 shows in which frequency range each predominates. In this book, we are almost exclusively concerned with LOS communication, but a short overview of each mode is given in this section.

Ground Wave Propagation

Ground wave propagation (Figure 5.6a) more or less follows the contour of the earth and can propagate considerable distances, well over the visual horizon. This effect is found in frequencies up to about 2 MHz. Several factors account for the

Table 5.3 Frequency Bands

Band	Frequency Range	Free-Space Wavelength Range	Propagation Characteristics	Typical Use
ELF (extremely low frequency)	30 to 300 Hz	10,000 to 1000 km	GW	Power line frequencies; used by some home control systems.
VF (voice frequency)	300 to 3000 Hz	1000 to 100 km	GW	Used by the telephone system for analog subscriber lines.
VLF (very low frequency)	3 to 30 kHz	100 to 10 km	GW; low attenuation day and night; high atmospheric noise level	Long-range navigation; submarine communication
LF (low frequency)	30 to 300 kHz	10 to 1 km	GW; slightly less reliable than VLF; absorption in daytime	Long-range navigation; marine communication radio beacons
MF (medium frequency)	300 to 3000 kHz	1000 to 100 m	GW and night SW; attenuation low at night, high in day; atmospheric noise	Maritime radio; direction finding; AM broadcasting.
HF (high frequency)	3 to 30 MHz	100 to 10 m	SW; quality varies with time of day, season, and frequency.	Amateur radio; international broadcasting, military communication; long-distance aircraft and ship communication
VHF (very high frequency)	30 to 300 MHz	10 to 1 m	LOS; scattering because of temperature inversion; cosmic noise	VHF television; FM broadcast and two-way radio, AM aircraft communication; aircraft navigational aids
UHF (ultra high frequency)	300 to 3000 MHz	100 to 10 cm	LOS; cosmic noise	UHF television; cellular telephone; radar; microwave links; personal communications systems
SHF (super high frequency)	3 to 30 GHz	10 to 1 cm	LOS; rainfall attenuation above 10 GHz; atmospheric attenuation due to oxygen and water vapor	Satellite communication; radar; terrestrial microwave links; wireless local loop
EHF (extremely high frequency)	30 to 300 GHz	10 to 1 mm	LOS; atmospheric attenuation due to oxygen and water vapor	Experimental; wireless local loop
Infrared	300 GHz to 400 THz	1 mm to 770 nm	LOS	Infrared LANs; consumer electronic applications
Visible light	400 THz to 900 THz	770 nm to 330 nm	LOS	Optical communication

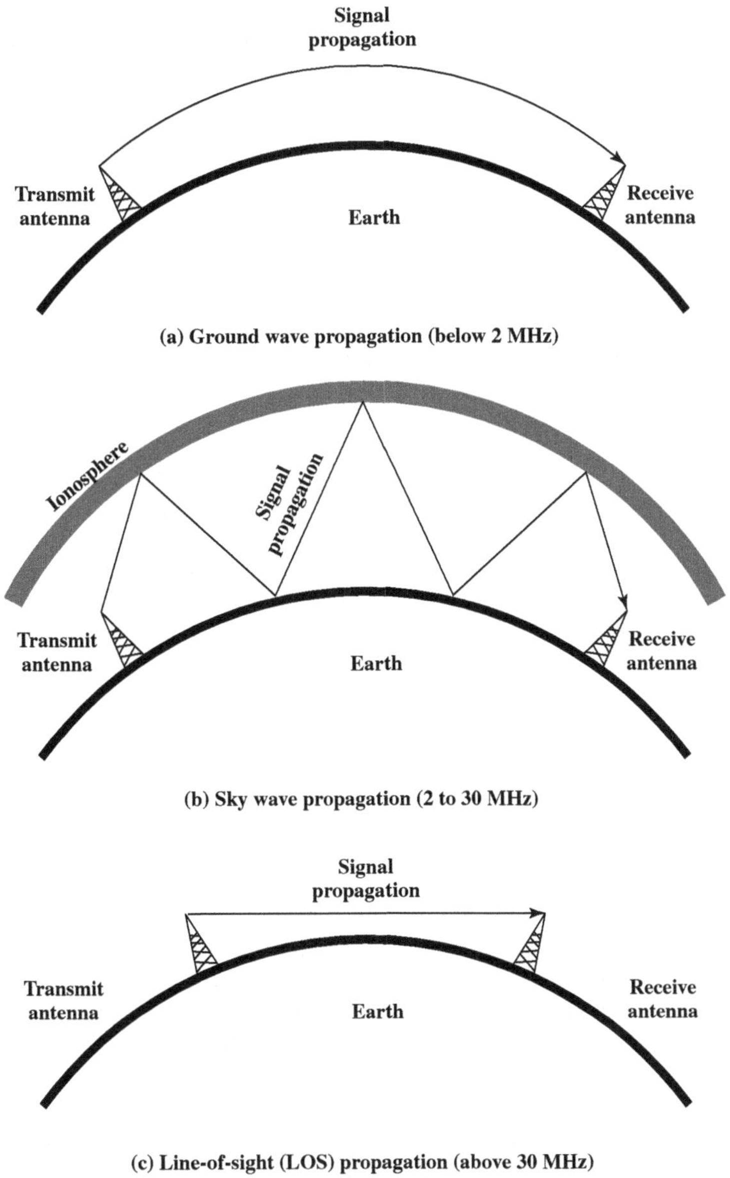

Figure 5.6 Wireless Propagation Modes

tendency of electromagnetic wave in this frequency band to follow the earth's curvature. One factor is that the electromagnetic wave induces a current in the earth's surface, the result of which is to slow the wavefront near the earth, causing the wavefront to tilt downward and hence follow the earth's curvature. Another factor is diffraction, which is a phenomenon having to do with the behavior of electromagnetic waves in the presence of obstacles.

Electromagnetic waves in this frequency range are scattered by the atmosphere in such a way that they do not penetrate the upper atmosphere.

The best-known example of ground wave communication is AM radio. The FCC provides an excellent discussion of this effect as follows:

> As many people are aware, many if not most AM radio stations reduce their signals at night. Ever been driving at night, perhaps on an interstate, and you notice that your AM station is slowly fading away? Well, it seems that most AM radio stations are required by the FCC to reduce their power or even cease operating at night. Why? This is in order to avoid interference to other AM stations. The issue centers around good ole physics. Because of the way in which the relatively long wavelengths of AM radio signals interact with the ionized layers of the ionosphere several miles above the earth's surface, the propagation of AM radio waves changes drastically from daytime to nighttime.[3]

Sky Wave Propagation

Sky wave propagation is used for amateur radio, CB radio, and international broadcasts such as BBC and Voice of America. With sky wave propagation, a signal from an earth-based antenna is reflected from the ionized layer of the upper atmosphere (ionosphere) back down to earth. Although it appears the wave is reflected from the ionosphere as if the ionosphere were a hard reflecting surface, the effect is in fact caused by refraction. Refraction is described subsequently.

A sky wave signal can travel through a number of hops, bouncing back and forth between the ionosphere and the earth's surface (Figure 5.6b). With this propagation mode, a signal can be picked up thousands of kilometers from the transmitter.

Line-of-Sight Propagation

Above 30 MHz, neither ground wave nor sky wave propagation modes operate, and communication must be by line of sight (Figure 5.6c). For satellite communication, a signal above 30 MHz is not reflected by the ionosphere and therefore can be transmitted between an earth station and a satellite overhead that is not beyond the horizon. For ground-based communication, the transmitting and receiving antennas must be within an *effective* line of sight of each other. The term *effective* is used because microwaves are bent or refracted by the atmosphere. The amount and even the direction of the bend depends on conditions, but generally microwaves are bent with the curvature of the earth and will therefore propagate farther than the optical line of sight. An excellent line of sight calculator can be found at http://www.calculatoredge.com/electronics/lineofsight.htm. And a calculator for line of sight based upon antenna heights can be found at http://www.bestdatasource.com/rad/horizon_calculator.htm.

Refraction Before proceeding, a brief discussion of refraction is warranted. Refraction occurs because the velocity of an electromagnetic wave is a function of the density of the medium through which it travels. In a vacuum, an electromagnetic wave (such as light or a radio wave) travels at approximately 3×10^8 m/s. This is the constant, c, commonly referred to as the speed of light, but actually referring to the speed of light

[3]http://transition.fcc.gov/mb/audio/bickel/daytime.html

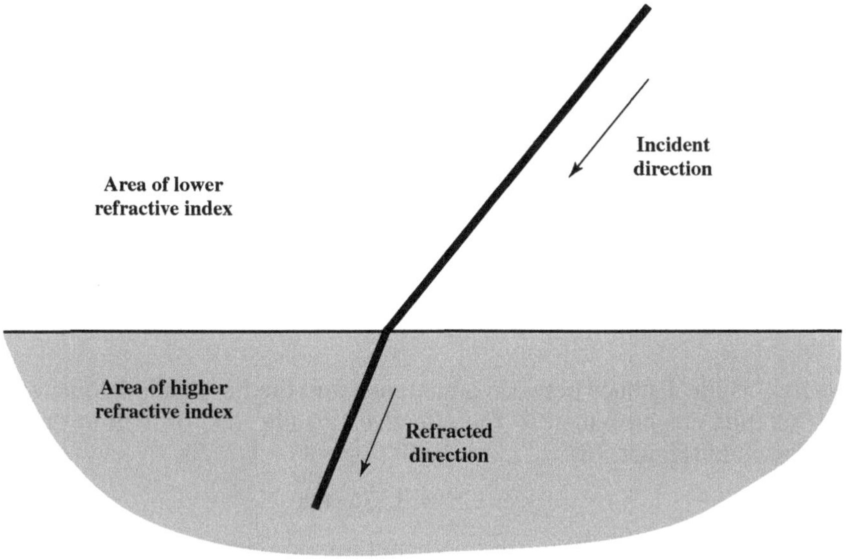

Figure 5.7 Refraction of an Electromagnetic Wave [POOL98]

in a vacuum. In air, water, glass, and other transparent or partially transparent media, electromagnetic waves travel at speeds less than c.

When an electromagnetic wave moves from a medium of one density to a medium of another density, its speed changes. The effect is to cause a one-time bending of the direction of the wave at the boundary between the two media. This is illustrated in Figure 5.7. If moving from a less dense to a more dense medium, the wave will bend toward the more dense medium. This phenomenon is easily observed by partially immersing a stick in water. The result will look much like Figure 5.7, with the stick appearing shorter and bent.

The index of refraction of one medium relative to another is the sine of the angle of incidence divided by the sine of the angle of refraction. The index of refraction is also equal to the ratio of the respective velocities in the two media. The absolute index of refraction of a medium is calculated in comparison with that of a vacuum. Refractive index varies with wavelength, so that refractive effects differ for signals with different wavelengths.

Although Figure 5.7 shows an abrupt, one-time change in direction as a signal moves from one medium to another, a continuous, gradual bending of a signal will occur if it is moving through a medium in which the index of refraction gradually changes. Under normal propagation conditions, the refractive index of the atmosphere decreases with height so that radio waves travel more slowly near the ground than at higher altitudes. The result is a slight bending of the radio waves toward the earth.

Optical and Radio Line of Sight With no intervening obstacles, the optical line of sight can be expressed as

$$d = 3.57\sqrt{h}$$

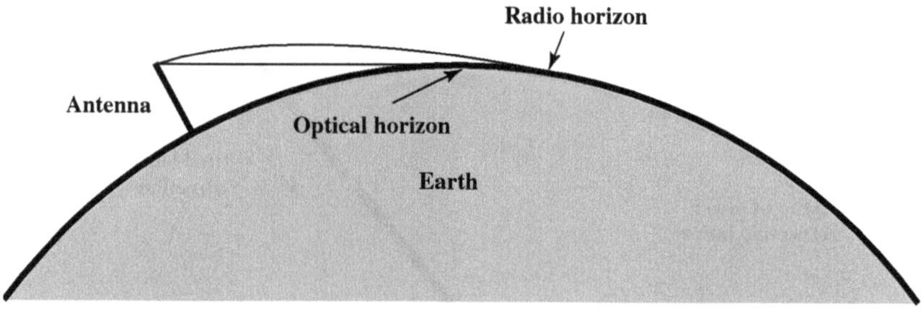

Figure 5.8 Optical and Radio Horizons

where d is the distance between an antenna and the horizon in kilometers and h is the antenna height in meters. The effective, or radio, line of sight to the horizon is expressed as (Figure 5.8):

$$d = 3.57\sqrt{Kh}$$

where K is an adjustment factor to account for the refraction. A good rule of thumb is $K = 4/3$. Thus, the maximum distance between two antennas for LOS propagation is $3.57(\sqrt{Kh_1} + \sqrt{Kh_2})$, where h_1 and h_2 are the heights of the two antennas.

Example 5.2 The maximum distance between two antennas for LOS transmission if one antenna is 100 m high and the other is at ground level is:

$$d = 3.57\sqrt{Kh} = 3.57\sqrt{133} = 41 \text{ km}$$

Now suppose that the receiving antenna is 10 m high. To achieve the same distance, how high must the transmitting antenna be? The result is:

$$41 = 3.57(\sqrt{Kh_1} + \sqrt{13.3})$$

$$\sqrt{Kh_1} = \frac{41}{3.57} - \sqrt{13.3} = 7.84$$

$$h_1 = 7.84^2/1.33 = 46.2 \text{ m}$$

This is a savings of over 50 m in the height of the transmitting antenna. This example illustrates the benefit of raising receiving antennas above ground level to reduce the necessary height of the transmitter.

5.3 LINE-OF-SIGHT TRANSMISSION

With any communications system, the signal that is received will differ from the signal that is transmitted, due to various transmission impairments. For analog signals, these impairments introduce various random modifications that degrade the signal quality. For digital data, bit errors are introduced: A binary 1 is transformed into a binary 0, and vice versa. In this section we examine the various impairments and comment on their effect on the information-carrying capacity of a communications

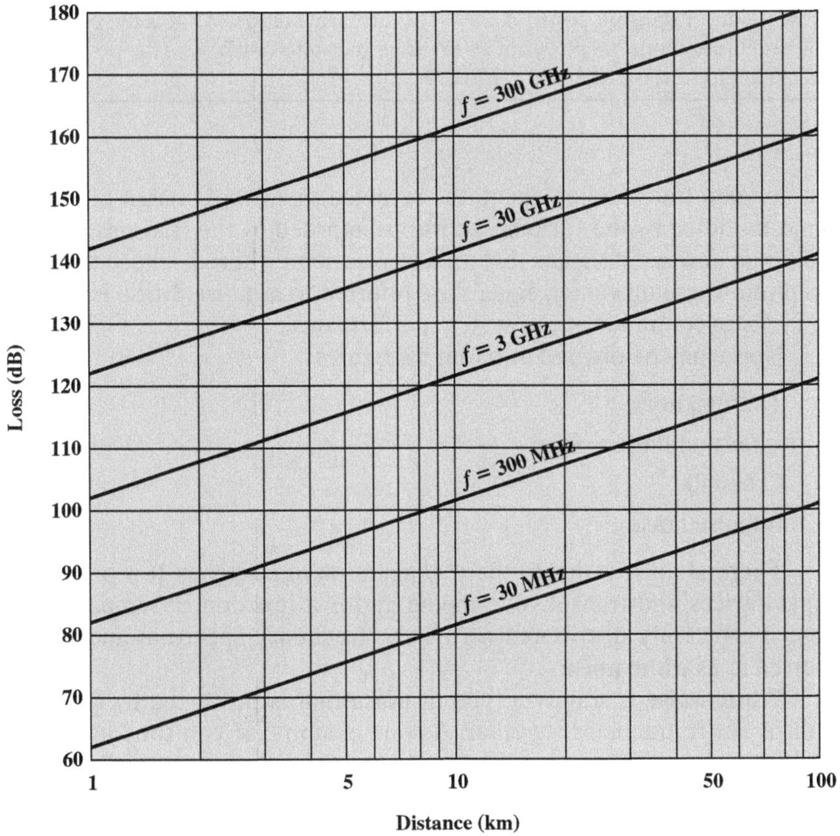

Figure 5.9 Free Space Loss

the frequency increases, the free space loss also increases, which would suggest that at higher frequencies, losses become more burdensome. However, Equation (5.3) shows that we can easily compensate for this increased loss with antenna gains. In fact, there is a net gain at higher frequencies, other factors remaining constant. Equation (5.2) shows that at a fixed distance an increase in frequency results in an increased loss measured by 20 log (f). However, if we take into account antenna gain, and fix antenna area, then the change in loss is measured by $-20 \log(f)$; that is, there is actually a decrease in loss at higher frequencies.

Example 5.3 Determine the isotropic free space loss at 4 GHz for the shortest path to a synchronous satellite from earth (35,863 km). At 4 GHz, the wavelength is $(3 \times 10^8)/(4 \times 10^9) = 0.075$ m. Then,

$$L_{dB} = -20 \log(0.075) + 20 \log(35.853 \times 10^6) + 21.98 = 195.6 \text{ dB}$$

Now consider the antenna gain of both the satellite- and ground-based antennas. Typical values are 44 dB and 48 dB respectively. The free space loss is:

$$L_{dB} = 195.6 - 44 - 48 = 103.6 \text{ dB}$$

Now assume a transmit power of 250 W at the earth station. What is the power received at the satellite antenna? A power of 250 W translates into 24 dBW, so the power at the receiving antenna is 24 − 103.6 = −79.6 dBW.

Noise

For any data transmission event, the received signal will consist of the transmitted signal, modified by the various distortions imposed by the transmission system, plus additional unwanted signals that are inserted somewhere between transmission and reception. These unwanted signals are referred to as noise. Noise is the major limiting factor in communications system performance.

Noise may be divided into four categories:

- Thermal noise
- Intermodulation noise
- Crosstalk
- Impulse noise

Thermal noise is due to thermal agitation of electrons. It is present in all electronic devices and transmission media and is a function of temperature. Thermal noise is uniformly distributed across the frequency spectrum and hence is often referred to as **white noise**.

White noise is simply a type of noise that is produced by grouping sounds of different frequencies together. As one example, if you took all of the imaginable tones that a human can *hear* and combined them together, you would have white noise.

The adjective "white" is used to describe this type of noise because of the way white light works. White light is light that is made up of all of the different colors (frequencies) of light combined together (a prism or a rainbow separates white light back into its component colors). In the same way, white noise is a combination of all of the different frequencies of sound. You can think of white noise as 20,000 tones all playing at the same time.

Because white noise contains all frequencies, it is frequently used to **mask** other sounds. If you are in a hotel and voices from the room next door are leaking into your room, you might turn on a fan to drown out the voices. The fan produces a good approximation of white noise. Why does that work? Why does white noise drown out voices?

Here is one way to think about it. Let's say two people are talking at the same time. Your *brain* can normally "pick out" one of the two voices and actually listen to it and understand it. If three people are talking simultaneously, your brain can probably still pick out one voice. However, if 1,000 people are talking simultaneously, there is no way that your brain can pick out one voice. It turns out that 1,000 people talking together sounds a lot like white noise. So when you turn on a fan to create white noise, you are essentially creating a source of 1,000 voices. The voice next door makes it 1,001 voices, and your brain can't pick it out anymore.[4]

[4]http://www.howstuffworks.com/question47.htm

Thermal noise cannot be eliminated and therefore places an upper bound on communications system performance. Because of the weakness of the signal received by satellite earth stations, thermal noise is particularly significant for satellite communication.

The amount of thermal noise to be found in a bandwidth of 1 Hz in any device or conductor is

$$N_0 = \mathrm{k}T(\mathrm{W/Hz})$$

where[5]

N_0 = noise power density in watts per 1 Hz of bandwidth
k = Boltzmann's constant = 1.38×10^{-23} J/K
T = temperature, in kelvins (absolute temperature)

Example 5.4 Room temperature is usually specified as $T = 17°\mathrm{C}$, or 290 K. At this temperature, the thermal noise power density is

$$N_0 = (1.3803 \times 10^{-23}) \times 290 = 4 \times 10^{-21}\ \mathrm{W/Hz} = -204\ \mathrm{dBW/Hz}$$

where dBW is the decibel-watt.

The noise is assumed to be independent of frequency. Thus the thermal noise in watts present in a bandwidth of B Hertz can be expressed as

$$N = \mathrm{k}TB$$

or, in decibel-watts,

$$\begin{aligned} N &= 10 \log \mathrm{k} + 10 \log T + 10 \log B \\ &= -228.6\ \mathrm{dBW} + 10 \log T + 10 \log B \end{aligned}$$

Example 5.5 Given a receiver with an effective noise temperature of 294 K and a 10-MHz bandwidth, the thermal noise level at the receiver's output is

$$\begin{aligned} N &= -228.6\ \mathrm{dBW} + 10 \log(294) + 10 \log 10^7 \\ &= -228.6 + 24.7 + 70 \\ &= -133.9\ \mathrm{dBW} \end{aligned}$$

When signals at different frequencies share the same transmission medium, the result may be **intermodulation noise**. Intermodulation noise produces signals at a frequency that is the sum or difference of the two original frequencies or multiples of those frequencies. For example, the mixing of signals at frequencies f_1 and f_2

[5]A Joule (J) is the International System (SI) unit of electrical, mechanical, and thermal energy. A watt is the SI unit of power, equal to one joule per second. The kelvin (K) is the SI unit of thermodynamic temperature. For a temperature in degrees kelvin of T, the corresponding temperature in degrees Celsius is equal to $T - 273.15$.

might produce energy at the frequency $f_1 + f_2$. This derived signal could interfere with an intended signal at the frequency $f_1 + f_2$.

Intermodulation noise is produced when there is some nonlinearity in the transmitter, receiver, or intervening transmission system. Normally, these components behave as linear systems; that is, the output is equal to the input times a constant. In a nonlinear system, the output is a more complex function of the input. Such nonlinearity can be caused by component malfunction, the use of excessive signal strength, or just the nature of the amplifiers used. It is under these circumstances that the sum and difference frequency terms occur.

Crosstalk has been experienced by anyone who, while using the telephone, has been able to hear another conversation; it is an unwanted coupling between signal paths. It can occur by electrical coupling between nearby twisted pairs or, rarely, coax cable lines carrying multiple signals. Crosstalk can also occur when unwanted signals are picked up by microwave antennas; although highly directional antennas are used, microwave energy does spread during propagation. Typically, crosstalk is of the same order of magnitude as, or less than, thermal noise. However, in the unlicensed ISM bands, crosstalk often dominates.

In structured cabling, crosstalk can refer to electromagnetic interference from one unshielded twisted pair to another twisted pair, normally running in parallel. And, several types exist.

Near End Crosstalk (NEXT) Interference between two pairs in a cable measured at the same end of the cable as the transmitter.

Far End Crosstalk (FEXT) Interference between two pairs of a cable measured at the other end of the cable from the transmitter.

Alien Crosstalk (AXT) Interference caused by other cables routed close to the cable of interest.[6]

In wireless communication, crosstalk is often called co-channel interference. As the land mobile radio frequency spectrum has become overcrowded, interference has become the rule, rather than the exception, I'm afraid.[7] The FCC is working to address this in its frequency spectrum reallocations and subsequent auctions.

All of the types of noise discussed so far have reasonably predictable and relatively constant magnitudes. Thus it is possible to engineer a transmission system to cope with them. **Impulse noise**, however, is noncontinuous, consisting of irregular pulses or noise spikes of short duration and of relatively high amplitude. It is generated from a variety of causes, including external electromagnetic disturbances, such as lightning, and faults and flaws in the communications system.

Impulse noise is generally only a minor annoyance for analog data. For example, voice transmission may be corrupted by short clicks and crackles with no

[6]*Eliminating alien crosstalk,* Communications News, February 2009, http://www.comnews.com/features/2009_february/0209_web3_eliminating.aspx, retrieved 2011-08-02.

[7]http://urgentcomm.com/mag/radio_cochannel_interference_bad/

loss of intelligibility. However, impulse noise is the primary source of error in digital data transmission. For example, a sharp spike of energy of 0.01 s duration would not destroy any voice data but would wash out about 560 bits of data being transmitted at 56 kbps.

The Expression E_b/N_0

There is a parameter related to signal-to-noise ratio (SNR) that is more convenient for determining digital data rates and error rates and that is the standard quality measure for digital communication system performance. The parameter is the ratio of signal energy per bit to noise power density per Hertz, E_b/N_0. Consider a signal, digital or analog, that contains binary digital data transmitted at a certain bit rate R. Recalling that 1 watt = 1 J/s, the energy per bit in a signal is given by $E_b = ST_b$, where S is the signal power and T_b is the time required to send one bit. The data rate R is just $R = 1/T_b$. Thus

$$\frac{E_b}{N_0} = \frac{S/R}{N_0} = \frac{S}{\mathrm{k}TR} \tag{5.4}$$

or, in decibel notation,

$$\begin{aligned}\left(\frac{E_b}{N_0}\right)_{\mathrm{dB}} &= S_{\mathrm{dBW}} - 10\log R - 10\log k - 10\log T \\ &= S_{\mathrm{dBW}} - 10\log R + 228.6\ \mathrm{dBW} - 10\log T\end{aligned}$$

The ratio E_b/N_0 is important because the bit error rate (BER) for digital data is a (decreasing) function of this ratio. Figure 5.10 illustrates the typical shape of a plot of BER versus E_b/N_0. Such plots are commonly found in the literature and several examples appear in this text. For any particular curve, as the signal strength relative to the noise increases (increasing E_b/N_0), the BER performance at the receiver decreases. This makes intuitive sense. However, there is not a single unique curve that expresses the dependence of BER on E_b/N_0. Instead the performance of a transmission/reception system, in terms of BER versus E_b/N_0, also depends on the way in which the data is encoded onto the signal. Thus, Figure 5.10 shows two curves, one of which gives better performance than the other. A curve below and to the left of another curve defines superior performance. Chapter 6 explores the relationship of signal encoding to performance. A more detailed discussion of E_b/N_0 is found in [SKLA01].

Given a value of E_b/N_0 needed to achieve a desired error rate, the parameters in Equation (5.4) may be selected. Note that as the bit rate R increases, the transmitted signal power, relative to noise, must increase to maintain the required E_b/N_0.

Let us try to grasp this result. The signal here is digital, but the reasoning would be the same for an analog signal. In several instances, the noise is sufficient to alter the value of a bit. If the data rate were doubled, the bits would be more tightly packed together, and the same passage of noise might destroy two bits. Thus, for constant signal and noise strength, an increase in data rate increases the error rate.

The advantage of E_b/N_0 compared to SNR is that the latter quantity depends on the bandwidth.

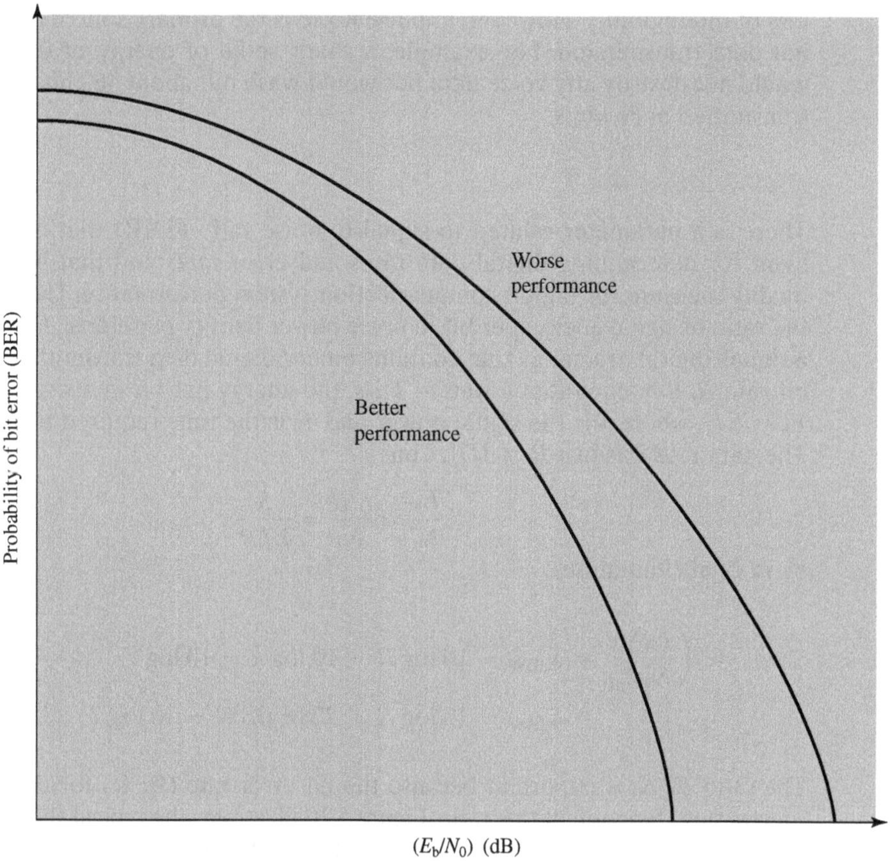

Figure 5.10 General Shape of BER Versus E_b/N_0 Curves

Example 5.6 Suppose a signal encoding technique requires that $E_b/N_0 = 8.4$ dB for a bit error rate of 10^{-4} (one bit error out of every 10,000). If the effective noise temperature is 290°K (room temperature) and the data rate is 2400 bps, what received signal level is required to overcome thermal noise?

We have

$$\begin{aligned} 8.4 &= S_{dBW} - 10 \log 2400 + 228.6 \text{ dBW} - 10 \log 290 \\ &= S_{dBW} - (10)(3.38) + 228.6 - (10)(2.46) \\ S &= -161.8 \text{ dBW} \end{aligned}$$

We can relate E_b/N_0 to SNR as follows. We have

$$\frac{E_b}{N_0} = \frac{S}{N_0 R}$$

The parameter N_0 is the noise power density in watts/hertz. Hence, the noise in a signal with bandwidth B_T is $N = N_0 B_T$. Substituting, we have

$$\frac{E_b}{N_0} = \frac{S}{N}\frac{B_T}{R} \tag{5.5}$$

Another formulation of interest relates to E_b/N_0 spectral efficiency. Recall, Shannon's result that the maximum channel capacity, in bits per second, obeys the equation

$$C = B \log_2(1 + S/N)$$

where C is the capacity of the channel in bits per second and B is the bandwidth of the channel in Hertz. This can be rewritten as:

$$\frac{S}{N} = 2^{C/B} - 1$$

Using Equation (5.5), and equating B_T with B and R with C, we have

$$\frac{E_b}{N_0} = \frac{B}{C}(2^{C/B} - 1)$$

This is a useful formula that relates the achievable spectral efficiency C/B to E_b/N_0.

> **Example 5.7** Suppose we want to find the minimum E_b/N_0 required to achieve a spectral efficiency of 6 bps/Hz. Then $E_b/N_0 = (1/6)(2^6 - 1) = 10.5 = 10.21$ dB.

Atmospheric Absorption

An additional loss between the transmitting and receiving antennas is atmospheric absorption. Water vapor and oxygen contribute most to attenuation. A peak attenuation occurs in the vicinity of 22 GHz due to water vapor. At frequencies below 15 GHz, the attenuation is less. The presence of oxygen results in an absorption peak in the vicinity of 60 GHz but contributes less at frequencies below 30 GHz. Rain and fog (suspended water droplets) cause scattering of radio waves that results in attenuation. This can be a major cause of signal loss. Thus, in areas of significant precipitation, either path lengths have to be kept short or lower-frequency bands should be used.

Multipath

For wireless facilities where there is a relatively free choice of where antennas are to be located, they can be placed so that if there are no nearby interfering obstacles, there is a direct line-of-sight path from transmitter to receiver. This is generally the case for many satellite facilities and for point-to-point microwave. In other cases, such as mobile telephony, there are obstacles in abundance. The signal can be reflected by such obstacles so that multiple copies of the signal with varying delays can be received. In fact, in extreme cases, the receiver may capture only reflected signals and not the direct signal. Depending on the differences in the path lengths of the direct and reflected waves, the composite signal can be either larger or smaller than the direct signal. Reinforcement and cancellation of the signal resulting from the signal following multiple paths can be controlled for communication between fixed, well-sited antennas, and between satellites and fixed ground stations. One exception is when the path goes across water, where the wind keeps the reflective surface of the water in motion. For mobile telephony and communication to antennas that are not well sited, multipath considerations can be paramount.

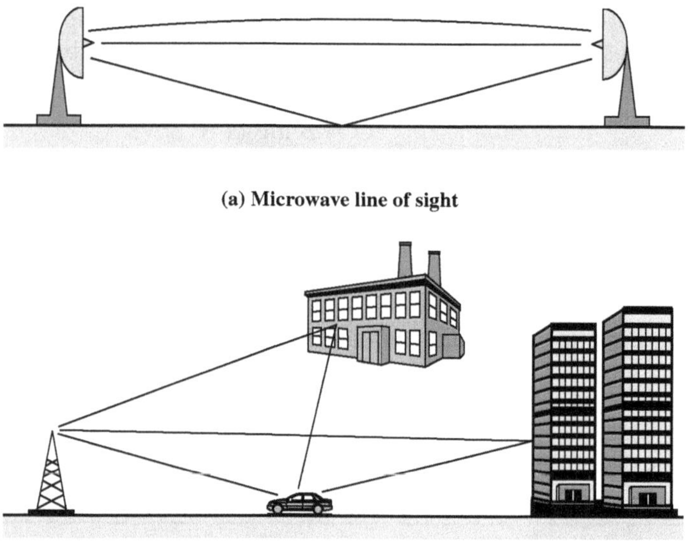

(a) Microwave line of sight

(b) Mobile radio

Figure 5.11 Examples of Multipath Interference

Figure 5.11 illustrates in general terms the types of multipath interference typical in terrestrial, fixed microwave and in mobile communications. For fixed microwave, in addition to the direct line of sight, the signal may follow a curved path through the atmosphere due to refraction and the signal may also reflect from the ground. For mobile communications, structures and topographic features provide reflection surfaces.

Refraction

Radio waves are refracted (or bent) when they propagate through the atmosphere. The refraction is caused by changes in the speed of the signal with altitude or by other spatial changes in the atmospheric conditions. Normally, the speed of the signal increases with altitude, causing radio waves to bend downward. However, on occasion, weather conditions may lead to variations in speed with height that differ significantly from the typical variations. This may result in a situation in which only a fraction or no part of the line-of-sight wave reaches the receiving antenna.

Refraction on the troposphere relies on the variations in space of the refractive index n. Typically, the refractive index falls with increasing height. The refractive index governs the speed of propagation in a medium.

5.4 FADING IN THE MOBILE ENVIRONMENT

Perhaps the most challenging technical problem facing communications systems engineers is fading in a mobile environment. The term *fading* refers to the time variation of received signal power caused by changes in the transmission medium or

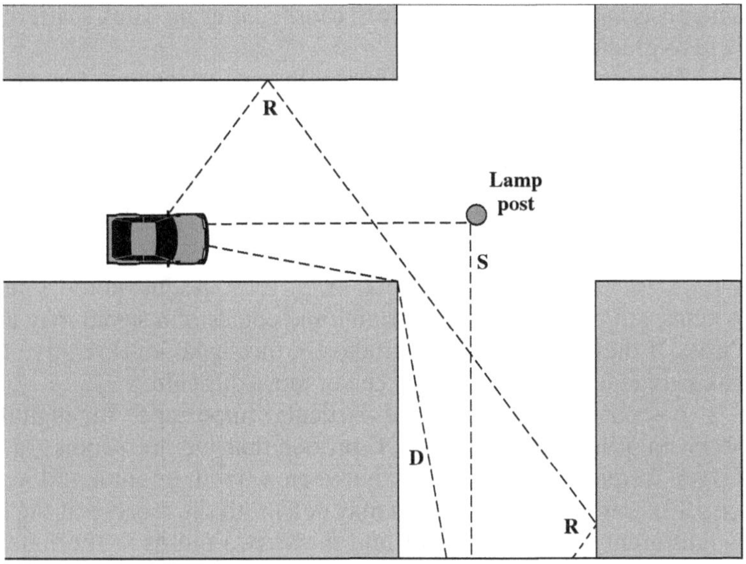

Figure 5.12 Sketch of Three Important Propagation Mechanisms: Reflection (R), Scattering (S), Diffraction (D) [ANDE95]

path(s). In a fixed environment, fading is affected by changes in atmospheric conditions, such as rainfall. But in a mobile environment, where one of the two antennas is moving relative to the other, the relative location of various obstacles changes over time, creating complex transmission effects.

Multipath Propagation

Three propagation mechanisms, illustrated in Figure 5.12, play a role. **Reflection** occurs when an electromagnetic signal encounters a surface that is large relative to the wavelength of the signal. For example, suppose a ground-reflected wave near the mobile unit is received. Because the ground-reflected wave has a 180° phase shift after reflection, the ground wave and the line-of-sight (LOS) wave may tend to cancel, resulting in high signal loss.[8] Further, because the mobile antenna is lower than most human-made structures in the area, multipath interference occurs. These reflected waves may interfere constructively or destructively at the receiver.

Diffraction occurs at the edge of an impenetrable body that is large compared to the wavelength of the radio wave. When a radio wave encounters such an edge, waves propagate in different directions with the edge as the source. Thus, signals can be received even when there is no unobstructed LOS from the transmitter.

If the size of an obstacle is on the order of the wavelength of the signal or less, **scattering** occurs. An incoming signal is scattered into several weaker outgoing signals. At typical cellular microwave frequencies, there are numerous objects, such as

[8]On the other hand, the reflected signal has a longer path, which creates a phase shift due to delay relative to the unreflected signal. When this delay is equivalent to half a wavelength, the two signals are back in phase.

lamp posts and traffic signs, that can cause scattering. Thus, scattering effects are difficult to predict.

These three propagation effects influence system performance in various ways depending on local conditions and as the mobile unit moves within a cell. If a mobile unit has a clear LOS to the transmitter, then diffraction and scattering are generally minor effects, although reflection may have a significant impact. If there is no clear LOS, such as in an urban area at street level, then diffraction and scattering are the primary means of signal reception.

The Effects of Multipath Propagation As just noted, one unwanted effect of multipath propagation is that multiple copies of a signal may arrive at different phases. If these phases add destructively, the signal level relative to noise declines, making signal detection at the receiver more difficult.

A second phenomenon, of particular importance for digital transmission, is intersymbol interference (ISI). Consider that we are sending a narrow pulse at a given frequency across a link between a fixed antenna and a mobile unit. Figure 5.13 shows what the channel may deliver to the receiver if the impulse is sent at two different times. The upper line shows two pulses at the time of transmission. The lower line shows the resulting pulses at the receiver. In each case the first received pulse is the desired LOS signal. The magnitude of that pulse may change because of changes in atmospheric attenuation. Further, as the mobile unit moves farther away from the fixed antenna, the amount of LOS attenuation increases. But in addition to this primary pulse, there may be multiple secondary pulses due to reflection, diffraction, and scattering. Now suppose that this pulse encodes one or more bits of data. In that case, one or more delayed copies of a pulse may arrive at the same time as the primary pulse for a subsequent bit. These delayed pulses act as a form of noise to the subsequent primary pulse, making recovery of the bit information more difficult.

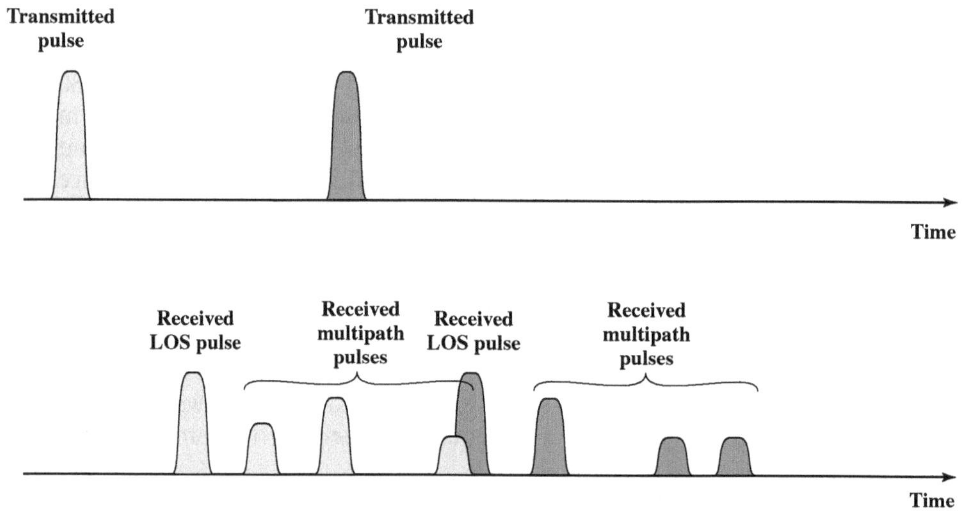

Figure 5.13 Two Pulses in Time-Variant Multipath

As the mobile antenna moves, the location of various obstacles changes; hence the number, magnitude, and timing of the secondary pulses change. This makes it difficult to design signal processing techniques that will filter out multipath effects so that the intended signal is recovered with fidelity.

Types of Fading Fading effects in a mobile environment can be classified as either fast or slow. Referring to Figure 5.12, as the mobile unit moves down a street in an urban environment, rapid variations in signal strength occur over distances of about one-half a wavelength. At a frequency of 900 MHz, which is typical for mobile cellular applications, a wavelength is 0.33 m. The rapidly changing waveform in Figure 5.14 shows an example of the spatial variation of received signal amplitude at 900 MHz in an urban setting. Note that changes of amplitude can be as much as 20 or 30 dB over a short distance. This type of rapidly changing fading phenomenon, known as **fast fading**, affects not only mobile phones in automobiles, but even a mobile phone user walking down an urban street.

As the mobile user covers distances well in excess of a wavelength, the urban environment changes, as the user passes buildings of different heights, vacant lots, intersections, and so forth. Over these longer distances, there is a change in the average received power level about which the rapid fluctuations occur. This is indicated by the slowly changing waveform in Figure 5.14 and is referred to as **slow fading**.

Fading effects can also be classified as flat or selective. **Flat fading**, or nonselective fading, is that type of fading in which all frequency components of the received signal fluctuate in the same proportions simultaneously. **Selective fading** affects unequally the different spectral components of a radio signal. The term *selective fading* is usually significant only relative to the bandwidth of the overall communications channel. If attenuation occurs over a portion of the bandwidth of the signal, the fading is considered to be selective; nonselective fading implies that the signal bandwidth of interest is narrower than, and completely covered by, the spectrum affected by the fading.

The Fading Channel In designing a communications system, the communications engineer needs to estimate the effects of multipath fading and noise on the mobile channel. The simplest channel model, from the point of view of analysis, is the

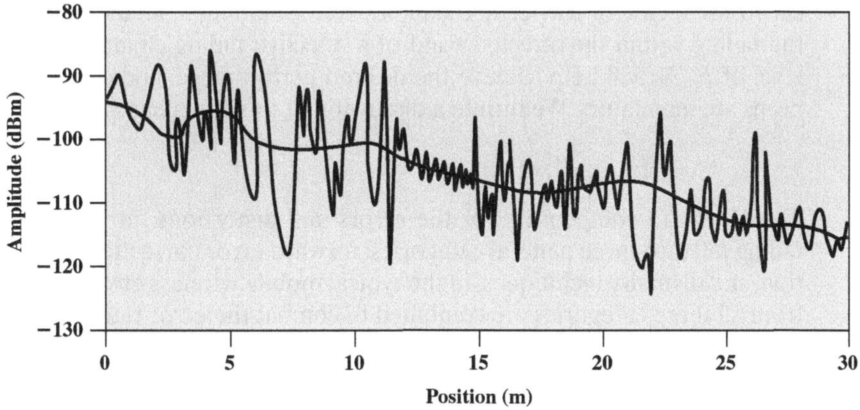

Figure 5.14 Typical Slow and Fast Fading in an Urban Mobile Environment

additive white Gaussian noise (AWGN) channel. In this channel, the desired signal is degraded by thermal noise associated with the physical channel itself as well as electronics at the transmitter and receiver (and any intermediate amplifiers or repeaters). This model is fairly accurate in some cases, such as space communications and some wire transmissions, such as coaxial cable. For terrestrial wireless transmission, particularly in the mobile situation, AWGN is not a good guide for the designer.

Rayleigh fading occurs when there are multiple indirect paths between transmitter and receiver and no distinct dominant path, such as an LOS path. This represents a worst case scenario. Fortunately, Rayleigh fading can be dealt with analytically, providing insights into performance characteristics that can be used in difficult environments, such as downtown urban settings.

Rician fading best characterizes a situation where there is a direct LOS path in addition to a number of indirect multipath signals. The Rician model is often applicable in an indoor environment whereas the Rayleigh model characterizes outdoor settings. The Rician model also becomes more applicable in smaller cells or in more open outdoor environments. The channels can be characterized by a parameter K, defined as follows:

$$K = \frac{\text{power in the dominant path}}{\text{power in the scattered paths}}$$

When $K = 0$ the channel is Rayleigh (i.e., numerator is zero) and when $K = \infty$, the channel is AWGN (i.e., denominator is zero). Figure 5.15, based on [FREE98a] and [SKLA01], shows system performance in the presence of noise. Here bit error rate is plotted as a function of the ratio E_b/N_0. Of course, as that ratio increases, the bit error rate drops. The figure shows that with a reasonably strong signal, relative to noise, an AWGN exhibit provides fairly good performance, as do Rician channels with larger values of K, roughly corresponding to microcells or an open country environment. The performance would be adequate for a digitized voice application, but for digital data transfer efforts to compensate would be needed. The Rayleigh channel provides relatively poor performance; this is likely to be seen for flat fading and for slow fading; in these cases, error compensation mechanisms become more desirable. Finally, some environments produce fading effects worse than the so-called worst case of Rayleigh. Examples are fast fading in an urban environment and the fading within the affected band of a selective fading channel. In these cases, no level of E_b/N_0 will help achieve the desired performance, and compensation mechanisms are mandatory. We turn to a discussion of those mechanisms next.

Error Compensation Mechanisms

The efforts to compensate for the errors and distortions introduced by multipath fading fall into three general categories: forward error correction, adaptive equalization, and diversity techniques. In the typical mobile wireless environment, techniques from all three categories are combined to combat the error rates encountered.

Forward Error Correction Forward error correction is applicable in digital transmission applications: those in which the transmitted signal carries digital data or digitized voice or video data. The term *forward* refers to procedures whereby a

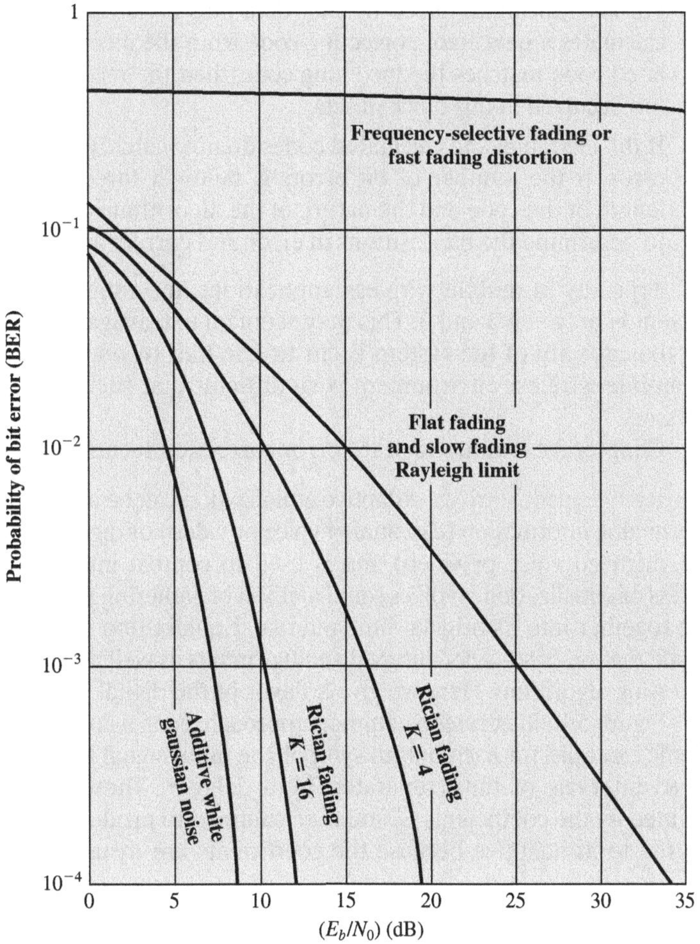

Figure 5.15 Theoretical Bit Error Rate for Various Fading Conditions

receiver, using only information contained in the incoming digital transmission, corrects bit errors in the data. This is in contrast to backward error correction, in which the receiver merely detects the presence of errors and then sends a request back to the transmitter to retransmit the data in error. Backward error correction is not practical in many wireless applications. For example, in satellite communications, the amount of delay involved makes retransmission undesirable. In mobile communications, the error rates are often so high that there is a high probability that the retransmitted block of bits will also contain errors. In these applications, forward error correction is required. In essence, forward error correction is achieved as follows:

1. Using a coding algorithm, the transmitter adds a number of additional, redundant bits to each transmitted block of data. These bits form an **error-correcting code** and are calculated as a function of the data bits.

2. For each incoming block of bits (data plus error-correcting code), the receiver calculates a new error-correcting code from the incoming data bits. If the calculated code matches the incoming code, then the receiver assumes that no error has occurred in this block of bits.
3. If the incoming and calculated codes do not match, then one or more bits are in error. If the number of bit errors is below a threshold that depends on the length of the code and the nature of the algorithm, it is possible for the receiver to determine the bit positions in error and correct all errors.

Typically in mobile wireless applications, the ratio of total bits sent to data bits sent is between 2 and 3. This may seem an extravagant amount of overhead, in that the capacity of the system is cut to one-half or one-third of its potential, but the mobile wireless environment is so difficult that such levels of redundancy are necessary.

Chapter 8 examines forward error correction techniques in detail.

Adaptive Equalization Adaptive equalization can be applied to transmissions that carry analog information (e.g., analog voice or video) or digital information (e.g., digital data, digitized voice or video) and is used to combat intersymbol interference. The process of equalization involves some method of gathering the dispersed symbol energy back together into its original time interval. Equalization is a broad topic; techniques include the use of so-called lumped analog circuits as well as sophisticated digital signal processing algorithms. Here we give a flavor of the digital signal processing approach.

Figure 5.16 illustrates a common approach using a linear equalizer circuit. In this specific example, for each output symbol, the input signal is sampled at five uniformly spaced intervals of time, separated by a delay τ. These samples are individually weighted by the coefficients C_i and then summed to produce the output. The circuit is referred to as adaptive because the coefficients are dynamically adjusted. Typically,

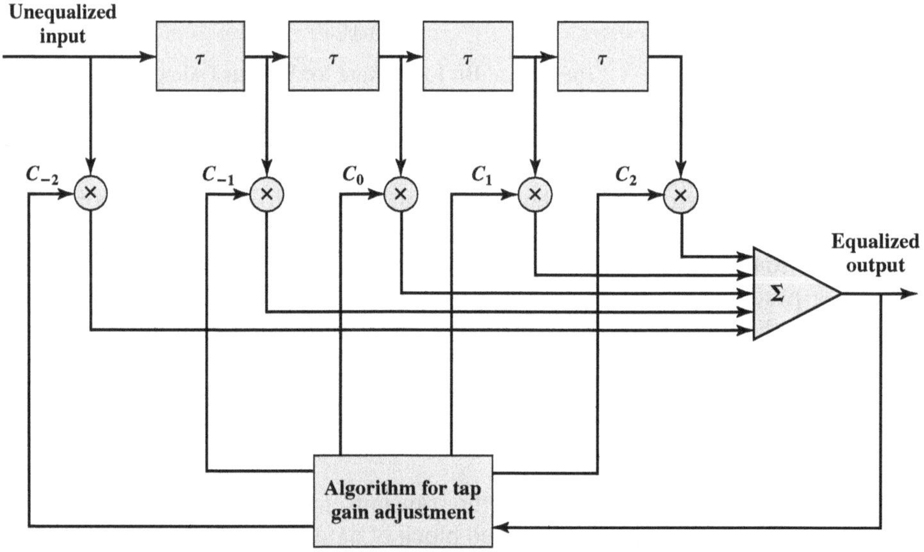

Figure 5.16 Linear Equalizer Circuit [PROA01]

the coefficients are set using a *training sequence*, which is a known sequence of bits. The training sequence is transmitted. The receiver compares the received training sequence with the expected training sequence and on the basis of the comparison calculates suitable values for the coefficients. Periodically, a new training sequence is sent to account for changes in the transmission environment.

For Rayleigh channels, or worse, it may be necessary to include a new training sequence with every single block of data. Again, this represents considerable overhead but is justified by the error rates encountered in a mobile wireless environment.

Diversity Techniques Diversity is based on the fact that individual channels experience independent fading events. We can therefore compensate for error effects by providing multiple logical channels in some sense between transmitter and receiver and sending part of the signal over each channel. This technique does not eliminate errors but it does reduce the error rate, since we have spread the transmission out to avoid being subjected to the highest error rate that might occur. The other techniques (equalization, forward error correction) can then cope with the reduced error rate.

Some diversity techniques involve the physical transmission path and are referred to as **space diversity**. For example, multiple nearby antennas may be used to receive the message, with the signals combined in some fashion to reconstruct the most likely transmitted signal. Another example is the use of collocated multiple directional antennas, each oriented to a different reception angle with the incoming signals again combined to reconstitute the transmitted signal.

More commonly, the term *diversity* refers to frequency diversity or time diversity techniques. With **frequency diversity**, the signal is spread out over a larger frequency bandwidth or carried on multiple frequency carriers. The most important example of this approach is spread spectrum, which is examined in Chapter 7.

Time diversity techniques aim to spread the data out over time so that a noise burst affects fewer bits. Time diversity can be quite effective in a region of slow fading. If a mobile unit is moving slowly, it may remain in a region of a high level of fading for a relatively long interval. The result will be a long burst of errors even though the local mean signal level is much higher than the interference. Even powerful error correction codes may be unable to cope with an extended error burst. If digital data is transmitted in a time division multiplex (TDM) structure, in which multiple users share the same physical channel by the use of time slots, then block interleaving can be used to provide time diversity. Figure 5.17a, based on one in [JONE93], illustrates the concept. Note that the same number of bits are still affected by the noise surge, but they are spread out over a number of logical channels. If each channel is protected by forward error correction, the error-correcting code may be able to cope with the fewer number of bits that are in error in a particular logical channel. If TDM is not used, time diversity can still be applied by viewing the stream of bits from the source as a sequence of blocks and then shuffling the blocks. In Figure 5.17b, blocks are shuffled in groups of four. Again, the same number of bits is in error, but the error correcting code is applied to sets of bits that are spread out in time. Even greater diversity is achieved by combining TDM interleaving with block shuffling.

The tradeoff with time diversity is delay. The greater the degree of interleaving and shuffling used, the longer the delay in reconstructing the original bit sequence at the receiver.

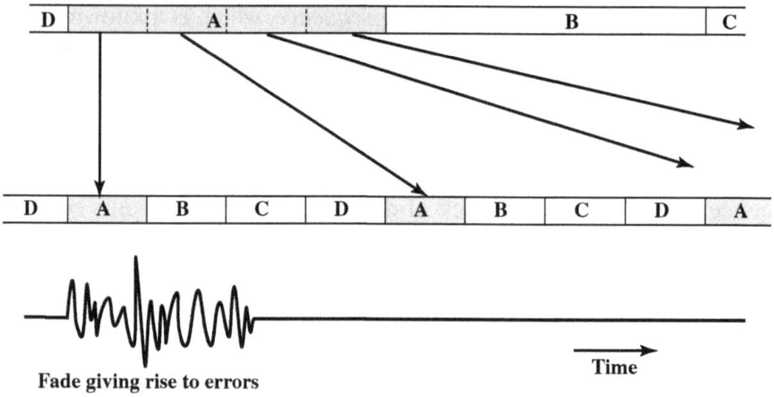

(a) TDM stream

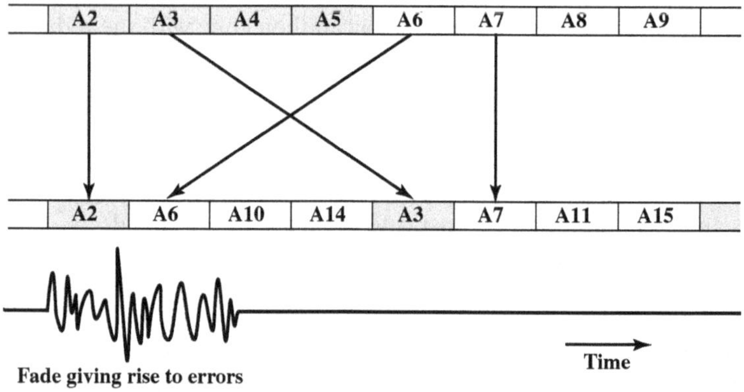

(b) Interleaving without TDM

Figure 5.17 Interleaving Data Blocks to Spread the Effects of Error Bursts

5.5 RECOMMENDED READINGS AND WEB SITES

[FREE97] provides good coverage of all of the topics in this chapter. A rigorous treatment of antennas and propagation is found in [BERT00]. [THUR00] provides an exceptionally clear discussion of antennas.

BERT00 Bertoni, H. *Radio Propagation for Modern Wireless Systems.* Upper Saddle River, NJ: Prentice Hall, 2000.

FREE97 Freeman, R. *Radio System Design for Telecommunications.* New York: Wiley, 1997.

THUR00 Thurwachter, C. *Data and Telecommunications: Systems and Applications.* Upper Saddle River, NJ: Prentice Hall, 2000.

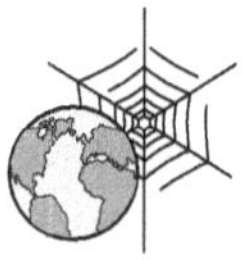

Recommended Web Site:

- **About Antennas:** Good source of information and links.

5.6 KEY TERMS, REVIEW QUESTIONS, AND PROBLEMS

Key Terms

adaptive equalization	flat fading	parabolic reflective antenna
antenna	forward error correction (FEC)	radiation pattern
antenna gain	free space loss	radio LOS
atmospheric absorption	ground wave propagation	reception pattern
attenuation	Hertz antenna	reflection
beam width	impulse noise	refraction
crosstalk	intermodulation noise	scattering
diffraction	isotropic antenna	selective fading
dipole	line of sight (LOS)	sky wave propagation
diversity	multipath	slow fading
fading	noise	thermal noise
fast fading	optical LOS	

Review Questions

5.1 What two functions are performed by an antenna?
5.2 What is an isotropic antenna?
5.3 What information is available from a radiation pattern? Graphical representation
5.4 What is the advantage of a parabolic reflective antenna?
5.5 What factors determine antenna gain?
5.6 What is the primary cause of signal loss in satellite communications?
5.7 Name and briefly define four types of noise.
5.8 What is refraction?
5.9 What is fading?
5.10 What is the difference between diffraction and scattering?
5.11 What is the difference between fast and slow fading?
5.12 What is the difference between flat and selective fading?
5.13 Name and briefly define three diversity techniques.

Problems

5.1 For radio transmission in free space, signal power is reduced in proportion to the square of the distance from the source, whereas in wire transmission, the attenuation is a fixed number of dB per kilometer. The following table is used to show the dB reduction relative to some reference for free space radio and uniform wire. Fill in the missing numbers to complete the table.

Distance (km)	Radio (dB)	Wire (dB)
1	−6	−3
2		
4		
8		
16		

5.2 Find the optimum wavelength and frequency for a half-wave dipole of length 10 m.

5.3 It turns out that the depth in the ocean to which airborne electromagnetic signals can be detected grows with the wavelength. Therefore, the military got the idea of using very long wavelengths corresponding to about 30 Hz to communicate with submarines throughout the world. If we want to have an antenna that is about one-half wavelength long, how long would that be?

5.4 The audio power of the human voice is concentrated at about 300 Hz. Antennas of the appropriate size for this frequency are impracticably large, so that to send voice by radio the voice signal must be used to modulate a higher (carrier) frequency for which the natural antenna size is smaller.

a. What is the length of an antenna one-half wavelength long for sending radio at 300 Hz?

b. An alternative is to use a modulation scheme, as described in Chapter 6, for transmitting the voice signal by modulating a carrier frequency, so that the bandwidth of the signal is a narrow band centered on the carrier frequency. Suppose we would like a half-wave antenna to have a length of 1 m. What carrier frequency would we use?

5.5 Stories abound of people who receive radio signals in fillings in their teeth. Suppose you have one filling that is 2.5 mm (0.0025 m) long that acts as a radio antenna. That is, it is equal in length to one-half the wavelength. What frequency do you receive?

5.6 Section 5.1 states that if a source of electromagnetic energy is placed at the focus of the paraboloid, and if the paraboloid is a reflecting surface, then the wave will bounce back in lines parallel to the axis of the paraboloid. To demonstrate this, consider the parabola $y^2 = 2px$ shown in Figure 5.18. Let $P(x_1, y_1)$ be a point on the parabola and PF be the line from P to the focus. Construct the line L through P parallel to the x-axis and the line M tangent to the parabola at P. The angle between L and M is β, and the angle between PF and M is α. The angle α is the angle at which a ray from F strikes

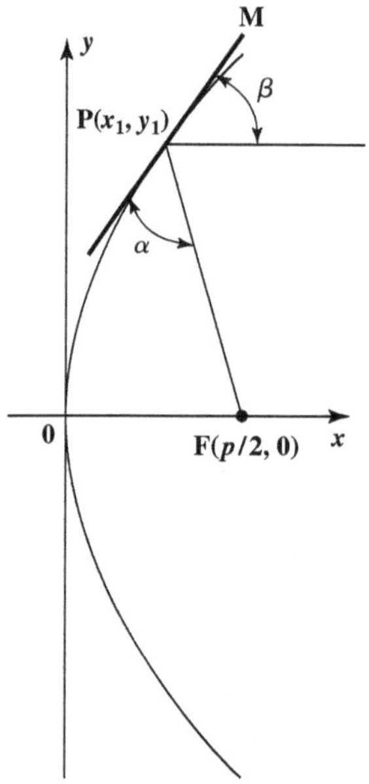

Figure 5.18 Parabolic Reflection

the parabola at P. Because the angle of incidence equals the angle of reflection, the ray reflected from P must be at an angle α to M. Thus, if we can show that $\alpha = \beta$, we have demonstrated that rays reflected from the parabola starting at F will be parallel to the x-axis.

a. First show that $\tan \beta = (p/y_1)$. *Hint:* Recall from trigonometry that the slope of a line is equal to the tangent of the angle the line makes with the positive x direction. Also recall that the slope of the line tangent to a curve at a given point is equal to the derivative of the curve at that point.

b. Now show that $\tan \alpha = (p/y_1)$, which demonstrates that $\alpha = \beta$. *Hint:* Recall from trigonometry that the formula for the tangent of the difference between two angles α_1 and α_2 is $\tan(\alpha_2 - \alpha_1) = (\tan \alpha_2 - \tan \alpha_1)/(1 + \tan \alpha_2 \times \tan \alpha_1)$.

5.7 For each of the antenna types listed in Table 5.2, what is the effective area and gain at a wavelength of 30 cm? Repeat for a wavelength of 3 mm. Assume that the actual area for the horn and parabolic antennas is πm^2.

5.8 It is often more convenient to express distance in km rather than m and frequency in MHz rather than Hz. Rewrite Equation (5.2) using these dimensions.

5.9 Assume that two antennas are half-wave dipoles and each has a directive gain of 3 dB. If the transmitted power is 1 W and the two antennas are separated by a distance of 10 km, what is the received power? Assume that the antennas are aligned so that the directive gain numbers are correct and that the frequency used is 100 MHz.

5.10 Suppose a transmitter produces 50 W of power.

a. Express the transmit power in units of dBm and dBW.

b. If the transmitter's power is applied to a unity gain antenna with a 900-MHz carrier frequency, what is the received power in dBm at a free space distance of 100 m?

c. Repeat (b) for a distance of 10 km.

d. Repeat (c) but assume a receiver antenna gain of 2.

5.11 A microwave transmitter has an output of 0.1 W at 2 GHz. Assume that this transmitter is used in a microwave communication system where the transmitting and receiving antennas are parabolas, each 1.2 m in diameter.

a. What is the gain of each antenna in decibels?

b. Taking into account antenna gain, what is the effective radiated power of the transmitted signal?

c. If the receiving antenna is located 24 km from the transmitting antenna over a free space path, find the available signal power out of the receiving antenna in dBm units.

5.12 Show that doubling the transmission frequency or doubling the distance between transmitting antenna and receiving antenna attenuates the power received by 6 dB.

5.13 Section 5.2 states that with no intervening obstacles, the optical line of sight can be expressed as $d = 3.57\sqrt{h}$, where d is the distance between an antenna and the horizon in kilometers and h is the antenna height in meters. Using a value for the earth's radius of 6370 km, derive this equation. *Hint:* Assume that the antenna is perpendicular to the earth's surface, and note that the line from the top of the antenna to the horizon forms a tangent to the earth's surface at the horizon. Draw a picture showing the antenna, the line of sight, and the earth's radius to help visualize the problem.

5.14 Determine the height of an antenna for a TV station that must be able to reach customers up to 80 km away.

5.15 What is the thermal noise level of a channel with a bandwidth of 10 kHz carrying 1000 watts of power operating at 50°C? Compare the noise level to the operating power.

5.16 A square wave with $T = 1$ ms is passed through a low-pass filter that passes frequencies up to 8 kHz with no attenuation.

a. Find the power in the output waveform.

b. Assuming that at the filter input there is a thermal noise voltage with $N_0 = 0.1\ \mu W/Hz$, find the output signal to noise ratio in dB.

5.17 If the received signal level for a particular digital system is −151 dBW and the receiver system effective noise temperature is 1500 K, what is E_b/N_0 for a link transmitting 2400 bps?

5.18 Suppose a ray of visible light passes from the atmosphere into water at an angle to the horizontal of 30°. What is the angle of the ray in the water? *Note:* At standard atmospheric conditions at the earth's surface, a reasonable value for refractive index is 1.0003. A typical value of refractive index for water is 4/3.

CHAPTER 6

SIGNAL ENCODING TECHNIQUES

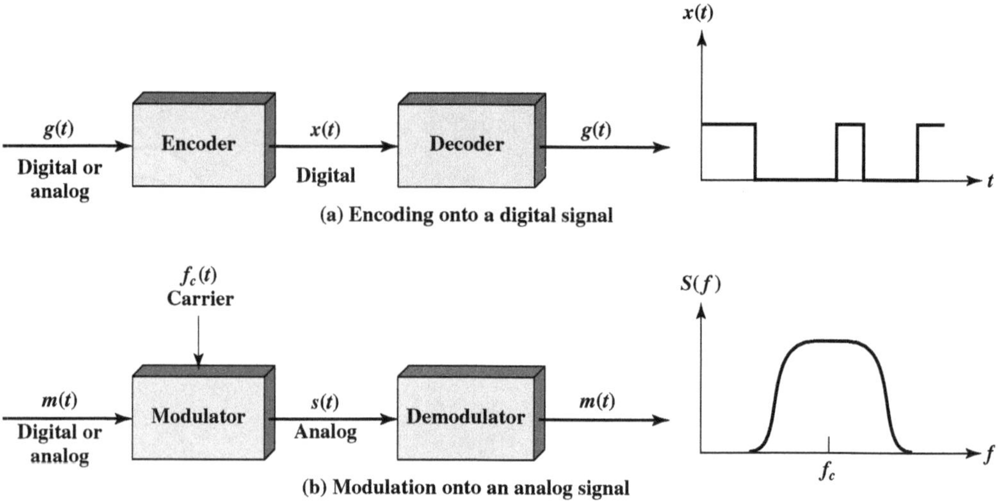

Figure 6.1 Encoding and Modulation Techniques

A distinction can be made between analog and digital data and analog and digital signals. Either form of data can be encoded into either form of signal.

Figure 6.1 is another depiction that emphasizes the process involved. For **digital signaling**, a data source $g(t)$, which may be either digital or analog, is encoded into a digital signal $x(t)$. The actual form of $x(t)$ depends on the encoding technique and is chosen to optimize use of the transmission medium. For example, the encoding may be chosen to conserve bandwidth or to minimize errors.

The basis for **analog signaling** is a continuous constant-frequency signal known as the carrier signal. The frequency of the carrier signal is chosen to be compatible with the transmission medium being used. Data may be transmitted using a carrier signal by modulation. Modulation is the process of encoding source data onto a carrier signal with frequency f_c. All modulation techniques involve operation on one or more of the three fundamental frequency domain parameters: amplitude, frequency, and phase.

The input signal $m(t)$ may be analog or digital and is called the modulating signal or baseband signal. The result of modulating the carrier signal is called the modulated signal $s(t)$. As Figure 6.1b indicates, $s(t)$ is a bandlimited (bandpass) signal. The location of the bandwidth on the spectrum is related to f_c and is often centered on f_c. Again, the actual form of the encoding is chosen to optimize some characteristic of the transmission.

Figure 6.1 suggests four different mappings, or encodings: digital-to-digital, digital-to-analog, analog-to-analog, and analog-to-digital. The latter three techniques are all relevant in the context of wireless communication and are in widespread use in that context:

- **Digital-to-analog:** Digital data and digital signals must be converted to analog signals for wireless transmission.

- **Analog-to-analog:** Typically, a baseband analog signal, such as voice or video, must be modulated onto a higher-frequency carrier for transmission.
- **Analog-to-digital:** It is common to digitize voice signals prior to transmission over either guided or unguided media to improve quality and to take advantage of TDM schemes. For wireless transmission, the resulting digital data must be modulated onto an analog carrier.

These three techniques are examined in this chapter. First we look at some criteria that can be used in evaluating various approaches in each category. Chapter 7 examines spread spectrum, which combines techniques from several categories.

6.1 SIGNAL ENCODING CRITERIA

To begin, we need to define some terms. Recall that a digital signal is a sequence of discrete, discontinuous voltage pulses. Each pulse is a signal element. Binary data are transmitted by encoding each data bit into signal elements. In the simplest case, there is a one-to-one correspondence between bits and signal elements. An example can be where binary 0 is represented by a higher voltage level and binary 1 by a lower voltage level. Similarly, a digital bit stream can be encoded onto an analog signal as a sequence of signal elements, with each signal element being a pulse of constant frequency, phase, and amplitude. There may be a one-to-one correspondence between data elements (bits) and analog signal elements. For both analog and digital signals, there may be a one-to-multiple or multiple-to-one correspondence between data elements and signal elements, as will be shown.

The data signaling rate, or just **data rate**, of a signal is the rate, in bits per second, that data are transmitted. The duration or length of a bit is the amount of time it takes for the transmitter to emit the bit; for a data rate R, the bit duration is $1/R$. The **modulation rate**, in contrast, is the rate at which the signal level is changed. This will depend on the nature of the encoding. The modulation rate is expressed in baud, which means signal elements per second. The data signaling rate is given by $\sum_{i=1}^{m} \frac{\log_2 n_i}{T_i}$ where m is the number of parallel channels, n_i is the number of significant conditions of the *modulation* in the i-th *channel*, and T_i is the *unit interval*, expressed in seconds, for the i-th channel.

Table 6.1 summarizes key terms; these should be clearer when we see an example later in this chapter.

The tasks involved in interpreting digital signals at the receiver can be summarized by the following steps. First, the receiver must know the timing of each bit. That is, the receiver must know with some accuracy when a bit begins and ends. Second, the receiver must determine whether the signal level for each bit position is high (0) or low (1). These tasks can be performed by sampling each bit position in the middle of an interval and comparing the value to a threshold. Because of noise and other impairments, there will be errors.

Table 6.1 Key Data Transmission Terms

Term	Units	Definition
Data element	Bits	A single binary one or zero
Data rate	Bits per second (bps)	The rate at which data elements are transmitted
Signal element	Digital: a voltage pulse of constant amplitude Analog: a pulse of constant frequency, phase, and amplitude	That part of a signal that occupies the shortest interval of a signaling code
Signaling rate or modulation rate	Signal elements per second (baud)	The rate at which signal elements are transmitted

What factors determine how successful the receiver will be in interpreting the incoming signal? Three factors are important: the signal-to-noise ratio (or, better, E_b/N_0), the data rate, and the bandwidth. With other factors held constant, the following statements are true:

- An increase in data rate increases bit error rate (BER).[1]
- An increase in SNR decreases bit error rate.
- An increase in bandwidth allows an increase in data rate.

There is another factor that can be used to improve performance, and that is the encoding scheme. The encoding scheme is simply the mapping from data bits to signal elements. A variety of approaches are in use. Before describing these techniques, let us consider the following ways of evaluating or comparing the various techniques.

- **Signal spectrum:** Several aspects of the signal spectrum are important. A lack of high-frequency components means that less bandwidth is required for transmission. In addition, lack of a direct current (dc) component is also desirable. With a dc component to the signal, there must be direct physical attachment of transmission components. With no dc component, alternating current (ac) coupling via transformer is possible; this provides excellent electrical isolation, reducing interference. Finally, the magnitude of the effects of signal distortion and interference depend on the spectral properties of the transmitted signal. In practice, it usually happens that the transfer function of a channel is worse near the band edges. Therefore, a good signal design should concentrate the transmitted power in the middle of the transmission bandwidth. In such a case, less distortion should be present in the received signal. To meet this objective, codes can be designed with the aim of shaping the spectrum of the transmitted signal.

---

[1]The BER is the most common measure of error performance on a data circuit and is defined as the probability that a bit is received in error. It is also called the *bit error ratio*. This latter term is clearer, because the term *rate* typically refers to some quantity that varies with time. Unfortunately, most books and standards documents refer to the R in BER as *rate*.

- **Clocking:** The receiver must determine the beginning and end of each bit position. This is no easy task. One rather expensive approach is to provide a separate clock channel to synchronize the transmitter and receiver. The alternative is to provide some synchronization mechanism that is based on the transmitted signal. This can be achieved with suitable encoding.
- **Signal interference and noise immunity:** Certain codes exhibit superior performance in the presence of noise. This is usually expressed in terms of a BER.
- **Cost and complexity:** Although digital logic continues to drop in price, this factor should not be ignored. In particular, the higher the signaling rate to achieve a given data rate, the greater the cost. We will see that some codes require a signaling rate that is in fact greater than the actual data rate.

We now turn to a discussion of various techniques.

6.2 DIGITAL DATA, ANALOG SIGNALS

We start with the case of transmitting digital data using analog signals. The most familiar use of this transformation is for transmitting digital data through the public telephone network. The telephone network was designed to receive, switch, and transmit analog signals in the voice-frequency range of about 300 to 3400 Hz. It is not at present suitable for handling digital signals from the subscriber locations (although this is beginning to change). Thus digital devices are attached to the network via a modem (modulator-demodulator), which converts digital data to analog signals, and vice versa.

For the telephone network, modems are used that produce signals in the voice-frequency range.The sounds of a normal speaking voice contain fundamental frequencies between 100 and 300 hertz. The overtones contained in these sounds extend the range of frequencies to approximately 5,000 hertz. Of course, voices of different people differ in their frequency content. Men typically have voices with lower fundamental and harmonic frequencies than those of women and children. The range of fundamental frequencies of the singing voice is greater than that of the speaking voice; it varies from about 80 hertz for a deep bass to about 1,200 hertz for a high soprano. The overtones contained in the sounds of the singing voice reach as high as 10,000 hertz. For purposes of comparison, the frequency range of the instruments of a typical symphony orchestra includes fundamental of about 16 to 4,000 hertz with overtones ranging to 12,000 hertz or higher.

Due to the greater range of frequencies contained in musical sounds—voice and instrument—telephone circuits designed for their transmission must have more firm specifications to prevent distortion. This increases both the initial cost of the equipment and the expense of maintaining it over time. For transmission or ordinary conversation, however, it can be noted that a acceptably high degree of intelligibility can be attained if the frequencies transmitted are restricted to those between approximately 200 and 2,700 Hertz. This is the range of frequencies with which the various circuits and equipment to be discussed in this manual are concerned.[2]

---

[2]http://www.tpub.com/content/armycomsystems/SS0330/SS03300019.htm

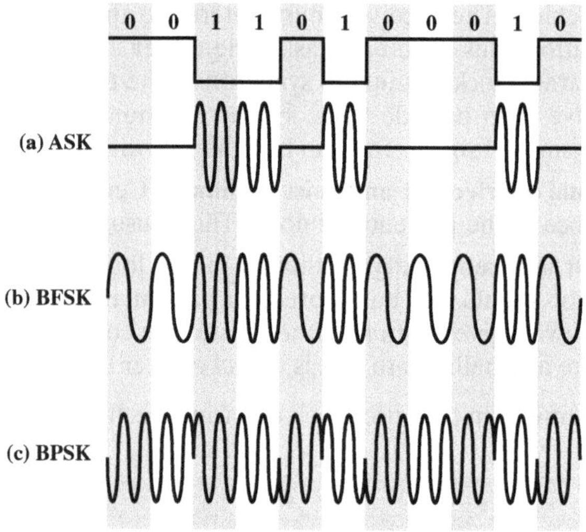

Figure 6.2 Modulation of Analog Signals for Digital Data

The same basic techniques are used for modems that produce signals at higher frequencies (e.g., microwave). This section introduces these techniques and provides a brief discussion of the performance characteristics of the alternative approaches.

We mentioned that modulation involves operation on one or more of the three characteristics of a carrier signal: amplitude, frequency, and phase. Accordingly, there are three basic encoding or modulation techniques for transforming digital data into analog signals, as illustrated in Figure 6.2: amplitude-shift keying (ASK), frequency-shift keying (FSK), and phase-shift keying (PSK). In all these cases, the resulting signal occupies a bandwidth centered on the carrier frequency.

Amplitude-Shift Keying

In ASK, the two binary values are represented by two different amplitudes of the carrier frequency. Commonly, one of the amplitudes is zero; that is, one binary digit is represented by the presence, at constant amplitude, of the carrier, the other by the absence of the carrier (Figure 6.2a). The resulting transmitted signal for one bit time is

$$\textbf{ASK} \qquad s(t) = \begin{cases} A\cos(2\pi f_c t) & \text{binary 1} \\ 0 & \text{binary 0} \end{cases} \tag{6.1}$$

where the carrier signal is $A\cos(2\pi f_c t)$. ASK is susceptible to sudden gain changes and is a rather inefficient modulation technique. On voice-grade lines, it is typically used only up to 1200 bps.

The ASK technique is used to transmit digital data over optical fiber. For LED (light-emitting diode) transmitters, Equation (6.1) is valid. That is, one signal element is represented by a light pulse while the other signal element is represented by the absence of light. Laser transmitters normally have a fixed "bias" current that causes the device to emit a low light level. This low level represents one signal element, while a higher-amplitude lightwave represents another signal element.

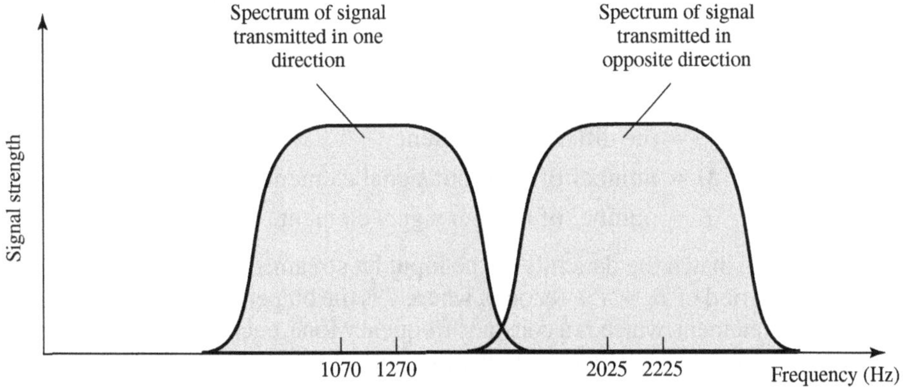

Figure 6.3 Full-Duplex FSK Transmission on a Voice-Grade Line

Frequency-Shift Keying

The most common form of FSK is binary FSK (BFSK), in which the two binary values are represented by two different frequencies near the carrier frequency (Figure 6.2b). The resulting transmitted signal for one bit time is:

$$\textbf{BFSK} \qquad s(t) = \begin{cases} A\cos(2\pi f_1 t) & \text{binary 1} \\ A\cos(2\pi f_2 t) & \text{binary 0} \end{cases} \qquad (6.2)$$

where f_1 and f_2 are typically offset from the carrier frequency f_c by equal but opposite amounts.

Figure 6.3 shows an example of the use of BFSK for full-duplex operation over a voice-grade line. The figure is a specification for the Bell System 108 series modems. A voice-grade line will pass frequencies in the approximate range 300 to 3400 Hz. *Full duplex* means that signals are transmitted in both directions at the same time. To achieve full-duplex transmission, this bandwidth is split. In one direction (transmit or receive), the frequencies used to represent 1 and 0 are centered on 1170 Hz, with a shift of 100 Hz on either side. The effect of alternating between those two frequencies is to produce a signal whose spectrum is indicated as the shaded area on the left in Figure 6.3. Similarly, for the other direction (receive or transmit) the modem uses frequencies shifted 100 Hz to each side of a center frequency of 2125 Hz. This signal is indicated by the shaded area on the right in Figure 6.3. Note that there is little overlap and thus little interference.

BFSK is less susceptible to error than ASK. On voice-grade lines, it is typically used up to 1200 bps. It is also commonly used for high-frequency (3 to 30 MHz) radio transmission. It can also be used at even higher frequencies on local area networks that use coaxial cable.

A signal that is less susceptible to error, is multiple FSK (MFSK), in which more than two frequencies are used. In this case each signaling element represents more than one bit. The transmitted MFSK signal for one signal element time can be defined as follows:

$$\textbf{MFSK} \qquad s_i(t) = A\cos 2\pi f_i t, \qquad 1 \le i \le M \qquad (6.3)$$

where

$$\begin{aligned} f_i &= f_c + (2i - 1 - M)f_d \\ f_c &= \text{the carrier frequency} \\ f_d &= \text{the difference frequency} \\ M &= \text{number of different signal elements} = 2^L \\ L &= \text{number of bits per signal element} \end{aligned}$$

To match the data rate of the input bit stream, each output signal element is held for a period of $T_s = LT$ seconds, where T is the bit period (data rate $= 1/T$). Thus, one signal element, which is a constant-frequency tone, encodes L bits. The total bandwidth required is $2Mf_d$. It can be shown that the minimum frequency separation required is $2f_d = 1/T_s$. Therefore, the modulator requires a bandwidth of $W_d = 2Mf_d = M/T_s$.

Example 6.1 With $f_c = 250$ kHz, $f_d = 25$ kHz, and $M = 8$ ($L = 3$ bits), we have the following frequency assignments for each of the 8 possible 3-bit data combinations:

$f_1 = 75$ kHz 000	$f_2 = 125$ kHz 001	$f_3 = 175$ kHz 010	$f_4 = 225$ kHz 011
$f_5 = 275$ kHz 100	$f_6 = 325$ kHz 101	$f_7 = 375$ kHz 110	$f_8 = 425$ kHz 111

This scheme can support a data rate of $1/T = 2Lf_d = 150$ kbps.

Example 6.2 Figure 6.4 shows an example of MFSK with $M = 4$. An input bit stream of 20 bits is encoded 2 bits at a time, with each of the four possible 2-bit combinations transmitted as a different frequency. The display in the figure shows the frequency transmitted (y-axis) as a function of time (x-axis). Each column represents a time unit T_s in which a single 2-bit signal element is transmitted. The shaded rectangle in the column indicates the frequency transmitted during that time unit.

Phase-Shift Keying

In PSK, the phase of the carrier signal is shifted to represent data.

Two-Level PSK The simplest scheme uses two phases to represent the two binary digits (Figure 6.2c) and is known as binary phase-shift keying. The resulting transmitted signal for one bit time is:

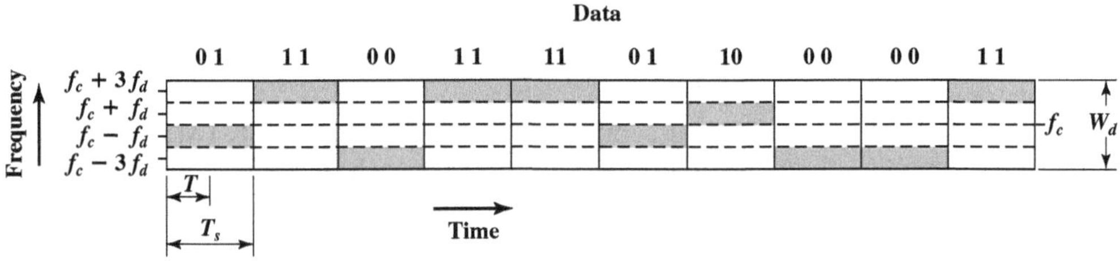

Figure 6.4 MFSK Frequency Use ($M = 4$)

$$\textbf{BPSK} \quad s(t) = \begin{cases} A\cos(2\pi f_c t) \\ A\cos(2\pi f_c t + \pi) \end{cases} = \begin{cases} A\cos(2\pi f_c t) & \text{binary 1} \\ -A\cos(2\pi f_c t) & \text{binary 0} \end{cases} \quad (6.4)$$

Because a phase shift of 180° (π) is equivalent to flipping the sine wave or multiplying it by -1, the rightmost expressions in Equation (6.4) can be used. This leads to a convenient formulation. If we have a bit stream, and we define $d(t)$ as the discrete function that takes on the value of +1 for one bit time if the corresponding bit in the bit stream is 1 and the value of -1 for one bit time if the corresponding bit in the bit stream is 0, then we can define the transmitted signal as:

$$\textbf{BPSK} \quad s_d(t) = Ad(t)\cos(2\pi f_c t) \quad (6.5)$$

An alternative form of two-level PSK is differential PSK (DPSK). Figure 6.5 shows an example. In this scheme, a binary 0 is represented by sending a signal burst of the same phase as the previous signal burst sent. A binary 1 is represented by sending a signal burst of opposite phase to the preceding one. This term *differential* refers to the fact that the phase shift is with reference to the previous bit transmitted rather than to some constant reference signal. In differential encoding, the information to be transmitted is represented in terms of the changes between successive data symbols rather than the signal elements themselves. DPSK avoids the requirement for an accurate local oscillator phase at the receiver that is matched with the transmitter. As long as the preceding phase is received correctly, the phase reference is accurate.

Four-Level PSK More efficient use of bandwidth can be achieved if each signaling element represents more than one bit. For example, instead of a phase shift of 180°, as allowed in PSK, a common encoding technique, known as quadrature phase-shift keying (QPSK), uses phase shifts separated by multiples of $\pi/2$ (90°).

$$\textbf{QPSK} \quad s(t) = \begin{cases} A\cos\left(2\pi f_c t + \frac{\pi}{4}\right) & 11 \\ A\cos\left(2\pi f_c t + \frac{3\pi}{4}\right) & 01 \\ A\cos\left(2\pi f_c t - \frac{3\pi}{4}\right) & 00 \\ A\cos\left(2\pi f_c t - \frac{\pi}{4}\right) & 10 \end{cases} \quad (6.6)$$

Thus each signal element represents two bits rather than one.

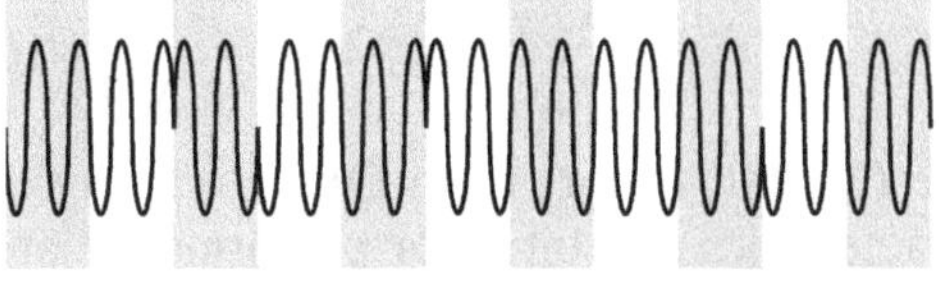

Figure 6.5 Differential Phase Shift Keying (DPSK)

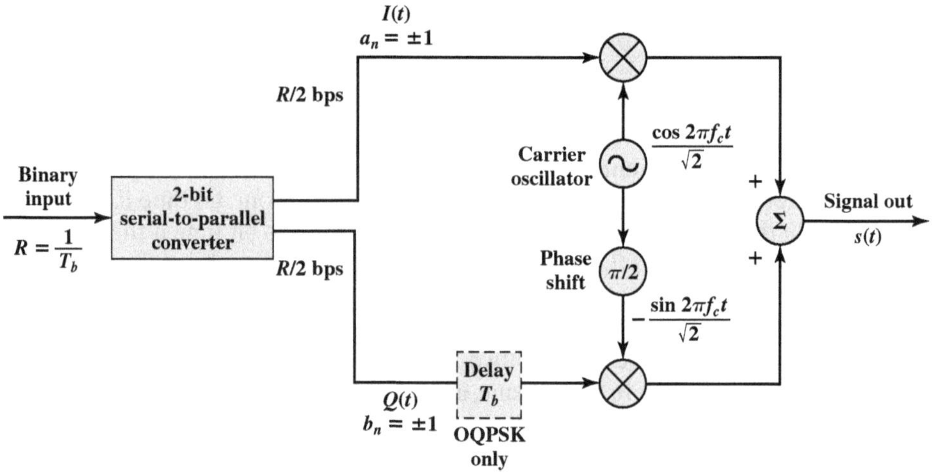

Figure 6.6 QPSK and OQPSK Modulators

Figure 6.6 shows the QPSK modulation scheme in general terms. The input is a stream of binary digits with a data rate of $R = 1/T_b$, where T_b is the width of each bit. This stream is converted into two separate bit streams of $R/2$ bps each, by taking alternate bits for the two streams. The two data streams are referred to as the I (in-phase) and Q (quadrature phase) streams. In the diagram, the upper stream is modulated on a carrier of frequency f_c by multiplying the bit stream by the carrier. For convenience of modulator structure we map binary 1 to $\sqrt{1/2}$ and binary 0 to $-\sqrt{1/2}$. Thus, a binary 1 is represented by a scaled version of the carrier wave and a binary 0 is represented by a scaled version of the negative of the carrier wave, both at a constant amplitude. This same carrier wave is shifted by 90° and used for modulation of the lower binary stream. The two modulated signals are then added together and transmitted. The transmitted signal can be expressed as follows:

$$\textbf{QPSK} \qquad s(t) = \frac{1}{\sqrt{2}} I(t) \cos 2\pi f_c t - \frac{1}{\sqrt{2}} Q(t) \sin 2\pi f_c t$$

Figure 6.7 shows an example of QPSK coding. Each of the two modulated streams is a BPSK signal at half the data rate of the original bit stream. Thus, the combined signals have a symbol rate that is half the input bit rate. Note that from one symbol time to the next, a phase change of as much as 180° (π) is possible.

Figure 6.6 also shows a variation of QPSK known as offset QPSK (OQPSK), or orthogonal QPSK. The difference is that a delay of one bit time is introduced in the Q stream, resulting in the following signal:

$$\textbf{OQPSK} \qquad s(t) = \frac{1}{\sqrt{2}} I(t) \cos 2\pi f_c t - \frac{1}{\sqrt{2}} Q(t - T_b) \sin 2\pi f_c t$$

Because OQPSK differs from QPSK only by the delay in the Q stream, its spectral characteristics and bit error performance are the same as that of QPSK. From Figure 6.7, we can observe that only one of two bits in the pair can change

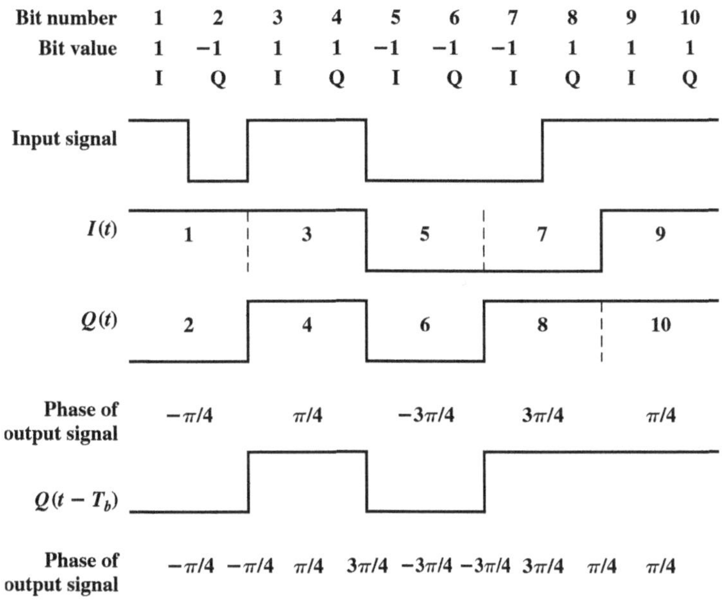

Figure 6.7 Example of QPSK and OQPSK Waveforms

sign at any time and thus the phase change in the combined signal never exceeds 90° ($\pi/2$). This can be an advantage because physical limitations on phase modulators make large phase shifts at high transition rates difficult to perform. OQPSK also provides superior error performance when the transmission channel (including transmitter and receiver) has significant nonlinear components. The effect of nonlinearities is a spreading of the signal bandwidth, which may result in adjacent channel interference. It is easier to control this spreading if the phase changes are smaller, hence the advantage of OQPSK over QPSK.

Multilevel PSK The use of multiple levels can be extended beyond taking bits two at a time. It is possible to transmit bits three at a time using eight different phase angles. Further, each angle can have more than one amplitude. For example, a standard 9600-bps modem uses 12 phase angles, four of which have two amplitude values, for a total of 16 different signal elements.

This latter example points out very well the difference between the data rate R (in bps) and the modulation rate D (in baud) of a signal. Let us assume that this scheme is being employed with digital input in which each bit is represented by a constant voltage pulse, one level for binary one and one level for binary zero. The data rate is $R = 1/T_b$. However, the encoded signal contains $L = 4$ bits in each signal element using $M = 16$ different combinations of amplitude and phase. The modulation rate can be seen to be $R/4$, because each change of signal element communicates four bits. Thus the line signaling speed is 2400 baud, but the data rate is 9600 bps. This is the reason that higher bit rates can be achieved over voice-grade lines by employing more complex modulation schemes.

In general,

$$D = \frac{R}{L} = \frac{R}{\log_2 M} \tag{6.7}$$

where

D = modulation rate, baud
R = data rate, bps
M = number of different signal elements = 2^L
L = number of bits per signal element

Performance

In looking at the performance of various digital-to-analog modulation schemes, the first parameter of interest is the bandwidth of the modulated signal. This depends on a variety of factors, including the definition of bandwidth used and the filtering technique used to create the bandpass signal. We will use some straightforward results from [COUC01].

The transmission bandwidth B_T for ASK is of the form

$$\textbf{ASK} \qquad B_T = (1 + r)R \tag{6.8}$$

where R is the bit rate and r is related to the technique by which the signal is filtered to establish a bandwidth for transmission; typically $0 < r < 1$. Thus the bandwidth is directly related to the bit rate. The preceding formula is also valid for PSK and, under certain assumptions, FSK.

With multilevel PSK (MPSK), significant improvements in bandwidth can be achieved. In general

$$\textbf{MPSK} \qquad B_T = \left(\frac{1 + r}{L}\right)R = \left(\frac{1 + r}{\log_2 M}\right)R \tag{6.9}$$

where L is the number of bits encoded per signal element and M is the number of different signal elements.

For multilevel FSK (MFSK), we have

$$\textbf{MFSK} \qquad B_T = \left(\frac{(1 + r)M}{\log_2 M}\right)R \tag{6.10}$$

Table 6.2 shows the ratio of data rate to transmission bandwidth (R/B_T) for various schemes. This ratio is also referred to as the bandwidth efficiency. As the name suggests, this parameter measures the efficiency with which bandwidth can be used to transmit data.

Of course, the preceding discussion refers to the spectrum of the input signal to a communications line. Nothing has yet been said of performance in the presence of noise. Figure 6.8 summarizes some results based on reasonable assumptions concerning the transmission system [COUC01]. Here bit error rate

Table 6.2 Data Rate to Transmission Bandwidth Ratio for Various Digital-to-Analog Encoding Schemes

	$r = 0$	$r = 0.5$	$r = 1$
ASK	1.0	0.67	0.5
FSK	0.5	0.75	1.00
Multilevel FSK			
$M = 4, L = 2$	0.5	0.75	1.00
$M = 8, L = 3$	0.375	0.56	0.75
$M = 16, L = 4$	0.25	0.375	0.5
$M = 32, L = 5$	0.156	0.234	0.312
PSK	1.0	0.67	0.5
Multilevel PSK			
$M = 4, L = 2$	2.00	1.33	1.00
$M = 8, L = 3$	3.00	2.00	1.50
$M = 16, L = 4$	4.00	2.67	2.00
$M = 32, L = 5$	5.00	3.33	2.50

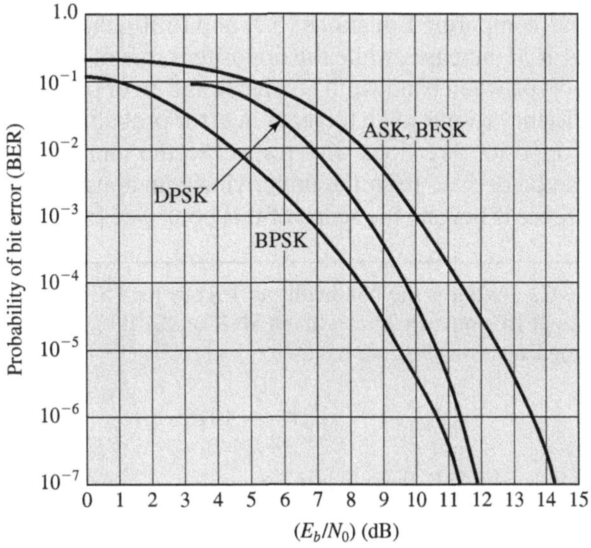

Figure 6.8 Theoretical Bit Error Rate for Various Encoding Schemes

is plotted as a function of the ratio E_b/N_0 defined in Chapter 5. Of course, as that ratio increases, the bit error rate drops. Further, DPSK and BPSK are about 3 dB superior to ASK and BFSK.

Figure 6.9 shows the same information for various levels of M for MFSK and MPSK. There is an important difference. For MFSK, the error probability for a given

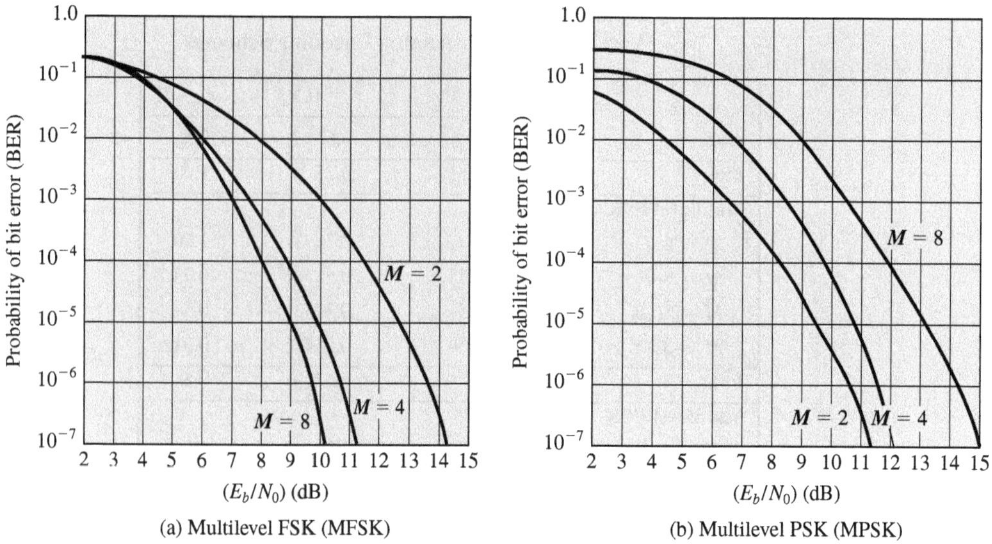

Figure 6.9 Theoretical Bit Error Rate for Multilevel FSK and PSK

value E_b/N_0 of decreases as M increases, while the opposite is true for MPSK. On the other hand, comparing Equations (6.9) and (6.10), the bandwidth efficiency of MFSK decreases as M increases, while the opposite is true of MPSK. Thus, in both cases, there is a tradeoff between bandwidth efficiency and error performance: an increase in bandwidth efficiency results in an increase in error probability. The fact that these tradeoffs move in opposite directions with respect to the number of levels M for MFSK and MPSK can be derived from the underlying equations. A discussion of the reasons for this difference is beyond the scope of this book. See [SKLA01] for a full treatment.

Example 6.3 What is the bandwidth efficiency for FSK, ASK, PSK, and QPSK for a bit error rate of 10^{-7} on a channel with an SNR of 12 dB?

Using Equation (5.4), we have

$$\left(\frac{E_b}{N_0}\right)_{\text{dB}} = 12\text{ dB} - \left(\frac{R}{B_T}\right)_{\text{dB}}$$

For FSK and ASK, from Figure 6.8,

$$\left(\frac{E_b}{N_0}\right)_{\text{dB}} = 14.2\text{ dB}$$

$$\left(\frac{R}{B_T}\right)_{\text{dB}} = -2.2\text{ dB}$$

$$\frac{R}{B_T} = 0.6$$

For PSK, from Figure 6.8

$$\left(\frac{E_b}{N_0}\right)_{\text{dB}} = 11.2\text{ dB}$$

$$\left(\frac{R}{B_T}\right)_{\text{dB}} = 0.8 \text{ dB}$$

$$\frac{R}{B_T} = 1.2$$

The result for QPSK must take into account that the baud rate $D = R/2$. Thus

$$\frac{R}{B_T} = 2.4$$

As the preceding example shows, ASK and FSK exhibit the same bandwidth efficiency, PSK is better, and even greater improvement can be achieved with multilevel signaling.

Minimum-Shift Keying

Minimum-shift keying (MSK) is a form of modulation that is found in some mobile commutations system. It provides superior bandwidth efficiency to BFSK with only a modest decrease in error performance. MFSK can be considered to be a form of BFSK. For MFSK, the transmitted signal for one bit time is:

$$\textbf{MSK} \qquad s(t) = \begin{cases} \sqrt{\dfrac{2E_b}{T_b}}\cos(2\pi f_1 t + \theta(0)) & \text{binary 1} \\ \sqrt{\dfrac{2E_b}{T_b}}\cos(2\pi f_2 t + \theta(0)) & \text{binary 0} \end{cases}$$

where E_b is the transmitted signal energy per bit, and T_b is the bit duration. The phase $\theta(0)$ denotes the value of the phase at time $t = 0$. An important characteristic of MSK is that it is a form of FSK known as continuous-phase FSK (CPFSK), in which the phase is continuous during the transition from one bit time to the next. The BFSK signal shown in Figure 6.2b is in fact an example of CPFSK. Note that the signal is smooth between bit times. In contrast, in Figure 6.2c, there is sometimes an abrupt change in phase.

For MSK, the two frequencies satisfy the following equations:

$$f_1 = f_c + \frac{1}{4T_b} \qquad f_2 = f_c - \frac{1}{4T_b}$$

It can be shown that this spacing between the two frequencies is the minimum that can be used and permit successful detection of the signal at the receiver. This is the reason for the term *minimum* in MSK.

It can also be shown that MSK can be thought of as a special case of OQPSK. In OQPSK, the carrier is multiplied by either $I(t)$ or $Q(t)$, both of which are rectangular pulse functions, taking on the values plus and minus 1. For MSK, the carrier is multiplied by a sinusoidal function, as follows:

$$\textbf{MSK} \qquad s(t) = I(t)\cos\left(\frac{\pi t}{2T_b}\right)\cos 2\pi f_c t + Q(t - T_b)\sin\left(\frac{\pi t}{2T_b}\right)\sin 2\pi f_c t$$

An analysis of MSK is beyond the scope of this book. For more details, see [PASU79] and [XION94].

Quadrature Amplitude Modulation

QAM is a popular analog signaling technique that is used in some wireless standards. This modulation technique is a combination of ASK and PSK. QAM can also be considered a logical extension of QPSK. QAM takes advantage of the fact that it is possible to send two different signals simultaneously on the same carrier frequency, by using two copies of the carrier frequency, one shifted by 90° with respect to the other. For QAM, each carrier is ASK modulated. The two independent signals are simultaneously transmitted over the same medium. At the receiver, the two signals are demodulated and the results combined to produce the original binary input.

Figure 6.10 shows the QAM modulation scheme in general terms. The input is a stream of binary digits arriving at a rate of R bps. This stream is converted into two separate bit streams of $R/2$ bps each, by taking alternate bits for the two streams. In the diagram, the upper stream is ASK modulated on a carrier of frequency f_c by multiplying the bit stream by the carrier. Thus, a binary zero is represented by the absence of the carrier wave and a binary one is represented by the presence of the carrier wave at a constant amplitude. This same carrier wave is shifted by 90° and used for ASK modulation of the lower binary stream. The two modulated signals are then added together and transmitted. The transmitted signal can be expressed as follows:

$$\textbf{QAM} \qquad s(t) = d_1(t)\cos 2\pi f_c t + d_2(t)\sin 2\pi f_c t$$

If two-level ASK is used, then each of the two streams can be in one of two states and the combined stream can be in one of $4 = 2 \times 2$ states. This is essentially QPSK. If four-level ASK is used (i.e., four different amplitude levels), then the combined stream can be in one of $16 = 4 \times 4$ states. Systems using 64 and even 256 states have been implemented. The greater the number of states, the higher the data rate that is possible within a given bandwidth. Of course, as discussed previously, the greater the number of states, the higher the potential error rate due to noise and attenuation.

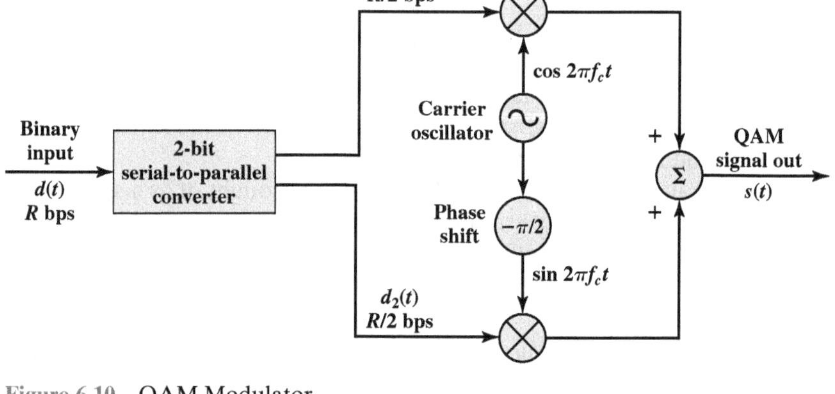

Figure 6.10 QAM Modulator

6.3 ANALOG DATA, ANALOG SIGNALS

Modulation has been defined as the process of combining an input signal $m(t)$ and a carrier at frequency f_c to produce a signal $s(t)$ whose bandwidth is (usually) centered on f_c. For digital data, the motivation for modulation should be clear: When only analog transmission facilities are available, modulation is required to convert the digital data to analog form. The motivation when the data are already analog is less clear. After all, voice signals are transmitted over telephone lines at their original spectrum (referred to as baseband transmission). There are two principal reasons for analog modulation of analog signals:

- A higher frequency may be needed for effective transmission. For unguided transmission, it is virtually impossible to transmit baseband signals; the required antennas would be many kilometers in diameter.
- Modulation permits frequency division multiplexing.

In this section we look at the principal techniques for modulation using analog data: amplitude modulation (AM), frequency modulation (FM), and phase modulation (PM). As before, the three basic characteristics of a signal are used for modulation.

Amplitude Modulation

Amplitude modulation (AM) is depicted in Figure 6.11. Mathematically, the process can be expressed as

$$\textbf{AM} \qquad s(t) = [1 + n_a x(t)]\cos 2\pi f_c t \tag{6.11}$$

where $\cos 2\pi f_c t$ is the carrier and $x(t)$ is the input signal (carrying data), both normalized to unity amplitude. The parameter n_a, known as the modulation index, is the ratio of the amplitude of the input signal to the carrier. Corresponding to our previous notation, the input signal is $m(t) = n_a x(t)$. The "1" in Equation (6.11) is a dc component that prevents loss of information, as explained subsequently. This scheme is also known as double sideband transmitted carrier (DSBTC).

Example 6.4 Derive an expression for $s(t)$ if $x(t)$ is the amplitude-modulating signal $\cos 2\pi f_m t$.

We have

$$s(t) = [1 + n_a \cos 2\pi f_m t]\cos 2\pi f_c t$$

By trigonometric identity, this may be expanded to

$$s(t) = \cos 2\pi f_c t + \frac{n_a}{2}\cos 2\pi(f_c - f_m)t + \frac{n_a}{2}\cos 2\pi(f_c + f_m)t$$

The resulting signal has a component at the original carrier frequency plus a pair of components each spaced f_m hertz from the carrier.

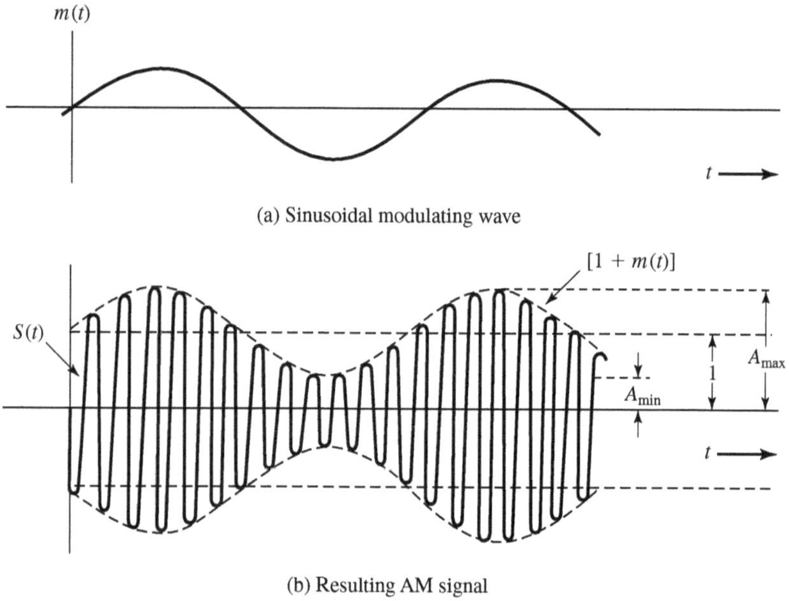

Figure 6.11 Amplitude Modulation

From Equation (6.11) and Figure 6.10, it can be seen that AM involves the multiplication of the input signal by the carrier. The envelope of the resulting signal is $[1 + n_a x(t)]$ and, as long as $n_a < 1$, the envelope is an exact reproduction of the original signal. If $n_a > 1$, the envelope will cross the time axis and information is lost.

It is instructive to look at the spectrum of the AM signal. An example is shown in Figure 6.12. The spectrum consists of the original carrier plus the spectrum of the input signal translated to f_c. The portion of the spectrum for $|f| > |f_c|$ is the *upper sideband*, and the portion of the spectrum for $|f| < |f_c|$ is the *lower sideband*. Both the upper and lower sidebands are replicas of the original spectrum $M(f)$, with the lower sideband being frequency reversed. As an example, consider a voice signal with a bandwidth that extends from 300 to 3000 Hz being modulated on a 60-kHz carrier. The resulting signal contains an upper sideband of 60.3 to 63 kHz, a lower sideband of 57 to 59.7 kHz, and the 60-kHz carrier. An important relationship is

$$P_t = P_c\left(1 + \frac{n_a^2}{2}\right)$$

where P_t is the total transmitted power in $s(t)$ and P_c is the transmitted power in the carrier. We would like n_a as large as possible so that most of the signal power is used to carry information. However, n_a must remain below 1.

It should be clear that $s(t)$ contains unnecessary components, because each of the sidebands contains the complete spectrum of $m(t)$. A popular variant of AM, known as single sideband (SSB), takes advantage of this fact by sending only one of

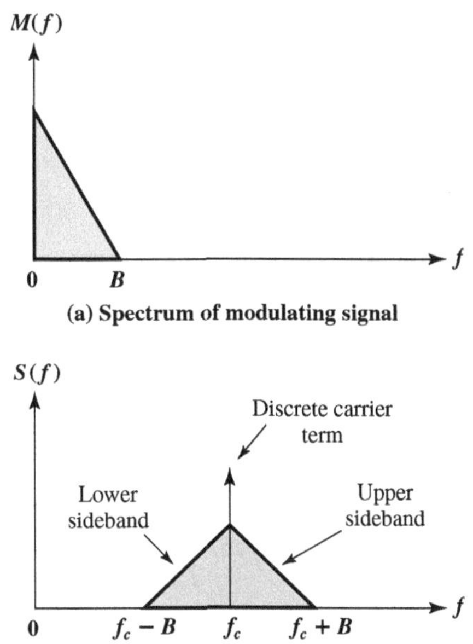

(a) Spectrum of modulating signal

(b) Spectrum of AM signal with carrier at f_c

Figure 6.12 Spectrum of an AM Signal

the sidebands, eliminating the other sideband and the carrier. The principal advantages of this approach are

- Only half the bandwidth is required, that is, $B_T = B$, where B is the bandwidth of the original signal. For DSBTC, $B_T = 2B$.
- Less power is required because no power is used to transmit the carrier or the other sideband. Another variant is double sideband suppressed carrier (DSBSC), which filters out the carrier frequency and sends both sidebands. This saves some power but uses as much bandwidth as DSBTC.

The disadvantage of suppressing the carrier is that the carrier can be used for synchronization purposes. For example, suppose that the original analog signal is an ASK waveform encoding digital data. The receiver needs to know the starting point of each bit time to interpret the data correctly. A constant carrier provides a clocking mechanism by which to time the arrival of bits. A compromise approach is vestigial sideband (VSB), which uses one sideband and a reduced-power carrier.

Angle Modulation

Frequency modulation (FM) and phase modulation (PM) are special cases of angle modulation. The modulated signal is expressed as

$$\textbf{Angle Modulation} \qquad s(t) = A_c \cos[2\pi f_c t + \phi(t)] \tag{6.12}$$

For phase modulation, the phase is proportional to the modulating signal:

$$\textbf{PM} \qquad \phi(t) = n_p m(t) \tag{6.13}$$

where n_p is the phase modulation index.

For frequency modulation, the derivative of the phase is proportional to the modulating signal:

$$\textbf{FM} \qquad \phi'(t) = n_f m(t) \tag{6.14}$$

where n_f is the frequency modulation index.

For those who wish a more detailed mathematical explanation of the preceding, consider the following. The phase of $s(t)$ at any instant is just $2\pi f_c t + \phi(t)$. The instantaneous phase deviation from the carrier signal is $\phi(t)$. In PM, this instantaneous phase deviation is proportional to $m(t)$. Because frequency can be defined as the rate of change of phase of a signal, the instantaneous frequency of $s(t)$ is

$$2\pi f_i(t) = \frac{d}{dt}[2\pi f_c t + \phi(t)]$$

$$f_i(t) = f_c + \frac{1}{2\pi}\phi'(t)$$

and the instantaneous frequency deviation from the carrier frequency is $\phi'(t)$, which in FM is proportional to $m(t)$.

Figure 6.13 illustrates amplitude, phase, and frequency modulation by a sine wave. The shapes of the FM and PM signals are very similar. Indeed, it is impossible to tell them apart without knowledge of the modulation function.

Several observations about the FM process are in order. The peak deviation ΔF can be seen to be

$$\Delta F = \frac{1}{2\pi} n_f A_m \text{ Hz}$$

where A_m is the maximum value of $m(t)$. Thus an increase in the magnitude of $m(t)$ will increase ΔF, which, intuitively, should increase the transmitted bandwidth B_T. However, as should be apparent from Figure 6.13, this will not increase the average power level of the FM signal, which is $A_c^2/2$. This is distinctly different from AM, where the level of modulation affects the power in the AM signal but does not affect its bandwidth.

Example 6.5 Derive an expression for $s(t)$ if $\phi(t)$ is the phase-modulating signal $n_p \cos 2\pi f_m t$. Assume that $A_c = 1$. This can be seen directly to be

$$s(t) = \cos[2\pi f_c t + n_p \cos 2\pi f_m t]$$

The instantaneous phase deviation from the carrier signal is $n_p \cos 2\pi f_m t$. The phase angle of the signal varies from its unmodulated value in a simple sinusoidal fashion, with the peak phase deviation equal to n_p.

The preceding expression can be expanded using Bessel's trigonometric identities:

$$s(t) = \sum_{n=-\infty}^{\infty} J_n(n_p)\cos\left(2\pi f_c t + 2\pi n f_m t + \frac{n\pi}{2}\right)$$

where $J_n(n_p)$ is the nth order Bessel function of the first kind. Using the property

$$J_{-n}(x) = (-1)^n J_n(x)$$

this can be rewritten as

$$s(t) = J_0(n_p)\cos 2\pi f_c t + \sum_{n=1}^{\infty} J_n(n_p)\left[\cos\left(2\pi(f_c + nf_m)t + \frac{n\pi}{2}\right) + \cos\left(2\pi(f_c - nf_m)t + \frac{(n+2)\pi}{2}\right)\right]$$

The resulting signal has a component at the original carrier frequency plus a set of sidebands displaced from f_c by all possible multiples of f_m. For $n_p \ll 1$, the higher-order terms fall off rapidly.

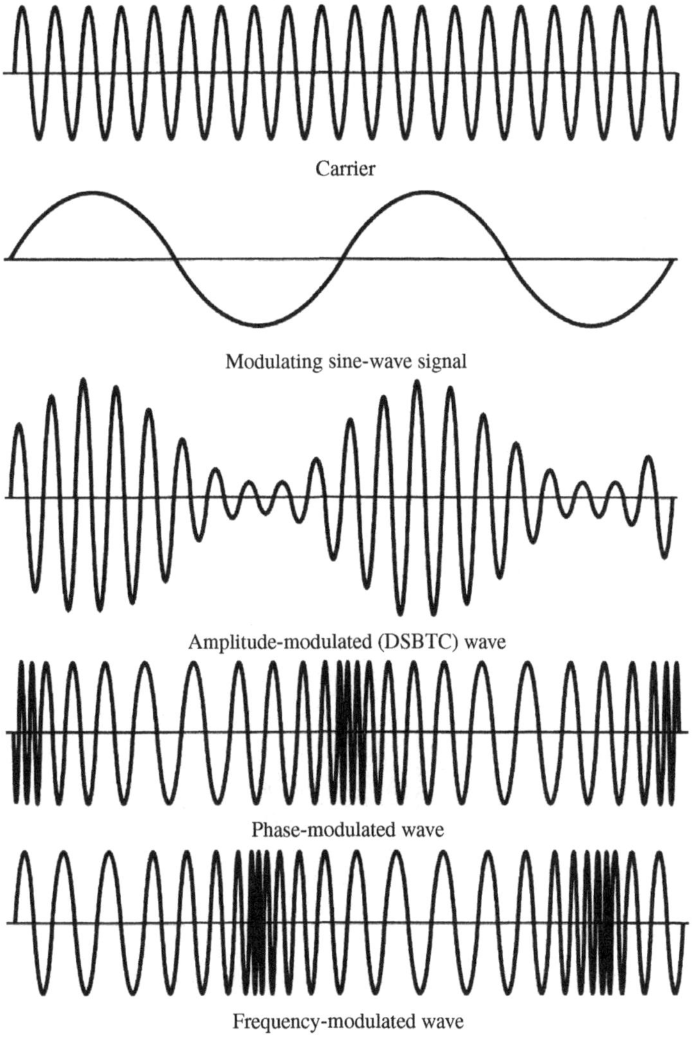

Figure 6.13 Amplitude, Phase, and Frequency Modulation of a Sine-Wave Carrier by a Sine-Wave Signal

Example 6.6 Derive an expression for $s(t)$ if $\phi'(t)$ is the frequency-modulating signal $-n_f \sin 2\pi f_m t$. The form of $\phi'(t)$ was chosen for convenience. We have

$$\phi(t) = -\int n_f \sin 2\pi f_m t \, dt = \frac{n_f}{2\pi f_m} \cos 2\pi f_m t$$

Thus

$$s(t) = \cos\left[2\pi f_c t + \frac{n_f}{2\pi f_m} \cos 2\pi f_m t\right]$$
$$= \cos\left[2\pi f_c t + \frac{\Delta F}{f_m} \cos 2\pi f_m t\right]$$

The instantaneous frequency deviation from the carrier signal is $-n_f \sin 2\pi f_m t$. The frequency of the signal varies from its unmodulated value in a simple sinusoidal fashion, with the peak frequency deviation equal to n_f radians/second.

The equation for the FM signal has the identical form as for the PM signal, with $\Delta F/f_m$ substituted for n_p. Thus the Bessel expansion is the same.

As with AM, both FM and PM result in a signal whose bandwidth is centered at f_c. However, we can now see that the magnitude of that bandwidth is very different. Amplitude modulation is a linear process and produces frequencies that are the sum and difference of the carrier signal and the components of the modulating signal. Hence, for AM,

$$B_T = 2B$$

However, angle modulation includes a term of the form $\cos(\phi(t))$, which is nonlinear and will produce a wide range of frequencies. In essence, for a modulating sinusoid of frequency f_m, $s(t)$ will contain components at $f_c + f_m$, $f_c + 2f_m$, and so on. In the most general case, infinite bandwidth is required to transmit an FM or PM signal. As a practical matter, a very good rule of thumb, known as Carson's rule [COUC01], is

$$B_T = 2(\beta + 1)B$$

where

$$\beta = \begin{cases} n_p A_m & \text{for PM} \\ \dfrac{\Delta F}{B} = \dfrac{n_f A_m}{2\pi B} & \text{for FM} \end{cases}$$

We can rewrite the formula for FM as

$$B_T = 2\Delta F + 2B \qquad (6.15)$$

Thus both FM and PM require greater bandwidth than AM.

6.4 ANALOG DATA, DIGITAL SIGNALS

In this section we examine the process of transforming analog data into digital signals. Strictly speaking, it might be more correct to refer to this as a process of converting analog data into digital data; this process is known as digitization. Once analog data have been converted into digital data, a number of things can happen. The three most common are as follows:

1. The digital data can be transmitted using NRZ-L.[3] In this case, we have in fact gone directly from analog data to a digital signal.
2. The digital data can be encoded as a digital signal using a code other than NRZ-L. Thus an extra step is required.
3. The digital data can be converted into an analog signal, using one of the modulation techniques discussed in Section 6.2.

This last, seemingly curious, procedure is illustrated in Figure 6.14, which shows voice data that are digitized and then converted to an analog ASK signal. This allows digital transmission. The voice data, because they have been digitized, can be treated as digital data, even though transmission requirements (e.g., use of microwave) dictate that an analog signal be used.

The device used for converting analog data into digital form for transmission, and subsequently recovering the original analog data from the digital, is known as a codec (coder-decoder). In this section we examine the two principal techniques used in codecs, pulse code modulation and delta modulation. The section closes with a discussion of comparative performance.

Pulse Code Modulation

Pulse code modulation (PCM) is based on the sampling theorem, which states that

> If a signal $f(t)$ is sampled at regular intervals of time and at a rate higher than twice the highest signal frequency, then the samples contain all the information of the original signal. The function $f(t)$ may be reconstructed from these samples by the use of a low-pass filter.

For the interested reader, a proof is provided in a supporting document at this book's Web site. If voice data are limited to frequencies below 4000 Hz, a conservative procedure for intelligibility, 8000 samples per second would be sufficient to characterize the voice signal completely. Note, however, that these are analog samples, called **pulse amplitude modulation (PAM)** samples. To convert to digital, each of these analog samples must be assigned a binary code.

[3]NRZ-L (nonreturn to zero, level) is the most common, and easiest, way to transmit digital signals. It uses two different voltage levels for the two binary digits: A negative voltage represents binary 1 and a positive voltage represents binary 0. NRZ-L is generally the code used to generate or interpret digital data by terminals and other devices. If a different code is to be used for transmission, it is typically generated from an NRZ-L signal by the transmission system.

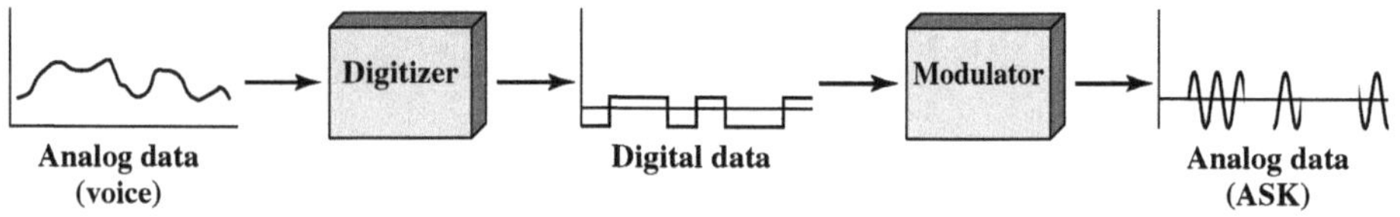

Figure 6.14 Digitizing Analog Data

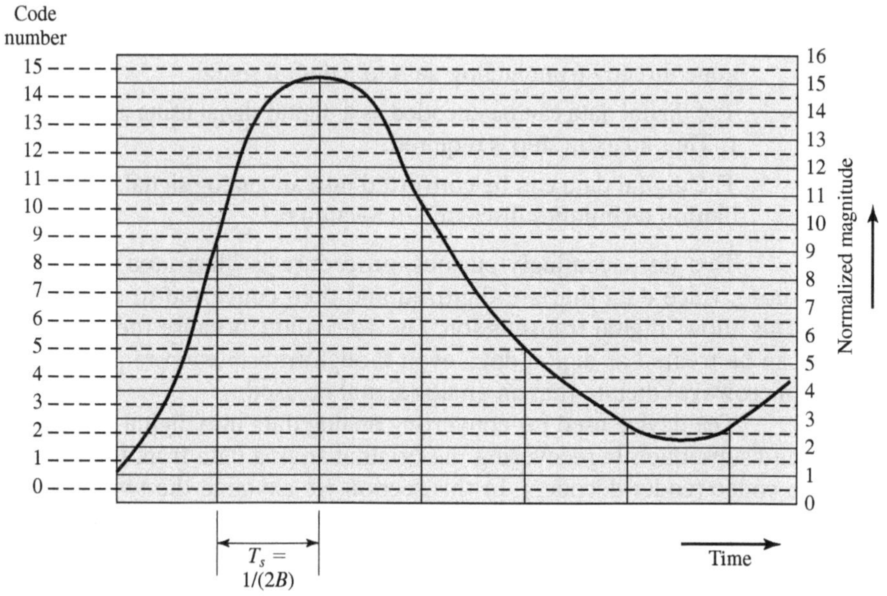

PAM value	1.1	9.2	15.2	10.8	5.6	2.8	2.7
Quantized code number	1	9	15	10	5	2	2
PCM code	0001	1001	1111	1010	0101	0010	0010

Figure 6.15 Pulse Code Modulation Example

Figure 6.15 shows an example in which the original signal is assumed to be bandlimited with a bandwidth of B. PAM samples are taken at a rate of $2B$, or once every $T_s = 1/2B$ seconds. Each PAM sample is approximated by being *quantized* into one of 16 different levels. Each sample can then be represented by 4 bits. But because the quantized values are only approximations, it is impossible to recover the original signal exactly. By using an 8-bit sample, which allows 256 quantizing levels, the quality of the recovered voice signal is comparable with that achieved via analog transmission. Note that this implies that a data rate of (8000 samples per second) $\times$ (8 bits per sample) = 64 kbps is needed for a single voice signal.

Thus, PCM starts with a continuous-time, continuous-amplitude (analog) signal, from which a digital signal is produced. The digital signal consists of blocks of n bits, where each n-bit number is the amplitude of a PCM pulse. On reception, the process is reversed to reproduce the analog signal. Notice, however, that this process violates the terms of the sampling theorem. By quantizing the PAM pulse, the original signal is now only approximated and cannot be recovered exactly. This effect is known as quantizing error or quantizing noise. The signal-to-noise ratio for quantizing noise can be expressed as [GIBS93]

$$\text{SNR}_{\text{dB}} = 20 \log 2^n + 1.76 \text{ dB} = 6.02n + 1.76 \text{ dB}$$

Thus each additional bit used for quantizing increases SNR by about 6 dB, which is a factor of 4.

Typically, the PCM scheme is refined using a technique known as nonlinear encoding, which means, in effect, that the quantization levels are not equally spaced. The problem with equal spacing is that the mean absolute error for each sample is the same, regardless of signal level. Consequently, lower amplitude values are relatively more distorted. By using a greater number of quantizing steps for signals of low amplitude and a smaller number of quantizing steps for signals of large amplitude, a marked reduction in overall signal distortion is achieved (e.g., see Figure 6.16).

The same effect can be achieved by using uniform quantizing but companding (compressing-expanding) the input analog signal. Companding is a process that compresses the intensity range of a signal by imparting more gain to weak signals than to strong signals on input. At output, the reverse operation is performed. Figure 6.17 shows typical companding functions. Note that the effect on the input side is to compress the sample so that the higher values are reduced with respect to the lower values. Thus, with a fixed number of quantizing levels, more levels are available for lower-level signals. On the output side, the compander expands the samples so the compressed values are restored to their original values.

Nonlinear encoding can significantly improve the PCM SNR ratio. For voice signals, improvements of 24 to 30 dB have been achieved.

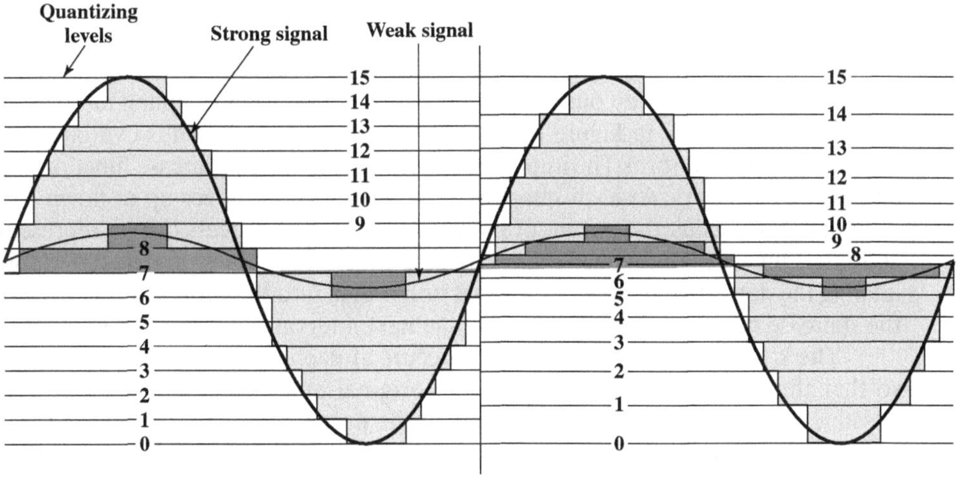

(a) Without nonlinear encoding (b) With nonlinear encoding

Figure 6.16 Effect of Nonlinear Coding

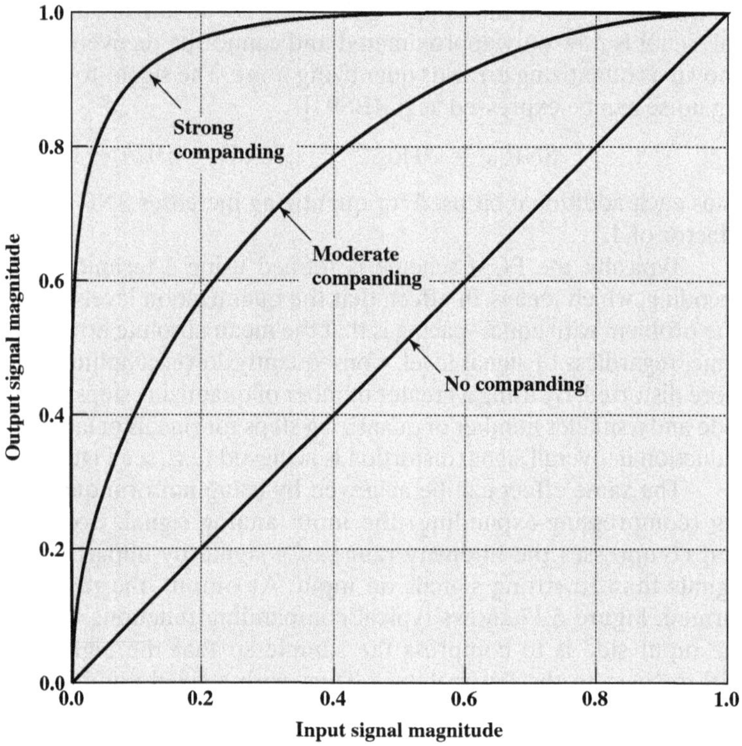

Figure 6.17 Typical Companding Functions

Delta Modulation (DM)

A variety of techniques have been used to improve the performance of PCM or to reduce its complexity. One of the most popular alternatives to PCM is delta modulation (DM).

With delta modulation, an analog input is approximated by a staircase function that moves up or down by one quantization level (δ) at each sampling interval (T_s). An example is shown in Figure 6.18, where the staircase function is overlaid on the original analog waveform. The important characteristic of this staircase function is that its behavior is binary: At each sampling time, the function moves up or down a constant amount δ. Thus, the output of the delta modulation process can be represented as a single binary digit for each sample. In essence, a bit stream is produced by approximating the derivative of an analog signal rather than its amplitude: A 1 is generated if the staircase function is to go up during the next interval; a 0 is generated otherwise.

The transition (up or down) that occurs at each sampling interval is chosen so that the staircase function tracks the original analog waveform as closely as possible. Figure 6.19 illustrates the logic of the process, which is essentially a feedback mechanism. For transmission, the following occurs: At each sampling time, the analog input is compared to the most recent value of the approximating staircase function. If the value of the sampled waveform exceeds that of the staircase function, a 1 is generated; otherwise, a 0 is generated. Thus, the staircase is always

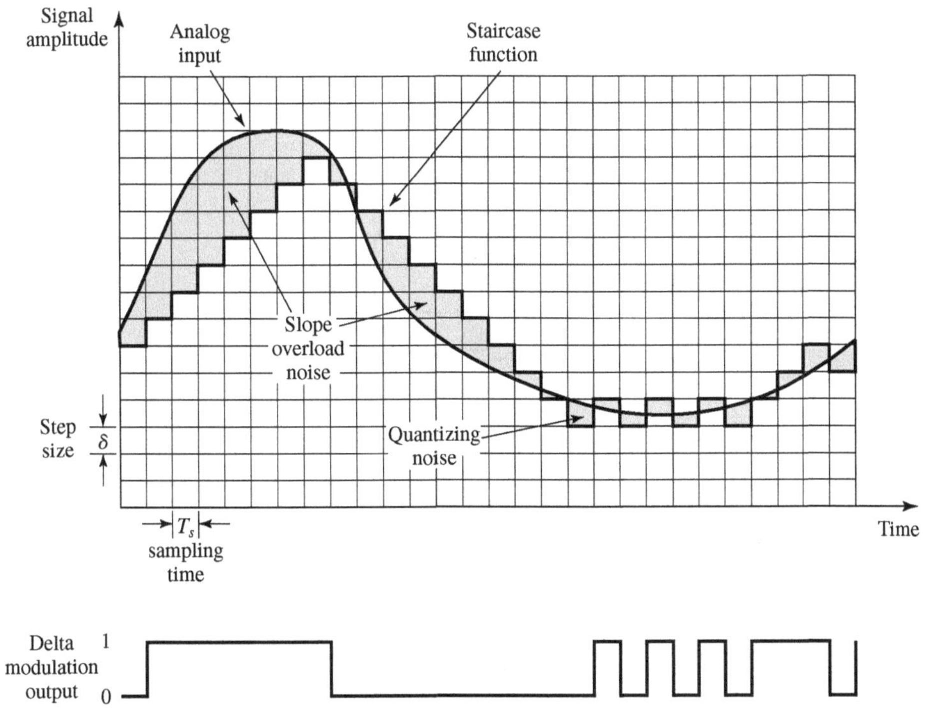

Figure 6.18 Example of Delta Modulation

changed in the direction of the input signal. The output of the DM process is therefore a binary sequence that can be used at the receiver to reconstruct the staircase function. The staircase function can then be smoothed by some type of integration process or by passing it through a low-pass filter to produce an analog approximation of the analog input signal.

There are two important parameters in a DM scheme: the size of the step assigned to each binary digit, δ, and the sampling rate. As Figure 6.18 illustrates, δ must be chosen to produce a balance between two types of errors or noise. When the analog waveform is changing very slowly, there will be quantizing noise. This noise increases as δ is increased. On the other hand, when the analog waveform is changing more rapidly than the staircase can follow, there is slope overload noise. This noise increases as δ is decreased.

It should be clear that the accuracy of the scheme can be improved by increasing the sampling rate. However, this increases the data rate of the output signal.

The principal advantage of DM over PCM is the simplicity of its implementation. In general, PCM exhibits better SNR characteristics at the same data rate.

Performance

Good voice reproduction via PCM can be achieved with 128 quantization levels, or 7-bit coding ($2^7 = 128$). A voice signal, conservatively, occupies a bandwidth of 4 kHz. Thus, according to the sampling theorem, samples should be taken at a rate of

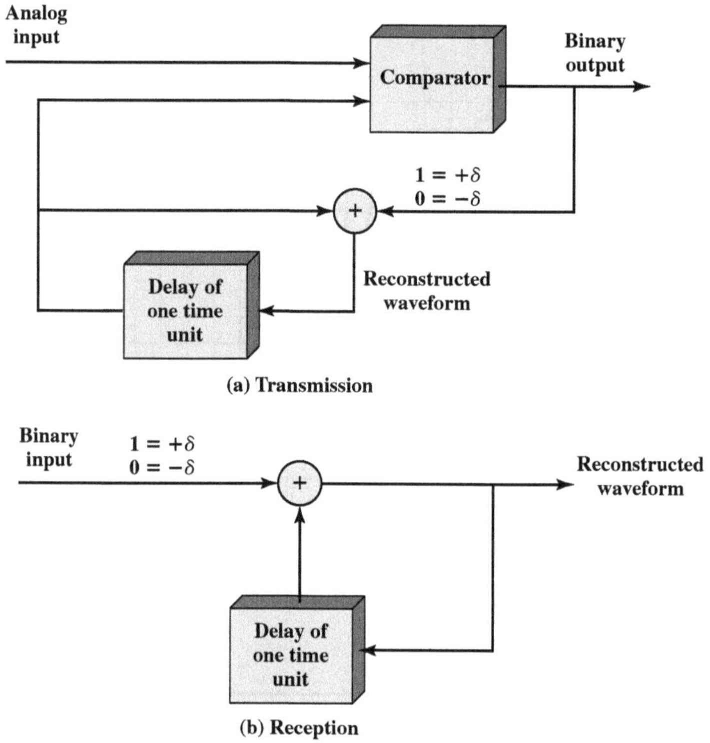

Figure 6.19 Delta Modulation

8000 samples per second. This implies a data rate of $8000 \times 7 = 56$ kbps for the PCM-encoded digital data.

Consider what this means from the point of view of bandwidth requirement. An analog voice signal occupies 4 kHz. Using PCM this 4-kHz analog signal can be converted into a 56-kbps digital signal. But using the Nyquist criterion, this digital signal could require on the order of 28 kHz of bandwidth. Even more severe differences are seen with higher bandwidth signals. For example, a common PCM scheme for color television uses 10-bit codes, which works out to 92 Mbps for a 4.6-MHz bandwidth signal. In spite of these numbers, digital techniques continue to grow in popularity for transmitting analog data. The principal reasons for this are as follows:

- Because repeaters are used instead of amplifiers, there is no additive noise.
- As we shall see, time division multiplexing (TDM) is used for digital signals instead of the frequency division multiplexing (FDM) used for analog signals. With TDM, there is no intermodulation noise, whereas we have seen that this is a concern for FDM.
- The conversion to digital signaling allows the use of the more efficient digital switching techniques.

Furthermore, techniques have been developed to provide more efficient codes. In the case of voice, a reasonable goal appears to be in the neighborhood of

4 kbps. With video, advantage can be taken of the fact that from frame to frame, most picture elements will not change. Interframe coding techniques should allow the video requirement to be reduced to about 15 Mbps, and for slowly changing scenes, such as found in a video teleconference, down to 64 kbps or less.

As a final point, we mention that in many instances, the use of a telecommunications system will result in both digital-to-analog and analog-to-digital processing. The overwhelming majority of local terminations into the telecommunications network is analog, and the network itself uses a mixture of analog and digital techniques. Thus digital data at a user's terminal may be converted to analog by a modem, subsequently digitized by a codec, and perhaps suffer repeated conversions before reaching its destination.

Thus, telecommunication facilities handle analog signals that represent both voice and digital data. The characteristics of the waveforms are quite different. Whereas voice signals tend to be skewed to the lower portion of the bandwidth, analog encoding of digital signals has a more uniform spectral content over the bandwidth and therefore contains more high-frequency components. Studies have shown that, because of the presence of these higher frequencies, PCM-related techniques are preferable to DM-related techniques for digitizing analog signals that represent digital data.

6.5 RECOMMENDED READINGS

There are many good references on analog modulation schemes for digital data. Good choices are [COUC01], [XION00], and [PROA02]; these three also provide comprehensive treatment of digital and analog modulation schemes for analog data.

An exceptionally clear exposition that covers digital-to-analog, analog-to-digital, and analog-to-analog techniques is [PEAR92]. Another comprehensive treatment of the topics in this chapter is [SKLA01].

An instructive treatment of the concepts of bit rate, baud, and bandwidth is [FREE98]. A recommended tutorial that expands on the concepts treated in this chapter relating to bandwidth efficiency and encoding schemes is [SKLA93].

COUC01 Couch, L. *Digital and Analog Communication Systems.* Upper Saddle River, NJ: Prentice Hall, 2001.

FREE98 Freeman, R. "Bits, Symbols, Baud, and Bandwidth." *IEEE Communications Magazine*, April 1998.

PEAR92 Pearson, J. *Basic Communication Theory.* Englewood Cliffs, NJ: Prentice Hall, 1992.

PROA02 Proakis, J. *Communication Systems Engineering.* Upper Saddle River, NJ: Prentice Hall, 2002.

SKLA93 Sklar, B. "Defining, Designing, and Evaluating Digital Communication Systems." *IEEE Communications Magazine*, November 1993.

SKLA01 Sklar, B. *Digital Communications: Fundamentals and Applications.* Upper Saddle River, NJ: Prentice Hall, 2001.

XION00 Xiong, F. *Digital Modulation Techniques.* Boston: Artech House, 2000.

6.6 KEY TERMS, REVIEW QUESTIONS, AND PROBLEMS

Key Terms

amplitude modulation (AM) amplitude shift keying (ASK) angle modulation bit error rate (BER) carrier frequency delta modulation (DM)	differential PSK (DPSK) frequency modulation (FM) frequency shift keying (FSK) modulation phase modulation (PM) phase shift keying (PSK)	pulse code modulation (PCM) quadrature amplitude modulation (QAM) quadrature PSK (QPSK)

Review Questions

6.1 What is differential encoding?

6.2 What function does a modem perform?

6.3 Indicate three major advantages of digital transmission over analog transmission.

6.4 How are binary values represented in amplitude shift keying, and what is the limitation of this approach?

6.5 What is NRZ-L? What is a major disadvantage of this data encoding approach?

6.6 What is the difference between QPSK and offset QPSK?

6.7 What is QAM?

6.8 What does the sampling theorem tell us concerning the rate of sampling required for an analog signal?

6.9 What are the differences among angle modulation, PM, and FM?

Problems

6.1 Figure 6.20 shows the QAM demodulator corresponding to the QAM modulator of Figure 6.10. Show that this arrangement does recover the two signals $d_1(t)$ and $d_2(t)$, which can be combined to recover the original input.

6.2 A sine wave is to be used for two different signaling schemes: (a) PSK; (b) QPSK. The duration of a signal element is 10^{-5} s. If the received signal is of the following form

$$s(t) = 0.005 \sin(2\pi\, 10^6 t + \theta) \text{ volts}$$

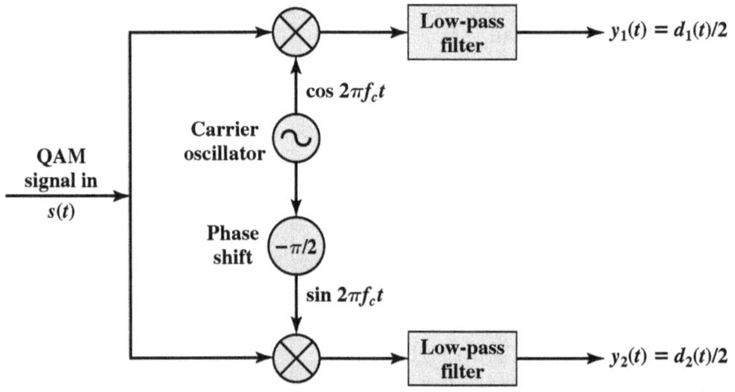

Figure 6.20 QAM Demodulator

and if the measured noise power at the receiver is 2.5×10^{-8} watts, determine the E_b/N_0 (in dB) for each case.

6.3 Derive an expression for baud rate D as a function of bit rate R for QPSK using the digital encoding techniques of Table 6.2.

6.4 What SNR ratio is required to achieve a bandwidth efficiency of 1.0 for ASK, FSK, PSK, and QPSK? Assume that the required bit error rate is 10^{-6}.

6.5 An NRZ-L signal is passed through a filter with $r = 0.5$ and then modulated onto a carrier. The data rate is 2400 bps. Evaluate the bandwidth for ASK and FSK. For FSK assume that the two frequencies used are 50 kHz and 55 kHz.

6.6 Assume that a telephone line channel is equalized to allow bandpass data transmission over a frequency range of 600 to 3000 Hz. The available bandwidth is 2400 Hz. For $r = 1$, evaluate the required bandwidth for 2400 bps QPSK and 4800-bps, eight-level multilevel signaling. Is the bandwidth adequate?

6.7 Why should PCM be preferable to DM for encoding analog signals that represent digital data?

6.8 Are the modem and the codec functional inverses (i.e., could an inverted modem function as a codec, or vice versa)?

6.9 A signal is quantized using 10-bit PCM. Find the signal-to-quantization noise ratio.

6.10 Consider an audio signal with spectral components in the range 300 to 3000 Hz. Assume that a sampling rate of 7000 samples per second will be used to generate a PCM signal.
   a. For SNR = 30 dB, what is the number of uniform quantization levels needed?
   b. What data rate is required?

6.11 Find the step size δ required to prevent slope overload noise as a function of the frequency of the highest-frequency component of the signal. Assume that all components have amplitude A.

6.12 A PCM encoder accepts a signal with a full-scale voltage of 10 V and generates 8-bit codes using uniform quantization. The maximum normalized quantized voltage is $1 - 2^{-8}$. Determine (a) normalized step size, (b) actual step size in volts, (c) actual maximum quantized level in volts, (d) normalized resolution, (e) actual resolution, and (f) percentage resolution.

6.13 The analog waveform shown in Figure 6.21 is to be delta modulated. The sampling period and the step size are indicated by the grid on the figure. The first DM output

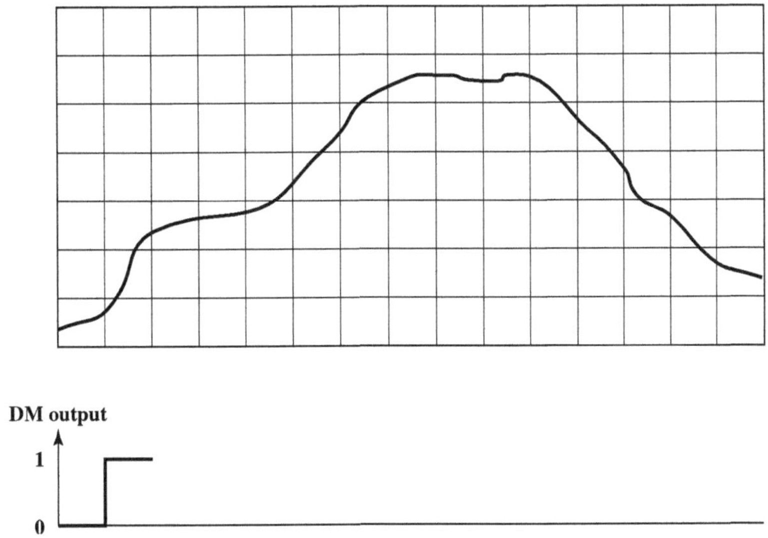

Figure 6.21 Delta Modulation Example

and the staircase function for this period are also shown. Show the rest of the staircase function and give the DM output. Indicate regions where slope overload distortion exists.

6.14 Consider the angle-modulated signal

$$s(t) = 10 \cos[(10^8)\pi t + 5 \sin 2\pi(10^3)t]$$

Find the maximum phase deviation and the maximum frequency deviation.

6.15 Consider the angle-modulated signal

$$s(t)\pi = 10 \cos[2\pi(10^6)t + 0.1 \sin(10^3)\pi t]$$

a. Express $s(t)$ as a PM signal with $n_p = 10$.

b. Express $s(t)$ as an FM signal with $n_f = 10\pi$.

6.16 Let $m_1(t)$ and $m_2(t)$ be message signals and let $s_1(t)$ and $s_2(t)$ be the corresponding modulated signals using a carrier frequency of f_c.

a. Show that if simple AM modulation is used, then $m_1(t) + m_2(t)$ produces a modulated signal equal that is a linear combination of $s_1(t)$ and $s_2(t)$. This is why AM is sometimes referred to as linear modulation.

b. Show that if simple PM modulation is used, then $m_1(t) + m_2(t)$ produces a modulated signal that is not a linear combination of $s_1(t)$ and $s_2(t)$. This is why angle modulation is sometimes referred to as nonlinear modulation.

CHAPTER 7

SPREAD SPECTRUM

An increasingly important form of communications is known as spread spectrum. This technique does not fit neatly into the categories defined in the preceding chapter, as it can be used to transmit either analog or digital data, using an analog signal.

The spread spectrum technique was developed initially for military and intelligence requirements. The essential idea is to spread the information signal over a wider bandwidth to make jamming and interception more difficult. The first type of spread spectrum developed is known as frequency hopping.[1] A more recent type of spread spectrum is direct sequence. Both of these techniques are used in various wireless communications standards and products.

After a brief overview, we look at these two spread spectrum techniques. We then examine a multiple access technique based on spread spectrum.

7.1 THE CONCEPT OF SPREAD SPECTRUM

Figure 7.1 highlights the key characteristics of any spread spectrum system. Input is fed into a channel encoder that produces an analog signal with a relatively narrow bandwidth around some center frequency. This signal is further modulated using a sequence of digits known as a spreading code or spreading sequence. Typically, but not always, the spreading code is generated by a pseudonoise, or pseudorandom number, generator. The effect of this modulation is to increase significantly the bandwidth (spread the spectrum) of the signal to be transmitted. On the receiving end, the same digit sequence is used to demodulate the spread spectrum signal. Finally, the signal is fed into a channel decoder to recover the data.

Several things can be gained from this apparent waste of spectrum:

- We can gain immunity from various kinds of noise and multipath distortion. The earliest applications of spread spectrum were military, where it was used for its immunity to jamming.

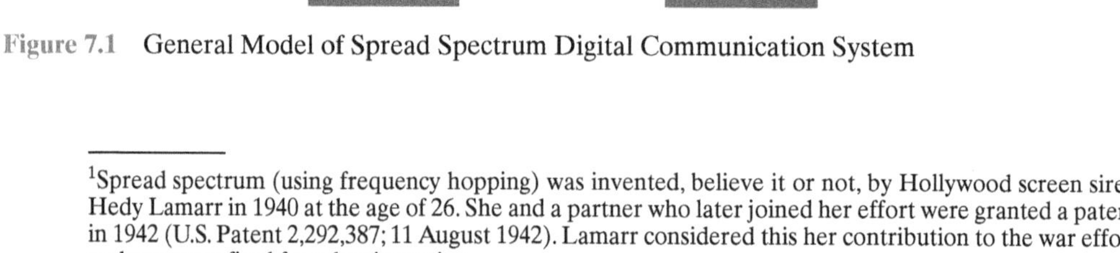

Figure 7.1 General Model of Spread Spectrum Digital Communication System

[1]Spread spectrum (using frequency hopping) was invented, believe it or not, by Hollywood screen siren Hedy Lamarr in 1940 at the age of 26. She and a partner who later joined her effort were granted a patent in 1942 (U.S. Patent 2,292,387; 11 August 1942). Lamarr considered this her contribution to the war effort and never profited from her invention.

- It can also be used for hiding and encrypting signals. Only a recipient who knows the spreading code can recover the encoded information.
- Several users can independently use the same higher bandwidth with very little interference. This property is used in cellular telephony applications, with a technique know as code division multiplexing (CDM) or code division multiple access (CDMA).

7.2 FREQUENCY HOPPING SPREAD SPECTRUM

With frequency hopping spread spectrum (FHSS), the signal is broadcast over a seemingly random series of radio frequencies, hopping from frequency to frequency at fixed intervals. A receiver, hopping between frequencies in synchronization with the transmitter, picks up the message. Would-be eavesdroppers hear only unintelligible blips. Attempts to jam the signal on one frequency succeed only at knocking out a few bits of it.

Basic Approach

Figure 7.2 shows an example of a frequency hopping signal. A number of channels are allocated for the FH signal. Typically, there are 2^k carrier frequencies forming 2^k channels. The spacing between carrier frequencies and hence the width of each channel usually corresponds to the bandwidth of the input signal. The transmitter operates in one channel at a time for a fixed interval; for example, the IEEE 802.11 wireless LAN standard uses a 300-ms interval. During that interval, some number of bits (possibly a fraction of a bit, as discussed subsequently) is transmitted using some encoding scheme. The sequence of channels used is dictated by a spreading code. Both transmitter and receiver use the same code to tune into a sequence of channels in synchronization.

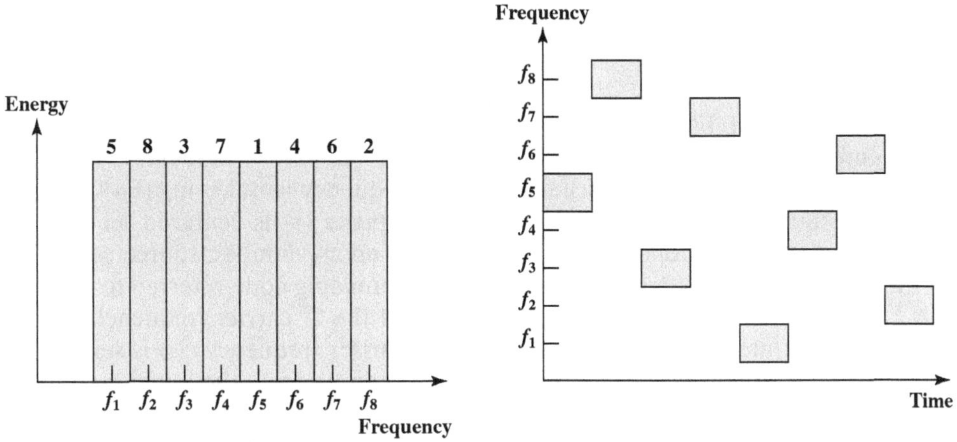

(a) Channel assignment (b) Channel use

Figure 7.2 Frequency Hopping Example

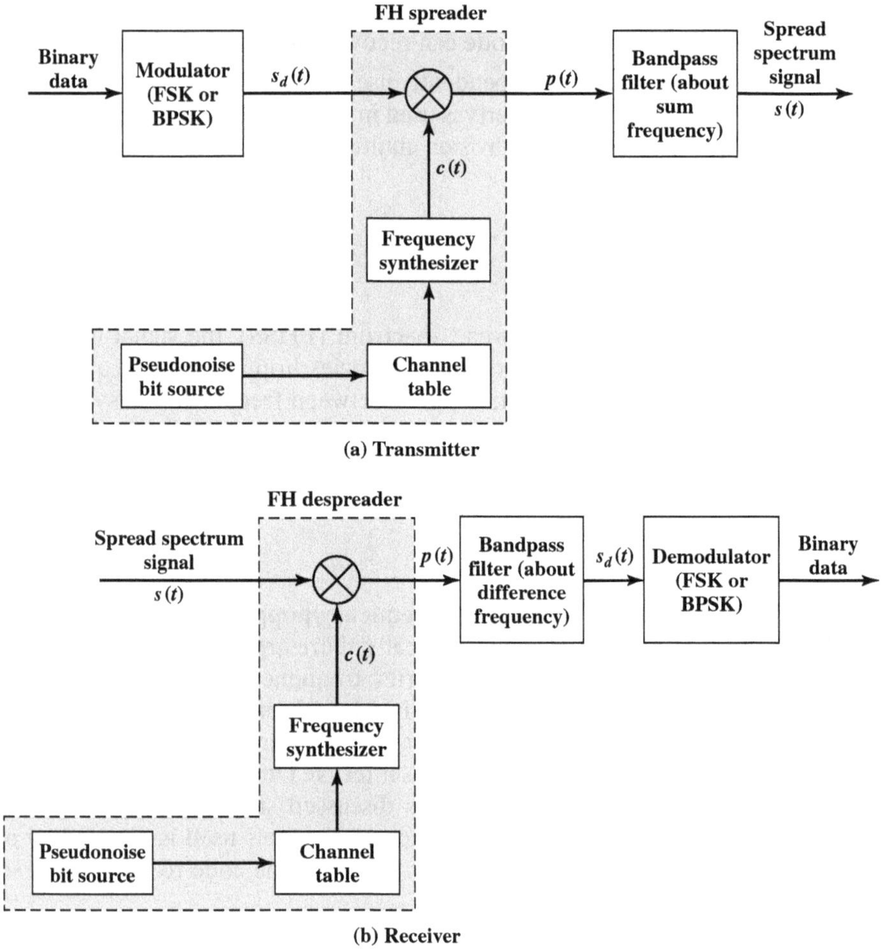

Figure 7.3 Frequency Hopping Spread Spectrum System

A typical block diagram for a frequency hopping system is shown in Figure 7.3. For transmission, binary data are fed into a modulator using some digital-to-analog encoding scheme, such as frequency-shift keying (FSK) or binary phase-shift keying (BPSK). The resulting signal $s_d(t)$ is centered on some base frequency. A pseudonoise (PN), or pseudorandom number, source serves as an index into a table of frequencies; this is the spreading code referred to previously. Each k bits of the PN source specifies one of the 2^k carrier frequencies. At each successive interval (each k PN bits), a new carrier frequency $c(t)$ is selected. This frequency is then modulated by the signal produced from the initial modulator to produce a new signal $s(t)$ with the same shape but now centered on the selected carrier frequency. On reception, the spread spectrum signal is demodulated using the same sequence of PN-derived frequencies and then demodulated to produce the output data.

Figure 7.3 indicates that the two signals are multiplied. Let us give an example of how this works, using BFSK as the data modulation scheme. We can define the FSK input to the FHSS system as [compare to Equation (6.2)]:

$$s_d(t) = A\cos(2\pi(f_0 + 0.5(b_i + 1)\Delta f)t) \qquad \text{for } iT < t < (i+1)T \tag{7.1}$$

where

A = amplitude of signal
f_0 = base frequency
b_i = value of the ith bit of data (+1 for binary 1, −1 for binary 0)
Δf = frequency separation
T = bit duration; data rate = $1/T$

Thus, during the ith bit interval, the frequency of the data signal is f_0 if the data bit is −1 and $f_0 + \Delta f$ if the data bit is +1.

The frequency synthesizer generates a constant-frequency tone whose frequency hops among a set of 2^k frequencies, with the hopping pattern determined by k bits from the PN sequence. For simplicity, assume the duration of one hop is the same as the duration of one bit and we ignore phase differences between the data signal $s_d(t)$ and the spreading signal, also called a chipping signal, $c(t)$. Then the product signal during the ith hop (during the ith bit) is

$$p(t) = s_d(t)c(t) = A\cos(2\pi(f_0 + 0.5(b_i + 1)\Delta f)t)\cos(2\pi f_i t)$$

where f_i is the frequency of the signal generated by the frequency synthesizer during the ith hop. Using the trigonometric identity[2] $\cos(x)\cos(y) = (1/2)(\cos(x + y) + \cos(x - y))$, we have

$$p(t) = 0.5A[\cos(2\pi(f_0 + 0.5(b_i + 1)\Delta f + f_i)t) + \cos(2\pi(f_0 + 0.5(b_i + 1)\Delta f - f_i)t)]$$

A bandpass filter (Figure 7.3) is used to block the difference frequency and pass the sum frequency, yielding an FHSS signal of

$$s(t) = 0.5A\cos(2\pi(f_0 + 0.5(b_i + 1)\Delta f + f_i)t) \tag{7.2}$$

Thus, during the ith bit interval, the frequency of the data signal is $f_0 + f_i$ if the data bit is −1 and $f_0 + f_i + \Delta f$ if the data bit is +1.

At the receiver, a signal of the form $s(t)$ just defined will be received. This is multiplied by a replica of the spreading signal to yield a product signal of the form

$$p(t) = s(t)c(t) = 0.5A\cos(2\pi(f_0 + 0.5(b_i + 1)\Delta f + f_i)t)\cos(2\pi f_i t)$$

[2]See the math refresher document at WilliamStallings.com/StudentSupport.html for a summary of trigonometric identities.

Again using the trigonometric identity, we have

$$p(t) = s(t)c(t) = 0.25A[\cos(2\pi(f_0 + 0.5(b_i + 1)\Delta f + f_i + f_i)t) + \cos(2\pi(f_0 + 0.5(b_i + 1)\Delta f)t)]$$

A bandpass filter (Figure 7.3) is used to block the sum frequency and pass the difference frequency, yielding a signal of the form of $s_d(t)$, defined in Equation (7.1):

$$0.25A \cos(2\pi(f_0 + 0.5(b_i + 1)\Delta f)t)$$

FHSS Using MFSK

A common modulation technique used in conjunction with FHSS is multiple FSK (MFSK). Recall from Chapter 6 that MFSK uses $M = 2^L$ different frequencies to encode the digital input L bits at a time. The transmitted signal is of the form [Equation (6.3)]:

$$s_i(t) = A \cos 2\pi f_i t, \qquad 1 \le i \le M$$

where

$f_i = f_c + (2i - 1 - M)f_d$
f_c = denotes the carrier frequency
f_d = denotes the difference frequency
M = number of different signal elements = 2^L
L = number of bits per signal element

For FHSS, the MFSK signal is translated to a new frequency every T_c seconds by modulating the MFSK signal with the FHSS carrier signal. The effect is to translate the MFSK signal into the appropriate FHSS channel. For a data rate of R, the duration of a bit is $T = 1/R$ seconds and the duration of a signal element is $T_s = LT$ seconds. If T_c is greater than or equal to T_s, the spreading modulation is referred to as **slow-frequency-hop spread spectrum**; otherwise it is known as **fast-frequency-hop spread spectrum**.[3] To summarize,

Slow-frequency-hop spread spectrum	$T_c \ge T_s$
Fast-frequency-hop spread spectrum	$T_c < T_s$

Figure 7.4 shows an example of slow FHSS, using the MFSK example from Figure 6.4. That is, $M = 4$, and the same sequence of input bits is used in both examples. The display in the figure shows the frequency transmitted (y-axis) as a function of time (x-axis). Each column represents a time unit T_s in which a single 2-bit signal element is transmitted. The shaded rectangle in the column indicates the frequency transmitted during that time unit. Each pair of columns corresponds to the selection of a frequency band based on a 2-bit PN sequence. Thus, for the first pair of

[3]Some authors use a somewhat different definition (e.g., [PICK82]) of multiple hops per bit for fast frequency hop, multiple bits per hop for slow frequency hop, and one hop per bit if neither fast nor slow. The more common definition, which we use, relates hops to signal elements rather than bits.

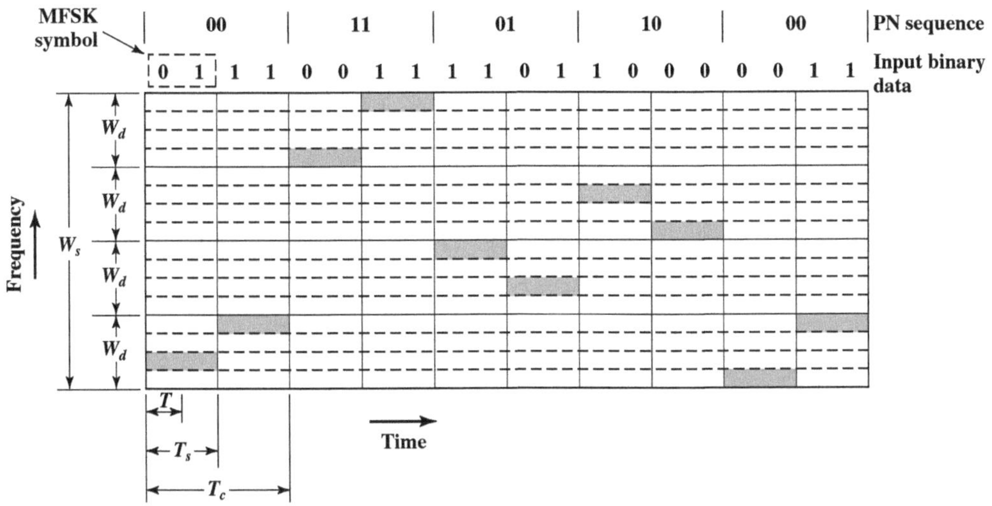

Figure 7.4 Slow-Frequency-Hop Spread Spectrum Using MFSK ($M = 4, k = 2$)

columns, governed by PN sequence 00, the lowest band of frequencies is used. For the second pair of columns, governed by PN sequence 11, the highest band of frequencies is used.

Here we have $M = 4$, which means that four different frequencies are used to encode the data input 2 bits at a time. Each signal element is a discrete frequency tone, and the total MFSK bandwidth is $W_d = Mf_d$. We use an FHSS scheme with $k = 2$. That is, there are $4 = 2^k$ different channels, each of width W_d. The total FHSS bandwidth is $W_s = 2^k W_d$. Each 2 bits of the PN sequence is used to select one of the four channels. That channel is held for a duration of two signal elements, or four bits ($T_c = 2T_s = 4T$).

Figure 7.5 shows an example of fast FHSS, using the same MFSK example. Again, $M = 4$ and $k = 2$. In this case, however, each signal element is represented by two frequency tones. Again, $W_d = Mf_d$ and $W_s = 2^k W_d$. In this example $T_s = 2T_c = 2T$. In general, fast FHSS provides improved performance compared to slow FHSS in the face of noise or jamming. For example, if 3 or more frequencies (chips) are used for each signal element, the receiver can decide which signal element was sent on the basis of a majority of the chips being correct.

FHSS Performance Considerations

Typically, a large number of frequencies are used in FHSS so that W_s is much larger than W_d. One benefit of this is that a large value of k results in a system that is quite resistant to noise and jamming. For example, suppose we have an MFSK transmitter with bandwidth W_d and noise jammer of the same bandwidth and fixed power S_j on the signal carrier frequency. Then we have a ratio of signal energy per bit to noise power density per Hertz of

$$\frac{E_b}{N_j} = \frac{E_b W_d}{S_j}$$

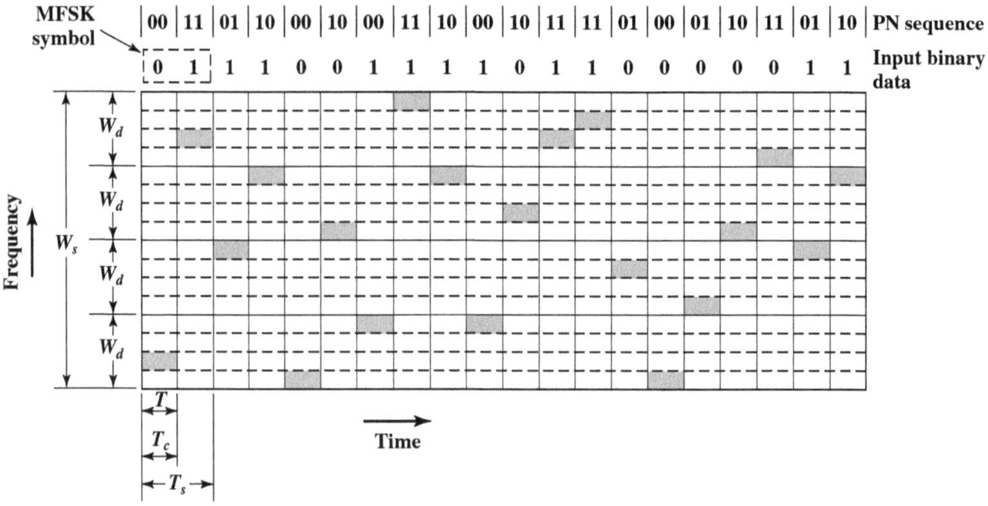

Figure 7.5 Fast-Frequency-Hop Spread Spectrum Using MFSK ($M = 4, k = 2$)

If frequency hopping is used, the jammer must jam all 2^k frequencies. With a fixed power, this reduces the jamming power in any one frequency band to $S_j/2^k$. The gain in signal-to-noise ratio, or processing gain, is

$$G_P = 2^k = \frac{W_s}{W_d} \tag{7.3}$$

7.3 DIRECT SEQUENCE SPREAD SPECTRUM

For direct sequence spread spectrum (DSSS), each bit in the original signal is represented by multiple bits in the transmitted signal, using a spreading code. The spreading code spreads the signal across a wider frequency band in direct proportion to the number of bits used. Therefore, a 10-bit spreading code spreads the signal across a frequency band that is 10 times greater than a 1-bit spreading code.

One technique for direct sequence spread spectrum is to combine the digital information stream with the spreading code bit stream using an exclusive-OR (XOR). The XOR obeys the following rules:

$$0 \oplus 0 = 0 \qquad 0 \oplus 1 = 1 \qquad 1 \oplus 0 = 1 \qquad 1 \oplus 1 = 0$$

Figure 7.6 shows an example. Note that an information bit of one inverts the spreading code bits in the combination, while an information bit of zero causes the spreading code bits to be transmitted without inversion. The combination bit stream has the data rate of the original spreading code sequence, so it has a wider bandwidth than the information stream. In this example, the spreading code bit stream is clocked at four times the information rate.

DSSS Using BPSK

To see how this technique works out in practice, assume that a BPSK modulation scheme is to be used. Rather than represent binary data with 1 and 0, it is more

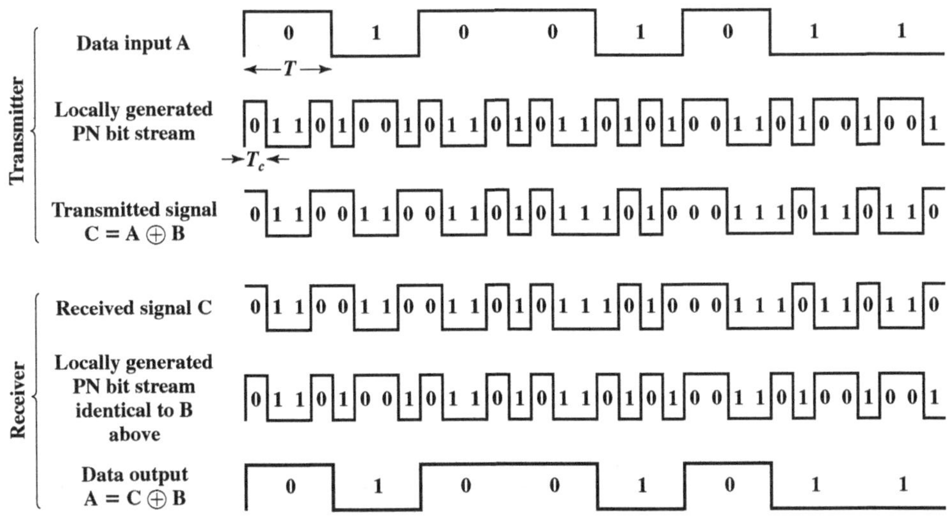

Figure 7.6 Example of Direct Sequence Spread Spectrum

convenient for our purposes to use +1 and −1 to represent the two binary digits. In that case, a BPSK signal can be represented as was shown in Equation (6.5):

$$s_d(t) = Ad(t)\cos(2\pi f_c t) \tag{7.4}$$

where

A = amplitude of signal
f_c = carrier frequency
$d(t)$ = the discrete function that takes on the value of +1 *for one bit time* if the corresponding bit in the bit stream is 1 and the value of −1 *for one bit time* if the corresponding bit in the bit stream is 0

To produce the DSSS signal, we multiply the preceding by $c(t)$, which is the PN sequence taking on values of +1 and −1:

$$s(t) = Ad(t)c(t)\cos(2\pi f_c t) \tag{7.5}$$

At the receiver, the incoming signal is multiplied again by $c(t)$. But $c(t) \times c(t) = 1$ and therefore the original signal is recovered:

$$s(t)c(t) = Ad(t)c(t)c(t)\cos(2\pi f_c t) = s_d(t)$$

Equation (7.5) can be interpreted in two ways, leading to two different implementations. The first interpretation is to first multiply $d(t)$ and $c(t)$ together and then perform the BPSK modulation. That is the interpretation we have been discussing. Alternatively, we can first perform the BPSK modulation on the data stream $d(t)$ to generate the data signal $s_d(t)$. This signal can then be multiplied by $c(t)$.

An implementation using the second interpretation is shown in Figure 7.7. Figure 7.8 is an example of this approach.

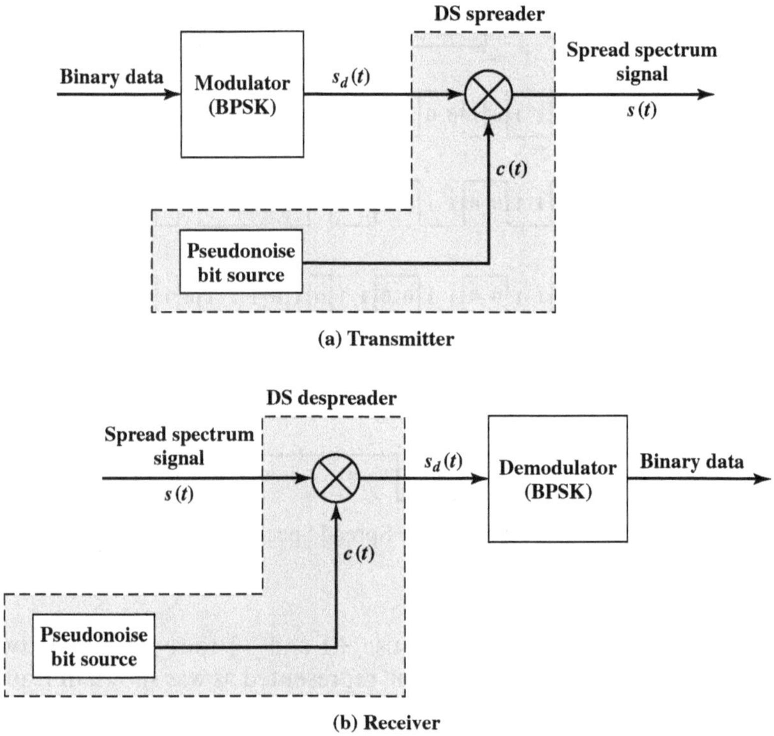

Figure 7.7 Direct Sequence Spread Spectrum System

DSSS Performance Considerations

The spectrum spreading achieved by the direct sequence technique is easily determined (Figure 7.9). In our example, the information signal has a bit width of T, which is equivalent to a data rate of $1/T$. In that case, the spectrum of the signal, depending on the encoding technique, is roughly $2/T$. Similarly, the spectrum of the PN signal is $2/T_c$. Figure 7.9c shows the resulting spectrum spreading. The amount of spreading that is achieved is a direct result of the data rate of the PN stream.

As with FHSS, we can get some insight into the performance of DSSS by looking at its effectiveness against jamming. Let us assume a simple jamming signal at the center frequency of the DSSS system. The jamming signal has the form

$$s_j(t) = \sqrt{2S_j}\cos(2\pi f_c t)$$

and the received signal is

$$s_r(t) = s(t) + s_j(t) + n(t)$$

where

$$s(t) = \text{transmitted signal}$$
$$s_j(t) = \text{jamming signal}$$

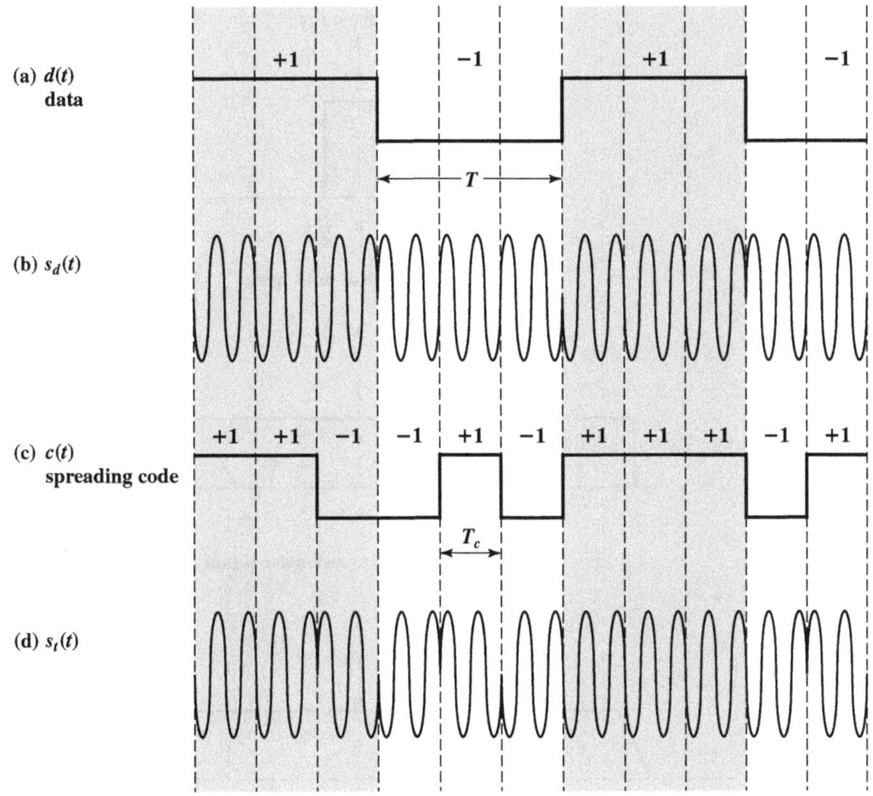

Figure 7.8 Example of Direct Sequence Spread Spectrum Using BPSK

$$n(t) = \text{additive white noise}$$
$$S_j = \text{jammer signal power}$$

The despreader at the receiver multiplies $s_r(t)$ by $c(t)$, so the signal component due to the jamming signal is

$$y_j(t) = \sqrt{2S_j}c(t)\cos(2\pi f_c t)$$

This is simply a BPSK modulation of the carrier tone. Thus, the carrier power S_j is spread over a bandwidth of approximately $2/T_c$. However, the BPSK demodulator (Figure 7.7) following the DSSS despreader includes a bandpass filter matched to the BPSK data, with bandwidth of $2/T$. Thus, most of the jamming power is filtered. Although a number of factors come into play, as an approximation, we can say that the jamming power passed by the filter is

$$S_{jF} = S_j(2/T)/(2/T_c) = S_j(T_c/T)$$

The jamming power has been reduced by a factor of (T_c/T) through the use of spread spectrum. The inverse of this factor is the gain in signal-to-noise ratio:

$$G_P = \frac{T}{T_c} = \frac{R_c}{R} \approx \frac{W_s}{W_d} \tag{7.6}$$

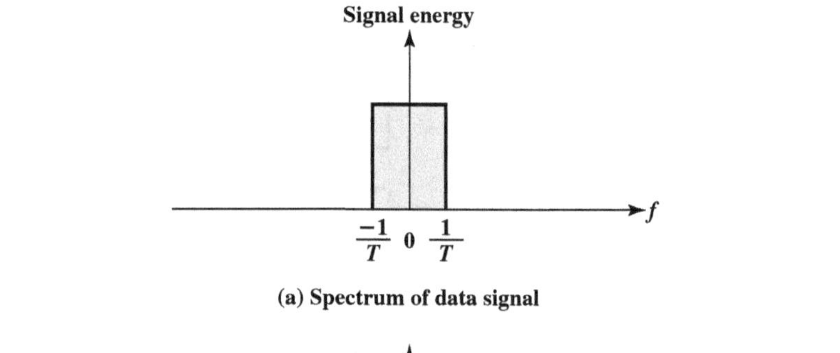

Figure 7.9 Approximate Spectrum of Direct Sequence Spread Spectrum Signal

where R_c is the spreading bit rate, R is the data rate, W_d is the signal bandwidth, and W_s is the spread spectrum signal bandwidth. The result is similar to the result for FHSS [Equation 7.3)].

7.4 CODE DIVISION MULTIPLE ACCESS

Basic Principles

CDMA is a multiplexing technique used with spread spectrum. The scheme works in the following manner. We start with a data signal with rate D, which we call the bit data rate. We break each bit into k *chips* according to a fixed pattern that is specific to each user, called the user's code. The new channel has a chip data rate of kD chips per second. As an illustration we consider a simple example[4] with $k = 6$. It is simplest to

[4]This example was provided by Prof. Richard Van Slyke of the Polytechnic University of Brooklyn.

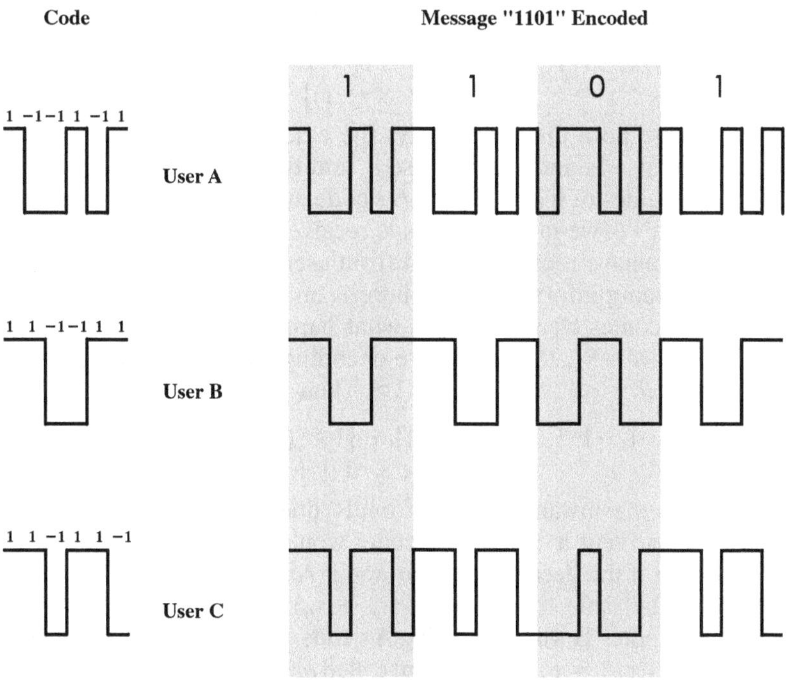

Figure 7.10 CDMA Example

characterize a code as a sequence of 1s and −1s. Figure 7.10 shows the codes for three users, A, B, and C, each of which is communicating with the same base station receiver, R. Thus, the code for user A is $c_A = <1, -1, -1, 1, -1, 1>$. Similarly, user B has code $c_B = <1, 1, -1, -1, 1, 1>$, and user C has $c_C = <1, 1, -1, 1, 1, -1>$.

We now consider the case of user A communicating with the base station. The base station is assumed to know A's code. For simplicity, we assume that communication is already synchronized so that the base station knows when to look for codes. If A wants to send a 1 bit, A transmits its code as a chip pattern $<1, -1, -1, 1, -1, 1>$. If a 0 bit is to be sent, A transmits the complement (1s and −1s reversed) of its code, $<-1, 1, 1, -1, 1, -1>$. At the base station the receiver decodes the chip patterns. In our simple version, if the receiver R receives a chip pattern $d = <d1, d2, d3, d4, d5, d6>$, and the receiver is seeking to communicate with a user u so that it has at hand u's code, $<c1, c2, c3, c4, c5, c6>$, the receiver performs electronically the following decoding function:

$$S_u(d) = (d1 \times c1) + (d2 \times c2) + (d3 \times c3) + (d4 \times c4) + (d5 \times c5) + (d6 \times c6)$$

The subscript u on S simply indicates that u is the user that we are interested in. Let's suppose the user u is actually A and see what happens. If A sends a 1 bit, then d is $<1, -1, -1, 1, -1, 1>$ and the preceding computation using S_A becomes

$$S_A(1, -1, -1, 1, -1, 1) = [1 \times 1] + [(-1) \times (-1)] + [(-1) \times (-1)] + [(-1) \times (-1)] + [1 \times 1] = 6$$

If A sends a 0 bit that corresponds to $d = \langle -1, 1, 1, -1, 1, -1 \rangle$, we get

$$S_A(-1, 1, 1, -1, 1, -1) = [-1 \times 1] + [1 \times (-1)] + [1 \times (-1)] + [(-1) \times 1] + [1 \times (-1)] + [1 \times (-1)] + [(-1) \times 1] = -6$$

Please note that it is always the case that $-6 \leq S_A(d) \leq 6$ no matter what sequence of -1s and 1s comprise d, and that the only values of d resulting in the extreme values of 6 and -6 are A's code and its complement, respectively. So if S_A produces a $+6$, we say that we have received a 1 bit from A; if S_A produces a -6, we say that we have received a 0 bit from user A; otherwise, we assume that someone else is sending information or there is an error. So why go through all this?. The reason becomes clear if we see what happens if user B is sending and we try to receive it with S_A, that is, we are decoding with the wrong code, A's. If B sends a 1 bit, then $d = \langle 1, 1, -1, -1, 1, 1 \rangle$. Then

$$S_A(1, 1, -1, -1, 1, 1) = [1 \times 1] + [1 \times (-1)] + [(-1) \times (-1)] + [(-1) \times 1] + [1 \times (-1)] + [1 \times 1] = 0$$

Thus, the unwanted signal (from B) does not show up at all. You can easily verify that if B had sent a 0 bit, the decoder would produce a value of 0 for S_A again. This means that if the decoder is linear and if A and B transmit signals s_A and s_B, respectively, at the same time, then $S_A(s_A + s_B) = S_A(s_A) + S_A(s_B) = S_A(s_A)$ since the decoder ignores B when it is using A's code. The codes of A and B that have the property that $S_A(c_B) = S_B(c_A) = 0$ are called *orthogonal*. Such codes are very nice to have but there are not all that many of them. More common is the case when $S_X(c_Y)$ is small in absolute value when $X \times Y$. Then it is easy to distinguish between the two cases when $X = Y$ and when $X \neq Y$. In our example $S_A(c_C) = S_c(c_A) = 0$, but $S_B(c_C) = S_C(c_B) = 2$. In the latter case the C signal would make a small contribution to the decoded signal instead of 0. Using the decoder, S_u, the receiver can sort out transmission from u even when there may be other users broadcasting in the same cell.

Table 7.1 summarizes the example from the preceding discussion.

In practice, the CDMA receiver can filter out the contribution from unwanted users or they appear as low-level noise. However, if there are many users competing for the channel with the user the receiver is trying to listen to, or if the signal power of one or more competing signals is too high, perhaps because it is very near the receiver (the "near/far" problem), the system breaks down.

CDMA for Direct Sequence Spread Spectrum

Let us now look at CDMA from the viewpoint of a DSSS system using BPSK. Figure 7.11 depicts a configuration in which there are n users, each transmitting using a different, orthogonal, PN sequence (compare Figure 7.7). For each user, the data stream to be transmitted, $d_i(t)$, is BPSK modulated to produce a signal with a bandwidth of W_s and then multiplied by the spreading code for that user, $c_i(t)$. All of the signals, plus noise, are received at the receiver's antenna. Suppose that the receiver is attempting to recover the data of user 1. The incoming signal is multiplied by the spreading code of user 1 and then demodulated. The effect of this is to narrow the bandwidth of that portion of the incoming signal corresponding to user 1 to the original bandwidth of the unspread signal, which is proportional to the data rate. Because the remainder of the incoming signal is orthogonal to the spreading code of user 1,

Table 7.1 CDMA Example

(a) User's codes

User A	1	−1	−1	1	−1	1
User B	1	1	−1	−1	1	1
User C	1	1	−1	1	1	−1

(b) Transmission from A

Transmit (data bit = 1)	1	−1	−1	1	−1	1	
Receiver codeword	1	−1	−1	1	−1	1	
Multiplication	1	1	1	1	1	1	= 6

Transmit (data bit = 0)	−1	1	1	−1	1	−1	
Receiver codeword	1	−1	−1	1	−1	1	
Multiplication	−1	−1	−1	−1	−1	−1	= −6

(c) Transmission from B, receiver attempts to recover A's transmission

Transmit (data bit = 1)	1	1	−1	−1	1	1	
Receiver codeword	1	−1	−1	1	−1	1	
Multiplication	1	−1	1	−1	−1	1	= 0

(d) Transmission from C, receiver attempts to recover B's transmission

Transmit (data bit = 1)	1	1	−1	1	1	−1	
Receiver codeword	1	1	−1	−1	1	1	
Multiplication	1	1	1	−1	1	−1	= 2

(e) Transmission from B and C, receiver attempts to recover B's transmission

B (data bit = 1)	1	1	−1	−1	1	1	
C (data bit = 1)	1	1	−1	1	1	−1	
Combined signal	2	2	−2	0	2	0	
Receiver codeword	1	1	−1	−1	1	1	
Multiplication	2	2	2	0	2	0	= 8

that remainder still has the bandwidth W_s. Thus the unwanted signal energy remains spread over a large bandwidth and the wanted signal is concentrated in a narrow bandwidth. The bandpass filter at the demodulator can therefore recover the desired signal.

7.5 GENERATION OF SPREADING SEQUENCES

As was mentioned, the spreading sequence, $c(t)$, is a sequence of binary digits shared by transmitter and receiver. Spreading consists of multiplying (XOR) the input data by the spreading sequence, where the bit rate of the spreading sequence is higher than that of the input data. When the signal is received, the spreading is

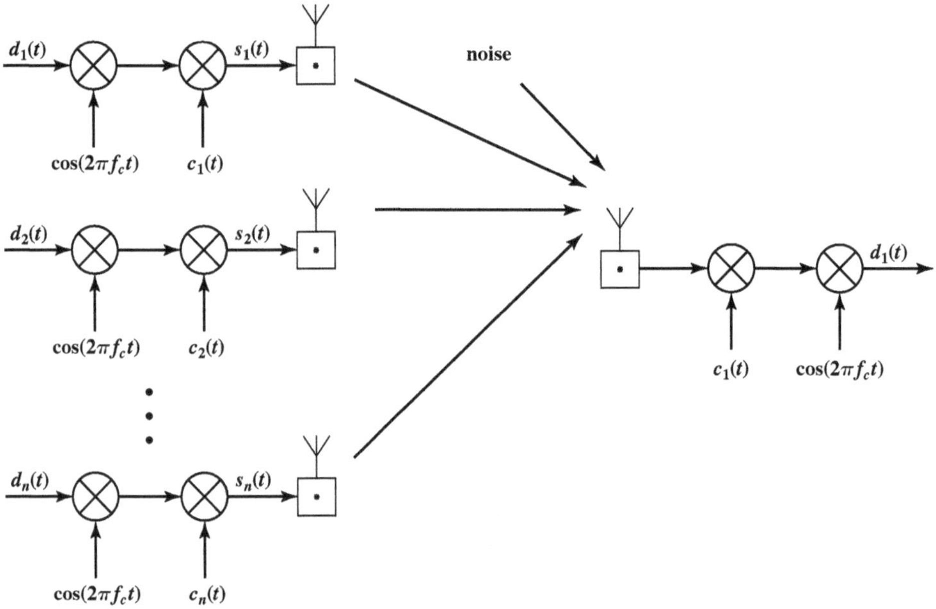

Figure 7.11 CDMA in a DSSS Environment

removed by multiplying with the same spreading code, exactly synchronized with the received signal.

The resulting data rate is consequently that of the spreading sequence. This increases the transmitted data rate and therefore increases the required bandwidth. The redundancy of the system is also increased. The spreading codes are chosen so that the resulting signal is noiselike; therefore, there should be an approximately equal number of ones and zeros in the spreading code and few or no repeated patterns. When spreading codes are used in a CDMA application, there is the further requirement of lack of correlation. When multiple signals are received, each spread with a different spreading code, the receiver should be able to pick out any individual signal using that signal's spreading code. The spread signals should behave as if they were uncorrelated with each other, so that other signals will appear as noise and not interfere with the despreading of a particular signal. Because of the high degree of redundancy provided by the spreading operation, the despreading operation is able to cope with the interference of other signals in the same bandwidth.

Two general categories of spreading sequences have been used: PN sequences and orthogonal codes. PN sequences are the most common ones used in FHSS systems and in DSSS systems not employing CDMA. In DSSS CDMA systems, both PN and orthogonal codes have been used. We examine each of these approaches in turn.

PN Sequences

An ideal spreading sequence would be a random sequence of binary ones and zeros. However, because it is required that transmitter and receiver must have a copy of the random bit stream, a predictable way is needed to generate the same bit stream at transmitter and receiver and yet retain the desirable properties of a random bit stream. This requirement is met by a PN generator. A PN generator will produce a periodic sequence that eventually repeats but that appears to be random. The **period** of a sequence is the length of the sequence before it starts repeating.

PN sequences are generated by an algorithm using some initial value called the **seed**. The algorithm is deterministic and therefore produces sequences of numbers that are not statistically random. However, if the algorithm is good, the resulting sequences will pass many reasonable tests of randomness. Such numbers are often referred to as **pseudorandom numbers**, or **pseudonoise sequences**. An important point is that unless you know the algorithm and the seed, it is impractical to predict the sequence. Hence, only a receiver that shares this information with a transmitter will be able to decode the signal successfully.

PN sequences find a number of uses in computers and communications, and the principles involved are well developed. We begin with a general description of desirable properties of PNs and then look at the generation method typically used for spread spectrum applications.

PN Properties Two important properties for PNs are randomness and unpredictability.

Traditionally, the concern in the generation of a sequence of allegedly random numbers has been that the sequence of numbers be random in some well-defined statistical sense. The following two criteria are used to validate that a sequence of numbers is random:

- **Uniform distribution:** The distribution of numbers in the sequence should be uniform; that is, the frequency of occurrence of each of the numbers should be approximately the same. For a stream of binary digits, we need to expand on this definition because we are dealing with only 2 numbers (0 and 1). Generally, we desire the following two properties:
  - **Balance property:** In a long sequence the fraction of binary ones should approach 1/2.
  - **Run property:** A run is defined as a sequence of all 1s or a sequence of all 0s. The appearance of the alternate digit marks the beginning of a new run. About one-half of the runs of each type should be of length 1, one-fourth of length 2, one-eighth of length 3, and so on.
- **Independence:** No one value in the sequence can be inferred from the others.

Although there are well-defined tests for determining that a sequence of numbers matches a particular distribution, such as the uniform distribution, there is no such test to "prove" independence. Rather, a number of tests can be applied to demonstrate that a sequence does not exhibit independence. The general strategy is to apply a number of such tests until the confidence that independence exists is sufficiently strong.

In applications such as spread spectrum, there is also the following requirement:

- **Correlation property:** If a period of the sequence is compared term by term with any cycle shift of itself, the number of terms that are the same differs from those that are different by at most 1.

Linear Feedback Shift Register Implementation The PN generator for spread spectrum is usually implemented as a circuit consisting of XOR gates and a shift register, called a linear feedback shift register (LFSR). The LFSR is a string of 1-bit storage devices. Each device has an output line, which indicates the value currently stored, and an input line. At discrete time instants, known as clock times, the value in the storage device is replaced by the value indicated by its input line. The entire LFSR is clocked simultaneously, causing a 1-bit shift along the entire register.

The circuit is implemented as follows:

1. The LFSR contains n bits.
2. There are from 1 to $(n - 1)$ XOR gates.
3. The presence or absence of a gate corresponds to the presence or absence of a term in the generator polynomial (explained subsequently), $P(X)$, excluding the X^n term.

Two equivalent ways of characterizing the PN LFSR are used. We can think of the generator as implementing a sum of XOR terms:

$$B_n = A_0B_0 \oplus A_1B_1 \oplus A_2B_2 \oplus \cdots \oplus A_{n-1}B_{n-1} \tag{7.7}$$

Figure 7.12 illustrates this equation. An actual implementation would not have the multiply circuits; instead, for $A_i = 0$, the corresponding XOR circuit is eliminated. Figure 7.13a is an example of a 4-bit LFSR that implements the equation

$$B_3 = B_0 \oplus B_1 \tag{7.8}$$

The shift register technique has several important advantages. The sequences generated by an LFSR can be nearly random with long periods, which aids in making the spread signal appear noiselike. In addition, LFSRs are easy to implement in hardware and can run at high speeds; this is important because the spreading rate is higher than the data rate.

It can be shown that the output of an LFSR is periodic with maximum period $N = 2^n - 1$. The all-zeros sequence occurs only if either the initial contents of the LFSR are all zero or the coefficients in Equation (7.7) are all zero (no feedback). A feedback configuration can always be found that gives a period of N; the resulting

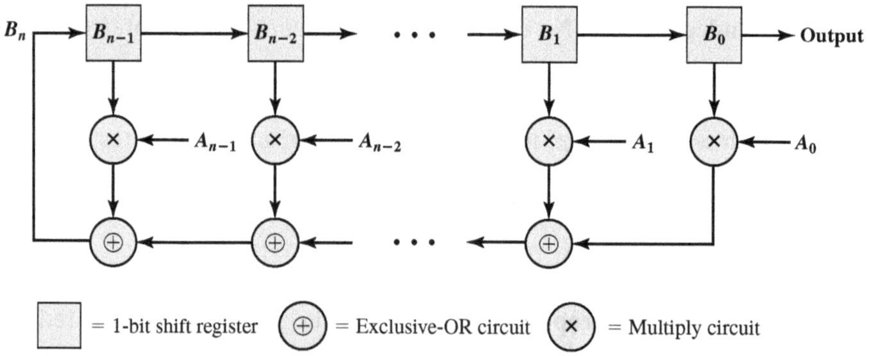

Figure 7.12 Binary Linear Feedback Shift Register Sequence Generator

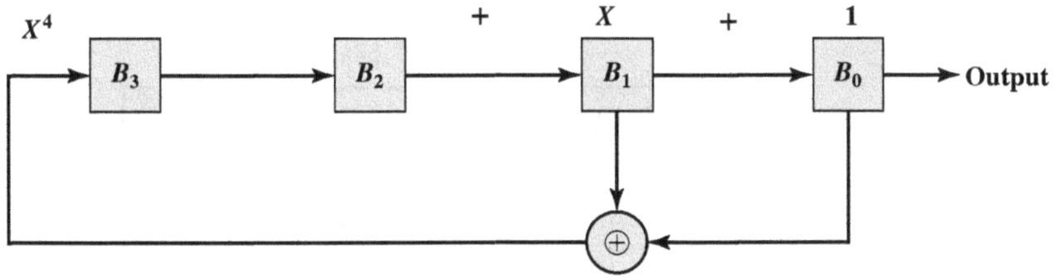

(a) Shift register implementation

State	B_3	B_2	B_1	B_0	$B_0 \oplus B_1$	Output
Initial = 0	1	0	0	0	0	0
1	0	1	0	0	0	0
2	0	0	1	0	1	0
3	1	0	0	1	1	1
4	1	1	0	0	0	0
5	0	1	1	0	1	0
6	1	0	1	1	0	1
7	0	1	0	1	1	1
8	1	0	1	0	1	0
9	1	1	0	1	1	1
10	1	1	1	0	1	0
11	1	1	1	1	0	1
12	0	1	1	1	0	1
13	0	0	1	1	0	1
14	0	0	0	1	1	1
15 = 0	1	0	0	0	0	0

(b) Example with initial state of 1000

Figure 7.13 Circuit with Shift Registers for Generating PN Sequence

sequences are called **maximal-length sequences**, or **m-sequences**. The m-sequences are important in enabling synchronization by the receiver and in use in multiple access techniques, such as CDMA, as will be explained.

Figure 7.13b shows the generation of an m-sequence for the LFSR of Figure 7.13a. The LFSR implements Equation (7.8) with an initial state of 1000 ($B_3 = 1, B_2 = 0, B_1 = 0, B_0 = 0$). Figure 7.13b is a table that shows the step-by-step operation as the LFSR is clocked one bit at a time. Each row of the table shows the values currently stored in the four shift register elements. In addition, the row shows the values that appear at the output of the exclusive-OR circuit. Finally, the row shows the value of the output bit, which is just B_0. Note that the output repeats after 15 bits. That is, the period of the sequence, or the length of the m-sequence, is $15 = 2^4 - 1$. This same periodic m-sequence is generated regardless of the initial state of the LFSR (except for 0000), as shown in Table 7.2. With each different initial state, the m-sequence begins at a different point in its cycle, but it is the same sequence.

Table 7.2 The 15 PN Sequences Obtained From Figure 7.13a

Initial State	Output Sequence
1000	000100110101111
0100	001001101011110
0010	010011010111100
1001	100110101111000
1100	001101011110001
0110	011010111100010
1011	110101111000100
0101	101011110001001
1010	010111100010011
1101	101111000100110
1110	011110001001101
1111	111100010011010
0111	111000100110101
0011	110001001101011
0001	100010011010111

For any given size of LFSR, a number of different unique m-sequences can be generated by using different values for the A_i in Equation (7.7). Table 7.3 shows the sequence length and number of unique m-sequences that can be generated for LFSRs of various sizes.

An equivalent definition of an LFSR configuration is a generator polynomial. The generator polynomial *P(X)* that corresponds to Equation (7.7) has the form

$$P(X) = A_0 + A_1X + A_2X^2 + \cdots + A_{n-1}X^{n-1} + X^n \tag{7.9}$$

One useful attribute of the generator polynomial is that it can be used to find the sequence generated by the corresponding LFSR, by taking the reciprocal of the polynomial. For example, for the three bit LSFR with $P(X) = 1 + X + X^3$, we perform the division $1/(1 + X + X^3)$. Figure 7.14 depicts the long division. The result is

$$1 + X + X^2 + (0 \times X^3) + X^4 + (0 \times X^5) + (0 \times X^6)$$

after which the pattern repeats. This means that the shift register output is

1 1 1 0 1 0 0

Because the period of this sequence is $7 = 2^3 - 1$, this is an m-sequence. Notice that we are doing division somewhat differently from the normal method. This is because the subtractions are done modulo 2, or using the XOR function, and in this system, subtraction produces the same result as addition.

Table 7.3 lists a generator polynomial that produces an m-sequence for LFSRs of various sizes.

Table 7.3 Maximal-Length Shift Register Sequences

Number of shift register stages N	Sequence length $L = 2^N - 1$	Number of m-sequences	Example generating polynomial	B_n in Figure 7.12 for example polynomial
2	3	1	$X^2 + X + 1$	$B_1 \oplus B_0$
3	7	2	$X^3 + X + 1$	$B_1 \oplus B_0$
4	15	2	$X^4 + X + 1$	$B_1 \oplus B_0$
5	31	6	$X^5 + X2 + 1$	$B_2 \oplus B_0$
6	63	6	$X^6 + X + 1$	$B_1 \oplus B_0$
7	127	18	$X^7 + X + 1$	$B_1 \oplus B_0$
8	255	16	$X^8 + X^6 + X^5 + X + 1$	$B_6 \oplus B_5 \oplus B_1 \oplus B_0$
9	511	48	$X^9 + X^4 + 1$	$B_4 \oplus B_0$
10	1023	60	$X^{10} + X^3 + 1$	$B_3 \oplus B_0$
11	2047	176	$X^{11} + X^2 + 1$	$B_2 \oplus B_0$
12	4095	144	$X^{12} + X^7 + X^4 + X^3 + 1$	$B_7 \oplus B_4 \oplus B_3 \oplus B_0$
13	8191	630	$X^{13} + X^4 + X^3 + X + 1$	$B_4 \oplus B_3 \oplus B_1 \oplus B_0$
14	16,383	756	$X^{14} + X^{12} + X^{11} + X + 1$	$B_{12} \oplus B_{11} \oplus B_1 \oplus B_0$
15	32,767	1800	$X^{15} + X + 1$	$B_1 \oplus B_0$
20	1,048,575	2400	$X^{20} + X3 + 1$	$B_3 \oplus B_0$

$$
\begin{array}{r|l}
 & 1 + X + X^2 + \quad X^4 + \quad\quad X^7 + X^8 + \cdots \\
\hline
1 + X + X^3 & 1 \\
 & \underline{1 + X + \quad X^3} \\
 & \quad X \quad\; X^3 \\
 & \quad \underline{X + X^2 + \quad X^4} \\
 & \qquad X^2 + X^3 + X^4 \\
 & \qquad \underline{X^2 + X^3 + \quad X^5} \\
 & \qquad\qquad X^4 + X^5 \\
 & \qquad\qquad \underline{X^4 + X^5 + \quad X^7} \\
 & \qquad\qquad\qquad\quad X^7 \\
 & \qquad\qquad\qquad\quad \underline{X^7 + X^8 \;+ X^{10}} \\
 & \qquad\qquad\qquad\qquad X^8 + \; X^{10} \\
 & \qquad\qquad\qquad\qquad \underline{X^8 + X^9 \;+ X^{11}}
\end{array}
$$

Figure 7.14 $1/(1 + X + X^3)$

Properties of M-Sequences M-sequences have several properties that make them attractive for spread spectrum applications:

- **Property 1.** An m-sequence has 2^{n-1} ones and $2^{n-1} - 1$ zeros.
- **Property 2.** If we slide a window of length n along the output sequence for N shifts, where $N = 2^n - 1$, each n-tuple, except the all-zeros sequence, appears exactly once.
- **Property 3.** There is one run of ones of length n; one run of zeros of length $n - 1$; one run of ones and one run of zeros of length $n - 2$; two runs of ones and two runs of zeros of length $n - 3$; and, in general, 2^{n-3} runs of ones and 2^{n-3} runs of zeros of length 1.

For many communications applications, the 0, 1 sequence is changed to a ± 1 sequence by representing a binary 1 with 1 and a binary 0 with -1.[5] We define the periodic autocorrelation of the resulting sequence as

$$R(\tau) = \frac{1}{N}\sum_{k=1}^{N} B_k B_{k-\tau} \tag{7.10}$$

Then,

- **Property 4.** The periodic autocorrelation of a ± 1 m-sequence is

$$R(\tau) = \begin{cases} 1 & \tau = 0, N, 2N, \ldots \\ -\dfrac{1}{N} & \text{otherwise} \end{cases}$$

[5]In some of the literature, the opposite convention is used, representing binary 0 by 1 and binary 1 by -1. It makes no difference so long as the convention is consistently followed.

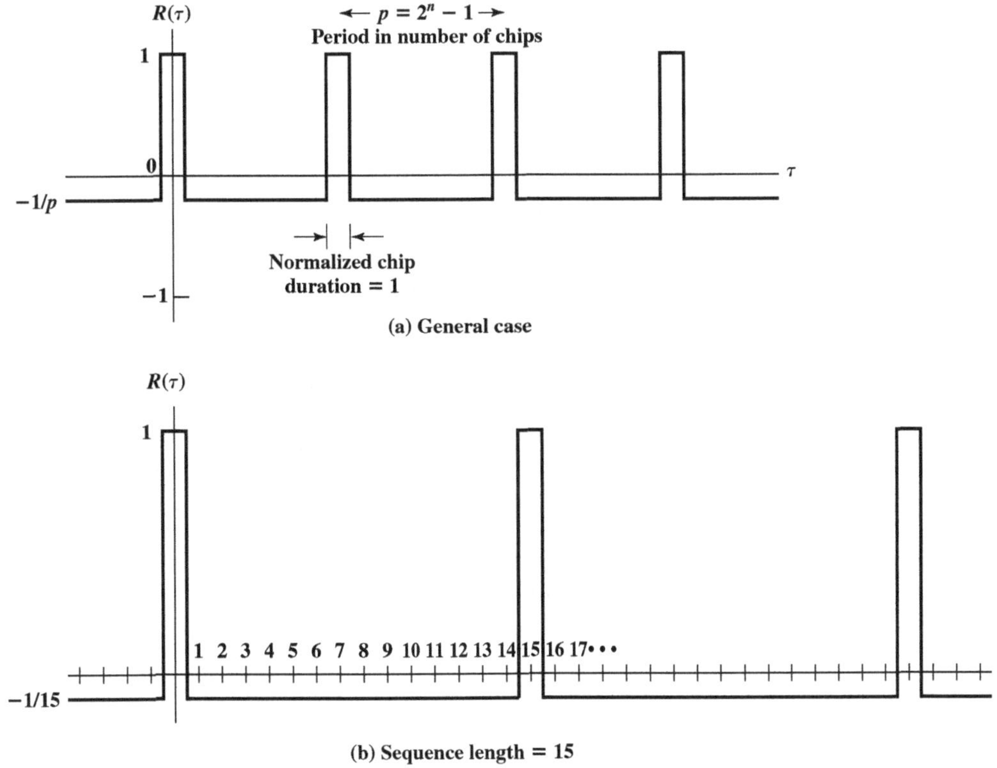

Figure 7.15 PN Autocorrelation Function

Figure 7.15 shows the general autocorrelation case for m-sequences and the autocorrelation function for m-sequences generated by a 4-bit LFSR.

In essence, correlation is the concept of determining how much similarity one set of data has with another. **Correlation** is defined with a range between −1 and 1 with the following meanings:

Correlation Value	Interpretation
1	The second sequence matches the first sequence exactly.
0	There is no relation at all between the two sequences.
−1	The two sequences are mirror images of each other.

Other values indicate a partial degree of correlation. **Autocorrelation**, which is defined in Equation (7.10), is the correlation of a sequence with all phase shifts of itself. Pure random data should have a correlation value close to 0 for all autocorrelations with a phase shift other than 0. The m-sequences have this property. It can be shown that the autocorrelation function of an m-sequence, with its single sharp peak, is a powerful aid to synchronization by the receiver.

A related function, also important in the spread spectrum context, is the **cross correlation** function. In this case, the comparison is made between two sequences from different sources rather than a shifted copy of a sequence with itself. The cross correlation between two sources, A and B, is defined as:

$$R_{A,B}(\tau) = \frac{1}{N}\sum_{k=1}^{N} A_k B_{k-\tau} \tag{7.11}$$

In general, the cross correlation value produced by matching a sequence with a random sequence is low, which has two advantages:

1. The cross correlation between an m-sequence and noise is low, and this property is useful to the receiver in filtering out noise.
2. The cross correlation between two different m-sequences is low, and this property is useful for CDMA applications because it enables a receiver to discriminate among spread spectrum signals generated by different m-sequences.

Gold Sequences M-sequences are easy to generate and are very useful for FHSS and DSSS systems not used for CDMA. However, for CDMA DSSS, m-sequences are not optimal. For CDMA, we need to construct a family of spreading sequences, one for each user, in which the codes have well-defined cross correlation properties. In general, m-sequences do not satisfy this criterion. One popular set of sequences that does is the Gold sequences. Gold sequences are attractive because only simple circuitry is needed to generate a large number of unique codes.

A Gold sequence is constructed by the XOR of two m-sequences with the same clocking. Figure 7.16a shows an example; in this example the two shift registers

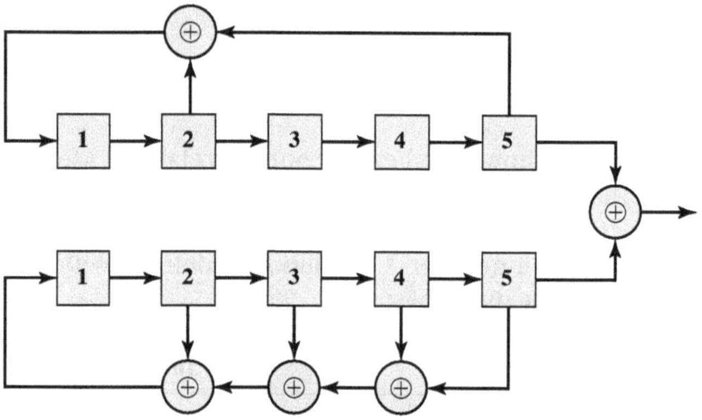

(a) Shift register implementation

Sequence 1: 1111100011011101010000100101100
Sequence 2: 1111100100110000101101010001110
0 shift XOR: 0000000111101101111101110100010
1 shift XOR: 0000101010111100001010000110001
•
•
30 shift XOR: 1000010001000101000110001101011

(b) Resulting Gold sequences

Figure 7.16 Example of Generating a Set of Gold Sequences [DINA98] generate the two m-sequences and these are then bitwise XORed. In general, the length of the resulting sequence is not maximal. Further, the desired Gold sequences can only be generated by **preferred pairs** of m-sequences. These preferred pairs can be selected from tables of pairs or generated by an algorithm. [DIXO94] lists sets of preferred pairs and describes the algorithm. Here, we summarize the mathematical conditions that lead to a Gold code.

Suppose we take an m-sequence represented by a binary vector **a** of length N, and generate a new sequence $\mathbf{a}'$ by sampling every qth symbol of **a**. We use multiple copies of **a** until we have enough samples to produce a sequence of $\mathbf{a}'$ of length N. The sequence $\mathbf{a}'$ is said to be a **decimation** of the sequence **a** and is written as $\mathbf{a}' = \mathbf{a}[q]$. The sequence $\mathbf{a}'$ does not necessarily have a period N and is therefore not necessarily an m-sequence. It can be shown that $\mathbf{a}'$ will be an m-sequence, with period N, if and only if $\gcd(n, q) = 1$, where gcd stands for greatest common divisor; in other words, n and q have no common factor except 1. For Gold sequences, we need to start with a preferred pair **a** and $\mathbf{a}' = \mathbf{a}[q]$ that are both m-sequences and that meet the following conditions:

1. $n \bmod 4 \neq 0$; that is, all n except 0, 4, 8, 12, ...
2. q is odd and $q = (2^k + 1)$ or $q = (2^{2k} - 2^k + 1)$ for some k.
3. $\gcd(n, k) = \begin{cases} 1 & \text{for } n \text{ odd} \\ 2 & \text{for } n \bmod 4 = 2 \end{cases}$

For shift registers of length n, the cross correlation of the Gold sequences produced by a preferred pair is bounded by $|R| \leq 2^{(n+1)/2} + 1$ for n odd and $|R| \leq 2^{(n+2)/2} + 1$ for n even.

Starting with a preferred pair, a set of Gold codes consists of the sequences $\{\mathbf{a}, \mathbf{a}', \mathbf{a} \oplus \mathbf{a}', \mathbf{a} \oplus \mathrm{D}\mathbf{a}', \mathbf{a} \oplus \mathrm{D}^2\mathbf{a}', \ldots, \mathbf{a} \oplus \mathrm{D}^{N-1}\mathbf{a}'\}$, where D is the delay element; that is, D represents a one-bit shift of $\mathbf{a}'$ relative to **a**. To generate the Gold codes from shift registers, we start with the all-ones vector set in both registers as an initial condition. The resulting sequences are XORed to produce one Gold sequence. This yields the first three sequences in the set. To generate the remaining sequences, the second of the first two sequences is shifted by one bit and the XOR operation performed again. This process continues through all possible shifts, with each additional one-bit shift followed by an XOR producing a new sequence in the set. For a preferred pair of 5-bit shift registers, it can be shown that for any shift in the initial condition from 0 to 30, a new Gold sequence is generated (a 31-bit shift is the same as a 0 shift). The Gold sequences are the two initial m-sequences plus the generated sequences for a total of 33 sequences. This is illustrated in Figure 7.16b.

In general, the period of any code in a Gold set generated with 2 n-bit shift registers is $N = 2^n - 1$, which is the same as the period of the m-sequences. There is a total of $N + 2$ codes in any family of Gold codes. As an example of the effectiveness of Gold codes, for $n = 13$ ($N = 2^{13} - 1 = 8191$), there are 630 m-sequences (Table 7.3) and there exist pairs of these sequences whose correlation values are at $R = 703$, while Gold sequence guarantee the selection of pairs such that $R \leq (2^{(n+1)/2} + 1) = 129$.

Kasami Sequences Another important set of PN sequences are the Kasami sequences, which are used in some third-generation wireless schemes. Kasami sequences are defined by a procedure similar to that for Gold codes. There are two sorts of sequences, small sets and large sets.

For n even, we can generate a **small set** of Kasami sequences containing $M = 2^{n/2}$ distinct sequences each with period $N = 2^n - 1$. A set is defined by starting with an m-sequence **a** with period N and decimating the sequence by $q = 2^{n/2} + 1$. It can be shown that the resulting sequence **a**′ has a period $2^{n/2} - 1$. Now we replicate a single period of **a**′ q times to produce a sequence of length $(2^{n/2} - 1)(2^{n/2} + 1) = N$. For example, for $n = 10$, the period of **a** is $2^{10} - 1 = 1023$ and the period of **a**′ is $2^5 - 1 = 31$. If we observe 1023 bits of sequence **a**′, we see 33 repetitions of the 31-bit sequence. Finally, we generate the Kasami set by taking N bits of **a** and N bits of **a**′ and forming a new set of sequences by XORing the bits from **a** and the bits from **a**′ as well as all $2^{n/2} - 1$ cyclic shifts of the bits from **a**′.

It can be shown that the maximum cross correlation value for the set is $2^{n/2} - 1$. This is smaller than for Gold sequences and in fact is optimal.

The **large set** of Kasami sequences also consists of certain sequences, each with period $N = 2^n - 1$ for n even, and contains both Gold sequences and the small set of Kasami sequences as subsets. A set is defined by starting with an m-sequence **a** with period N and decimating the sequence by $q = 2^{n/2} + 1$ to form **a**′ and decimating the sequence by $q = 2^{(n+2)/2} + 1$ to form **a**″. A set is then formed by taking the XOR of **a**, **a**′, and **a**″ with different shifts of **a**′ and **a**″. It can be shown that the maximum cross correlation value for a large set is $2^{(n+2)/2}$.

Orthogonal Codes

Unlike PN sequences, an orthogonal codes is a set of sequences in which all pairwise cross correlations are zero. An orthogonal set of sequences is characterized by the following equality:

$$\sum_{k=0}^{M-1} \varphi_i(k\tau)\varphi_j(k\tau) = 0, \qquad i \neq j$$

where M is the length of each of the sequences in the set, ϕ_i and ϕ_j are the ith and jth members of the set, and τ is the bit duration.

Both fixed- and variable-length orthogonal codes have been used in CDMA systems. For the CDMA application, each mobile user uses one of the sequences in the set as a spreading code, providing zero cross correlation among all users.

Walsh Codes

Walsh codes are the most common orthogonal codes used in CDMA applications. A set of Walsh codes of length n consists of the n rows of an $n \times n$ Walsh matrix. That is, there are n codes, each of length n. The matrix is defined recursively as follows:

$$W_1 = (0) \qquad W_{2n} = \begin{pmatrix} W_n & W_n \\ W_n & \overline{W_n} \end{pmatrix}$$

where n is the dimension of the matrix and the overscore denotes the logical NOT of the bits in the matrix. The Walsh matrix has the property that every row is orthogonal to every other row and to the logical NOT of every other row.

Figure 7.17 shows the Walsh matrices of dimensions 2, 4, and 8. Note that in each matrix, three of the four quadrants replicate the next smaller matrix, while the lower

$W_1 = (0)$

(a) 1×1

$$W_2 = \begin{pmatrix} 0 & 0 \\ 0 & 1 \end{pmatrix}$$

(b) 2×2

$$W_4 = \begin{pmatrix} 0 & 0 & 0 & 0 \\ 0 & 1 & 0 & 1 \\ 0 & 0 & 1 & 1 \\ 0 & 1 & 1 & 0 \end{pmatrix}$$

(c) 4×4

$$W_8 = \begin{pmatrix} 0 & 0 & 0 & 0 & 0 & 0 & 0 & 0 \\ 0 & 1 & 0 & 1 & 0 & 1 & 0 & 1 \\ 0 & 0 & 1 & 1 & 0 & 0 & 1 & 1 \\ 0 & 1 & 1 & 0 & 0 & 1 & 1 & 0 \\ 0 & 0 & 0 & 0 & 1 & 1 & 1 & 1 \\ 0 & 1 & 0 & 1 & 1 & 0 & 1 & 0 \\ 0 & 0 & 1 & 1 & 1 & 1 & 0 & 0 \\ 0 & 1 & 1 & 0 & 1 & 0 & 0 & 1 \end{pmatrix}$$

(d) 8×8

Figure 7.17 Walsh Matrices

right quadrant (shaded) is the complement of the next smaller matrix. In each case, the first row consists entirely of 0s and each of the other rows contains n 0s and n 1s.

Recall that to compute the cross correlation, we replace 1 with +1 and 0 with −1.

Orthogonal spreading codes such as the Walsh sequences can only be used if all of the users in the same CDMA channel are synchronized to the accuracy of a small fraction of one chip. Because the cross correlation between different shifts of Walsh sequences is not zero, if tight synchronization is not provided, PN sequences are needed.

Variable-Length Orthogonal Codes Third-generation mobile CDMA systems are designed to support users at a number of different data rates. Thus, effective support can be provided by using spreading codes at different rates while maintaining orthogonality. Suppose that the minimum data rate to be supported is R_{min} and that all other data rates are related by powers of 2. If a spreading sequence of length N is used for the R_{min} data rate, such that each bit of data is spread by $N = 2^n$ bits of the spreading sequence (transmit the sequence for data bit 0; transmit the complement of the sequence for data bit 1), then the transmitted data rate is NR_{min}. For a data rate of $2\,R_{min}$, a spreading sequence of length $N/2 = 2^{n-1}$ will produce the same output rate of $N \times R_{min}$. In general, a code length of 2^{n-k} is needed for a bit rate of $2^k R_{min}$.

A set of variable-length orthogonal sequences is readily generated from Walsh matrices of different dimensions. For example, see [DINA98] for a description.

Multiple Spreading

When sufficient bandwidth is available, a multiple spreading technique can prove highly effective. A typical approach is to spread the data rate by an orthogonal code to provide mutual orthogonality among all users in the same cell and to further spread the result by a PN sequence to provide mutual randomness (low cross correlation) between users in different cells. In such a two-stage spreading, the orthogonal codes are referred to as **channelization codes**, and the PN codes are referred to as **scrambling codes**. We show an example of this technique in Chapter 10, with the IS-95 standard.

7.6 RECOMMENDED READINGS AND WEB SITES

Both [PETE95] and [DIXO94] provide comprehensive treatment of spread spectrum. [TANT98] contains reprints of many important papers in the field, including [PICK82], which provides an excellent introduction to spread spectrum.

A good survey of PN sequences for spread spectrum is [MACW76], and a good survey of CDMA is [PRAS98].

DIXO94 Dixon, R. *Spread Spectrum Systems with Commercial Applications.* New York: Wiley, 1994.

MACW76 Macwilliams, F., and Sloane, N. "Pseudo-Random Sequences and Arrays." *Proceedings of the IEEE,* December 1976. Reprinted in [TANT98].

PETE95 Peterson, R.; Ziemer, R.; and Borth, D. *Introduction to Spread Spectrum Communications.* Englewood Cliffs, NJ: Prentice Hall, 1995.

PICK82 Pickholtz, R.; Schilling, D.; and Milstein, L. "Theory of Spread Spectrum Communications—A Tutorial." *IEEE Transactions on Communications,* May 1982. Reprinted in [TANT98].

PRAS98 Prasad, R., and Ojanpera, T. "An Overview of CDMA Evolution: Toward Wideband CDMA." *IEEE Communications Surveys,* Fourth Quarter 1998. Available at www.comsoc.org.

TANT98 Tantaratana, S, and Ahmed, K., eds. *Wireless Applications of Spread Spectrum Systems: Selected Readings.* Piscataway, NJ: IEEE Press, 1998.

Recommended Web Site:

- **Spread Spectrum Scene:** Excellent source of information and links.

7.7 KEY TERMS, REVIEW QUESTIONS, AND PROBLEMS

Key Terms

autocorrelation	fast FHSS	pseudorandam numbers
chip	frequency hopping spread spectrum (FHSS)	seed
code division multiple access (CDMA)	linear feedback shift register (LFSR)	slow FHSS
correlation	m-sequence	spread spectrum
cross correlation	orthogonal pseudonoise (PN)	spreading code
decimation	pseudonoise (PN) sequence	spreading sequence
direct sequence spread spectrum (DSSS)		

Review Questions

7.1 What is the relationship between the bandwidth of a signal before and after it has been encoded using spread spectrum?

7.2 List three benefits of spread spectrum.

7.3 What is frequency hopping spread spectrum?

7.4 Explain the difference between slow FHSS and fast FHSS.

7.5 What is direct sequence spread spectrum?

7.6 What is the relationship between the bit rate of a signal before and after it has been encoded using DSSS?

7.7 What is CDMA?

7.8 Explain the difference between autocorrelation and cross correlation.

Problems

7.1 Assume we wish to transmit a 56-kbps data stream using spread spectrum.

a. Find the channel bandwidth required when SNR = 0.1, 0.01, and 0.001.

b. In an ordinary (not spread spectrum) system, a reasonable goal for bandwidth efficiency might be 1 bps/Hz. That is, to transmit a data stream of 56 kbps, a bandwidth of 56 kHz is used. In this case, what is the minimum SNR that can be endured for transmission without appreciable errors? Compare to the spread spectrum case.

7.2 An FHSS system employs a total bandwidth of $W_s = 400$ MHz and an individual channel bandwidth of 100 Hz. What is the minimum number of PN bits required for each frequency hop?

7.3 An FHSS system using MFSK with $M = 4$ employs 1000 different frequencies. What is the processing gain?

7.4 The following table illustrates the operation of an FHSS system for one complete period of the PN sequence.

Time	0	1	2	3	4	5	6	7	8	9	10	11
Input data	0	1	1	1	1	1	1	0	0	0	1	0
Frequency	f_1		f_3		f_{23}		f_{22}		f_8		f_{10}	
PN sequence	001				110				011			

Time	12	13	14	15	16	17	18	19
Input data	0	1	1	1	1	0	1	0
Frequency	f_1		f_3		f_2		f_2	
PN sequence	001				001			

a. What is the period of the PN sequence?

b. The system makes use of a form of FSK. What form of FSK is it?

c. What is the number of bits per symbol?

d. What is the number of FSK frequencies?

e. What is the length of a PN sequence per hop?

f. Is this a slow or fast FH system?

g. What is the total number of possible hops?

h. Show the variation of the dehopped frequency with time.

7.5 The following table illustrates the operation of a FHSS system using the same PN sequence as Problem 7.4.

Time	0	1	2	3	4	5	6	7	8	9	10	11
Input data	0	1	1	1	1	1	1	0	0	0	1	0
Frequency	f_1	f_{21}	f_{11}	f_3	f_3	f_3	f_{22}	f_{10}	f_0	f_0	f_2	f_{22}
PN sequence	001	110	011	001	001	001	110	011	001	001	001	110

Time	12	13	14	15	16	17	18	19
Input data	0	1	1	1	1	0	1	0
Frequency	f_9	f_1	f_3	f_3	f_{22}	f_{10}	f_2	f_2
PN sequence	011	001	001	001	110	011	001	001

a. What is the period of the PN sequence?
b. The system makes use of a form of FSK. What form of FSK is it?
c. What is the number of bits per symbol?
d. What is the number of FSK frequencies?
e. What is the length of a PN sequence per hop?
f. Is this a slow or fast FH system?
g. What is the total number of possible hops?
h. Show the variation of the dehopped frequency with time.

7.6 Consider an MFSK scheme with $f_c = 250$ kHz, $f_d = 25$ kHz, and $M = 8$ ($L = 3$ bits).
a. Make a frequency assignment for each of the eight possible 3-bit data combinations.
b. We wish to apply FHSS to this MFSK scheme with $k = 2$; that is, the system will hop among four different carrier frequencies. Expand the results of part (a) to show the $4 \times 8 = 32$ frequency assignments.

7.7 Figure 7.18, based on one in [BELL00], depicts a simplified scheme for CDMA encoding and decoding. There are seven logical channels, all using DSSS with a spreading code of 7 bits. Assume that all sources are synchronized. If all seven sources transmit a data bit, in the form of a 7-bit sequence, the signals from all sources combine at the receiver so that two positive or two negative values reinforce and a positive and negative value cancel. To decode a given channel, the receiver multiplies the incoming composite signal by the spreading code for that channel, sums the result, and assigns binary 1 for a positive value and binary 0 for a negative value.
a. What are the spreading codes for the seven channels?
b. Determine the receiver output measurement for channel 1 and the bit value assigned.
c. Repeat part b for channel 2.

7.8 For the spreading codes of the preceding problem, determine the cross correlation between channel 0 and each of the other 6 channels.

7.9 By far, the most widely used technique for pseudorandom number generation is the linear congruential method. The algorithm is parameterized with four numbers, as follows:

m the modulus $m > 0$
a the multiplier $0 \le a < m$
c the increment $0 \le c < m$
X_0 the starting value, or seed $0 \le X_0 < m$

The sequence of pseudorandom numbers $\{X_n\}$ is obtained via the following iterative equation:

$$X_{n+1} = (aX_n + c) \bmod m$$

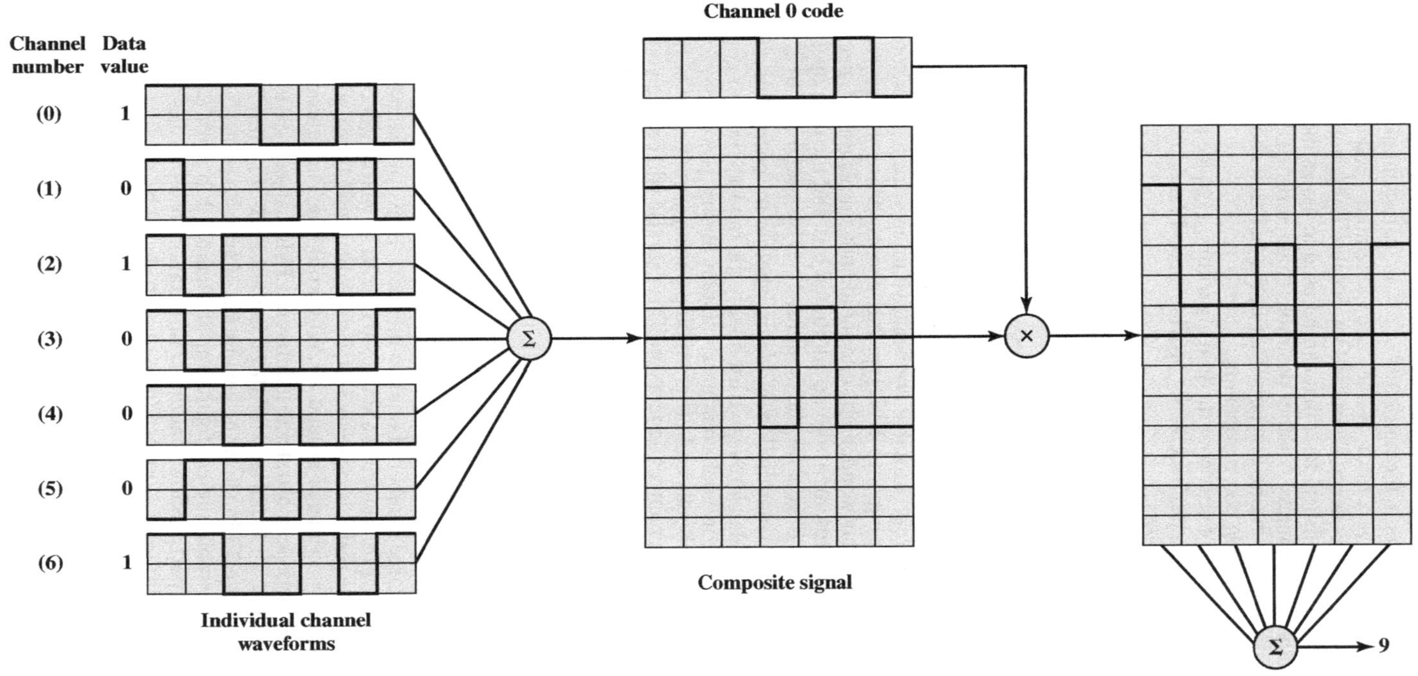

Figure 7.18 Example Seven-Channel CDMA Encoding and Decoding

If m, a, c, and X_0 are integers, then this technique will produce a sequence of integers with each integer in the range $0 \leq X_n < m$. An essential characteristic of a pseudorandom number generator is that the generated sequence should appear random. Although the sequence is not random, because it is generated deterministically, there is a variety of statistical tests that can be used to assess the degree to which a sequence exhibits randomness. Another desirable characteristic is that the function should be a full-period generating function. That is, the function should generate all the numbers between 0 and m before repeating.

With the linear congruential algorithm, a choice of parameters that provides a full period does not necessarily provide a good randomization. For example, consider the two generators:

$$X_{n+1} = (6X_n)\bmod 13$$
$$X_{n+1} = (7X_n)\bmod 13$$

Write out the two sequences to show that both are full period. Which one appears more random to you?

7.10 We would like m to be very large so that there is the potential for producing a long series of distinct random numbers. A common criterion is that m be nearly equal to the maximum representable nonnegative integer for a given computer. Thus, a value of m near to or equal to 2^{31} is typically chosen. Many experts recommend a value of $2^{31} - 1$. You may wonder why one should not simply use 2^{31}, because this latter number can be represented with no additional bits, and the mod operation should be easier to perform. In general, the modulus $2^k - 1$ is preferable to 2^k. Why is this so?

7.11 In any use of pseudorandom numbers, whether for encryption, simulation, or statistical design, it is dangerous to trust blindly the random number generator that happens to be available in your computer's system library. [PARK88] found that many contemporary textbooks and programming packages make use of flawed algorithms for pseudorandom number generation. This exercise will enable you to test your system.

The test is based on a theorem attributed to Ernesto Cesaro (see [KNUT98] for a proof), which states that the probability is equal to $\frac{6}{\pi^2}$ that the greatest common divisor of two randomly chosen integers is 1. Use this theorem in a program to determine statistically the value of π. The main program should call three subprograms: the random number generator from the system library to generate the random integers; a subprogram to calculate the greatest common divisor of two integers using Euclid's algorithm; and a subprogram that calculates square roots. If these latter two programs are not available, you will have to write them as well. The main program should loop through a large number of random numbers to give an estimate of the aforementioned probability. From this, it is a simple matter to solve for your estimate of π.

If the result is close to 3.14, congratulations! If not, then the result is probably low, usually a value of around 2.7. Why would such an inferior result be obtained?

7.12 This problem demonstrates that different LFSRs can be used to generate an m-sequence.

a. Assume an initial state of 10000 in the LFSR of Figure 7.19a. In a manner similar to Figure 7.13b, show the generation of an m-sequence.

b. Now assume the configuration of Figure 7.19b, with the same initial state, and repeat part a. Show that this configuration also produces an m-sequence, but that it is a different sequence from that produced by the first LFSR.

7.13 Demonstrate that the codes in an 8×8 Walsh matrix are orthogonal to each other by showing that multiplying any code by any other code produces a result of zero.

7.14 Consider a CDMA system in which users A and B have the Walsh codes $(-1\ 1\ -1\ 1\ -1\ 1\ -1\ 1)$ and $(-1\ -1\ 1\ 1\ -1\ -1\ 1\ 1)$, respectively.

a. Show the output at the receiver if A transmits a data bit 1 and B does not transmit.

b. Show the output at the receiver if A transmits a data bit 0 and B does not transmit.

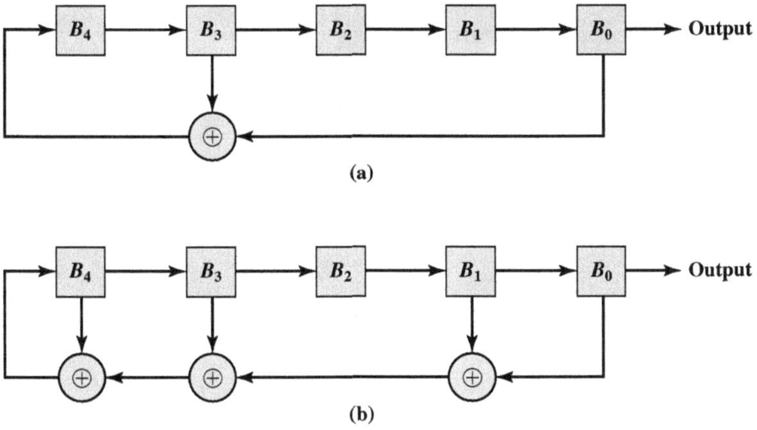

Figure 7.19 Two Different Configurations of LFSRs of Length 5

c. Show the output at the receiver if A transmits a data bit 1 and B transmits a data bit 1. Assume the received power from both A and B is the same.
d. Show the output at the receiver if A transmits a data bit 0 and B transmits a data bit 1. Assume the received power from both A and B is the same.
e. Show the output at the receiver if A transmits a data bit 1 and B transmits a data bit 0. Assume the received power from both A and B is the same.
f. Show the output at the receiver if A transmits a data bit 0 and B transmits a data bit 0. Assume the received power from both A and B is the same.
g. Show the output at the receiver if A transmits a data bit 1 and B transmits a data bit 1. Assume the received power from B is twice the received power from A. This can be represented by showing the received signal component from A as consisting of elements of magnitude $1(+1, -1)$ and the received signal component from B as consisting of elements of magnitude $2(+2, -2)$.
h. Show the output at the receiver if A transmits a data bit 0 and B transmits a data bit 1. Assume the received power from B is twice the received power from A.

CHAPTER 8

CODING AND ERROR CONTROL

In earlier chapters, we talked about transmission impairments and the effect of data rate and signal-to-noise ratio on bit error rate. Regardless of the design of the transmission system, there will be errors, resulting in the change of one or more bits in a transmitted frame.

Three approaches are in common use for coping with data transmission errors:

- Error detection codes
- Error correction codes, also called forward error correction (FEC) codes
- Automatic repeat request (ARQ) protocols

An error detection code simply detects the presence of an error. Typically, such codes are used in conjunction with a protocol at the data link or transport level (see Figure 4.4) that uses an ARQ scheme. With an ARQ scheme, a receiver discards a block of data in which an error is detected and the transmitter retransmits that block of data. FEC codes are designed not just to detect but correct errors, avoiding the need for retransmission. FEC schemes are frequently used in wireless transmission, where retransmission schemes are highly inefficient and error rates may be high.

This chapter looks at all three approaches in turn.

8.1 ERROR DETECTION

In what follows, we assume that data are transmitted as one or more contiguous sequences of bits, called *frames*. Let us define these probabilities with respect to errors in transmitted frames:

P_b: Probability of a single bit error; also known as the bit error rate (BER)

P_1: Probability that a frame arrives with no bit errors

P_2: Probability that, with an error detection algorithm in use, a frame arrives with one or more undetected errors

P_3: Probability that, with an error detection algorithm in use, a frame arrives with one or more detected bit errors but no undetected bit errors

First consider the case when no means are taken to detect errors. Then the probability of detected errors (P_3) is zero. To express the remaining probabilities, assume the probability that any bit is in error (P_b) is constant and independent for each bit. Then we have

$$P_1 = (1 - P_b)^F$$
$$P_2 = 1 - P_1$$

where F is the number of bits per frame. In words, the probability that a frame arrives with no bit errors decreases when the probability of a single bit error increases, as you would expect. Also, the probability that a frame arrives with no bit errors decreases with increasing frame length; the longer the frame, the more bits it has and the higher the probability that one of these is in error.

Example 8.1 A defined objective for ISDN (Integrated Services Digital Network) connections is that the BER on a 64-kbps channel should be less than 10^{-6} on at least 90% of observed 1-minute intervals. Suppose now that we have the rather modest user requirement that on average one frame with an undetected bit error should occur per day on a continuously used 64-kbps channel, and let us assume a frame length of 1000 bits. The number of frames that can be transmitted in a day comes out to 5.529×10^6, which yields a desired frame error rate of $P_2 = 1/(5.529 \times 10^6) = 0.18 \times 10^{-6}$. But if we assume a value of P_b of 10^{-6}, then $P_1 = (0.999999)^{1000} = 0.999$ and therefore $P_2 = 10^{-3}$, which is about three orders of magnitude too large to meet our requirement.

This is the kind of result that motivates the use of error detection techniques. All of these techniques operate on the following principle (Figure 8.1). For a given frame of bits, the transmitter adds additional bits that constitute an error-detecting code. This code is calculated as a function of the other transmitted bits. Typically, for a data block of k bits, the error detection algorithm yields an error detection code of $n - k$ bits, where $(n - k) < k$. The error detection code, also referred to as the **check bits**, is appended to the data block to produce a frame of n bits, which is then transmitted. For more on check bits see "Design of Parallel Concatenated Convolutional Codes" *IEEE Transactions on Communications–TCOM,* 1995. The receiver separates the incoming frame into the k bits of data and $(n - k)$ bits of the error detection code. The receiver performs the same error detection calculation on the data bits and compares this value with the value of the incoming error detection code. A detected error occurs if and only if there is a mismatch. Thus P_3 is the probability that a frame contains errors and that the error detection scheme will detect that fact. P_2 is known as the *residual error rate* and is the probability that an error will be undetected despite the use of an error detection scheme.

Parity Check

The simplest error detection scheme is to append a parity bit to the end of a block of data. A typical example is character transmission, in which a parity

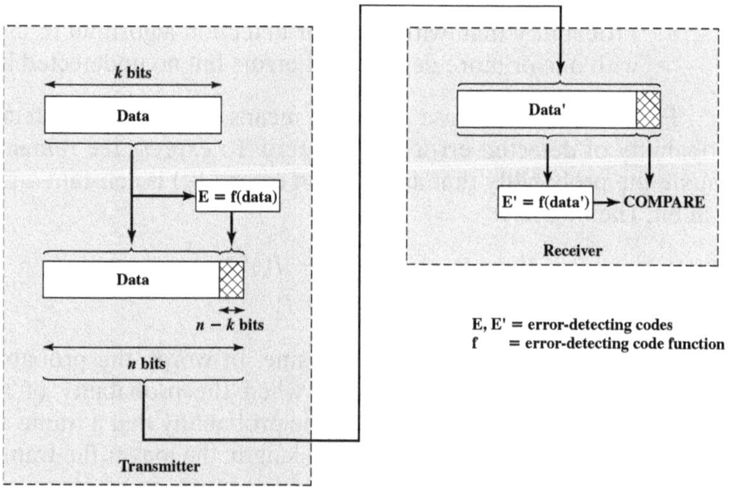

Figure 8.1 Error Detection Process

bit is attached to each 7-bit character. The value of this bit is selected so that the character has an even number of 1s (even parity) or an odd number of 1s (odd parity).

Example 8.2 If the transmitter is transmitting 1110001 and using odd parity, it will append a 1 and transmit 11110001. The receiver examines the received character and, if the total number of 1s is odd, assumes that no error has occurred. If one bit (or any odd number of bits) is erroneously inverted during transmission (for example, 11100001), then the receiver will detect an error.

Note, however, that if two (or any even number) of bits are inverted due to error, an undetected error occurs. Typically, even parity is used for synchronous transmission and odd parity for asynchronous transmission.

The use of the parity bit is not foolproof, as noise impulses are often long enough to destroy more than one bit, particularly at high data rates. This is particularly true in older copper-based lines. Newer fiber optic lines do not suffer from this problem. For more information on noise, see MIMO Detection Schemes with Interference and Noise Estimation Enhancement.

Cyclic Redundancy Check

One of the most common, and one of the most powerful, error-detecting codes is the cyclic redundancy check (CRC), which can be described as follows. Given a k bit block of bits, or message, the transmitter generates an $(n - k)$-bit sequence, known as a frame check sequence (FCS), such that the resulting frame, consisting of n bits, is exactly divisible by some predetermined number. The receiver then divides the incoming frame by that number and, if there is no remainder, assumes there was no error.[1] CRCs are based on the theory of *cyclic error-correcting codes*. The use of *systematic* cyclic codes, which encode messages by adding a fixed-length check value, for the purpose of error detection in communication networks was first proposed by W. Wesley Peterson in 1961.

To clarify this, we present the procedure in three ways: modulo 2 arithmetic, polynomials, and digital logic.

Modulo 2 Arithmetic Modulo 2 arithmetic uses binary addition with no carries, which is just the exclusive-OR (XOR) operation. Binary subtraction with no carries is also interpreted as the XOR operation: For example,

$$\begin{array}{r} 1111 \\ +\ \underline{1010} \\ 0101 \end{array} \qquad \begin{array}{r} 1111 \\ -\ \underline{0101} \\ 1010 \end{array} \qquad \begin{array}{r} 11001 \\ \underline{\times\ 11} \\ 11001 \\ \underline{11001\ \ } \\ 101011 \end{array}$$

[1]This procedure is slightly different from that of Figure 8.1. As shall be seen, the CRC process could be implemented as follows. The receiver could perform a division operation on the incoming k data bits and compare the result to the incoming $(n - k)$ check bits.

Now define

T = n-bit frame to be transmitted

D = k-bit block of data, or message, the first k bits of T

F = $(n - k)$-bit FCS, the last $(n - k)$ bits of T

P = pattern of $n - k + 1$ bits; this is the predetermined divisor

We would like T/P to have no remainder. It should be clear that

$$T = 2^{n-k}D + F$$

That is, by multiplying D by 2^{n-k}, we have in effect shifted it to the left by $n - k$ bits and padded out the result with zeroes. Adding F yields the concatenation of D and F, which is T. We want T to be exactly divisible by P. Suppose that we divide $2^{n-k}D$ by P:

$$\frac{2^{n-k}D}{P} = Q + \frac{R}{P} \tag{8.1}$$

There is a quotient and a remainder. Because division is modulo 2, the remainder is always at least one bit shorter than the divisor. We will use this remainder as our FCS. Then

$$T = 2^{n-k}D + R \tag{8.2}$$

Does this R satisfy our condition that T/P have no remainder? To see that it does, consider

$$\frac{T}{P} = \frac{2^{n-k}D + R}{P} = \frac{2^{n-k}D}{P} + \frac{R}{P}$$

Substituting Equation (8.1), we have

$$\frac{T}{P} = Q + \frac{R}{P} + \frac{R}{P}$$

However, any binary number added to itself modulo 2 yields zero. Thus

$$\frac{T}{P} = Q + \frac{R + R}{P} = Q$$

There is no remainder, and therefore T is exactly divisible by P. Thus, the FCS is easily generated: Simply divide $2^{n-k}D$ by P and use the $(n - k)$-bit remainder as the FCS. On reception, the receiver will divide T by P and will get no remainder if there have been no errors.

Example 8.3

1. Given

Message D = 1010001101 (10 bits)

Pattern P = 110101 (6 bits)

FCS R = to be calculated (5 bits)

Thus, $n = 15$, $k = 10$, and $(n - k) = 5$.

2. The message is multiplied by 2^5, yielding 101000110100000.
3. This product is divided by P:

```
                       1 1 0 1 0 1 0 1 1 0 ← Q
P → 1 1 0 1 0 1 / 1 0 1 0 0 0 1 1 0 1 0 0 0 0 0 ← 2^(n-k)D
                  1 1 0 1 0 1
                    1 1 1 0 1 1
                    1 1 0 1 0 1
                        1 1 1 0 1 0
                        1 1 0 1 0 1
                            1 1 1 1 1 0
                            1 1 0 1 0 1
                                1 0 1 1 0 0
                                1 1 0 1 0 1
                                  1 1 0 0 1 0
                                  1 1 0 1 0 1
                                      0 1 1 1 0 ← R
```

4. The remainder is added to 2^5D to give T = 101000110101110, which is transmitted.
5. If there are no errors, the receiver receives T intact. The received frame is divided by P:

```
                       1 1 0 1 0 1 0 1 1 0 ← Q
P → 1 1 0 1 0 1 / 1 0 1 0 0 0 1 1 0 1 0 1 1 1 0 ← T
                  1 1 0 1 0 1
                    1 1 1 0 1 1
                    1 1 0 1 0 1
                        1 1 1 0 1 0
                        1 1 0 1 0 1
                            1 1 1 1 1 0
                            1 1 0 1 0 1
                                1 0 1 1 1 1
                                1 1 0 1 0 1
                                  1 1 0 1 0 1
                                  1 1 0 1 0 1
                                              0 ← R
```

Because there is no remainder, it is assumed that there have been no errors.

The pattern P is chosen to be one bit longer than the desired FCS, and the exact bit pattern chosen depends on the type of errors expected. At minimum, both the high- and low-order bits of P must be 1.

There is a concise method for specifying the occurrence of one or more errors. An error results in the reversal of a bit. This is equivalent to taking the XOR of the bit and 1 (modulo 2 addition of 1 to the bit): $0 + 1 = 1$; $1 + 1 = 0$. Thus, the errors in an n-bit frame can be represented by an n-bit field with 1s in each error position. The resulting frame T_r can be expressed as

$$T_r = T \oplus E$$

where

T = transmitted frame

E = error pattern with 1s in positions where errors occur

T_r = received frame

If there is an error ($E \neq 0$), the receiver will fail to detect the error if and only if T_r is divisible by P, which is equivalent to E divisible by P. Intuitively, this seems an unlikely occurrence.

Polynomials A second way of viewing the CRC process is to express all values as polynomials in a dummy variable X, with binary coefficients. The coefficients correspond to the bits in the binary number. Arithmetic operations are again modulo 2. The CRC process can now be described as

$$\frac{X^{n-k}D(X)}{P(X)} = Q(X) + \frac{R(X)}{P(X)}$$

$$T(X) = X^{n-k}D(X) + R(X)$$

Compare these equations with Equations (8.1) and (8.2).

> **Example 8.4** Continuing with Example (8.3), for $D = 1010001101$, we have $D(X) = X^9 + X^7 + X^3 + X^2 + 1$, and for $P = 110101$, we have $P(X) = X^5 + X^4 + X^2 + 1$. We should end up with $R = 01110$, which corresponds to $R(X) = X^3 + X^2 + X$. Figure 8.2 shows the polynomial division that corresponds to the binary division in the preceding example.

An error $E(X)$ will only be undetectable if it is divisible by $P(X)$. It can be shown [PETE61, RAMA88] that all of the following errors are not divisible by a suitably chosen $P(X)$ and hence are detectable:

- All single-bit errors, if $P(X)$ has more than one nonzero term
- All double-bit errors, as long as $P(X)$ has a factor with at least three terms
- Any odd number of errors, as long as $P(X)$ contains a factor $(X + 1)$
- Any burst error[2] for which the length of the burst is less than or equal to $n - k$; that is, less than or equal to the length of the FCS
- A fraction of error bursts of length $n - k + 1$; the fraction equals $1 - 2^{-(n-k-1)}$
- A fraction of error bursts of length greater than $n - k + 1$; the fraction equals $1 - 2^{-(n-k)}$

In addition, it can be shown that if all error patterns are considered equally likely, then for a burst error of length $r + 1$, the probability of an undetected error [i.e., $E(X)$ is divisible by $P(X)$] is $1/2^{r-1}$, and for a longer burst, the probability is $1/2^r$, where r is the length of the FCS.

---

[2]A burst error of length B is a contiguous sequence of B bits in which the first and last bits and any number of intermediate bits are received in error.

$$X^9 + X^8 + X^6 + X^4 + X^2 + X \quad \leftarrow Q(X)$$
$$P(X) \rightarrow X^5 + X^4 + X^2 + 1 \,/\, X^{14} \quad X^{12} \quad X^8 + X^7 + \quad X^5 \quad \leftarrow X^5D(X)$$
$$X^{14} + X^{13} + \quad X^{11} + \quad X^9$$
$$X^{13} + X^{12} + X^{11} + \quad X^9 + X^8$$
$$X^{13} + X^{12} + \quad X^{10} + \quad X^8$$
$$X^{11} + X^{10} + X^9 + \quad X^7$$
$$X^{11} + X^{10} + \quad X^8 + \quad X^6$$
$$X^9 + X^8 + X^7 + X^6 + X^5$$
$$X^9 + X^8 + \quad X^6 + \quad X^4$$
$$X^7 + \quad X^5 + X^4$$
$$X^7 \quad X^6 + \quad X^4 + \quad X^2$$
$$X^6 \quad X^5 + \quad X^2$$
$$X^6 + X^5 + \quad X^3 + \quad X$$
$$X^3 + X^2 + X \leftarrow R(X)$$

Figure 8.2 Polynomial Division for Example 8.4

Four versions of $P(X)$ have been widely used:

$$\text{CRC-12} = X^{12} + X^{11} + X^3 + X^2 + X + 1$$
$$\text{CRC-16} = X^{16} + X^{15} + X^2 + 1$$
$$\text{CRC-CCITT} = X^{16} + X^{12} + X^5 + 1$$
$$\text{CRC-32} = X^{32} + X^{26} + X^{23} + X^{22} + X^{16} + X^{12} + X^{11} + X^{10} + X^8 + X^7 + X^5 + X^4 + X^2 + X + 1$$

The CRC-12 system is used for transmission of streams of 6-bit characters and generates a 12-bit FCS. Both CRC-16 and CRC-CCITT are popular for 8-bit characters, in the United States and Europe, respectively, and both result in a 16-bit FCS. This would seem adequate for most applications, although CRC-32 is specified as an option in some point-to-point synchronous transmission standards.

Digital Logic The CRC process can be represented by, and indeed implemented as, a dividing circuit consisting of XOR gates and a shift register. The shift register is a string of 1-bit storage devices. Each device has an output line, which indicates the value currently stored, and an input line. At discrete time instants, known as clock times, the value in the storage device is replaced by the value indicated by its input line. The entire register is clocked simultaneously, causing a 1-bit shift along the entire register.

The circuit is implemented as follows:

1. The register contains $n - k$ bits, equal to the length of the FCS.
2. There are up to $n - k$ XOR gates.
3. The presence or absence of a gate corresponds to the presence or absence of a term in the divisor polynomial, $P(X)$, excluding the terms 1 and X^{n-k}.

Example 8.5 The architecture of this circuit is best explained by first considering an example, which is illustrated in Figure 8.3. In this example, we use:

Data D = 1010001101;	$D(X) = X^9 + X^7 + X^3 + X^2 + 1$
Divisor P = 110101;	$P(X) = X^5 + X^4 + X^2 + 1$

which were used in Examples (8.3) and (8.4).

Figure 8.3a shows the shift register implementation. The process begins with the shift register cleared (all zeros). The message, or dividend, is then entered, one bit at a time, starting with the most significant bit. Figure 8.3b is a table that shows the step-by-step operation as the input is applied one bit at a time. Each row of the table shows the values currently stored in the five shift-register elements. In addition, the row shows the values that appear at the outputs of the three XOR circuits. Finally, the row shows the value of the next input bit, which is available for the operation of the next step.

Note that the XOR operation affects C_4, C_2, and C_0 on the next shift. This is identical to the binary long division process illustrated earlier. The process continues through all the bits of the message. To produce the proper output, two switches are used. The input data bits are fed in with both switches in the A position. As a result, for the first 10 steps, the input bits are fed into the shift register and also used as output bits. After the last data bit is processed, the shift register contains the remainder (FCS) (shown shaded). As soon as the last data bit is provided to the shift register, both switches are set to the B position. This has two effects: (1) all of the XOR gates become simple pass-throughs; no bits are changed, and (2) as the shifting process continues, the 5 CRC bits are output.

At the receiver, the same logic is used. As each bit of M arrives, it is inserted into the shift register. If there have been no errors, the shift register should contain the bit pattern for R at the conclusion of M. $$$ the transmitted bits of R now begin to arrive, and the effect is to zero out the register so that, at the conclusion of reception, the register contains all 0s.

Figure 8.4 indicates the general architecture of the shift register implementation of a CRC for the polynomial $P(X) = \sum_{i=0}^{n-k} A_i X^i$, where $A_0 = A_{n-k} = 1$ and all other A_i equal either 0 or 1.[3]

8.2 BLOCK ERROR CORRECTION CODES

Error detection is a useful technique, found in data link control protocols, such as HDLC, and in transport protocols, such as TCP. However, correction of errors using an error detection code, requires that block of data be retransmitted, using the ARQ discipline explained in Section 8.4. For wireless applications this approach is inadequate for two reasons.

[3]It is common for the CRC register to be shown shifting to the right, which is the reverse of the analogy to binary division. Because binary numbers are usually shown with the most significant bit on the left, a left-shifting register is more appropriate.

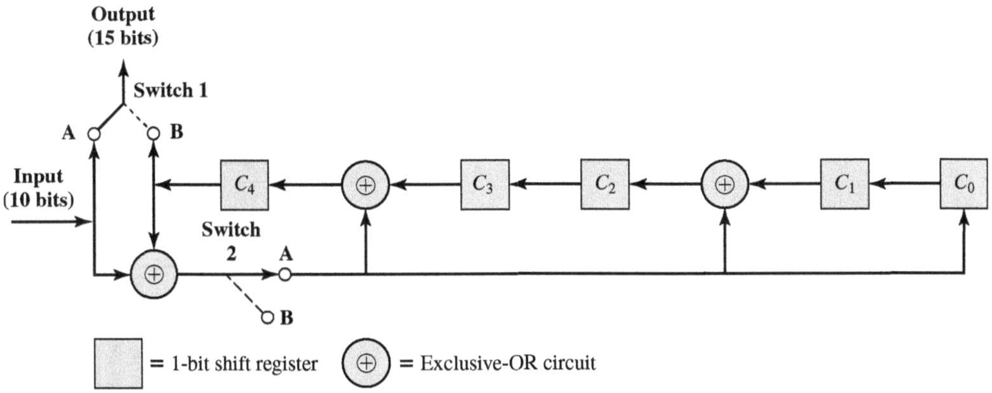

(a) Shift register implementation

	C_4	C_3	C_2	C_1	C_0	$C_4 \oplus C_3 \oplus I$	$C_4 \oplus C_1 \oplus I$	$C_4 \oplus I$	I = input
Initial	0	0	0	0	0	1	1	1	1
Step 1	1	0	1	0	1	1	1	1	0
Step 2	1	1	1	1	1	1	1	0	1
Step 3	1	1	1	1	0	0	0	1	0
Step 4	0	1	0	0	1	1	0	0	0
Step 5	1	0	0	1	0	1	0	1	0
Step 6	1	0	0	0	1	0	0	0	1
Step 7	0	0	0	1	0	1	0	1	1
Step 8	1	0	0	0	1	1	1	1	0
Step 9	1	0	1	1	1	0	1	0	1
Step 10	0	1	1	1	0				

Message to be sent

(b) Example with input of 1010001101

Figure 8.3 Circuit with Shift Registers for Dividing by the Polynomial $X^5 + X^4 + X^2 + 1$

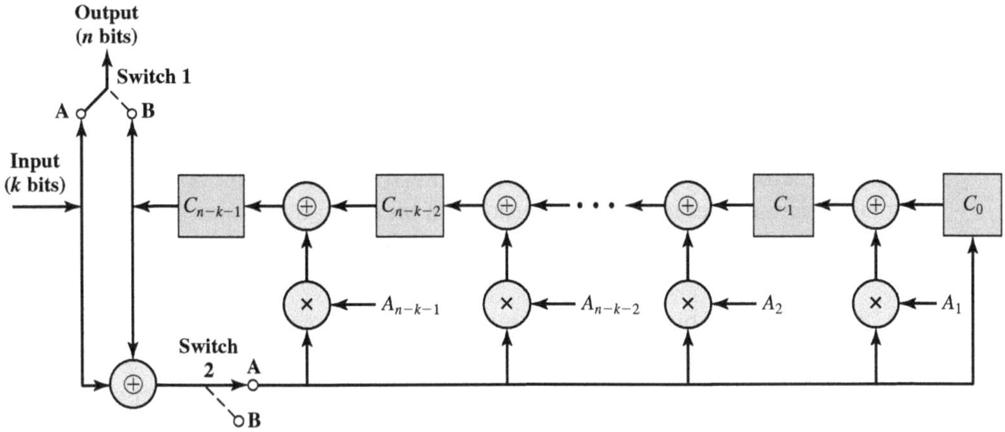

Figure 8.4 General CRC Architecture to Implement Divisor
$1 + A_1X + A_2X^2 + \cdots + A_{n-1}X^{n-k-1} + X^{n-k}$

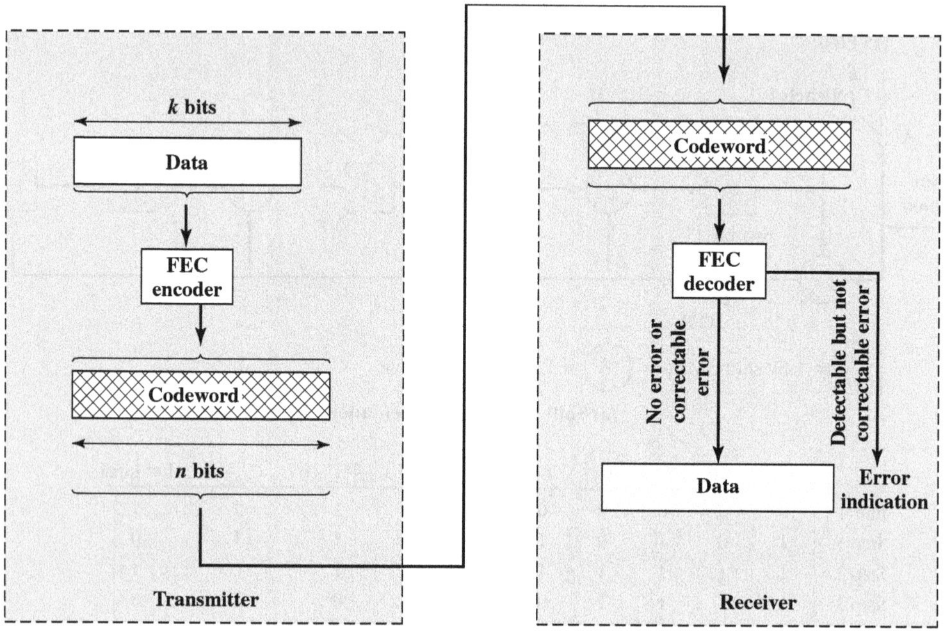

Figure 8.5 Forward Error Correction Process

1. The bit error rate on a wireless link can be quite high, which would result in a large number of retransmissions.
2. In some cases, especially satellite links, the propagation delay is very long compared to the transmission time of a single frame. The result is a very inefficient system. As is discussed in Section 8.4, the common approach to retransmission is to retransmit the frame in error plus all subsequent frames. With a long data link, an error in a single frame necessitates retransmitting many frames.

Instead, it would be desirable to enable the receiver to correct errors in an incoming transmission on the basis of the bits in that transmission. Figure 8.5 shows in general how this is done. On the transmission end, each k-bit block of data is mapped into an n-bit block $(n > k)$ called a **codeword**, using an FEC (forward error correction) encoder. The codeword is then transmitted; in the case of wireless transmission a modulator produces an analog signal for transmission. During transmission, the signal is subject to noise, which may produce bit errors in the signal. At the receiver, the incoming signal is demodulated to produce a bit string that is similar to the original codeword but may contain errors. This block is passed through an FEC decoder, with one of four possible outcomes:

1. If there are no bit errors, the input to the FEC decoder is identical to the original codeword, and the decoder produces the original data block as output.
2. For certain error patterns, it is possible for the decoder to detect and correct those errors. Thus, even though the incoming data block differs from the transmitted codeword, the FEC decoder is able to map this block into the original data block.

3. For certain error patterns, the decoder can detect but not correct the errors. In this case, the decoder simply reports an uncorrectable error.
4. For certain, typically rare, error patterns, the decoder does not detect that any errors have occurred and maps the incoming n-bit data block into a k-bit block that differs from the original k-bit block.

How is it possible for the decoder to correct bit errors? In essence, error correction works by adding redundancy to the transmitted message. The redundancy makes it possible for the receiver to deduce what the original message was, even in the face of a certain level of error rate. In this section we look at a widely used form of error correction code known as a block error correction code. We begin with a discussion of general principles and then look at some specific codes.

Before proceeding, we note that in many cases, the error correction code follows the same general layout as shown for error detection codes in Figure 8.1. That is, the FEC algorithm takes as input a k-bit block and adds $(n - k)$ check bits to that block to produce an n-bit block; all of the bits in the original k-bit block show up in the n-bit block. For some FEC algorithms, such as the convolutional code discussed in Section 8.3, the FEC algorithm maps the k-bit input into an n-bit codeword in such a way that the original k bits do not appear in the codeword.

Block Code Principles

To begin, we define a term that shall be of use to us. The **Hamming distance** $d(\mathbf{v}_1, \mathbf{v}_2)$ between two n-bit binary sequences $\mathbf{v}_1$ and $\mathbf{v}_2$ is the number of bits in which $\mathbf{v}_1$ and $\mathbf{v}_2$ disagree. For example, if

$$\mathbf{v}_1 = 011011, \qquad \mathbf{v}_2 = 110001$$

then

$$d(\mathbf{v}_1, \mathbf{v}_2) = 3$$

Suppose we wish to transmit blocks of data of length k bits. Instead of transmitting each block as k bits, we map each k-bit sequence into a unique n-bit codeword.

Example 8.6 For $k = 2$ and $n = 5$, we can make the following assignment:

Data block	Codeword
00	00000
01	00111
10	11001
11	11110

Now, suppose that a codeword block is received with the bit pattern 00100. This is not a valid codeword and so the receiver has detected an error. Can the error be corrected? We can not be sure which data block was sent because 1, 2, 3, 4, or even all 5 of the bits that were transmitted may have been corrupted by noise. However, notice that it would require only a single bit change to transform the valid codeword 00000 into 00100. It would take two bit changes to transform 00111 to 00100, three bit changes to transform 11110 to 00100, and it would take four bit changes to transform 11001 into 00100. Thus, we can deduce that the most likely codeword that was sent was 00000 and that therefore the desired data block is 00. This is error correction. In terms of Hamming distances, we have

$$d(00000, 00100) = 1; \quad d(00111, 00100) = 2; \quad d(11001, 00100) = 4; \quad d(11110, 00100) = 3$$

So the rule we would like to impose is that if an invalid codeword is received, then the valid codeword that is closest to it (minimum distance) is selected. This will only work if there is a unique valid codeword at a minimum distance from each invalid codeword.

For our example, it is not true that for every invalid codeword there is one and only one valid codeword at a minimum distance. There are $2^5 = 32$ possible codewords of which 4 are valid, leaving 28 invalid codewords. For the invalid codewords, we have the following:

Invalid Codeword	Minimum distance	Valid codeword	Invalid codeword	Minimum distance	Valid codeword
00001	1	00000	10000	1	00000
00010	1	00000	10001	1	11001
00011	1	00111	10010	2	00000 or 11110
00100	1	00000	10011	2	00111 or 11001
00101	1	00111	10100	2	00000 or 11110
00110	1	00111	10101	2	00111 or 11001
01000	1	00000	10110	1	11110
01001	1	11001	10111	1	00111
01010	2	00000 or 11110	11000	1	11001
01011	2	00111 or 11001	11010	1	11110
01100	2	00000 or 11110	11011	1	11001
01101	2	00111 or 11001	11100	1	11110
01110	1	11110	11101	1	11001
01111	1	00111	11111	1	11110

There are eight cases in which an invalid codeword is at a distance 2 from two different valid codewords. Thus, if one such invalid codeword is received, an error in 2 bits could have caused it and the receiver has no way to choose between the two alternatives. An error is detected but cannot be corrected. However, in every case in which a single bit error occurs, the resulting codeword is of distance 1 from only one valid codeword and the decision can be made. This code is therefore capable of correcting all single-bit errors but cannot correct double bit errors. Another way to see this is to look at the pairwise distances between valid codewords:

$$d(00000, 00111) = 3; \quad d(00000, 11001) = 3; \quad d(00000, 11110) = 4;$$
$$d(00111, 11001) = 4; \quad d(00111, 11110) = 3; \quad d(11001, 11110) = 3;$$

The minimum distance between valid codewords is 3. Therefore, a single bit error will result in an invalid codeword that is a distance 1 from the original valid codeword but a distance at least 2 from all other valid codewords. As a result, the code can always correct a single-bit error. Note that the code also will always detect a double-bit error.

The preceding example illustrates the essential properties of a block error-correcting code. An (n, k) block code encodes k data bits into n-bit codewords. Thus the design of a block code is equivalent to the design of a function of the form $\mathbf{v_c} = f(\mathbf{v_d})$, where $\mathbf{v_d}$ is a vector of k data bits and $\mathbf{v_c}$ is a vector of n codeword bits.

With an (n, k) block code, there are 2^k valid codewords out of a total of 2^n possible codewords. The ratio of redundant bits to data bits, $(n - k)/k$, is called the **redundancy** of the code, and the ratio of data bits to total bits, k/n, is called the **code rate**. The code rate is a measure of how much additional bandwidth is required to carry data at the same data rate as without the code. For example, a code rate of 1/2 requires double the bandwidth of an uncoded system to maintain the same data rate. Our example has a code rate of 2/5 and so requires a bandwidth 2.5 times the bandwidth for an uncoded system. For example, if the data rate input to the encoder is 1 Mbps, then the output from the encoder must be at a rate of 2.5 Mbps to keep up.

For a code consisting of the codewords $\mathbf{w}_1, \mathbf{w}_2, \ldots, \mathbf{w}_s$, where $s = 2^k$, the minimum distance $d_{\min}$ of the code is defined as:

$$d_{\min} = \min_{i \neq j}[d(\mathbf{w}_i, \mathbf{w}_j)]$$

It can be shown that the following conditions hold. For a given positive integer t, if a code satisfies $d_{\min} \geq 2t + 1$, then the code can correct all bit errors up to and including errors of t bits. If $d_{\min} \geq 2t$, then all errors $\leq t - 1$ bits can be corrected and errors of t bits can be detected but not, in general, corrected. Conversely, any code for which all errors of magnitude $\leq t$ are corrected must satisfy $d_{\min} \geq 2t + 1$, and any code for which all errors of magnitude $\leq t - 1$ are corrected and all errors of magnitude t are detected must satisfy $d_{\min} \geq 2t$.

Another way of putting the relationship between $d_{\min}$ and t is to say that the maximum number of guaranteed correctable errors per codeword satisfies:

$$t = \left\lfloor \frac{d_{\min} - 1}{2} \right\rfloor$$

where $\lfloor x \rfloor$ means the largest integer not to exceed x (e.g., $\lfloor 6.3 \rfloor = 6$). Furthermore, if we are concerned only with error detection and not error correction, then the number of errors, t, that can be detected satisfies

$$t = d_{\min} - 1$$

To see this, consider that if $d_{\min}$ errors occur, this could change one valid codeword into another. Any number of errors less than $d_{\min}$ cannot result in another valid codeword.

The design of a block code involves a number of considerations.

1. For given values of n and k, we would like the largest possible value of $d_{\min}$.
2. The code should be relatively easy to encode and decode, requiring minimal memory and processing time.
3. We would like the number of extra bits, $(n - k)$, to be small, to reduce bandwidth.
4. We would like the number of extra bits, $(n - k)$, to be large, to reduce error rate.

Clearly, the last two objectives are in conflict, and tradeoffs must be made.

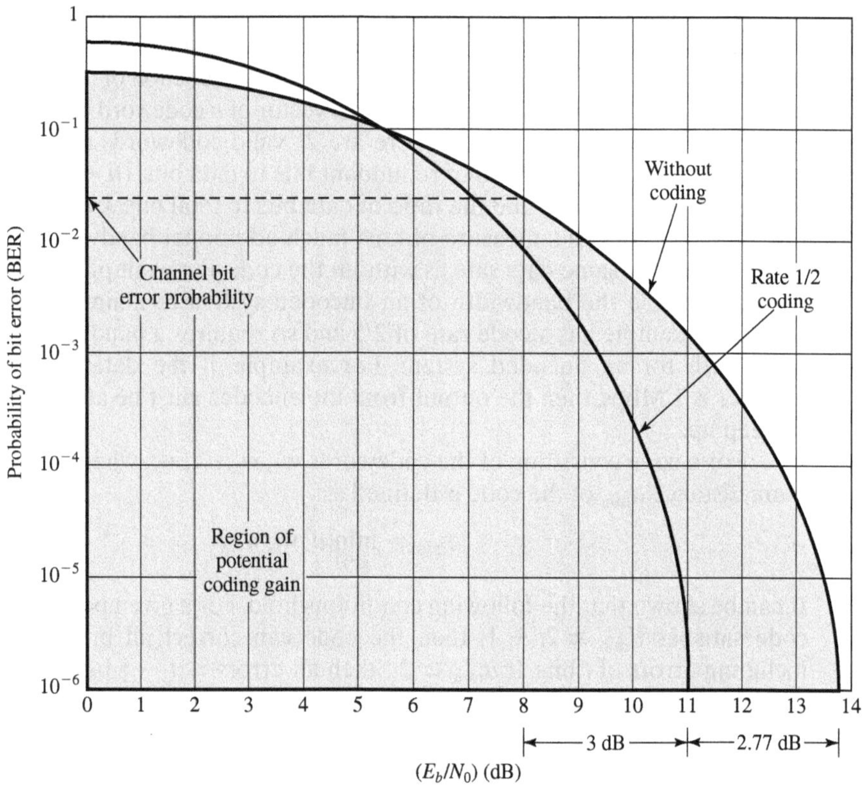

Figure 8.6 How Coding Improves System Performance

Before looking at specific codes, it will be useful to examine Figure 8.6, based on one in [LEBO98]. The literature on error-correcting codes frequently includes graphs of this sort to demonstrate the effectiveness of various encoding schemes. Recall from Chapter 6 that coding can be used to reduce the required E_b/N_0 value to achieve a given bit error rate.[4] The coding discussed in Chapter 6 has to do with the definition of signal elements to represent bits. The coding discussed in this chapter also has an effect on E_b/N_0. In Figure 8.6, the curve on the right is for an uncoded modulation system; the shaded region represents the area in which potential improvement can be achieved. In this region, a smaller BER (bit error rate) is achieved for a given E_b/N_0, and conversely, for a given BER, a smaller E_b/N_0 is required. The other curve is a typical result of a code rate of one-half (equal number of data and check bits). Note that at an error rate of 10^{-5}, the use of coding allows a reduction in E_b/N_0 of 2.77 dB. This reduction is referred to as the **coding gain**, which is defined as the reduction, in decibels, in the required E_b/N_0 to achieve a specified BER of an error-correcting coded system compared to an uncoded system using the same modulation.

[4] E_b/N_0 is the ratio of signal energy per bit to noise power density per Hertz; it is defined and discussed in Chapter 5.

It is important to realize that the BER for the second rate 1/2 curve refers to the rate of uncorrected errors and that the E_b value refers to the energy per data bit. Because the rate is 1/2, there are two bits on the channel for each data bit, and the energy per coded bit is half that of the energy per data bit, or a reduction of 3 dB. If we look at the energy per coded bit for this system, then we see that the channel bit error rate is about 2.4×10^{-2}, or 0.024.

Finally, note that below a certain threshold of E_b/N_0, the coding scheme actually degrades performance. In our example of Figure 8.6, the threshold occurs at about 5.4 dB. Below the threshold, the extra check bits add overhead to the system that reduces the energy per data bit causing increased errors. Above the threshold, the error-correcting power of the code more than compensates for the reduced E_b, resulting in a coding gain.

We now turn to a look at some specific block error correction codes.

Hamming Code

Hamming codes are a family of (n, k) block error-correcting codes that have the following parameters:

Block length:	$n = 2^m - 1$
Number of data bits:	$k = 2^m - m - 1$
Number of check bits:	$n - k = m$
Minimum distance:	$d_{\min} = 3$

where $m \geq 3$. Hamming codes are straightforward and easy to analyze but are rarely used. We begin with these codes because they illustrate some of the fundamental principles of block codes.

Hamming codes are designed to correct single bit errors. To start, let us determine how long the code must be. The Hamming code process has the same structure as the error detection logic shown in Figure 8.1; that is, the encoding process preserves the k data bits and adds $(n - k)$ check bits. For decoding, the comparison logic receives as input two $(n - k)$-bit values, one from the incoming codeword and one from a calculation performed on the incoming data bits. A bit-by-bit comparison is done by taking the XOR of the two inputs. The result is called the **syndrome word**. Thus, each bit of the syndrome is 0 or 1 according to whether there is or is not a match in that bit position for the two inputs.

The syndrome word is therefore $(n - k)$ bits wide and has a range between 0 and $2^{(n-k)} - 1$. The value 0 indicates that no error was detected, leaving $2^{(n-k)} - 1$ values to indicate, if there is an error, which bit was in error. Now, because an error could occur on any of the k data bits or $(n - k)$ check bits, we must have

$$2^{(n-k)} - 1 \geq k + (n - k) = n$$

This equation gives the number of bits needed to correct a single bit error in a word containing k data bits. Table 8.1 lists the number of check bits required for various data lengths.

Table 8.1 Hamming Code Requirements

	Single-Error Correction		Single-Error Correction/ Double-Error Detection	
Data Bits	**Check Bits**	**% Increase**	**Check Bits**	**% Increase**
8	4	50	5	62.5
16	5	31.25	6	37.5
32	6	18.75	7	21.875
64	7	10.94	8	12.5
128	8	6.25	9	7.03
256	9	3.52	10	3.91

For convenience, we would like to generate a syndrome with the following characteristics:

- If the syndrome contains all 0s, no error has been detected.
- If the syndrome contains one and only one bit set to 1, then an error has occurred in one of the check bits. No correction is needed.
- If the syndrome contains more than one bit set to 1, then the numerical value of the syndrome indicates the position of the data bit in error. This data bit is inverted for correction.

To achieve these characteristics, the data and check bits are arranged into an n-bit block as follows. Counting from the least-significant (rightmost) position, the Hamming check bits are inserted at positions that are a power of 2 [i.e., positions $1, 2, 4, \ldots, 2^{(n-k)}$]. The remaining bits are data bits. To calculate the check bits, each data position which has a value 1 is represented by a binary value equal to its position; thus if the 9th bit is 1, the corresponding value is 1001. All of the position values are then XORed together to produce the bits of the Hamming code. At the receiver all bit position values where there is 1 are XORed. In this case, the XOR includes both data bits and check bits. Because the check bits occur at bit positions that are a power of 2, we can simply XOR all data bit positions with a value of 1, plus the Hamming code formed by the check bits. If the result of the XOR is zero, no error is detected. If the result is nonzero, then the result is the syndrome, and its value equals the bit position that is in error.

Example 8.7 An (8, 4) Hamming code has the assignment shown in Table 8.2. The 8-bit data block is 00111001. Four of the data bits have a value 1 (shaded in the table), and their bit position values are XORed to produce the Hamming code 0111, which forms the four check digits. The entire block that is transmitted is 001101001111. Suppose now that data bit 3, in bit position 6, sustains an error and is changed from 0 to 1. Then the received block is 001101101111. The received Hamming code is still 0111. The receiver performs an XOR of the Hamming code and all of the bit position values for nonzero data bits, with a result of 0110. The nonzero result detects an error and indicates that the error is in bit position 6.

Table 8.2 Layout of Data Bits and Check Bits

(a) Transmitted block

Bit Position	12	11	10	9	8	7	6	5	4	3	2	1
Position Number	1100	1011	1010	1001	1000	0111	0110	0101	0100	0011	0010	0001
Data Bit	D8	D7	D6	D5		D4	D3	D2		D1		
Check Bit					C8				C4		C2	C1
Transmitted Block	0	0	1	1	0	1	0	0	1	1	1	1
Codes			1010	1001		0111				0011		

(b) Check bit calculation prior to transmission

Position	Code
10	1010
9	1001
7	0111
3	0011
XOR = C8 C4 C2 C1	0111

(c) Received block

Bit Position	12	11	10	9	8	7	6	5	4	3	2	1
Position Number	1100	1011	1010	1001	1000	0111	0110	0101	0100	0011	0010	0001
Data Bit	D8	D7	D6	D5		D4	D3	D2		D1		
Check Bit					C8				C4		C2	C1
Received Block	0	0	1	1	0	1	1	0	1	1	1	1
Codes			1010	1001		0111	0110			0011		

(d) Check bit calculation after reception

Position	Code
Hamming	0111
10	1010
9	1001
7	0111
6	0110
3	0011
XOR = syndrome	0110

The code just described is known as a *single-error-correcting* (SEC) code. A variation is a single-error-correcting, double-error-detecting (SEC-DED) code. As Table 8.1 shows, such codes require one additional bit compared with SEC codes. The extra bit is a parity bit over the entire code block.

Cyclic Codes

Most of the error-correcting block codes that are in use are in a category called cyclic codes. For such codes, if the n-bit sequence $\mathbf{c} = (c_0, c_1, \ldots, c_{n-1})$ is a valid codeword, then $(c_{n-1}, c_0, c_1, \ldots, c_{n-2})$, which is formed by cyclically shifting $\mathbf{c}$ one place to the right, is also a valid codeword. This class of codes can be easily encoded and decoded using linear feedback shift registers (LFSRs). Examples of cyclic codes include the Bose-Chaudhuri-Hocquenhem (BCH) and Reed-Solomon codes.

The LFSR implementation of a cyclic error-correcting encoder is the same as that of the CRC error-detecting code, illustrated in Figure 8.4. The key difference is that the CRC code takes an input of arbitrary length and produces a fixed-length CRC check code, while a cyclic error-correcting code takes a fixed-length input (k bits) and produces a fixed-length check code ($n - k$ bits).

Figure 8.7 shows the LFSR implementation of the decoder for a cyclic block code. Compare this to the encoder logic in Figure 8.4. Note that for the encoder, the k data bits are treated as input to produce an $(n - k)$ code of check bits in the shift register. For the decoder, the input is the received bit stream of n bits, consisting of k data bits followed by $(n - k)$ check bits. If there have been no errors, after the first k steps, the shift register contains the pattern of check bits that were transmitted. After the remaining $(n - k)$ steps, the shift register contains a syndrome code.

For decoding of a cyclic code, the following procedure is used:

1. Process received bits to compute the syndrome code in exactly the same fashion as the encoder processes the data bits to produce the check code.
2. If the syndrome bits are all zero, no error has been detected.
3. If the syndrome is nonzero, perform additional processing on the syndrome for error correction.

To understand the significance of the syndrome, let us examine the block code using polynomials. As in the case of the CRC, a particular cyclic code can be

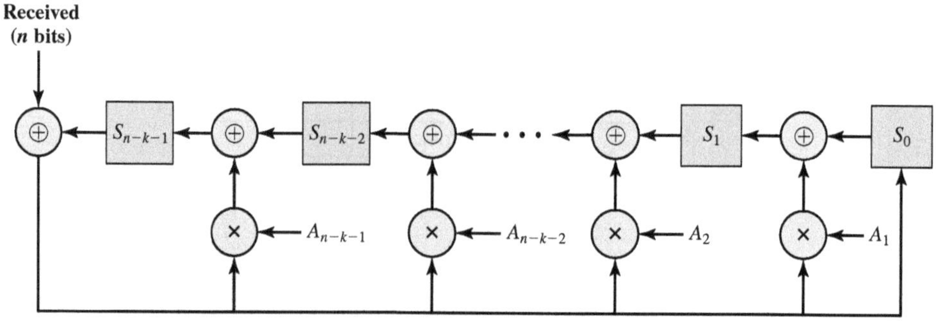

Figure 8.7 Block Syndrome Generator for Divisor $1 + A_1X + A_2X^2 + \cdots + A_{n-1}X^{n-k-1} + X^{n-k}$

represented by a polynomial divisor, called the generator polynomial. For an (n, k) code, the generator polynomial has the form

$$P(X) = 1 + \sum_{i=1}^{n-k-1} A_i X^i + X^{n-k}$$

where each coefficient A_i is either 0 or 1, corresponding to one bit position in the divisor. For example, for $P = 11001$, we have $P(X) = X^4 + X^3 + 1$. Similarly, the set of data bits is represented by the polynomial $D(X)$ and the check code by the polynomial $C(X)$. Recall from the CRC discussion that a check code is determined in the following way:

$$\frac{X^{n-k}D(X)}{P(X)} = Q(X) + \frac{C(X)}{P(X)}$$

That is, the data block $D(X)$ is shifted to the left by $(n - k)$ bits and divided by $P(X)$. This produces a quotient $Q(X)$ and a remainder $C(X)$ of length $(n - k)$ bits. The transmitted block is formed by concatenating $D(X)$ and $C(X)$:

$$T(X) = X^{n-k}D(X) + C(X) \tag{8.3}$$

If there is no error on reception, $T(X)$ will be exactly divisible by $P(X)$ with no remainder. This is easily demonstrated:

$$\begin{aligned} \frac{T(X)}{P(X)} &= \frac{X^{n-k}D(X)}{P(X)} + \frac{C(X)}{P(X)} \\ &= \left(Q(X) + \frac{C(X)}{P(X)}\right) + \frac{C(X)}{P(X)} = Q(X) \end{aligned} \tag{8.4}$$

The last equality is valid because of the rules of modulo 2 arithmetic ($a + a = 0$, whether $a = 1$ or $a = 0$). Thus, if there are no errors, the division of $T(X)$ by $P(X)$ produces no remainder.

If one or more bit errors occur, then the received block $Z(X)$ will be of the form

$$Z(X) = T(X) + E(X)$$

where $E(X)$ is an n-bit error polynomial with a value of 1 in each bit position that is in error in $Z(X)$. If we pass $Z(X)$ through the LFSR of Figure 8.7, we are performing the division $Z(X)/P(X)$, which produces the $(n - k)$ bit syndrome $S(X)$:

$$\frac{Z(X)}{P(X)} = B(X) + \frac{S(X)}{P(X)} \tag{8.5}$$

where $B(X)$ is the quotient and $S(X)$ is the remainder. Thus, $S(X)$ is a function of $Z(X)$. But how does this help us perform error correction? To see this, let us expand Equation (8.5).

$$\frac{Z(X)}{P(X)} = B(X) + \frac{S(X)}{P(X)}$$

$$\frac{T(X) + E(X)}{P(X)} = B(X) + \frac{S(X)}{P(X)}$$

$$Q(X) + \frac{E(X)}{P(X)} = B(X) + \frac{S(X)}{P(X)} \tag{8.6}$$

$$\frac{E(X)}{P(X)} = [Q(X) + B(X)] + \frac{S(X)}{P(X)}$$

What we see is that $E(X)/P(X)$ produces the same remainder as $Z(X)/P(X)$. Therefore, regardless of the initial pattern of bits (transmitted value of $T(X)$), the syndrome value $S(X)$ depends only on the error bits. If we can recover the error bits, $E(X)$, from $S(X)$, then we can correct the errors in $Z(X)$ by simple addition:

$$Z(X) + E(X) = T(X) + E(X) + E(X) = T(X)$$

Because $S(X)$ depends only on $E(X)$, we can easily determine the power of a cyclic block code. The syndrome pattern consists of $n - k$ bits and therefore takes on 2^{n-k} possible values. A value of all zeros indicates no errors. Therefore, a total of $2^{n-k} - 1$ different error patterns can be corrected. To be able to correct all possible single bit errors with an (n, k) code, we must have $n \le (2^{n-k} - 1)$. To be able to correct all single and double bit errors, the relationship is $\left(n + \frac{n(n-1)}{2}\right) \le (2^{n-k} - 1)$.

The way in which $E(X)$ is recovered from $S(X)$ may depend on the specific code involved. The most straightforward approach is to develop a table of all possible values of $E(X)$ with the corresponding value of $S(X)$ of each. Then a simple table lookup is required.

Example 8.8[5] Consider a (7, 4) code with the generator polynomial $P(X) = X^3 + X^2 + 1$. We have $7 = 2^3 - 1$, so this code is capable of correcting all single-bit errors. Table 8.3a lists all of the valid codewords; note that d_{min} is 3, confirming that this is a single-error-correcting code. For example, for the data block 1010, we have $D(X) = X^3 + X$ and $X^{n-k}D(X) = X^6 + X^4$. Dividing as in Equation (8.4):

$$\begin{array}{rl}
 & X^3 + X^2 + 1 \quad \leftarrow Q(X) \\
P(X) \rightarrow X^3 + X^2 + 1 \,\big/ & X^6 \qquad\quad X^4 \quad \leftarrow 2^3D(X) \\
 & X^6 + X^5 + \qquad X^3 \\
 & \quad X^5 + X^4 + X^3 \\
 & \quad X^5 + X^4 + \qquad X^2 \\
 & \qquad\quad X^3 + X^2 \\
 & \qquad\quad X^3 + X^2 + \quad 1 \\
 & \qquad\qquad\qquad 1 \leftarrow C(X)
\end{array}$$

Then, using Equation (8.3), we have $T(X) = X^6 + X^4 + 1$, which is the code word 1010001. For error correction, we need to construct the syndrome table shown in Table **8.3b**. For example, for an error pattern of 1000000, $E(X) = X^6$. Using the last line of Equation **(8.6)**, we calculate:

[5]This example is taken from [LATH98].

$$
\begin{array}{rll}
 & X^3 + X^2 + X & \leftarrow Q(X) + B(X) \\
P(X) \rightarrow X^3 + X^2 + 1 \,/ & X^6 & \leftarrow E(X) \\
 & \underline{X^6 + X^5 + \qquad X^3} & \\
 & \quad X^5 + \qquad X^3 & \\
 & \quad \underline{X^5 + X^4 + \qquad X^2} & \\
 & \qquad X^4 + X^3 + X^2 & \\
 & \qquad \underline{X^4 + X^3 + \qquad X} & \\
 & \qquad\qquad X^2 + X & \leftarrow S(X)
\end{array}
$$

Therefore, S = 110. The remaining entries in Table 8.3b are calculated similarly. Now suppose the received block is 1101101, or $Z(X) = X^6 + X^5 + X^3 + X^2 + 1$. Using Equation (8.5):

$$
\begin{array}{rll}
 & X^3 & \leftarrow B(X) \\
P(X) \rightarrow X^3 + X^2 + 1 \,/ & X^6 + X^5 + \qquad X^3 + X^2 + 1 & \leftarrow Z(X) \\
 & \underline{X^6 + X^5 + \qquad X^3 \qquad\qquad} & \\
 & \qquad\qquad\qquad X^2 + 1 & \leftarrow S(X)
\end{array}
$$

Thus $S = 101$. Using Table 8.3b, this yields E = 0001000. Then,

$$T = 1101101 \mid 0001000 = 1100101$$

Then, from Table 8.3a, the transmitted data block is 1100.

Table 8.3 A Single-Error-Correcting (7, 4) Cyclic Code

(a) Table of valid codewords

Data Block	Codeword
0000	0000000
0001	0001101
0010	0010111
0011	0011010
0100	0100011
0101	0101110
0110	0110100
0111	0111001
1000	1000110
1001	1001011
1010	1010001
1011	1011100
1100	1100101
1101	1101000
1110	1110010
1111	1111111

(b) Table of syndromes for single-bit errors

Error pattern E	Syndrome S
0000001	001
0000010	010
0000100	100
0001000	101
0010000	111
0100000	011
1000000	110

Table 8.4 BCH Code Parameters

n	*k*	*t*	*n*	*k*	*t*	*n*	*k*	*t*	*n*	*k*	*t*	*n*	*k*	*t*
7	4	1	63	30	6	127	64	10	255	207	6	255	99	23
15	11	1		24	7		57	11		199	7		91	25
	7	2		18	10		50	13		191	8		87	26
	5	3		16	11		43	14		187	9		79	27
31	26	1		10	13		36	15		179	10		71	29
	21	2		7	15		29	21		171	11		63	30
	16	3	127	120	1		22	23		163	12		55	31
	11	5		113	2		15	27		155	13		47	42
	6	7		106	3		8	31		147	14		45	43
63	57	1		99	4	255	247	1		139	15		37	45
	51	2		92	5		239	2		131	18		29	47
	45	3		85	6		231	3		123	19		21	55
	39	4		78	7		223	4		115	21		13	59
	36	5		71	9		215	5		107	22		9	63

BCH Codes

BCH codes are among the most powerful cyclic block codes and are widely used in wireless applications. For any positive pair of integers m and t, there is a binary (n, k) BCH code with the following parameters:

Block length:	$n = 2^m - 1$
Number of check bits:	$n - k \leq mt$
Minimum distance:	$d_{\min} \geq 2t + 1$

This code can correct all combinations of t or fewer errors. The generator polynomial for this code can be constructed from the factors of $(X^{2^m-1} + 1)$. The BCH codes provide flexibility in the choice of parameters (block length, code rate). Table 8.4 lists the BCH parameters for code lengths up to $2^8 - 1$. Table 8.5 lists some of the BCH generator polynomials.

Table 8.5 BCH Polynomial Generators

n	*k*	*t*	*P(X)*
7	4	1	$X^3 + X + 1$
15	11	1	$X^4 + X + 1$
15	7	2	$X^8 + X^7 + X^6 + X^4 + 1$
15	5	3	$X^{10} + X^8 + X^5 + X^4 + X^2 + X + 1$
31	26	1	$X^5 + X^2 + 1$
31	21	2	$X^{10} + X^9 + X^8 + X^6 + X^5 + X^3 + 1$

A number of techniques have been designed for BCH decoding that require less memory than a simple table lookup. One of the simplest was proposed by Berlekamp [BERL80]. The central idea is to compute an error-locator polynomial and solve for its roots. The complexity of the algorithm increases only as the square of the number of errors to be corrected.

Reed-Solomon Codes

Reed-Solomon (RS) codes are a widely used subclass of nonbinary BCH codes. With RS codes, data are processed in chunks of m bits, called symbols. An (n, k) RS code has the following parameters:

Symbol length:	m bits per symbol
Block length:	$n = 2^m - 1$ symbols $= m(2^m - 1)$ bits
Data length:	k symbols
Size of check code:	$n - k = 2t$ symbols $= m(2t)$ bits
Minimum distance:	$d_{\min} = 2t + 1$ symbols

Thus, the encoding algorithm expands a block of k symbols to n symbols by adding $n - k$ redundant check symbols. Typically, m is a power of 2; a popular value of m is 8.

Example 8.9 Let $t = 1$ and $m = 2$. Denoting the symbols as 0, 1, 2, 3 we can write their binary equivalents as 0 = 00; 1 = 01; 2 = 10; 3 = 11. The code has the following parameters.

$$n = 2^2 - 1 = 3 \text{ symbols} = 6 \text{ bits}$$
$$(n - k) = 2 \text{ symbols} = 4 \text{ bits}$$

This code can correct any burst error that spans a symbol of 2 bits.

RS codes are well suited for burst error correction. They make highly efficient use of redundancy, and block lengths and symbol sizes can be easily adjusted to accommodate a wide range of message sizes. In addition, efficient coding techniques are available for RS codes.

Block Interleaving

Block interleaving is a common technique used with block codes in wireless systems; we saw an example of this in Figure 5.16. The advantage of interleaving is that a burst error that affects a sequence of bits is spread out over a number of separate blocks at the receiver so that error correction is possible. Interleaving is accomplished by reading and writing data from memory in different orders. Figure 8.8 illustrates a simple and common interleaving technique. In this case, the data to be transmitted are stored in a rectangular array in which each row consists of n bits, equal to the block size. Data are then read out one column at a time. The result is that the k data bits and their corresponding $(n - k)$ check bits, which form a single n-bit block, are spread out and interspersed with bits from other blocks. At the receiver, the data are deinterleaved to recover the original order. If, during transmission, a burst of noise affects a consecutive sequence of bits, those bits belong to

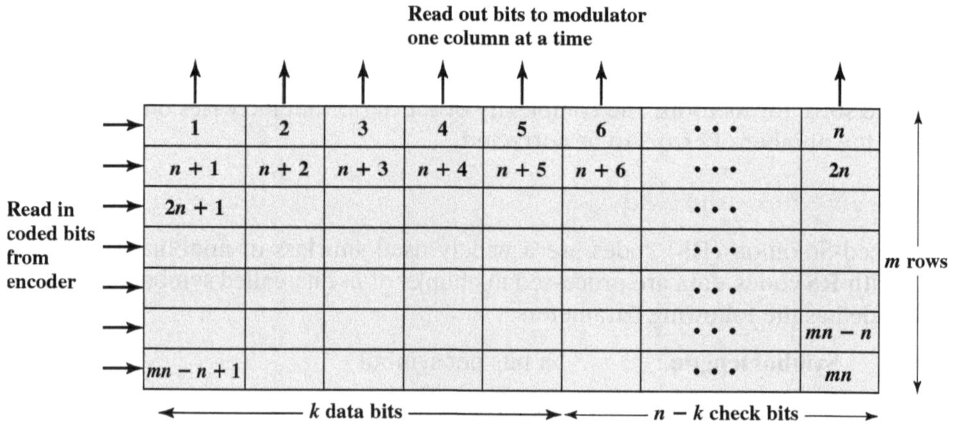

Note: The numbers in the matrix indicate the order in which bits are read in.
Interleaver output sequence: $1, n + 1, 2n + 1, \ldots$

Figure 8.8 Block Interleaving

different blocks and hence only a fraction of the bits in error need to be corrected by any one set of check bits. Specifically, a burst of length $l = mb$ is broken up into m bursts of length b. Some thought should convince you of the following assertion: Suppose we have an (n, k) code that can correct all combinations of t or fewer errors, where $t = \lfloor (n - k)/2 \rfloor$. Then if we use an interleaver of degree m, then the result is an (mn, mk) code that can correct burst errors of up to mt bits.

8.3 CONVOLUTIONAL CODES

Block codes are one of the two widely used categories of error correcting codes for wireless transmission; the other is convolutional codes. An (n, k) block code process data in blocks of k bits at a time, producing a block of n bits $(n > k)$ as output for every block of k bits as input. If data are transmitted and received in a more or less continuous stream, a block code, particularly one with a large value of n, may not be as convenient as a code that generates redundant bits continuously so that error checking and correcting are carried out continuously. This is the function of convolution codes.

A convolutional code is defined by three parameters: n, k, and K. An (n, k, K) code processes input data k bits at a time and produces an output of n bits for each incoming k bits. So far this is the same as the block code. In the case of a convolutional code, n and k are generally quite small numbers. The difference is that convolutional codes have memory, which is characterized by the *constraint factor* K. In essence, the current n-bit output of an (n, k, K) code depends not only on the value of the current block of k input bits but also on the previous $K - 1$ blocks of k input bits. Hence, the current output of n bits is a function of the last $K \times k$ input bits.

Convolutional codes are best understood by looking at a specific example. We use the example shown in Figure 8.9. There are two alternative representations of

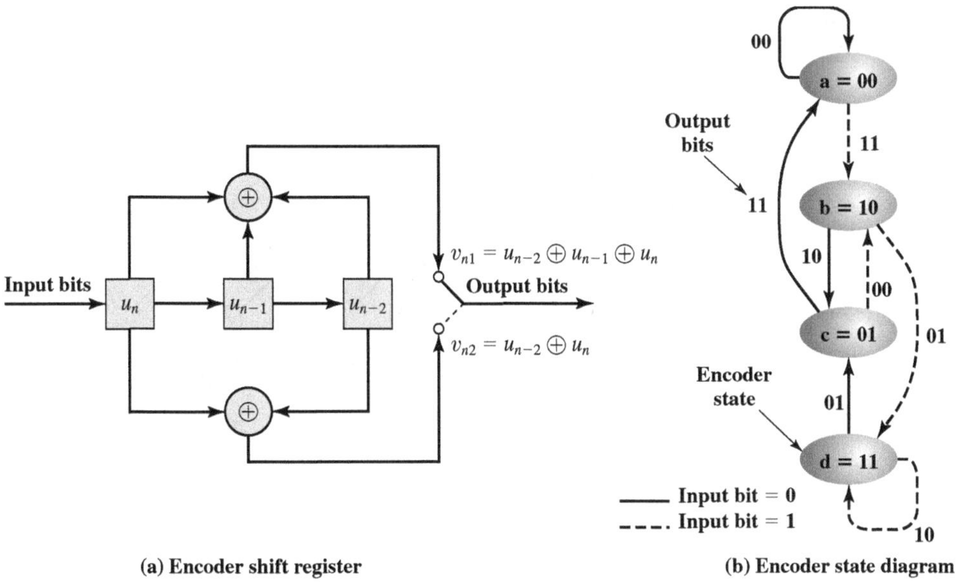

Figure 8.9 Convolutional Encoder with $(n, k, K) = (2, 1, 3)$

the code shown in the figure. Figure 8.9a is a shift register, which is most convenient for describing and implementing the encoding process. Figure 8.9b is an equivalent representation that is useful in discussing the decoding process.

For an *(n, k, K)* code, the shift register contains the most recent $K \times k$ input bits; the register is initialized to all zeros.[6] The encoder produces *n* output bits, after which the oldest *k* bits from the register are discarded and *k* new bits are shifted in. Thus, although the output of *n* bits depends on $K \times k$ input bits, the rate of encoding is *n* output bits per *k* input bits. As in a block code, the code rate is therefore *k/n*. The most commonly used binary encoders have $k = 1$ and hence a shift register length of *K*. Our example is of a (2, 1, 3) code (Figure 8.9a). In this example, the encoder converts an input bit u_n into two output bits v_{n1} and v_{n2}, using the three most recent bits. The first output bit produced is from the upper logic circuit $(v_{n1} = u_n \oplus u_{n-1} \oplus u_{n-2})$, and the second output bit from the lower logic circuit $(v_{n2} = u_n \oplus u_{n-2})$.

For any given input of *k* bits, there are $2^{k(K-1)}$ different functions that map the *k* input bits into *n* output bits. Which function is used depends on the history of the last $(K - 1)$ input blocks of *k* bits each. We can therefore represent a convolutional code using a finite-state machine. The machine has $2^{k(K-1)}$ states, and the transition from one state to another is determined by the most recent *k* bits of inputs and produces *n* output bits. The initial state of the machine corresponds to the all-zeros state. For our example (Figure 8.9b) there are 4 states, one for each possible pair of values for the last two bits. The next input bit causes a transition and produces an output of two bits. For example, if the last two bits were 10 $(u_{n-1} = 1, u_{n-2} = 0)$ and

[6]In some of the literature, the shift register is shown with one less storage cell and with the input bits feeding the XOR circuits as well as a storage cell; the depictions are equivalent.

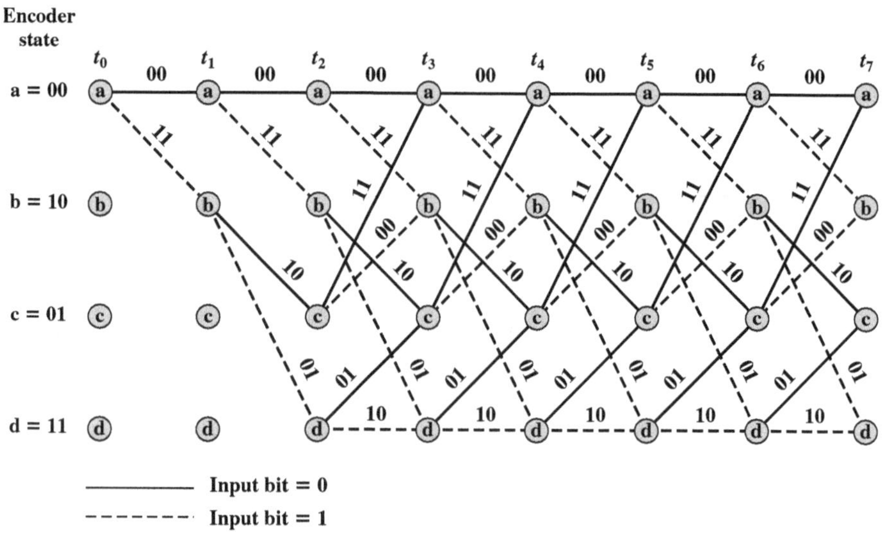

Figure 8.10 Trellis Diagram for Encoder of Figure 8.9

the next bit is 1 ($u_n = 1$), then the current state is state b (10) and the next state is d (11). The output is

$$v_{n1} = u_{n-2} \oplus u_{n-1} \oplus u_n = 0 \oplus 1 \oplus 1 = 0$$
$$v_{n2} = 0 \oplus 1 = 1$$

Decoding

To understand the decoding process, it simplifies matters to expand the state diagram to show the time sequence of the encoder. If the state diagram is laid out vertically, as shown in Figure 8.9b, then the expanded diagram, called a **trellis**, is constructed by reproducing the states horizontally and showing the state transitions going from left to right corresponding to time, or data input (Figure 8.10). If the constraint length K is large, then the trellis diagram becomes unwieldy. In that case, 2^{K-2} simplified trellis fragments can be used to depict the transitions. Figure 8.11 demonstrates this for a (2,1,7) code. Each of the states of the encoder is shown, along with the branch definition.

Any valid output is defined by a path through the trellis. In our example, the path a-b-c-b-d-c-a-a produces the output 11 10 00 01 01 11 00 and was generated by the input 1011000. If an invalid path occurs, such as a-c, then the decoder attempts error correction. In essence, the decoder must determine what data input was most likely to have produced the invalid output.

A number of error correction algorithms have been developed for convolutional codes. Perhaps the most important is the Viterbi code. In essence, the Viterbi technique compares the received sequence with all possible transmitted sequences. The algorithm chooses a path through the trellis whose coded sequence differs from the received sequence in the fewest number of places. Once a valid path is selected as the correct path, the decoder can recover the input data bits from the output code bits.

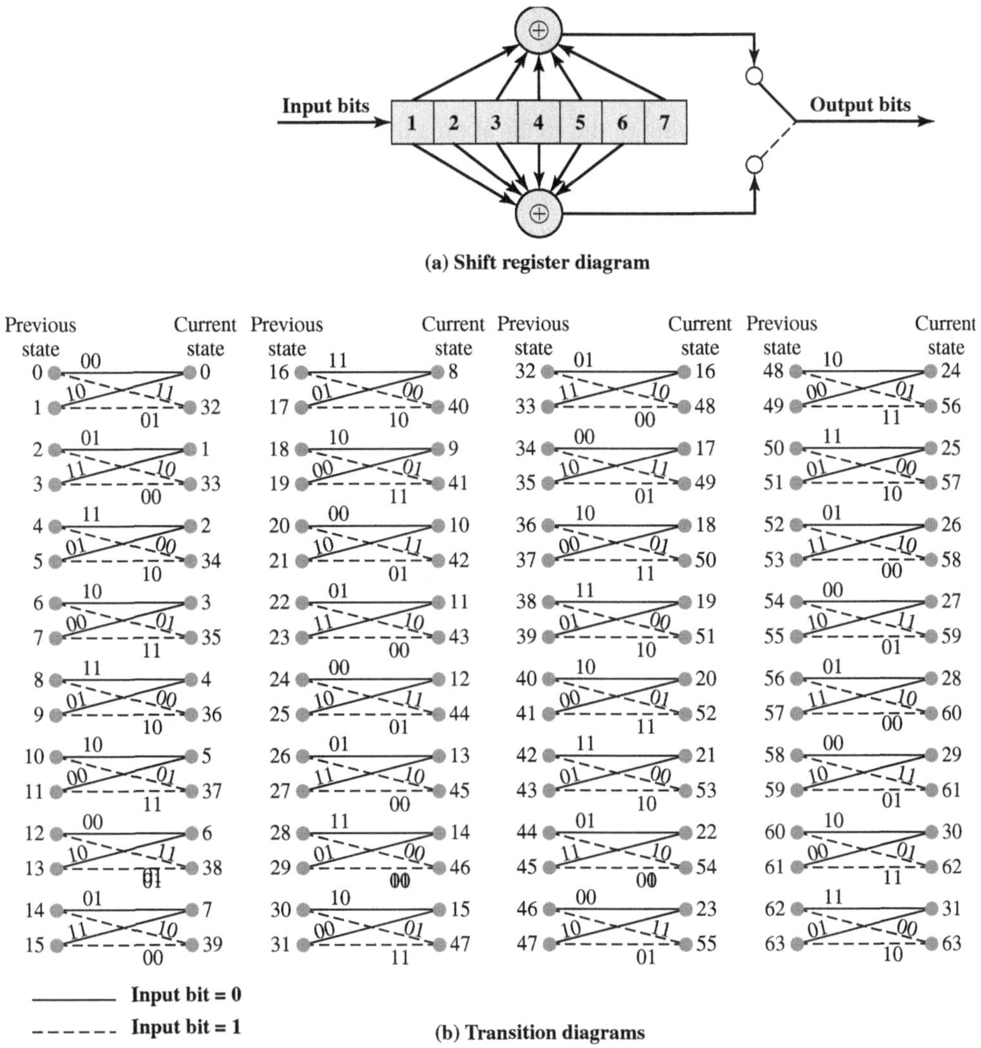

(a) Shift register diagram

(b) Transition diagrams

Figure 8.11 Trellis Diagrams for Encoder with $(n, k, K) = (2, 1, 7)$ [JAIN90]

There are several variations on the Viterbi algorithm, depending on which metric is used to measure differences between received sequences and valid sequences. To give an idea of the operation of the algorithm, we use the common metric of Hamming distance. We represent a received coded sequence as the word $\mathbf{w} = w_0 w_1 w_2 \ldots$, and attempt to find the most likely valid path through the trellis. At each time i and for each state we list the *active path* (or paths) through the trellis to the state. An active path is a valid path through the trellis whose Hamming distance from the received word up to time i is minimal. We label each state at time i by the distance of its active path from the received word. The following relationship is used:

$$\text{(distance of a path)} = \text{(distance of the last edge)} + \text{(distance of the last-but-one state)} \tag{8.7}$$

The algorithm proceeds in $b + 1$ steps, where b is a prechosen window size. For an (n, k, K) code, the first output block of n bits, $w_0w_1w_2 \ldots w_{n-1}$, is decoded in the following steps.

Step 0: The initial state of the trellis at time 0 is labeled 0, because there is so far no discrepancy.

Step $i + 1$: For each state S at time $i + 1$, find all active paths leading to S [using Equation (8.7)]. Label S by the distance of that path or paths.

Step b: The algorithm terminates at time b. If all the active paths at that time have the same first edge and the label of that edge is $x_0x_1x_2 \ldots x_{n-1}$, then the first code block $w_0w_1w_2 \ldots w_{n-1}$ is corrected to $x_0x_1x_2 \ldots x_{n-1}$. If the are two active first edges, the error is not correctable.

After accepting and, if necessary, correcting, the first code block, the decoding window is moved n bits to the right and the decoding of the next block is performed.

> **Example 8.10** [7] Using the encoder defined in Figures 8.9 and 8.10, Figure 8.12 shows the application of the Viterbi algorithm to the sequence 10010100101100..., with a decoding window of length $b = 7$. The lines in the figure represent valid paths through the trellis. The bold lines indicate the current active paths. At step 1, we have a received sequence of $w_0w_1 = 10$. The two valid sequences are 00 and 11. For both of these sequences, there is a distance of 1 from the received sequence. Two active paths are defined, each with a state label of 1. For the next step, we have $w_2w_3 = 01$. Using Equation (8.7), we compute the differences for the four possible valid states (from top to bottom) as 2, 2, 3, and 1. So far, all possible valid paths are included as active paths. In Step 3, we see that some valid paths do not survive as active paths. This is because each such path terminates on a state for which there is another valid path that has a smaller distance. For example, the state sequence a-a-a-a has a discrepancy of 3, while the state sequence a-b-c-a has the discrepancy of 4. At the conclusion of step 7, all active paths pass through the first edge a-b, which has the output 11. The algorithm corrects w_0w_1 to 11 and continues with the next block w_2w_3. Note that if the window size b was 5, the error would not have been correctable.

Convolutional codes provide good performance in noisy channels where a high proportion of the bits are in error. Thus, they have found increasing use in wireless applications.

Turbo Coding

As higher and higher speeds are used in wireless applications, error correction continues to pose a major design challenge. Recently, a new class of codes, called turbo codes, has emerged as a popular choice for third-generation wireless systems. Turbo codes exhibit performance, in terms of bit error probability, that is very close to the Shannon limit and can be efficiently implemented for high-speed use. A number of different turbo encoders and decoders have been introduced, most of which are based on convolutional encoding. In this subsection, we give a general overview.

[7] This example is based on one in [ADAM91].

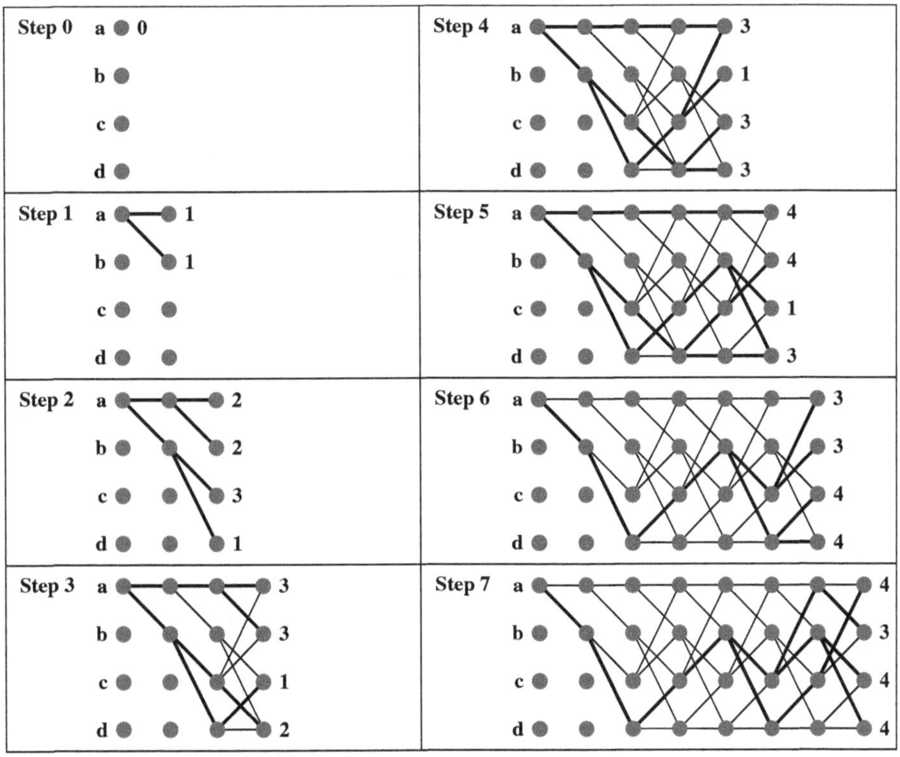

Figure 8.12 Viterbi Algorithm for $w = 10010100101100\ldots$ with decoding window $b = 7$

Figure 8.13a depicts a turbo encoder. In this scheme, the encoder is replicated. One copy of the encoder receives a stream of input bits and produces a single output check bit C_1 for each input bit. The input to the other encoder is an interleaved version of the input bit stream, producing a sequence of C_2 check bits. The initial input bit plus the two check bits are then multiplexed to produce the sequence $I_1C_{11}C_{21}I_2C_{12}C_{22}\ldots$, that is, the first input bit followed by the first bit from encoder one, followed by the first bit from encoder 2, and so on. The resulting sequence has a code rate of 1/3. A code rate of 1/2 can be achieved by taking only half of the check bits, alternating between outputs from the two encoders; this process is called *puncturing*. Rates of 1/3 and 1/2 are both found in third-generation systems.

Note that each encoder only produces a single check bit for each input bit and that the input bit is preserved. In the convolutional encoders we have discussed so far (e.g., Figure 8.9a), the input bits are not preserved, and there are multiple output bits (n output check bits for k input bits). For turbo coding, a variation of the convolutional code, known as a recursive systematic convolutional code (RSC), is used. In a $(2, 1, K)$ RSC encoder, which is typical, one of the two check bit calculations is fed back to the shift register, and the other check bit calculation produces an output bit (Figure 8.14). The output of the encoder consists of alternating input and check bits. The RSC encoder has the same trellis structure as a conventional convolutional encoder and similar statistical properties.

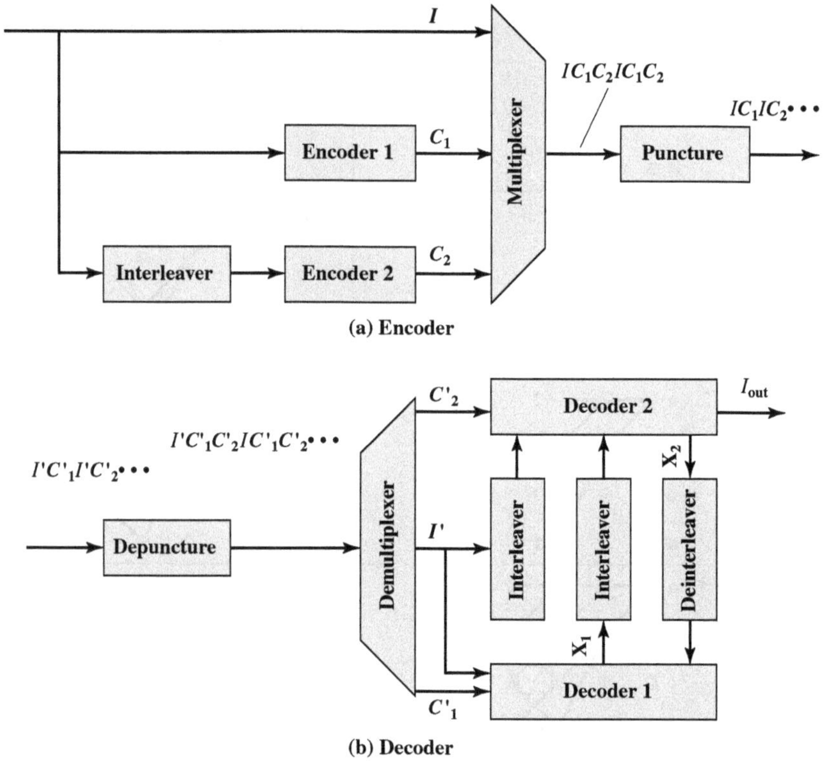

Figure 8.13 Turbo Encoding and Decoding [COTT00]

Figure 8.15 shows how a turbo encoder can be implemented using two RSC coders, where the switch is used to puncture the code, producing a code rate of 1/2. Without the switch, the code rate is 1/3.

Figure 8.13b is a general diagram of a turbo decoder. The received data is depunctured, if necessary, by estimating the missing check bits or by setting the missing bits to 0. Decoder 1 operates first, using the I′ and C'_1 values to produce

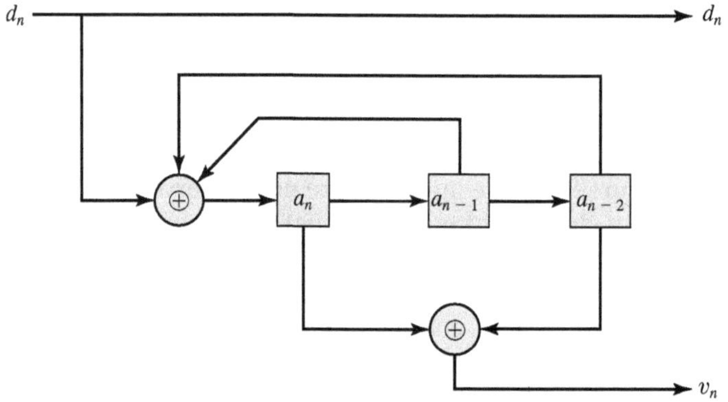

Figure 8.14 Recursive Systematic Concolutional (RSC) Encoder

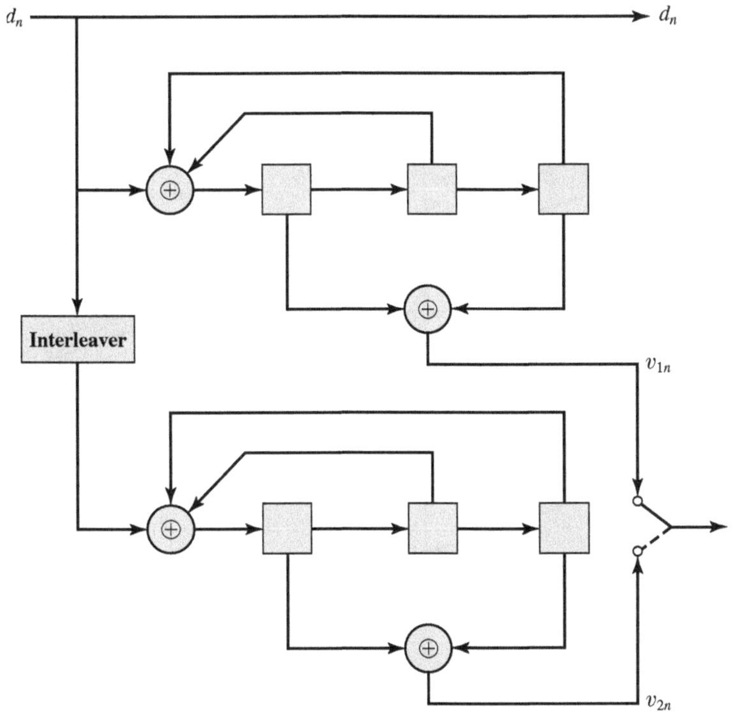

Figure 8.15 Parallel Concatenation of Two RSC Encoders [SKLA97b]

correction (X_1) bits. The I′ and X_1 bits are fed into decoder 2, together with the C'_2 values. Interleaving must be performed to align bits properly. Decoder 2 uses all of its input to produce correction values X_2. These are fed back to decoder 1 for a second iteration of the decoding algorithm, being first deinterleaved for alignment. After sufficient iterations, an output bit is generated from I′ and X_2.

8.4 AUTOMATIC REPEAT REQUEST

Automatic repeat request (ARQ) is a mechanism used in data link control and transport protocols and relies on the use of an error detection code, such as the cyclic redundancy check (CRC) described in Section 8.1. The ARQ error control mechanism is closely related to a flow control mechanism that is also a part of these protocols. We first examine flow control and then go on to look at ARQ. In what follows, we refer to the block of data that is transmitted from one protocol entity to another as a protocol data unit (PDU); this term was introduced in Chapter 4.

Flow Control

Flow control is a technique for assuring that a transmitting entity does not overwhelm a receiving entity with data. The receiving entity typically allocates a data buffer of some maximum length for a transfer. When data are received, the

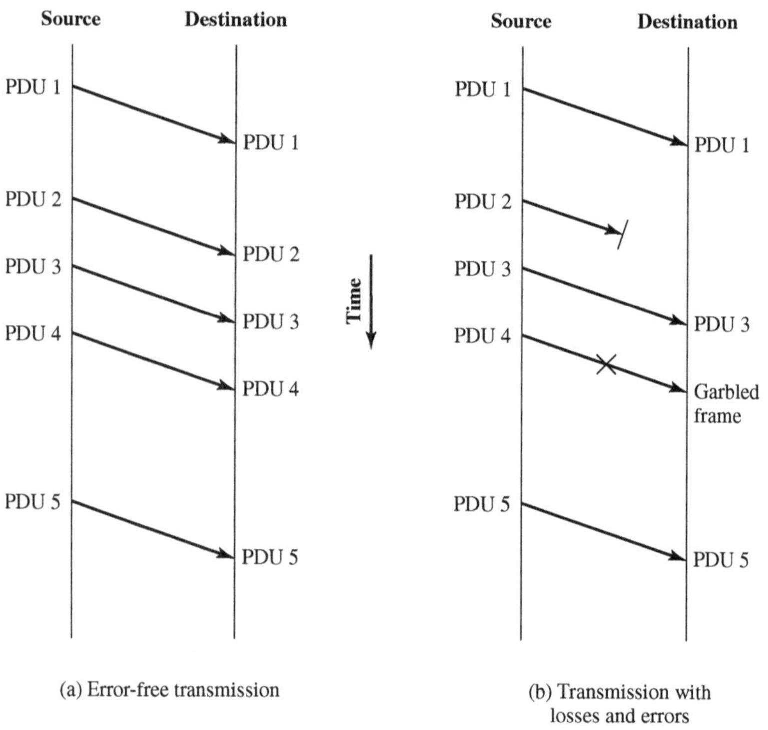

Figure 8.16 Model of PDU Transmission

receiver must do a certain amount of processing (e.g., examine the header and strip it off the PDU) before passing the data to the higher-level software. In the absence of flow control, the receiver's buffer may fill up and overflow while it is processing old data.

To begin, we examine mechanisms for flow control in the absence of errors. The model we will use is depicted in Figure 8.16a, which is a vertical-time sequence diagram. It has the advantages of showing time dependencies and illustrating the correct send-receive relationship. Each arrow represents a single PDU traversing a data link between two stations. The data are sent in a sequence of PDUs, with each PDU containing a portion of the data and some control information. For now, we assume that all PDUs that are transmitted are successfully received; no PDUs are lost and none arrive with errors. Furthermore, PDUs arrive in the same order in which they are sent. However, each transmitted PDU suffers an arbitrary and variable amount of delay before reception.

Typically, when a source has a block or stream of data to transmit, the source will break up the block of data into smaller blocks and transmit the data in many PDUs. This is done for the following reasons:

- The buffer size of the receiver may be limited.
- The longer the transmission, the more likely that there will be an error, necessitating retransmission of the entire PDU. With smaller PDUs, errors are detected sooner, and a smaller amount of data needs to be retransmitted.

- On a shared medium, such as a LAN, it is usually desirable not to permit one station to occupy the medium for an extended period, thus causing long delays at the other sending stations.

Typically, protocols that have a flow control mechanism allow multiple PDUs to be in transit at the same time. Let us examine how this might work for two stations, A and B, connected via a full-duplex link. Station B allocates buffer space for W PDUs. Thus B can accept W PDUs, and A is allowed to send W PDUs without waiting for any acknowledgments. To keep track of which PDUs have been acknowledged, each is labeled with a sequence number. B acknowledges a PDU by sending an acknowledgment that includes the sequence number of the next PDU expected. This acknowledgment also implicitly announces that B is prepared to receive the next W PDUs, beginning with the number specified. This scheme can also be used to acknowledge multiple PDUs. For example, B could receive PDUs 2, 3, and 4 but withhold acknowledgment until PDU 4 has arrived. By then returning an acknowledgment with sequence number 5, B acknowledges PDUs 2, 3, and 4 at one time. A maintains a list of sequence numbers that it is allowed to send, and B maintains a list of sequence numbers that it is prepared to receive. Each of these lists can be thought of as a *window* of PDUs. The operation is referred to as **sliding-window flow control.**

Several additional comments need to be made. Because the sequence number to be used occupies a field in the PDU, it is clearly of bounded size. For example, for a 3-bit field, the sequence number can range from 0 to 7. Accordingly, PDUs are numbered modulo 8; that is, after sequence number 7, the next number is 0. In general, for a k-bit field the range of sequence numbers is 0 through $2^k - 1$, and PDUs are numbered modulo 2^k.

Figure 8.17 is a useful way of depicting the sliding-window process. It assumes the use of a 3-bit sequence number, so that PDUs are numbered sequentially from 0 through 7, and then the same numbers are reused for subsequent PDUs. The shaded rectangle indicates the PDUs that may be sent; in this figure, the sender may transmit five PDUs, beginning with PDU 0. Each time a PDU is sent, the shaded window shrinks; each time an acknowledgment is received, the shaded window grows. PDUs between the vertical bar and the shaded window have been sent but not yet acknowledged. As we shall see, the sender must buffer these PDUs in case they need to be retransmitted.

The window size need not be the maximum possible size for a given sequence number length. For example, using a 3-bit sequence number, a window size of 4 could be configured for the stations using the sliding-window flow control protocol.

Example 8.11 An example is shown in Figure 8.18. The example assumes a 3-bit sequence number field and a maximum window size of seven PDUs. Initially, A and B have windows indicating that A may transmit seven PDUs, beginning with PDU 0 (P0). After transmitting three PDUs (P0, P1, P2) without acknowledgment, A has shrunk its window to four PDUs and maintains a copy of the three transmitted PDUs. The window indicates that A may transmit four PDUs, beginning with PDU number 3. B then transmits an RR (Receive Ready) 3, which means "I have received all PDUs up through PDU number 2 and am ready to receive PDU number 3; in fact, I am prepared to receive seven PDUs, beginning

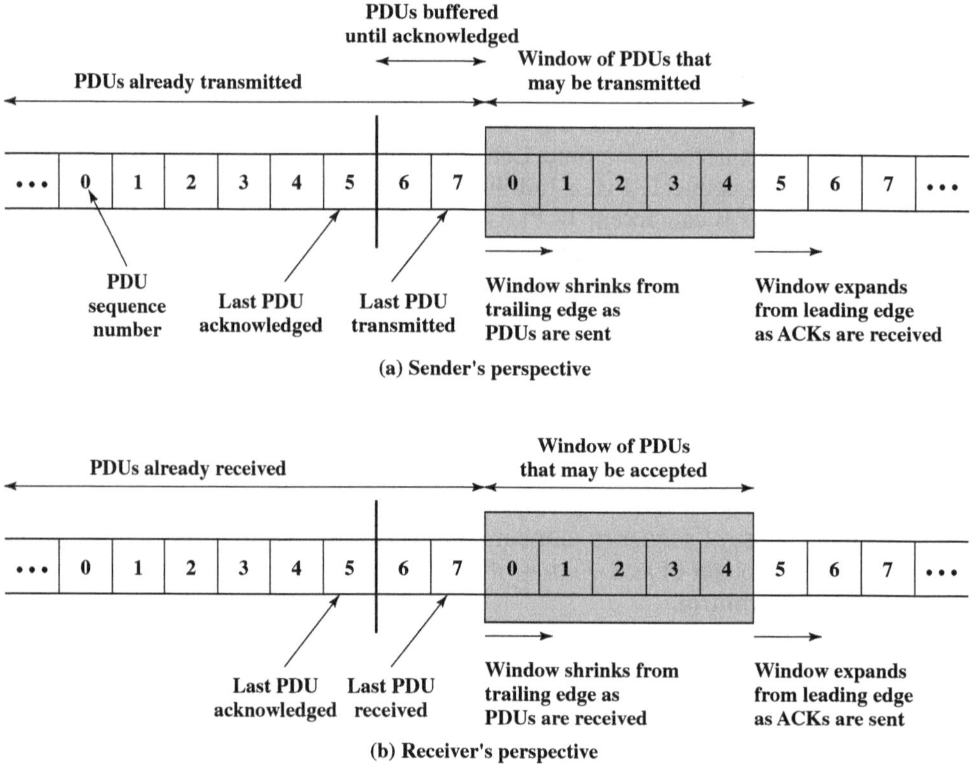

Figure 8.17 Sliding-Window Depiction

with PDU number 3." With this acknowledgment, A is back up to permission to transmit seven PDUs, still beginning with PDU 3; also A may discard the buffered PDUs that have now been acknowledged. A proceeds to transmit PDUs 3, 4, 5, and 6. B returns RR 4, which acknowledges P3, and allows transmission of P4 through the next instance of P2. By the time this RR reaches A, it has already transmitted P4, P5, and P6, and therefore A may only open its window to permit sending four PDUs beginning with P7.

The mechanism so far described does indeed provide a form of flow control: The receiver must only be able to accommodate seven PDUs beyond the one it has last acknowledged. Most protocols also allow a station to cut off the flow of PDUs from the other side by sending a Receive Not Ready (RNR) message, which acknowledges former PDUs but forbids transfer of future PDUs. Thus, RNR 5 means "I have received all PDUs up through number 4 but am unable to accept any more." At some subsequent point, the station must send a normal acknowledgment to reopen the window.

So far, we have discussed transmission in one direction only. If two stations exchange data, each needs to maintain two windows, one for transmit and one for receive, and each side needs to send the data and acknowledgments to the other. To provide efficient support for this requirement, a feature known as *piggybacking*

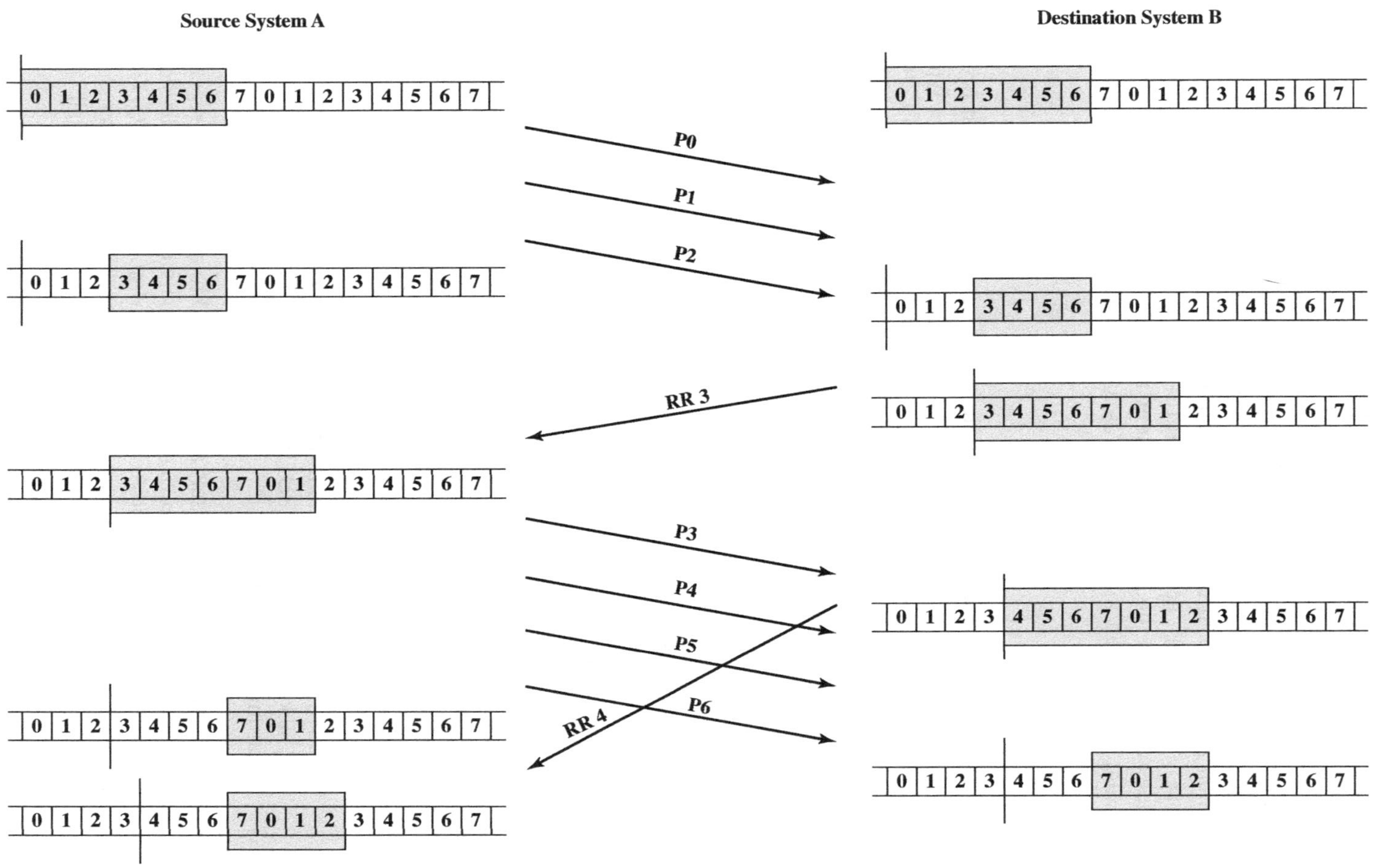

Figure 8.18 Example of a Sliding-Window Protocol

is typically provided. Each *data PDU* includes a field that holds the sequence number of that PDU plus a field that holds the sequence number used for acknowledgment. Thus, if a station has data to send and an acknowledgment to send, it sends both together in one PDU, saving communication capacity. Of course, if a station has an acknowledgment but no data to send, it sends a separate *acknowledgment PDU*. If a station has data to send but no new acknowledgment to send, it must repeat the last acknowledgment that it sent. This is because the data PDU includes a field for the acknowledgment number, and some value must be put into that field. When a station receives a duplicate acknowledgment, it simply ignores it.

Error Control

Error control refers to mechanisms to detect and correct errors that occur in the transmission of PDUs. The model that we will use, which covers the typical case, is illustrated in Figure 8.16b. As before, data are sent as a sequence of PDUs; PDUs arrive in the same order in which they are sent; and each transmitted PDU suffers an arbitrary and variable amount of delay before reception. In addition, we admit the possibility of two types of errors:

- **Lost PDU:** A PDU fails to arrive at the other side. For example, a noise burst may damage a PDU to the extent that the receiver is not aware that a PDU has been transmitted.
- **Damaged PDU:** A recognizable PDU does arrive, but some of the bits are in error (have been altered during transmission).

The most common techniques for error control are based on some or all of the following ingredients:

- **Error detection:** The receiver detects errors and discards PDUs that are in error.
- **Positive acknowledgment:** The destination returns a positive acknowledgment to successfully received, error-free PDUs.
- **Retransmission after timeout:** The source retransmits a PDU that has not been acknowledged after a predetermined amount of time.
- **Negative acknowledgment and retransmission:** The destination returns a negative acknowledgment to PDUs in which an error is detected. The source retransmits such PDUs.

Collectively, these mechanisms are all referred to as **automatic repeat request** (ARQ); the effect of ARQ is to turn an unreliable data link into a reliable one. The most commonly used versions of ARQ is known as go-back-N ARQ. Go-back-N ARQ is based on the sliding-window flow control mechanism just discussed.

In go-back-N ARQ, a station may send a series of PDUs sequentially numbered modulo some maximum value. The number of unacknowledged PDUs outstanding is determined by window size, using the sliding-window flow control technique. While no errors occur, the destination will acknowledge incoming PDUs as usual

(RR = receive ready, or piggybacked acknowledgment). If the destination station detects an error in a PDU, it sends a negative acknowledgment (REJ = reject) for that PDU. The destination station will discard that PDU and all future incoming PDUs until the PDU in error is correctly received. Thus the source station, when it receives a REJ, must retransmit the PDU in error plus all succeeding PDUs that had been transmitted in the interim.

Consider that station A is sending PDUs to station B. After each transmission, A sets an acknowledgment timer for the PDU just transmitted. Suppose that B has previously successfully received PDU $(i - 1)$ and A has just transmitted PDU i. The go-back-N technique takes into account the following contingencies:

1. **Damaged PDU.** If the received PDU is invalid (i.e., B detects an error), B discards the PDU and takes no further action as the result of that PDU. There are two subcases:
   a. Within a reasonable period of time, A subsequently sends PDU $(i + 1)$. B receives PDU $(i + 1)$ out of order and sends a REJ i. A must retransmit PDU i and all subsequent PDUs.
   b. A does not soon send additional PDUs. B receives nothing and returns neither an RR nor a REJ. When A's timer expires, it transmits an RR PDU that includes a bit known as the P bit, which is set to 1. B interprets the RR PDU with a P bit of 1 as a command that must be acknowledged by sending an RR indicating the next PDU that it expects, which is PDU i. When A receives the RR, it retransmits PDU i.
2. **Damaged RR.** There are two subcases:
   a. B receives PDU i and sends RR $(i + 1)$, which suffers an error in transit. Because acknowledgments are cumulative (e.g., RR 6 means that all PDUs through 5 are acknowledged), it may be that A will receive a subsequent RR to a subsequent PDU and that it will arrive before the timer associated with PDU i expires.
   b. If A's timer expires, it transmits an RR command as in Case 1b. It sets another timer, called the P-bit timer. If B fails to respond to the RR command, or if its response suffers an error in transit, then A's P-bit timer will expire. At this point, A will try again by issuing a new RR command and restarting the P-bit timer. This procedure is tried for a number of iterations. If A fails to obtain an acknowledgment after some maximum number of attempts, it initiates a reset procedure.
3. **Damaged REJ.** If a REJ is lost, this is equivalent to Case 1b.

Figure 8.19 is an example of the PDU flow for go-back-N ARQ. Because of the propagation delay on the line, by the time that an acknowledgment (positive or negative) arrives back at the sending station, it has already sent two additional PDUs beyond the one being acknowledged. Thus, when a REJ is received to PDU 5, not only PDU 5 but PDUs 6 and 7 must be retransmitted. Thus, the transmitter must keep a copy of all unacknowledged PDUs.

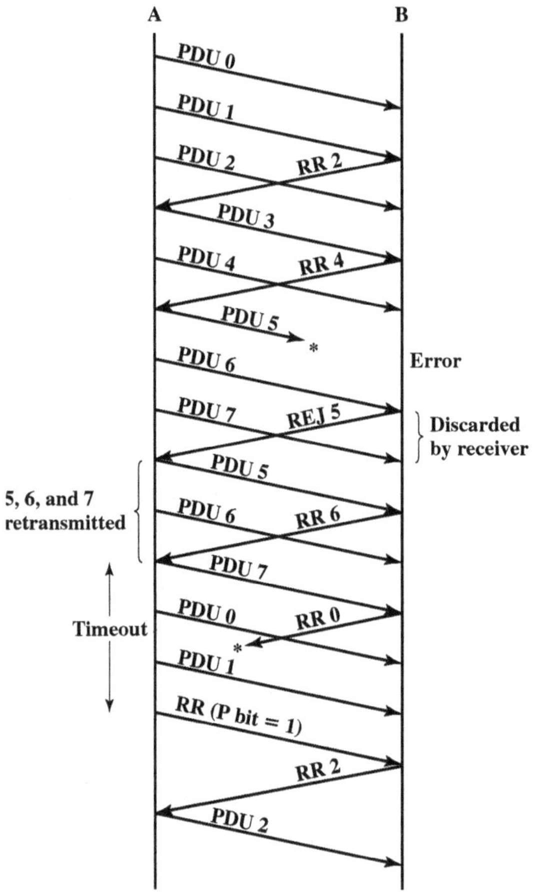

Figure 8.19 Go-back-N ARQ

8.5 RECOMMENDED READINGS

The classic treatment of error detecting codes and CRC is [PETE61]. [RAMA88] is an excellent tutorial on CRC.

[ADAM91] provides comprehensive treatment of error-correcting codes. [SKLA01] contains a clear, well-written section on the subject. Two useful survey articles are [BERL87] and [BHAR83]. A quite readable theoretical and mathematical treatment of error-correcting codes is [ASH90].

Two good treatments of turbo codes are [SKLA97] and [BERR96]. A more detailed analysis is [VUCE00].

ADAM91 Adamek, J. *Foundations of Coding.* New York: Wiley, 1991.

ASH90 Ash, R. *Information Theory.* New York: Dover, 1990.

BERL87 Berlekamp, E.; Peile, R.; and Pope, S. "The Application of Error Control to Communications." *IEEE Communications Magazine,* April 1987.

BERR96 Berrou, C., and Glavieux, A. "Near Optimum Error Correcting Codes and Decoding: Turbo Codes." *IEEE Transactions on Communications*, October 1996.

BHAR83 Bhargava, V. "Forward Error Correction Schemes for Digital Communications." *IEEE Communications Magazine*, January 1983.

PETE61 Peterson, W., and Brown, D. "Cyclic Codes for Error Detection." *Proceedings of the IEEE*, January 1961.

Peterson, W. W. and Brown, D. T. (January 1961). "Cyclic Codes for Error Detection." *Proceedings of the IRE*.

RAMA88 Ramabadran, T., and Gaitonde, S. "A Tutorial on CRC Computations." *IEEE Micro*, August 1988.

SKLA97 Sklar, B. "A Primer on Turbo Code Concepts." *IEEE Communications Magazine*, December 1997.

SKLA01 Sklar, B. *Digital Communications: Fundamentals and Applications*. Upper Saddle River, NJ: Prentice Hall, 2001.

VUCE00 Vucetic, B., and Yuan, J. *Turbo Codes: Principles and Applications*. Boston: Kluwer Academic Publishers, 2000.

HYPERLINK http://academic.research.microsoft.com/Author/322223/sergio-benedetto *Sergio Benedetto*

HYPERLINK http://academic.research.microsoft.com/Author/2959664/colin-f-n-cowan *Colin F. N. Cowan*

HYPERLINK http://academic.research.microsoft.com/Author/439660/guido-montorsi *Guido Montorsi*

HYPERLINK http://academic.research.microsoft.com/Author/2216417/juriaan-simonis *Juriaan Simonis*

HYPERLINK http://academic.research.microsoft.com/Author/667026/jinsong-wu *Jinsong Wu*

HYPERLINK http://academic.research.microsoft.com/Author/2299062/pei-xiao *Pei Xiao*

Journal: HYPERLINK ../../Journal/433/tit-ieee-transactions-on-information-theory *IEEE Transactions on Information Theory–TIT*, vol. 46, no. 4, pp. 1544–1545, 2000.

Journal: HYPERLINK ../../Journal/855/twc-ieee-transactions-on-wireless-communications *IEEE Transactions on Wireless Communications–TWC*, vol. 59, no. 1, pp. 26–32, 2011.

8.6 KEY TERMS, REVIEW QUESTIONS, AND PROBLEMS

Key Terms

automatic repeat request (ARQ)	convolutional code	error correction code (ECC)
block ECC	cyclic code	error detection
block interleaving	cyclic redundancy check (CRC)	error detection code
check bits	error control	flow control
codeword	error correction	forward error correction (FEC)

frame check sequence (FCS)	parity bit	sliding-window flow control
go-back-N ARQ	parity check	trellis
Hamming code	protocol data unit (PDU)	turbo code
Hamming distance		

Review Questions

8.1 What is a parity bit?

8.2 What is the CRC?

8.3 Why would you expect a CRC to detect more errors than a parity bit?

8.4 List three different ways in which the CRC algorithm can be described.

8.5 Is it possible to design an ECC that will correct some double bit errors but not all double bit errors? Why or why not?

8.6 In an (n, k) block ECC, what do n and k represent?

8.7 In an (n, k, K) convolutional code, what to n, k, and K represent?

8.8 What is a trellis in the context of a convolutional code?

8.9 What two key elements comprise error control?

8.10 Explain how Go-back-N ARQ works.

Problems

8.1 What is the purpose of using modulo 2 arithmetic rather than binary arithmetic in computing an FCS?

8.2 Consider a frame consisting of two characters of four bits each. Assume that the probability of bit error is 10^{-3} and that it is independent for each bit.
  a. What is the probability that the received frame contains at least one error?
  b. Now add a parity bit to each character. What is the probability?

8.3 Using the CRC-CCITT polynomial, generate the 16-bit CRC code for a message consisting of a 1 followed by 15 0s.
  a. Use long division.
  b. Use the shift register mechanism shown in Figure 8.4.

8.4 Explain in words why the shift register implementation of CRC will result in all 0s at the receiver if there are no errors. Demonstrate by example.

8.5 For $P = 110011$ and $M = 11100011$, find the CRC.

8.6 A CRC is constructed to generate a 4-bit FCS for an 11-bit message. The generator polynomial is $X^4 + X^3 + 1$.
  a. Draw the shift register circuit that would perform this task (see Figure 8.4).
  b. Encode the data bit sequence 10011011100 (leftmost bit is the least significant) using the generator polynomial and give the codeword.
  c. Now assume that bit 7 (counting from the LSB) in the code word is in error and show that the detection algorithm detects the error.

8.7 A modified CRC procedure is commonly used in communications standards such as HDLC. It is defined as follows:

$$\frac{X^{16}M(X) + X^k L(X)}{P(X)} = Q + \frac{R(X)}{P(X)}$$

$$\text{FCS} = L(X) + R(X)$$

where

$$L(X) = X^{15} + X^{14} + X^{13} + \cdots + X + 1$$

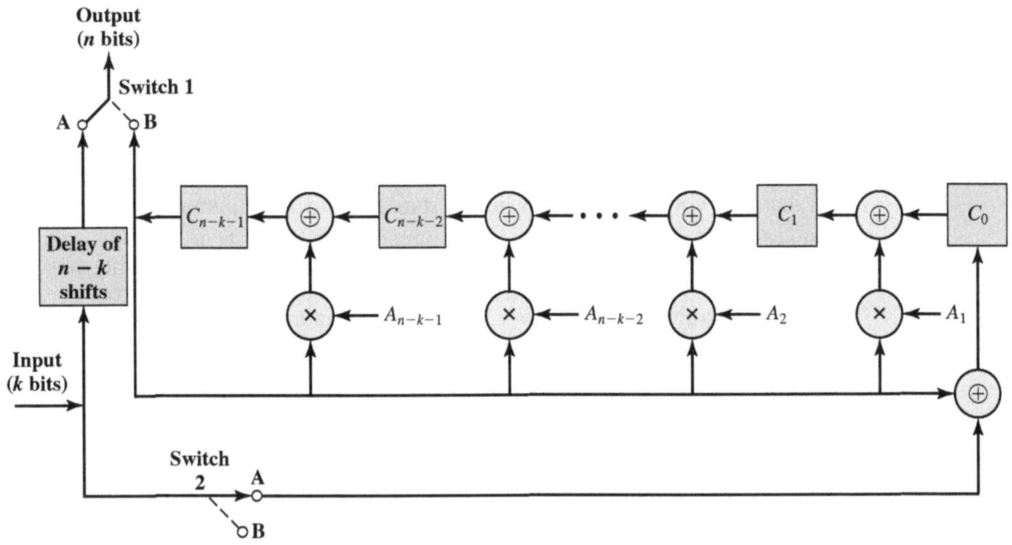

Figure 8.20 Another CRC Architecture to Implement Divisor $1 + A_1X + A_2X^2 + \cdots + A_{n-1}X^{n-k-1} + X^{n-k}$

and k is the number of bits being checked (address, control, and information fields).

a. Describe in words the effect of this procedure.
b. Explain the potential benefits.
c. Show a shift register implementation for $P(X) = X^{16} + X^{12} + X^5 + 1$.

8.8 Figure 8.20 shows a polynomial division circuit that produces a result equivalent to that of the circuit in Figure 8.4.

a. Using this alternative structure, draw a LFSR for dividing by $X^5 + X^4 + X^2 + 1$ that is equivalent to that of Figure 8.3a.
b. Show the sequence of steps that produces the resulting CRC, following the method of Figure 8.3. You should end up with the same pattern, 01110, in the shift register at the end of the operation. *Hint:* Note that there is a delay in outputting the input bits of $(n - k)$ bits, so you need to perform $(n - k)$ additional shifts to produce the final result.
c. An advantage of the structure in Figure 8.20, compared to that in Figure 8.4, is that it shows the correspondence with the long division process more clearly. Explain.
d. What is a disadvantage of the structure in Figure 8.20?

8.9 Calculate the Hamming pairwise distances among the following codewords:

a. 00000, 10101, 01010
b. 000000, 010101, 101010, 110110

8.10 Section 8.2 discusses block error correction codes that make a decision on the basis of minimum distance. That is, given a code consisting of s equally likely code words of length n, for each received sequence $\mathbf{v}$, the receiver selects the codeword $\mathbf{w}$ for which the distance $d(\mathbf{w}, \mathbf{v})$ is a minimum. We would like to prove that this scheme is "ideal" in the sense that the receiver always selects the codeword for which the probability of $\mathbf{w}$ given $\mathbf{v}$, $p(\mathbf{w}|\mathbf{v})$, is a maximum. Because all codewords are assumed equally likely, the codeword that maximizes $p(\mathbf{w}|\mathbf{v})$ is the same as the codeword that maximizes $p(\mathbf{v}|\mathbf{w})$.

a. In order that $\mathbf{w}$ be received as $\mathbf{v}$, there must be exactly $d(\mathbf{w}, \mathbf{v})$ errors in transmission, and these errors must occur in those bits where $\mathbf{w}$ and $\mathbf{v}$ disagree. Let β be the probability that a given bit is transmitted incorrectly and n be the length of a codeword. Write an expression for $p(\mathbf{v}|\mathbf{w})$ as a function of β, $d(\mathbf{w}, \mathbf{v})$, and n. *Hint:* The number of bits in error is $d(\mathbf{w}, \mathbf{v})$ and the number of bits not in error is $n - d(\mathbf{w}, \mathbf{v})$.

b. Now compare $p(\mathbf{v}|\mathbf{w}_1)$ and $p(\mathbf{v}|\mathbf{w}_2)$ for two different codewords $\mathbf{w}_1$ and $\mathbf{w}_2$ by calculating $p(\mathbf{v}|\mathbf{w}_1)/p(\mathbf{v}|\mathbf{w}_2)$.

c. Assume that $0 < \beta < 0.5$ and show that $p(\mathbf{v}|\mathbf{w}_1) > p(\mathbf{v}|\mathbf{w}_2)$ if and only if $d(\mathbf{v}, \mathbf{w}_1) < d(\mathbf{v}, \mathbf{w}_2)$. This proves that the codeword $\mathbf{w}$ that gives the largest value of $p(\mathbf{v}|\mathbf{w})$ is that word whose distance from $\mathbf{v}$ is a minimum.

8.11 Section 8.2 states that for a given positive integer t, if a code satisfies $d_{min} \geq 2t + 1$, then the code can correct all bit errors up to and including errors of t bits. Prove this assertion. *Hint:* Start by observing that for a codeword $\mathbf{w}$ to be decoded as another codeword $\mathbf{w}'$, the received sequence must be at least as close to $\mathbf{w}'$ as to $\mathbf{w}$.

8.12 For the Hamming code shown in Table 8.2, show the formulas used to calculate the check bits as functions of the data bits.

8.13 For the Hamming code shown in Table 8.2, show what happens when a check bit rather than a data bit is received in error.

8.14 Suppose an 8-bit data word stored in memory is 11000010. Using the Hamming algorithm, determine what check bits would be stored in memory with the data word. Show how you got your answer.

8.15 For the 8-bit word 00111001, the check bits stored with it would be 0111. Suppose when the word is read from memory, the check bits are calculated to be 1101. What is the data word that was read from memory?

8.16 How many check bits are needed if the Hamming error correction code is used to detect single bit errors in a 1024-bit data word?

8.17 Divide $f(X) = X^6 + 1$ by $g(X) = X^4 + X^3 + X + 1$. Verify the result by multiplying the quotient by $g(X)$ to recover $f(X)$.

8.18 For the example related to Table 8.3:

a. Draw the LFSR.

b. Using a layout similar to Figure 8.3b, show that the check bits for the data block 1010 are 001.

8.19 Using an interleaving structure of $n = 4$, $m = 6$ (Figure 8.8), demonstrate each of the following block interleaving characteristics:

a. Any burst of m contiguous channel bit errors results in isolated errors at the deinterleaver output that are separated from each other by at least n bits.

b. Any bm bursts of errors ($b > 1$) results in output bursts from the deinterleaver of no more than $\lceil b \rceil$ errors. Each output burst is separated from the other bursts by no less than $\lfloor b \rfloor$ bits. The notation $\lceil b \rceil$ means the smallest integer no less than b, and $\lfloor b \rfloor$ means the largest integer no greater than b.

c. A periodic sequence of single bit errors spaced m bits apart results in a single burst of errors of length n at the deinterleaver output.

d. Not including channel propagation delay, the interleaver end-to-end delay is $2(n(m - 1) + 1)$. Only $(n(m - 1) + 1)$ cells need to be filled before transmission can begin and a corresponding number needs to be filled at the receiver before deinterleaving can begin.

8.20 Consider a convolutional encoder defined by $(v_{n1} = u_n \oplus u_{n-2})$ and $(v_{n2} = u_{n-1} \oplus u_{n-2})$.

a. Draw a shift register implementation for this encoder similar to Figure 8.9a.

b. Draw an state diagram for this encoder similar to Figure 8.9b.

c. Draw a Trellis diagram for this encoder similar to Figure 8.10.

8.21 For the encoder of Problem 8.20, assume that the shift register is initialized to all zeros and that after the transmission of the last information bit, two zero bits are transmitted.

a. Why are the two extra bits needed?

b. What is the encoded sequence corresponding to the information sequence 1101011, where the leftmost bit is the first bit presented to the encoder?

8.22 The simplest form of flow control, known as **stop-and-wait flow control**, works as follows. A source entity transmits a frame. After the destination entity receives the frame, it indicates its willingness to accept another frame by sending back an acknowledgment to the frame just received. The source must wait until it receives the acknowledgment before sending the next frame. The destination can thus stop the flow of data simply by withholding acknowledgment. Consider a half-duplex point-to-point link using a stop-and-wait scheme, in which a series of messages is sent, with each message segmented into a number of frames. Ignore errors and frame overhead.
a. What is the effect on line utilization of increasing the message size so that fewer messages will be required? Other factors remain constant.
b. What is the effect on line utilization of increasing the number of frames for a constant message size?
c. What is the effect on line utilization of increasing frame size?

8.23 In Figure 8.21, frames are generated at node A and sent to node C through node B. Determine the minimum data rate required between nodes B and C so that the buffers of node B are not flooded, based on the following:
- The data rate between A and B is 100 kbps.
- The propagation delay is 5 μs/km for both lines.
- There are full duplex lines between the nodes.
- All data frames are 1000 bits long; ACK frames are separate frames of negligible length.
- Between A and B, a sliding-window protocol with a window size of 3 is used.
- Between B and C, stop-and-wait is used.
- There are no errors.

Hint: In order not to flood the buffers of B, the average number of frames entering and leaving B must be the same over a long interval.

8.24 A channel has a data rate of R bps and a propagation delay of t seconds per kilometer. The distance between the sending and receiving nodes is L kilometers. Nodes exchange fixed-size frames of B bits. Find a formula that gives the minimum sequence field size of the frame as a function of R, t, B, and L (considering maximum utilization). Assume that ACK frames are negligible in size and the processing at the nodes is instantaneous.

8.25 Two neighboring nodes (A and B) use a sliding-window protocol with a 3-bit sequence number. As the ARQ mechanism, Go-back-N is used with a window size of 4. Assuming A is transmitting and B is receiving, show the window positions for the following succession of events:
a. Before A sends any frames
b. After A sends frames 0, 1, 2 and receives acknowledgment from B for 0 and 1
c. After A sends frames 3, 4, and 5 and B acknowledges 4 and the ACK is received by A

8.26 Two stations communicate via a 1-Mbps satellite link with a propagation delay of 270 ms. The satellite serves merely to retransmit data received from one station to another, with negligible switching delay. Using frames of 1024 bits with 3-bit sequence numbers, what is the maximum possible data throughput; that is, what is the throughput of data bits carried in frames?

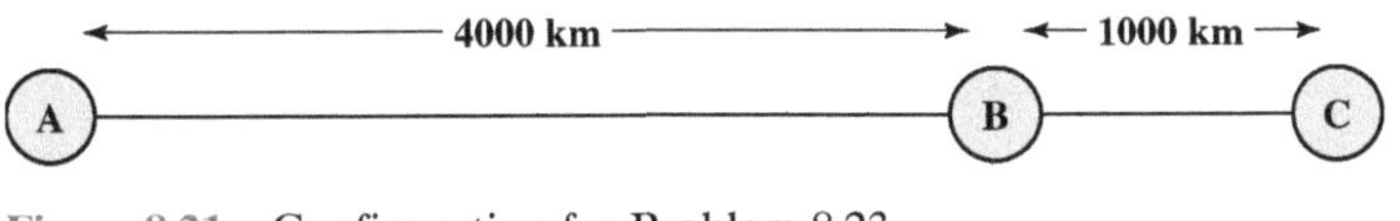

Figure 8.21 Configuration for Problem 8.23

PART THREE

Wireless Networking

CHAPTER 9

Satellite Communications

9.1 SATELLITE COMMUNICATIONS

Objectives

After reading this section and completing the exercises, you will be able to:

- Learn the various types of satellite-based systems
- Learn the various uses for satellite-based systems
- Learn a few basics about orbits and how satellites get into orbit
- Learn examples of satellite systems in use today and those planned for the near future

Background

Satellites are generally categorized by the altitude or geometry of their orbit around earth. The types of services these satellites provide are the determining factors in choosing what type of earth orbit each of the satellite systems will use. The different orbits allow for multiple paths and better use of the space around earth, as well as facilitate the specific needs of different satellite systems.

Following are the basic types of satellite systems and their ranges:

- LEO—low earth orbit (500–1,500 km)
- MEO—medium earth orbit (5,000–15,000 km)
- GEO—geostationary earth orbit (35,786 km)
- Polar orbits (variable heights)
- HEO—highly elliptical earth orbit (variable generally apogee = GEO altitude)

Each of these systems has their own advantages and disadvantages, and each is configured to make the best use of its associated attributes while minimizing detriments. Our discussion will begin with a brief history of satellites and then address some general concepts on satellites. Lastly, we will discuss the LEO satellite system configurations. Discussions on the other types will follow.

History

On October 4, 1957, the first artificial satellite, named **Sputnik**, was successfully launched and achieved orbit.[1] This Russian satellite was designed to measure and transmit information about the density of the upper atmosphere as it circled the earth. Before then, all atmospheric information that meteorologists had was based on "looking up" instead of "looking down." Since Sputnik, the science of satellites has advanced significantly. Specialized satellites now orbit the earth for telecommunications, global broadcasting, oceanic observations, scientific research, and military purposes, as well as for atmospheric observation. It is amazing to consider the rapid progress and evolution of satellite technology.

---

[1]Courtesy of www.nauts.com.

Figure 9.1 Sputnik
(Courtesy of www.nauts.com)

The first Soviet satellite program consisted of four Sputnik, or fellow traveler, satellites. As shown in Figure 9.1, Sputnik had a mass of 83.6 kg. As mentioned, it was designed to determine the density of the upper atmosphere and return data about the earth's ionosphere. However, its two radio transmitters only returned signals to earth for 21 days.

Meteorological satellites themselves have changed considerably since Sputnik. Weather observation and forecasting have become much more reliable today, thanks to the sophisticated satellites currently orbiting the earth. In 1947, an unmanned American rocket carried a camera into outer space and recorded pictures of Earth from space.[2] The pictures showed how the atmosphere appeared from above. Cloud formations were clearly visible. These pictures gave scientists proof that weather observations could be made from space on a regular basis.

[2]Courtesy of nauts.com.

In 1960, the first weather satellite was launched into orbit around the earth. Called the television infrared observational satellite (Tiros), it carried a video camera to make regular observations of the atmosphere below. For the first time, meteorologists were able to compare their localized ground-based weather observations with broader pictures of the weather system. Weather forecasting took a dramatic leap forward. Figure 9.2 depicts the Tiros-1 satellite. After the initial successes, nine more Tiros satellites were put into orbit during the 1960s.

In 1966, the United States placed its first weather satellite in high, geostationary orbit. Called the applications technology satellite (ATS), it traveled at the same speed the earth rotates, appearing to remain stationary with respect to the earth below. From this GEO location 22,300 miles above the equator, ATS took the first pictures showing a whole hemisphere of the earth at once. With ATS images, meteorologists saw how clouds moved and storms formed over wide regions. The development of satellite weather technology had an enormous impact on the field of meteorology. The "big pictures" came into focus, and weather forecasting became more accurate.

Communicating with a Satellite

Transmission to and from a satellite are performed in select frequency bands. These bands are:

Frequency Band	Downlink	Uplink
C	3,700–4,200 MHz	5,925–6,425 MHz
Ku	11.7–12.2 GHz	14.0–14.5 GHz
Ka	17.7–21.2 GHz	27.5–31.0 GHz

Figure 9.2 Tiros-1 Measures 42 Inches in Diameter by 19 Inches High *(Courtesy of NASA)*

9.2 LAUNCHING A SATELLITE

Let us discuss how satellites are launched into orbit. Satellites are launched by being carried on a rocket into space. The rocket is simply a huge canister or tube filled with either liquid or solid rocket fuel. If not carried on a rocket, satellites can sometimes be carried by the space shuttle (Figure 9.3).

After a rocket is launched with the satellite onboard, the rocket control mechanism uses an inertial guidance system to calculate any necessary modifications to the rocket's nozzles to tilt the rocket to the course described in the approved flight plan. In most cases, the flight plan calls for the rocket to head east because the earth rotates to the east, giving the launch vehicle a free boost. The strength of this boost depends on the rotational velocity of the earth at the launch location. The boost is greatest at the equator where the distance around the earth is greatest, and is therefore rotating at the fastest rate.

Just how big is the boost from an equatorial launch? To make a rough estimate, we can determine earth's circumference by multiplying its diameter times pi (3.1416). The diameter of earth is approximately 7,926 miles (12,753 km). Multiplying times pi yields a circumference of about 24,900 miles (40,065 km). To travel around that circumference in 24 hours, a point on the earth's surface has to move at 1,038 mph (1,669 km/h). A launch from Cape Canaveral, Florida, does not get as big a boost from the earth's rotational speed as it would on the equator. The Kennedy Space Center's Launch Complex 39-A, one of its launch facilities, is located at 28 degrees 36 minutes 29.7014 seconds north latitude. There the earth's rotational

Figure 9.3 Space Shuttle
(Courtesy of NASA)

speed is about 894 mph (1,440 km/h). The difference in the earth's surface speed between the equator and Kennedy Space Center, then, is about 144 mph (229 km/h). This 144 mph is truly significant.

The reason the lower speed is important is the weight of the rocket. As an example, the space shuttle can weigh over 4.5 million pounds (2 million kg), depending on its payload (its load, such as a satellite, equipment, or space station component). This requires a great deal of energy to accelerate such a mass to 144 mph, and therefore a significant amount of fuel; thus, launching from the equator makes a significant difference. This issue is one that most people rarely think about.

9.3 ESCAPE AND ORBITAL VELOCITY

Whether a rocket wants to simply orbit the earth or escape its gravitational pull is determined by its velocity. To completely escape the earth's gravitational pull, and therefore enter space, a rocket must accelerate to at least 25,039 mph (40,320 km/h). This happens when NASA sends probes to the outer reaches of the solar system or when missions such as the Apollo moon mission transpire. Figure 9.4 shows the latest Titan rocket, the Titan 4. This rocket is used to send many of the latest satellites into orbit.

However, in the case of orbital velocity, or how much velocity is required to simply orbit the earth, it is a different issue, because earth's escape velocity is much greater than what is required to place an earth satellite into orbit. With satellites, the object is not to escape earth's gravity, but to balance it. This centers around orbital velocity. **Orbital velocity** is the velocity needed to achieve balance between gravity's pull on the satellite and the inertia of the satellite's motion—the satellite's tendency

Figure 9.4 Titan-4
(Courtesy of NASA)

to keep going. This tendency to keep moving is due to the fact that space is a vacuum and an object, and once it is going in a direction, will continue in that direction indefinitely. This differs from an atmosphere in which an object will slow down until it finally stops. As far as orbital velocity, this is approximately 17,000 mph at an altitude of 150 miles (242 km). Gravity also enters the picture. Without gravity, the satellite's inertia would carry it off into space. Even with gravity, if the intended satellite goes too fast, it will eventually fly away. However, if the satellite goes too slowly, gravity will pull it back to earth. At the correct orbital velocity, gravity exactly balances the satellite's inertia, pulling down toward earth's center just enough to keep the path of the satellite curving like earth's curved surface, rather than flying off in a straight line.

The issue of orbital velocity is a little more complicated than it may seem on the surface. The orbital velocity of a satellite depends on its altitude above earth. The nearer the satellite is to the earth, the faster the *required* orbital velocity must be. At an altitude of 124 miles (200 km), the required orbital velocity is just over 17,000 mph (27,400 km/h). To maintain an orbit of 22,223 miles (35,786 km) above earth, the satellite must orbit at a speed of about 7,000 mph (11,300 km/h). That specific orbital speed and distance permits the satellite to make one revolution in 24 hours. Because the earth also rotates once in 24 hours, a satellite at 22,223 miles

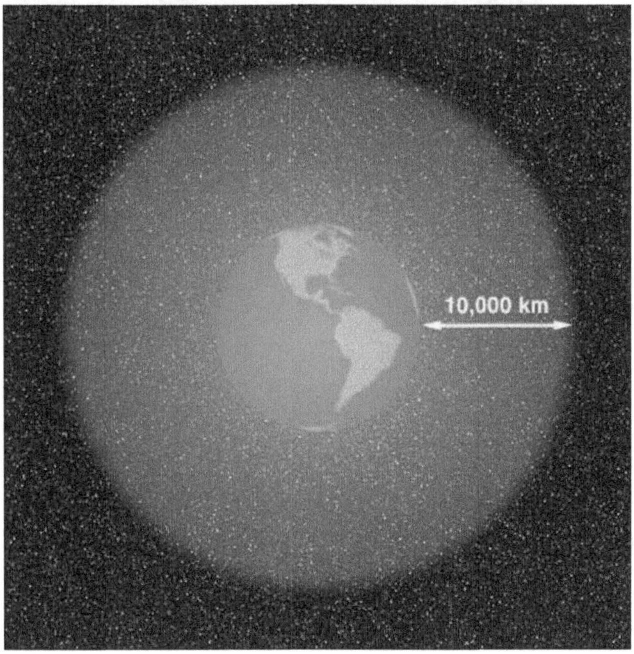

Figure 9.5 The Exosphere
(Courtesy of www.noaa.gov)

(35,786 km) altitude will stay in a fixed position relative to a point on the earth's surface. Because the satellite stays directly over the same spot all the time, this kind of orbit is called geostationary. Geostationary orbits are ideal for weather satellites and communications satellites.

In general, the rule is *the higher the orbit, the longer the satellite can stay in orbit.* At lower altitudes, a satellite runs into traces of the earth's atmosphere, which creates drag on the satellite. This drag causes the orbit of the satellite to decay until the satellite falls back into the atmosphere and burns up. At higher altitudes, where the vacuum of space is nearly complete, there is almost no drag and a satellite can stay in orbit almost indefinitely.

LEOs are actually in the two outer layers of the atmosphere. The outermost layer is called the exosphere. The exosphere is the most distant atmospheric region from the earth's surface, as shown in Figure 9.5. The upper boundary of the layer extends to heights of perhaps 960 to 1,000 km and is relatively undefined. The exosphere is a transitional zone between the earth's atmosphere and interplanetary space. The next lower layer is the thermosphere (literally "heat sphere"), as shown in Figure 9.6. Most LEOs orbit in the thermosphere. Figure 9.7 depicts graphically the earth's atmosphere.

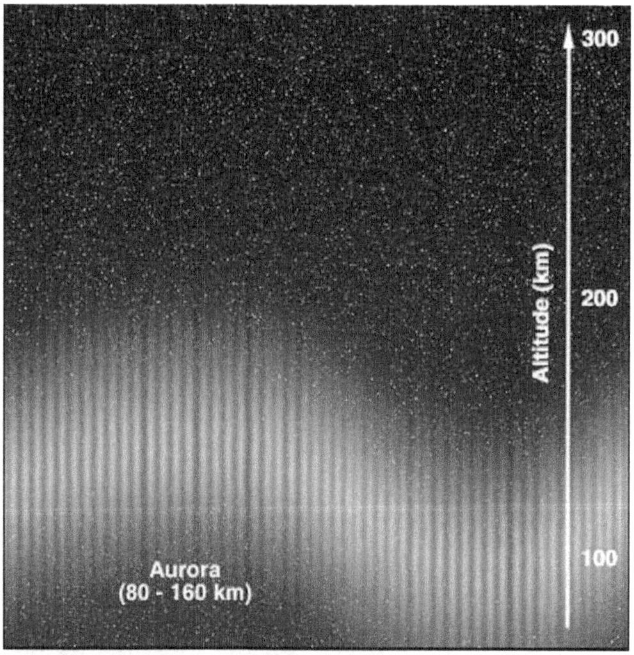

Figure 9.6 The Thermosphere
(Courtesy of www.noaa.gov)

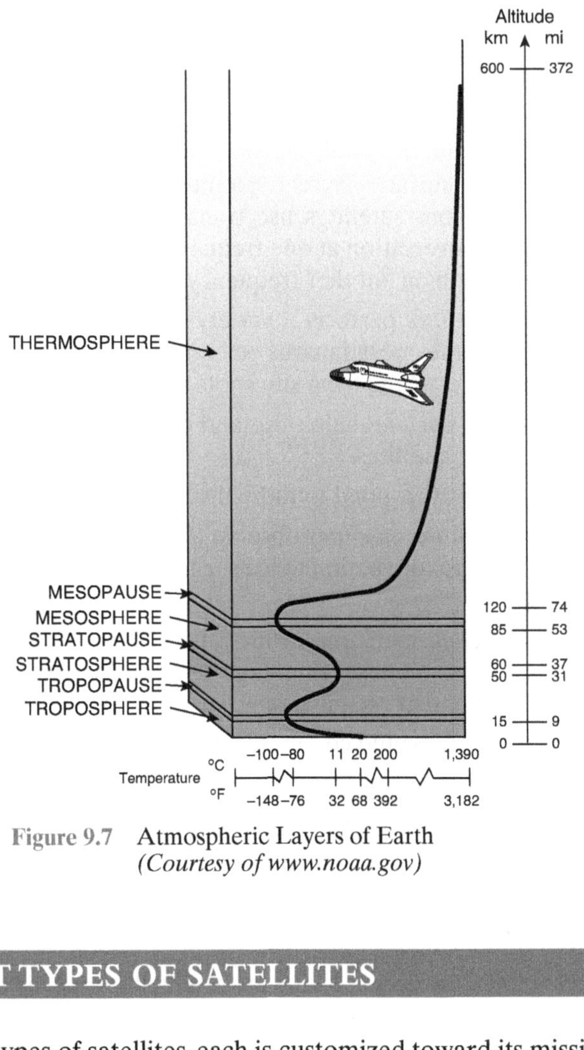

Figure 9.7 Atmospheric Layers of Earth
(Courtesy of www.noaa.gov)

9.4 DIFFERENT TYPES OF SATELLITES

Of the several types of satellites, each is customized toward its mission.[3]

- *Weather satellites* pinpoint weather conditions and provide data for meteorologists to determine future weather conditions. Typical weather satellites include the Tiros, COSMOS, and GOES satellites. These satellites usually contain cameras that can return photos of the earth's weather, either from fixed geostationary positions or from polar orbits, as well as sensitive barometric and environmental sensors.

[3]www.howstuffworks.com

- *Broadcast satellites* broadcast television signals from a ground station to another ground station. These include a cable TV antenna and a home DirecTV/DishTV antenna.
- *Communications satellites* allow telephone and data conversations to be relayed through the satellite from one point on the earth's surface to another point on the surface. Typical satellites include Iridium, Telstar, and Intelsat. Communications satellites use transponders. A **transponder** is a radio that receives a conversation at one frequency and then amplifies it and retransmits it back to earth on another frequency.
- *Scientific satellites* perform a variety of scientific missions. The Hubble space telescope is the most famous scientific satellite, but there are many others looking at everything from sun spots to gamma rays.
- *Navigational satellites* help ships and planes navigate. The most famous are the GPS Navstar satellites.
- *Rescue satellites* respond to radio distress signals.
- *Earth observation satellites* observe the planet for changes in everything from temperature to forestation to ice sheet coverage. The most famous is the Landsat series.
- *Military satellites* perform a wide range of surveillance activities. Intelligence-gathering possibilities using high-tech electronic and sophisticated photographic equipment reconnaissance are endless. Applications may include:
  - Relaying encrypted communications
  - Nuclear monitoring
  - Observing enemy movements
  - Early warning of missile launches
  - Eavesdropping on terrestrial radio links
  - Radar imaging
- *Photography satellites* use what are essentially large telescopes to take pictures of militarily interesting areas as well as a wide range of civilian photography uses.[4]

All satellites, regardless of their mission, have several basic components. First, they have a metal or composite frame and body. This is usually very thin, because structural integrity is not as much of an issue in gravity-less space. Second, satellites have a source of power (usually solar cells) and batteries for storage. Arrays of solar cells provide power to charge rechargeable batteries. Newer designs include using fuel cells. Power on most satellites is precious and very limited, because the technology relating to solar cells is not very advanced (i.e., solar cells cannot accumulate very much power). Nuclear power has also been used on space probes to other planets. Nuclear-powered spacecraft do not suffer this power shortage, but, due to environmental concerns, nuclear power is only used for spacecraft that will *not* be cir-

---

[4]See www.howstuffworks.com/framed.htm?parent=satellite.htm&url=http://spacelink.nasa.gov/Instructional.Materials/Multimedia/Satellite.Tracking/.index.html to see what satellites will pass over your location at any given time.

cling the earth. Third, satellites have an onboard computer to control and monitor the different systems. This onboard computer system can be more or less advanced, depending on what it is expected to control. Fourth, satellites hold a radio system and antenna. Some satellites contain multiple antennas of varying strengths. Finally, they have an attitude control system to keep the satellite pointed in the right direction.

Also, here are several other attributes that affect satellite orbit such as a satellite's speed, the solar wind and the gravitational fields of the Earth, moon and sun. Each one of these factors can speed up or slow down a satellite depending on which axis the force and direction is applied to the satellite.

Over time, and left on its own, this speeding up and slowing down will cause a satellite to drift away from its operational box. To counteract these undesired forces, early engineers designed small thruster systems placed onboard the satellite for station-keeping purposes. These thruster systems have built-in redundancies to ensure satellites can be controlled at all times. The history surrounding the use of nuclear power in satellites is an interesting, if brief, one. While nuclear airplanes and rockets were being designed and then eventually shelved, the most successful application of nuclear energy in space was born a safe, effective and reliable power source known as the Radioisotope Thermoelectric Generator (RTG) has powered satellites to the far reaches of the solar system and beyond.[5] In the early years of space research scientists knew they needed a long-lived power source that would also be compact and able to endure a rocket ride into space. Chemical batteries, fuel cells and solar panels were all tried. Batteries and fuel cells were limited by their fuel, and solar panels took up large amounts of space and would not be effective for missions far from the sun. A new concept was investigated, namely a power generator that worked from the heat given off by a decaying radioactive source.

An RTG consists of two pieces: a radioactive element used as a heat source (such as Plutonium-238, which becomes physically hot as it decays) and a way to convert heat into electricity. The heat is converted to electricity by a thermoelectric converter which takes advantage of the Seebeck Effect.

The Seebeck Effect is a principle of thermoelectricity discovered in 1822, where a voltage is produced when electrons move across the junction of two different types of material, usually metals or semiconductors, when the materials are at different temperatures.

On June 29, 1961, the United States Navy launched the first satellite powered by an RTG that generated 3 watts of electricity. Since that time the U.S. has launched a total of 26 spacecraft using RTGs (with these satellites or spacecraft often using more than one RTG to generate the needed electricity). RTGs provided power on the moon's surface during the Apollo missions, kept the Pioneer and Voyager satellites going on their long trips through the solar system and most recently have powered the Galileo mission to Jupiter, the Ulysses mission to the Sun and the Cassini mission to Saturn.

A Radioisotope Thermoelectric Generator. *(Courtesy of NASA)*

The Cassini mission, in particular, has experienced its share of controversy.[6] Previous missions as mentioned above utilized nuclear power but activists, for a

[5]http://www.aboutnuclear.org/view.cgi?fC=Space,History

[6]http://motherjones.com/politics/1997/09/cassini-controversy

variety of reasons, concentrated their efforts on stopping the launch of the Cassini spacecraft.

Cassini completed its initial four-year mission to explore the Saturn System in June 2008 and the first extended mission, called the Cassini Equinox Mission in September 2010. Now, the spacecraft is seeking to make exciting new discoveries in a second extended mission called the Cassini Solstice Mission.[7]

Cassini launched in October 1997 with the European Space Agency's Huygens probe. The probe was equipped with six instruments to study Titan, Saturn's largest moon. It landed on Titan's surface on Jan. 14, 2005, and returned spectacular results.

Meanwhile, Cassini's 12 instruments have returned a daily stream of data from Saturn's system since arriving at Saturn in 2004.

As the launch date neared, Cassini's radioactive cargo attracted increased scrutiny from the mainstream press. It had all the elements of a sensational story: A nerve-racking flyby of Earth two years after launch will bring it 500 scant miles from the planet's surface; scientists disagree wildly over the consequences of a potential accident; and activists claim that NASA could, but refuses to, use solar energy instead. NASA defends the mission. By its calculations, the chances of an accident that could release plutonium are incredibly slim—less than 1 in 1,400 at launch (this is when the space shuttle *Challenger* exploded in 1986), 1 in 476 just after launch, and less than 1 in a million during Cassini's flyby of Earth in August 1999.

If a worst-case-scenario accident occurs—if the probe re-enters Earth's atmosphere and spews vaporized plutonium—NASA's 1995 environmental impact statement estimates that up to 5 billion people could be "exposed." But the individual doses of radiation would be so small—1 millirem per year—that at most 120 humans could die from Cassini-caused cancer over 50 years. It wouldn't be possible to distinguish those fatalities from the umpteen-thousand deaths caused by other sources of radiation.

But critics disagree with NASA's calculations. "Give me a break. They're making these numbers up," says Michio Kaku, a professor of nuclear physics at the City University of New York, adding that by his calculations of NASA's own accident scenario, some 200,000 people could die if Cassini crashed in an urban area. "This is a science experiment, and we are the guinea pigs."

What transpired at and after launch? Nothing but success. No "disaster" occurred; no nuclear fallout from an explosion, etc. NASA's position is that no power source other than nuclear power can be successful as a power source on voyages so far away from the sun since solar power will be useless at that distance (not enough sunshine to provide power) and battery technology is not advanced enough to provide necessary power for extended missions.

To be clear, there have been accidents involving RTG-powered satellites. These were all caused by rocket failure or by a satellite dropping back to earth. The RTG power supplies were never a cause of the accident as there are no parts that would explode, rupture or otherwise affect a spacecraft and no nuclear fallout has been ever recorded.

---

[7]http://saturn.jpl.nasa.gov/mission/introduction

9.5 ORBITAL MECHANICS

Think about what happens when you throw a ball. Imagine that you are standing in a big field and throw a baseball as hard as you can. The ball may go 100 feet (30 m) and then hit the ground, but you put the ball in orbit. It's just that a ball's orbit is very short! Now imagine that you shot a rifle straight and level instead of throwing a ball. The bullet might travel 1 mile (1.6 km) before succumbing to gravity and hitting the ground. Now imagine that you shoot a very large cannon that is able to give its shell an extremely high initial velocity. Also imagine that our world is completely covered in water to remove any worries about hills, and that the cannon is shot straight and level. Its path might look like this:

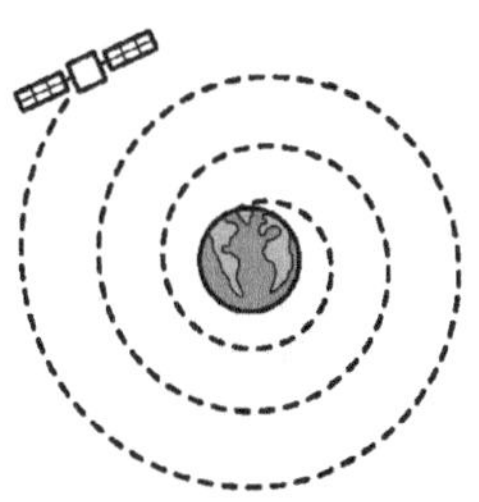

In this diagram you can see that the shell is going far enough to actually follow the curve of the earth for a period of time before hitting the ground. One thing that needs to be considered is air resistance, or drag. Imagine that you took the cannon to the moon and mounted it on top of the highest mountain. The moon has no atmosphere and is completely surrounded by the vacuum of space. If you adjusted the speed of the shell just right and shot the cannon, the shell would follow the curve of the moon perfectly. The shell would fall at exactly the same rate that the curve of the moon falls away from it, so it would never hit the ground. Eventually the shell would curve all the way around the moon and ram right into the back of the cannon! On the moon you could actually have satellites in extremely low orbits like that—just a couple of miles off the ground to avoid the mountains. In addition, satellites could conceivably be launched from cannons.

On the earth it is not so easy, because satellites have to get up above the atmosphere and into the vacuum of space to orbit for any length of time. The minimum to avoid atmospheric interference is about 200 miles (320 km). The Hubble space telescope orbits at an altitude of about 380 miles (600 km). The principle, however, is exactly the same. The speed of the satellite is adjusted so that it falls to earth at the same rate that the curve of the earth falls away from the satellite. The satellite is perpetually falling, but it never hits the ground.

LEO satellites are generally used for communications services or surveillance activities. In the communications arena, these services are satellite telephony; in the surveillance arena, LEOs are used primarily by the military to determine the activities of surface-based entities such as ships and troop formations. LEO satellites have certain advantages when compared with the more widely used GEO satellites. The LEO satellites' nearer proximity to the earth allow them the ability to communicate with earth stations using much less power than GEO satellites are required to use. This is because the satellite does not require as much power to send messages back and forth since the distance is not great. To transmit data over longer distances, much more powerful transmitters are required. The exception to this is the NASA space probes. These probes utilize low-power transmitters because the timeliness of the transmission is not as much of an issue as opposed to a businessperson talking to colleagues on a satellite telephone network. Therefore, a LEO satellite can be built much smaller than a GEO satellite that supplies the same type of service. These satellites range from over 1,000 kg (2,200 lb) to less than 10 kg (22 lb). Due to their smaller size, LEOs can be launched at around $50 million, as opposed to some GEO launches that costs in the neighborhood of $400 million in 1998 and over $500 million in 2002 (Goldin 1998). This cost also does not account for the price of the payload about the rocket. For example, hurricane watch satellites can cost $300 million, and missile warning satellites can cost $700 million, as in the case of the Defense Support Program (DSP) missile warning satellite launched in 2000.[8] The DSP satellite is a heat-sensing telescope that, from its vantage point high above the planet, looks down on earth in a constant vigil to detect missile launches or nuclear detonations. Another important factor with satellites is the cost of the launch. According to some reports[9], a satellite launch can cost anywhere between $50 million and $400 million. However, the increased participation of emerging-market economies such as India and China in the overall space market will continue to exert downward pressure on launch and satellite prices[10] since launches here are less expensive.

Typically, a LEO satellite uses 20 dB (100 times) less power than a GEO satellite. The propagation delay for the LEO is much less than either GEO or MEO. **Propagation delay** is the amount of time it takes for a signal to go from one point to another. In fact, the propagation delay is about 13 microseconds (ms) for a round-trip, two-way conversation. How does this compare to a GEO? The propagation delay for a LEO is about 13 ms, while this same trip takes 0.25 seconds and almost 0.5 seconds for GEO satellites.

Now that we have discussed the advantages of LEOs, there are a few disadvantages.

A LEO, at an altitude of 1,000 km on an equatorial orbit, will circle the earth in about 100 minutes. This speed makes it difficult to locate, track, and communicate with. This, in turn, results in the need for highly sophisticated communications equipment, because it is a moving target and it is much more difficult to track and communicate with a moving target than a stationary one like a GEO. Another disadvantage of LEOs is that more satellites are needed to achieve the desired coverage of the earth's surface. The footprint of the LEO signal coverage is much less than satellites with higher orbits. For complete earth coverage, it requires forty to sixty (depending on exact orbital height) LEOs working together, while all-over earth coverage from GEOs requires only three to six satellites due to their higher altitude from the earth's surface. Finally, there exists a serious drawback concerning LEOs that is directly related to their orbital height. LEOs, because of their low orbital height, are actually in the upper ranges of the earth's atmosphere. This produces a drag effect and their orbits slowly decay. As their orbit decays, they fall into denser atmospheric layers and the decay increases. Eventually, the LEO satellite will crash. To forestall this eventuality as long as possible, LEOs typically use rocket motors which attempt to counter the orbital decay scenario. This works to delay the crash until the fuel runs out.

---

[8]For updates on the cost of satellites, go to www.howstuffworks.com/satellite7.htm or the official NASA govt site: www.nasa.gov.

[9]http://www.howstuffworks.com/framed.htm?parent=satellite.htm&url=http://www.hq.nasa.gov/office/legaff/9-23gold.html

[10]http://www.space.com/news/090615-satellite-futures.html

LEO Systems

Most LEOs are used as communications satellites. A key factor in the success of many LEO systems is personal communications services. To succeed, LEOs have to compete with terrestrial cellular phone systems. To see a comparison of terrestrial-based versus satellite-based cellular calls, see Figure 9.8.

The rapidly increasing quality of terrestrial PCS puts a huge burden on satellite systems to perform better. To compete with current terrestrial communications systems, a satellite system cannot offer substandard services, especially at the high prices of $1.50 to $7.00 per minute. Satellite systems have the problem of overcoming technological barriers, such as the interference caused by storms on the earth's surface, solar flare activity, and the sheer distance over which they must transmit information from people's telephone conversations to messaging data as in the case of WAP telephony.

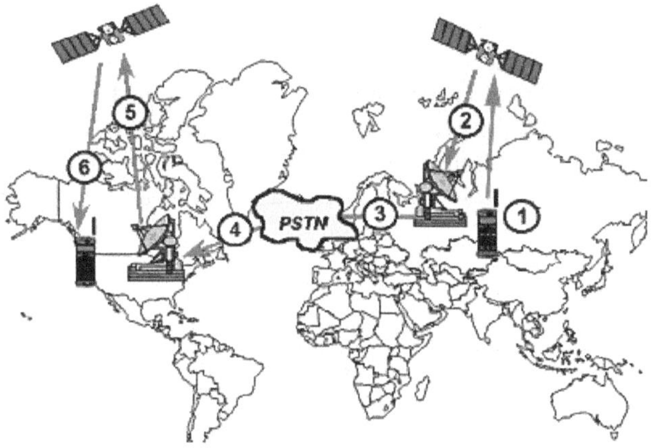

Making a Call via Satellite versus Cellular

1. A subscriber in Russia calls a friend in San Francisco on a Globalstar satellite phone. The signal is handled by a passing satellite.
2. The satellite relays the call to a gateway in its footprint.

3–4. The gateway converts the signal to work with the local PSTN and passes on the call. Depending on the distance between the callers, a Globalstar satellite call might pass through several gateways and PSTNs before locating the receiving phone. The PSTN uses the call's routing information to connect to another gateway that knows where the receiving phone is located.

5. The gateway located closest to the receiving phone converts the signal to Globalstar format and uplinks it to a satellite. This gateway knows that the receiving phone is in its contact area, because an earlier satellite relayed that phone's power-on registration message to the gateway. This information was stored in the gateway's visitor location register (VLR).
6. The call is relayed to the receiving phone and the call linkage is complete.

Figure 9.8 Satellite versus Terrestrial Cellular Calling
(Courtesy of www.globalstar.com)

History and current events also play a key role in understanding the unique environment of LEOs. When Iridium and Globalstar were first being conceived in the late 1980s and early 1990s, worldwide cellular phone coverage was sparse. Gaining the necessary international government approvals to launch dozens of satellites in space and to establish on-ground base stations in hundreds of nations took years. By then, wireless services widely proliferated; prices for cellular telephone calls fell dramatically, and the handsets became smaller and easier to use. By the time the satellites were ready (meaning launched, set into orbit, established connectivity between the satellites and ground stations, and worked out all anomalies), cell phones had captured most of the market Globalstar and Iridium were targeting. In addition, initial satellite phones were large and bulky with sizable antennas which made them awkward to use. They were also the size of a medium suitcase. Now they are smaller, just a little larger than a typical cellular phone, as shown in Figure 9.9. These phones were costly, too, with first generation Iridium handsets going for as much as $3,000. The original Iridium services cost the user as much as $5 to $7 per minute, quickly relegating satellite phones to the wealthy international business traveler and government agencies that needed communications in remote locations.

The mass-market consumer had hardly heard of Iridium or Globalstar[11] and was certainly unwilling to pay their costly per-minute fees. Some analysts say satellite phone systems amounted to overkill for most consumers, limiting them to a small target audience. If you are part of that limited audience, however, then a satellite phone is a must.

Figure 9.9 Typical Iridium Phone *(Courtesy of www.iridium.com)*

[11]For more information on Globalstar, go to www.globalstar.com.

9.6 IRIDIUM

The first and probably the most recognized name in LEO satellite constellations is Iridium.[12] Motorola first proposed this system in 1987 and applied for an FCC license in 1990. These Iridium satellites, when set into orbit, can handle over 2,000 simultaneous full-duplex connections, or over 140,000 connections system wide (see Figure 9.10).

Originally when launched in the early 1990s, this system was famous for being on the cutting edge of communications technology. The idea of using LEO satellites for cellular telephony, anywhere in the world, was a bold initiative. Advantages to a satellite-based telephony system include having no cellular towers every 5 miles and no building permits.

With this advantage, why has Iridium failed to capture a profitable market share? Basically, it is an issue of sheer economics on the consumer side. Phone sets can be expensive, especially when compared to a typical cell phone. For example, handsets were once priced well over $3,000. Now, in 2011, they still sell around $1300 as shown here:

Iridium 9555 Satellite Phone[13]
$1349.00 Standard Phone Kit W/ All Accessories
$1249.00 Phone and Basic Accessories (Phone,Bat,Wall Charger)

Check out the new iridium 9555 satellite phone at GlobalCom. This is the smallest and lightest of the Iridium handsets.

The Iridium 9555 satellite phone is designed to withstand the toughest environments and will work from anywhere on the planet to anywhere. All that is required is a clear view of sky.

Users can choose from prepaid service plans or monthly service plans to complete the package.

With Iridium there are no roaming and no long distance charges, just one simple rate. Act now, there is a limited supply.

Iridium 9555 Product Brochure

Technical Specifications for Iridium Phones:

- Dimensions: 143 mm (L) × 55 mm (W) × 30 mm (D)
- Weight: 266g (9.4 oz)
- Standby time: Up to 30 hours
- Talk time: Up to 4 hours
- 200 character illuminated graphic display
- Volume, signal and battery strength meters
- Illuminated weather-resistant keypad
- Integrated speakerphone
- Quick-connect to Iridium voicemail
- Two-way SMS and short email capability
- Pre-programmable International Access Code (00 or +)
- Mailbox for voice, numeric & text messages
- Selectable ring and alert tones (8 choices)

[12]Information on the new Iridium system can be found at www.iridium.com.

[13]http://www.globalcomsatphone.com/iridium/9555_phone.html

- 100 entry internal address book, with capacity for multiple phone numbers, email addresses and notes
- SIM-based address book with 155 entry capacity
- Call history retains received, missed and dialed calls
- User-configurable call timers to manage costs
- Keypad lock and PIN lock for additional security

GlobalCom's Standard Iridium 9555 Satellite Phones Include:

- Iridium 9555 Hand Held Phone
- AC Wall Charger
- One High Capacity Battery
- International Adapters
- Cigarette Lighter Adapter
- Ear Piece
- Auxiliary Antenna
- Auxiliary Antenna Adapter
- Leather Case
- Instruction Manual
- One Year Warranty
- Price $1349.00

These were the size of a large briefcase and included a foldout antenna. In addition, the user would pay about $7 per minute for airtime use, which is also more than most nonglobal wireless services at $0.10 per minute (Grice 2000).

Iridium's design also posed a problem. There were sixty-six Iridium satellites launched so that the entire planet could be covered; but most of the users of wireless telephony do not particularly need global coverage, especially for the costs they would incur. There is little commercial need to provide coverage over the oceans or in deep forests or other inaccessible locations.

Figure 9.10 Typical Iridium Satellites *(Courtesy of www.iridium.com)*

Governments and scientists may need such coverage, but that target audience is too small to provide any positive return on investments for a system this large. The initial start-up costs for Iridium 66 are estimated at $7 billion.

The market situation of terrestrial-based cellular telephony systems has improved dramatically. The growth of the market for wireless communications has been staggering, and the subscriber base has increased as well. Government involvement by subsidizing the expansion of cellular telephony systems, particularly in Europe, has also been a factor.

The Iridium system has had an interesting history. It began in January 1999 and with billions of dollars from Motorola, its primary backer, Iridium has struggled toward profitability. A firm called Iridium Satellite7 is now in charge of the Iridium system and has found some success (Grice 2000). In December 2000, the U.S. Defense Department signed a $72 million, 2-year deal to use Iridium Satellite's space-based phone network to provide secure voice communications for the navy and other government users (Grice 2000). The contract calls for Iridium Satellite to provide unlimited use for up to 20,000 government workers. Expected rates for nondefense users are in the $1.50 per minute range. This is comparable with Globalstar, a major competitor (see below).

One reason the cost per minute is lower than the initial Iridium system backed by Motorola is that the new firm purchased the Iridium system from the bankruptcy court at $25 million. This compares with the $5 billion Motorola put into the original Iridium system to get it going.

Despite the rosy market projections that have yet to pan out, the original (and now the new) Iridium's service has found a niche among industrial, personal, and military users: mining operators, offshore drilling rigs, Iditarod dog sled racers in Alaska, and CNN international correspondents. The ability to deliver service nearly anywhere on the globe has made satellite phones an attractive alternative to spotty cellular service for those willing to pay a hefty premium (Grice 2000).

9.7 GLOBALSTAR

The Globalstar satellite system began in January 2000. It is another LEO-based satellite system attempting to be commercially successful in the satellite-based telephony market. Unlike the original Iridium, which ceased operations with 63,000 customers (though this is difficult to ascertain), the Globalstar system has 75,000 subscribers as of August 2002. (Globalstar Reports 2001).

The Globalstar system is similar to Iridium. Unlike the primarily voice-oriented Iridium, Globalstar offers voice, fax, and paging services worldwide using a constellation of LEO satellites. Globalstar's market is mainly remote areas. The company hopes to create a profitable niche market by offering services to remote areas around the world.

Globalstar handsets were priced at around $1000 with per minute rates at 17¢/minute as of August 2002 but have been reduced in price to under $500 in 2011 with very reasonable pricing plans.[14] Figure 9.11 displays a typical Globalstar phone and pricing plan. The implementation costs are $2.5 billion, which is just about half as much as Iridium, but is configured to manage 3 to 4 times the call volume.

---

[14]http://www.globalstar.com/shop/index.php?main_page=product_info&cPath=1&products_id=39

Figure 9.11 The GSP-1700 Handheld Satellite Phone

Loaded with Features:

- Compact size: 5.3"H x 2.2"W x 1.5"D
- Lightweight: 7.05 ounces
- Optimal voice clarity
- Backlit color display optimized for outdoor daytime viewing
- Long-life battery: 4 hours talk time, 36 hours standby
- Ergonomic design
- Lighted keypad

GSP-1700 Satellite Phone for **$499** with unlimited airtime voice plan at **$19.99** per month.

Small Phone, Huge Advantages

Enjoy crystal-clear voice quality. Whisper and be heard with CDMA digital voice quality. Fast data speeds at 9.6 Kbps. Position Location Service—get your Latitude and Longitude directly from your Globalstar phone. Enjoy locally based phone numbers where available.

This increased volume is mainly due to the use of the advanced digital compression technique CDMA, which also allows for far higher voice quality.

Globalstar is a consortium of leading international telecommunications companies originally established in 1991 to deliver satellite telephony services through a network of exclusive service providers. The consortium is a partnership of the world's leading telecommunications service providers and equipment manufacturers, including cofounders Loral Space & Communications, Qualcomm Incorporated, Alenia, China Telecom (HK), DACOM, DaimlerChrysler Aerospace, Elsacom (a Finmeccanica Company), Hyundai, TE.SA.M (a France Telecom/Alcatel company), Space Systems/Loral; and Vodafone Group PLC.

Specifically, the Globalstar system is designed to provide high-quality satellite-based telephony services to a broad range of users:

- Cellular users who roam outside of conventional coverage areas
- People who work in remote areas where terrestrial systems do not exist
- Residents of underserved markets who can use Globalstar's fixed-site phones to satisfy their needs for basic telephony
- International travelers who need to keep in constant touch

The Globalstar system offers the following services to users.

- One phone for both cellular and satellite calls
- Voice calling
- Short messaging service
- Global roaming
- Facsimile
- Data transmission

Globalstar's constellation of LEO satellites transmits calls from a Globalstar wireless phone or fixed phone station to a terrestrial gateway, where the calls are passed on to existing fixed and cellular telephone networks in more than 100 countries on six continents.

Gateways

Gateways are an integral part of the Globalstar ground segment, which also includes ground operations control centers (GOCCs), satellite operations control centers (SOCCs), and the Globalstar Data Network (GDN).

Each gateway, which is owned and managed by the service provider for the region (i.e., one gateway may serve several countries) in which the gateway is located, receives transmissions from orbiting satellites, processes calls, and switches them to the appropriate ground network. An individual gateway may service more than one country. Gateways consist of three or four dish antennas, a switching station, and remote operating controls. Because all of the switches and

Figure 9.12 Typical Globalstar Satellites *(Courtesy of www.globalstar.com)*

complex hardware are located on the ground, it is easier for Globalstar to maintain and upgrade its system than it is for systems that handle switching in orbit.

Gateways offer seamless integration with local and regional telephony and wireless networks. They utilize a standard high-speed, or T-1, interface to the existing PSTN. Encryption ensures voice and signaling security for individual transmissions.

The GOCCs are responsible for planning and controlling the use of the satellites by the gateway terminals and for coordinating with the SOCC. GOCCs plan the communications schedules for the gateways and control the allocation of satellite resources to each gateway. Figure 9.12 shows typical Globalstar satellites.

The SOCC manages the Globalstar satellite constellation. It tracks satellites, controls their orbits, and provides telemetry and command (T&C) services for 9 Eight orbital planes of six satellites each, inclined at 52 degrees to provide service on earth from 70 degrees North latitude to 70 degrees South.

Globalstar satellites continuously transmit spacecraft telemetry data that provide onboard diagnostic and status reports for the satellites. The SOCC also oversees each satellite launch and any deployment activities. The SOCC and GOCC facilities remain in constant contact through the GDN. The GDN is the connective network that provides wide-area intercommunications facilities for the gateways, GOCCs, and SOCCs.

As a wholesaler, Globalstar sells access to its system to regional and local telecom service providers around the world. These Globalstar partners, such as Qualcomm Inc., in turn form alliances with additional providers. This lets Globalstar leverage the marketing, operating, and technical capabilities of the world's premier communications service providers. A typical Globalstar phone can be seen in Figure 9.13.

The Globalstar constellation consists of forty-eight LEO satellites, plus an additional four satellites in orbit as spares. Each consists of an antenna, a trapezoidal body, two solar arrays, and a magnetometer, and operates at an altitude of 876 miles (1,414 km). The satellites are placed in such an orbit that the polar

Figure 9.13 Typical Globalstar Satellite Phone *(Courtesy of www.globalstar.com)*

regions—including most of Greenland, small parts of Alaska, Canada, Scandinavia, Siberia, and regions in the Southern Hemisphere, including Antarctica and parts of South America—are not covered. This is entirely acceptable because these areas are not considered to be profitable. The Globalstar constellation of satellites can then pick up signals from over 80 percent of the earth's surface. Several satellites pick up a call, and this "path diversity" ensures that the call does not get dropped even if one of the phones moves out of sight of one of the satellites. If buildings or terrain block the phone signal, a "soft handover" takes place, and the call's transmission is switched to an alternate satellite with no interruption.

Satellite Footprint

The satellite coverage beams for satellite phone communication links are large, as shown in Figure 9.14. Try to imagine the scale for the coverage of a typical 3,600-mile-diameter beam footprint. Each footprint moves rapidly across the earth's surface. A satellite that passes directly overhead of a specific point on the earth's surface is visible to that spot for only about 15 minutes.

When a user places a Globalstar satellite call, the nearest satellite picks up the signal. Globalstar satellite phones can operate with a single satellite in view, though typically two to four satellites will be overhead. This simultaneous coverage by multiple satellites is called path diversity, which enhances the quality of the Globalstar satellite call.

Path Diversity

Path diversity is a method of signal reception that combines multiple signals of varying power strengths into a single coherent signal, as shown in Figure 9.15. Satellite

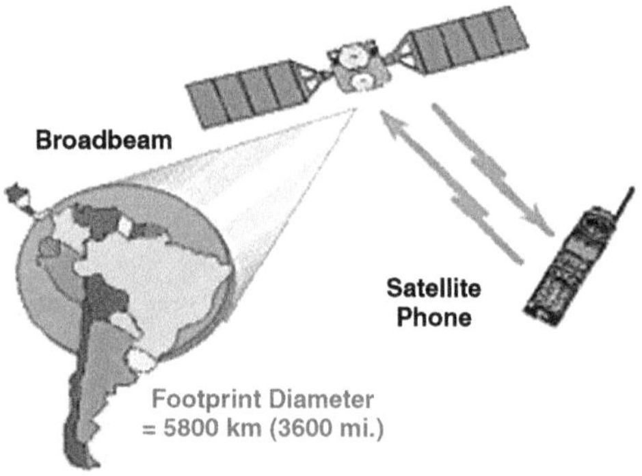

Figure 9.14 Footprint of a Satellite
(Courtesy of www.globalstar.com)

Figure 9.15 Path Diversity
(Courtesy of www.globalstar.com)

phones communicate with as many as three satellites simultaneously, combining those signals into a single, static-free signal. Globalstar satellite phones also alter power levels to compensate for shadowing and interference as needed.

As satellites move in and out of view, they will be seamlessly added to and removed from the calls in progress, reducing call interruption. This enables the Globalstar system to provide superior service to a wide variety of locations with less potential for signal blockage from buildings, terrain, or other natural features. A coverage map can be seen in Figure 9.16.

The first satellites were launched in February 1998, but system deployment was delayed due to a launch failure in September 1998 that resulted in the loss of 12 satellites in a launch by the Russian Space Agency (used due to the reduced costs charged). In February 2000, it launched the last of 52 satellites—48 satellites and four spares (reduced from the original plan of eight spares).

The first call on the original Globalstar system was placed on November 1, 1998, from Qualcomm chairman Irwin Jacobs in San Diego to Loral Space & Communications CEO and chairman Bernard Schwartz in New York.

In December 1999, the system began limited commercial service for 200 users with the full 48 satellites (no spares in orbit). In February 2000, it began full

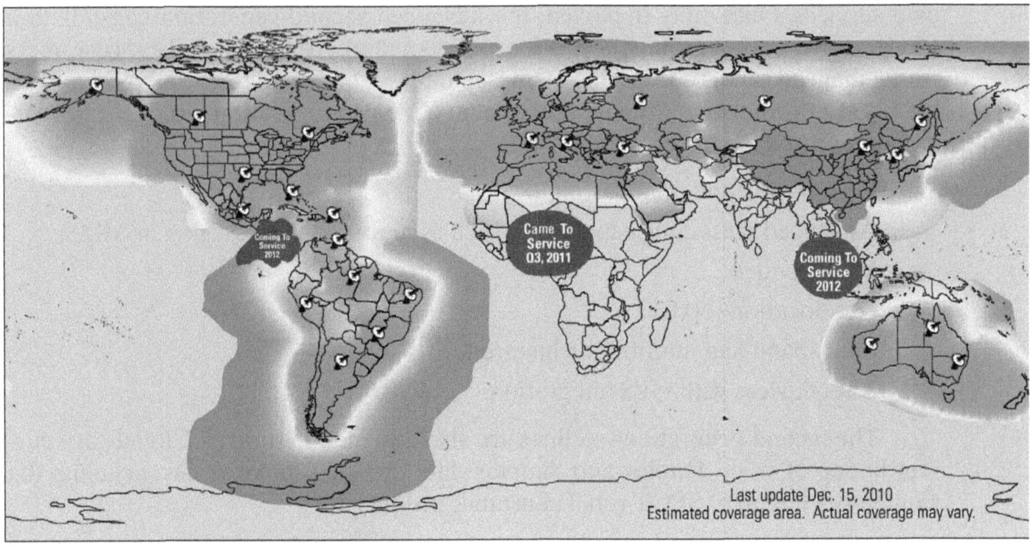

Figure 9.16 Globalstar Coverage Map
(Courtesy of www.globalstar.com)

commercial service with its 48 satellites and 4 spares in North America, Europe and Brazil.

On February 15, 2002, the predecessor company Globalstar (old Globalstar) and three of its subsidiaries filed voluntary petitions under Chapter 11 of the United States Bankruptcy Code.

In 2004, restructuring of the old Globalstar was completed. The first stage of the restructuring was completed on December 5, 2003, when Thermo Capital Partners LLC was deemed to obtain operational control of the business, as well as certain ownership rights and risks. Thermo Capital Partners, became the principal owner.

Globalstar LLC was formed as a Delaware limited liability company in November 2003, and was converted into Globalstar, Inc., on March 17, 2006.

In 2007 Globalstar launched eight additional first-generation spare satellites into space.[15] These second-generation satellites are expected to provide Globalstar customers with satellite voice and data services until at least 2025. Eighteen more satellite Launches are scheduled in February, April and June 2011.[16]

Globalstar, had approximately 315,000 customers reported in 2008 and 350,000 in 2010 and is still struggling to be profitable.

On October 19th, 2010 Globalstar launched its second-generation satellite constellation designed to restore its industry leading commercial voice and duplex

[15]http://en.wikipedia.org/wiki/Globalstar

[16]http://www.spaceflightnow.com/tracking/index.html

data services. Once fully deployed, the advanced second-generation constellation and next-generation ground network are designed to provide Globalstar customers with enhanced services featuring increased data speeds of up to 256 Kbps in a flexible Internet protocol multimedia subsystem (IMS) configuration. Products and services supported are expected to include:

- Push-to-talk and multicasting.
- Advanced messaging capabilities such as multimedia messaging or MMS.
- Mobile video.
- Geo-location services.
- Multi-band and multi-mode handsets.
- Data devices with GPS integration.

The second-generation satellites are also designed to support Globalstar's current lineup of voice, Duplex and Simplex data products and services including the Company's lineup of SPOT retail consumer products.

9.8 ORBCOMM

ORBCOMM advertises itself as the world's first commercial provider of global LEO satellite data communication services.[17] The ORBCOMM system enables businesses to track remote and mobile assets such as trailers, railcars, locomotives, and heavy equipment; to monitor remote utility meters and oil and gas storage tanks, wells, and pipelines; and to stay in touch with remote workers anywhere on the globe.

Frequency Allocation

The ORBCOMM system uses 137 to 138 MHz and 400 MHz frequencies for transmissions down to mobile or fixed data communications devices, and 148 to 150 MHz frequencies for transmissions up to the satellites. These frequencies, approved for use by LEO satellite systems at the World Administrative Radio Conference in February 1992, were allocated by the FCC to little LEO mobile satellite services in January 1993. The FCC granted ORBCOMM a U.S. commercial license in October 1994.

Description

The ORBCOMM system uses LEO satellites instead of terrestrial fixed-site relay repeaters to provide worldwide geographic coverage as can be seen in Figure 9.17. The system is capable of sending and receiving two-way alphanumeric packets, similar to two-way paging or e-mail. The three main components of the ORBCOMM system are (1) the **space segment**, the constellation of satellites; (2) the **ground segment**,

[17]http://www.orbcomm.com

gateways that include the gateway control centers (GCCs) and gateway earth stations (GESs) and the network control center (NCC) located in the United States; and (3) **subscriber communicators** (SCs), handheld devices for personal messaging as well as fixed and mobile units for remote monitoring and tracking.

ORBCOMM satellites are relatively small in size, weighing less than one hundred pounds and measuring only forty-two inches in diameter and six inches in height before deployment. Their compact profile is a result of the fact that they do not require a propulsion system to maintain the appropriate orbit, and they have significantly lower power requirements, giving them more reliable travel patterns and a longer functional lifecycle than geostationary satellites.

Each satellite is equipped with a VHF and Ultra High Frequency, or UHF, communication payload capable of operation in the 137.0–150.05 MHz and the 400.075–400.125 MHz bands. The use of the system uplink (earth-to-space) spectrum is managed by an on-board computer that employs the ORBCOMM-pioneered Dynamic Channel Activity Assignment System, or DCAAS. DCAAS continuously scans the authorized spectrum, identifies frequencies already in use and dynamically assigns your uplink channel to minimize interference. DCAAS changes the uplink frequency at least every 15 seconds, which allows our system to coexist with the current users of the VHF frequency band, and limits its interference.

The gateway earth stations and the subscriber communicators communicate with the satellites in the same VHF band, thus reducing complexity, size, power and cost of supporting multiple communications on a single satellite—reductions that are reflected in our affordable subscription rates.

Similar to the other LEO-based systems, ORBCOMM has experienced financial difficulties. In fact, it changed hands in mid-2000 when International

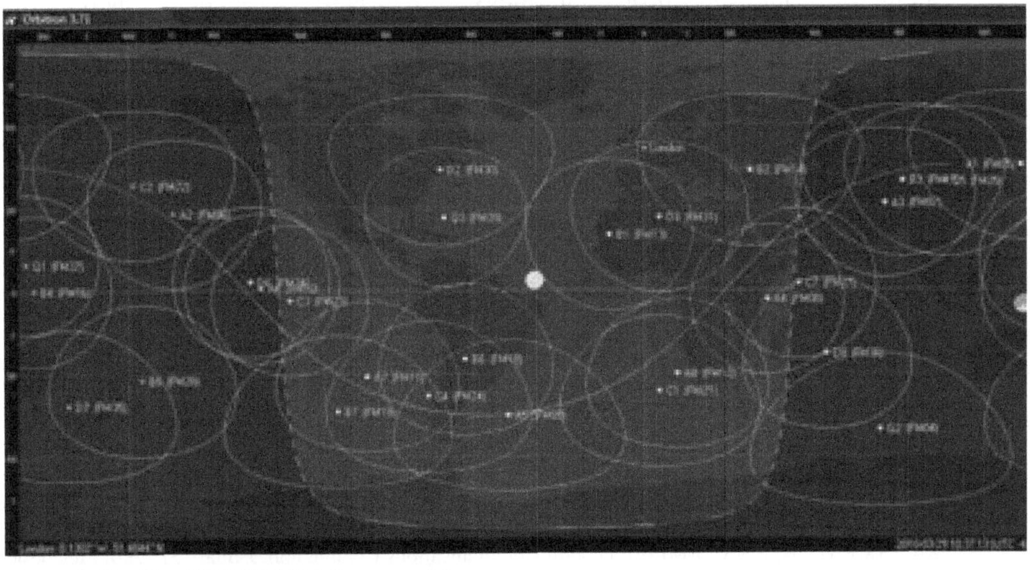

Figure 9.17 The ORBCOMM Coverage Map
(Courtesy of www.orbcomm.com)

Licensees purchased the firm in bankruptcy court. These new owners are believed to have bought the assets of the firm for a fraction of the $810 million that investors sank into it (the company did not disclose the purchase price) (Reuters 2001). This should help ORBCOMM because it will allow the company to offer lower rates to its customers. However, times have still been difficult. ORBCOMM's operating loss for the third quarter ending September 30, 2010 was $0.4 million loss in the third quarter of 2009. As of September 30, 2010, there were about 556,000 billable subscriber communicators, a 9.2% increase over the third quarter of 2009. Total net additions during the quarter were 16,000, with net satellite subscriber additions of approximately 13,000 and terrestrial subscribers increasing more than 3,000. "We are encouraged by the continued improvement in subscriber growth during the quarter, as many of our resellers and OEMs in particular have been benefiting from improving trends," said Marc Eisenberg, ORBCOMM's Chief Executive Officer.[18]

LEO satellites have had a turbulent time. After all, this frontier was a new one and has required a great deal of technological advance and patience. There have been failures such as Teledesic. Teledesic was a company founded in the 1990s to build a commercial broadband satellite constellation for Internet services. Using low-earth orbiting satellites small antennas could be used to provide uplinks of as much as 100 Mbit/second and downlinks of up to 720 Mbit/second.[19] The original 1995 proposal was extremely ambitious, costing over US$9 billion and originally planning 840 active satellites with in-orbit spares at an altitude of 700 km. In 1997 the scheme was scaled back to 288 active satellites at 1400 km[20] and was later scaled back further in complexity and number of satellites as the projected market demand continued to decrease.

The commercial failure of the similar Iridium and Globalstar ventures (composed of 66 and 48 operational satellites, respectively) and other systems, along with bankruptcy protection filings, were primary factors in halting the project, and Teledesic officially suspended its satellite construction work on October 1, 2002.[21]

Teledesic was notable for gaining early funding from Microsoft (investing US$30 million for an 8.5% stake), Craig McCaw, Bill Gates, Paul Allen, and Saudi prince Alwaleed bin Talal, and for achieving allocation on the Ka-band frequency spectrum for non-geostationary services.

Other ventures have followed similar paths. For example, **1worldspace** is a satellite radio network that provides service to over 170,000 subscribers in eastern and southern Africa, the Middle East, and much of Asia with 96% coming from

---

[18]http://www.orbcomm.com/Collateral/Documents/English-US/ORBCOMM_FY_2010_Q3_Earnings_Release.pdf

[19]In the Matter of Teledesic Corporation: Application for Authority to Construct, Launch, and Operate a Low Earth Orbit Satellite System in the Domestic and International Fixed Satellite Service. File Nos. 22-DSS-P/LA-94, 43-SAT-AMEND-95, 127 SAT-AMEND-95. Federal Communications Commission, March 14, 1997. (Initial Teledesic FCC authorization.) Accessed March 15, 2010.

[20]In the Matter of Teledesic LLC Application for Authority to Construct, Launch, and Operate a Ka-band Satellite System in the Fixed-Satellite Service. File Nos. 22-DSS-P/LA-94, 43-SAT-AMEND-95, 127 SAT-AMEND-95, 195-SAT-ML-97. Federal Communications Commission, January 31, 2001. (Teledesic FCC Modification.) Accessed March 15, 2010.

[21]de Selding, Peter B. "Teledesic Plays Its Last Card, Leaves the Game." Space News, July 14, 2003.

India. 1worldspace claimed to be the only company with rights to the world's globally allocated spectrum for digital satellite radio.[22] However, it never made use of its license to broadcast to the Americas or the Caribbean. The company gained attention around 2000 because of its willingness to invest in impoverished areas and from 2006 to the present due to its financial difficulties and bankruptcy proceedings.

The company filed for bankruptcy in October 2008. For a while Liberty Media sought to buy the assets, but in June 2010, a company called Yazmi USA owned by former WorldSpace founder, chairman, and CEO Noah Samara purchased the remains for US$5.5M.[23]

European operations were liquidated in the spring of 2009.

On December 25, 2009, the company issued notices to all of its subscribers in India that WorldSpace service in India would officially be terminated from December 31, 2009, with no refunds given to its subscribers, on account of bankruptcy.[24]

The company was known as "WorldSpace" until July 2008.

Globalstar and other ventures will find their place, figuratively and financially, in orbit. It is expected that new and imaginative ideas and technologies will allow LEOs to become a valuable piece of the overall telecommunications pie.

9.9 MEOs

MEO systems operate at between 1,500 and 6,500 miles (10,000 km) above the earth, which is lower than GEO and higher than most LEOs. The MEO orbit is a compromise between the LEO and the GEO. Compared with LEOs, MEOs with their more distant orbit require fewer satellites to provide all-over global coverage than LEOs, because each satellite may be in view of any particular location for several hours. Compared with GEOs, MEOs can operate effectively with smaller mobile equipment and with less latency (signal delay). Their signal takes from 50 to 150 ms to make the round trip, compared with 1 to 2 seconds for a GEO. MEO satellites cover more earth area than LEO satellites but have a higher latency due to their higher orbit.

MEO satellites are in view of any point on the earth for a longer period of time than LEOs; therefore, they can be effectively used for communications, but they must be reachable. To combat the reachability problem, MEO systems often feature significant footprint coverage overlap from satellite to satellite, which in turn requires more sophisticated tracking and switching schemes than GEOs (which are stationary). Typically, MEO constellations have ten to seventeen satellites distributed over two or three orbital planes.

MEO systems plan to include AstroLink, KaStar, and CyberStar. Several systems in particular have helped form the use and development of MEO satellites. These are briefly discussed.

---

[22]http://en.wikipedia.org/wiki/1worldspace

[23]http://www.webcitation.org/5qtvGXToh

[24]http://www.worldspace.com/index_wsmsg.html

Telstar 1

The Telstar 1 was one of the first and most famous experimental satellites orbited in MEO. Figure 9.18 depicts this satellite. On July 10, 1962, NASA launched the Telstar satellite. It was the first satellite to give television signals across the Atlantic. Its orbit was such that it was visible to both Europe and the United States simultaneously during one part of its orbit and both the United States and Japan during another orbit.

The Telstar satellite was in an orbit quite a distance from the earth, outside the Van Allen belts, which protect satellites and space shuttles in low orbits from most of the harmful effects of cosmic rays and geomagnetic storms. The satellite was also in a low orbit and thus carried the same disadvantage as before, only for a few minutes each hour.

Telstar was a 170-pound experimental satellite, created by AT&T's Bell Labs and launched into elliptical orbit by NASA. It transmitted international phone calls, television programs, radio signals, and newspaper stories. The first transatlantic transmission occurred on July 11, 1962, from a twin station in Andover, Maine, via the Telstar satellite. The success of Telstar and the earth stations, the first built for active satellite communications, illustrated the potential of a future worldwide satellite system to provide communications between continents.

It is interesting to note that Telstar 1 was the first privately sponsored space launch. A MEO satellite, Telstar was placed in an elliptical orbit completed once every 2 hours and 37 minutes, inclined at an angle of approximately 45 degrees to the equator, with perigee about 1000 km from Earth and apogee about 6000 km from Earth. (This is in contrast to most of today's broadcast communications satellites, which are placed in circular geostationary orbits.)

Due to its non-geosynchronous orbit, Telstar's availability for transatlantic signals was limited to 20 minutes in each orbit that passed over the Atlantic Ocean. Ground antennas had to track the satellite as it came around the earth approximately every two and a half hours. Since the transmitting and receiving radio systems on board Telstar were not nearly as powerful or capable as those of today's

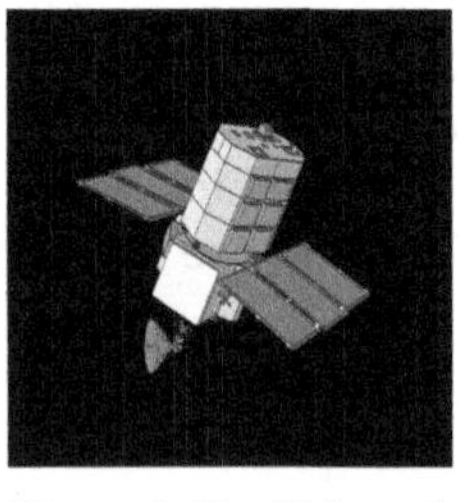

Figure 9.18 Telstar 1
(Courtesy of www.telstar.com)

satellites, the ground antennas had to be huge. The antennas were 177 feet (54 m) long and weighed 380 tons. The antennas were housed in structures the size of a 14-story office building. The challenge was to accurately steer the huge antennas to track the satellite that moved up to 1.5 degrees per second.

Telstar was considered an unqualified success for AT&T; but then, without warning, the satellite fell silent. Broadcast from the satellite ended February 1963 after radiation damaged its transistors. Telstar 1, which had ushered in a new age of the benevolent use of technology, became a victim of technology during the Cold War. The day before Telstar 1 was launched, the United States had tested a high-altitude nuclear bomb (called Starfish Prime) which energized the Earth's Van Allen Belt where Telstar 1 went into orbit. This vast increase in radiation, combined with subsequent high-altitude blasts, including a Soviet test in October, overwhelmed Telstar's fragile transistors;[25] it went out of service in early December 1962, but was restarted by a workaround in early January 1963.[26] The additional radiation associated with its return to full sunlight ("shock") once again caused a transistor failure, this time irreparably, and Telstar 1 went out of service on February 21, 1963.

The satellite that captured the world's imagination was suddenly nothing more than an expensive piece of space junk. Telstar ushered in broadcasting from space, a "first." For more "satellite firsts," please see http://en.wikipedia.org/wiki/List_of_communications_satellite_firsts.

Since then, more than ten Telnet satellites have been launched, several unsuccessfully. Currently, as of January 2011, there are seven Telstar satellites operating in orbit that provide the following services:

- Television broadcasting
- Cable and direct to home
- Sports and events
- Data transmission
- Internet applications
- Satellite news gathering
- Business television
- Distance learning
- Video conferencing

Telstar provides many services. For example, Telstar provides TV relay and broadcasting services for over 100 TV channels including:

- HBO-HDTV
- A&E Television Network
- Time Warner Cable

---

[25]Daniel R. Glover (2005-04-12). "TELSTAR." *NASA Experimental Communications Satellites.* http://roland.lerc.nasa.gov/~dglover/sat/telstar.html.

[26]Ralph D. Lorenz, David Michael Harland (2005). *Space Systems Failures: Disasters and Rescues of Satellites,* Rocket and Space Probes. Springer. ISBN 0387215190. http://books.google.com/books?id=g-UOdh34utQC&pg=RA2-PA266&dq=telstar+transistors+radiation+starfish&ei=Cc3ZRsr6FIKmowKO3eySCw&ie=ISO-8859-1&sig=WUcdA_54_3BVeGJNPokAmRrhBYk.

- AthenaTV
- InDemand
- OlympuSAT
- Playboy Television

Landsat The Landsat Program is the longest running enterprise for acquisition of imagery of the earth from space. The first Landsat satellite was launched in 1972; the most recent, Landsat 7, was launched on April 15, 1999. Landsat satellites have gradually grown in size as more capabilities have been added, with the latest, Landsat 7, weighing approximately 4,800 pounds (2,200 kg). The spacecraft is about 14 feet long (4.3 m) and 9 feet (2.8 m) in diameter.

Figure 9.19 depicts a typical Landsat satellite.

The instruments on the Landsat satellites have acquired millions of images of points on the earth's surface. The images, archived in the United States and at Landsat receiving stations around the world, are a unique resource for global change research and applications in agriculture, geology, forestry, regional planning, education, and national security.

The value of the Landsat Program was recognized by Congress in October 1992, when it passed the Land Remote Sensing Policy Act (Public Law 102-555), authorizing the procurement of Landsat 7 and assuring the continued availabilty of Landsat digital data and images, at the lowest possible cost, to traditional and new users of the data. Table 9.1 provides a summary of the Landsat satellites.

The Landsat Program has provided over almost fifty years of calibrated high spatial resolution data of the Earth's surface to a broad and varied user community, including agribusiness, global change researchers, academia, state and local governments, commercial users, military, and the international community. Landsat images provide information meeting the broad and diverse needs of business, science, education, government, and national security.

The mission of the Landsat Program is to provide repetitive acquisition of high resolution multispectral data of the Earth's surface on a global basis. Landsat represents the only source of global, calibrated, high spatial resolution measure-

Figure 9.19 Landsat 7 Satellite
(Courtesy of NASA)

Table 9.1 Landsat Program–System Summary

System	Launch (End of service)
Landsat 1	7/23/72 (1/6/78)
Landsat 2	1/22/75 (2/25/82)
Landsat 3	3/5/78 (3/31/83)
Landsat 4	7/16/82
Landsat 5	3/1/84
Landsat 6	10/5/93 (10/5/93)
Landsat 7	4/99

(Courtesy of NASA)

ments of the Earth's surface that can be compared to previous data records. The data from the Landsat spacecraft constitute the longest record of the Earth's continental surfaces as seen from space. It is a record unmatched in quality, detail, coverage, and value.

The Landsat platforms carry multiple remote sensor systems and data relay systems along with attitude-control and orbit-adjust subsystems, power supply, receivers for ground station commands and transmitters to send the data to ground receiving stations.

Landsat satellites have been providing multispectral images of the Earth continuously since the early 1970's. A unique almost fifty years data record of the Earth's land surface now exists. This unique retrospective portrait of the Earth's surface has been used across disciplines to achieve improved understanding of the Earth's land surfaces and the impact of humans on the environment. Landsat data have been utilized in a variety of government, public, private, and national security applications. Examples include land and water management, global change research, oil and mineral exploration, agricultural yield forecasting, pollution monitoring, land surface change detection, and cartographic mapping.

Landsat 7, launched in 1999, is the latest satellite in this series and can be seen in Figure 9.20. The first Landsat satellite, Landsat 1, was launched in 1972 with two Earth-viewing imagers. Landsat 2 and 3, launched in 1975 and 1978 respectively, were configured similarly. In 1984, Landsat 4 was launched the MSS and a new instrument called the Thematic Mapper (TM). Instrument upgrades included improved ground resolution (30 meters) and 3 new channels or bands. Landsat 5, a duplicate of 4, was launched in 1984. Landsat 6 was unfortunately lost immediately after launch in 1993.

Landsat 7 is a 5000 pound-class satellite designed for a 705 km, sun synchronous, earth mapping orbit with a 16-day repeat cycle. It's orbit can be seen in Figure 9.21. It's mapper camera is the most advanced ever used in space.

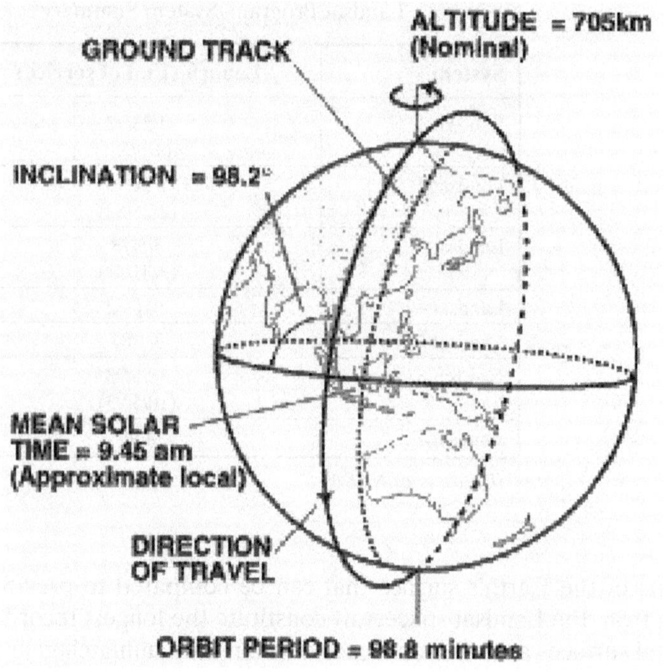

Figure 9.20 Landsat 7 Orbit
(Courtesy of NASA)

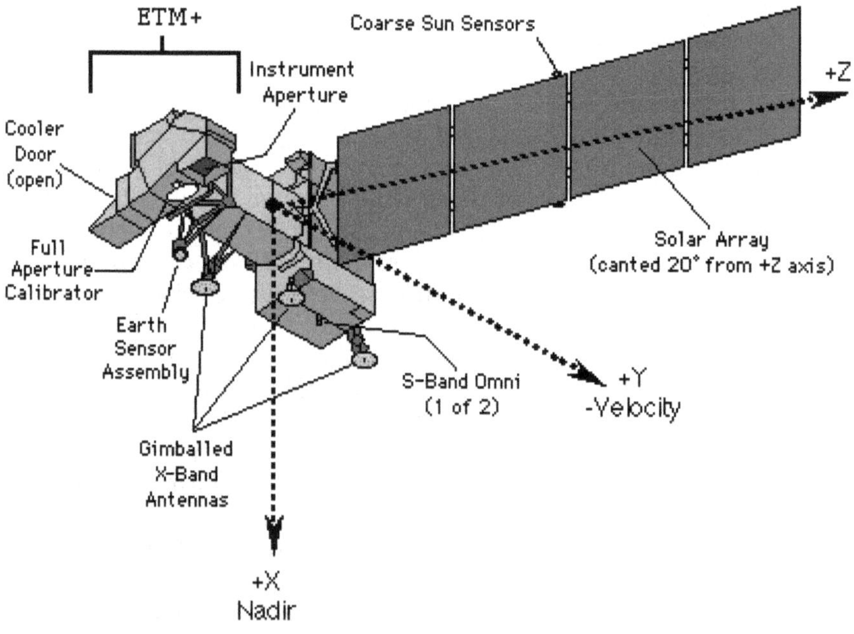

Figure 9.21 Landsat 7
(Courtesy of NASA)

The Landsat program is continuing. The Landsat Data Continuity Mission, scheduled to launch in 2012, will be the next satellite in the series. Other MEO satellite systems are planned, but none are in orbit at this time. Examples of proposed or partially deployed MEO systems include ICO Global Communications and proposed Orblink from Orbital Sciences. The MEO market is yet to meet its potential.

9.10 GEOs

A geostationary orbit can only be achieved at an altitude very close to 35,786 km (22,236 mi), and directly above the equator. This equates to an orbital velocity of 3.07 km/s (1.91 mi/s) or a period of 1,436 minutes, which equates to almost exactly one sidereal day or 23.934461223 hours (a **sidereal day** is a time period corresponding to the time it takes for the Earth to complete one rotation relative to the vernal equinox). This makes sense considering that the satellite must be locked to the Earth's rotational period in order to have a stationary footprint (the **footprint** of a communications satellite is the ground area that its transponders offer coverage, and determines the satellite dish diameter required to receive each transponder's signal) on the ground. In practice, this means that all geostationary satellites have to exist on this ring or "orbital trough").

As noted, geostationary satellites are stationed at approximately 22,300 miles (36,000 kilometers) from Earth and located directly over the equator. Given the equator is offset by 22.5 degrees, the sun aligns directly with satellites and receiving earth stations twice a year—once in the spring and once in the autumn (Figure 9.22). This event is called a **sun outage**, and is also known as sun fade or sun transit.

The heat emitted by the sun is an intense source of noise radiated at all frequencies, including the frequency range communication satellites use. That noise is called **thermal noise**. When the sun—and its thermal noise—aligns perfectly with a satellite and the receive antenna on the ground (line-of-sight), the **noise floor**, as seen by the receive earth station, is significant enough that it rises above the satellite's carrier signal and causes a temporary loss of reception.

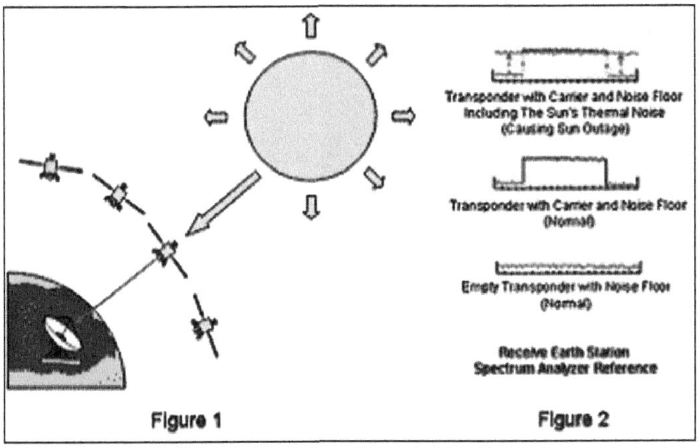

Figure 9.22 The Sun's Thermal Noise Overpowers the Signal Coming from the Satellite

A sun outage occurs because the earth station cannot distinguish between the energy from the sun and its intended communication signal. This is similar to when one is listening to a person talk immediately adjacent to them and a loud noise suddenly drowns out the voice of the person speaking, such that all that can be heard is that loud noise, until the noise either stops or moves far enough away to again hear the speaking person's voice.

The duration of the solar interference depends on the receive antenna's location on the Earth, the satellite's orbital location above the equator, the size of the receive antenna and the reception frequency. These **sun outages** start with a signal loss of only a few minutes. The outages start small—when the sun is very near alignment with the satellite and the earth station.

The sun's thermal energy is strong enough to temporarily interfere with the satellite signal and cause an outage as it approaches direct alignment. Each day as the sun moves further north, the sun's alignment with the satellite and earth station move ever so slightly. As the sun becomes more aligned with the satellite and the earth station on the ground, the outage duration increases. **Peak outage time** occurs when the sun, satellite and the earth station are **exactly aligned** with each other. The interference declines gradually as the sun starts moving away from the satellite and earth station alignment, until it is no longer a factor—until the next interference season when the sun starts heading south (northern hemispheric in autumn).

Given that all geostationary satellites are over the same geographic plane—the equator—and orbiting at the same distance, 22,300 miles or 36,000 kilometers, the sun outage will apply to every antenna at a given location. For instance, if there are four antennas looking at four different satellites (assuming the dishes are of the same size and same frequency reception), the solar outage will travel through all four satellites and antennas at that location in the same day. The four events will happen at different times of day for each satellite, as Earth's rotation creates alignment.

The duration of the outage is inversely related to the size and frequency of the satellite receive dish. The larger the antenna, the shorter the duration and intensity of the outage. Similarly, the smaller the dish, the great the duration and intensity.

For example, a 3.8 meter C-band receive antenna located in Toronto, Ontario, Canada, receiving from Intelsat's Galaxy 16 satellite will have the following outages for the spring of 2010.

Spring Interference

Date	Time (UTC)	Duration
1 March 2010	18:55	5 minutes
2 March 2010	18:53	7 minutes
3 March 2010	18:53	8 minutes
4 March 2010	18:53	7 minutes
5 March 2010	18:54	4 minutes

Using the same example, when the dish size increases to 9 meters, the outage time decreases in both minutes and number of days.

Spring Interference

Date	Time (UTC)	Duration
2 March 2010	18:55	4 minutes
3 March 2010	18:55	4 minutes
4 March 2010	18:55	3 minutes

Using the same 3.8 meter dish and C-band frequency noted above, the sun interference in Los Angeles is noted in the below chart. The interference starts four days later than in Toronto due to Los Angeles being lower in latitude than Toronto, but has very similar outage durations.

Spring Interference

Date	Time (UTC)	Duration
4 March 2010	18:34	5 minutes
5 March 2010	18:33	7 minutes
6 March 2010	18:32	8 minutes
7 March 2010	18:32	7 minutes
8 March 2010	18:33	4 minutes[27]

Every once in a great while, a report surfaces about a communications satellite which has been partially or completed disabled as the result of a sudden knockout blow delivered by the sun. The first thing to keep in mind is that these things do happen. The second thing to keep in mind is that they happen very rarely.

Out of the hundreds of satellites successfully launched over the past 5 decades, only a mere handful have succumbed to any form of so-called "solar weather" which satellites are designed and built to withstand.

The study of solar weather is ongoing, and, operators are constantly monitoring the sun's activities and improving their ability to respond to the impact of solar events.

Satellite operators focus on four elements of solar weather that can affect satellite communications: solar wind, coronal holes, coronal mass ejections (CME's) and solar flares.

The solar wind is constant but varies in intensity, while the other three solar phenomena come and go. The goal in terms of space infrastructure has been to identify and effectively counter the sun's link to so-called single-event upsets (SEUs) which happen whenever the performance of one or more spacecraft components abruptly changes without warning.

SEU's are not apt to be caused by the solar wind itself which is relatively low in energy and seldom penetrates the outer layers or protective skin of a spacecraft. Instead, solar flares, CME's and coronal holes—their powerful reach often extends beyond the orbit of Mars—can be disruptive.

When solar storms erupt, they can bombard a satellite with highly charged particles and increase the amount of charging on a spacecraft's surfaces. When

[27]http://www.intelsat.com/resources/tech-talk/satellite-sun-interference.asp

CMEs occur in the Sun's corona or outer atmosphere, for example, a huge amount of plasma and magnetic energy is emitted.

The huge and quite visible explosions on the sun are known as solar flares the most extreme form of solar storms. They discharge large amounts of radiation and a highly charged cloud of protons in particular. X-ray observations provide an important early warning for astronauts in orbit, while slower - moving CMEs often trail behind subject to the sun's magnetic field.

CME's follow a curving path as they leave the sun. Because of this, the CME may not actually impact satellites at all. When a CME impacts the earth, the earth's magnetic field compresses on one side and stretches out on the other. This can result in dazzling auroral displays over the poles, for example. Fortunately, most CMEs last only 3 days or less.

Thankfully, the sun is fairly predictable in this regard, and sunspot activity takes place in 11-year cycles with the maximum or most intense stage lasting about 2 years, and the least intense stage lasting about 5 years.

Since 2006, we have experienced the least active period of major solar weather events in recent history. In other words, the sun has been very quiet lately.

Coping with electrostatic discharges from the sun that can potentially disrupt satellite services are part of the everyday reality of the satellite world. Losing solar power is not a serious concern whereas losing total control and command of a satellite as the result of solar weather is the most severe effect.

Solar panels on satellites are the most affected components, and normal erosion rates for solar panels are usually 0.3% to 1% per year.

A solar storm can reduce solar panel performance by 3% to 5% in a day, but since this phenomenon is well understood, spacecraft manufacturers increase the tolerances by design, and attach larger than needed solar panels to satellite in order to allow for losses during the anticipated solar storms.

The body of a communications satellite, which contains vital control and communication components, is specially adapted using special materials as well as active and passive measures so as to be highly resilient. A so-called "Faraday Cage" protects the satellite's internal equipment from external electrical charges. High - energy particles discharged by the sun rapidly lose strength as they pass through the multiple layers of a spacecraft's body or bus as well. There, they encounter a series of specially designed circuit dividers, individual compartments, and other unique structural elements that act as barriers.

The disruptive nature of solar weather impacts far more than satellite operations, and adversely affects terrestrial power and communications grids.

For these and other reasons, a considerable amount of manpower and money has been devoted to monitoring the sun's activity, and more research into solar phenomena in general is planned in the future. Among other things, one benefit has been a steady improvement in our ability to rapidly detect and track these solar events using powerful observation and detection systems both on the ground and in space.

NASA, the U.S. National Oceanic and Atmospheric Administration and the U.S. Department of Defense oversee much of this activity. For example, besides NASA's twin Solar Terrestrial Relations Observatory (STEREO) spacecraft, the Air Force Research Laboratory launched the Communication/Navigation Outage Forecasting System (C/NOFS) satellite several years ago to forecast the presence of ionospheric irregularities caused by the sun that adversely impact communication and navigation systems. Space and ground-based measurements have been taken to help determine how the plasma irregularities affect the propagation of electromagnetic waves, among other things.

Satellites depend upon the sun, and satellite operators have steadily developed tools and techniques which allow them to ensure the operational integrity of all satellites in the face of all forms of solar weather. That weather changes over time, while satellite performance and design gets better and better. Thanks to proper planning, design and execution, the survival rate of satellites is quite remarkable.[28]

GEOs are the earliest and the most prevalent type of satellite system to date. GEOs have been launched and placed into orbit since the mid-1970s. They are circular orbits orientated in the plane of the earth's equator. In a geosynchronous orbit, the satellite appears stationary (i.e., in a fixed position) to an observer on earth. More technically, a geosynchronous orbit is a circular prograde orbit in the equatorial plane with an orbital period equal to that of the earth; this is achieved with an orbital radius of 6.6107 (equatorial) earth radii, or an orbital height of 35,786 km. A satellite in a geosynchronous orbit will appear fixed above the surface of the earth (i.e., at a fixed latitude and longitude).

The footprint, or service area, of a geosynchronous satellite covers almost one-third of the earth's surface (from about 75 degrees south to about 75 degrees north latitude), so that near-global coverage can be achieved with a minimum of three to four satellites in orbit.

By placing the satellite at an altitude where its orbital period exactly matches the rotation of the earth (approximately 35,800 km), the satellite appears to hover over one spot on the earth's equator and thus appears to stay stationary over the same point.

A geosynchronous satellite completes one orbit revolution in circular orbit, around the earth, every 24 hours. If the orbit is in the equatorial plane, and if rotation is in the same direction as the earth (rotating at the same angular velocity as the Earth) and it overlies the same point on the globe permanently, then the satellite is termed geosynchronous.

Geosynchronous means that a satellite makes one orbit every 24 hours so that it is synchronized with the rotation period of the earth. As stated, this will happen when a satellite is in a circular orbit at a rough distance of 36,000 km above the surface of the earth, or roughly 42,000 km from the center of the earth. The orbital location of geosynchronous satellites is called the Clarke Belt, in honor of Arthur C. Clarke who first published the theory of locating geosynchronous satellites in earth's equatorial plane for use in fixed communications purposes. For brevity, the term *geosynchronous satellite* is often shortened to *geo satellite.*

Earth stations transmit a signal to a satellite in orbit; this act is called an **uplink**. Geosynchronous satellites receive the uplinked signal, amplify it, shift it to a lower frequency, and then couple the outgoing signal to the transmitting array of onboard satellite antenna where the signal is focused into a narrow beam and sent back to earth. The act of sending the signal back to earth is called a **downlink**. The onboard satellite electronics, which receive the uplinked signal, amplify it, and shift the frequencies, is called a transponder. See Figure 9.23.

---

[28]http://www.intelsat.com/resources/tech-talk/solar-weather.asp

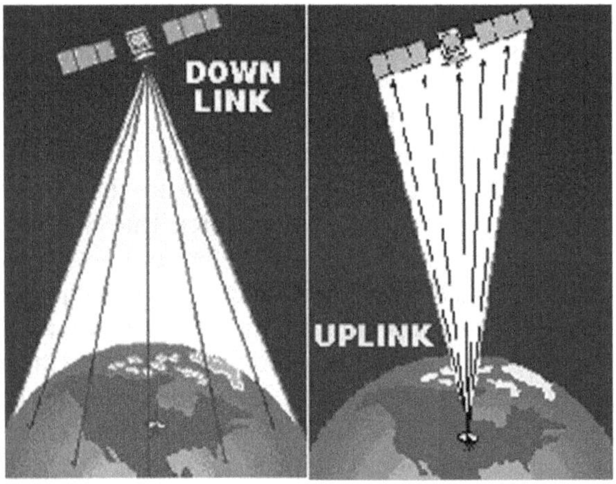

Figure 9.23 Uplink and Downlink Process

In the transponder layout (i.e., configuration) of a satellite, the channels are arranged with a band of frequencies between each one, typically 4 MHz. This is known as a guard band and its purpose is to provide isolation between each channel. Note also that there are usually at least two sets of frequencies per transponder and they are at opposite polarities; this is known as frequency reuse. Frequency reuse is a technique in which two transponders share the same frequency; however, by handling signals at opposite polarities, the two signals will not interfere with each other, so each frequency is reused. This fact is especially important because satellites cost from between $150 million to $1 billion to build and launch (this includes the cost to launch plus the satellite itself). Without finding ways to reuse frequencies in each satellite, the orbits would quickly fill up, and too many resources would be pumped into less efficient programs.

To further avoid co-channel interference, each set of polarities is typically offset from each other by an amount equal to one-half of their bandwidth (i.e., the band ends of one set of polarities fall on the center frequencies of the other set of polarities). In the current age of digital compression, frequency reuse is further obtained by digitally compressing multiple channels per transponder (i.e., more use of each frequency is obtained by using compression techniques to cram more information into each uplink/downlink signal).

On newer satellites, some individual transponders can be reconfigured from earth control stations to be combined to provide a customer with more bandwidth or can be divided to lessen the bandwidth to customer specifications (for instance, a 72 MHz transponder can be broken into two 36 MHz bandwidth units).

Whereas a low altitude orbiting satellite is hidden for part of its orbit around the earth, at least one GEO satellite is always directly visible from the same earth geographical area, day or night. The field of view of a satellite in GEO is fixed. A GEO is essential for a permanent satellite communications system between two points and is ideal for repeat observations to a fixed geographical global area. Examples of GEO satellite systems follow.

Direct Broadcast Services

There are several providers of direct broadcast services (DBS)—DirecTV, DishTV and WildBlue, among others.

DirecTV DirecTV Inc., provider of the nation's leading digital satellite television service, uses seven DirecTV-owned satellites that deliver the high-power DirecTV programming service to millions of customers in the United States. DirecTV has launched five satellites and obtained in 2000 the two Primestar satellites from that defunct system.

DirecTV currently has a license for forty-six high-power frequencies at three orbital slots, all of which provide full coverage of the continental United States. DirecTV is the nation's leading provider of digital television entertainment service with more than 8.7 million customers.

Along with broadcasting more than 500 television channels, DirecTV has broadened out into the Internet services arena by providing Internet access to home or business-based users via arrangements with land-based DSL providers such as AT&T. Also, subscribers can receive movies to their home TV and/or PC. DirecTV reports a substantial subscriber base as seen in the table on the below.[29]

Subscribers

1994	320,000
1995	1,200,000
1996	2,300,000
1997	3,301,000
1998	4,458,000
1999	6,679,000
2000	9,554,000
2001	10,218,000
2002	11,181,000
2003	12,290,000
2004	13,000,000
2005	15,000,000
2006	15,950,000
2007	16,830,000
2008	17,620,000
2009	18,081,000
2010	18,542,194

DishTV DirecTV is not the only satellite-based provider of Internet services to home and business-based subscribers. The other provider is DishTV, provided by EchoStar Communications. DISH Network's rapid growth continued into 2010 when the provider announced it had reached 15 million customers in January.[30] Internet connectivity is provided by a local DSL provider similar to DirecTV.

---

[29]www.directv.com

[30]www.dishtv.com

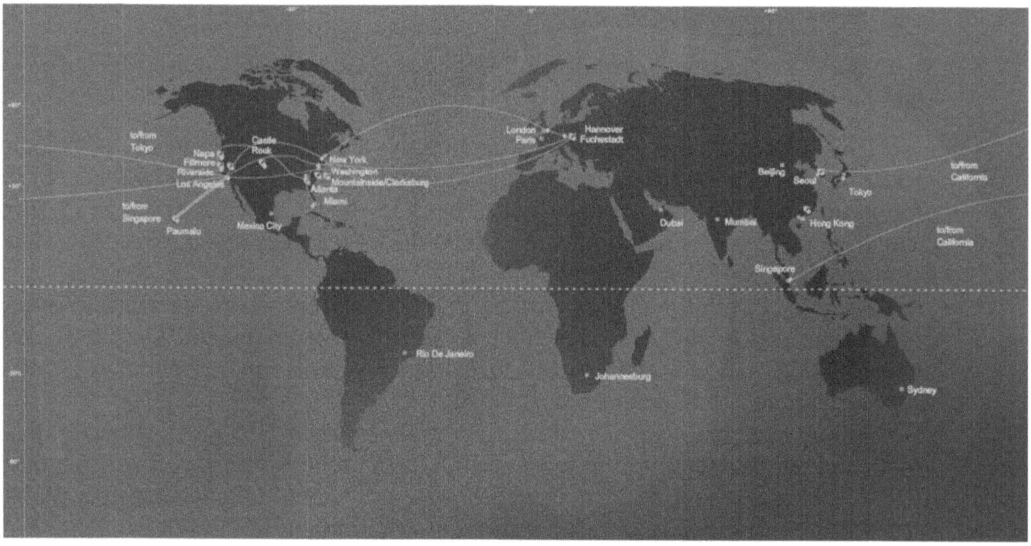

Figure 9.24 Intelsat Satellite Coverage Map: World View
(Courtesy of www.intelsat.com)

Intelsat

Intelsat serves approximately 1,800 customers around the world, including the world's largest Internet service providers,[31] telecommunications companies, broadcasters and corporate network service providers. Figure 9.24 shows Intelsat Satellite Coverage.

Intelsat (Figure 9.25) operates a fleet of approximately fifty satellites. In contrast to the direct broadcast services, Intelsat offers Internet, broadcast, telephony, and corporate network services to leading companies in more than 200 countries and territories worldwide. In an expansion mode, Intelsat has launched satellites regularly, with Intelsat 16 (IS-16)'s successfully launched by International Launch

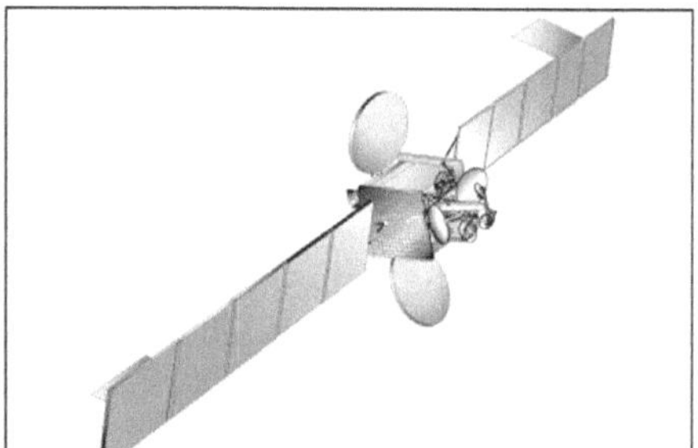

Figure 9.25 Intelsat Satellite
(Courtesy of www.intelsat.com)

[31]http://www.intelsat.com/press/company-facts/

Services (ILS) on a Proton Breeze M vehicle from Kazahkstan's Baikonur Cosmodrome in February, 2010. All are in geostationary orbit at a distance of 22,300 miles (36,000 km). Figure 9.26 shows that the coverage of the earth's surface by the Intelsat fleet of satellites is extensive.

Intelsat's customer base includes hundreds of Internet service providers, telecommunications companies, broadcasters, and corporate network service providers worldwide. As compared with systems such as Iridium, which are primarily U.S. based, Intelsat is international in scope. The headquarters are in Washington, D.C., but other major offices are in several locations as listed below.

Total Revenue $2.5 billion in 2009

Employees Staff of 1,100

Offices Intelsat has offices in Brazil, China (Hong Kong), France, Germany, India, Singapore, South Africa, the United Arab Emirates, the United Kingdom and the United States.

Inmarsat Inmarsat was the world's first global mobile satellite communications operator and advertises itself as the only one to offer a mature range of modern communications services to maritime, land mobile, aeronautical, and other users.[32]

- Formed as a maritime-focused intergovernmental organization over 20 years ago, Inmarsat has been a limited company since 1999, serving a broad range of

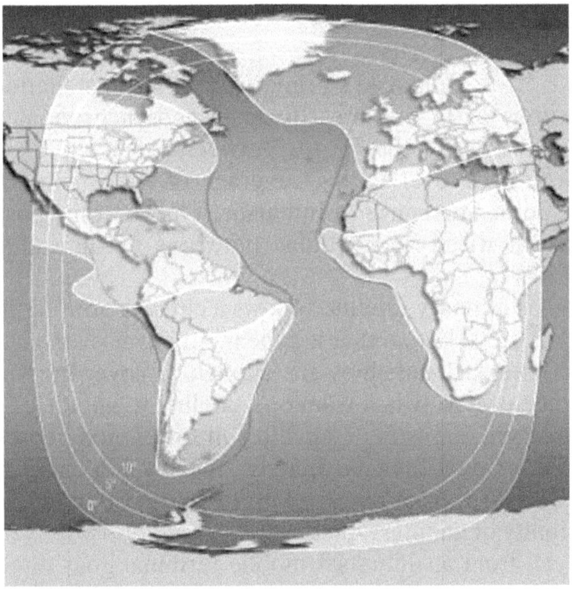

Figure 9.26 Intelsat Coverage of the Earth's Surface
(Courtesy of www.intelsat.com)

[32]Information courtesy of INMARSAT at http://www.inmarsat.com.

markets. Starting with a user base of 900 ships in the early 1980s, it now supports links for phone, fax, and data communications at up to 64 Kbps to more than 210,000 ship, vehicle, aircraft, and portable terminals.

- Inmarsat Ltd. is a subsidiary of the Inmarsat Ventures PLC holding company. It operates a constellation of geostationary satellites designed to extend phone, fax, and data communications worldwide. The constellation comprises five third-generation satellites backed by four earlier spacecraft. These satellites are controlled from Inmarsat's headquarters in London, which is also home to Inmarsat Ventures, as well as the small IGO created to supervise the company's public service duties for the maritime community (Global Maritime Distress and Safety System) and aviation (air traffic control communications). Inmarsat has regional offices in Dubai, Singapore, and India.

  Users of the Inmarsat system of satellites include ship owners and managers, journalists and broadcasters, health and disaster relief workers, land transport fleet operators, airlines, airline passengers and air traffic controllers, government workers, national emergency and civil defense agencies, and peacekeeping forces.
- The central aspect of the strategy is the new Inmarsat I-4 satellite system, which, beginning in 2004, will support the Inmarsat Broadband Global Area Network (B-GAN). This system will be capable of handling mobile data communications at up to 432 Kbps for Internet access, mobile multimedia, and many other advanced applications.

The Satellites Inmarsat's primary satellite constellation consists of three global constellations of 11 satellites flying in geosynchronous orbit 37,786 km (22,240 statute miles) above the Earth. Between them, the main (global) beams of the satellites provide overlapping coverage of the whole surface of the earth apart from the poles. So, thanks to Inmarsat, it has become possible to extend the reach of terrestrial wired and cellular networks to almost anywhere on earth (see Figure 9.27).

A geostationary satellite follows a circular orbit in the plane of the equator at a height of 35,600 km, so that it appears to hover over a chosen point on the earth's surface. Three such satellites are enough to cover most of the globe, and mobile users rarely have to switch from one satellite to another. Other mobile satellite systems use larger numbers of satellites in lower, non-geostationary orbits. From the user's point of view, they move across the sky at a comparatively high speed, often requiring a switch from one satellite to another in mid-communication and risking the possibility of an interrupted call.

A call from an Inmarsat mobile terminal goes directly to the satellite overhead, which routes it back down to a gateway on the ground called a land earth station (LES). From there the call is passed into the public phone network. The Inmarsat-3 satellites are backed up by a fifth Inmarsat-3 and four previous generation Inmarsat-2s, also in geostationary orbit.

Figure 9.27 A Typical Inmarsat Satellite
(Courtesy of www.inmarsat.com)

The Network To deliver its services, Inmarsat operates a worldwide network of ground stations in addition to the satellite constellation.

- The satellites are controlled from the satellite control center (SCC) at Inmarsat HQ in London. The control teams there are responsible for keeping the satellites in position above the equator, and for ensuring that the onboard systems are fully functional at all times.
- Data on the status of the nine Inmarsat satellites are supplied to the SCC by four tracking, telemetry, and control (TT&C) stations located at Fucino, Italy; Beijing, China; Lake Cowichan, western Canada; and Pennant Point, eastern Canada. There is also a backup station at Eik, Norway.
- Data from a user terminal are transmitted to a satellite and then down to a LES, which acts as a gateway into the terrestrial telecom networks. There are about forty LESs, located in thirty countries.
- The flow of communications traffic through the Inmarsat network is monitored and managed by the network operations center (NOC) at Inmarsat HQ in London.
- The NOC is supported by network coordination stations (NCSs). Their primary role is to help set up each call by assigning a channel to the MES and the appropriate LES. There is one NCS for each ocean region and for each Inmarsat system (Inmarsat A, B, C, and so on). Each NCS communicates with all the land earth station operators in its ocean region, the other NCS, and the NOC, making it possible to distribute operational information throughout the system. Figure 9.28 shows Inmarsat global coverage.

Geostationary Operational Environmental Satellite

Another GEO system used extensively is the geostationary operational environmental satellite (GOES) system. Like many weather satellites, GOES was developed and

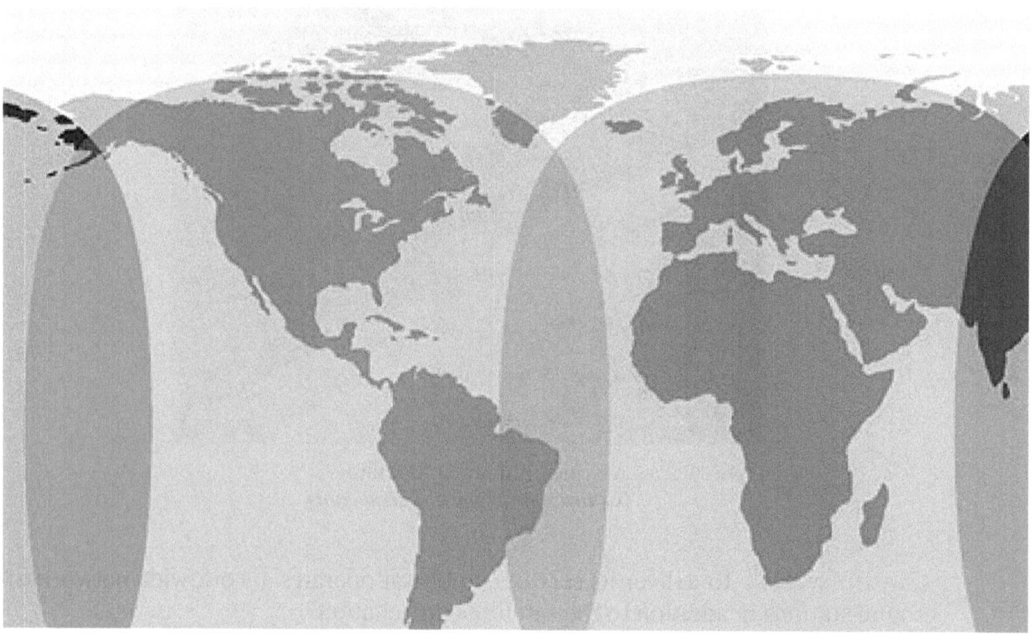

Figure 9.28 Inmarsat Global Coverage
(Courtesy of www.inmarsat.com)

launched by NASA. Since 1968, there have been twelve GOES satellites launched; nine are still operational. Figure 9.29 depicts the latest GOES satellite—GOES 12. The GOES mission is to provide timely global weather information. GOES imagery is commonly featured on many TV weather reports across the United States and the world. For example, the hurricane images during hurricane season are provided via the GOES system. The GOES Program maintains two satellites operating in conjunction to provide observational coverage of 60 percent of the earth. The GOES satellite system has remained an essential cornerstone of weather observations and forecasting for 25 years. Operating the country's system of environmental satellites is one of the major responsibilities of the National Oceanic and Atmospheric Administration's (NOAA's) National Environmental Satellite, Data, and Information Service (NESDIS). NESDIS operates the satellites and manages the processing and distribution of the millions of bits of data and images theses satellites produce daily. The primary customer is NOAA's National Weather Service, which uses satellite data to create forecasts for the public, television, radio, and weather advisory services. Satellite information is also shared with various Federal agencies, such as the Departments of Agriculture, Interior, Defense, and Transportation; with other countries, such as Japan, India, and Russia, and members of the European Space Agency (ESA) and the United Kingdom Meteorological Office; and with the private sector.

NOAA's operational weather satellite system is composed of two types of satellites: geostationary operational environmental satellites (GOES) for short-range warning and "now-casting" and polar-orbiting satellites for longer-term fore-

Figure 9.29 Typical GOES Satellite
(Courtesy of NASA)

casting. Both types of satellite are necessary for providing a complete global weather monitoring system.

A new series of GOES and polar-orbiting satellites has been developed for NOAA by the National Aeronautics and Space Administration (NASA). The new GOES-R series provide higher spatial and temporal resolution images and full-time operational soundings (vertical temperature and moisture profiles of the atmosphere). The newest polar-orbiting meteorological satellites (National Polar-orbiting Operational Environmental Satellite System in 2014) will provide improved atmospheric temperature and moisture data in all weather situations. This new technology will help provide the National Weather Service the most advanced weather forecast system in the world.

GOES satellites provide the kind of continuous monitoring necessary for intensive data analysis. They circle the Earth in a geosynchronous orbit, which means they orbit the equatorial plane of the Earth at a speed matching the Earth's rotation. This allows them to hover continuously over one position on the surface. The geosynchronous plane is about 35,800 km (22,300 miles) above the Earth, high enough to allow the satellites a full-disc view of the Earth. Because they stay above a fixed spot on the surface, they provide a constant vigil for the atmospheric "triggers" for severe weather conditions such as tornadoes, flash floods, hail storms, and hurricanes. When these conditions develop the GOES satellites are able to monitor storm development and track their movements.

GOES satellite imagery is also used to estimate rainfall during the thunderstorms and hurricanes for flash flood warnings, as well as estimates snowfall accumulations and overall extent of snow cover. Such data help meteorologists issue winter storm warnings and spring snow melt advisories. Satellite sensors also detect ice fields and map the movements of sea and lake ice.

NASA launched the first GOES for NOAA in 1975 and followed it with another in 1977. Currently, the United States is operating GOES-11 and GOES-12. (GOES-10, which is partially operational, supports Central and South America to prevent data outages during the GOES-12 rapid scan operations.) GOES-13 is being stored in orbit as a replacement for GOES-12 or GOES-11 in the event of failure.

GOES-11 and GOES-12

The United States normally operates two meteorological satellites in geostationary orbit over the equator. Each satellite views almost a third of the Earth's surface: one monitors North and South America and most of the Atlantic Ocean, the other North America and the Pacific Ocean basin. GOES-12 (or GOES-East) is positioned at 75 W longitude and the equator, while GOES-11 (or GOES-West) is positioned at 135 W longitude and the equator. The two operate together to produce a full-face picture of the Earth, day and night. Coverage extends approximately from 20 W longitude to 165 E longitude. This figure shows the coverage provided by each satellite.

GOES 13, known as **GOES-N** before becoming operational, was launched in 2006. Since April 14, 2010, GOES-13 has been the operational weather satellite for GOES-EAST. At launch, the satellite had a mass of 3,133 kilograms (6,910 lb), and an expected operational lifespan of ten years, although it carries fuel for longer.[33] It was built by Boeing and was the first of three GOES-N series satellites to be launched. It is currently in a geostationary orbit at a longitude of 75° West. It has been serving actively as GOES-East since April 2010. In December 2007, it was called up to provide coverage of the east coast of the United States during an outage of GOES 12 due to a thruster leak. After the problem with GOES 12 cleared, it resumed operations, and GOES 13 was deactivated again.[34] It was also briefly activated in mid May 2009, when GOES 12 developed another thruster problem, however it did not need to take over operations, and was deactivated by the end of the month.[35]

The main mission of these GOES satellites is carried out by the primary instruments, the Imager and the Sounder. The imager is a multichannel instrument that senses radiant energy and reflected solar energy from the Earth's surface and atmosphere. The Sounder provides data to determine the vertical temperature and moisture profile of the atmosphere, surface and cloud top temperatures, and ozone distribution.

---

[33]Krebs, Gunter. "GOES N, O, P, Q." Gunter's Space Page. http://space.skyrocket.de/doc_sdat/goes-n.htm.

[34]"GOES-M Status." NOAA. http://goes.gsfc.nasa.gov/text/goesmstatus.html.

[35]http://en.wikipedia.org/wiki/GOES_13

GOES WEST

GOES EAST

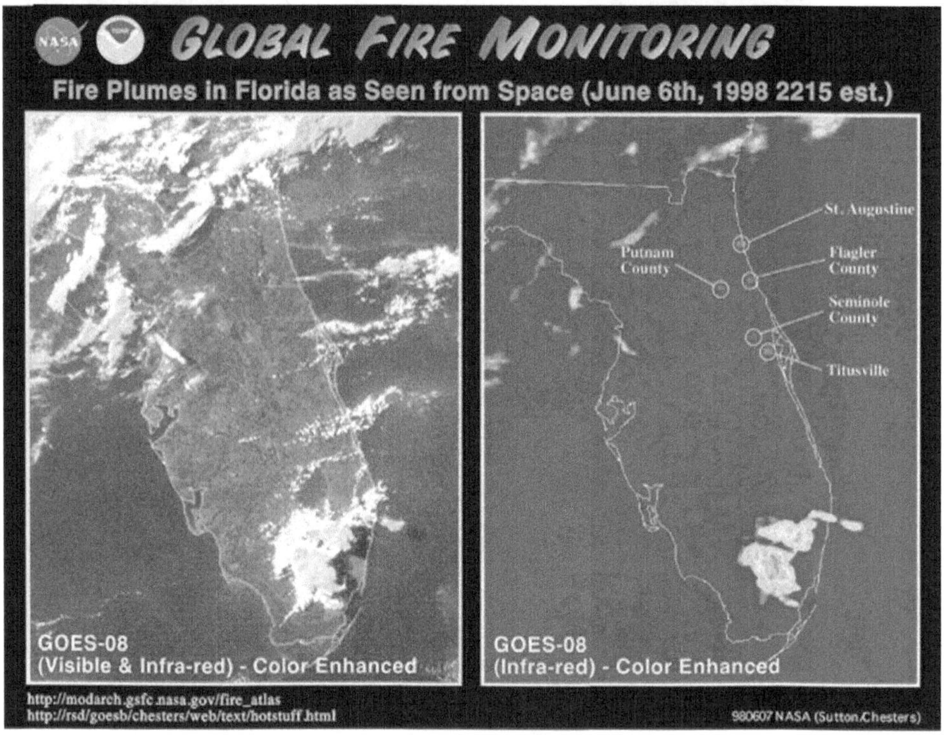

Figure 9.30 Fires Seen from GOES Satellite Images: NASA-GSFC, Data from NOAA GOES *(Courtesy of NASA)*

The GOES satellites also carry a space environment monitor (SEM), which investigates solar particle emissions and helps study the effect of solar activity on the earth's telecommunications systems. The SEM detects solar protons, alpha particles, solar electrons, solar x-rays, and magnetic fields. In addition to observations, the GOES platform (the satellite stationed over the Pacific Ocean) has been used to create and operate PEACESAT (Pan-Pacific Educational and Cultural Experiments by Satellite). PEACESAT provides satellite telecommunications to serve the educational, economic development, medical, and cultural needs of many Pacific island nations and territories.

GOES observations have proven helpful in monitoring dust storms, volcano eruptions, and even the spread of forest fires (see Figure 9.30). A data collection system added to GOES allows it to receive and relay environmental data.

Polar-Orbiting Satellites

Complementing the geostationary satellites are two polar-orbiting satellites known as Advanced Television Infrared Observation Satellite (TIROS-N or ATN), as seen in Figure 9.31, are constantly circling the Earth in an almost north-south orbit, passing close to both poles. The orbits are circular, with an altitude between 830 (morning orbit) and 870 (afternoon orbit) km, and are sun synchronous. One satellite crosses the equator at 7:30 a.m. local time, the other at 1:40 p.m.

Figure 9.31 A TIROS satellite
(Courtesy of NASA)

local time. The circular orbit permits uniform data acquisition by the satellite and efficient control of the satellite by the NOAA Command and Data Acquisition (CDA) stations located near Fairbanks, Alaska and Wallops Island, Virginia. Operating as pair, these satellites ensure that data for any region of the Earth are no more than six hours old.

A suite of instruments is able to measure many parameters of the Earth's atmosphere, its surface, cloud cover, incoming solar protons, positive ions, electron-flux density, and the energy spectrum at the satellite altitude. As a part of the mission, the satellites can receive, process and retransmit data from Search and Rescue beacon transmitters, and automatic data collection platforms on land, ocean buoys, or aboard free-floating balloons.[36]

PEACESAT PEACESAT is best known as a public service satellite telecommunications network that links educational institutions, regional organizations, and governments in the Pacific Islands.[37] The capabilities of PEACESAT are provided via the GOES satellite system.

The capability of PEACESAT, via GOES, to provide telecommunications services to this region is crucial. In more developed economies, telecommunications is far less of a cost and technology barrier than it is in developing or emerging economies. For example, it is possible for residents in Hawaii to call New York at $0.15 a minute, but the same call would cost many of the Pacific island economies over $3 per minute.

[36]http://noaasis.noaa.gov/NOAASIS/ml/genlsatl.html

[37]Read the entire PEACESAT Mission at www.obake.peacesat.hawaii.edu/info/2-miss.htm.

In addition, while access to information via the Internet is provided at a very small cost in Hawaii and in other developed economies, the same service for a user spending 10 hours per month in other Pacific islands could cost over $100 per month.

PEACESAT also provides information to these islands in the areas of education, health and medical emergencies, emergency management, and technology transfer. Some of the projects that PEACESAT is working on to support these program areas include the development of digital voice, data, and compressed video teleconferencing capabilities within the region; building collaborative relationships to support these levels of technology; developing an electronic mail system for health and emergency operations; and developing a network interface among emergency agencies in Hawaii.

Meteosat

The **Meteosat** series of satellites are geostationary meteorological satellites operated by EUMETSAT under the Meteosat Transition Programme (MTP) and the Meteosat Second Generation (MSG) program. See Figure 9.32 to see a typical Meteosat First Generation satellite. EUMETSAT was formed in 1986 with the objective to provide, from space, information that can be used in weather forecasting and climate applications. The success story of satellite meteorology in Europe is closely linked to two organisations. One is EUMETSAT itself which in just two decades has become one of the worlds pre-eminent meteorological and environmental satellite organisations, serving the interests of Europe's National Meteorological Services, the citizens of Europe and way beyond. The other is the European Space Agency (ESA). ESA research expertise was required for the conception and development of the first Meteosat back in the 1970s and ESA was also the driving force behind the original formation of EUMETSAT. Over the past 20 years the relationship between the two

Figure 9.32 Meteosat First Generation satellite *(Courtesy of NASA)*

organisations has evolved and ESA has now become an established and important cooperation partner and procurement agency for EUMETSAT.

Meteosat-4, EUMETSAT's first operational satellite, was launched in 1989. The first generation of Meteosat satellites, Meteosat-1 to Meteosat-7, provide continuous and reliable meteorological observations from space to a large user community.

Meteosat Second Generation (MSG) was designed in response to user requirements, particularly climate monitoring and research. The MSG satellites are 3.2 m in diameter and 2.4 m high. The first was launched on January 29, 2004.

In 2010, Meteosat-6, -7, -8 and -9 are all operational. Meteosat-6 and -7 are stationed over the Indian Ocean. Meteosat-8, and -9 are both located over Africa with various differences in operational configuration. Meteosat-6 provides a DCP service and is a backup to Meteosat-7, where Meteosat-7 provides the primary imagery coverage over the Indian Ocean (with images every 30 minutes). Meteosat-8 is a backup to Meteosat-9 (and Meteosat-8 also provides an operational European 'rapid scan' mode service, which commenced in the second quarter of 2008 (with images of Europe every 5 minutes)). Meteosat-9 provides the main full earth imagery service over Europe and Africa (with images every 15 minutes).

The launch of MSG-3 is tentatively planned for 2012 and MSG-4 tentatively planned for 2014.

9.11 POLAR ORBITS

Because geosynchronous satellites cannot cover the poles of the planet, another method for providing satellite coverage is required. Polar synchronous satellites are a solution to the challenge, as shown in Figure 9.33. Polar orbits are a type of LEO orbit. They are much closer to the earth than GEOs (GEOs are at 35,800 km altitude; polar orbiting satellites are at 850 km altitude). By definition, a polar satellite has an inclination of 90 degrees to the equator. By placing a polar orbit satellite at an altitude of about 850 km above the earth's surface, a polar orbit of roughly 100 minutes can be achieved. This will allow the earth to rotate beneath the satellite

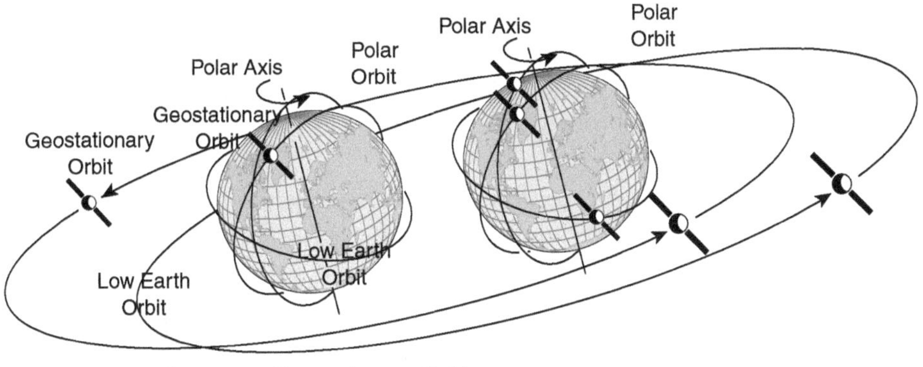

Figure 9.33 Polar versus Geostationary Orbit
(Courtesy of NASA)

so that one polar satellite is used per application. For more continuous coverage, more than one polar orbiting satellite may be used.

Polar orbit satellites can be used for one of two applications or uses—to view only the poles (to fill in gaps of GEO coverage) or to view the same place on earth at the same time each 24-hour day. The critical design goal is to place a polar satellite in an orbit that is low enough to allow a relatively short orbital period, but at the same time keep its orbit altitude sufficient to permit observation of a sufficiently wide path. This would enable the satellite instrumentation time to scan the earth below, because the earth will be rotating more slowly in relation to the satellite.

With the two applications of polar satellites come many uses. Polar satellites can carry sensors that are sensitive to both visible light and infrared radiation. They can measure the temperature and humidity in the Earth's atmosphere. They can sense and record surface ground and surface seawater temperatures, and monitor cloud cover and water or ice boundaries. When *Discovery* airs programs about the theory of global warming, the pictures shown are from polar satellites. Polar satellites are also able to receive, measure, process, and retransmit data from various scientific platforms such as balloons, buoys, and remote automatic stations. Polar satellites can carry emergency search-and-rescue transponders to help locate downed airplanes or ships in distress.

Usually a polar orbit is fixed in space, and the earth rotates underneath, so it travels from the North Pole to the South Pole. Atypical polar satellite can cover the entire globe every 14 days.

Sun-Synchronous Orbits

A special polar orbit that crosses the equator and each latitude at the same time each day is called a sun-synchronous orbit. Sun-synchronous orbits are also called helio-synchronous orbits, and the timeliness of their crossing a certain latitude at almost the same time every day can come in handy when wanting to do comparative studies or provide a regular interval of communication each day. The timing of the orbital period is caused by the centripetal force of the spinning earth.

One of the reasons to use this type of orbit, also called a dawn-to-dusk orbit, is that it enables the satellite to always have its solar panels in the sun. An example of a dawn-to-dusk satellite orbit is the one occupied by the "Radarsat" satellite. Radarsat is only 798 km above the earth, and circles the globe from the North Pole to the South Pole. Because Radarsat can keep its solar panels pointed toward the sun almost constantly, it does not have to rely much on batteries. Radarsat takes pictures that are useful for agriculture, oceanography, forestry, hydrology, geology, cartography, and meteorology.

9.12 HEOs

Highly elliptical orbits are very different from the other orbits because of their shape. Instead of orbiting the earth at a relatively constant distance, they dip and dive, then shoot out further than most satellites. The top of an orbit is called the apogee, and the lower end is the perigee. The apogees and perigees of HEOs range from 50,000 km to 500 km above the earth's surface, respectively.

HEOs for earth applications were initially used by the Russians to provide communications to their northern regions not covered by GEO satellite networks.

The Russians, for example, used the Molnya satellite system over Siberia. The area of interest would be one with a major population center or an arena otherwise necessary to cover. After the apogee period of orbit, a handoff must occur between the satellite about to descend and the rising satellite after it. Without the handoff, any communication being transmitted will be lost.

An example of a HEO is the Russian Molnya system, which employs three satellites in three 12-hour orbits around the earth. Each satellite is separated from the next by 120 degrees, with the **apogee** distance at 39,354 km above the earth's surface and the **perigee** at 1,000 km. The timing of the satellites in their orbits (especially having more than one satellite in the same orbit) is crucial, and if for some reason the timing is shot, there could be loss of service for any given amount of time. Another example of an HEO is the Russian Tundra satellite system. Unlike the Molnya, the Tundra only employs two satellites. Each satellite is separated by 180 degrees around the earth, and is responsible for its own 24-hour orbit. The Tundra satellites have their perigees and apogees at 17,951 km and 53,622 km, respectively.

Next we discuss probably one of the more well-known satellite systems, the Global Positioning System or GPS. This satellite system is used daily by literally millions throughout the world for positioning purposes. In fact, NASA estimates over 1 billion people use GPS services yearly.[38]

9.13 HISTORICAL PRECEDENTS OF GPS

Throughout history, one of the most critical issues for travelers has been how to get from location to location without becoming lost. Use of landmarks, compasses, dead reckoning, and celestial navigation has been common in the past. In the recent past, more accurate means of navigation have been used such as radar, sonar, and satellites. The development of a computer with the ability to make rapid complex computations enabled the U.S. Department of Defense (DOD) to launch a system of twenty-four satellites. From this system, we can calculate the exact position of a person, ship, or other object anywhere in the world. The uses of this system are broad, ranging from military to civilian services. GPS is easily used by experts and novices on both land and sea.

The beginnings of GPS, however, began many centuries ago. To ancient travelers on land and sea, landmarks and crude estimations of the location of stars and other celestial bodies were the main ways of navigation. The main problems with landmarks were they were only usable by the local population, and they were subject to destruction. One of the most famous landmarks in the ancient world was the Lighthouse of Alexandria. Built around 280 b.c., the lighthouse served as a guide to ships coming to harbor on an otherwise unmarked coast. It was destroyed in the fourteenth century after being damaged by several earthquakes.

[38]www.nasa.gov

The development of the compass freed navigators from landmarks. Although the phenomenon of magnetism was known to the ancient Greeks, Romans, and Chinese, it was not until the thirteenth century that people discovered a free-floating magnet aligns itself with the earth's magnetic field. This discovery led to the invention of the compass, which revolutionized travel by reducing the reliance on landmarks and stars for navigation.

A few centuries later, Columbus used a navigation method called deduced (or dead) reckoning to chart his way to the New World. Dead reckoning works by starting from a known position, such as a port, and calculating the distance traveled in a day and marking that spot on a chart. Each day's ending position would be the starting point for the next day's measurements. Speed was measured by throwing a piece of flotsam over the side of the ship and counting out how long the flotsam took to pass preset points on the ship. Use of a compass and this process allowed the navigator to keep a course and measure the distance traveled. This method was tedious and difficult, but until the Renaissance it was the best method available.

Developments during the fifteenth, sixteenth, and seventeenth centuries in the fields of astronomy, geometry, trigonometry, and physics led to the development of celestial navigation, a method of navigation utilizing the stars, moon, and sun. To calculate one's position on earth by looking at various objects in the sky, however, a few facts are needed. One needed to know the exact time, which at sea meant knowing the longitude. In 1762, English clockmaker John Harrison invented a chronometer, the first accurate mechanical clock in existence. After one knew the local time and could reference it to another time such as Greenwich mean time, an almanac describing the positions of stars at certain times could be used at sea. Another necessary item discovered for celestial navigation was the **sextant**, a system that consisted of two mirrors and a telescope mounted on a metal frame. It was a way to measure the position and angle of a celestial body in relation to the apparent horizon. As a star or other body was brought into view, light was reflected by one mirror, then another, before entering the telescope. By lining up the star with the horizon, the altitude of the star could be measured by examining where the lower part of the sextant listed the angles from 0 to 90 degrees. After the angle was obtained from the arc on the sextant, a process was then performed to eliminate several errors. Once this occurred, the sextant had a true measurement, including an error in the sextant itself (sextants are not scientifically precise), the error caused by the inability to see the true horizon due to the height of the eye and the curve of the earth, atmospheric refraction error, parallax error (the difference between the image seen through the viewfinder and the image seen by the taking lens), and errors caused by the semidiameter of objects closer to the earth such as the moon and planets. After these corrections were made, travelers could then determine their position on the edge of a circle whose radius was defined by the altitude of the celestial body observed. This procedure must be performed at least one more, and preferably two more, times to accurately locate one's position on the globe, because of natural human error. Typically, a traveler would take these measurements several times and then average the results. This is why it generally took many hours to do this centuries ago. Unfortunately, the most accurate measurements taken in this manner can only pinpoint a position within 60 miles. Although this is good enough for crossing an ocean, it does not work for more accurate calculations needed for surveying and mapmaking.

9.14 DESIGN AND PRINCIPLES OF OPERATION

The U.S. DoD developed a system of satellites for finding an exact position anywhere on the globe, for such purposes as finding locations of nuclear submarines when they surface. The DoD has allowed civilian use of the GPS free of charge; however, they introduced an error called selective availability, which limits GPS to approximately 100 m of accuracy for reasons of national security. This selective availability was eliminated by President Bill Clinton in May 2000, providing a current accuracy of approximately 10 m.

The U.S. national policy is that all radionavigation systems operated for public use by the USG will remain available for peaceful use subject to direction by the President in the event of a war or threat to national security. It is said the DoD has developed other ways of degrading performance in time of war; for example, they could conceivably switch SA back on or off. According to the *Federal Radionavigation Plan,* operating agencies may cease operations or change characteristics and signal formats of radionavigation systems during a dire national emergency. All communications links, including those used to transmit differential GPS corrections and other GPS augmentations, are also subject to the direction of the President. This plan, the FRP, preface states that it is prepared jointly by the Department of Defense, Department of Homeland Security, and Department of Transportation with assistance from other government agencies. The document covers radionavigation systems used by both the civilian and military communities. It does not cover radionavigation systems used exclusively by the U.S. military.

To provide global coverage, twenty-four satellites must orbit the earth every 12 hours. These Navstar satellites, made by Rockwell International, have an orbital plane 55 degrees to the equatorial plane. It would have been possible to place them in a geosynchronous orbit, the advantage being that it would take much fewer than twenty-four satellites to provide global coverage. This placement, however, would provide much less accuracy as one moved farther from the equator—a phenomenon known as dilution of precision. It should be noted that there are often more than twenty-four operational satellites as new ones are launched to replace older satellites. For example, as of January 2001, there are currently a total of thirty GPS satellite in orbit.[39] The satellite orbits repeat almost the same ground track (as the earth turns beneath them) once each day. The orbit altitude is such that the satellites repeat the same track and configuration over any point approximately each 24 hours (4 minutes earlier each day). There are six orbital planes (with nominally four SVs in each), equally spaced (60 degrees apart), and inclined at about 55 degrees with respect to the equatorial plane. This constellation provides the user with between five and eight SVs visible from any point on the earth (see Figures 9.34 and 9.35 for these orbits). Another issue is that if you were to reposition the satellites into a geosynchronous orbit (geosynchronous orbits are generally twice as high as the current GPS orbits), then another range of issues would arise such as signal strength. This would mean that a GPS receiver would have to be much more powerful than current

[39]http://en.wikipedia.org/wiki/Global_Positioning_System#cite_note-10

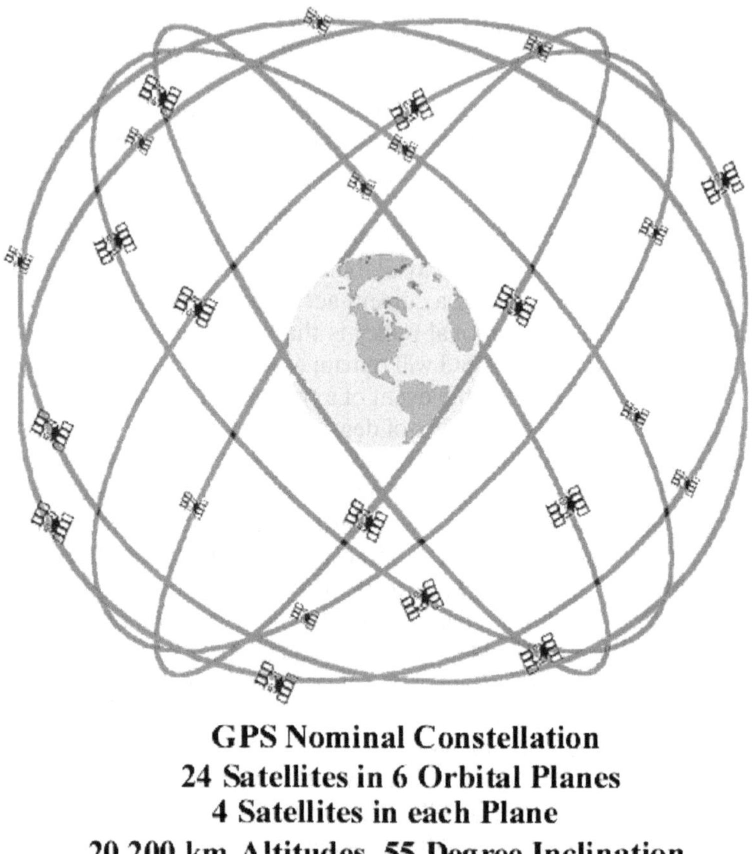

Figure 9.34 GPS Orbits

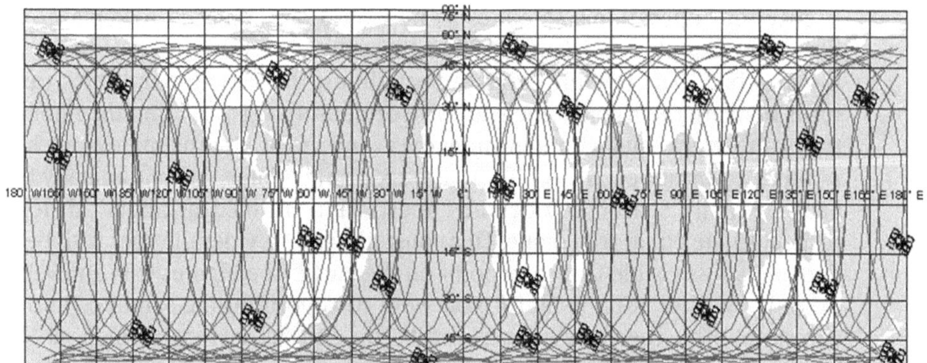

Figure 9.35 Global GPS Orbits

models, to accurately contact a geosynchronous GPS satellite. This would increase price and potentially raise health issues and a range of other issues.

Although the calculations involved are similar in some ways, the complexity of calculating one's position using GPS would be extremely difficult without the use of the microprocessor. The satellites in the GPS form a set of reference points other than celestial bodies which receivers can use to locate a position on earth. They form one segment of the three parts that comprise the GPS system. The other two parts consist of the users and their receivers, and the control stations on the ground that monitor the satellites and update information about their position. The information these ground control stations collect is put into an almanac or catalog such as the *Yuma Almanac.* The information these ground control stations collect is also in the pseudorandom code sent out by the satellites. To find an exact position, receivers use the catalogs to discover the location of the satellite from which it is receiving. They also need to know the exact time, triangulate a position based on the information received from the satellites, and correct for any errors caused by the atmosphere. The satellites send out a signal, which is called a pseudorandom code. It is easy for the receivers to pick up due to the amplification of the signal using **information theory**.[40]

Information theory is a concept invented by Claude Shannon and presented to the world in 1948. He proposed a linear schematic model of a communications system. This was a novel idea. At the time, communication was then thought of as requiring electromagnetic waves to be transmitted down a wire. The idea that one could transmit pictures, words, sounds and so on by sending a stream of 1s and 0s down a wire was fundamentally new. In defining information, Shannon identified the critical relationships among the elements of a communication system: the power at the source of a signal, the bandwidth or frequency range of an information channel through which the signal travels, and the noise of the **channel**, such as unpredictable static on a radio, which will alter the signal by the time it reaches the last element of the system, the receiver, which must decode the signal. In telecommunications, a channel is the path over a wire or fiber, or in wireless systems, the slice of radiospectrum used to transmit the message through free space. In short, Shannon's equations told engineers how much information could be transmitted over the channels of an ideal system.[41]

This pseudorandom code is a highly complex, non-repeating signal that is known to both the satellites and the receivers. Since the signal is essentially the same as the background noise, the receiver can measure where the signal boosts the background noise and pick up on the original signal instead of the background noise. Receivers pick up on this signal and calculate the distance from the receiver by multiplying the velocity of the signal, which is the speed of light by the

[40]This is a general discussion. To be specific, as Peter Dana of the University of Texas correctly points out: "We don't triangulate [no measured angles are used in the position solution]. You might say we quadralaterate [four ranges], but really it is a hyperbolic solution using four [or more] relative ranges [the receiver clock bias is unknown]. From that we find the position that minimizes the residuals. The satellites do each send an Almanac, a catalog of positions for the constellation, but what we use in position determination is the Ephemeris Data, sent by each satellite only for itself. The Almanacs are far from exact."

[41]For updates, see www.lucent.com/minds/infotheory/what5.html.

time it took to get there. To calculate the time it took to travel that distance, the receiver must measure the difference between the code it expects and the code it is receiving. The difference in the timing of the code is the time it took the signal to travel from the satellite to the position where the receiver is located. Once the receiver does this with three separate satellites it can combine these measurements to deduce its location down to two points, one of which can usually be thrown away. A fourth satellite measurement is also required to determine the exact time. The satellites have atomic clocks to measure the time precisely, which is necessary because the signals they are sending out are moving at the speed of light. Even a small time error here would cause a large error in distance. The receiver does not have an atomic clock due to the costs involved. A measurement from the fourth satellite allows the imperfect clock on the GPS receiver to discover exactly how different it is from the atomic clock. It does this using a simple application of algebra, solving for four variables using four equations. Besides the complicated math involved in solving for four variables, the receiver must take into account other errors caused by the atmosphere. This is done by applying a general mathematical model which estimates the error caused by the atmosphere. Another error that the receiver must deal with is caused by the GPS signal bouncing off other objects before coming to the receiver. Even with all these errors which can be corrected, the DoD introduces another error referred to as selective availability. This is done to make sure no terrorist or enemy groups can use GPS to make super accurate weapons. Differential GPS can overcome even this forced error, so the U.S. government is looking into discontinuing the policy of selective availability.

Differential GPS came into being as a result of techniques implemented to get around the errors caused by selective availability. Differential GPS has had a profound effect on GPS as a resource. Using differential GPS allows GPS to become much more than a system for navigation. It becomes a precise measuring tool for everyone. Differential GPS works using two receivers, one that is stationary and one that is mobile. Because the satellites are so far away, the stationary and mobile receivers have essentially the same errors. The idea behind differential GPS is to have one receiver measure the timing errors and then provide correction information to the other receivers that are roving around. In this way, nearly all errors are eliminated from the system, including selective availability error. With differential GPS, even more possibilities for the use of the technology become available.

The applications for GPS and differential GPS are as different as the people using them. GPS was developed for and by the military and as such still has a multitude of applications. It is used to find locations of units in the field so they can avoid friendly fire. Submarines that surface in the middle of the ocean can find their exact position quickly. These uses and others continue to allow the U.S. military to safely deploy and operate their mission throughout the world. GPS is not limited to the military world though. Many civilian application technologies have exploded onto the scene in recent years, with the promise of many more to come. One such idea is a technology known as free flight. This system would use GPS and other technologies to create and manage airplane flight paths. The pilot would be able to chart a course using GPS and information from other planes with GPS coordinated by stations on the ground to chart a shorter, more fuel-efficient flight plan. Another GPS application technology that would be useful for everyone would be an automatic vehicle location system. This system would use GPS to find a car's position and tie that information into the geographic information system, which is a database storing a map in a computer. These maps are much more complex than paper maps, as they show terrain in three dimensions. Using this software with a car would allow people to plot a course from city to city and within cities with ease. GPS technologies have found their way into many other fields as well, such as surveying, mining, and oil drilling. The applications possible for GPS are only limited by the imagination of the human mind. In the near future, GPS may be as vital to our lives as gasoline and electricity.

9.15 THE CONTROVERSIES

As mentioned, GPS was not accurate enough for many civilian applications, partly because of the DoD's encryption, and partly because of atmospheric conditions and other errors. Even after President Clinton addressed this issue of encryption in 2000, controversies still abounded. As various commercial GPS applications developed, such as for use in surveying, investors remained skeptical about being able to rely on a system which was both encrypted and operated by the U.S. government. President Clinton addressed this issue years earlier when, in 1996, he signed the Presidential Decision Directive on GPS, guaranteeing that GPS signals, although government controlled, would be permanently available for civilian use. Today, applications employing the knowledge of precision location are giving rise to new innovations, with promise for more in the future.

Russia has developed its own satellite navigation system, **Glonass**, and Europe objects strongly to using the U.S. system (as a sole means system), preferring to create its own rather than being subject to the whims of the U.S. government. This situation is currently being negotiated.

GLONASS ("**GLO**bal **NA**vigation **S**atellite **S**ystem" in English) is a radio-based satellite navigation system operated for the Russian government by the Russian Space Forces. It is an alternative and complementary to the United States' Global Positioning System (GPS), the Chinese Compass navigation system, and the Galileo positioning system of the European Union (EU).

Development on the GLONASS began in the Soviet Union in 1976, with a goal of global coverage by 1991. Beginning on 12 October 1982, numerous rocket launches added satellites to the system until the constellation was completed in 1995. Following completion, the system fell into disrepair with the collapse of the Russian economy.

Beginning in 2003, Russia committed to restoring the system and by mid-2010 it has achieved 100% coverage of the Russia's territory. Currently 20 satellites are operational, while 4 other satellites are in maintainance and 2 more are spare ones. The constellation is short of a few operational satellites needed to achieve a total number of 24 satellites which will provide continuous global coverage.[42]

---

[42]http://en.wikipedia.org/wiki/GLONASS

The system requires 18 satellites for continuous navigation services covering the entire territory of the Russian Federation, and 24 satellites to provide services worldwide. The GLONASS system currently covers 100% of Russian territory.[43]

Galileo is a global navigation satellite system (GNSS) currently being built by the European Union (EU) and European Space Agency (ESA). The €3.4 billion project is named after the famous Italian astronomer Galileo Galilei. One of the political aims with Galileo is to provide a high-accuracy positioning system upon which European nations can rely independent from the Russian GLONASS and US GPS systems which can be disabled for commercial users in times of war or conflict.

China's GPS system is called Compass. This new system will be a constellation of 35 satellites, which include 5 geostationary orbit (GEO) satellites and 30 medium Earth orbit (MEO) satellites, that will offer complete coverage of the globe. The ranging signals are based on the CDMA principle and have complex structure typical to Galileo or modernized GPS. Similarly to the other GNSS, there will be two levels of positioning service: open and restricted (military). The public service shall be available globally to general users. When all the currently planned GNSS systems are deployed, the users will benefit from the use of a total constellation of 75+ satellites, which will significantly improve all the aspects of positioning, especially availability of the signals in so-called "urban canyons."[44]

When in operation, it will use the two ground operations centers, one near Munich, Germany, and another in Fucino, Italy and will consist of 30 satellites (27 operational + 3 active spares). The first experimental satellite, GIOVE-A, was launched in 2005 and was followed by a second test satellite, GIOVE-B, launched in 2008. The first four operational satellites for navigation will be launched in 2011 and once this In-Orbit Validation (IOV) phase has been completed, additional satellites will be launched. On 30 November 2007 the 27 EU transportation ministers involved reached an agreement that it should be operational by 2013, but later press releases suggest it was delayed to 2014.

The navigation system is intended to provide measurements down to the meter range as a free service including the height (altitude) above sea level, and better positioning services at high latitudes compared to GPS and GLONASS. Though with recent upgrades on GPS similar accuracy levels are reached. As a further feature, Galileo will provide a global Search and Rescue (SAR) function. To do so, each satellite will be equipped with a transponder, which is able to transfer the distress signals from the user transmitters to the Rescue Co-ordination Centre, which will then initiate the rescue operation. At the same time, the system will provide a signal to the user, informing him that his situation has been detected and that help is under way. This latter feature is new and is considered a major upgrade compared to the existing GPS and GLONASS navigation systems which do not provide feedback to the user. The use of basic (low-accuracy) Galileo services will be free and open to everyone. The high-accuracy capabilities will be available for paying commercial users and for military use.[45]

---

[43]http://www.interfax.ru/society/news.asp?id=62659

[44]http://en.wikipedia.org/wiki/Compass_navigation_system

[45]http://en.wikipedia.org/wiki/Galileo_(satellite_navigation)

While business is rushing to develop new products using the GPS-enabled chip sets, there has been some concerns expressed about their privacy. Many people do not want the government and businesses to have access to their whereabouts at any given moment. Examples abound concerning how this advancement of technology can be disconcerting. For example, in August of 2010, Adam Savage, of "MythBusters," took a photo of his vehicle using his smartphone. He then posted the photo to his Twitter account including the phrase "off to work." Since the photo was taken by his smartphone, the image contained metadata revealing the exact geographical location the photo was taken. So by simply taking and posting a photo, Savage revealed the exact location of his home, the vehicle he drives, and the time he leaves for work.[46]

Also, in 2009, Wired magazine posted this article: "I ran a little experiment. On a sunny Saturday, I spotted a woman in Golden Gate Park taking a photo with a 3G iPhone. Because iPhones embed geodata into photos that users upload to Flickr or Picasa, iPhoneshots can be automatically placed on a map. At home I searched the Flickrmap, and score—a shot from today. I clicked through to the user's photo stream and determined it was the woman I had seen earlier. After adjusting the settings so that only her shots appeared on the map, I saw a cluster of images in one location. Clicking on them revealed photos of an apartment interior—a bedroom, a kitchen, a filthy living room. Now I know where she lives."[47]

Speaking of smartphones, GPS on smartphones is no longer an emerging trend. It's almost a must-have feature nowadays, and more and more handsets are offering it. With the embedded GPS receiver and a mapping service, you can get real-time position tracking, text- and voice-guided directions, and points of interest. However, taking advantage of GPS, and the navigation powers that come with it, sometimes come at a price. If you want features, such as voice-guided directions, you often have to subscribe to a location-based service (LBS), such as TeleNav or VZ Navigator, which require a subscription fee. However, Google and Nokia are shaking things up by offering the premium features for free on such devices as the HTC Droid Incredible and Nokia 5800 Navigation Edition. Microsoft has even jumped on the bandwagon by offering free, voice-guided directions with an updated Bing app for its Windows phones.[48]

A review of GPS-enabled smartphones can be found at the following website: http://reviews.cnet.com/gps-systems/?tag=mncol;srt&sort= edRating7+desc.

A review of GPS-in-your-car systems can be found at the following website: http://reviews.cnet.com/4321-3430_7-6544608.html?tag=mncol;2n.

With a GPS card in consumers' computers, Internet advertising agencies can target their customers within a geographical area, say a distance of 3 miles. Knowing that government agencies and commercial businesses alike will know their every move, as is currently the case with commercial truck drivers, customers

[46]http://nyti.ms/917hRh

[47]http://www.wired.com/gadgets/wireless/magazine/17-02/lp_guineapig?currentPage=all

[48]http://reviews.cnet.com/4321-6452_7-6564140.html

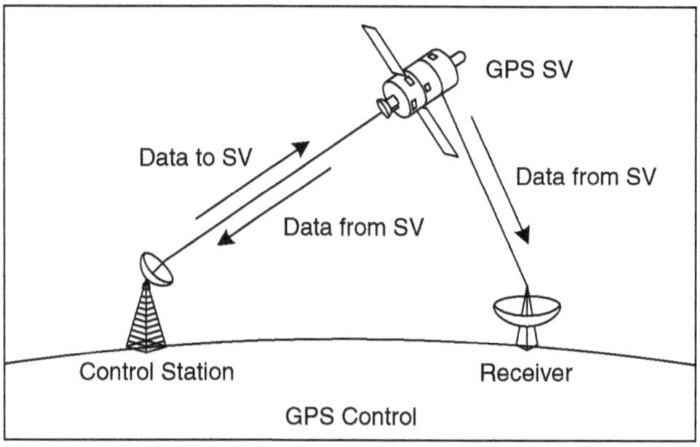

Figure 9.36 The Segments of GPS

believe the system is an invasion of privacy. The government recently mandated that the FCC put a system in place which will accurately pinpoint the location of a cellular phone calling 911 for an emergency. This is currently being implemented. As of December 2010, the FCC reports over 77% of counties in the U.S. implement some form of this system. Some believe this is another attempt at "Big Brother" tracking private citizens.

All of this is made possible at no charge by the government to commercial interests and with no access fees to the end user.

The GPS consists of three segments—satellite, control, and user. We will now address each in some detail. Figure 9.36 graphically depicts this configuration.

9.16 SATELLITE SEGMENT

The Navstar GPS contains twenty-four satellites, maintaining an altitude of approximately 12,500 miles above the earth. These satellites are divided into six planes of four satellites each, spaced equally around the equator, and the ascending nodes of each has an inclination of 55¡. There are several types of satellites: Block I, launched from 1976 to 1982 (used to demonstrate the feasibility of the GPS system).; Blocks II and IIA, launched from 1989 to 1993, demonstrating increased power from Block I's 400 W to 710.0 W; and the newer Block IIR satellites, which have improved nuclear explosion detection and onboard computer memories. New Block IIR Navstar satellites replace the older models when they are no longer functional. The clocks on board each satellite are synchronized with an accuracy of three billionths of a second. Block IIR-M versions, launched from 2005–2009, have three more frequency channels (with two more military and one more civilian), and are more secure against jamming and radiation than all older models. Navstar-2F (Navigation System using Timing And Ranging) or GPS-2F satellites are the fourth evolution stage of the Navstar GPS satellites. Improvements included an extended design life of 12 years (earlier Navstar satellites has

Figure 9.37 Block I GPS Satellite circa 1989–1990 *(Courtesy of NASA)*

a design life of 7.5 years), faster processors with more memory, and a new civil signal on a third frequency. The first Block IIF satellite was launched in May, 2010 and is now fully operational. Unlike earlier GPS satellites, which were launched on Atlas E/F and Delta II rockets, GPS IIF SV-1 was placed directly into its operational orbit, eliminating the need for an apogee motor. In addition to broadcasting the same signals as previous satellites, it will also broadcast the L5 signal, and a military signal known as M-code. Its signal accuracy is approximately twice that of its predecessors.[49] An apogee motor is basically a rocket motor that is regularly employed on artificial satellites destined for higher orbits such as GPS. It is more more-effective to launch from the ground with a large booster rocket and then use this smaller rocket motor for final orbital adjustment for several reasons, one being that the largest rocket boosters are prohibitively expensive and so reserved for use only when priority is utmost. Figures 9.37 thru 9.41 show these satellites.

All of the GPS satellites are stabilized in orbit on three axes through the use of reaction wheels and magnetic torque. The satellites must deal with forces such as solar pressure; the gravitational fields of the sun, earth, and moon; and thermal radiation from the satellite itself. Orbit predictions must take these factors into consideration, in addition to the rotation rate and axis of the earth. The orbit maintained by each satellite allows it to repeat the same path once every 24 hours, completing it 4 minutes earlier every day. Each satellite orbits the earth with its solar panels facing the sun at right angles and its antennas facing earth. Each satellite broadcasts pseudorandom noise (PRN) codes to modulate the signal, allowing receivers to cal-

[49]See http://en.wikipedia.org/wiki/GPS_IIF_SV-1

Figure 9.38 Block IIA GPS Satellite (circa 1990–1997)

Figure 9.39 Block IIR GPS Satellite (circa 1997–2004)

Figure 9.40 Block IIR-M GPS Satellite (circa 2005–2009)
(Courtesy of NASA)

Figure 9.41 Block IIF GPS Satellite circa 2011
(Courtesy of NASA)

culate the signal arrival time compared with the receiving unit's local clock. The satellites each transmit their signal at two frequencies, the L1 (1575.42 MHz) and L2 (1227.60 MHz) signals. The PRN codes are superimposed on the data in the L1 signal. The precision (P) code and a data message are contained in the L2 signal. Although all the satellites are broadcasting on the same frequency, each satellite's PRN is unique, allowing a receiver to track each satellite separately. This process is known as code division multiple access (CDMA).

Other factors can interfere with the satellite-originated signal arriving on time to the receiver; therefore, the satellites broadcast over two frequencies to allow correction for them. Some of these factors include interference from the **troposphere** and the total electron content in the **ionosphere**, along the path the signal travels from the satellite to the receiver. The arrival time difference of the two signals can be computed by the receiver, allowing a more accurate prediction of its position. To understand this process, it is necessary to discuss the earth's atmosphere.[50]

Layers of the Atmosphere

The atmosphere of the earth may be divided into several distinct layers, as shown in Figure 9.42.

Troposphere Layer The troposphere is where all weather takes place; it is the region of rising and falling packets of air. The air pressure at the top of the tropos-

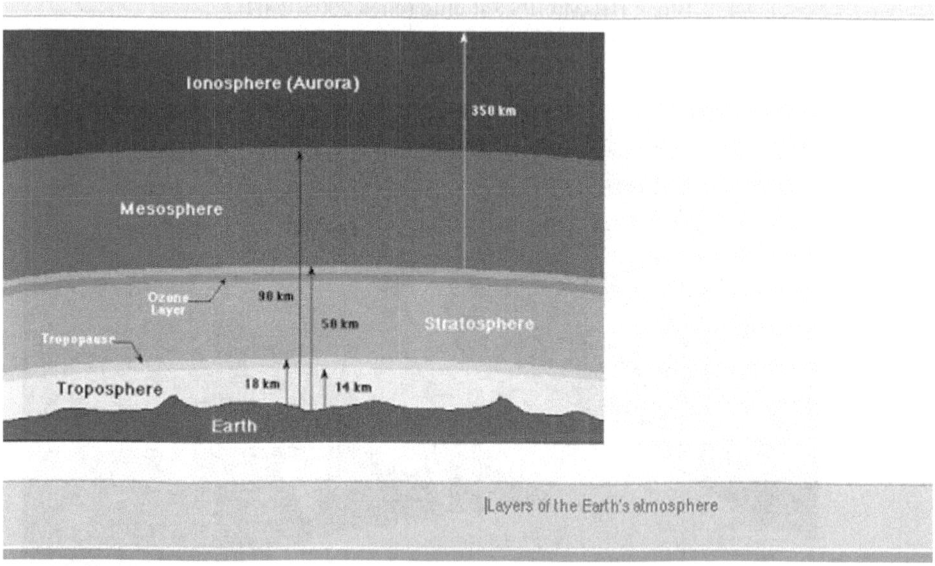

Figure 9.42 Layers of the Earth's Atmosphere

[50]For additional information on the earth's atmosphere, see www.csep10.phys.utk.edu/astr161/lect/earth/atmosphere.html.

phere is only 10 percent of that at sea level (0.1 atmosphere). A thin buffer zone lies between the troposphere and the next layer called the tropopause.

Stratosphere and Ozone Layers Above the troposphere is the **stratosphere**, where airflow is mostly horizontal. The thin ozone layer in the upper stratosphere has a high concentration of ozone, a particularly reactive form of oxygen. This layer is primarily responsible for absorbing the ultraviolet radiation from the sun. The formation of this layer is a delicate matter, because only when oxygen is produced in the atmosphere can an ozone layer form and prevent an intense flux of ultraviolet radiation from reaching the surface, where it is quite hazardous to the evolution of life.

Mesosphere and Ionosphere Layers Above the stratosphere is the **mesosphere** and above that is the ionosphere (or thermosphere), where many atoms are ionized (have gained or lost electrons so they have a net electrical charge). The ionosphere is very thin, but it is where aurorae take place, and it is responsible for absorbing the most energetic photons from the sun and for reflecting radio waves, thereby making long-distance radio communications possible. The structure of the ionosphere is strongly influenced by the charged particle wind from the sun (solar wind), which is in turn governed by the level of solar activity.

9.17 CONTROL SEGMENT

The accuracy of the Navstar satellites is maintained by the master control station, located at Schriever Air Force Base in Colorado Springs, by five unmanned monitor stations and four antenna stations situated around the world. There are two stations in the Pacific, located in Hawaii and Kwajalein; one unmanned station in the Atlantic, on Ascension Island; and the other in the Indian Ocean at Diego Garcia. The monitor stations gather information from all the satellites and relay it to the master control station. It is at the master control station that the information is calculated for accuracy and relayed back to the satellites to update their navigation messages.

9.18 USER SEGMENT

A minimum of four GPS satellites are required for a receiver to calculate its three-dimensional position. The twenty-four-satellite constellation configuration ensures a minimum of six satellites within view of any receiver at any point on the globe at any given moment. It is possible for twelve satellites to be within range of a single receiver. The greater the number of satellites in range, the greater the accuracy of the position solution calculated by the GPS receiver. Hand-held GPS units are compact, typically the size of a cell phone or smaller. Major U.S. manufacturers include Trimble Navigation, Ltd., Ashtech-Magellan Corp., and Novatel.

How a GPS Receiver Works

First, the antenna on each GPS receiver converts the satellite's radio signals into an electric current which is then filtered, amplified, and processed according to the capabilities of the particular receiver used. Until recently, the hand-held units have been considered more of a specialized gadget or an executive novelty as the cost was significant (usually over $1,000). Now these devices are around $200 and are also incorporated into many devices such as smartphones.

The media news website CNETR provides product reviews, specifications, and pricing information on GPS receivers.[51]

To correct the inaccuracies inherent in the system, an earth-based solution known as the differential system helps to improve GPS calculations. The differential system employs the use of ground-based receiver/transmitters situated on surveyed points. These provide accurate, reliable readings, which are used in differential receivers to compute a position solution much closer to the actual location. These locations read the satellite position, compare it with the ground-base known location, and broadcast an accurate signal for use in differential receivers, creating an accuracy level within a few meters. The lower price and the improved accuracy level of the GPS receivers are spurring new applications which, in turn, increase consumer demand.

Although GPS and its technology have been available for some time now, the costs, inaccuracy, government ownership, and privacy issues have prevented this useful and practical service from being utilized fully. These issues have slowly been working themselves out and are mostly resolved. For example, most smartphones of today incorporate GPS capability and many people in the developed nations have GPS devices in their automobiles, many for a price less than $200. Future prospects are more promising and there is not another system of its type likely to take its place for personal, commercial, and military use.

As GPS cards have become commonplace technology, consumers express privacy concerns and yet still purchase the devices. object to the government or to commercial enterprises knowing their exact location? If your computer's IP address includes the precise geographic location, it would be available to anyone on the Internet. Is this good business or is it an invasion of privacy? The courts will have to determine the legal issues involved with this technology. The lives of many are enhanced through GPS already. The safe and speedy navigation of ships and boats of all sizes, the ability to track a package from the distributor to the consumer, or pinpointing the yield effects of fertilizer application down to the square meter, thus reducing fertilizer pollution runoff, are all practical applications of today's GPS. Many new cars can combine the information from their GPS card, cell phone connections with a central assistance location, and onboard maps provided on CD-ROM to plot directions to the next location. If the car is stolen, the GPS locator can relay its location to assist the police in returning the stolen vehicle. Do you know precisely where you are? Whether you are ready or not, GPS can tell you precisely where you stand.

---

[51]http://www.cnet.com/1770-5_1-0.html?query=gps+receiver&tag=srch

More GPS products are coming on the market as vendors see a viable market for these devices and software, for example, GPS receivers, GPS software for the PC, and even GPS software for the iPhone and Droid as well as other lesser known smartphones.

9.19 SUMMARY

With the advances in satellite technology, we find ourselves with the same struggle as always: unlimited wants and needs, and limited resources. Thus far we have been able to find different orbits in which to launch satellites and calculate distances and forces in the atmosphere and beyond. We are able to measure more accurately, from outer space, aspects of our planet that would have remained unknown to us had we not traveled there. We have come a long way since Sputnik, and we are ever finding more ways to use our knowledge and technology. One thing throughout is certain: We continue to find new limits and we continue to break them.

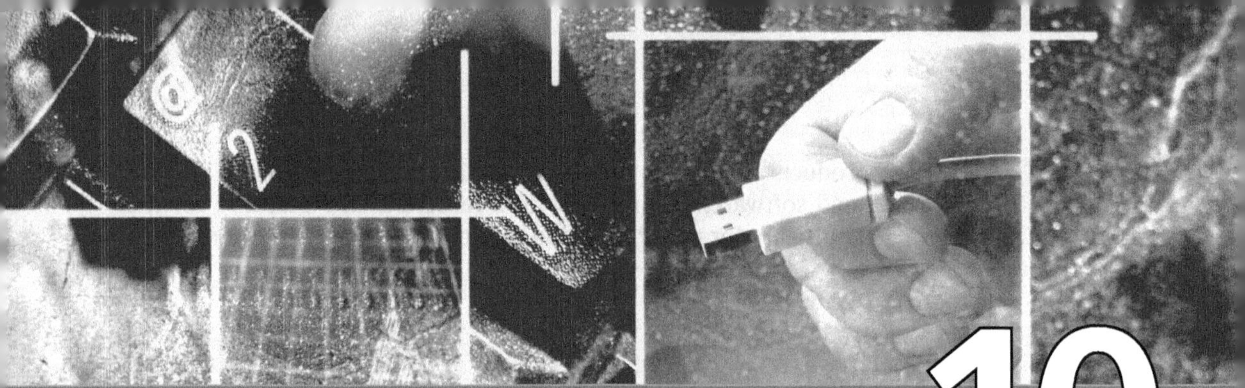

CHAPTER 10

Cellular Wireless Networks

Of all the tremendous advances in data communications and telecommunications, perhaps the most revolutionary is the development of cellular networks. Cellular technology is the foundation of mobile wireless communications and supports users in locations that are not easily served by wired networks. Cellular technology is the underlying technology for mobile telephones, personal communications systems, wireless Internet and wireless Web applications, and much more.

We begin this chapter with a look at the basic principles used in all cellular networks. Then we look at specific cellular technologies and standards, which are conveniently grouped into three generations. The first generation is analog based and is passing from the scene. The dominant technology today is the digital second-generation systems. Finally, third-generation high-speed digital systems have begun to emerge.

10.1 PRINCIPLES OF CELLULAR NETWORKS

Cellular radio is a technique that was developed to increase the capacity available for mobile radio telephone service. Prior to the introduction of cellular radio, mobile radio telephone service was only provided by a high-power transmitter/receiver. A typical system would support about 25 channels with an effective radius of about 80 km. The way to increase the capacity of the system is to use lower-power systems with shorter radius and to use numerous transmitters/receivers. We begin this section with a look at the organization of cellular systems and then examine some of the details of their implementation.

Cellular Network Organization

The essence of a cellular network is the use of multiple low-power transmitters, on the order of 100 W or less. Because the range of such a transmitter is small, an area can be divided into cells, each one served by its own antenna. Each cell is allocated a band of frequencies and is served by a **base station**, consisting of transmitter, receiver, and control unit. Adjacent cells are assigned different frequencies to avoid interference or crosstalk. However, cells sufficiently distant from each other can use the same frequency band.

The first design decision to make is the shape of cells to cover an area. A matrix of square cells would be the simplest layout to define (Figure 10.1a). However, this geometry is not ideal. If the width of a square cell is d, then a cell has four neighbors at a distance d and four neighbors at a distance $\sqrt{2}d$. As a mobile user within a cell moves toward the cell's boundaries, it is best if all of the adjacent antennas are equidistant. This simplifies the task of determining when to switch the user to an adjacent antenna and which antenna to choose. A hexagonal pattern provides for equidistant antennas (Figure 10.1b). The radius of a hexagon is defined to be the radius of the circle that circumscribes it (equivalently, the distance from the center to each vertex; also equal to the length of a side of a hexagon). For a cell radius R, the distance between the cell center and each adjacent cell center is $d = \sqrt{3}R$.

In practice, a precise hexagonal pattern is not used. Variations from the ideal are due to topographical limitations, local signal propagation conditions, and practical limitation on siting antennas.

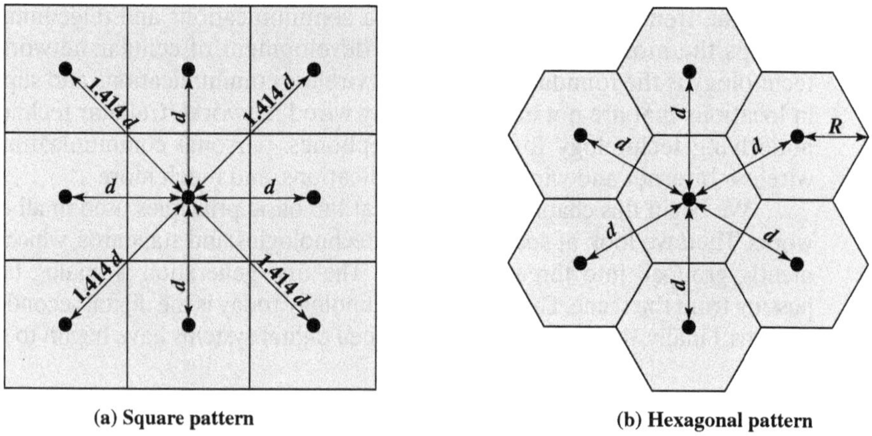

Figure 10.1 Cellular Geometries

Frequency Reuse In a cellular system, each cell has a base transceiver. The transmission power is carefully controlled (to the extent that it is possible in the highly variable mobile communication environment) to allow communication within the cell using a given frequency band while limiting the power at that frequency that escapes the cell into adjacent cells. Nevertheless, it is not practical to attempt to use the same frequency band in two adjacent cells.[1] Instead, the objective is to use the same frequency band in multiple cells at some distance from one another. This allows the same frequency band to be used for multiple simultaneous conversations in different cells. Within a given cell, multiple frequency bands are assigned, the number of bands depending on the traffic expected.

A key design issue is to determine the minimum separation between two cells using the same frequency band, so that the two cells do not interfere with each other. Various patterns of frequency reuse are possible. Figure 10.2 shows some examples. If the pattern consists of N cells and each cell is assigned the same number of frequencies, each cell can have K/N frequencies, where K is the total number of frequencies allotted to the system. For AMPS, $K = 395$, and $N = 7$ is the smallest pattern that can provide sufficient isolation between two uses of the same frequency. This implies that there can be at most 57 frequencies per cell on average.

In characterizing frequency reuse, the following parameters are commonly used:

D = minimum distance between centers of cells that use the same frequency band (called cochannels)

R = radius of a cell

d = distance between centers of adjacent cells $\left(d = \sqrt{3}R\right)$

N = number of cells in a repetitious pattern (each cell in the pattern uses a unique set of frequency bands), termed the **reuse factor**

[1]The exception is CDMA systems, described subsequently.

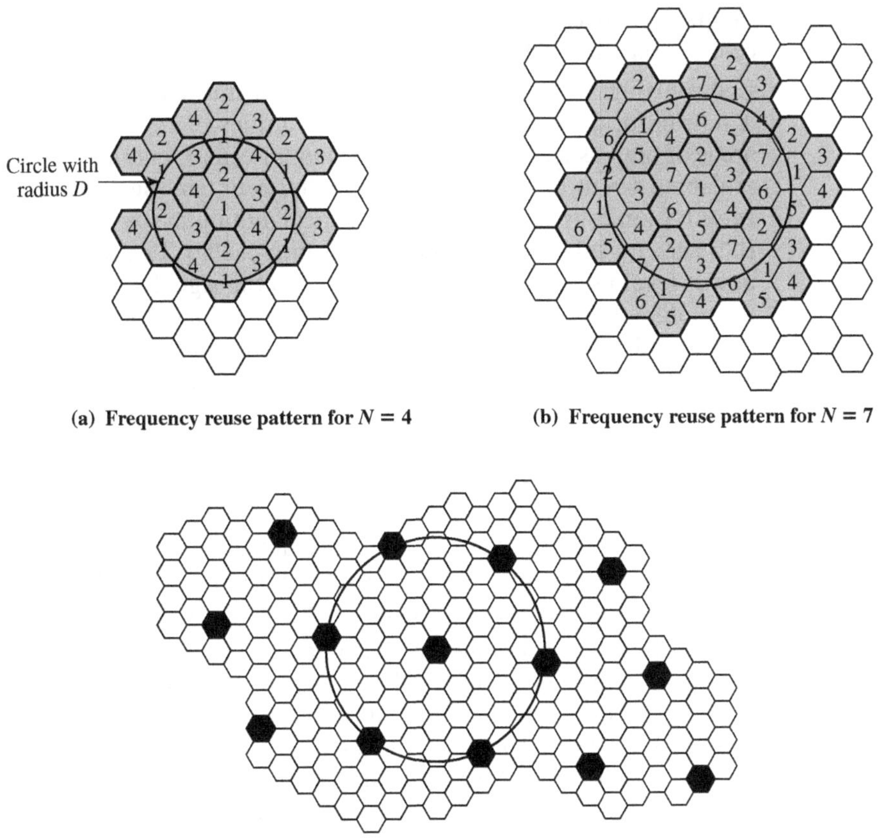

(a) Frequency reuse pattern for $N = 4$

(b) Frequency reuse pattern for $N = 7$

(c) Black cells indicate a frequency reuse for $N = 19$

Figure 10.2 Frequency Reuse Patterns

In a hexagonal cell pattern, only the following values of N are possible:

$$N = I^2 + J^2 + (I \times J), \quad I, J = 0, 1, 2, 3, \ldots$$

Hence, possible values of N are 1, 3, 4, 7, 9, 12, 13, 16, 19, 21, and so on. The following relationship holds:

$$\frac{D}{R} = \sqrt{3N}$$

This can also be expressed as $D/d = \sqrt{N}$.

Increasing Capacity In time, as more customers use the system, traffic may build up so that there are not enough frequency bands assigned to a cell to handle its calls. A number of approaches have been used to cope with this situation, including the following:

- **Adding new channels:** Typically, when a system is set up in a region, not all of the channels are used, and growth and expansion can be managed in an orderly fashion by adding new channels.

- **Frequency borrowing:** In the simplest case, frequencies are taken from adjacent cells by congested cells. The frequencies can also be assigned to cells dynamically.
- **Cell splitting:** In practice, the distribution of traffic and topographic features is not uniform, and this presents opportunities of capacity increase. Cells in areas of high usage can be split into smaller cells. Generally, the original cells are about 6.5 to 13 km in size. The smaller cells can themselves be split; however, 1.5-km cells are close to the practical minimum size as a general solution (but see the subsequent discussion of microcells). To use a smaller cell, the power level used must be reduced to keep the signal within the cell. Also, as the mobile units move, they pass from cell to cell, which requires transferring of the call from one base transceiver to another. This process is called a *handoff*. As the cells get smaller, these handoffs become much more frequent. Figure 10.3 indicates schematically how cells can be divided to provide more capacity. A radius reduction by a factor of F reduces the coverage area and increases the required number of base stations by a factor of F^2.
- **Cell sectoring:** With cell sectoring, a cell is divided into a number of wedge-shaped sectors, each with its own set of channels, typically 3 or 6 sectors per cell. Each sector is assigned a separate subset of the cell's channels, and directional antennas at the base station are used to focus on each sector.
- **Microcells:** As cells become smaller, antennas move from the tops of tall buildings or hills, to the tops of small buildings or the sides of large buildings, and finally to lamp posts, where they form microcells. Each decrease in cell size is accompanied by a reduction in the radiated power levels from the base stations and the mobile units. Microcells are useful in city streets in congested areas, along highways, and inside large public buildings.

Table 10.1 suggests typical parameters for traditional cells, called macrocells, and microcells with current technology. The average delay spread refers to multipath delay spread; that is, the same signal follows different paths and there is a time delay between the earliest and latest arrival of the signal at the receiver. As indicated, the use of smaller cells enables the use of lower power and provides superior propagation conditions.

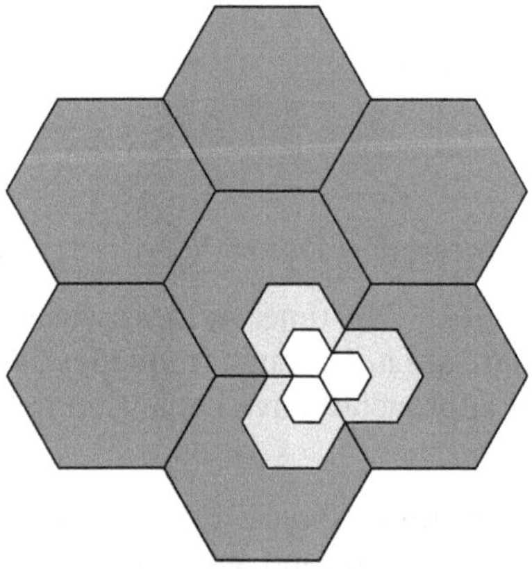

Figure 10.3 Cell Splitting

Table 10.1 Typical Parameters for Macrocells and Microcells [ANDE95]

	Macrocell	Microcell
Cell radius	1 to 20 km	0.1 to 1 km
Transmission power	1 to 10 W	0.1 to 1 W
Average delay spread	0.1 to 10 μs	10 to 100 ns
Maximum bit rate	0.3 Mbps	1 Mbps

Example 10.1 [HAAS00]. Assume a system of 32 cells with a cell radius of 1.6 km, a total of 32 cells, a total frequency bandwidth that supports 336 traffic channels, and a reuse factor of $N = 7$. If there are 32 total cells, what geographic area is covered, how many channels are there per cell, and what is the total number of concurrent calls that can be handled? Repeat for a cell radius of 0.8 km and 128 cells.

Figure 10.4a shows an approximately square pattern. The area of a hexagon of radius R is $1.5R^2\sqrt{3}$. A hexagon of radius 1.6 km has an area of 6.65 km^2, and the total area covered is $6.65 \times 32 = 213$ km^2. For $N = 7$, the number of channels per cell is $336/7 = 48$, for a total channel capacity of $48 \times 32 = 1536$ channels. For the layout of Figure 10.4b, the area covered is $1.66 \times 128 = 213$ km^2. The number of channels per cell is $336/7 = 48$, for a total channel capacity of $48 \times 128 = 6144$ channels.

Operation of Cellular Systems

Figure 10.5 shows the principal elements of a cellular system. In the approximate center of each cell is a base station (BS). The BS includes an antenna, a controller, and a number of transceivers, for communicating on the channels assigned to that cell. The controller is used to handle the call process between the mobile unit and the rest of the network. At any time, a number of mobile units may be active and moving about within a cell, communicating with the BS. Each BS is connected to a mobile telecommunications switching office (MTSO), with one MTSO serving

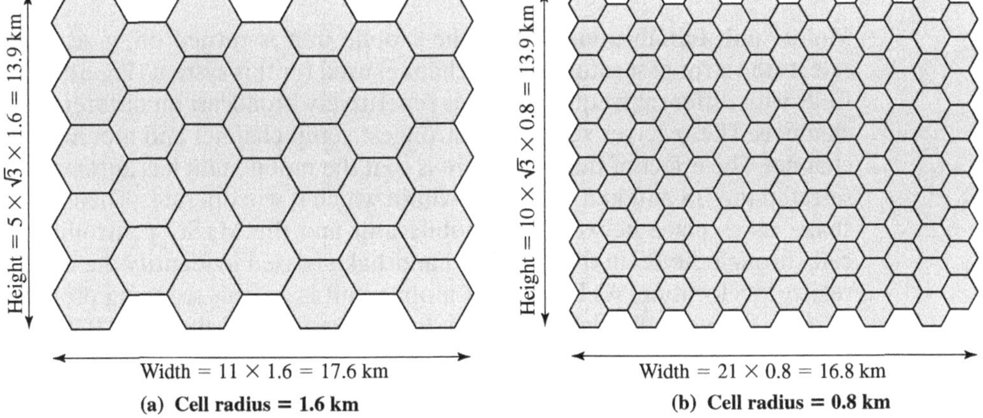

Figure 10.4 Frequency Reuse Example

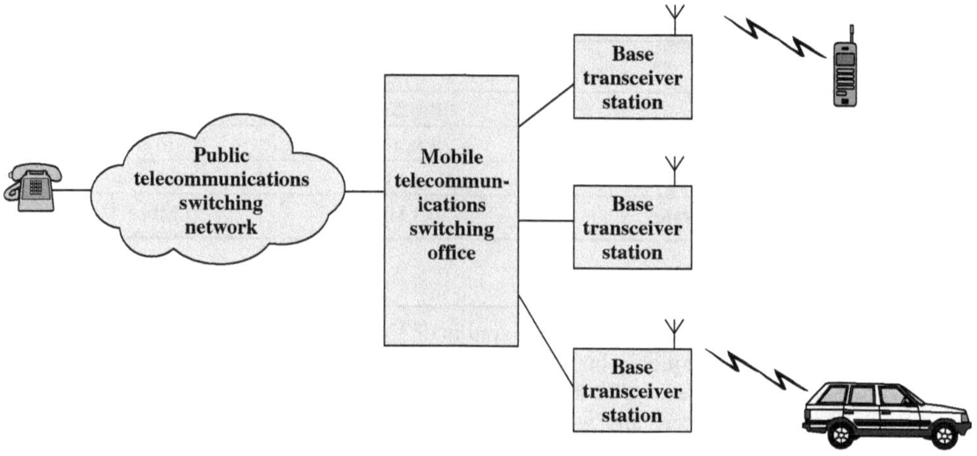

Figure 10.5 Overview of Cellular System

multiple BSs. Typically, the link between an MTSO and a BS is by a wire line, although a wireless link is also possible. The MTSO connects calls between mobile units. The MTSO is also connected to the public telephone or telecommunications network and can make a connection between a fixed subscriber to the public network and a mobile subscriber to the cellular network. The MTSO assigns the voice channel to each call, performs handoffs (discussed subsequently), and monitors the call for billing information.

The use of a cellular system is fully automated and requires no action on the part of the user other than placing or answering a call. Two types of channels are available between the mobile unit and the base station (BS): control channels and traffic channels. **Control channels** are used to exchange information having to do with setting up and maintaining calls and with establishing a relationship between a mobile unit and the nearest BS. **Traffic channels** carry a voice or data connection between users. Figure 10.6 illustrates the steps in a typical call between two mobile users within an area controlled by a single MTSO:

- **Mobile unit initialization:** When the mobile unit is turned on, it scans and selects the strongest setup control channel used for this system (Figure 10.6a). Cells with different frequency bands repetitively broadcast on different setup channels. The receiver selects the strongest setup channel and monitors that channel. The effect of this procedure is that the mobile unit has automatically selected the BS antenna of the cell within which it will operate.[2] Then a handshake takes place between the mobile unit and the MTSO controlling this cell, through the BS in this cell. The handshake is used to identify the user and register its location. As long as the mobile unit is on, this scanning procedure is repeated periodically to account for the motion of the unit. If the unit

[2]Usually, but not always, the antenna and therefore the base station selected is the closest one to the mobile unit. However, because of propagation anomalies, this is not always the case.

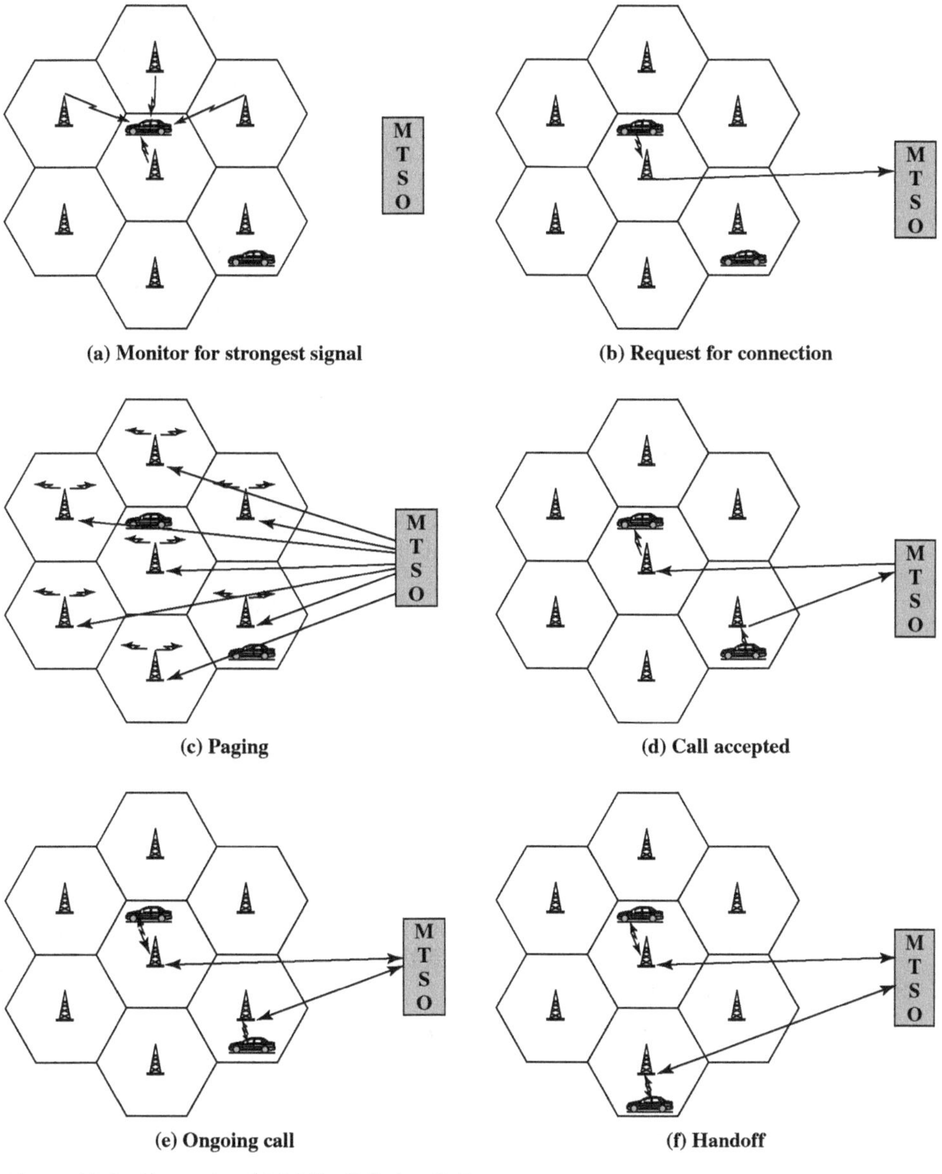

Figure 10.6 Example of Mobile Cellular Call

enters a new cell, then a new BS is selected. In addition, the mobile unit is monitoring for pages, discussed subsequently.

- **Mobile-originated call:** A mobile unit originates a call by sending the number of the called unit on the preselected setup channel (Figure 10.6b). The receiver at the mobile unit first checks that the setup channel is idle by examining information in the forward (from the BS) channel. When an idle is detected, the mobile unit may transmit on the corresponding reverse (to BS) channel. The BS sends the request to the MTSO.

- **Paging:** The MTSO then attempts to complete the connection to the called unit. The MTSO sends a paging message to certain BSs depending on the called mobile unit number (Figure 10.6c). Each BS transmits the paging signal on its own assigned setup channel.
- **Call accepted:** The called mobile unit recognizes its number on the setup channel being monitored and responds to that BS, which sends the response to the MTSO. The MTSO sets up a circuit between the calling and called BSs. At the same time, the MTSO selects an available traffic channel within each BS's cell and notifies each BS, which in turn notifies its mobile unit (Figure 10.6d). The two mobile units tune to their respective assigned channels.
- **Ongoing call:** While the connection is maintained, the two mobile units exchange voice or data signals, going through their respective BSs and the MTSO (Figure 10.6e).
- **Handoff:** If a mobile unit moves out of range of one cell and into the range of another during a connection, the traffic channel has to change to one assigned to the BS in the new cell (Figure 10.6f). The system makes this change without either interrupting the call or alerting the user.

Other functions performed by the system but not illustrated in Figure 10.6 include the following:

- **Call blocking:** During the mobile-initiated call stage, if all the traffic channels assigned to the nearest BS are busy, then the mobile unit makes a preconfigured number of repeated attempts. After a certain number of failed tries, a busy tone is returned to the user.
- **Call termination:** When one of the two users hangs up, the MTSO is informed and the traffic channels at the two BSs are released.
- **Call drop:** During a connection, because of interference or weak signal spots in certain areas, if the BS cannot maintain the minimum required signal strength for a certain period of time, the traffic channel to the user is dropped and the MTSO is informed.
- **Calls to/from fixed and remote mobile subscriber:** The MTSO connects to the public switched telephone network. Thus, the MTSO can set up a connection between a mobile user in its area and a fixed subscriber via the telephone network. Further, the MTSO can connect to a remote MTSO via the telephone network or via dedicated lines and set up a connection between a mobile user in its area and a remote mobile user.

Mobile Radio Propagation Effects

Mobile radio communication introduces complexities not found in wire communication or in fixed wireless communication. Two general areas of concern are signal strength and signal propagation effects.

- **Signal strength:** The strength of the signal between the base station and the mobile unit must be strong enough to maintain signal quality at the receiver but not so strong as to create too much cochannel interference with channels in another cell using the same frequency band. Several complicating factors exist. Human-made noise varies considerably, resulting in a variable noise level. For example, automobile ignition noise in the cellular frequency range is greater in the city than in a suburban area. Other signal sources vary from place to place. The signal strength varies as a function of distance from the BS to a point within its cell. Moreover, the signal strength varies dynamically as the mobile unit moves.

- **Fading:** Even if signal strength is within an effective range, signal propagation effects may disrupt the signal and cause errors. Section 5.4 discussed fading and various countermeasures.

In designing a cellular layout, the communications engineer must take account of these various propagation effects, the desired maximum transmit power level at the base station and the mobile units, the typical height of the mobile unit antenna, and the available height of the BS antenna. These factors will determine the size of the individual cell. Unfortunately, as just described, the propagation effects are dynamic and difficult to predict. The best that can be done is to come up with a model based on empirical data and to apply that model to a given environment to develop guidelines for cell size. One of the most widely used models was developed by Okumura et al. [OKUM68] and subsequently refined by Hata [HATA80]. The original was a detailed analysis of the Tokyo area and produced path loss information for an urban environment. Hata's model is an empirical formulation that takes into account a variety of environments and conditions. For an urban environment, predicted path loss is

$$L_{dB} = 69.55 + 26.16 \log f_c - 13.82 \log h_t - A(h_r) + (44.9 - 6.55 \log h_t)\log d \tag{10.1}$$

where

f_c = carrier frequency in MHz from 150 to 1500 MHz
h_t = height of transmitting antenna (base station) in m, from 30 to 300 m
h_r = height of receiving antenna (mobile unit) in m, from 1 to 10 m
d = propagation distance between antennas in km, from 1 to 20 km
$A(h_r)$ = correction factor for mobile unit antenna height

For a small or medium sized city, the correction factor is given by

$$A(h_r) = (1.1 \log f_c - 0.7)h_r - (1.56 \log f_c - 0.8) \text{ dB}$$

And for a large city it is given by

$$A(h_r) = 8.29[\log(1.54\, h_r)]^2 - 1.1 \text{ dB} \quad \text{for } f_c \le 300 \text{ MHz}$$
$$A(h_r) = 3.2[\log(11.75\, h_r)]^2 - 4.97 \text{ dB} \quad \text{for } f_c \ge 300 \text{ MHz}$$

To estimate the path loss in a suburban area, the formula for urban path loss in Equation (10.1) is modified as

$$L_{dB}(\text{suburban}) = L_{dB}(\text{urban}) - 2[\log(f_c/28)]^2 - 5.4$$

And for the path loss in open areas, the formula is modified as

$$L_{dB}(\text{open}) = L_{dB}(\text{urban}) - 4.78(\log f_c)^2 - 18.733(\log f_c) - 40.98$$

The Okumura/Hata model is considered to be among the best in terms of accuracy in path loss prediction and provides a practical means of estimating path loss in a wide variety of situations [FREE97, RAPP02].

Example 10.2 [FREE97]. Let $f_c = 900$ MHz, $h_t = 40$ m, $h_r = 5$ m, and $d = 10$ km. Estimate the path loss for a medium-size city.

$$\begin{aligned} A(h_r) &= (1.1 \log 900 - 0.7)5 - (1.56 \log 900 - 0.8) \text{ dB} \\ &= 12.75 - 3.8 = 8.95 \text{ dB} \end{aligned}$$

$$\begin{aligned} L_{dB} &= 69.55 + 26.16 \log 900 - 13.82 \log 40 - 8.95 + (44.9 - 6.55 \log 40)\log 10 \\ &= 69.55 + 77.28 - 22.14 - 8.95 + 34.4 = 150.14 \text{ dB} \end{aligned}$$

Handoff

Handoff[3] is the procedure for changing the assignment of a mobile unit from one BS to another as the mobile unit moves from one cell to another. Handoff is handled in different ways in different systems and involves a number of factors. Here we give a brief overview.

Handoff may be network initiated, in which the decision is made solely by the network measurements of received signals from the mobile unit. Alternatively, mobile unit assisted handoff schemes enable the mobile unit to participate in the handoff decision by providing feedback to the network concerning signals received at the mobile unit. In either case, a number of different performance metrics may be used to make the decision. [HAAS00] lists the following:

- **Cell blocking probability:** The probability of a new call being blocked, due to heavy load on the BS traffic capacity. In this case, the mobile unit is handed off to a neighboring cell based not on signal quality but on traffic capacity.
- **Call dropping probability:** The probability that, due to a handoff, a call is terminated.
- **Call completion probability:** The probability that an admitted call is not dropped before it terminates.
- **Probability of unsuccessful handoff:** The probability that a handoff is executed while the reception conditions are inadequate.
- **Handoff blocking probability:** The probability that a handoff cannot be successfully completed.
- **Handoff probability:** The probability that a handoff occurs before call termination.
- **Rate of handoff:** The number of handoffs per unit time.

[3]The term *handoff* is used in U.S. cellular standards documents. ITU documents use the term *handover*, and both terms appear in the technical literature. The meanings are the same.

- **Interruption duration:** The duration of time during a handoff in which a mobile unit is not connected to either base station.
- **Handoff delay:** The distance the mobile unit moves from the point at which the handoff should occur to the point at which it does occur.

The principal parameter used to make the handoff decision is measured signal strength from the mobile unit at the BS. Typically, the BS averages the signal over a moving window of time to remove the rapid fluctuations due to multipath effects. Figure 10.7a, based on one in [POLL96], shows the average received power level at two adjacent base stations as a mobile unit moves from BS A, at L_A, to BS B, at L_B. This figure is useful in explaining various handoff strategies that have been used to determine the instant of handoff:

- **Relative signal strength:** The mobile unit is handed off from BS A to BS B when the signal strength at B first exceeds that at A. If the signal strength at B subsequently falls below that of A, the mobile unit is handed back to A. In Figure 10.7a, handoff occurs at point L_1. At this point, signal strength to BS A is still adequate but is declining. Because signal strength fluctuates due to multipath effects, even with power averaging, this approach can lead to a ping-pong effect in which the unit is repeatedly passed back and forth between two BSs.
- **Relative signal strength with threshold:** Handoff only occurs if (1) the signal at the current BS is sufficiently weak (less than a predefined threshold) and (2) the other signal is the stronger of the two. The intention is that so long as the signal at the current BS is adequate, handoff is unnecessary. If a high threshold is used, such as Th_1, this scheme performs the same as the relative signal strength scheme. With a threshold of Th_2, handoff occurs at L_2. If the threshold is set

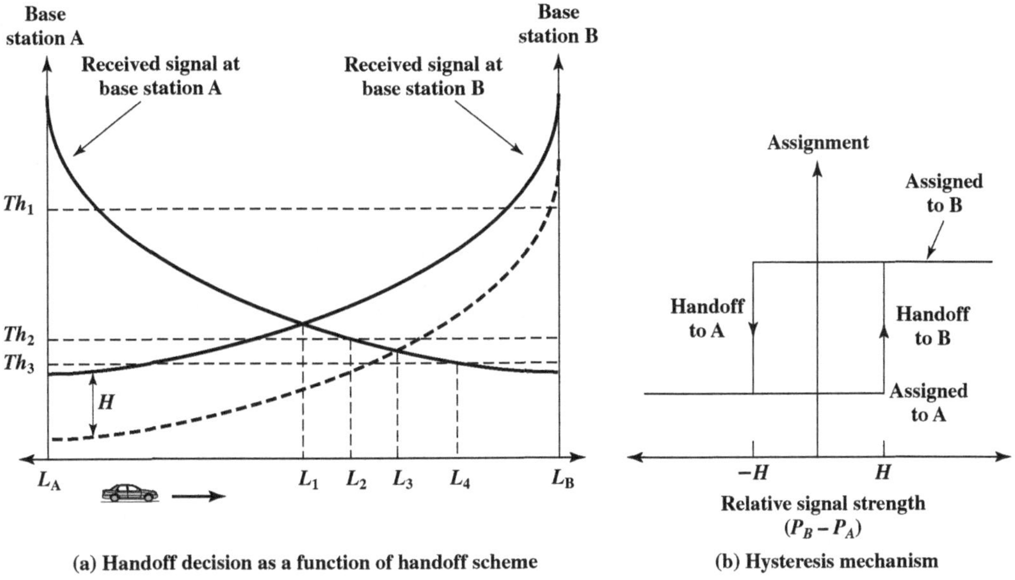

Figure 10.7 Handoff between Two Cells

quite low compared to the crossover signal strength (signal strength at L_1), such as Th_3, the mobile unit may move far into the new cell (L_4) before handoff. This reduces the quality of the communication link and may result in a dropped call. A threshold should not be used alone because its effectiveness depends on prior knowledge of the crossover signal strength between the current and candidate base stations.

- **Relative signal strength with hysteresis:** Handoff occurs only if the new base station is sufficiently stronger (by a margin H in Figure 10.7a) than the current one. In this case, handoff occurs at L_3. This scheme prevents the ping-pong effect, because once handoff occurs, the effect of the margin H is reversed. The term *hysteresis* refers to a phenomenon known as relay hysteresis and can be appreciated with the aid of Figure 10.7b. We can think of the handoff mechanism as having two states. While the mobile unit is assigned to BS A, the mechanism will generate a handoff when the relative signal strength reaches or exceeds the H. Once the mobile unit is assigned to B, it remains so until the relative signal strength falls below $-H$, at which point it is handed back to A. The only disadvantage of this scheme is that the first handoff may still be unnecessary if BS A still has sufficient signal strength.
- **Relative signal strength with hysteresis and threshold:** Handoff occurs only if (1) the current signal level drops below a threshold, and (2) the target base station is stronger than the current one by a hysteresis margin H. In our example, handoff occurs at L_3 if the threshold is either Th_1 or Th_2 and at L_4 if the threshold is at Th_3.
- **Prediction techniques:** The handoff decision is based on the expected future value of the received signal strength.

The handoff decision is complicated by the use of power control techniques, which enable the BS to dynamically adjust the power transmitted by the mobile unit. This topic is discussed next.

Power Control

A number of design issues make it desirable to include a dynamic power control capability in a cellular system:

1. The received power must be sufficiently above the background noise for effective communication, which dictates the required transmitted power. As the mobile unit moves away from the transmitter, the received power declines due to normal attenuation. In addition, the effects of reflection, diffraction, and scattering can cause rapid changes in received power levels over small distances. This is because the power level is the sum from signals coming from a number of different paths and the phases of those paths are random, sometimes adding and sometimes subtracting. As the mobile unit moves, the contributions along various paths change.
2. At the same time, it is desirable to minimize the power in the transmitted signal from the mobile unit, to reduce cochannel interference (interference with channels on the same frequency in remote cells), alleviate health concerns, and save battery power.

3. In spread spectrum (SS) systems using code division multiple access (CDMA), it is desirable to equalize the received power level from all mobile units at the BS. This is crucial to system performance because all users have the same frequency allocation.

Cellular systems use the two kinds of power control. **Open-loop power control** depends solely on the mobile unit, with no feedback from the BS, and is used in some SS systems. In SS systems, the BS continuously transmits an unmodulated signal, known as a pilot. The pilot allows a mobile unit to acquire the timing of the forward (BS to mobile) CDMA channel and provides a phase reference for demodulation. It can also be used for power control. The mobile unit monitors the received power level of the pilot and sets the transmitted power in the reverse (mobile to BS) channel inversely proportional to it. This approach assumes that the forward and reverse link signal strengths are closely correlated, which is generally the case. The open-loop approach is not as accurate as the closed-loop approach. However, the open-loop scheme can react more quickly to rapid fluctuations in signal strength, such as when a mobile unit emerges from behind a large building. This fast action is required in the reverse link of a CDMA system where the sudden increase in received strength at the BS may suppress all other signals.

Closed-loop power control adjusts signal strength in the reverse (mobile to BS) channel based on some metric of performance in that reverse channel, such as received signal power level, received signal-to-noise ratio, or received bit error rate. The BS makes the power adjustment decision and communicates a power adjustment command to the mobile unit on a control channel. Closed-loop power control is also used to adjust power in the forward channel. In this case, the mobile unit provides information about received signal quality to the BS, which then adjusts transmitted power.

Table 10.2 shows the power classes used in the GSM standard, which is a TDMA standard and is discussed in Section 10.3. GSM defines eight classes of base station channels and five classes of mobile stations, according to their power output. Adjustments in both directions are made using closed-loop power control.

Table 10.2 GSM Transmitter Classes

Power Class	Base Station Power (watts)	Mobile Station Power (watts)
1	320	20
2	160	8
3	80	5
4	40	2
5	20	0.8
6	10	
7	5	
8	2.5	

Traffic Engineering

For an FDMA system, the capacity of a cell is equal to the number of frequency channels allocated to it. Ideally, the number of available channels in a cell would equal the total number of subscribers who could be active at any time. In practice, it is not feasible to have the capacity to handle any possible load at all times. Fortunately, not all subscribers place calls at the same time and so it is reasonable to size the network to be able to handle some expected level of load. This is the discipline of traffic engineering.

Traffic engineering concepts were developed in the design of telephone switches and circuit-switching telephone networks, but the concepts equally apply to cellular networks. Consider a cell that has L potential subscribers (L mobile units) and that is able to handle N simultaneous users (capacity of N channels). If $L \leq N$, the system is referred to as *nonblocking*; all calls can be handled all the time. If $L > N$, the system is *blocking*; a subscriber may attempt a call and find the capacity fully in use and therefore be blocked. For a blocking system, the fundamental performance questions we wish to answer are

1. What is the degree of blocking; that is, what is the probability that a call request will be blocked? Alternatively, what capacity (N) is needed to achieve a certain upper bound on the probability of blocking?
2. If blocked calls are queued for service, what is the average delay? Alternatively, what capacity is needed to achieve a certain average delay?

In this subsection, we briefly introduce the relevant traffic engineering concepts and give an example of their use. Appendix B examines the subject in more detail.

Two parameters determine the amount of load presented to a system:

λ = the mean rate of calls (connection requests) attempted per unit time

h = the mean holding time per successful call

The basic measure of traffic is the **traffic intensity**, expressed in a dimensionless unit, the erlang:

$$A = \lambda h$$

A can be interpreted in several ways. It is a normalized version of λ: A equals the average number of calls arriving during the average holding period. We can also view the cell as a multiserver queuing system where the number of servers is equal to the channel capacity N. The average service time at a server is h. A basic relationship in a multiserver queue is $\lambda h = \rho N$, where ρ is server utilization, or the fraction of time that a server is busy. Therefore, $A = \rho N$ and is a measure of the average number of channels required.

Example 10.3 If the calling rate averages 20 calls per minute and the average holding time is 3 minutes, then $A = 60$. We would expect a cell with a capacity of 120 channels to be about half utilized at any given time. A switch of capacity 50 would clearly be inadequate. A capacity of 60 would meet the average demand but, because of fluctuations around the mean rate A, this capacity would at times be inadequate.

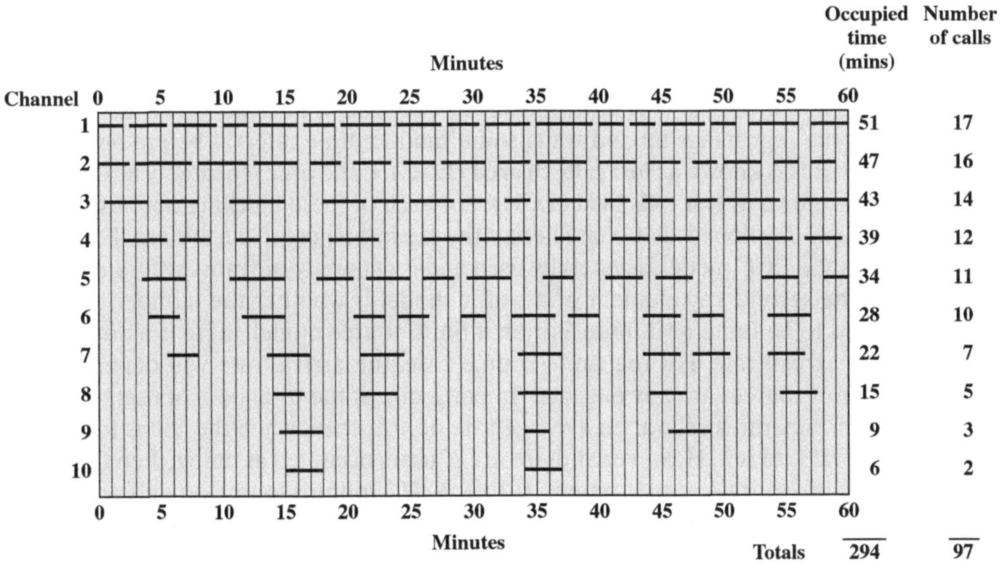

Note: **Horizontal lines indicate occupied periods to the nearest 1/2 minute**

Figure 10.8 Example Distribution of Traffic in a Cell with Capacity 10

Example 10.4 To clarify these concepts, consider Figure 10.8, which shows the pattern of activity in a cell of capacity 10 channels over a period of 1 hour. The rate of calls per minute is 97/60. The average holding time per call, in minutes, is 294/97. Thus $A = (97/60) \times (294/97) = 4.9$ erlangs. Another way of viewing the parameter A is that it is the mean number of calls in progress. Thus, on average, 4.9 channels are engaged. The latter interpretation, however, is true only in the nonblocking case. The parameter λ was defined as the rate of calls attempted, not carried traffic.

Typically, a blocking system is sized to deal with some upper limit of traffic intensity. It is generally thought unreasonable to size for the highest surge of traffic anticipated; rather, the common practice is to size the system to meet the average rate encountered during a busy hour. The busy hour is the 60-minute period during the day when the traffic is highest, in the long run. ITU-T recommends taking the average of the busy hour traffic on the 30 busiest days of the year, called the "mean busy-hour traffic," and using that quantity to size the system. The North American practice is to take the average over the 10 busiest days. These are typically measurements of carried rather than offered traffic and can only be used to estimate the true load.

The parameter A, as a measure of busy-hour traffic, serves as input to a traffic model. The model is then used to answer questions such as those posed in the beginning of this subsection. There are two key factors that determine the nature of the model:

- The manner in which blocked calls are handled
- The number of traffic sources

Blocked calls may be handled in one of two ways. First, blocked calls can be put in a queue awaiting a free channel; this is referred to as **lost calls delayed** (LCD), although in fact the call is not lost, merely delayed. Second, a blocked call can be rejected and dropped. This in turn leads to two assumptions about the action of the user. If the user hangs up and waits some random time interval before another call attempt, this is known as **lost calls cleared** (LCC). If the user repeatedly attempts calling, it is known as **lost calls held** (LCH). For each of these blocking options, formulas have been developed that characterize the performance of the system. For cellular systems, the LCC model is generally used and is generally the most accurate.

The second key element of a traffic model is whether the number of users is assumed to be finite or infinite. For an infinite source model, there is assumed to be a fixed arrival rate. For the finite source case, the arrival rate will depend on the number of sources already engaged. In particular, if the total pool of users is L, each of which generates calls at an average rate of λ/L, then, when the cell is totally idle, the arrival rate is λ. However, if there are K users occupied at time t, then the instantaneous arrival rate at that time is $\lambda(L - K)/L$. Infinite source models are analytically easier to deal with. The infinite source assumption is reasonable when the number of sources is at least 5 to 10 times the capacity of the system.

Infinite Sources, Lost Calls Cleared For an infinite source LCC model, the key parameter of interest is the probability of loss, or **grade of service**. Thus a grade of service of 0.01 means that, during a busy hour, the probability that an attempted call is blocked is 0.01. Values in the range 0.01 to 0.001 are generally considered quite good.

The equation of infinite source LCC, known as Erlang B, has the following form:

$$P = \frac{\dfrac{A^N}{N!}}{\displaystyle\sum_{x=0}^{N} \frac{A^x}{x!}}$$

where

A = offered traffic, erlangs

N = number of servers

P = probability of blocking (grade of service)

This equation is easily programmed, and tables of values are readily available. Table 10.3 is an extract from such a table. Given the offered load and number of servers, the grade of service can be calculated or determined from a table. More often, the inverse problem is of interest: determining the amount of traffic that can be handled by a given capacity to produce a given grade of service. Another problem is to determine the capacity required to handle a given amount of traffic at a given grade of service. For both these problems, tables or suitable trial-and-error programs are needed.

Two important points can be deduced from Table 10.3:

1. A larger-capacity system is more efficient than a smaller-capacity one for a given grade of service.
2. A larger-capacity system is more susceptible to an increase in traffic.

Table 10.3 Erlang B Table

	Capacity (Erlangs) for Grade of Service of				
Number of Servers (N)	**P = 0.02 (1/50)**	**P = 0.01 (1/100)**	**P = 0.005 (1/200)**	**P = 0.002 (1/500)**	**P = 0.001 (1/1000)**
1	0.02	0.01	0.005	0.002	0.001
4	1.09	0.87	0.7	0.53	0.43
5	1.66	1.36	1.13	0.9	0.76
10	5.08	4.46	3.96	3.43	3.09
20	13.19	12.03	11.10	10.07	9.41
24	16.64	15.27	14.21	13.01	12.24
40	31.0	29.0	27.3	25.7	24.5
70	59.13	56.1	53.7	51.0	49.2
100	87.97	84.1	80.9	77.4	75.2

Example 10.5 To illustrate the first point, consider two cells, each with a capacity of 10 channels. They have a joint capacity of 20 channels and can handle a combined offered traffic intensity of 6.86 for a grade of service of 0.002. However, a single cell of capacity 20 channels will handle 10.07 erlangs at a grade of service of 0.002. To illustrate the second point, consider a cell of 10 channels giving a grade of service of 0.002 for a load of 3.43 erlangs. A 30% increase in traffic reduces the grade of service to 0.01. However, for a cell of capacity 70 channels, only a 10% increase in traffic reduces the grade of service from 0.002 to 0.01.

All of the preceding discussion deals with offered traffic. If sizing is done on the basis of system measurement, all that we are likely to have is carried traffic. A program can readily be developed that accepts carried traffic as input and then performs a seeking algorithm to work backward to offered traffic. The relationship between carried traffic C and offered traffic A is

$$C = A(1 - P)$$

For small values of P, A is a good approximation of C.

Effect of Handoff One complication in cellular traffic models not found in other such models is the effect of handoff. This is illustrated in Figure 10.9. The arrival rate of calls at a cell has two components: new calls placed by mobile units in the cell (λ_1), and calls handed off to the cell for mobile units entering the cell while connected (λ_2). The total arrival rate is $\lambda = \lambda_1 + \lambda_2$. Similarly, the completion rate consists of

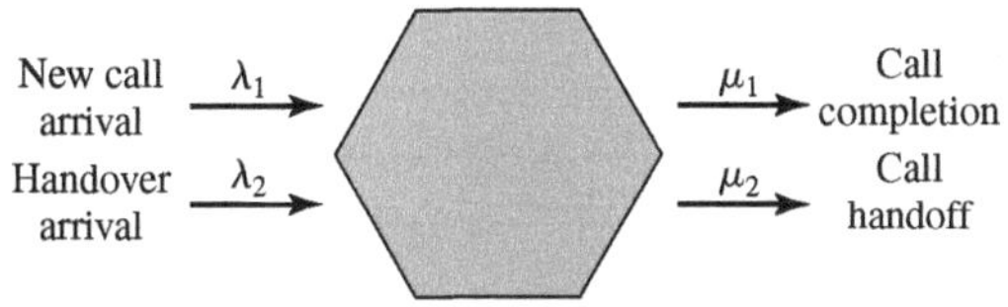

Figure 10.9 Cell Traffic Model

calls being terminated and calls being handed off. The model must be adjusted accordingly to obtain overall arrival rates and holding times.

10.2 FIRST-GENERATION ANALOG

The original cellular telephone networks provided analog traffic channels; these are now referred to as first-generation systems. Since the early 1980s the most common first-generation system in North America has been the **Advanced Mobile Phone Service (AMPS)** developed by AT&T. This approach is also common in South America, Australia, and China. Although it has been replaced, for the most part, by second-generation systems, AMPS is still in use. In this section, we provide an overview of AMPS.

Spectral Allocation

In North America, two 25-MHz bands are allocated to AMPS (Table 10.4), one for transmission from the base station to the mobile unit (869–894 MHz), the other for transmission from the mobile unit to the base station (824–849 MHz). Each of these bands is split in two to encourage competition (i.e., so that in each market two operators can be accommodated). An operator is allocated only 12.5 MHz in each direction for its system. The channels are spaced 30 kHz apart, which allows a total of 416 channels per operator. Twenty-one channels are allocated for control, leaving 395 to carry calls. The control channels are data channels operating at 10 kbps. The conversation channels carry the conversations in analog using frequency modulation. Control information is also sent on the conversation channels in bursts as data. This number of channels is inadequate for most major markets, so some way must be found either to use less bandwidth per conversation or to reuse frequencies. Both approaches have been taken in the various approaches to mobile telephony. For AMPS, frequency reuse is exploited.

Table 10.4 AMPS Parameters

Base station transmission band	869 to 894 MHz
Mobile unit transmission band	824 to 849 MHz
Spacing between forward and reverse channels	45 MHz
Channel bandwidth	30 kHz
Number of full-duplex voice channels	790
Number of full-duplex control channels	42
Mobile unit maximum power	3 watts
Cell size, radius	2 to 20 km
Modulation, voice channel	FM, 12-kHz peak deviation
Modulation, control channel	FSK, 8-kHz peak deviation
Data transmission rate	10 kbps
Error control coding	BCH (48, 36,5) and (40, 28,5)

Operation

Each AMPS-capable cellular telephone includes a *numeric assignment module* (NAM) in read-only memory. The NAM contains the telephone number of the phone, which is assigned by the service provider, and the serial number of the phone, which is assigned by the manufacturer. When the phone is turned on, it transmits its serial number and phone number to the MTSO (Figure 10.5); the MTSO maintains a database with information about mobile units that have been reported stolen and uses serial number to lock out stolen units. The MTSO uses the phone number for billing purposes. If the phone is used in a remote city, the service is still billed to the user's local service provider.

When a call is placed, the following sequence of events occurs [COUC01]:

1. The subscriber initiates a call by keying in the telephone number of the called party and presses the send key.
2. The MTSO verifies that the telephone number is valid and that the user is authorized to place the call; some service providers require the user to enter a PIN (personal identification number) as well as the called number to counter theft.
3. The MTSO issues a message to the user's cell phone indicating which traffic channels to use for sending and receiving.
4. The MTSO sends out a ringing signal to the called party. All of these operations (steps 2 through 4) occur within 10 s of initiating the call.
5. When the called party answers, the MTSO establishes a circuit between the two parties and initiates billing information.
6. When one party hangs up, the MTSO releases the circuit, frees the radio channels, and completes the billing information.

AMPS Control Channels

Each AMPS service includes 21 full-duplex 30-kHz control channels, consisting of 21 reverse control channels (RCCs) from subscriber to base station, and 21 forward channels base station to subscriber. These channels transmit digital data using FSK. In both channels, data are transmitted in frames.

Figure 10.10a shows the RCC frame structure. The frame begins with a 48-bit precursor, consisting of a 30-bit bit sync field of alternating ones and zeros, an 11-bit word sync field (11100010010), and a 7-bit digital color code (DCC). The DCC is used to distinguish transmissions in cochannel cells; it is a unique identifier of a base station and acts as a destination address for an RCC frame. Following the precursor, the frame contains from one to 6 words of data. Each word contains 36 data bits and is encoded using a shortened version of a $(n, k, t) = (63, 51, 5)$ BCH block code (see Table 8.4). In this shortened version, 12 check bits are added to the 36 data bits to form a 48-bit word. To further increase reliability, each word is transmitted five times in the same frame, and a majority logic is used to recover the word at the base station. When all the overhead is taken into account, the data rate is on the order of a few hundred bits per second. Examples of RCC messages include origination, page response, and order confirmation.

The FCC frame structure (Figure 10.10b) starts with a 10-bit bit sync and an 11-bit word sync. Each frame contains two words of data. Each word is encoded

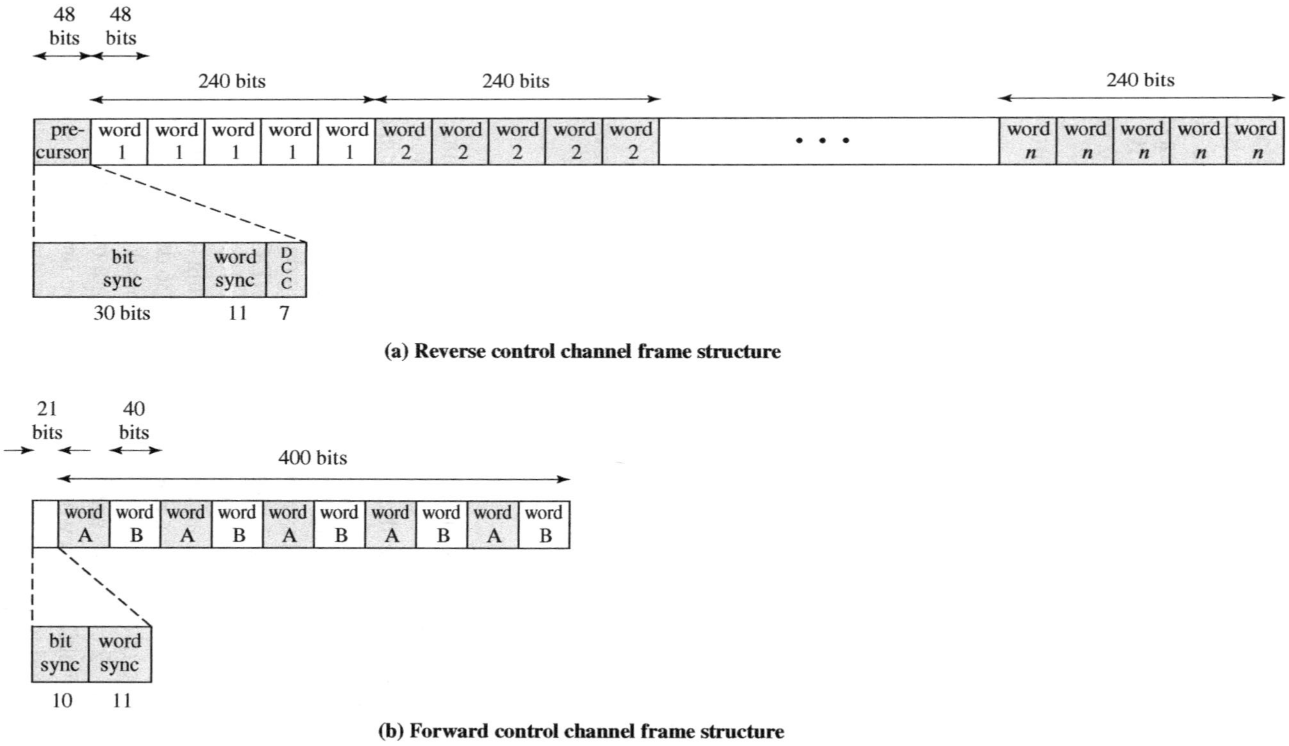

Figure 10.10 AMPS Control Channel Frame Formats

using BCH and contains 28 data bits and 12 check bits. Again, for reliability, each word is repeated five times. In addition, each FCC frame provides information about the status (idle or busy) of the corresponding RCC frame through the busy/idle bits that are inserted every tenth bit in the frame. This brings the total frame size to 463 bits. At the 10-kbps signaling rate, the data rate (excluding overhead) is about 1.2 kbps. FCC messages include paging messages and frequency assignment messages.

Finally, control information can be transmitted over a voice channel during a conversation. The mobile unit or the base station can insert a burst of data by turning off the voice FM transmission for about 100 ms and replacing it with an FSK-encoded message. These messages are used to exchange urgent messages, such as change power level and handoff.

10.3 SECOND-GENERATION TDMA

This section begins our study of second-generation cellular systems. We begin with an overview and then look in detail at one type of second-generation cellular system.

First- and Second-Generation Cellular Systems

First-generation cellular networks, such as AMPS, quickly became highly popular, threatening to swamp available capacity. Second-generation systems have been developed to provide higher quality signals, higher data rates for support of digital services, and greater capacity. [BLAC99a] lists the following as the key differences between the two generations:

- **Digital traffic channels:** The most notable difference between the two generations is that first-generation systems are almost purely analog, whereas second-generation systems are digital. In particular, the first-generation systems are designed to support voice channels using FM; digital traffic is supported only by the use of a modem that converts the digital data into analog form. Second-generation systems provide digital traffic channels. These readily support digital data; voice traffic is first encoded in digital form before transmitting. Of course, for second-generation systems, the user traffic (data or digitized voice) must be converted to an analog signal for transmission between the mobile unit and the base station (e.g., see Figure 6.14).
- **Encryption:** Because all of the user traffic, as well as control traffic, is digitized in second-generation systems, it is a relatively simple matter to encrypt all of the traffic to prevent eavesdropping. All second-generation systems provide this capability, whereas first-generation systems send user traffic in the clear, providing no security.
- **Error detection and correction:** The digital traffic stream of second-generation systems also lends itself to the use of error detection and correction techniques, such as those discussed in Chapter 8. The result can be very clear voice reception.

- **Channel access:** In first-generation systems, each cell supports a number of channels. At any given time a channel is allocated to only one user. Second-generation systems also provide multiple channels per cell, but each channel is dynamically shared by a number of users using time division multiple access (TDMA) or code division multiple access (CDMA). We look at TDMA-based systems in this section and CDMA-based systems in Section 10.4.

Beginning around 1990, a number of different second-generation systems have been deployed. Table 10.5 lists some key characteristics of three of the most important of these systems.

Time Division Multiple Access

First-generation cellular systems provide for the support of multiple users with frequency division multiple access (FDMA). FDMA was introduced in our discussion of satellite communications and the principle is the same here. FDMA for cellular systems can be described as follows. Each cell is allocated a total of $2M$ channels of bandwidth δ Hz each. Half the channels (the reverse channels) are used for transmission from the mobile unit to the base station: $f_c, f_c + \delta, f_c + 2\delta, \ldots, f_c + (M - 1)\delta$, where f_c is the center frequency of the lowest-frequency channel. The other half of the channels (the forward channels) are used for transmission from the base sta-

Table 10.5 Second-Generation Cellular Telephone Systems

	GSM	IS-136	IS-95
Year introduced	1990	1991	1993
Access method	TDMA	TDMA	CDMA
Base station transmission band	935 to 960 MHz	869 to 894 MHz	869 to 894 MHz
Mobile station transmission band	890 to 915 MHz	824 to 849 MHz	824 to 849 MHz
Spacing between forward and reverse channels	45 MHz	45 MHz	45 MHz
Channel bandwidth	200 kHz	30 kHz	1250 kHz
Number of duplex channels	125	832	20
Mobile unit maximum power	20 W	3 W	0.2 W
Users per channel	8	3	35
Modulation	GMSK	$\pi/4$ DQPSK	QPSK
Carrier bit rate	270.8 kbps	48.6 kbps	9.6 kbps
Speech coder	RPE-LTP	VSELP	QCELP
Speech coding bit rate	13 kbps	8 kbps	8, 4, 2, 1 kbps
Frame size	4.6 ms	40 ms	20 ms
Error control coding	Convolutional 1/2 rate	Convolutional 1/2 rate	Convolutional 1/2 rate forward; 1/3 rate reverse

tion to the mobile unit: $f_c + \Delta, f_c + \delta + \Delta, f_c + 2\delta + \Delta, \ldots, f_c + (M - 1)\delta + \Delta$, where Δ is the spacing between the reverse and forward channels. When a connection is set up for a mobile user, the user is assigned two channels, at f and $f + \Delta$, for full-duplex communication. This arrangement is quite wasteful, because much of the time one or both of the channels are idle.

TDMA for cellular systems can be described as follows. As with FDMA, each cell is allocated a number of channels, half reverse and half forward. Again, for full duplex communication, a mobile unit is assigned capacity on matching reverse and forward channels. In addition, each physical channel is further subdivided into a number of logical channels. Transmission is in the form of a repetitive sequence of frames, each of which is divided into a number of time slots. Each slot position across the sequence of frames forms a separate logical channel.

Mobile Wireless TDMA Design Considerations

Before turning to the specific example of GSM, it will be useful to consider some general design guidelines by looking at a simple analysis, based on one in [JONE93]. This analysis motivates some of the design decisions made for GSM. The overall objective is to determine the length and composition of the traffic channel time slot that will provide effective speech and data transmission with efficient use of the radio spectrum. Let us consider the following set of requirements:

- **Number of logical channels (number of time slots in TDMA frame):** 8; this appears to be the minimum to justify the additional costs of multiplexing.
- **Maximum cell radius (R):** 35 km, to give a sufficiently high traffic level in rural areas.
- **Frequency:** Region around 900 MHz; this is commonly allocated to mobile radio applications.
- **Maximum vehicle speed (V_m):** 250 km/hr, or 69.4 m/s, to accommodate mobile units on high-speed trains.
- **Maximum coding delay:** Approximately 20 ms, to avoid adding unduly to delays within the fixed network, which may involve satellite links. Above 20 ms, voice conversation becomes difficult.
- **Maximum delay spread (Δ_m):** 10 μs (in mountainous regions); this is the difference in propagation delay among different multipath signals arriving at the same antenna.
- **Bandwidth:** Not to exceed 200 kHz, corresponding to 25 kHz per channel (the current spacing for analog FM cellular systems in Europe).

Figure 10.11 suggests the steps to be considered in designing the TDMA time slot. We use this as a guide in the following discussion.

The speech coder must provide satisfactory speech quality at minimum data rate. The traditional form of speech coding to produce a digital bit stream is pulse code modulation (PCM), which, as we saw in Section 6.4, results in a data rate of 64 kbps. This rate is undesirably high for use in cellular radio. With current technology, a data rate of 12 kbps is reasonable for producing good-quality speech reproduction.

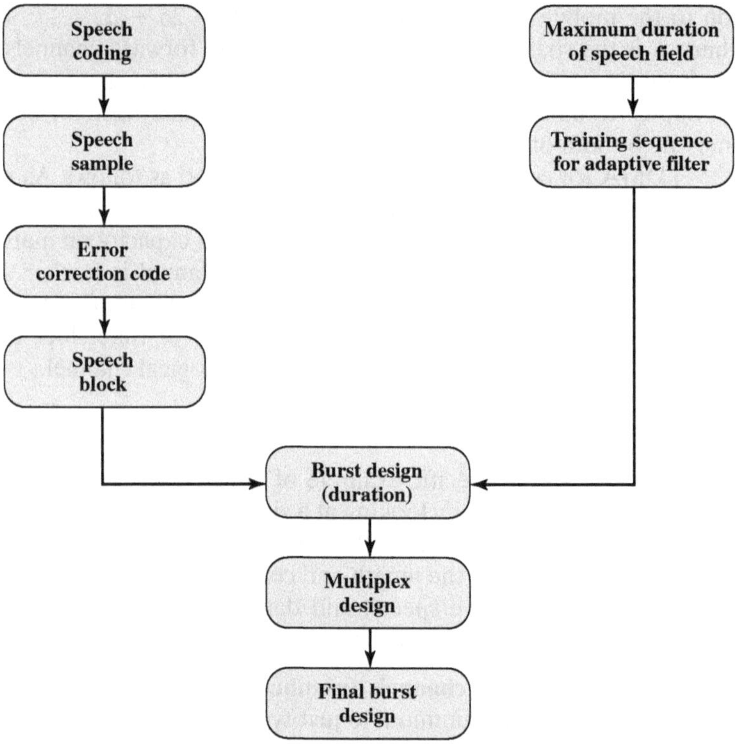

Figure 10.11 Steps in Design of TDMA Time Slot

If we restrict the coding delay to 20 ms, then it would be acceptable to form the encoded speech into blocks of 20 ms duration, or speech samples of 240 bits. Data at 12 kbps could also be blocked in 240-bit units. Error correction can then be applied to the 240-bit blocks.

For second-generation digital systems, convolutional error-correcting codes are commonly used with a code rate of 1/2. This overhead raises the number of bits in a block to 480. In addition, there is a constraint factor of 5, meaning that 4 bits must be added to the data block to account for the length of the shift register (see Section 8.3). This brings the speech block length to 488 bits.

With the parameters chosen so far, the minimum bit rate for an eight-channel system is

$$\frac{8 \text{ channels} \times 488 \text{ bits/channel}}{20 \times 10^{-3}\text{ s}} = 195.2 \text{ kbps}$$

In fact, the bit rate will be somewhat higher to take care of other design considerations, discussed subsequently. This means that a data rate of greater than 200 kbps will need to be carried in the available bandwidth of 200 kHz. In practice, such data rates cannot be achieved without the use of adaptive equalization. As was discussed in Section 5.4, in a mobile environment, adaptive equalization will require the inclusion of a new training sequence each time the mobile unit moves a distance sufficient to potentially cause changes in transmission path characteristics. Let us assume that a training sequence is included in each time slot. A rough criterion suggested in [JONE93] is that the phase angle of the carrier signal should be restricted to a change of 1/20th of a wavelength (an angle of $\eta/10$) after the training sequence. At 900 MHz, the wavelength is 0.333m. We can calculate

$$\text{Maximum transmission duration} = \frac{\lambda/20}{V_m} = \frac{0.333/20}{69.4} = 0.24 \text{ ms}$$

We can take better advantage of the training sequence by transmitting 0.24 ms of speech or data both before and after the training sequence and using the training sequence on the combined 0.48 ms of data.

Next, we need to determine the length of the training sequence. In the design of an equalizer for a multipath signal whose bandwidth is about equal to the bit rate (200 kHz, 200 kbps), a rule of thumb is that the number of taps on the equalizer (Figure 5.15) should be equal to 6 times the number of bits transmitted in the maximum dispersal time ($\Delta_m = 0.01$ ms). Thus, the amount of time in the time slot devoted to the training sequence is 0.06 ms.

Now consider that a guard interval is needed at the end of each time slot to account for the differing amounts of delay between different mobile units and the base station. Because eight mobile units share the same TDMA frame, it is necessary to adjust the timing of the transmissions of the mobile units so that the transmission from one unit does not interfere with adjacent time slots. It is the responsibility of the base station to provide synchronization information to each mobile unit to adjust relative delays to enforce the time slot structure of the TDMA frame. However, the mobile units may be moving relative to the base station and relative to each other, so a guard time is inserted in each time slot to account for these discrepancies. When a mobile unit first makes a connection through the base station, the base station can provide the mobile unit with timing information based on the current propagation delay between the mobile unit and the base station. We would also like to add a guard time sufficient to avoid the need to frequently update this synchronization information. We can calculate the guard time as follows. The average telephone call is about 130 seconds [JONE93], so the radial distance toward or away from the base station that a mobile unit could cover is $(130 \text{ s}) \times (69.4 \text{ m/s}) = 9022$ m. The change in propagation delay caused by a movement of this distance is $9022/(3 \times 10^8 \text{ m/s}) = 0.03$ ms.

Figure 10.12a shows the tentative time slot design. The next step is to fit a coded data block into a convenient number of time slots, together with the training sequence and guard bits. We have a maximum duration of a time slot of approximately 0.57 ms. With 8 time slots per frame, that gives a frame time of about 4.6 ms. We said that we wanted to send data with a coding delay of 20 ms, so if we round the frame time down to 4 ms (time slot = 0.5 ms), then we could conveniently send a block of speech in five successive slots on the same channel. A speech block consists of 488 bits, so each time slot would need to hold 488/5 or about 98 data bits. This yields a bit rate of $98/0.4 = 245$ kbps. At this data rate, the minimum number of training bits required is $(0.06 \text{ ms}) \times (245 \text{ kbps}) = 14.7$, which on rounding becomes 15 bits. Similarly, the minimum number of guard bits is $(0.03 \text{ ms}) \times (245 \text{ kbps}) = 7.35$, which on rounding becomes 8 bits.

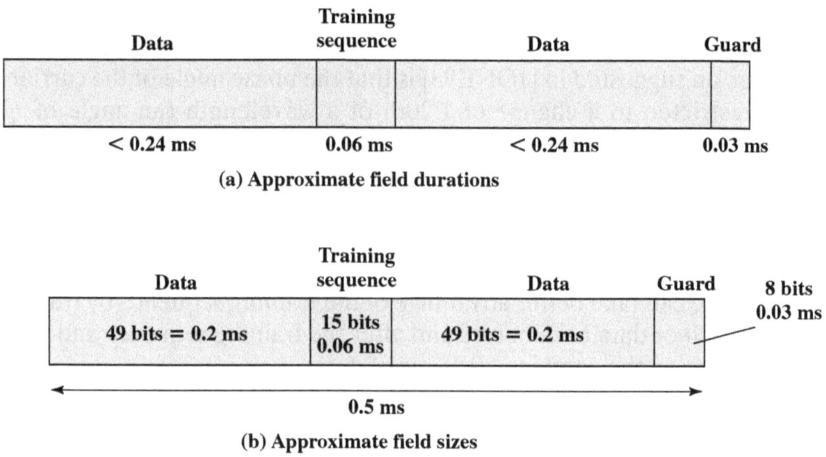

Figure 10.12 TDMA Time Slot

The resulting frame structure is shown in Figure 10.12b. We have 121 bits transmitted in 0.5 ms for a channel bit rate of 242 kbps.

Global System for Mobile Communications

Before the Global System for Mobile Communications (GSM) was developed, the countries of Europe used a number of incompatible first-generation cellular phone technologies. GSM was developed to provide a common second-generation technology for Europe so that the same subscriber units could be used throughout the continent. The technology has been extremely successful and is probably the most popular standard, worldwide, for new implementations. GSM first appeared in 1990 in Europe. Similar systems have now been implemented in North and South America, Asia, North Africa, the Middle East, and Australia. The GSM Association claimed over a billion subscribers worldwide by early 2004, the bulk of these in Europe and Asia Pacific, but with growing market share in North and South America.

GSM Network Architecture

Figure 10.13 shows the key functional elements in the GSM system. The boundaries at Um, Abis, and A refer to interfaces between functional elements that are standardized in the GSM documents. Thus, it is possible to buy equipment from different vendors with the expectation that they will successfully interoperate. Additional interfaces are also defined in the GSM standards, but need not concern us here.

Mobile Station A mobile station communicates across the Um interface, also known as the **air interface**, with a base station transceiver in the same cell in which the mobile unit is located. The **mobile equipment** (ME) refers to the physical terminal, such as a telephone or PCS (personal communications service) device, which includes the radio transceiver, digital signal processors, and the **subscriber identity module** (SIM). The SIM is a portable device in the form of a smart card or plug-in module that stores the subscriber's identification number, the networks the subscriber is

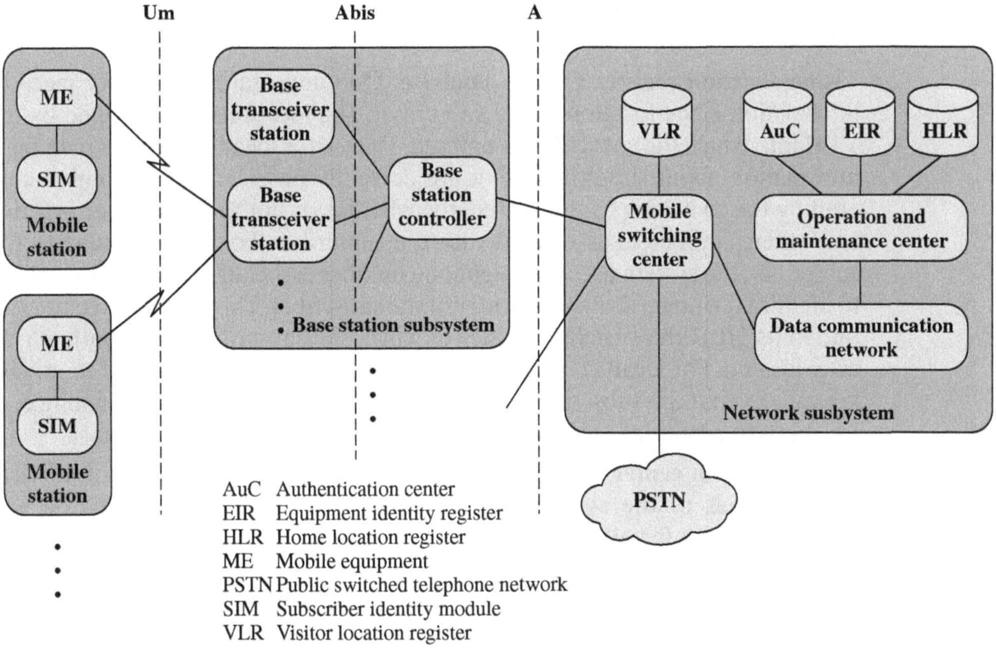

Figure 10.13 Overall GSM Architecture

authorized to use, encryption keys, and other information specific to the subscriber. The GSM subscriber units are totally generic until an SIM is inserted. Therefore, a subscriber need only carry his or her SIM to use a wide variety of subscriber devices in many countries simply by inserting the SIM in the device to be used. In fact, except for certain emergency communications, the subscriber units will not work without a SIM inserted. Thus, the SIMs roam, not necessarily the subscriber devices.

Base Station Subsystem A base station subsystem (BSS) consists of a base station controller and one or more base transceiver stations. Each **base transceiver station** (BTS) defines a single cell; it includes a radio antenna, a radio transceiver, and a link to a base station controller. A GSM cell can have a radius of between 100 m and 35 km, depending on the environment. A **base station controller** (BSC) may be collocated with a BTS or may control multiple BTS units and hence multiple cells. The BSC reserves radio frequencies, manages the handoff of a mobile unit from one cell to another within the BSS, and controls paging.

Network Subsystem The network subsystem (NS) provides the link between the cellular network and the public switched telecommunications networks. The NS controls handoffs between cells in different BSSs, authenticates users and validates their accounts, and includes functions for enabling worldwide roaming of mobile users. The central element of the NS is the **mobile switching center** (MSC). It is supported by four databases that it controls:

- **Home location register (HLR) database:** The HLR stores information, both permanent and temporary, about each of the subscribers that "belongs" to it (i.e., for which the subscriber has its telephone number associated with the switching center).

- **Visitor location register (VLR) database:** One important, temporary piece of information is the location of the subscriber. The location is determined by the VLR into which the subscriber is entered. The visitor location register maintains information about subscribers that are currently physically in the region covered by the switching center. It records whether or not the subscriber is active and other parameters associated with the subscriber. For a call coming to the subscriber, the system uses the telephone number associated with the subscriber to identify the home switching center of the subscriber. This switching center can find in its HLR the switching center in which the subscriber is currently physically located. For a call coming from the subscriber, the VLR is used to initiate the call. Even if the subscriber is in the area covered by its home switching center, it is also represented in the switching center's VLR, for consistency.
- **Authentication center database (AuC):** This database is used for authentication activities of the system; for example, it holds the authentication and encryption keys for all the subscribers in both the home and visitor location registers. The center controls access to user data as well as being used for authentication when a subscriber joins a network. GSM transmission is encrypted, so it is private. A stream cipher, A5, is used to encrypt the transmission from subscriber to base transceiver. However, the conversation is in the clear in the landline network. Another cipher, A3, is used for authentication.
- **Equipment identity register database (EIR):** The EIR keeps track of the type of equipment that exists at the mobile station. It also plays a role in security (e.g., blocking calls from stolen mobile stations and preventing use of the network by stations that have not been approved).

Radio Link Aspects

The GSM spectral allocation is 25 MHz for base transmission (935–960 MHz) and 25 MHz for mobile transmission (890–915 MHz). Other GSM bands have also been defined outside Europe. Users access the network using a combination of frequency division multiple access (FDMA) and time division multiple access (TDMA) (both are discussed in the next section). There are radio-frequency carriers every 200 kHz, which provide for 125 full-duplex channels. The channels are modulated at a data rate of 270.833 kbps. As with AMPS, there are two types of channels, traffic and control.

TDMA Format GSM uses a complex hierarchy of TDMA frames to define logical channels (Figure 10.14). Fundamentally, each 200-kHz frequency band is divided into 8 logical channels defined by the repetitive occurrence of time slots.

At the lowest level is the time slot, also called a burst period, which has a duration of 15/26 ms, or approximately 0.577 ms. With a bit rate of 270.833 kbps, each time slot has a length of 156.25 bits. The time slot includes the following fields:

- **Trail bits:** Allow synchronization of transmissions from mobile units located at different distances from the base station, as explained subsequently.

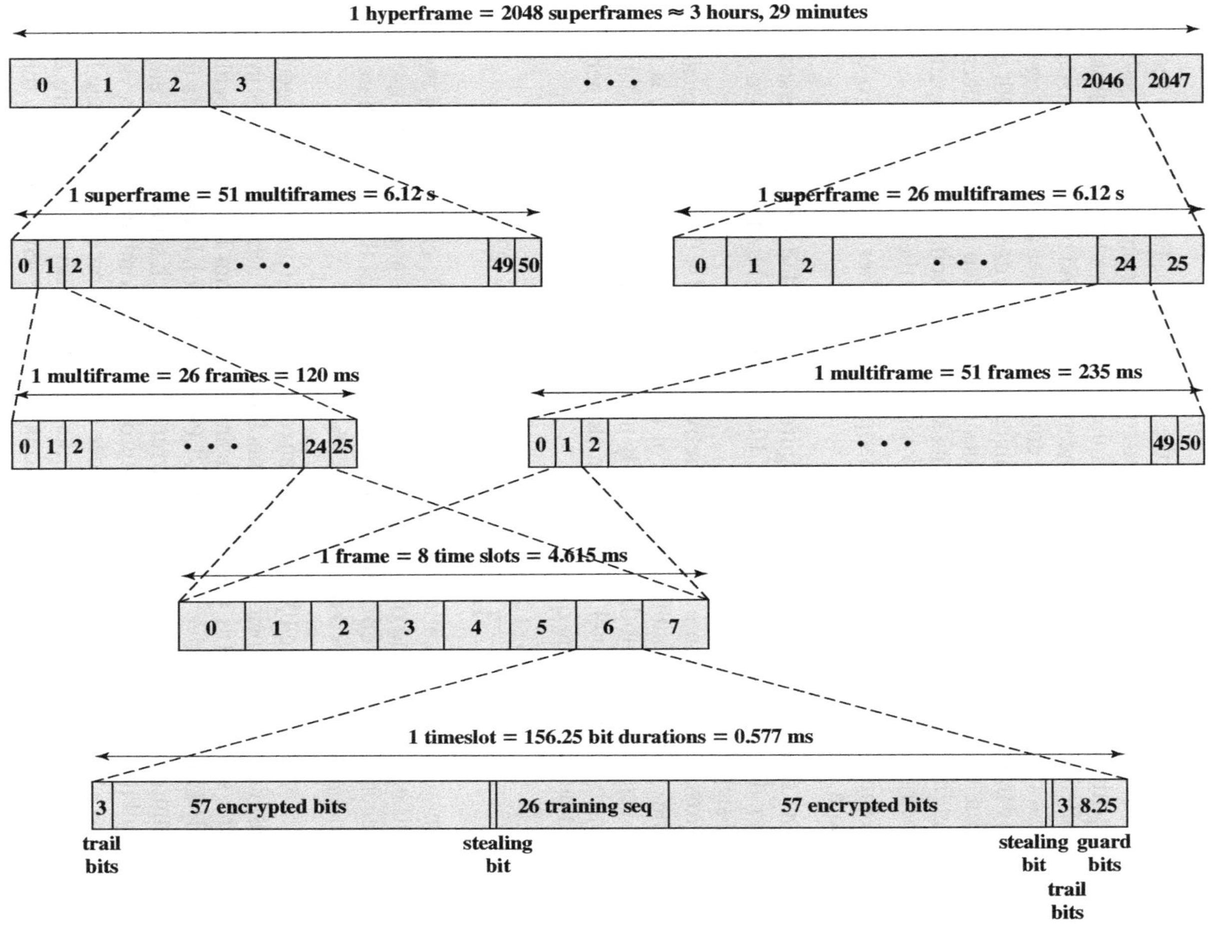

Figure 10.14 GSM Frame Format

- **Encrypted bits:** Data is encrypted in blocks by conventional encryption of 114 plaintext bits into 114 ciphertext bits; the encrypted bits are then placed in two 57-bit fields in the time slot.
- **Stealing bit:** Used to indicate whether this block contains data or is "stolen" for urgent control signaling.
- **Training sequence:** Used to adapt the parameters of the receiver to the current path propagation characteristics and to select the strongest signal in case of multipath propagation. The training sequence is a known bit pattern that differs for different adjacent cells. It enables the mobile units and base stations to determine that the received signal is from the correct transmitter and not a strong interfering transmitter. In addition, the training sequence is used for multipath equalization, which is used to extract the desired signal from unwanted reflections. By determining how the known training sequence is modified by multipath fading, the rest of the signal is processed to compensate for these effects.
- **Guard bits:** Used to avoid overlapping with other bursts due to different path delays.

The time slot format shown in Figure 10.14 is called a normal burst and carries user data traffic (compare Figure 10.12b). Other burst formats are used for control signaling.

Moving up the frame format hierarchy, 8-slot TDMA frames are typically organized into a 26-frame multiframe. One of the frames in the multiframe is used for control signaling and another is currently unused, leaving 24 frames for data traffic. Thus, each traffic channel receives one slot per frame and 24 frames per 120-ms multiframe. The resulting data rate is

$$\frac{114 \text{ bits / slot} \times 24 \text{ slots / multiframe}}{120\text{ms / multiframe}} = 22.8 \text{ kbps}$$

The GSM specification also allows half-rate traffic channels, with two traffic channels each occupying one time slot in 12 of the 26 frames. With the use of half-rate speech coders, this effectively doubles the capacity of the system. There is also a 51-frame multiframe used for control traffic.

Speech coding Figure 10.15 provides an overview of the processing of speech signals for transmission over a logical traffic channel. We look at each of these steps in turn.

The speech signal is compressed using an algorithm known as Regular Pulse Excited - Linear Predictive Coder (RPE-LPC) [KROO86]. In essence, data from previous samples are used to predict the current sample. Each sample is then encoded to consist of bits representing the coefficients of the linear combination of previous samples plus an encoded form of the difference between the predicted and actual sample. The result of the use of this code is to produce 260 bits every 20 ms, for a raw data rate of 13 kbps. From the point of view of the quality of the speech produced by this encoding, the bits in the 260-bit block can be divided into three classes:

- **Class Ia:** 50 bits, most sensitive to bit errors
- **Class Ib:** 132 bits, moderately sensitive to bit errors
- **Class II:** 78 bits, least sensitive to bit errors

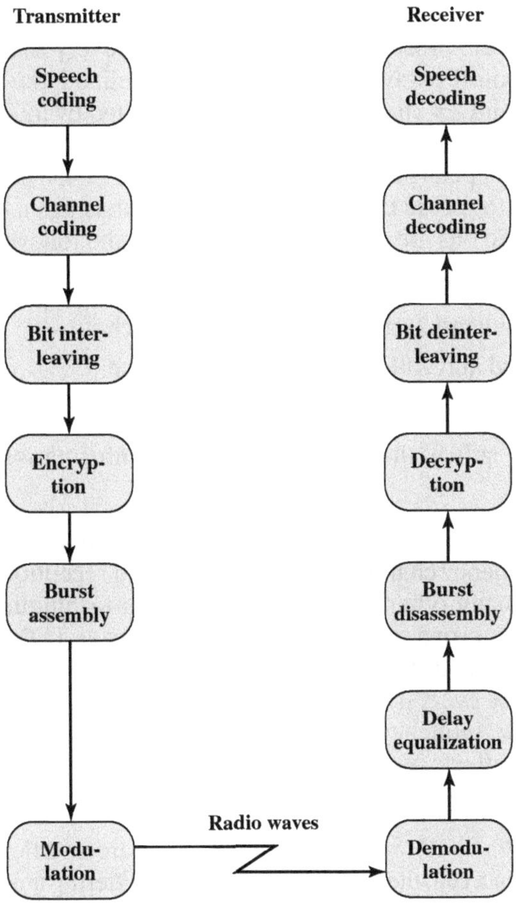

Figure 10.15 GSM Speech Signal Processing

The first 50 bits are protected by a 3-bit cyclic redundancy check (CRC) error detection code. If an error is detected, the entire sample is discarded and replaced by a modified version of the preceding block. These 53 bits plus the 132 class 1b bits, plus a 4-bit tail sequence, are then protected by a convolutional (2, 1, 5) error correcting code, resulting in $189 \times 2 = 378$ bits. The remaining 78 bits are unprotected and are appended to the protected bits to produce a block of 456 bits, with a resulting data rate of 456/20 ms = 22.8 kbps, which is the GSM traffic channel data rate.

To add protection against burst errors, each 456-bit block is divided into eight 57-bit blocks, which are transmitted in eight consecutive time slots. Because each time slot can carry two 57-bit blocks, each burst carries data from two different speech samples.

Following these steps, the speech data are encrypted 114 bits at a time, assembled into time slots (burst assembly), and finally modulated for transmission. The modulation scheme, Gaussian minimum shift keying (GMSK), is a form of frequency shift keying (FSK).

Data Encoding Digital data are processed in a similar fashion as applied to speech signals. Data are processed in blocks of 240 bits every 20 ms, for a data rate of 12 kbps. Depending on the way logical channels are defined, the actual supported data rates are 9.6, 4,8, and 2.4 kbps. Each block is augmented by four tail bits. A (2, 1, 5) convolutional code is used to produce a block of $244 \times 2 = 488$ bits. Then 32 bits of this block are dropped (puncturing) leaving a block of 456 bits. A bit interleaving scheme is then used to spread the data over multiple bursts, again to reduce the effects of burst noise. The 456 bits are spread over 22 bursts in the following fashion:

- The 1st and 22nd bursts carry 6 bits each.
- The 2nd and 21st bursts carry 12 bits each.
- The 3rd and 20th bursts carry 18 bits each.
- The 4th through 19th bursts carry 24 bits each.

The result is that each burst carries information from 5 or 6 consecutive data blocks.

Slow Frequency Hopping We have said that a given traffic channel is assigned a given frequency channel for transmission and reception. This is not strictly correct. GSM and many other cellular schemes use a technique known as slow frequency hopping to improve signal quality. Each successive TDMA frame in a given channel is carried on a different carrier frequency. Thus, the transmission frequency is changed once every 4.615 ms. Because multipath fading is dependent on carrier frequency, slow frequency hopping helps to compensate. Slow frequency hopping also reduces the effects of cochannel interference. Note that this is a form of spread spectrum communication.

Delay Equalization Because mobile units are at different distances from the base station within a cell, their transmissions suffer differing amounts of delay. This phenomenon creates a design issue, because up to eight mobile units share the same TDMA frame. Thus, the timing of frame slots is critical. The base station provides a control signal to synchronize the timing of the various mobile units. Within the slot format, the tail bits and guard bits provide a margin to prevent the overlap of data bits from one time slot to another. The base station can adjust the timing of any active mobile unit by control signals that instruct the mobile unit to increment or decrement its timing.

GSM Signaling Protocol Architecture

A number of control messages are exchanged between the key entities in Figure 10.13 that deal with mobility, radio resources, and connection management. A detailed look at the various message formats and semantics could fill a book. Here we give an overview of the structure, which suggests the complexity of second-generation design.

Figure 10.16 summarizes the protocols used between the main elements of the network architecture. The lowest layer of the architecture is tailored to the physical link between entities. Between the mobile station and the base transceiver station, the radio link discussed in preceding subsections carries higher-level data inside the TDMA format. Between other entities a standard 64-kbps digital channel is used.

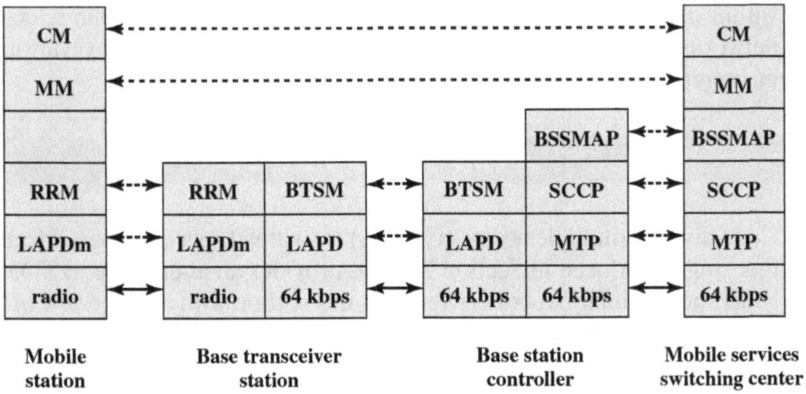

BSSMAP	= BSS mobile application part	MM	= mobility management
BTSM	= BTS management	MTP	= message transfer part
CM	= connection management	RRM	= radio resources management
LAPD	= link access protocol, D channel	SCCP	= signal connection control part

Figure 10.16 GSM Signaling Protocol Architecture

At the link layer, a data link control protocol (see Figure 4.3) known as LAPDm is used. This is a modified version of the LAPD protocol defined for the Integrated Services Digital Network (ISDN). The remaining links use the normal LAPD protocol. In essence, LAPD is designed to convert a potentially unreliable physical link into a reliable data link. It does this by using a cyclic redundancy check to perform error detection (discussed in Section 8.1) and automatic repeat request (ARQ) to retransmit damaged frames (discussed in Section 8.4).[4]

Above the link layer are a number of protocols that provide specific functions. These include

- **Radio resource management:** Controls the setup, maintenance, and termination of radio channels, including handoffs
- **Mobility management:** Manages the location updating and registration procedures, as well as security and authentication
- **Connection management:** Handles the setup, maintenance, and termination of calls (connections between end users)
- **Mobile application part (MAP):** Handles most of the signaling between different entities in the fixed part of the network, such as between the HLR and VLR
- **BTS management:** Performs various management and administrative functions at the base transceiver station, under the control of the base station controller

The MAP does not run directly on top of the link layer but rather on top of two intermediate protocols, SCCP and MTP. These latter protocols are part of Signaling System Number 7, which is a set of protocols designed to provide control signaling

[4]See Appendix C for a discussion of data link control protocols.

within digital circuit-switching networks, such as digital public telecommunications networks. These protocols provide general functions used by various applications, including MAP.

10.4 SECOND-GENERATION CDMA

Code division multiple access (CDMA) is a spread spectrum based technique for multiplexing, introduced in Section 7.4, that provides an alternative to TDMA for second-generation cellular networks. We begin this section with an overview of the advantages of the CDMA approach and then look at the most widely used scheme, IS-95.

Code Division Multiple Access

CDMA for cellular systems can be described as follows. As with FDMA, each cell is allocated a frequency bandwidth, which is split into two parts, half for reverse (mobile unit to base station) and half for forward (base station to mobile unit). For full duplex communication, a mobile unit uses both reverse and forward channels. Transmission is in the form of direct-sequence spread spectrum (DS-SS), which uses a chipping code to increase the data rate of the transmission, resulting in an increased signal bandwidth. Multiple access is provided by assigning orthogonal chipping codes to multiple users, so that the receiver can recover the transmission of an individual unit from multiple transmissions.

CDMA has a number of advantages for a cellular network:

- **Frequency diversity:** Because the transmission is spread out over a larger bandwidth, frequency-dependent transmission impairments, such as noise bursts and selective fading, have less effect on the signal.
- **Multipath resistance:** In addition to the ability of DS-SS to overcome multipath fading by frequency diversity, the chipping codes used for CDMA not only exhibit low cross correlation but also low autocorrelation. Therefore, a version of the signal that is delayed by more than one chip interval does not interfere with the dominant signal as much as in other multipath environments.
- **Privacy:** Because spread spectrum is obtained by the use of noiselike signals, where each user has a unique code, privacy is inherent.
- **Graceful degradation:** With FDMA or TDMA, a fixed number of users can access the system simultaneously. However, with CDMA, as more users access the system simultaneously, the noise level and hence the error rate increases; only gradually does the system degrade to the point of an unacceptable error rate.

A number of drawbacks of CDMA cellular should also be mentioned:

- **Self-jamming:** Unless all of the mobile users are perfectly synchronized, the arriving transmissions from multiple users will not be perfectly aligned on chip boundaries. Thus the spreading sequences of the different users are not orthogonal and there is some level of cross correlation. This is distinct from either TDMA or FDMA, in which for reasonable time or frequency guardbands, respectively, the received signals are orthogonal or nearly so.

- **Near-far problem:** Signals closer to the receiver are received with less attenuation than signals farther away. Given the lack of complete orthogonality, the transmissions from the more remote mobile units may be more difficult to recover. Thus, power control techniques are very important in a CDMA system.
- **Soft handoff:** As is discussed subsequently, a smooth handoff from one cell to the next requires that the mobile unit acquires the new cell before it relinquishes the old. This is referred to as a soft handoff and is more complex than the hard handoff used in FDMA and TDMA schemes.

Mobile Wireless CDMA Design Considerations

Before turning to the specific example of IS-95, it will be useful to consider some general design elements of a CDMA cellular system.

RAKE Receiver In a multipath environment, which is common in cellular systems, if the multiple versions of a signal arrive more than one chip interval apart from each other, the receiver can recover the signal by correlating the chip sequence with the dominant incoming signal. The remaining signals are treated as noise. However, even better performance can be achieved if the receiver attempts to recover the signals from multiple paths and then combine them, with suitable delays. This principle is used in the RAKE receiver.

Figure 10.17 illustrates the principle of the RAKE receiver. The original binary signal to be transmitted is spread by the exclusive-OR (XOR) operation with the transmitter's chipping code. The spread sequence is then modulated for transmission over the wireless channel. Because of multipath effects, the channel generates multiple copies of the signal, each with a different amount of time delay (τ_1, τ_2, etc.), and each with a different attenuation factors (a_1, a_2, etc.). At the receiver, the combined signal is demodulated. The demodulated chip stream is then fed into multiple correlators, each delayed by a different amount. These signals are then combined using weighting factors estimated from the channel.

Soft Handoff In an FDMA or TDMA system, neighboring cells use different portions of the available frequency spectrum (i.e., the frequency reuse factor N is greater than 1, typically 7). When the signal strength of a neighboring cell exceeds that of the current cell, plus a threshold, the mobile station is instructed to switch to a new frequency band that is within the allocation of the new cell. This is referred to as a **hard handoff**. In a typical CDMA cellular system, spatial separation of frequencies is not used (i.e., $N = 1$), because most of the time the interference from neighboring cells will not prohibit correct reception of a DS-SS signal.

In soft handoff, a mobile station is temporarily connected to more than one base station simultaneously. A mobile unit may start out assigned to a single cell. If the unit enters a region in which the transmissions from two base stations are comparable (within some threshold of each other), the mobile unit enters the soft handoff state in which it is connected to the two base stations. The mobile unit remains in this state until one base station clearly predominates, at which time it is assigned exclusively to that cell.

While in the soft handoff state, the transmissions from the mobile unit reaching the two base stations are both sent on to the mobile switching center, which estimates the quality of the two signals and selects one. The switch sends data or digitized

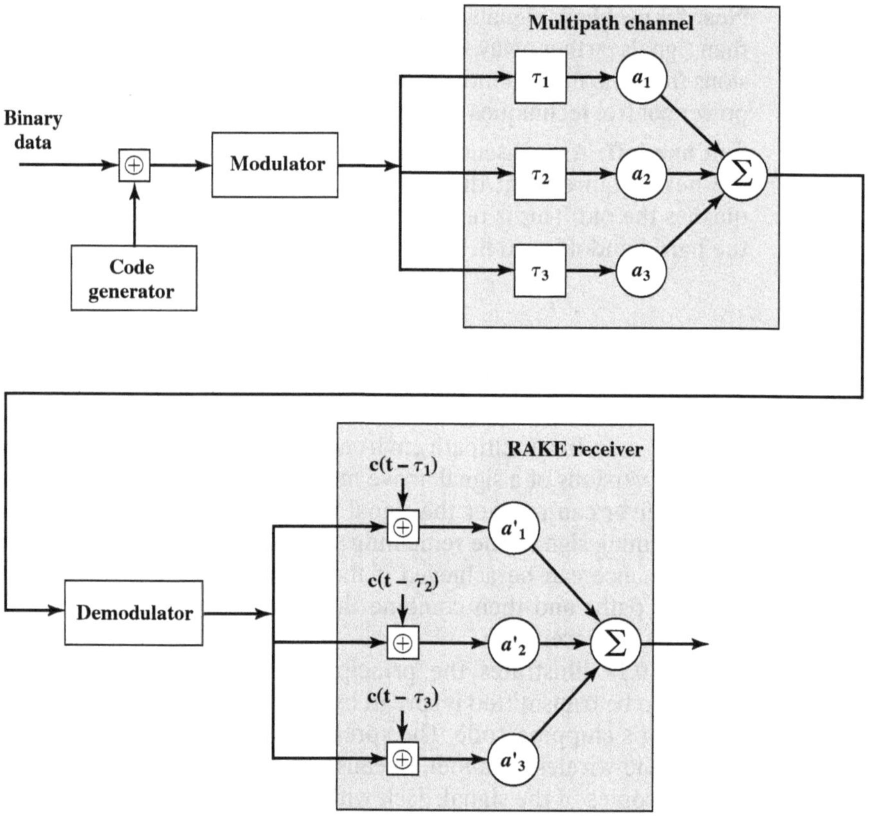

Figure 10.17 Principle of RAKE Receiver [PRAS98]

speech signals to both base stations, which transmit them to the mobile unit. The mobile unit combines the two incoming signals to recover the information.

IS-95

The most widely used second-generation CDMA scheme is IS-95, which is primarily deployed in North America. Table 10.5 lists some key parameters of the IS-95 system. The transmission structures on the forward and reverse links differ and are described separately.

IS-95 Forward Link

Table 10.6 lists forward link channel parameters. The forward link consists of up to 64 logical CDMA channels each occupying the same 1228-kHz bandwidth (Figure 10.18a). The forward link supports four types of channels:

- **Pilot (channel 0):** A continuous signal on a single channel. This channel allows the mobile unit to acquire timing information, provides phase reference for the demodulation process, and provides a means for signal strength comparison for the purpose of handoff determination. The pilot channel consists of all zeros.

Table 10.6 IS-95 Forward Link Channel Parameters

Channel	Sync	Paging		Traffic Rate Set 1				Traffic Rate Set 2			
Data rate (bps)	1200	4800	9600	1200	2400	4800	9600	1800	3600	7200	14400
Code repetition	2	2	1	8	4	2	1	8	4	2	1
Modulation symbol rate (sps)	4800	19,200	19,200	19,200	19,200	19,200	19,200	19,200	19,200	19,200	19,200
PN chips/ modulation symbol	256	64	64	64	64	64	64	64	64	64	64
PN chips/bit	1024	256	128	1024	512	256	128	682.67	341.33	170.67	85.33

- **Synchronization (channel 32):** A 1200-bps channel used by the mobile station to obtain identification information about the cellular system (system time, long code state, protocol revision, etc.).
- **Paging (channels 1 to 7):** Contain messages for one or more mobile stations.
- **Traffic (channels 8 to 31 and 33 to 63):** The forward channel supports 55 traffic channels. The original specification supported data rates of up to 9600 bps. A subsequent revision added a second set of rates up to 14,400 bps.

Note that all of these channels use the same bandwidth. The chipping code is used to distinguish among the different channels. For the forward channel, the chipping

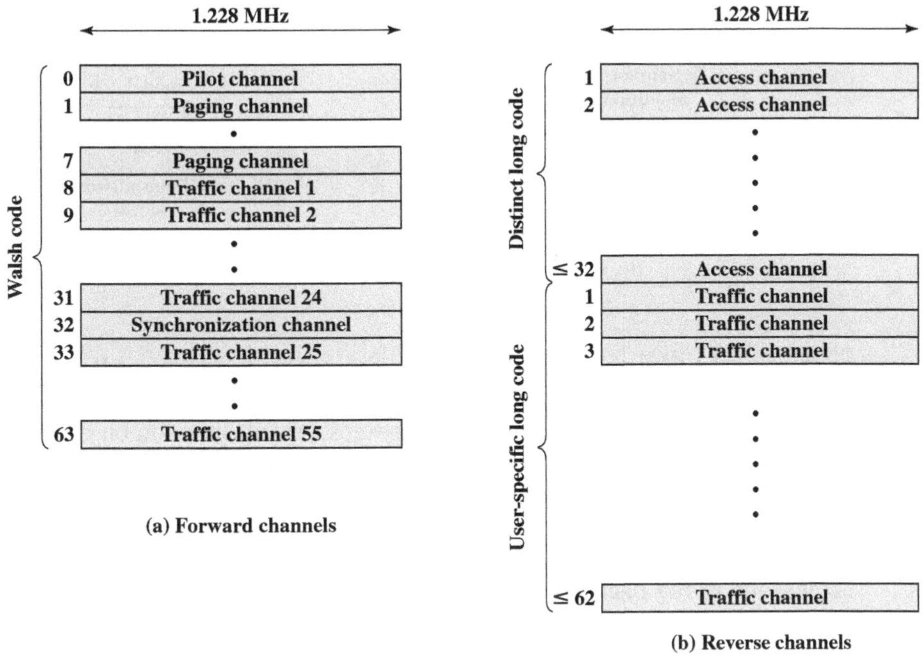

Figure 10.18 IS-95 Channel Structure

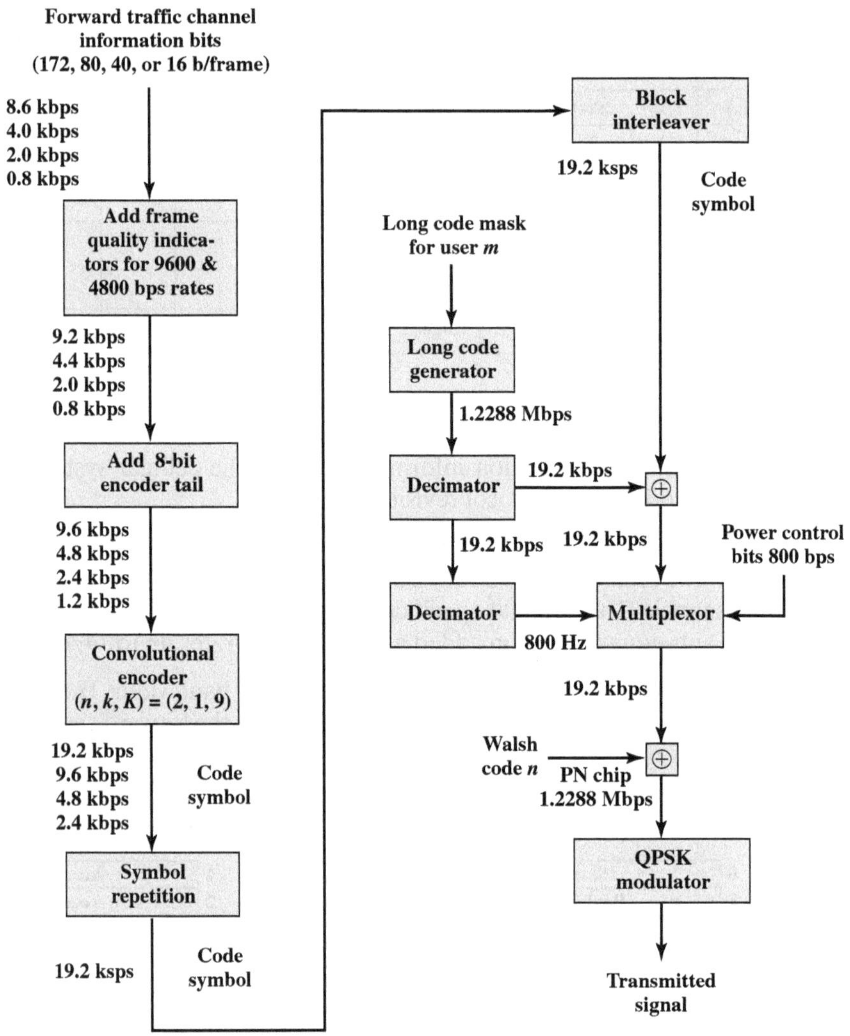

Figure 10.19 IS-95 Forward Link Transmission

codes are the 64 orthogonal 64-bit codes derived from a 64 × 64 Walsh matrix (discussed in Section 7.5; see Figure 7.17).

Figure 10.19 shows the processing steps for transmission on a forward traffic channel using rate set 1. For voice traffic, the speech is encoded at a data rate of 8550 bps. After additional bits are added for error detection, the rate is 9600 bps. The full channel capacity is not used when the user is not speaking. During quiet periods the data rate is lowered to as low as 1200 bps. The 2400-bps rate is used to transmit transients in the background noise, and the 4800 bps rate is used to mix digitized speech and signaling data.

The data or digitized speech is transmitted in 20-ms blocks with forward error correction provided by a convolutional encoder with rate 1/2, thus doubling the effective data rate to a maximum of 19.2 kbps. For lower data rates, the encoder output bits (called code symbols) are replicated to yield the 19.2-kbps rate. The data are then interleaved in blocks to reduce the effects of errors by spreading them out.

Following the interleaver, the data bits are scrambled. The purpose of this is to serve as a privacy mask and also to prevent the sending of repetitive patterns, which in turn reduces the probability of users sending at peak power at the same time. The scrambling is accomplished by means of a long code that is generated as a pseudorandom number from a 42-bit long shift register. The shift register is initialized with the user's electronic serial number. The output of the long code generator is at a rate of 1.2288 Mbps, which is 64 times the rate of 19.2 kbps, so only one bit in 64 is selected (by the decimator function). The resulting stream is XORed with the output of the block interleaver.

The next step in the processing inserts power control information in the traffic channel. The power control function of the base station robs the traffic channel of bits at a rate of 800 bps. These are inserted by stealing code bits. The 800-bps channel carries information directing the mobile unit to increment, decrement, or keep stable its current output level. This power control stream is multiplexed into the 19.2 kbps by replacing some of the code bits, using the long code generator to encode the bits.

The next step in the process is the DS-SS function, which spreads the 19.2 kbps to a rate of 1.2288 Mbps using one row of the 64 $\times$ 64 Walsh matrix. One row of the matrix is assigned to a mobile station during call setup. If a 0 bit is presented to the XOR function, then the 64 bits of the assigned row are sent. If a 1 is presented, then the bitwise XOR of the row is sent. Thus, the final bit rate is 1.2288 Mbps. This digital bit stream is then modulated onto the carrier using a QPSK modulation scheme. Recall from Chapter 6 that QPSK involves creating two bit streams that are separately modulated (see Figure 6.6). In the IS-95 scheme, the data are split into I and Q (in-phase and quadrature) channels; the data in each channel are XORed with a unique short code. The short codes are generated as pseudorandom numbers from a 15-bit long shift register.

IS-95 Reverse Link

Table 10.7 lists reverse link channel parameters. The reverse link consists of up to 94 logical CDMA channels each occupying the same 1228-kHz bandwidth (Figure 10.18b). The reverse link supports up to 32 access channels and up to 62 traffic channels.

The traffic channels in the reverse link are unique to each mobile unit. Each mobile unit has a unique long code mask based on its electronic serial number. The long code mask is a 42-bit number, so there are $2^{42} - 1$ different masks. The access channel is used by a mobile unit to initiate a call, to respond to a paging channel message from the base station, and for a location update.

Figure 10.20 shows the processing steps for transmission on a reverse traffic channel using rate set 1. The first few steps are the same as for the forward channel. For the reverse channel, the convolutional encoder has a rate of 1/3, thus tripling the effective data rate to a maximum of 28.8 kbps. The data are then block interleaved.

The next step is a spreading of the data using the Walsh matrix. The way in which the matrix is used, and its purpose, are different than that of the forward channel. In the reverse channel, the data coming out of the block interleaver are grouped in units of 6 bits. Each 6-bit unit serves as an index to select a row of the 64 $\times$ 64 Walsh matrix

Table 10.7 IS-95 Reverse Link Channel Parameters

Channel	Access	Traffic-Rate Set 1				Traffic-Rate Set 2			
Data rate (bps)	4800	1200	2400	4800	9600	1800	3600	7200	14400
Code rate	1/3	1/3	1/3	1/3	1/3	1/2	1/2	1/2	1/2
Symbol rate before repetition (sps)	14,400	3600	7200	14,400	28,800	3600	7200	14,400	28,800
Symbol repetition	2	8	4	2	1	8	4	2	1
Symbol rate after repetition (sps)	28,800	28,800	28,800	28,800	28,800	28,800	28,800	28,800	28,800
Transmit duty cycle	1	1/8	1/4	1/2	1	1/8	1/4	1/2	1
Code symbols/ modulation symbol	6	6	6	6	6	6	6	6	6
PN chips/ modulation symbol	256	256	256	256	256	256	256	256	256
PN chips/bit	256	128	128	128	128	256/3	256/3	256/3	256/3

($2^6 = 64$), and that row is substituted for the input. Thus the data rate is expanded by a factor of 64/6 to 307.2 kbps. The purpose of this encoding is to improve reception at the base station. Because the 64 possible codings are orthogonal, the block coding enhances the decision-making algorithm at the receiver and is also computationally efficient (see [PETE95] for details). We can view this Walsh modulation as a form of block error-correcting code with $(n, k) = (64, 6)$ and $d_{\min} = 32$. In fact, all distances are 32.

The data burst randomizer is implemented to help reduce interference from other mobile stations (see [BLAC99a] for a discussion). The operation involves using the long code mask to smooth the data out over each 20-ms frame.

The next step in the process is the DS-SS function. In the case of the reverse channel, the long code unique to the mobile unit is XORed with the output of the randomizer to produce the 1.2288-Mbps final data stream. This digital bit stream is then modulated onto the carrier using an orthogonal QPSK modulation scheme. This differs from the forward channel in the use of a delay element in the modulator (Figure 6.6) to produce orthogonality. The reason the modulators are different is that in the forward channel, the spreading codes are orthogonal, all coming from the Walsh matrix, whereas in the reverse channel, orthogonality of the spreading codes is not guaranteed.

10.5 THIRD-GENERATION SYSTEMS

The objective of the third-generation (3G) of wireless communication is to provide fairly high speed wireless communications to support multimedia, data, and video in addition to voice. The ITU's International Mobile Telecommunications for the year 2000 (IMT-2000) initiative has defined the ITU's view of third-generation capabilities as

- Voice quality comparable to the public switched telephone network
- 144 kbps data rate available to users in high-speed motor vehicles over large areas

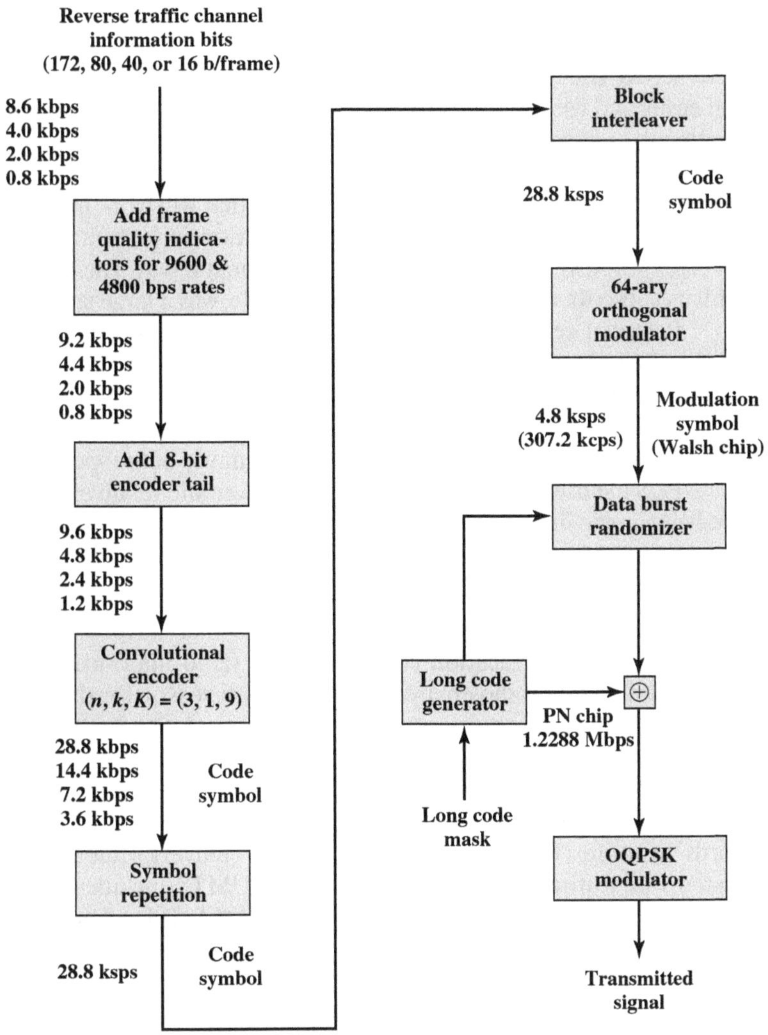

Figure 10.20 IS-95 Reverse Link Transmission

- 384 kbps available to pedestrians standing or moving slowly over small areas
- Support (to be phased in) for 2.048 Mbps for office use
- Symmetrical and asymmetrical data transmission rates
- Support for both packet switched and circuit switched data services
- An adaptive interface to the Internet to reflect efficiently the common asymmetry between inbound and outbound traffic
- More efficient use of the available spectrum in general
- Support for a wide variety of mobile equipment
- Flexibility to allow the introduction of new services and technologies

More generally, one of the driving forces of modern communication technology was the trend toward universal personal telecommunications and universal communications access. The first concept refers to the ability of a person to identify himself or herself easily and use conveniently any communication system in an entire country, over a continent, or even globally, in terms of a single account. The second refers to the capability of using one's terminal in a wide variety of environments to connect to information services (e.g., to have a portable terminal that will work in the office, on the street, and on airplanes equally well). This revolution in personal computing obviously involves wireless communication in a fundamental way. The GSM cellular telephony with its subscriber identity module, for example, was a large step toward these goals.

Personal communications services (PCSs) and personal communication networks (PCNs) are names attached to these concepts of global wireless communications, and they also form objectives for third-generation wireless.

Generally, the technology planned is digital using time division multiple access or code division multiple access to provide efficient use of the spectrum and high capacity.

PCS handsets are designed to be low power and relatively small and light. Efforts are being made internationally to allow the same terminals to be used worldwide.

Alternative Interfaces

Figure 10.21 shows the alternative schemes that have been adopted as part of IMT-2000. The specification covers a set of radio interfaces for optimized performance in different radio environments. A major reason for the inclusion of five alternatives was to enable a smooth evolution from existing first- and second-generation systems.

The five alternatives reflect the evolution from the second-generation. Two of the specifications grow out of the work at the European Telecommunications Standards Institute (ETSI) to develop a UMTS (universal mobile telecommunications system) as Europe's 3G wireless standard. UMTS includes two standards. One of these is known as Wideband CDMA, or W-CDMA. This scheme fully exploits CDMA

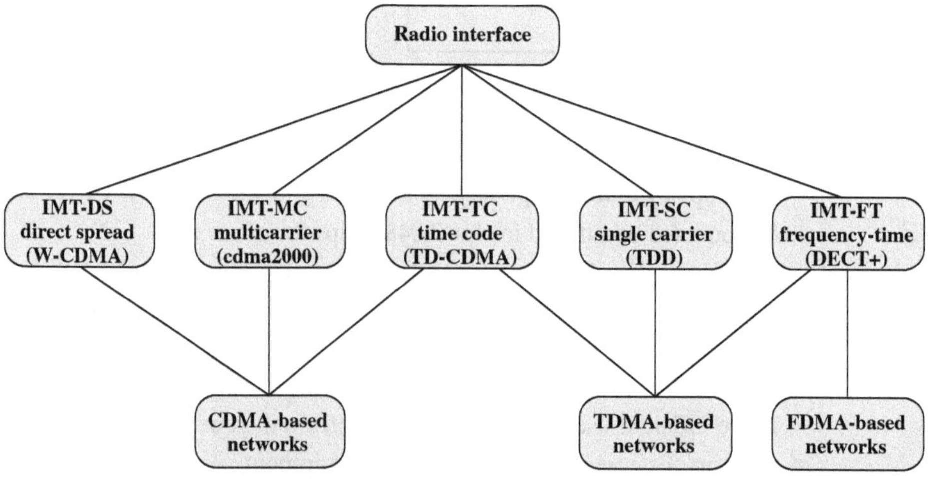

Figure 10.21 TMT-2000 Terrestrial Radio Interfaces

Table 10.8 W-CDMA Parameters

Channel bandwidth	5 MHz
Forward RF channel structure	Direct spread
Chip rate	3.84 Mcps
Frame length	10 ms
Number of slots/frame	15
Spreading modulation	Balanced QPSK (forward) Dual channel QPSK (reverse) Complex spreading circuit
Data modulation	QPSK (forward) BPSK (reverse)
Coherent detection	Pilot symbols
Reverse channel multiplexing	Control and pilot channel time multiplexed. I and Q multiplexing for data and control channels
Multirate	Various spreading and multicode
Spreading factors	4 t0 256
Power control	Open and fast closed loop (1.6 kHz)
Spreading (forward)	Variable length orthogonal sequences for channel separation. Gold sequences 2^{18} for cell and user separation.
Spreading (reverse)	Same as forward, different time shifts in I and Q channels.
Handover	Soft handover

technology to provide high data rates with efficient use of bandwidth. Table 10.8 shows some of the key parameters of W-CDMA. The other European effort under UMTS is known as IMT-TC, or TD-CDMA. This approach is a combination of W-CDMA and TDMA technology. IMT-TC is intended to provide an upgrade path for the TDMA-based GSM systems.

Another CDMA-based system, known as CDMA2000, has a North American origin. This scheme is similar to, but incompatible with, W-CDMA, in part because the standards use different chip rates. Also, CDMA2000 uses a technique known as multicarrier, not used with W-CDMA.

We have looked at some of the technologies that appear in these 3G systems elsewhere in the book. These include turbo codes (Section 8.3), and Gold codes and variable-length spreading codes (Section 7.5).

Two other interface specifications are shown in Figure 10.21. IMT-SC is primarily designed for TDMA-only networks. IMT-FT can be used by both TDMA and FDMA carriers to provide some 3G services; it is an outgrowth of the Digital European Cordless Telecommunications (DECT) standard, discussed in Chapter 11.

Figure 10.22 shows the evolution of wireless cellular systems. As the figure suggests, although 3G systems are in the early stages of commercial deployment, work on fourth generation is underway. Objectives for 4G systems include greater data rates and more flexible quality of service (QoS) capabilities.

In the remainder of this section, we present some general considerations for CDMA technology for 3G systems and then provide an overview of a specific 3G system.

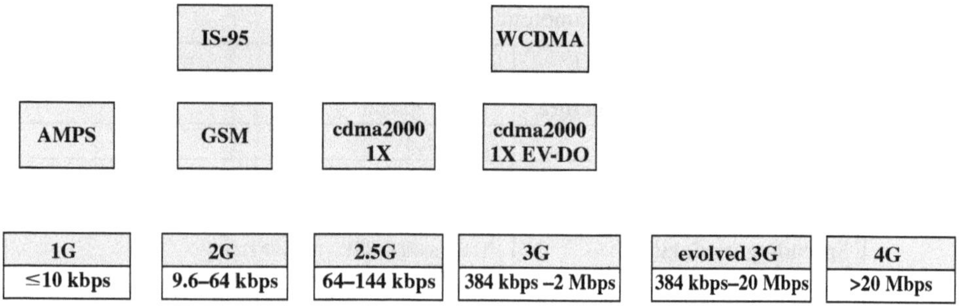

Figure 10.22 Evolution of Cellular Wireless Systems

CDMA Design Considerations

The dominant technology for 3G systems is CDMA. Although three different CDMA schemes have been adopted, they share some common design issues. [OJAN98] lists the following:

- **Bandwidth:** An important design goal for all 3G systems is to limit channel usage to 5 MHz. There are several reasons for this goal. On the one hand, a bandwidth of 5 MHz or more improves the receiver's ability to resolve multipath when compared to narrower bandwidths. On the other hand, available spectrum is limited by competing needs, and 5 MHz is a reasonable upper limit on what can be allocated for 3G. Finally, 5 MHz is adequate for supporting data rates of 144 and 384 kHz, the main targets for 3G services.
- **Chip rate:** Given the bandwidth, the chip rate depends on desired data rate, the need for error control, and bandwidth limitations. A chip rate of 3 Mcps (mega-chips per second) or more is reasonable given these design parameters.
- **Multirate:** The term *multirate* refers to the provision of multiple fixed-data-rate logical channels to a given user, in which different data rates are provided on different logical channels. Further, the traffic on each logical channel can be switched independently through the wireless and fixed networks to different destinations. The advantage of multirate is that the system can flexibly support multiple simultaneous applications from a given user and can efficiently use available capacity by only providing the capacity required for each service. Multirate can be achieved with a TDMA scheme within a single CDMA channel, in which a different number of slots per frame are assigned to achieve different data rates. All the subchannels at a given data rate would be protected by error correction and interleaving techniques (Figure 10.23a). An alternative is to use multiple CDMA codes, with separate coding and interleaving, and map them to separate CDMA channels (Figure 10.23b).

CDMA2000 1x EV-DO

The first 3G wireless system to be deployed commercially is known as CDMA2000 1x EV-DO, also known as CDMA/HDR (CDMA high data rate) and as IS-856. Its

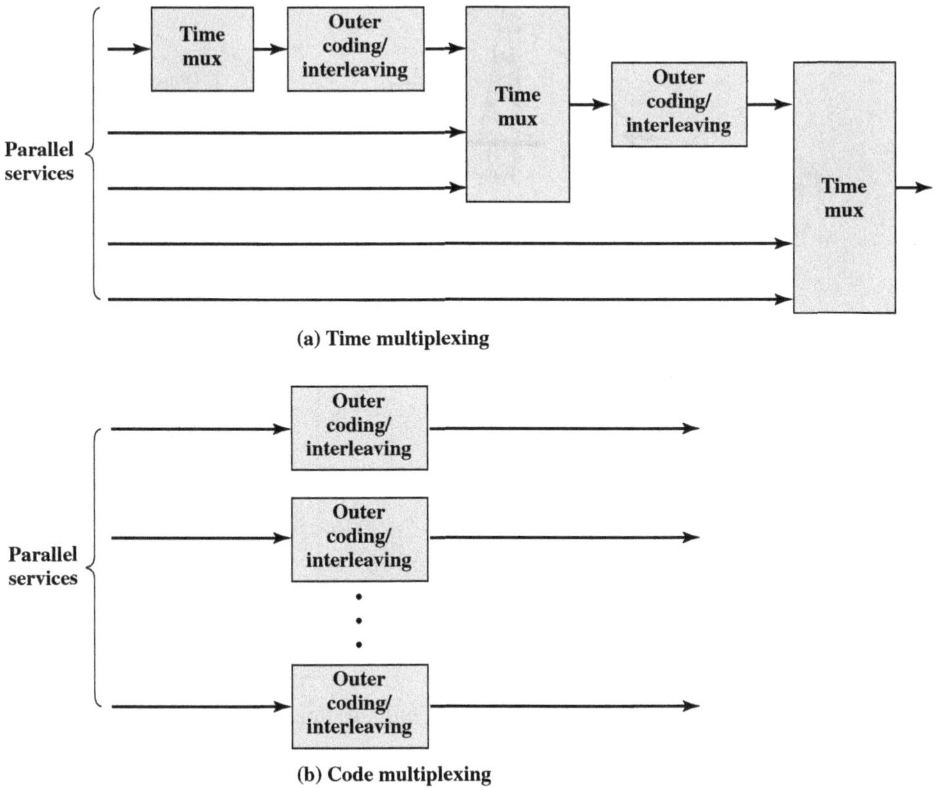

Figure 10.23 Time and Code Multiplexing Principles [OJAN98]

intent is to offer near-broadband packet data speeds for wireless access to the Internet. The 1x prefix refers to its use of 1x (1 times) the 1.2288 Mcps spreading rate of a standard IS-95 CDMA channel. EV signifies that it is an evolutionary technology built on the IS-95 standard. What differentiates this scheme from other 3G technologies is that it is designed for data only (DO) and is geared toward the use of IP for packet transmission and for Internet access. However, with voice over IP (VoIP) technology, CDMA2000 1xEV-DO can support voice traffic.

A well-engineered 1xEV-DO network delivers average download data rates of between 600 kbps and 1.2 Mbps during off-peak hours and between 150 kbps and 300 kbps during peak hours [EYUB02]. Instantaneous data rates are as high as 2.4 Mbps. These data rates are achieved using a bandwidth of only 1.25 MHz, one-quarter of what is required for WCDMA.

The 1xEV-DO design focuses on integration with IP-based networks. As a result, some vendors have built 1xEV-DO networks based entirely on IP technologies. Figure 10.24 shows the main elements in such an arrangement. Mobile users communicate with a base station in a nearby cell using the 1xEV-DO transmission scheme. Typically, the base station controller for a number of base stations is located

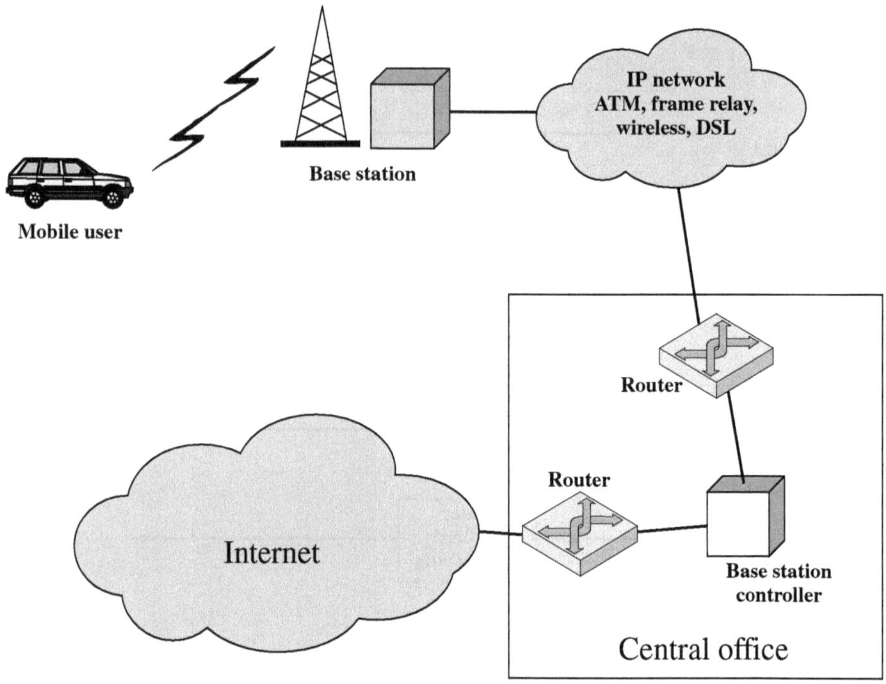

Figure 10.24 CDMA2000 1xEV-DO Configuration Elements

in a central office to provide switching, handoff, and other services. An IP transport service is used to connect the base station to the central office. Using IP transport lowers connection costs by giving operators a choice of connection services, including frame relay, ATM, broadband wireless links, and DSL. At the central office, the base station controller can route a call back out the IP network to another cellular subscriber or out over the Internet.

Because 1xEV-DO is specified as data-only, the transmission scheme can be optimized for data transfer and need not support voice requirements. Voice communications imposes restrictions that inhibit efficient use of bandwidth. For example, a delay of 100 ms makes voice communication difficult. Longer delays make useful communication impractical. For this reason, voice frames are short, typically on the order of 20 ms, in order to minimize delays. But the use of short frames increases overhead, resulting in reduced efficiency. In a data-only network, longer average delays can be tolerated, and QoS facilities can be used to accommodate a fraction of transmissions that require tight delay values. Accordingly, a data-only network can use longer frames, reducing overhead.

Another advantage to the longer frame is that it results in more efficient use of turbo codes. Whereas convolutional coding is well suited to the short voice frames, turbo coding is more powerful when frames are long (several hundred bits or more). Turbo coding with large frame sizes significantly improves performance by allowing the use of lower RF power while still achieving the same error rate.

In a typical data-only application, the amount of traffic from the network to the user significantly exceeds user-to-network traffic. Such applications include Web browsing and downloading e-mail. To optimize throughput and make the best use of the available bandwidth, 1xEV-DO sends and receives at different data rates. Download (forward channel) rates vary from 38.4 kbps to 2.4576 Mbps and upload (reverse channel) rates vary from 9.6 kbps to 156.3 kbps.

A major difference in a data-only design as compared to a voice-optimized design is the technique used to maintain continuous communication in a noisy and variable RF environment. Voice-optimized systems use power control: Users with weak signals increase their transmitting RF power to overcome path loss and/or fading while users close to the base station reduce power. In contrast, 1xEV-DO alters the data rate rather than the power when signal levels change. This is done in both directions (forward and reverse channels).

Let us consider the forward channel first. The base station always sends at full power, to assure that the mobile unit achieves the highest possible received SNR. If path loss increases, the resulting reduction in SNR yields a lower effective link capacity (using Shannon's formula) or, put another way, a higher error rate. The errors are reduced not by increasing RF power but by reducing the data rate. The data rate is reduced by increasing redundancy and altering the modulation method. Increasing the number of check bits reduces the data rate. Use of higher-order modulation methods (e.g., 16-QAM versus QPSK) increases the data rate. Table 10.9a shows the forward channel data rates. Although several data rates appear twice in the table, the number of 1.67-ms time slots used to send the same rate is different. The additional time slots provide redundant information. If the mobile unit can successfully decode a packet before all slots are sent, it sends an acknowledgement to the base station. This causes an early termination of the transmission, increasing effective throughput. The mobile unit provides continuous information about SNR conditions so that the base station can adjust its data rate.

Table 10.9b shows the data rates for the reverse channel. Because of the limited signal power on the reverse channel, only a simple BPSK modulation scheme is used, which is less affected by RF channel conditions than more complex modulation schemes.

Operators of these cellular networks are experiencing phenomenal growth and, due to market demand, are being forced to upgrade their networks from 2G to 2.5G to 3G to 4G. Figure 10.25 displays this process.

Table 10.9 CDMA2000 1xEV-DO Link Parameters

(a) Forward Link

Data rate (kbps)	38.4	76.8	153.6	307.2	307.2	614.4	614.4	921.6	1228.8	1228.8	1843.2	2457.6
Number of slots	16	8	4	2	4	1	2	2	1	2	1	1
Packet size (bytes)	128	128	128	128	256	128	256	384	256	512	384	512
Packet duration (ms)	26.67	13.33	6.67	3.33	6.67	1.67	3.33	3.33	1.67	3.33	1.67	1.67
Code rate	1/5	1/5	1/5	1/5	1/3	1/3	1/3	1/3	1/3	1/3	1/3	1/3
Modulation	QPSK	QPSK	QPSK	QPSK	QPSK	QPSK	QPSK	8PSK	QPSK	16QAM	8 PSK	16QAM

(b) Reverse Link

Data rate (kbps)	9.6	19.2	38.4	76.8	153.6
Number of slots	16	16	16	16	16
Packet size (bytes)	32	64	128	256	512
Packet duration (ms)	26.67	26.67	26.67	26.67	26.67
Code rate	1/4	1/4	1/4	1/4	1/2
Modulation	BPSK	BPSK	BPSK	BPSK	BPSK

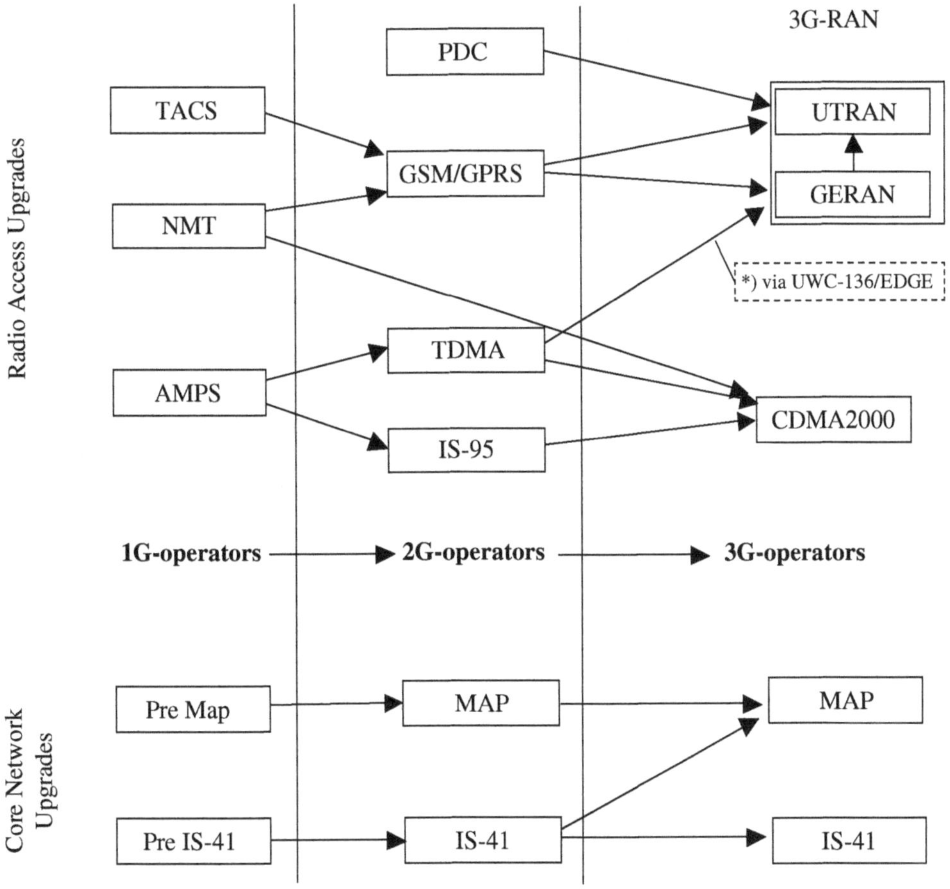

Figure 10.25 Observed Network Upgrades of Operators

10.6 4G

With the phenomenal growth of data services by mobile subscribers using handsets and laptops, data traffic has skyrocketed and 3G utilization rates are fast-approaching threshold levels and threatening the user experience.[5]

3G and 3.5G networks are increasingly proving incapable of handling data traffic, especially in urban areas and places with a high smartphone density. Facing a need for near constant enhancement of data transfer rates and mobile broadband network efficiency, MNOs are consequently planning to move to 4G technologies to accommodate the surge in data traffic and turn this challenge into an opportunity.

Long Term Evolution (LTE) and Worldwide Interoperability for Microwave Access (WiMAX) are the main pathways to 4G that MNOs have to pick between,

[5]http://www.researchandmarkets.com/reports/1295208/lte_and_the_road_to_4g_2010_2015

and on which they can build their data handling capacities. While WiMAX has enjoyed a first mover advantage and a clear head-start, LTE's benefits—not least that LTE is a natural progression for MNOs operating on GSM/UMTS networks, and offers the ability to lower the cost of delivering data services—are expected to drive a surge in LTE network deployments in the coming years.

The period 2009–2010 has already seen the announcement of numerous LTE trials and deployments the world-over, and both this ever-growing number of contracts, and the major MNOs involved who are favoring LTE over alternative technologies, strongly suggest that LTE deployment is gaining substantial momentum. It will be interesting to see if WiMax can survive several more years.

In fact, the worldwide LTE subscriber base is expected to grow at a phenomenal CAGR (Compound Annual Growth Rate) of 187.7 percent between 2010 and 2015.

This growth will see the worldwide LTE subscriber base pass the 200 million-mark by end-2015—within the first six years of its launch in late 2009; whereas the worldwide 3G subscriber base reached only the 100 million mark in the first six years after its launch.

Migrating to LTE technology is not just the preserve of the developed and saturated markets in North America and Western Europe, with MNOs in developing markets also proactively doing the same; though understandably LTE's scale and use will markedly vary between markets.

Description

IMT-Advanced, otherwise known as 4G, is intended to effectively handle the quality of service (QoS) and rate requirements set by further development of applications like mobile broadband access, Multimedia Messaging Service (MMS), video chat, mobile TV, but also new services like high-definition television (HDTV). 4G may allow roaming with wireless local area networks, and may interact with digital video broadcasting systems. It was meant to go beyond the International Mobile Telecommunications-2000 requirements, which specify mobile phones systems marketed as 3G.

Requirements

Specific requirements of the IMT-Advanced report included:

- Based on an all-Internet Protocol (IP) packet switched network.
- Interoperability with existing wireless standards.
- A nominal data rate of 100 Mbit/s while the client physically moves at high speeds relative to the station, and 1 Gbit/s while client and station are in relatively fixed positions.
- Dynamically share and use the network resources to support more simultaneous users per cell.
- Scalable channel bandwidth 5–20 MHz, optionally up to 40 MHz.

- Peak link spectral efficiency of 15 bit/s/Hz in the downlink, and 6.75 bit/s/Hz in the uplink (meaning that 1 Gbit/s in the downlink should be possible over less than 67 MHz bandwidth).
- System spectral efficiency of up to 3 bit/s/Hz/cell in the downlink and 2.25 bit/s/Hz/cell for indoor usage.
- Seamless connectivity and global roaming across multiple networks with smooth handovers.
- Ability to offer high quality of service for multimedia support[6].

While the ITU adopts requirements and recommendations for technologies that would be used for future communications, they do not actually perform the development work themselves, and countries do not consider them binding standards. Other trade groups and standards bodies such as the Institute of Electrical and Electronics Engineers (IEEE), the WiMAX Forum and 3GPP also have a role.

Long Term Evolution (LTE)

LTE has a theoretical net bit rate capacity of up to 100 Mbit/s in the downlink and 50 Mbit/s in the uplink if a 20 MHz channel is used—and more if multiple-input multiple-output (MIMO) antenna arrays, are used.

The CDMA spread spectrum radio technology used in 3G systems and IS-95 is abandoned and replaced by OFDMA and other frequency-domain equalization schemes. This is combined with MIMO (Multiple In Multiple Out), antenna arrays, dynamic channel allocation and channel-dependent scheduling.

The first publicly available LTE service was opened in Sweden and Norway in December 2009, and branded 4G. The user terminals were manufactured by Samsung. Currently, the two publicly available LTE services in the United States are provided by MetroPCS, and Verizon Wireless.

Mobile WiMAX (IEEE 802.16e)

The Mobile WiMAX (IEEE 802.16e-2005) mobile wireless broadband access (MWBA) standard (marketed as WiBro in South Korea) is sometimes branded 4G, and offers peak data rates of 128 Mbit/s downlink and 56 Mbit/s uplink over 20 MHz wide channels.

The first commercial mobile WiMAX service was opened in Seoul, South Korea in June 2006.

Sprint Nextel marketed Mobile WiMAX, in September 2008, branded as a "4G" network even though it did not fulfill the IMT Advanced requirements.

Data speeds of WiMAX	
	WiMAX
Peak Download	128 Mbit/s
Peak Upload	56 Mbit/s

[6]www.itu-r.int

Current Technology[7]

Most modern cellular phones are based on one of two transmission technologies: time-division multiple access (TDMA) or code-division multiple access (CDMA) (Riezenman 2000, 40). These two technologies are collectively referred to as second-generation, or 2G. Both systems make eavesdropping more difficult by digitally encoding the voice data and compressing it, then splitting up the resulting data into chunks upon transmission.

TDMA

TDMA, or Time Division Multiple Access, is a technique for dividing the time domain up into subchannels for use by multiple devices. Each device gets a single time slot in a procession of devices on the network. During that particular time slot, one device is allowed to utilize the entire bandwidth of the spectrum, and every other device is in the quiescent state.

The time is divided into frames in which each device on the network gets one timeslot. There are n timeslots in each frame, one each for n devices on the network. In practice, every device gets a timeslot in every frame. This makes the frame setup simpler and more efficient because there is no time wasted on setting up the order of transmission. This has the negative side effect of wasting bandwidth and capacity on devices that have nothing to send (Leon-Garcia and Widjaja 2000).

CDMA

CDMA, or Code Division Multiple Access, allows every device in a cell to transmit over the entire bandwidth at all times. Each mobile device has a unique and orthogonal code that is used to encode and recover the signal (Leon-Garcia and Widjaja 2000). The mobile phone digitizes the voice data as it is received, and encodes the data with the unique code for that phone. This is accomplished by taking each bit of the signal and multiplying it by all bits in the unique code for the phone. Thus, one data bit is transformed into a sequence of bits of the same length as the code for the mobile phone. This makes it possible to combine with other signals on the same frequency range and still recover the original signal from an arbitrary mobile phone as long as the code for that phone is known. Once encoded, the data is modulated for transmission over the bandwidth allocated for that transmission.

Once the signal is demodulated, a correlator and integrator pair recovers the signal based on the unique code from the cellular phone. The correlator recovers the original encoded signal for the device, and the integrator transforms the recovered signal into the actual data stream.

CDMA has been patented in the United States by Qualcomm, making it more expensive to implement due to royalty fees. This has been a factor for cellular phone providers when choosing which system to implement.

By keeping security in mind while designing the new system, the creators of 2G wireless were able to produce a usable system that is still in use today. Unfortunately, 2G technology is being superceded by 3G and 4G as more and more users realize the benefits of these more advanced technologies.

---

[7]http://ckdake.com/system/files/4gwireless.pdf

10.7 RECOMMENDED READINGS AND WEB SITES

[BERT94] and [ANDE95] are instructive surveys of cellular wireless propagation effects. [POLL96] covers the handoff problem in depth. [EVER94] and [ORLI98] provide good accounts of cellular traffic analysis. [BLAC99] is one of the best technical treatments of second-generation cellular systems. A good survey of GSM concepts is [RAHN93]; for more detail see [GARG99].

[TANT98] contains reprints of numerous important papers dealing with CDMA in cellular networks. [DINA98] provides an overview of both PN and orthogonal spreading codes for cellular CDMA networks.

[OJAN98] provides an overview of key technical design considerations for 3G systems. Another useful survey is [ZENG00]. [PRAS00] is a much more detailed analysis. For a discussion of CDMA2000 1xEV-DO, see [BEND00] and [BI03]. [BERE02] and [FROD01] are useful discussions of 4G networks.

ANDE95 Anderson, J.; Rappaport, T.; and Yoshida, S. "Propagation Measurements and Models for Wireless Communications Channels." *IEEE Communications Magazine*, January 1995.

BEND00 Bender. P., et al. "CDMA/HDR: A Bandwidth-Efficient High-Speed Wireless Data Service for Nomadic Users." *IEEE Communications Magazine*, July 2000.

BERE02 Berezdivin, R.; Breinig, R.; and Topp, R. "Next-Generation Wireless Communications Concepts and Technologies." *IEEE Communications Magazine*, March 2002.

BERT94 Bertoni, H.; Honcharenko, W.; Maciel, L.; and Xia, H. "UHF Propagation Prediction for Wireless Personal Communications." *Proceedings of the IEEE*, September 1994.

BI03 Bi, Q., et al. " Performance of 1xEV-DO Third-Generation Wireless High-Speed Data Systems." *Bell Labs Technical Journal*, Vol. 7, No. 3 2003.

BLAC99 Black, U. *Second-Generation Mobile and Wireless Networks*. Upper Saddle River, NJ: Prentice Hall, 1999.

DINA98 Dinan, E., and Jabbari, B. "Spreading Codes for Direct Sequence CDMA and Wideband CDMA Cellular Networks." *IEEE Communications Magazine*, September 1998.

EVER94 Everitt, D. "Traffic Engineering of the Radio Interface for Cellular Mobile Networks." *Proceedings of the IEEE*, September 1994.

FROD01 Frodigh, M., et al. "Future Generation Wireless Networks." *IEEE Personal Communications*, October 2001.

GARG99 Garg, V., and Wilkes, J. *Principles and Applications of GSM*. Upper Saddle River, NJ: Prentice Hall, 1999.

OJAN98 Ojanpera, T., and Prasad, G. "An Overview of Air Interface Multiple Access for IMT-2000/UMTS." *IEEE Communications Magazine*, September 1998.

ORLI98 Orlik, P., and Rappaport, S. "Traffic Performance and Mobility Modeling of Cellular Communications with Mixed Platforms and Highly Variable Mobilities." *Proceedings of the IEEE*, July 1998.

POLL96 Pollini, G. "Trends in Handover Design." *IEEE Communications Magazine*, March 1996.

PRAS00 Prasad, R.; Mohr, W.; and Konhauser, W., eds. *Third-Generation Mobile Communication Systems*. Boston: Artech House, 2000.

RAHN93 Rahnema, M. "Overview of the GSM System and Protocol Architecture." *IEEE Communications Magazine*, April 1993.

TANT98 Tantaratana, S, and Ahmed, K., eds. *Wireless Applications of Spread Spectrum Systems: Selected Readings*. Piscataway, NJ: IEEE Press, 1998.

ZENG00 Zeng, M.; Annamalai, A.; and Bhargava, V. "Harmonization of Global Third-Generation Mobile Systems. *IEEE Communications Magazine*, December 2000.

Recommended Web Sites:

- **Cellular Telecommunications and Internet Association:** An industry consortium that provides information on successful applications of wireless technology
- **GSM World:** Lots of information and links concerning GSM
- **CDMA Development Group:** Information and links for IS-95 and CDMA generally
- **3G Americas:** A trade group of Western Hemisphere companies supporting TDMA, GSM, GPRS, EDGE, and UMTS. Includes industry news, white papers, and other technical information
- **3G Today:** Contains a variety of information on 3G systems and providers

10.8 KEY TERMS, REVIEW QUESTIONS, AND PROBLEMS

Key Terms

Advanced Mobil Phone Service (AMPS)	frequency reuse	power control
base station	Global System for Mobile Communications (GSM)	reuse factor
blocking network	handoff	reverse channel
cellular network	handover	second-generation (2G) network
closed loop power control	hard handoff	soft handoff
code division multiple access (CDMA)	mobile radio	third-generation (3G) network
first-generation (1G) network	nonblocking network	time division multiple access (TDMA)
forward channel	open loop power control	

Review Questions

10.1 What geometric shape is used in cellular system design?

10.2 What is the principle of frequency reuse in the context of a cellular network?

10.3 List five ways of increasing the capacity of a cellular system.

10.4 Explain the paging function of a cellular system.

10.5 List and briefly define different performance metrics that may be used to make the handoff decision.

10.6 As a mobile unit in communication with a base station moves, what factors determine the need for power control and the amount of power adjustment?

10.7 Explain the difference between open-loop and closed-loop power control.

10.8 What is the difference between traffic intensity and the mean rate of calls in a system?

10.9 What are the key differences between first- and second-generation cellular systems?

10.10 What are the advantages of using CDMA for a cellular network?

10.11 What are the disadvantages of using CDMA for a cellular network?

10.12 Explain the difference between hard and soft handoff.

10.13 What are some key characteristics that distinguish third-generation cellular systems from second-generation cellular systems?

Problems

10.1 Consider four different cellular systems that share the following characteristics. The frequency bands are 825 to 845 MHz for mobile unit transmission and 870 to 890 MHz for base station transmission. A duplex circuit consists of one 30-kHz channel in each direction. The systems are distinguished by the reuse factor, which is 4, 7, 12, and 19, respectively.

a. Suppose that in each of the systems, the cluster of cells (4, 7, 12, 19) is duplicated 16 times. Find the number of simultaneous communications that can be supported by each system.

b. Find the number of simultaneous communications that can be supported by a single cell in each system.

c. What is the area covered, in cells, by each system?

d. Suppose the cell size is the same in all four systems and a fixed area of 100 cells is covered by each system. Find the number of simultaneous communications that can be supported by each system.

10.2 Describe a sequence of events similar to that of Figure 10.6 for

a. a call from a mobile unit to a fixed subscriber

b. a call from a fixed subscriber to a mobile unit

10.3 In the discussion of the handoff procedure based on relative signal strength with threshold, it was pointed out that if the threshold is set quite low, such as Th_3, the mobile unit may move far into the new cell (L_4). This reduces the quality of the communication link and may result in a dropped call. Can you suggest another drawback to this scheme?

10.4 Hysteresis is a technique commonly used in control systems. As an example, describe the hysteresis mechanism used in a household thermostat.

10.5 A telephony connection has a duration of 23 minutes. This is the only connection made by this caller during the course of an hour. How much is the amount of traffic, in Erlangs, of this connection?

10.6 Using Table 10.3, approximate the answers to the following. Also, in each case, give a description in words of the general problem being solved. *Hint*: Straight-line interpolation is adequate.

a. Given $N = 20, A = 10.5$, find P.

b. Given $N = 20, P = 0.015$, find A.

c. Given $P = 0.005, A = 6$, find N.

10.7 An analog cellular system has a total of 33 MHz of bandwidth and uses two 25-kHz simplex (one-way) channels to provide full duplex voice and control channels.

a. What is the number of channels available per cell for a frequency reuse factor of (1) 4 cells, (2) 7 cells, and (3) 12 cells?

b. Assume that 1 MHz is dedicated to control channels but that only one control channel is needed per cell. Determine a reasonable distribution of control channels and voice channels in each cell for the three frequency reuse factors of part (a).

10.8 As was mentioned, the one-way bandwidth available to a single operator in the AMPS system is 12.5 MHz with a channel bandwidth of 30 kHz and 21 control channels. We would like to calculate the efficiency with which this system utilizes bandwidth for a particular installation. Use the following parameters:

- Cell area $= 8\ \text{km}^2$
- Total coverage area $= 4000\ \text{km}^2$
- Frequency reuse factor $= 7$
- Average number of calls per user during the busy hour $= 1.2$

- Average holding time of a call = 100 s
- Call blocking probability = 2%

a. How many voice channels are there per cell?
b. Use Table 10.3 and a simple straight-line interpolation to determine the total traffic carried per cell, in Erlangs/cell. Then convert that to Erlangs/km^2.
c. Calculate the number of calls/hour/cell and the number of calls/hour/km^2.
d. Calculate the number of users/hour/cell and the number of users/hour/channel.
e. A common definition of spectral efficiency with respect to modulation, or modulation efficiency, in Erlangs/MHz/km^2, is

$$\eta_m = \frac{(\text{Total traffic carried by the system})}{(\text{Bandwidth})(\text{Total coverage area})}$$

Determine the modulation efficiency for this system.

10.9 A cellular system uses FDMA with a spectrum allocation of 12.5 MHz in each direction, a guard band at the edge of the allocated spectrum of 10 kHz, and a channel bandwidth of 30 kHz. What is the number of available channels?

10.10 If 8 speech channels are supported on a single radio channel, and if no guard band is assumed, what is the number of simultaneous users that can be accommodated in GSM?

10.11 a. What is the duration of a bit in GSM?
b. If a user is allocated one time slot per frame, what is the delay between successive transmissions in successive frames?

10.12 If we consider the trailing bits, stealing bits, guard bits, and training bits in a GSM frame as overhead, and the rest of the bits as data, then what is the percentage overhead in a GSM frame?

10.13 Using the definition of slow frequency hopping from Chapter 7, demonstrate that GSM uses slow frequency hopping.

10.14 For a cellular system, FDMA spectral efficiency is defined as $\eta_a = \frac{B_c N_T}{B_w}$, where

B_c = channel bandwidth
B_w = total bandwidth in one direction
N_T = total number of voice channels in the covered area

a. What is an upper bound on η_a?
b. Determine η_a for the system of Problem 8.

10.15 Consider a 7-cell system covering an area of 3100 km^2. The traffic in the seven cells is as follows:

Cell number	1	2	3	4	5	6	7
Traffic (Erlangs)	30.8	66.7	48.6	33.2	38.2	37.8	32.6

Each user generates an average of 0.03 Erlangs of traffic per hour, with a mean holding time of 120 s. The system consists of a total of 395 channels and is designed for a grade of service of 0.02.

a. Determine the number of subscribers in each cell.
b. Determine the number of calls per hour per subscriber.
c. Determine the number of calls per hour in each cell.
d. Determine the number of channels required in each cell. *Hint:* You will need to extrapolate using Table 10.3.
e. Determine the total number of subscribers.
f. Determine the average number of subscribers per channel.
g. Determine the subscriber density per km^2.
h. Determine the total traffic (total Erlangs).
i. Determine the Erlangs per km^2.
j. What is the radius of a cell?

CHAPTER 11

Cordless Systems and Wireless Local Loop

In this chapter, we look at two technologies that bring wireless access into the residence and office: cordless systems and wireless local loop (WLL).

11.1 CORDLESS SYSTEMS

Standardized cordless systems have evolved from cordless telephone technology. Originally, cordless telephones were developed to provide users with mobility within a residence or small office by separating the handset from the rest of the telephone (called the base station) and providing a simple analog wireless link. As technology improved, digital cordless telephones were developed. The products on the market used proprietary wireless interfaces. Because the same manufacturer sold the base station and the handset as a unit, there was no need for standards.

Standards-making bodies became interested in standardizing cordless technology to widen its range of applicability, in two directions. First, cordless systems can support multiple users from the same base station, which could include either multiple telephone handsets or both voice and data devices (e.g., fax or printer). Second, cordless systems can operate in a number of environments:

- **Residential:** Within a residence a single base station can provide voice and data support, enabling in-house communications as well as providing a connection to the public telephone network.
- **Office:** A small office can be supported by a single base station that provides service for a number of telephone handsets and data devices. In a larger office, multiple base stations can be used in a cellular configuration, with the base stations connected to a PBX (private branch exchange) switch. Such a configuration can serve hundreds or even thousands of users.
- **Telepoint:** Telepoint refers to the provision of a base station in a public place, such as a shopping mall or airport. This application has not succeeded in the marketplace.

A number of design considerations have driven the development of cordless standards. [WEBB00] lists the following:

1. The range of the handset from the base station is modest, up to about 200 m. Thus, low-power designs are used. Typically, the power output is one or two orders of magnitude lower than for cellular systems.
2. The handset and the base station need to be inexpensive. This dictates the use of simple technical approaches, such as in the area of speech coding and channel equalization.
3. Frequency flexibility is limited, because the user owns the base station as well as the mobile portion and can install these in a variety of environments. Hence, the system needs to be able to seek a low-interference channel wherever it is used.

Although a number of different standards have been proposed for cordless systems, the most prominent is DECT (digital enhanced cordless telecommunications),[1]

[1]DECT formerly stood for digital European cordless telephone.

Table 11.1 DECT and PWT Parameters

	DECT	PWT
Bandwidth	20 MHz	20 MHz
Band	1.88 to 1.9 GHz	1.91 to 1.92 GHz
Access method	TDD/TDMA/FDMA	TDD/TDMA/FDMA
Carrier bandwidth	1.728 MHz	1.25 MHz
Number of carriers	10	8
Channels per carrier	12	12
Number of channels	120	96
Handoff	Yes	Yes
Transmitted data rate	1.152 Mbps	1.152 Mbps
Speech rate	32 kbps	32 kbps
Speech coding technique	ADPCM	ADPCM
Modulation technique	Gaussian FSK	π/4 DQPSK
Peak output power	250 mW	90 mW
Mean output power	10 mW	10 mW
Maximum cell radius	30 to 100 m	30 to 100 m

developed in Europe. The U.S. equivalent is known as PWT (personal wireless telecommunications). Table 11.1 shows some of the key parameters for DECT and PWT. These systems use an approach referred to as time division duplex (TDD). We begin with a general discussion of TDD and then turn to the details of DECT.

Time Division Duplex

In the technique of TDD, also known as time-compression multiplexing (TCM), data are transmitted in one direction at a time, with transmission alternating between the two directions. We first look at simple TDD and then discuss TDMA/TDD.

Simple TDD To achieve the desired subscriber data rate with simple TDD, the transmitter's bit stream is divided into equal segments, compressed in time to a higher transmission rate, and transmitted in bursts, which are expanded at the other end to the original rate. A short quiescent period is used between bursts going in opposite directions to allow the channel to settle down. Thus, the actual data rate on the channel must be greater than twice the data rate required by the two end systems.

The timing implications are shown in Figure 11.1. The two sides alternate in the transmission of data. Each side sends blocks of some fixed length, which take a time T_b to transmit; this time is a linear function of the number of bits in a block. In addition, a time T_p is required for the propagation of a signal from transmitter to receiver; this time is a linear function of the distance between transmitter and receiver. Finally, a guard time T_g is introduced to turn the channel around. Thus, the time to send one block is $(T_p + T_b + T_g)$. However, because the two sides must alternate transmissions, the rate at which blocks

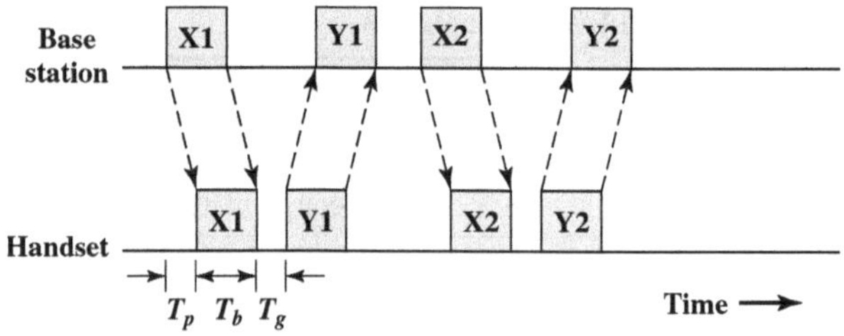

T_p = Propagation delay
T_b = Burst transmission time
T_g = Guard time

Figure 11.1 Transmission Using Time Division Duplex

can be transmitted by either side is only $1/[2(T_p + T_b + T_g)]$. We can relate this to the effective data rate, R, as seen by the two end points as follows. Let B be the size of a block in bits. Then the effective number of bits transmitted per second, or effective data rate, is

$$R = \frac{B}{2(T_p + T_b + T_g)}$$

The actual data rate, A, on the medium can easily be seen to be

$$A = B/T_b$$

Combining the two, we have

$$A = 2R\left(1 + \frac{T_p + T_g}{T_b}\right)$$

The choice of block size, B, is a compromise between competing requirements. For a larger block size, the value of T_b becomes larger compared to the values of T_p and T_g. Now consider that we have a fixed value of R, which is the data rate required for the link, and we need to determine the value of A. If B is increased, there is a decrease in the actual data rate, A. This makes the task of implementation easier. On the other hand, this is accompanied by an increase in the signal delay due to buffering, which is undesirable for voice traffic.

Example 11.1 One of the standard interfaces defined for ISDN (Integrated Services Digital Network) is the basic interface, which provides a data rate of 192 kbps and uses a frame size of 48 bits. Suppose we use TDD with a block size equal to the frame size. Assume the distance between the subscriber and the network switch is 1 km and a guard time 10 μs is used. What is the actual data rate?

The burst transmission time is (48 bits)/(192 kbps) = 250 μs. The propagation delay is (1 km)/(3×10^8 m/s) = 3.33 μs. Thus:

$$A = 2 \times 192 \times [1 + (3.33 + 10)/250)] = 404 \text{ kbps}$$

TDMA/TDD TDD was developed for use on wired subscriber systems but has now found application in wireless configurations. In a wireless configuration, TDD involves transmitting and receiving on the same carrier frequency but at different times. Wireless TDD is typically used with TDMA, in which a number of users receive forward (base to handset) channel signals in turn and then transmit reverse (handset to base) channel signals in turn, all on the same carrier frequency.

Two important advantages of TDD over using a TDMA system with two different carriers, one in each direction, are improved ability to cope with fast fading and improved capacity allocation.

With respect to **fast fading**, the pattern of fading changes as the frequency changes.[2] It is possible for a mobile unit receiving on one frequency and transmitting on another to experience strong fade in one direction only. One way to cope with fast fading is spatial diversity of the antennas. In this scheme, a receiver employs two antennas, spaced ideally at least one wavelength apart. With such a configuration there is a good chance that if one of the antennas is experiencing significant fade, the other is not. The receiver can then select the strongest incoming signal for demodulation. This approach is fine for the base station but is not practical for small, inexpensive handsets. Further, we wish to avoid complex adaptive equalization algorithms or forward error control algorithms. With TDD however, spatial diversity can still be used. For each forward channel burst arriving at the base station, the base station selects the antenna with the stronger signal for reception. The base station then uses that same antenna for the next transmission on the corresponding forward channel. Because the same frequency is used in both directions, this antenna should provide the strongest signal back at the handset.

The other advantage of TDMA/TDD over TDMA/FDMA is in the area of **capacity allocation**. For many data-oriented (as opposed to voice oriented) applications, it is likely that the volume of traffic will be greater in the forward direction than in the reverse direction. If a conventional FDMA scheme is used, with equal bandwidth on forward and reverse channels, then the system must be sized for the forward channel and capacity on the reverse channel is wasted. On a TDD system, it is possible for a controller to allocate dynamically the number of TDMA slots in each direction so that more slots are available on the forward channel when needed.

DECT Operation

Figure 11.2 indicates the protocol architecture that supports DECT operations. At the **physical layer**, data are transmitted in the TDMA-TDD frames over one of 10 RF carriers. The modulation method is Gaussian-filtered FSK, with a nominal deviation of 288 kHz. This is essentially the same as the GMSK technique used for GSM (Chapter 10). The ratio of data rate to transmission bandwidth is 2 (compare Table 6.2), and the data rate is 1.152 Mbps.

The **medium access control (MAC) layer** selects the physical channels and then establishes or releases connections on those channels. It also multiplexes

[2]See Section 5.4 for a discussion of fast fading.

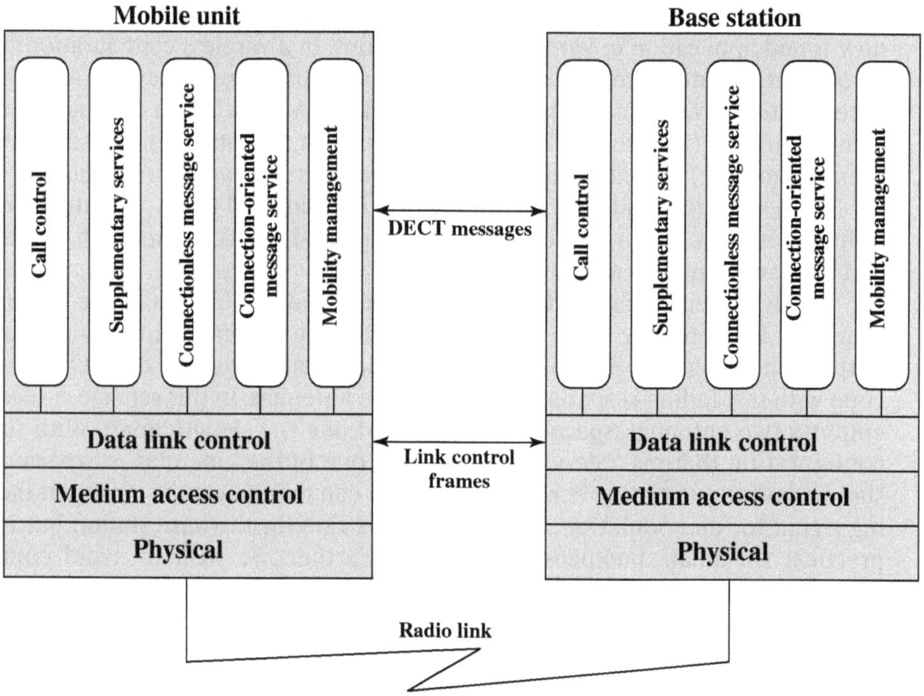

Figure 11.2 DECT Protocol Architecture

information into the TDMA-TDD frame format. The MAC layer supports three services:

- **Broadcast:** Broadcast messages sent in the A field
- **Connection oriented:** Transfer of user data in the B field
- **Connectionless:** Supports individual DECT messages sent in the A field

The data link control layer provides for the reliable transmission of messages using traditional data link control procedures, including error detection and automatic repeat request.[3]

Above the data link control layer are a set of services:

- **Call control:** Manages circuit-switched calls, including connection setup and release.
- **Supplementary services:** Services independent of any call that support operations.
- **Connectionless message service:** Support of connectionless messages. This service will segment longer messages into smaller blocks for transmission and reassemble at reception, if necessary.
- **Connection-oriented message service:** Support of connection-oriented messages.

[3]See Appendix C for a general discussion of data link control protocols.

- **Mobility management:** Handles functions necessary for the secure provision of DECT services. Mobility management is organized into seven groups of services:
  - **Identity procedures:** Used for the mobile unit to identify itself to the base station
  - **Authentication procedure:** Establishes that the mobile unit is a valid network user
  - **Location procedure:** Used in systems with multiple base stations to track the location of a mobile unit
  - **Access rights procedure:** Establishes that the mobile unit has the right to gain access to a specific type of local or global network
  - **Key allocation procedure:** Distributes encryption keys for protecting network control information and user information
  - **Parameter retrieval procedure:** Used to exchange information about the parameters of the mobile unit and network operation
  - **Ciphering-related procedure:** Encryption and decryption operations

Adaptive Differential Pulse Code Modulation

For voice digitization, DECT makes use of a procedure known as ADPCM. ADPCM has been standardized by ITU-T and is used in a number of applications, including digital circuit-switched networks such as ISDN, and in a number of wireless local loop implementations. We first look at the basic principles involved, then describe the simpler differential PCM (DPCM) scheme, and finally examine ADPCM.[4]

Differential Quantization Differential quantization is based on the principle that speech signals tend not to change much between two samples. Thus, with ordinary PCM, the quantized values of adjacent samples will generally be near to one another and the transmitted PCM values contain considerable redundancy. Hence, it might make sense to transmit only the difference value between adjacent samples rather than the actual value, leading to the use of fewer bits per sample (Figure 11.3). Thus, if $m(k)$ is the kth sample, we transmit the difference $d(k) = m(k) - m(k - 1)$. If the receiver starts with the correct initial value, then on the basis of the sequence of difference samples $d(k)$, it can reconstruct the sequence of samples $m(k)$.

However, if we merely transmit the difference between the current and the immediately preceding samples, using fewer bits, there is the danger that the output at the receiver will begin to drift away from the true value at an increasing amount. If the difference value between two samples exceeds that which can be represented by the bits transmitted, then the receiver will err in reproducing the input and there is no way to make a correction subsequently. As a way to address this problem, the encoder could not only transmit a difference value; it could also replicate the decoding function that takes place at the receiver. The encoder could then transmit the difference between the current sample and what the encoder knows is the receiver's output from the previous transmission. In effect, the encoder is instructing the decoder to make incremental adjustments to its previous output, thus automatically providing a correction.

---

[4]Before proceeding, the reader may wish to review the discussion of PCM in Section 6.4.

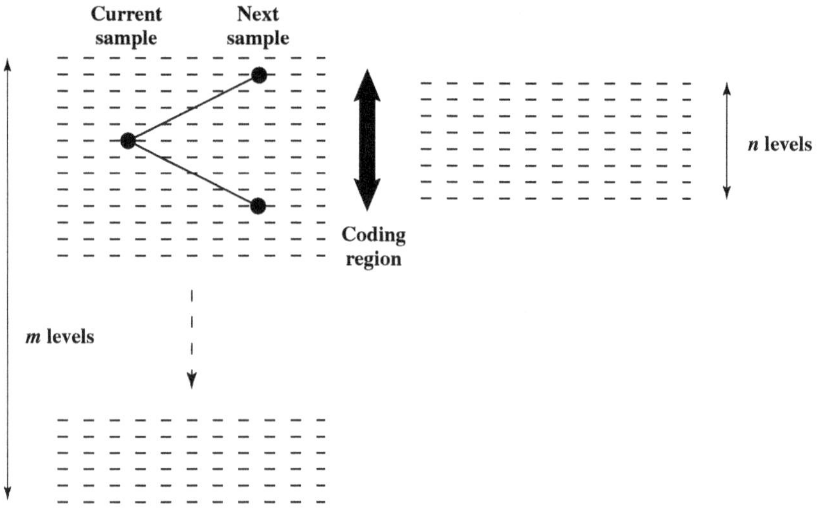

Figure 11.3 Normal and Differential Quantization

Differential PCM The scheme that has just been described is based on the assumption that difference values will be less than sample values. We can do even better than that by recognizing that voice signals change relatively slowly and therefore we can fairly accurately estimate, or predict, the value of the kth sample $m(k)$ from the values of the preceding samples. For an estimate of the kth sample, $\hat{m}(k)$, we then transmit the difference $d(k) = m(k) - \hat{m}(k)$. If we use an accurate estimator, this difference value should be less than the difference between successive samples. At the receiver, the same estimation function is used and the incoming difference value is added to the estimate of the current sample. This is the principle behind differential PCM (DPCM). Note that the simple difference scheme of the preceding paragraph is just a special case of DPCM in which we use the estimator $\hat{m}(k) = m(k - 1)$.

Figure 11.4a is a block diagram of the transmitter. An understanding of this diagram takes some discussion. To begin, an analog sample $m(k)$ is taken of the voice signal $g(t)$; this is a pulse amplitude modulation (PAM) sample. We are now faced with a difficulty. We could construct a predicted value $\hat{m}(k)$, take the difference, and transmit that. However, at the receiving end, instead of the past analog samples $m(k - 1), m(k - 2)$, and so on, what we have is the sequence of quantized differences from which we could construct a sequence of quantized samples, $m_q(k)$. So we cannot reconstruct $\hat{m}(k)$ but can only determine $\hat{m}_q(k)$, the estimate of the quantized sample $m_q(k)$, with the estimate based on the preceding quantized samples $m_q(k - 1)$, $m_q(k - 2)$, and so on. If the transmitter is basing its prediction on values of $m(k)$ and the receiver is basing its prediction on values of $m_q(k)$, there is an error introduced in reconstruction. Instead, the transmitter should also determine $m_q(k)$ and transmit the difference $d(k) = m(k) - \hat{m}_q(k)$. As we have just seen, the receiver can also generate $\hat{m}_q(k)$, and from the received $d_q(k)$, the receiver can reconstruct $m_q(k)$.

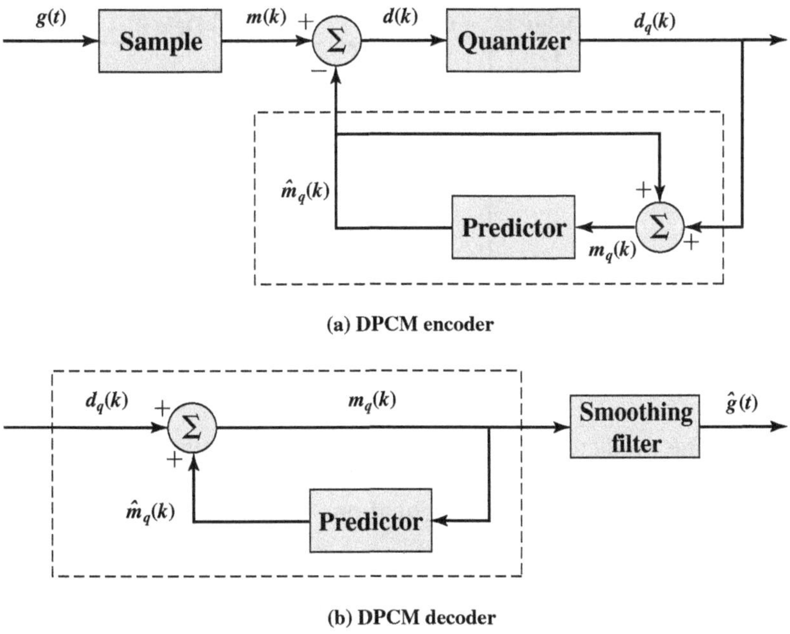

Figure 11.4 DPCM Transmitter and Receiver

It remains to show that Figure 11.4a produces the desired quantized differences. The output of the predictor is designated $\hat{m}_q(k)$, the predicted value of $m(k)$. The difference is taken to produce

$$d(k) = m(k) - \hat{m}_q(k)$$

This difference is then quantized to produce $d_q(k)$. We can express this as

$$d_q(k) = d(k) + e(k)$$

where $e(k)$ is the quantization error that results from approximating the analog $d(k)$ by the digital $d_q(k)$. The input to the predictor consists of this quantized difference plus the predictor output, which is fed back to become part of the input:

$$\begin{aligned} m_q(k) &= \hat{m}_q(k) + d_q(k) \\ &= [m(k) - d(k)] + [d(k) + q(k)] \\ &= m(k) + q(k) \end{aligned}$$

This demonstrates that $m_q(k)$ is a quantized version of $m(k)$. Therefore, the input to the predictor is the desired $m_q(k)$, which is what is needed for operation at the receiver. Figure 11.4b shows the logic at the receiver. The portion of the receiver in the dashed box is the same as the portion of the transmitter in the dashed box. The two dashed boxes have the same input, $d_q(k)$, and therefore produce the same output, $m_q(k)$. At the receiver, this output is passed through a filter to produce an analog output that is an estimate of the original analog source.

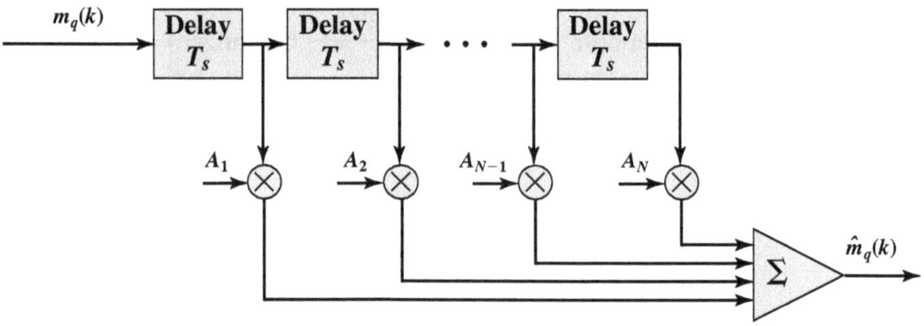

Figure 11.5 Linear Predictor Circuit

The predictor is often the linear weighted sum of previous samples, implemented using shift registers, and a delay equal to the sample interval (Figure 11.5). The predictor implements the equation

$$\hat{m}_q(k) = \sum_{i=1}^{N} A_i m_q(k - i) \tag{11.1}$$

For a further discussion of linear predictors, see Appendix 11A.

Adaptive Differential PCM The performance of DPCM can be improved by using adaptive prediction and quantization, so that the predictor and difference quantize adapt to the changing characteristics of the speech being coded. In this subsection, we describe the ADPCM scheme standardized by ITU-T in Recommendation G.726,[5] which is used in DECT and in a number of wireless local loop schemes.

Figure 11.6 shows the basic ADPCM logic. The transmitter converts a 64 kbps digitized voice stream into a compressed 32-kbps stream. The overall block diagram is the same as that for DPCM. In this case, the adaptive predictor makes use not only of previous predictor output values but also previous quantized difference values. In both the predictor and the quantizer, parameter values of the algorithms are dynamically adjusted based on the statistical properties of previous samples. As with DPCM, the heart of the decoder is a replication of part of the logic of the encoder.

The **adaptive quantizer** takes as input the difference $d(k)$ between the PCM signal $s(k)$ and the signal estimate $s_e(k)$ and produces a 4-bit (3 for the magnitude and 1 for the sign) output ADPCM $I(k)$. The first two columns of Table 11.2 show the mapping. Prior to quantization, $d(k)$ is converted to a base 2 logarithmic representation and scaled by $y(k)$, which is an adaptation factor based on the rate of change of the signal over recent samples. The result is then mapped into 4 bits for transmission as the ADPCM signal.

[5] *General Aspects of Digital Transmission Systems; Terminal Equipments: 40, 32, 20, 16 kbit/s ADPCM.* 1990.

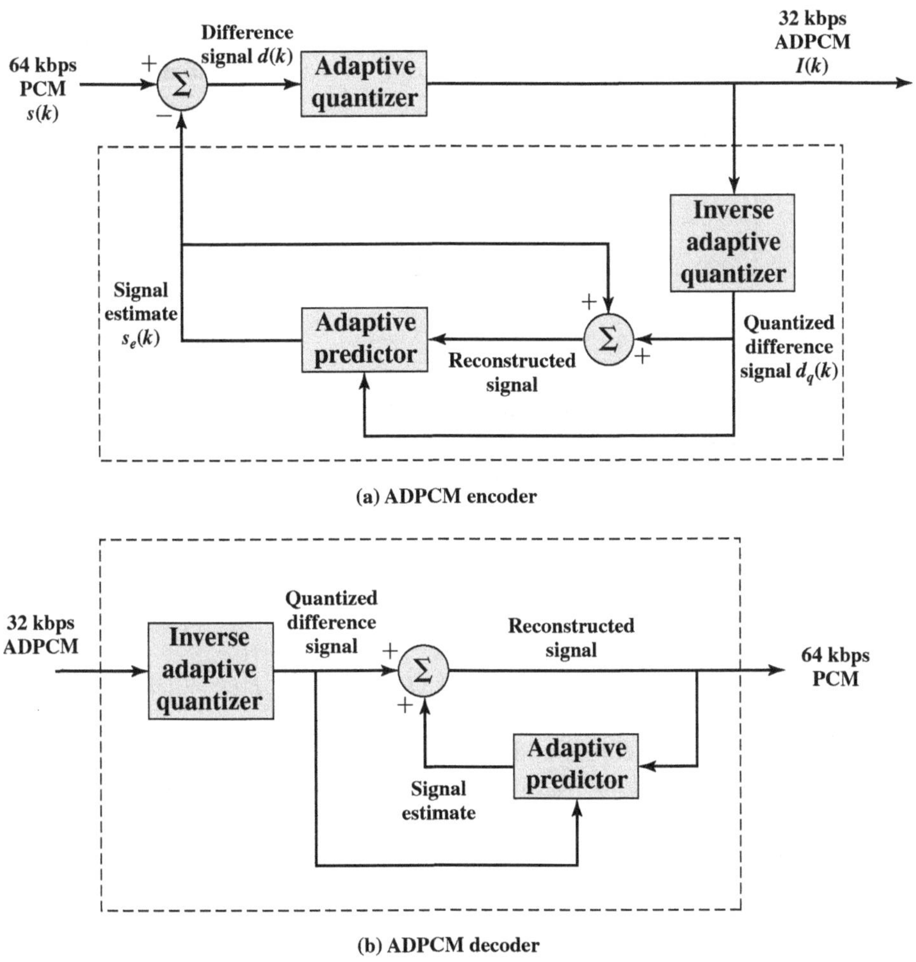

Figure 11.6 Simplified ADPCM Transmitter and Receiver

Table 11.2 ADPCM Quantizer Normalized Input/Output Characteristics

Normalized quantizer input range $\log_2\lvert d(k)\rvert - y(k)$	Adapter quantizer output $I(k)$	Inverse adapter quantizer output $d_q(k)$
$[3.12, +\infty)$	7	3.32
$[2.72, 3.12)$	6	2.91
$[2.34, 2.72)$	5	2.52
$[1.91, 2.34)$	4	2.13
$[1.38, 1.91)$	3	1.66
$[0.62, 1.38)$	2	1.05
$[-0.98, 0.62)$	1	0.031
$(-\infty, -0.98)$	0	$-\infty$

Table 11.3 Mean Opinion Score (MOS) Values

Number Score	Quality Scale	Impairment Scale
5	Excellent	Imperceptible
4	Good	(Just) perceptible but not annoying
3	Fair	(Perceptible and) slightly annoying
2	Poor	Annoying (but not objectionable)
1	Unsatisfactory	Very annoying (objectionable)

The **inverse adaptive quantizer** takes the 4-bit signal $I(k)$ and produces a difference signal $d_q(k)$, which serves as input to the adaptive predictor. The second and third columns of Table 11.3 show the mapping.

The **adaptive predictor** has the structure of a linear predictor (Figure 11.5) but is more complex than for DPCM. For ADPCM, the structure is a combination of a second-order recursive filter and a sixth-order nonrecursive filter. The equation is [compare Equation (11.1)]

$$s_e(k) = \sum_{i=1}^{2} A_i(k-i)s_e(k-i) + \sum_{i=1}^{6} B_i(k-i)d_q(k-i) \qquad (11.2)$$

where the coefficients A and B are updated using algorithms that adapt to the rate of change of the s_e and d_q samples. Thus, the adaptive predictor is adjusted to adapt to the rate of change of the difference samples as well as the rate of change of the signal estimates.

Subjective Measurement of Coder Performance The goal of speech coding is to exploit signal redundancies, signal structure, and knowledge of human perception to code the signal to various bit rates while maintaining as high a quality as possible. In assessing the performance of a speech coder, subjective measurements of quality are more relevant than objective measures such as SNR or the mean square error. However, reliable values of subjective measurements are in general more difficult to obtain.

The most widely used subjective measurement as a standard for determining quality of service is the mean opinion score (MOS), obtained from formal subjective testing [DAUM82]. For the MOS measurement, a group of subjects listens to a sample of coded speech, and each classifies the output on a 5-point scale. To enhance the reliability of the test, it is repeated with various speech samples and with various groups of subjects. The MOS scale is used in a number of specifications as a standard for quality (e.g., IEEE 802.16; described in Section 11.3).

Table 11.3 shows the scale that is used, with two alternative but equivalent interpretations. Figure 11.7 illustrates the MOS results reported in [RABI95] for various speech coders, including ADPCM. Note that even uncoded speech does not get a full rating of 5. This is because subjects may sometimes award a score of 4 to a

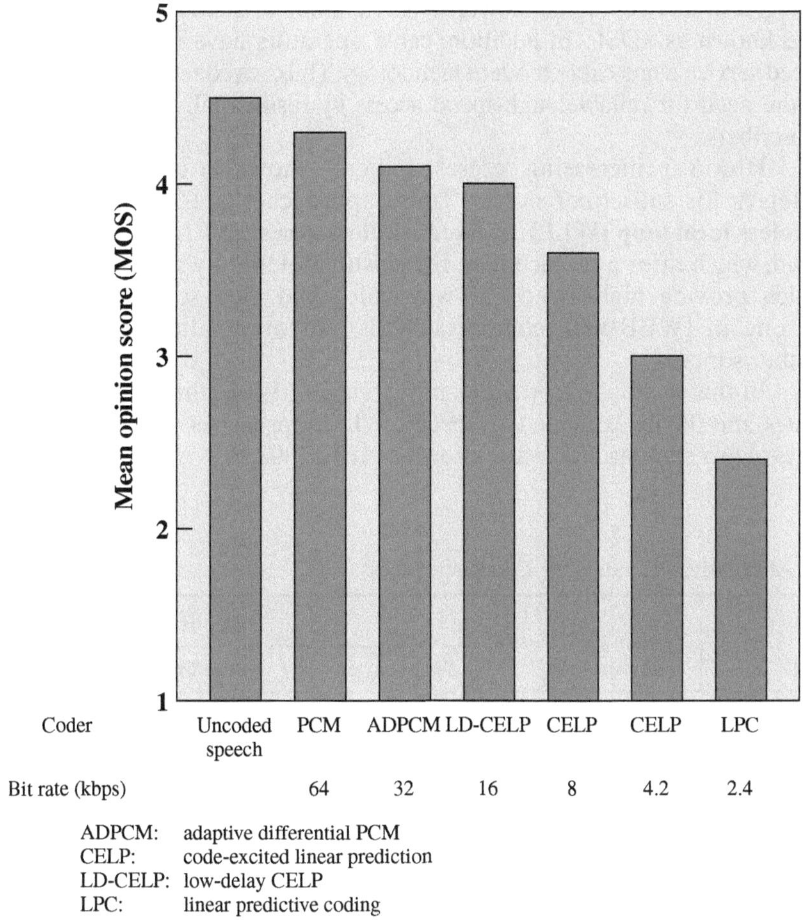

Figure 11.7 Subjective Speech Quality for Various Speech Coders

sample that ideally deserves a 5 [JAYA84]. With this phenomenon in mind, a score of 4.0 to 4.5 is a very useful indicator of high-quality digitization.

11.2 WIRELESS LOCAL LOOP

Traditionally, the provision of voice and data communications to the end user, over the local loop, or subscriber loop, has been provided by wired systems. For residential subscribers, twisted pair has been and continues to be the standard means of connection. For business and government subscribers, twisted pair, coaxial cable, and optical fiber are in use.

As subscribers have demanded greater capacity, particularly to support Internet use, traditional twisted pair technology has become inadequate. Telecommunications providers have developed a number of technologies to meet the need, including ISDN (integrated services digital network), and a family of digital subscriber loop technologies, known as xDSL. In addition, cable operators have introduced two-way high-speed service using cable modem technology. Thus, wired technologies are responding to the need for reliable, high-speed access by residential, business, and government subscribers.

However, increasing interest is being shown in competing wireless technologies for subscriber access. These approaches are generally referred to as **wireless local loop (WLL)**, or **fixed wireless access**. WLL alternatives are narrowband, which offer a replacement for existing telephony services, and broadband,[6] which provide high-speed two-way voice and data service. Table 11.4, based on one in [WEBB00], compares WLL and other alternatives for fixed subscriber support.

In this section, we provide an overview of WLL, then look at some technical issues, and finally examine two specific WLL approaches. Section 11.3 is devoted to an evolving standard for WLL known as IEEE 802.16.

Table 11.4 Alternative Providers for End User Access

		Application		
Entity	**Technology**	**Telephony**	**Broadcast**	**Computer**
Public telephone	Twisted pair, ISDN, xDSL	One and two lines	Video on demand	High-speed asymmetrical access
Cable operator	Coaxial cable	One and two lines	50+ channels	High-speed asymmetrical
Cellular provider	Cellular and cordless	One line	No	Limited but mobility
3G Cellular provider	Cellular	One line	No	High-speed asymmetrical access
Narrowband WLL operator	Wireless	Two lines	No	64-kbps access
Broadband WLL operator	Wireless	Yes	50+ channels	High-speed asymmetrical or symmetrical access
Terrestrial broadcast	Analog and digital TV	No	5 to 10 channels	Some download potential
Satellite broadcast	Analog and digital	No	50+ channels	No

[6]The term *broadband* is not precise. Generally, it refers to systems that provide user data rates of greater than 2 Mbps, up to 100s of Mbps.

The Role of WLL

Figure 11.8 illustrates a simple WLL configuration. A WLL provider services one or more cells. Each cell includes a base station antenna, mounted on top of a tall building or tower. Individual subscribers have a fixed antenna mounted on a building or pole that has an unobstructed line of sight to the base station antenna. From the base station, there is a link, which may either be wired or wireless, to a switching center. The switching center is typically a telephone company local office, which provides connections to the local and long-distance telephone networks. An Internet service provider (ISP) may be collocated at the switch or connected to the switch by a high-speed link.

Figure 11.8 shows what amounts to a two-level hierarchy. More complex configurations have also been implemented, in which a base station may serve a number of subordinate base station antennas, each of which supports a number of subscribers.

The WLL has a number of advantages over a wired approach to subscriber loop support:

- **Cost:** Wireless systems are less expensive than wired systems. Although the electronics of the wireless transmitter/receiver may be more expensive than those used for wired communications, with WLL the cost of installing kilometers of cable, either underground or on poles, is avoided, as well as the cost of maintaining the wired infrastructure.
- **Installation time:** WLL systems typically can be installed rapidly. The key stumbling blocks are obtaining permission to use a given frequency band and finding a suitable elevated site for the base station antennas. Once these hurdles are cleared, a WLL system can be installed in a small fraction of the time required for a new wired system.

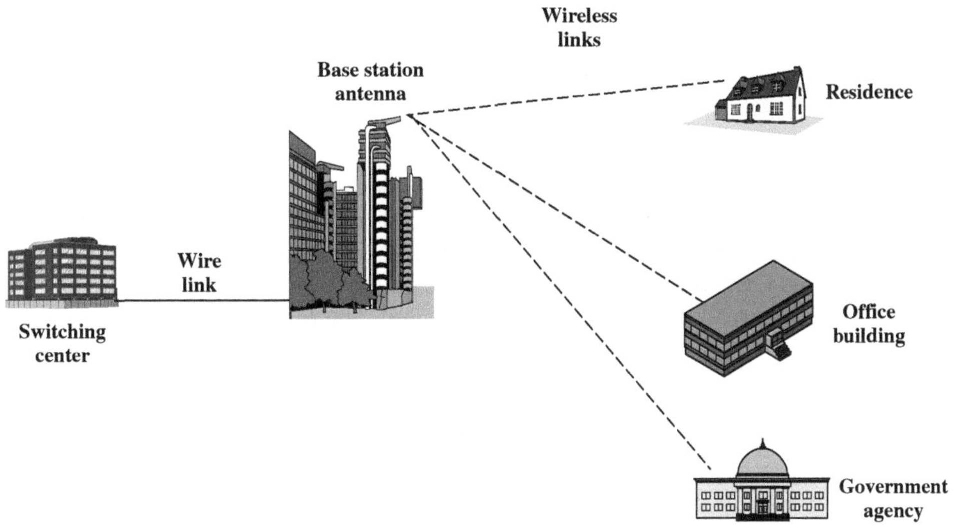

Figure 11.8 WLL Configuration

- **Selective installation:** Radio units are installed only for those subscribers who want the service at a given time. With a wired system, typically cable is laid out in anticipation of serving every subscriber in a local area.

WLL needs to be evaluated with respect to two alternatives:

- **Wired scheme using existing installed cable:** A large fraction of the earth's inhabitants do not have a telephone line. For high-speed applications, many subscribers with telephone lines do not have a line of sufficient quality or are too far from the central office to effectively use xDSL. Many of these same subscribers also do not have cable TV or their cable provider does not offer two-way data services. Finally, because WLL has become cost-competitive with wired schemes, new installations face a genuine choice between the wired and wireless approaches.
- **Mobile cellular technology:** Current cellular systems are too expensive and do not provide sufficient facilities to act as a realistic alternative to WLL. Even when 3G systems become available, they are likely to be more expensive and less functional than broadband WLL alternatives. A major advantage of WLL over mobile cellular is that, because the subscriber unit is fixed, the subscriber can use a directional antenna pointed at the base station antenna, providing improved signal quality in both directions.

In the United States, the Federal Communications Commission has set aside 15 frequency bands for use in commercial fixed wireless service, at frequencies of 2 to 40 GHz. In other countries, similar frequency bands have been allocated. Note that these frequencies are considerably higher than those used for cellular systems. At these frequencies, often referred to as millimeter wave frequencies, propagation characteristics are quite different from those in the MHz ranges. We look at propagation considerations next. Then we introduce a technique that is used in a number of WLL systems, known as orthogonal FDM (OFDM). Finally, we examine the two approaches of most interest for the WLL application: local multipoint distribution service (LMDS) and multichannel multipoint distribution service (MMDS).

Propagation Considerations for WLL

For most high-speed WLL schemes, frequencies in what is referred to as the millimeter wave region are used. Although the term *millimeter wave* is not precisely defined, a common boundary is 10 GHz; that is, frequencies above 10 GHz, up to about 300 GHz, are considered to be in the millimeter wave region.[7] The reasons for using frequencies in this range for WLL include the following:

1. There are wide unused frequency bands available above 25 GHz.
2. At these high frequencies, wide channel bandwidths can be used, providing high data rates.
3. Small size transceivers and adaptive antenna arrays can be used.

---

[7]The free space wavelength at 10 GHz is 30 mm, and at 300 GHz is 1 mm.

However, millimeter wave systems have some undesirable propagation characteristics:

1. Free space loss increases with the square of the frequency [Equation (5.2)]; thus losses are much higher in this range than in the ranges used for traditional microwave systems.
2. Generally, below 10 GHz, we can ignore attenuation due to rainfall and atmospheric or gaseous absorption. Above 10 GHz, these attenuation effects are large.
3. Multipath losses can be quite high. As was pointed out in Chapter 5, reflection occurs when an electromagnetic signal encounters a surface that is large relative to the wavelength of the signal; scattering occurs if the size of an obstacle is on the order of the wavelength of the signal or less; diffraction occurs when the wavefront encounters the edge of an obstacle that is large compared to the wavelength.

Because of these negative propagation characteristics, WLL systems can only serve cells of a limited radius, usually just a few kilometers. Also, obstructions, including foliage, must be avoided along or near the line of sight. Finally, rainfall and humidity effects limit the range and availability of WLL systems.

Fresnel Zone For effective communication at millimeter wavelengths, there should be an unobstructed line of sight between transmitter and receiver. The question then arises as to how much space around the direct path between transmitter and receiver should be clear of obstacles. A useful criterion relates to the concept of the Fresnel zone.

The definition of Fresnel zones is based on the theory that any small element of space in the path of an electromagnetic wave may be considered the source of secondary wavelet, and that the radiated field can be built up by the superposition of all these wavelets. On the basis of this theory, it can be shown that objects lying within a series of concentric circles around the direct line of sight between two transceivers have constructive or destructive effects on communication. Those that fall within the first circle, the first Fresnel zone, have the most serious negative effects.

Consider a point along the direct path between a transmitter and receiver, that is, a distance S from the transmitter and a distance D from the receiver, with the total distance along the path equal to $S + D$ (Figure 11.9). Then the radius of the first Fresnel zone at that point is

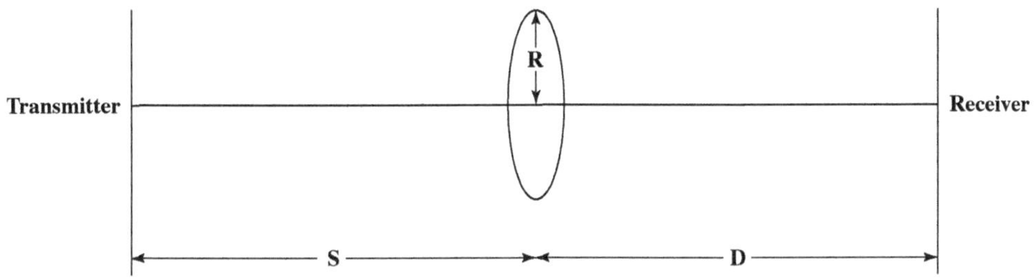

Figure 11.9 The First Fresnel Zone

$$R = \sqrt{\frac{\lambda SD}{S + D}}$$

where R, S, D, and λ are in the same units, and λ is the wavelength of the signal along the path. For convenience, this can be restated as

$$R_m = 17.3\sqrt{\frac{1}{f_{GHz}} \frac{S_{km}D_{km}}{S_{km} + D_{km}}}$$

where R is expressed in meters, the two distances are in kilometers, and the signal frequency is in gigahertz.

Example 11.2 Suppose the distance between the two transceivers is 10 km and the carrier frequency is 2.4 GHz. Then the radius of the first Fresnel zone at the midpoint between the two transceivers is 17.66 m. If the signal frequency is 28 GHz, then the radius at the same point is reduced to 5.17 m. Now consider a point along the path that is 1 km from one of the transceivers. Then, at 28 GHz, the radius is 3.1 m.

It has been found that if there is no obstruction within about 0.6 times the radius of the first Fresnel zone at any point between the two transceivers, then attenuation due to obstructions is negligible [FREE97]. One noteworthy example of an obstruction is the ground. Hence, the height of the two antennas must be such that there is no point along the path at which the ground is within 0.6 times the radius of the first Fresnel zone.

Atmospheric Absorption At frequencies above 10 GHz, radio waves propagating through the atmosphere are subject to molecular absorption. The absorption as a function of frequency is very uneven, as shown in Figure 11.10. There is a peak of water vapor absorption at around 22 GHz and a peak of oxygen absorption near 60 GHz. This figure suggests that there is a favorable window for communication roughly from 28 GHz to 42 GHz, where the attenuation is on the order of 0.13 dB/km, and another favorable window from 75 GHz to 95 GHz, where the attenuation is on the order of 0.4 dB/km.

However, Figure 11.10 only shows the absorption effects at a particular temperature, relative humidity, and atmospheric pressure. Although the shapes of these two curves remain the same, the actual values vary, especially with temperature and relative humidity. Table 11.5, taken from [DALK96], shows the effects of temperature and humidity.

Example 11.3 Consider a 6-km communication link at 28 GHz. What is the free space loss? What is the additional loss due to atmospheric absorption on a hot, muggy day with a temperature of 30° and a relative humidity of 100%?

From Equation (5.2), free space loss is $20\log(f) + 20\log(d) - 147.56 = 136.95$ dB. The additional loss due to atmospheric absorption is $6 \times 0.44 = 2.64$ dB.

Effect of Rain One of the most serious concerns for millimeter wave propagation is attenuation due to rain. The presence of raindrops can severely degrade the

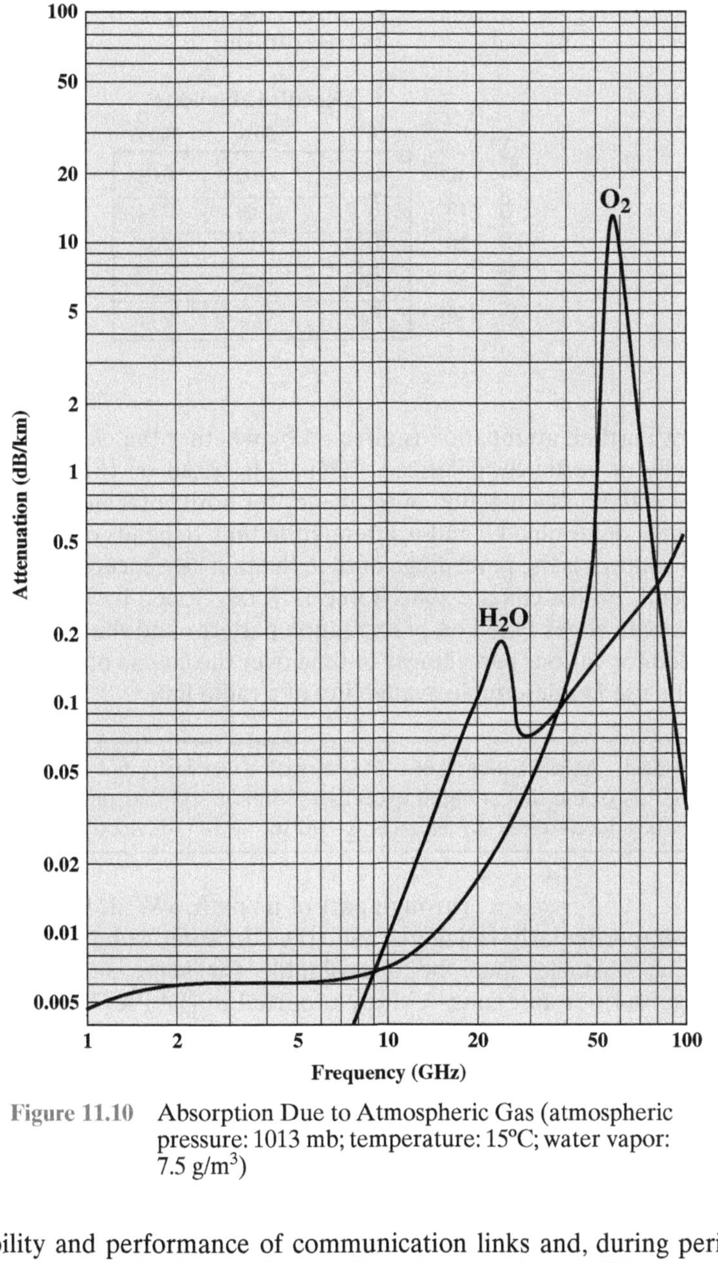

Figure 11.10 Absorption Due to Atmospheric Gas (atmospheric pressure: 1013 mb; temperature: 15ºC; water vapor: 7.5 g/m^3)

reliability and performance of communication links and, during periods of heavy rain, may outweigh all other factors. The effect of rain on millimeter wave propagation is complex, depending on drop shape, drop size, rain rate, and frequency. A widely used formula for estimating attenuation due to rain is

$$A = aR^b \tag{11.3}$$

where the attenuation is in units of dB/km, the rain rate R is measured in mm/hr, and the parameters a and b depend on the distribution of drop sizes and on

Table 11.5 Clear Air Absorption at 28 GHz (dB/km)

Temperature (°C)	Relative Humidity 0%	50%	100%
0°	0.02	0.05	0.08
10°	0.02	0.08	0.14
20°	0.02	0.12	0.25
30°	0.02	0.20	0.44
40°	0.01	0.33	0.79

frequency. Further, attenuation is affected by whether the electromagnetic wave is horizontally or vertically polarized. Table 11.6, based on [FREE97], gives typical values for a and b as a function of frequency for horizontal and vertical waves.

Having determined a and b, attenuation then depends on the rain rate R. The principal concern is the percentage of time the rain rate exceeds a certain threshold. This depends on the climate zone. Table 11.7, developed by ITU, divides the earth into 15 climate zones based on precipitation patterns and shows the value of R that is exceeded for various percentages of time over the course of a year. Such information can be used to determine availability of a radio link.

Example 11.4 At a frequency of 30 GHz, with a vertically polarized wave, in climate zone P, 0.01% of the time, rainfall exceeds 145 mm/hr. At that rain rate, the attenuation that must be added to free space loss is A = 0.167 × 145 = 24.2 dB/km.

Effects of Vegetation Through part of its path, a WLL link may run through vegetation, particularly foliage of tall trees. In some suburban and small town areas, such obstacles may be unavoidable for some subscribers, even with rooftop subscriber antennas. A study reported in [PAPA97] reached the following conclusions:

Table 11.6 Coefficients for Estimating Attenuation Due to Rain

Frequency (GHz)	a_h	a_v	b_h	b_v
1	0.0000387	0.0000352	0.912	0.880
2	0.000154	0.000138	0.963	0.923
6	0.00175	0.00155	1.308	1.265
10	0.0101	0.00887	1.276	1.264
20	0.0751	0.0691	1.099	1.065
30	0.187	0.167	1.021	1.000
40	0.350	0.310	0.939	0.929
50	0.536	0.479	0.873	0.868

Table 11.7 Rainfall Intensity Exceeded (mm/hr) for Various Rain Regions

Outage Percentage of Time	Rain Climate Zone														
	A	B	C	D	E	F	G	H	J	K	L	M	N	P	Q
1	0.1	0.5	1	2.1	0.6	2	3	2	8	1.5	2	4	5	12	24
0.3	0.8	2	3	4.5	2.4	5	7	4	13	4.2	7	11	15	34	49
0.1	2	3	5	8	6	8	12	10	20	12	15	22	35	64	72
0.01	8	12	15	19	22	28	30	32	35	42	60	63	95	145	115

1. The presence of trees near subscriber sites can lead to multipath fading.
2. The principal multipath effects from the tree canopy are diffraction and scattering.
3. Measurements in regularly planted orchards have found attenuation values between 12 and 20 dB per tree for deciduous trees and up to 40 dB for 1 to 3 coniferous trees, when the foliage is within 60% of the first Fresnel zone.
4. The multipath effects are highly variable due to wind.

Thus, when installing a WLL system, efforts should be made to avoid the presence of tree foliage within 60% of the first Fresnel zone for each subscriber. However, the presence of trees does not preclude communications, but means that adequate countermeasures, such as forward error correction, are required.

Orthogonal Frequency Division Multiplexing

OFDM, also called multicarrier modulation, uses multiple carrier signals at different frequencies, sending some of the bits on each channel. This is similar to FDM. However, in the case of OFDM, all of the subchannels are dedicated to a single data source.

Figure 11.11 illustrates OFDM. Suppose we have a data stream operating at R bps and an available bandwidth of Nf_b, centered at f_0. The entire bandwidth could be used to send the data stream, in which case each bit duration would be $1/R$. The alternative is to split the data stream into N substreams, using a serial-to-parallel converter. Each substream has a data rate of R/N bps and is transmitted on a separate subcarrier, with a spacing between adjacent subcarriers of f_b. Now the bit duration is N/R.

To gain a clearer understanding of OFDM, let us consider the scheme in terms of its base frequency, f_b. This is the lowest-frequency subcarrier. All of the other subcarriers are integer multiples of the base frequency, namely $2f_b$, $3f_b$, and so on, as shown in Figure 11.12a. The OFDM scheme uses advanced digital signal processing techniques to distribute the data over multiple carriers at precise frequencies. The precise relationship among the subcarriers is referred to as orthogonality. The result, as shown in Figure 11.12b, is that the peaks of the power spectral density of each subcarrier occurs at a point at which the power of other subcarriers is zero. With OFDM, the subcarriers can be packed tightly together because there is minimal interference between adjacent subcarriers.

Note that Figure 11.12 depicts the set of OFDM subcarriers in a frequency band beginning with the base frequency. For transmission, the set of OFDM

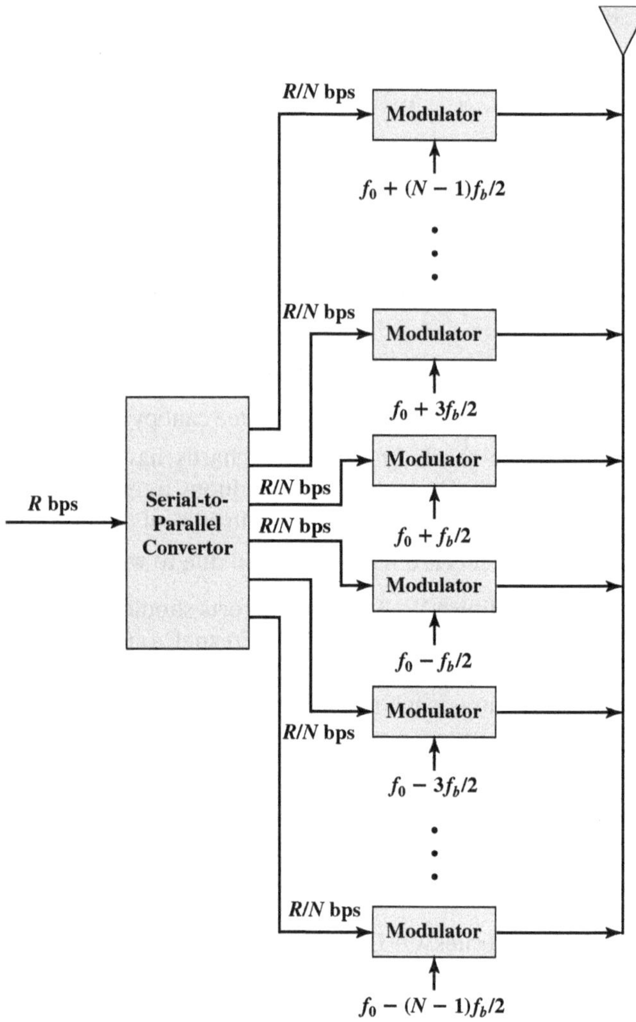

Figure 11.11 Orthogonal Frequency Division Multiplexing

subcarriers is further modulated to a higher frequency band. For example, for the IEEE 802.11a LAN standard, discussed in Chapter 14, the OFDM scheme consists of a set of 52 subcarriers with a base frequency of 0.3125 MHz. This set of subcarriers is then translated to the 5-GHz range for transmission.

OFDM has several advantages. First, frequency selective fading only affects some subchannels and not the whole signal. If the data stream is protected by a forward error-correcting code, this type of fading is easily handled. More important, OFDM overcome intersymbol interference (ISI) in a multipath environment. As discussed in Chapter 5, ISI has a greater impact at higher bit rates, because the distance between bits, or symbols, is smaller. With OFDM, the data rate is reduced by a factor of N, which increases the symbol time by a factor of N. Thus, if the symbol period is T_s for the source stream, the period for the OFDM signals is NT_s. This

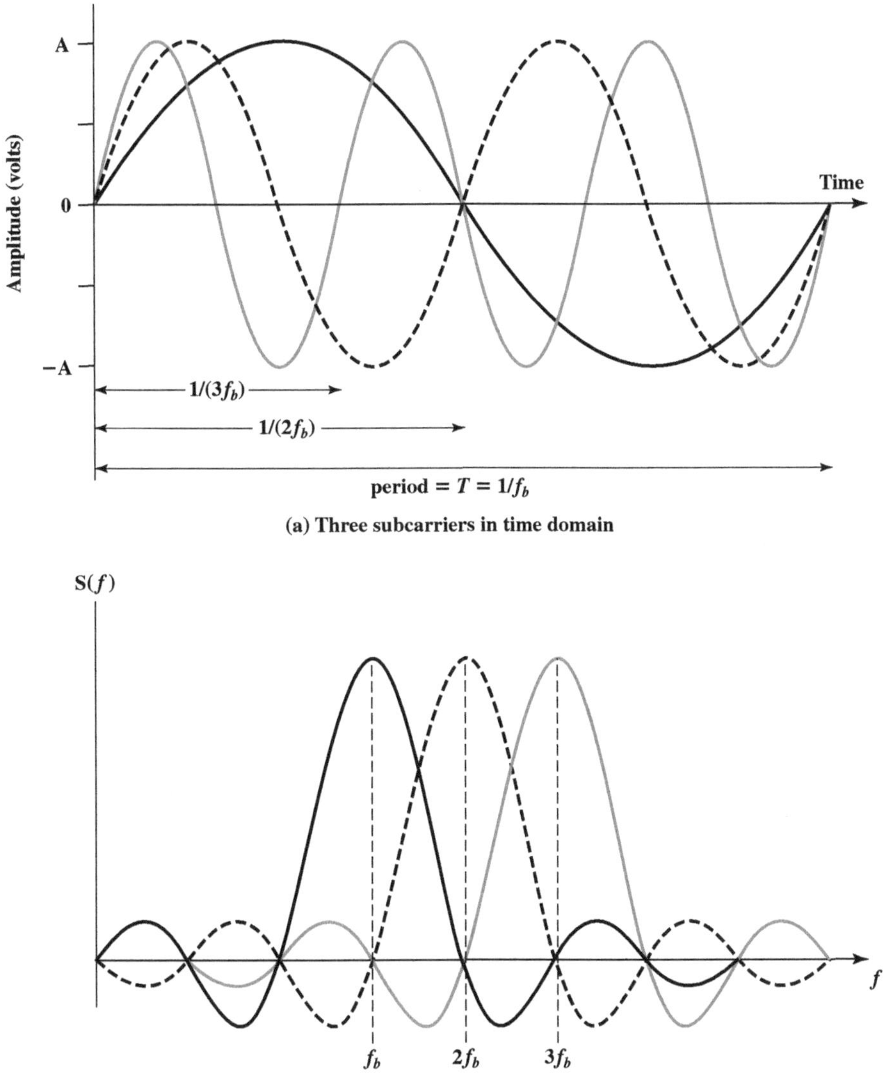

Figure 11.12 Illustration of Orthogonality of OFDM

dramatically reduces the effect of ISI. As a design criterion, N is chosen so that NT_s is significantly greater than the root-mean-square delay spread of the channel.

As a result of these considerations, with the use of OFDM, it may not be necessary to deploy equalizers, which are complex devices whose complexity increases with the number of symbols over which ISI is present.

A common modulation scheme used with OFDM is quadrature phase shift keying (QPSK). In this case, each transmitted symbol represents two bits. An example of an OFDM/QPSK scheme, used in a MMDS system [CISC00], occupies 6 MHz made up of 512 individual carriers, with a carrier separation of a little under 12 kHz. To minimize

ISI, data are transmitted in bursts, with each burst consisting of a cyclic prefix followed by data symbols. The cyclic prefix is used to absorb transients from previous bursts caused by multipath. For this system, 64 symbols constitute the cyclic prefix, followed by 512 QPSK symbols per burst. On each subchannel, therefore, QPSK symbols are separated by a prefix of duration 64/512 symbol times. In general, by the time the prefix is over, the resulting waveform created by the combined multipath signals is not a function of any samples from the previous burst. Hence there is no ISI.

Multichannel Multipoint Distribution Service

Table 11.8 shows five frequency bands in the range 2.15 GHz to 2.68 GHz that have been allocated in the United States for fixed wireless access using MMDS. The first two bands were licensed in the 1970s when they were called multipoint distributions services (MDSs), for broadcast of 6 MHz TV channels. In 1996, the FCC increased the allocation to its present range and allowed for multichannel services, called MMDS. MMDS has been used to compete with cable TV providers and to provide service in rural areas not reached by broadcast TV or cable. For this reason, MMDS is also referred to as *wireless cable.*

The transmitted power allowed by the FCC enables an MMDS base station to service an area with a radius of 50 km, but subscriber antennas must be in the line of

Table 11.8 Fixed Wireless Communications Bands, FCC Allocation

Frequency (GHz)	Usage
2.1500 to 2.1620	Licensed MDS and MMDS; two bands of 6 MHz each
2.4000 to 2.4835	Unlicensed ISM
2.5960 to 2.6440	Licensed MMDS; eight bands of 6 MHz each
2.6500 to 2.6560	Licensed MMDS
2.6620 to 2.6680	Licensed MMDS
2.6740 to 2.6800	Licensed MMDS
5.7250 to 5.8750	Unlicensed ISM-UNII
24.000 to 24.250	Unlicensed ISM
24.250 to 25.250	Licensed
27.500 to 28.350	Licensed LMDS (Block A)
29.100 to 29.250	Licensed LMDS (Block A)
31.000 to 31.075	Licensed LMDS (Block B)
31.075 to 31.225	Licensed LMDS (Block A)
31.225 to 31.300	Licensed LMDS (Block B)
38.600 to 40.000	Licensed

ISM = industrial, scientific, and medical

LMDS = local multipoint distribution service

MDS = multipoint distribution service

MMDS = multichannel multipointatribution service

UNII = unlicensed national information infrastructure

sight. MMDS can be used to support two-way services. MMDS is also used in other countries for two-way access. Thus, MMDS is an alternative for broadband data services, such as Internet access.

The principal disadvantage of MMDS, compared to LMDS, which we discuss next, is that at the lower frequency of MMDS, it offers much less bandwidth than LMDS. With current technology, a single MMDS channel can offer upstream (subscriber to base station) transfer rates of 27 Mbps, with individual subscriber rates of 300 kbps to 3 Mbps [ORTI00]. However, developments in OFDM may allow higher data rates or more subscriber support for upstream MMDS. In any case, because of its lesser bandwidth, MMDS is likely to be used mainly by residential subscribers and small businesses, whereas LMDS appeals to larger companies with greater bandwidth demands.

The advantages of MMDS over LMDS include the following:

1. MMDS signals have larger wavelengths (greater than 10 cm) and can travel farther without losing significant power. Hence MMDS can operate in considerably larger cells, thereby lowering base station equipment costs.
2. Equipment at lower frequencies is less expensive, yielding cost savings at both the subscriber and base station.
3. MMDS signals don't get blocked as easily by objects and are less susceptible to rain absorption.

Local Multipoint Distribution Service

LMDS is a relatively new WLL service to deliver TV signals and two-way broadband communications, operating at millimeter frequencies. In the United States, LMDS will be offered at frequencies near 30 GHz; in Europe and some other areas, frequencies near 40 GHz will be used. Table 11.8 shows frequency bands that have been allocated in the United States for fixed wireless access using LMDS.

LMDS has the following advantages:

- Relatively high data rates, in the Mbps range
- Capable of providing video, telephony, and data
- Relatively low cost in comparison with cable alternatives

The principal disadvantage of LMDS is the short range from the base station, requiring a relatively large number of base stations to service a given area.

In a typical system, the base station antenna is located on top of a tall building or high pole overlooking the service area, with line of sight to subscribers with the possible exception of tree canopies. The base station antenna covers a sector 60° to 90° wide. Thus, full coverage requires 4 to 6 antennas. A radius of 2 to 4 km is typical. With the bandwidths available, an upstream data rate from the subscriber of up to 1 Mbps is reasonable, with a downstream capacity of 36 Mbps.

An important consideration is that LMDS's short-wavelength signals cannot pass around or penetrate objects like buildings, walls, or thick foliage. A certain amount of foliage can be tolerated, as is discussed earlier in this section, but dense foliage may require other countermeasures. By overlapping cell coverage, it may be possible to obtain coverage in shielded areas in one cell from the base station of a neighboring cell. Use of repeaters or reflectors is another possibility.

11.3 WIMAX AND IEEE 802.16 BROADBAND WIRELESS ACCESS STANDARDS

With the growing interest in LMDS WLL services, a need was recognized within the industry to develop standards for this service. In response to this need the IEEE 802 committee set up the 802.16 working group in 1999 to develop broadband wireless standards. The charter for the group is to develop standards that [MARK99]

- Use wireless links with microwave or millimeter wave radios
- Use licensed spectrum (typically)
- Are metropolitan in scale
- Provide public network service to fee-paying customers (typically)
- Use point-to-multipoint architecture with stationary rooftop or tower-mounted antennas
- Provide efficient transport of heterogeneous traffic supporting quality of service (QoS)
- Are capable of broadband transmissions (>2 Mbps)

In essence, IEEE 802.16 standardizes the air interface and related functions associated with LMDS. As of this writing, standards have been developed in the areas indicated in Table 11.9. In addition, an industry group, the WiMAX (World-wide Interoperability for Microwave Access) Forum, has been formed to promote the 802.16 standards and to develop interoperability specifications.

The work on 802.16 in Table 11.9 is the farthest along and is the one most likely to generate the most industry interest, as it is targeted at available LMDS frequency bands. In this section, we provide an overview of 802.16 architecture and services and then look in more detail at the 802.16 specification. Finally, a summary of the 802.16a standard is presented.

IEEE 802.16 Architecture

System Reference Architecture The 802.16 standards are designed with respect to the abstract system reference model shown in Figure 11.13. An 802.16 wireless

Table 11.9 IEEE 802.16 Standards

Standard	Scope
IEEE 802.16	Medium access control (MAC): one common MAC for wireless MAN standards Physical layer: 10 to 66 GHz
IEEE 802.16a	MAC modifications to 802.16.1 Physical layer: 2 to 11 GHz
IEEE 802.16c	Detailed System Profiles for 10–66 GHz
IEEE 802.16e	Physical and Medium Access Control Layers for Combined Fixed and Mobile Operation in Licensed Bands
IEEE 802.16.2	Coexistence of Fixed Broadband Wireless Access Systems

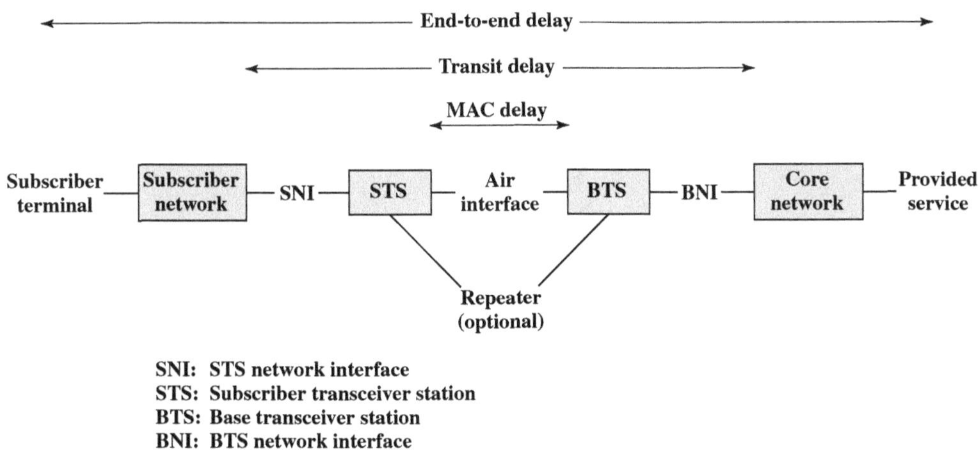

Figure 11.13 IEEE 802.16 System Reference Points

service provides a communications path between a subscriber site, which may be either a single subscriber device or a network on the subscriber's premises (e.g., a LAN, PBX, IP-based network) and a core network (the network to which 802.16 is providing access). Examples of a core network are the public telephone network and the Internet. Three interfaces are defined in this model. IEEE 802.16 standards are concerned with the air interface between the subscriber's transceiver station and the base transceiver station. The standards specify all the details of that interface, as discussed subsequently in this subsection. The system reference model also shows interfaces between the transceiver stations and the networks behind them (SNI and BNI). The details of these interfaces are beyond the scope of the 802.16 standards. The reason for showing these interfaces in the system reference model is that the subscriber and core network technologies (such as voice, ATM, etc.) have an impact on the technologies used in the air interface and the services provided by the transceiver stations over the air interface.

Finally, the system reference model includes the optional use of some sort of repeater. The air interface specification allows for the possibility of repeaters or reflectors to bypass obstructions and extend cell coverage.

Protocol Architecture Protocols defined specifically for wireless transmission address issues relating to the transmission of blocks of data over the network. In OSI terms, higher-layer protocols (layer 3 or 4 and above; see Figure 4.3) are independent of network architecture and are applicable to a variety of networks and communications interfaces. Thus, a discussion of 802.16 protocols is concerned with lowest two layers of the OSI model.

Figure 11.14 relates the four protocol layers defined in the 802.16 protocol architecture to the OSI model. Working from the bottom up, the lowest two layers of the 802.16 protocol model correspond to the physical layer of the OSI model and include such functions as

- Encoding/decoding of signals
- Preamble generation/removal (for synchronization)
- Bit transmission/reception

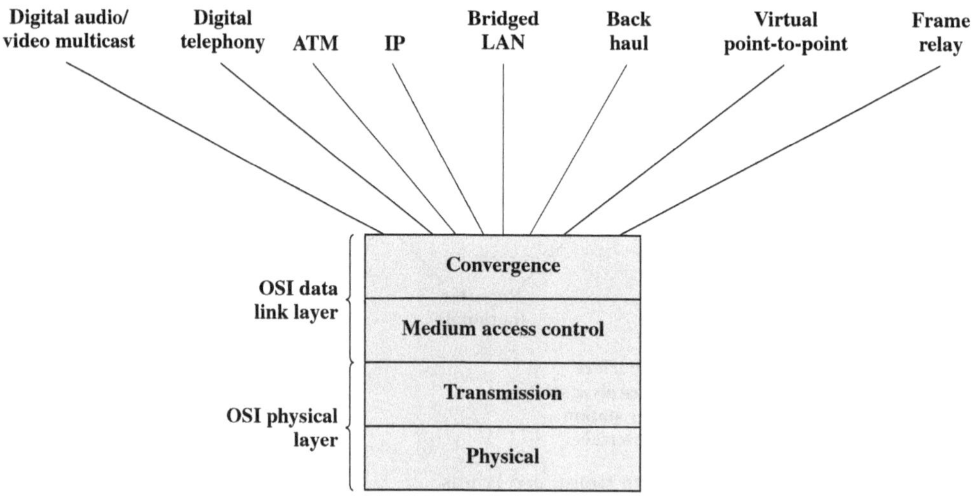

Figure 11.14 IEEE 802.16 Protocol Architecture

In addition, the physical layer of the 802 model includes a specification of the transmission medium and the frequency band. Generally, this is considered "below" the lowest layer of the OSI model. However, the choice of transmission medium and frequency band is critical in wireless link design, and so a specification of the medium is included. In general, the 802.16 physical layer is concerned with these medium-dependent issues, and the transmission layer is concerned with the bulleted items listed previously.

Above the physical and transmission layers are the functions associated with providing service to subscribers. These include

- On transmission, assemble data into a frame with address and error detection fields.
- On reception, disassemble frame, and perform address recognition and error detection.
- Govern access to the wireless transmission medium.

These functions are grouped into a medium access control (MAC) layer. The protocol at this layer, between the base station and the subscriber station, is responsible for sharing access to the radio channel. Specifically, the MAC protocol defines how and when a base station or subscriber station may initiate transmission on the channel. Because some of the layers above the MAC layer, such as ATM, require specified service levels (QoS), the MAC protocol must be able to allocate radio channel capacity so as to satisfy service demands. In the downstream direction (base station to subscriber stations), there is only one transmitter and the MAC protocol is relatively simple. In the upstream direction, multiple subscriber stations are competing for access, resulting in a more complex MAC protocol.

Above the MAC layer is a convergence layer that provides functions specific to the service being provided. A convergence layer protocol may do the following:

- Encapsulate PDU (protocol data unit) framing of upper layers into the native 802.16 MAC/PHY frames.
- Map an upper layer's addresses into 802.16 addresses.
- Translate upper layer QoS parameters into native 802.16 MAC format.
- Adapt the time dependencies of the upper layer traffic into the equivalent MAC service.

In some cases, such as digital audio and video, no convergence layer is needed and the stream of digital data is presented to the transmission layer. Upper-layer services that make use of a PDU structure do require a convergence layer.

An example of the protocol structure supported by the convergence layer is the handling of TCP/IP based traffic, as shown in Figure 11.15 (compare Figure 4.2). Higher-level data are passed down to LLC (logical link control), which appends control information as a header, creating an *LLC protocol data unit (PDU)*. This control information is used in the operation of the LLC protocol, which is a form of data link control protocol (see Appendix C). The entire LLC PDU is then passed down to the MAC layer, which appends control information at the front and back of the packet, forming a *MAC frame*. Again, the control information in the frame is needed for the operation of the MAC protocol. The figure shows the use of TCP/IP and an application layer above the 802.16 protocols.

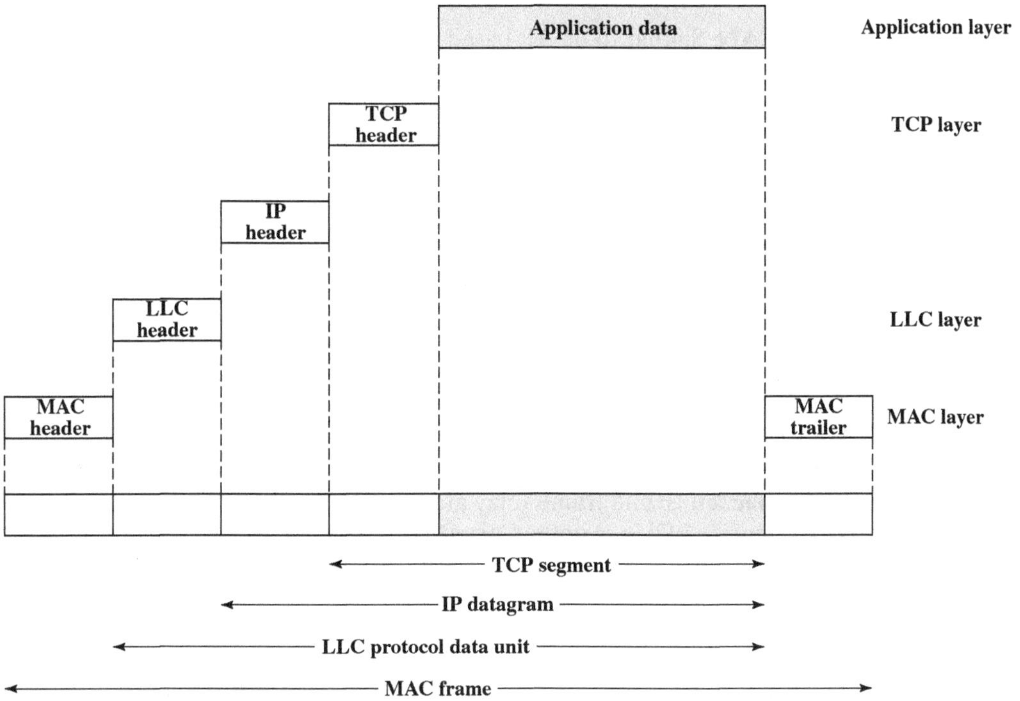

Figure 11.15 IEEE 802.16 Protocols in Context

Services

Requirements for the IEEE 802.16 standards are defined in terms of bearer services that the 802.16 systems must support. A bearer service refers to the type of traffic generated by a subscriber network or core network in Figure 11.13. For example, an 802.16 interface must be able to support the data rate and QoS required by an ATM network or an IP-based network, or support the data rate and delay requirements of voice or video transmissions.

IEEE 802.16 is designed to support the following bearer services:

- **Digital audio/video multicast:** Transports one-way digital audio/video streams to subscribers. The principal example of this service is a broadcast radio and video similar to digital broadcast cable TV and digital satellite TV. A special case of this service is two-way video such as in teleconferencing. In this latter case, delay requirements are stringent because of the interactivity involved.
- **Digital telephony:** Supports multiplexed digital telephony streams. This service is a classic WLL service that provides a replacement for wired access to the public telephone network.
- **ATM:** Provides a communications link that supports the transfer of ATM cells as part of an overall ATM network. The 802.16 link must support the various QoS services defined for ATM.
- **Internet protocol:** Supports the transfer of IP datagrams. The 802.16 link must provide efficient timely service. In addition, a variety of QoS services are now defined for IP-based networks, and 802.16 should support these.
- **Bridged LAN:** Similar to the IP-based support. A bridge LAN service enables transfer of data between two LANs with switching at the MAC layer.
- **Back-haul:** For cellular or digital wireless telephone networks. An 802.16 system may be a convenient means to provide wireless trunks for wireless telephony base stations.
- **Frame relay:** Similar to ATM. Frame relay uses variable-length frames in contrast to the fixed-length cells of ATM.

Another way of viewing the service requirements for 802.16 is shown in Table 11.10, which is taken from the 802.16 functional requirements document. Bearer services are grouped in three broad categories:

- **Circuit based:** These services provide a circuit-switching capability, in which connections are set up to subscribers across a core network.
- **Variable packet:** IP and frame relay are examples of services that make use of variable-length PDUs. Another example is MPEG video, which is a video compression scheme in which successive blocks of digital video information may be of varying sizes.
- **Fixed-length cell/packet:** This service is for ATM.

Table 11.10 summarizes requirements in three categories. The first category is the data rate that must be supported. The second category refers to error performance. For

Table 11.10 IEEE 802.16 Services and QoS Requirements

	Bearer Service	MAC Payload Rate	Maximum Ratio	Maximum Delay (one way)
Circuit Based	High-quality narrowband/ Voice frequency telephony (Vocoder MOS $\geq$ 4.0)	32 to 64 kbps	BER 10^{-6}	5 ms
Circuit Based	Lower quality narrowband/ Voice frequency telephony (Vocoder MOS < 4.0)	6 to 16 kbps	BER 10^{-4}	10 ms
Circuit Based	Trunking	≤155 Mbps	BER 10^{-6}	5 ms
Variable Packet	Time critical packet services	4 to 13 kbps (voice) 32 kbps to 1.5 Mbps (video)	BER 10^{-6}	10 ms
Variable Packet	Non-time-critical services: IP, IPX, frame relay, audio/video streaming, bulk data transfer, etc.	≤155 Mbps	BER 10^{-8}	N/A
Variable Packet	MPEG video	≤8 Mbps	BER 10^{-11}	TBD
Fixed-length Cell/Packet	ATM Cell Relay—CBR	16 kbps to 155 Mbps	CLR 3×10^{-8} CER 4×10^{-6} CMR 1/day SEBCR 10^{-4}	10 ms
Fixed-length Cell/Packet	ATM Cell Relay—rt-VBR	16 kbps to 155 Mbps	CLR 10^{-5} CER 4×10^{-6} CMR 1/day SEBCR 10^{-4}	10 ms
Fixed-length Cell/Packet	ATM Cell Relay—other	≤155 Mbps	CLR 10^{-5} CER 4×10^{-6} CMR 1/day SEBCR 10^{-4}	N/A

most services an upper limit on the bit error ration (BER) is defined. For ATM, various specific QoS error parameters are also used.

The final category is maximum one-way delay. To place this delay in context, Figure 11.13 shows three categories of delay defined in the 802.16 standards:

- **Medium access delay:** Once a transceiver station is ready to transmit, the medium access delay measures the amount of time that the station must wait before it can transmit.
- **Transit delay:** This is the delay from SNI to BNI or BNI to SNI. It includes the medium access delay plus the processing at the MAC layer for preparing transmission (from the STS or BTS) and at the MAC layer for reception (at the BTS or STS).
- **End-to-end delay:** The total delay between a terminal in the subscriber network, to the ultimate service beyond the core network. This includes the transit delay.

The maximum one-way delay category specified in Table 11.10 refers to transit delay.

IEEE 802.16 MAC Layer

Data transmitted over the 802.16 air interface from or to a given subscriber are structured as a sequence of MAC frames. The term **MAC frame** as used in this context refers to the PDU that includes MAC protocol control information and higher-level data. This is not to be confused with a **TDMA frame**, which consists of a sequence of time slots, each dedicated to a given subscriber. A TDMA time slot may contain exactly one MAC frame, a fraction of a MAC frame, or multiple MAC frames. The sequence of time slots across multiple TDMA frames that is dedicated to one subscriber forms a logical channel, and MAC frames are transmitted over that logical channel.

Connections and Service Flow The 802.16 MAC protocol is connection oriented. That is, a logical connection is set up between peer entities (MAC users) prior to the exchange of data between those entities. Each MAC frame includes a connection ID, which is used by the MAC protocol to deliver incoming data to the correct MAC user. In addition, there is a one-to-one correspondence between a connection ID and service flow. The service flow defines the QoS parameters for the PDUs that are exchanged on the connection.

The concept of a service flow on a connection is central to the operation of the MAC protocol. Service flows provide a mechanism for upstream and downstream QoS management. In particular, they are integral to the bandwidth allocation process. The base station allocates both upstream and downstream bandwidth on the basis of the service flow for each active connection. Examples of service flow parameters are latency (maximum acceptable delay), jitter (maximum acceptable delay variation), and throughput (minimum acceptable bit rate).

Frame Format A good way to get a grasp of the MAC protocol is to examine the frame format (Figure 11.16). The frame consists of three sections:

- **Header:** Contains protocol control information needed for the functioning of the MAC protocol.
- **Payload:** The payload may be either higher-level data (e.g., an ATM cell, an IP packet, a block of digital speech) or a MAC control message.
- **CRC:** The cyclic redundancy check field contains an error-detecting code (discussed in Section 8.1).

Three header formats are defined. There is a generic header format in both the uplink (toward the base station) and downlink (toward the subscriber) directions. These formats are used for frames that contain either higher-level data or a MAC control message. The third format is used for a bandwidth request frame.

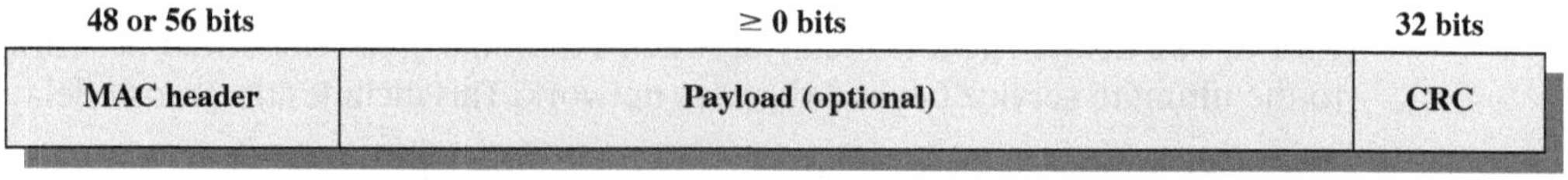

Figure 11.16 IEEE 802.16.1 Frame Format

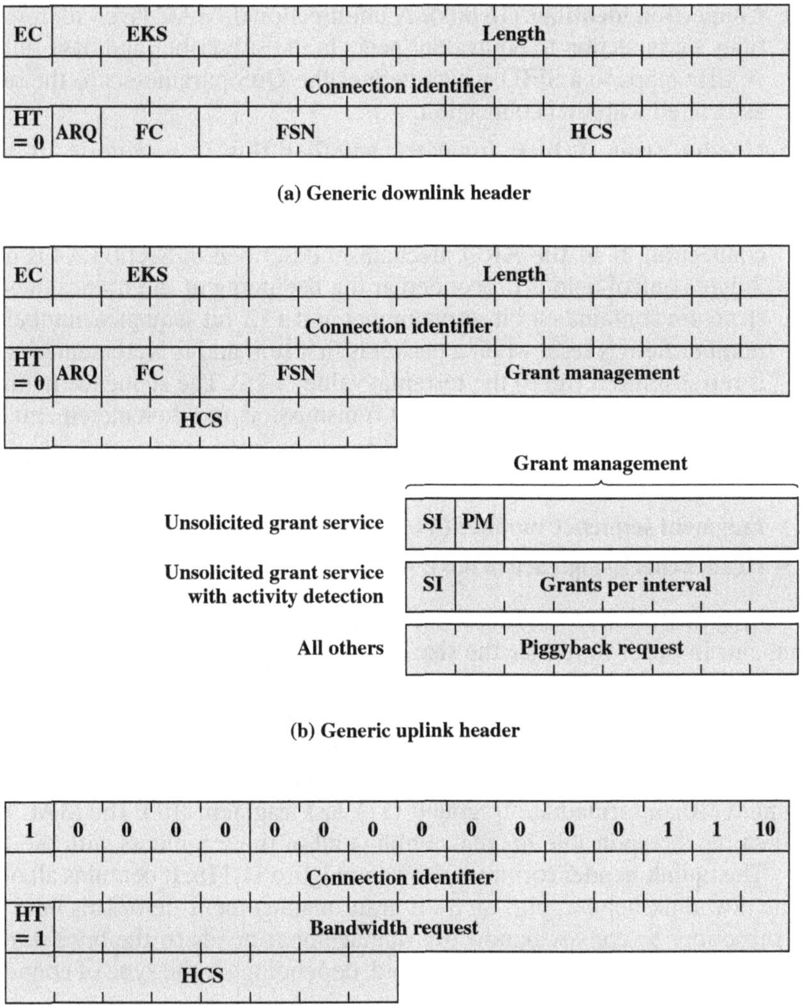

ARQ: Automatic repeat request
EC: Encryption control
EKS: Encryption key sequence
FC: Fragment control
FSN: Fragment sequence number
HCS: Header check sequence
HT: Header type
PM: Poll me bit
SI: Slip indicator

Figure 11.17 IEEE 802.16 MAC Header Formats

The **downlink header** format is shown in Figure 11.17a. It consists of the following fields:

- **Encryption control (1 bit):** Indicates whether the payload is encrypted.
- **Encryption key sequence (4 bits):** An index into a vector of encryption key information, to be used if the payload is encrypted.
- **Length (11 bits):** Length in bytes of the entire MAC frame.

- **Connection identifier (16 bits):** A unidirectional, MAC-layer address that identifies a connection to equivalent peers in the subscriber and base station MAC. A CID maps to a SFID, which defines the QoS parameters to the service flow associated with that connection.
- **Header type (1 bit):** Indicates whether this is a generic or bandwidth request header.
- **ARQ indicator (1 bit):** Indicates whether the frame belongs to an ARQ enabled connection. If so, the ARQ mechanism described in Section 8.4 is used, and a 2-byte control field is prepended at the beginning of the frame. The control bit structure contains a 4-bit retry number and a 12 -bit sequence number. The retry number field is reset when a packet is first sent and is incremented whenever it is retransmitted (up to the terminal value of 15). The sequence number field is assigned to each packet on its first transmission and then incremented.
- **Fragment control (2 bits):** Used in fragmentation and reassembly, as explained subsequently.
- **Fragment sequence number (4 bits):** Sequence number of the current fragment.
- **Header check sequence (8 bits):** An 8-bit CRC used to detect errors in the header.

Fragmentation is used to divide a higher-level block of data into two or more fragments in order to reduce the size of MAC frames. This is done to allow efficient use of available bandwidth relative to the QoS requirements of a connection's service flow. If fragmentation is not used, then the fragment control (FC) field is set to 00. If fragmentation is used, then the all of the fragments are assigned the same fragment sequence number (FSN) and the FC field has the following interpretation: first fragment (10); intermediate fragment (11); last fragment (01). The MAC user at the destination is responsible for reassembling all of the fragments with the same FSN.

The **uplink header** format is shown in Figure 11.17b. It contains all of the fields of the downlink header, plus an 8-bit grant management field. This field is used by the subscriber to convey bandwidth management needs to the base station. There are three different encodings of this field, depending on the type of connection. The subfields within the GM field include

- **Slip indicator (1 bit):** If set, indicates a slip of uplink grants relative to the uplink queue depth.
- **Poll-me (1 bit):** If set, requests a poll by the base station.
- **Grants per interval (7 bits):** The number of grants required by a connection.
- **Piggyback request (8 bits):** The number of bytes of uplink capacity requested by the subscriber for this connection.

The first two formats for the GM field are associated with the unsolicited grant service (UGS). This service is designed to support real-time service flows. In essence, the base station periodically, using MAC management messages, grants an allocation of bytes to the subscriber on a given connection. The allocation is designed to keep up with the real time demands. If a subscriber finds that its queue of data to send has exceeded a threshold, the subscriber sends a GM field with the SI bit set and either requests a poll for bandwidth by setting the PM bit or requests that a given number of bandwidth grants be executed in the next time interval. The latter technique is used if this is a UGS with activity detection; this simply means that the flow may become inactive for substantial periods of time. For other types of service, the GM field may be used to make a request for capacity. This is referred to as a piggyback request because the request is made as part of a MAC frame carrying user data rather than in a separate bandwidth request management MAC frame.

Finally, the **bandwidth request header** is used by the subscriber to request additional bandwidth. This header is for a MAC frame with no payload. The 15-bit bandwidth request field indicates the number of bytes of capacity requested for uplink transmission.

MAC Management Messages IEEE 802.16 defines a number of control messages that are used by the base station and the subscriber to manage the air interface and manage the exchange of data over the various connections. Messages are used to exchange operating parameters and status and encryption-related information and for capacity management. The following is a brief summary of the messages currently defined:

- **Uplink and downlink channel descriptor:** Transmits characteristics of the physical channel.
- **Uplink and downlink access definition:** Allocates access to the uplink and downlink channels.
- **Ranging request and response:** The request is used by the subscriber to determine network delay and to request power and/or modulation adjustment. The response from the BS contains the requested parameters.
- **Registration request, response, and acknowledge:** The request is transmitted by the subscriber at initialization time and contains various relevant parameters. The base station replies with a response, and the subscriber sends an acknowledge to complete the handshake.
- **Privacy key management request and response:** Used to exchange information about encryption keys.
- **Dynamic service addition request, response, and acknowledge:** The request is sent by a subscriber to request a new service flow.
- **Dynamic service change request, response, and acknowledge:** The request is sent by a subscriber or the base station to dynamically change the parameters of an existing service flow.
- **Dynamic service deletion request and response:** The request is sent by the base station or subscriber to delete an existing service flow.
- **Multicast polling assignment request and response:** Sent by a subscriber to request inclusion in a multicast polling group.
- **Downlink data grant type request:** Sent by the base station to the subscriber to dictate the modulation method and FEC technique to be used on a particular connection, to enhance performance.
- **ARQ acknowledgment:** Used to acknowledge successful receipt of one or more packets from the peer MAC entity.

Table 11.11 IEEE 801.16 Physical Layer Modes

	Upstream	Continuous Downstream (Mode A)	Burst Downstream (Mode B)
Access method	DAMA-TDMA	TDM	DAMA-TDMA
Duplexing technique	Matches downstream	FDD	FDD with adaptive modulation; FSDD; TDD

DAMA-TDMA: Demand assignement multiple access, time division multiple access
FDD: Frequency division duplexing
FSDD: Frequency shift division duplexing
TDD: Time division duplexing
TDM: Time division multiplexing

IEEE 802.16 Physical Layer

The 802.16 physical layer supports a different structure for the point-to-multipoint downstream channels and the multipoint-to-point upstream channels (Table 11.11). These structures reflect the differing requirements in the two directions. In general, most systems will require greater downstream capacity to individual subscribers to support asymmetric data connections such as Web applications over the Internet. For the upstream direction, the issue of medium access needs to be addressed, because there are a number of subscribers competing for the available capacity. These requirements are reflected in the physical layer specification.

Upstream Transmission Upstream transmission uses a DAMA-TDMA (demand assignment multiple access-time division multiple access) technique. DAMA is a capacity assignment technique that adapts as needed to optimally respond to demand changes among the multiple stations. TDMA is simply the technique of dividing time on a channel into a sequence of frames, each consisting of a number of slots, and allocating one or more slots per frame to form a logical channel. With DAMA-TDMA, the assignment of slots to channels varies dynamically.

Upstream transmission makes use of a Reed-Solomon code for error correction and a modulation scheme based on QPSK.

Downstream Transmission In the downstream direction, the standard specifies two modes of operation, one targeted to support a continuous transmission stream (mode A), such as audio or video, and one targeted to support a burst transmission stream (mode B), such as IP-based traffic.

For the **continuous downstream mode**, a simple TDM scheme is used for channel access. The duplexing technique that is used for allocating capacity between upstream and downstream traffic is known as FDD (frequency division duplex). FDD simply means that a different frequency band is used for transmission in each direction. This is equivalent to a FAMA-FDMA (fixed assignment multiple access-frequency division multiple access) scheme. FDD implies that all subscribers can transmit and receive simultaneously, each on their own assigned frequencies.

For the **burst downstream mode**, the DAMA-TDMA scheme is used for channel access. Three alternative techniques are available for duplexing traffic between upstream and downstream:

- **FDD with adaptive modulation:** This is the same FDD scheme used in the upstream mode, but with a dynamic capability to change the modulation and forward error correction schemes.
- **Frequency shift division duplexing (FSDD):** This is similar to FDD, but some or all of the subscribers are not capable of transmitting and receiving simultaneously.
- **Time division duplexing (TDD):** This technique is discussed in Section 11.1. A TDMA frame is used, with part of the time allocated for upstream transmission and part for downstream transmission.

The availability of these alternative techniques provides considerable flexibility in designing a system that optimizes the use of capacity.

IEEE 802.16a

The initial version of the 802.16 standard, ratified in 2002 and referred to simply as IEEE 802.16, operates in the 10-to-66-GHz frequency band and requires line-of-sight antennas. The IEEE 802.16a standard, ratified in 2003, does not require line-of-sight transmission and allows use of lower frequencies (2 to 11 GHz), many of which are unregulated. IEEE 802.16a can achieve a range of 50 km and data rates of over 70 Mbps.

IEEE 802.16a provides a new physical layer standard with some modifications to the 802.16 MAC layer. Compared to the higher frequencies, the 2-to-11-GHz range offers the opportunity to reach many more customers less expensively, though at generally lower data rates. This suggests that such services will be oriented toward individual homes or small- to medium-sized enterprises. Design of the 2-to-11-GHz physical layer is driven by the need for non-line-of-sight (NLOS) operation. This is essential to support residential applications since rooftops may be too low for a clear sight line to a BS antenna, possibly due to obstruction by trees. Therefore, significant multipath propagation must be expected. Furthermore, outdoor mounted antennas are expensive due to both hardware and installation costs. The 802.16a standard specifies that systems implement one of three air interface specifications, each of which provides for interoperability:

- **WirelessMAN-SCa:** This uses a single-carrier modulation format.
- **WirelessMAN-OFDM:** This uses orthogonal frequency division multiplexing with a 256-point transform. Access is by TDMA.
- **WirelessMAN-OFDMA:** This uses orthogonal frequency division multiple access with a 2048-point transform. In this system, multiple access is provided by addressing a subset of the multiple carriers to individual receivers

Table 11.12 Data Rates Achieved at Various 802.16a Bandwidths

Modulation	QPSK	QPSK	16QAM	16QAM	64QAM	64QAM
Code Rate	**1/2**	**3/4**	**1/2**	**3/4**	**2/3**	**3/4**
1.75 MHz	1.04	2.18	2.91	4.36	5.94	6.55
3.5 MHz	2.08	4.37	5.82	8.73	11.88	13.09
7.0 MHz	4.15	8.73	11.64	17.45	23.75	26.18
10.0 MHz	8.31	12.47	16.63	24.94	33.25	37.40
20.0 MHz	16.62	24.94	33.25	49.87	66.49	74.81

Because of the propagation requirements, the use of advanced antenna systems is supported. To accommodate the more demanding physical environment and different service requirements found at frequencies between 2 and 11 GHz, the 802.16a project upgrades the MAC to provide automatic repeat request (ARQ). Also, an optional mesh topology is defined to expand the basic point-to-multipoint architecture.

IEEE 802.16a supports both TDD and FDD modes of operation, along with a range of channel bandwidths. Table 11.12 shows the data rates that can be achieved at various 802.16a channel bandwidths.

The Latest Version of IEEE 802.16: 802.16m[8]

The IEEE 802.16e-2005 amendment to the IEEE Std 802.16-2004 Air Interface Standard which added Scalable-Orthogonal Frequency Division Multiple Access (S-OFDMA) and many other features for support of mobility has provided the basis for WiMAX System Release 1. Further specification enhancements for Release 1 were provided with IEEE Std 802.16e-2009. The first WiMAX System Release 1 deployments took place in 2006. Estimates by the WiMAX Forum indicate that as of the end of 2009, WiMAX service providers have covered more than 600 million people with over 500 deployments in over 140 telecommunications markets worldwide.[9]

In December 2006 the IEEE launched an effort to further evolve the IEEE 802.16 Wireless MAN-OFDMA specification. This amendment, known as 802.16m, is designed to meet or exceed the requirements of IMT-Advanced (the 4th generation of cellular systems). This relates to other terms mentioned in this book, namely IMT and 4G.

IMT-Advanced International Mobile Telecommunications-Advanced (IMT-Advanced) is a term used by the ITU to describe mobile communication systems which go further than that of IMT-2000. Previously, IMT-Advanced was known as "systems beyond IMT-2000" and is often referred to as 4G. 4G is heard frequently

[8]http://www.wimaxforum.org/sites/wimaxforum.org/files/document_library/wimax_802.16m.pdf used with permisison.

[9]www.wimaxforum.org

by vendors such as Verizon and AT&T when promoting their "advanced" cellular networks. In baselining the requirements for IMT-Advanced, the ITU has attempted to anticipate the wide range of application and service demands required for future mobile networks that would need to be widely deployed in many countries in the 2012–2015 timeframe. In addition to being the driving force for IEEE 802.16m, IMT-Advanced is also the basis for LTE, and LTE-Advanced.

IEEE 802.16e is already included in IMT-2000 while IEEE 802.16m and LTE-Advanced are the only two technologies submitted for IMT-Advanced. Both are expected to be included.

With a number of constraints for backwards compatibility, the 802.16m amendment provides the basis for WiMAX System Release 2 and provides existing WiMAX operators a graceful migration path to gain performance enhancements and add new services.

The IEEE 802.16m task group has more than 300 participating individuals from approximately 100 organizations from two dozen countries. As was the case for 802.16e-2005, 802.16m is designed to support frequencies in all licensed IMT bands below 6 GHz and include TDD and FDD duplexing schemes as well as half-duplex FDD (H-FDD) terminal operation to ensure applicability to the wide range of worldwide spectrum assignments.

The IEEE 802.16m specification was approved in March, 2011. Initial availability of WiMAX System Release 2 products based on 802.16m is anticipated in the 2012 timeframe.

The enhancements incorporated in the IEEE 802.16m amendment and subsequently, WiMAX can be grouped into the following six categories:

- Increased Coverage and Spectral Efficiency
- Increased Capacity for Data and VoIP
- Lower Latency and QoS Enhancements
- Interworking with other Wireless Networks
- Power Conservation
- Other Advanced Features and Supported Services

Example 11.5 Example of 802.11 in action here: http://www.wimaxforum.org/sites/wimaxforum.org/files/P1_case_study_intel.PDF

WiMAX Success Story: How Packet One Did It

P1 is Malaysia's first and leading WiMAX telecommunications company with the country's widest WiMAX network. Launched on August 19, 2008, P1 W1MAX™ represents the first large-scale commercial deployment of Mobile WiMAX in Southeast Asia, as well as the first large-scale deployment of an 802.16e 2.3GHz WiMAX network outside Korea. P1's goal is to bridge the digital divide by making access to the Internet universal, ubiquitous, and affordable for every Malaysian.

Release Date: Monday, November 9, 2009

11.4 RECOMMENDED READINGS AND WEB SITES

[PHIL98] is a detailed treatment of DECT and PWT.

A thorough analysis of propagation effects at millimeter wavelengths is found in [FREE97]. A briefer but useful survey of the same topic is [DALK96].

[NORD00] is a general overview of LMDS technology and applications. [FUNG98] focuses on some detailed transmitter/receiver design issues for MMDS. [WEBB00] is a good overall survey of wireless local loop technology. [KELL00] provides a thorough analysis of OFDM. [BOLC01] surveys design issues related to broadband wireless access. [MORA04] provides a detailed technical treatment of broadband wireless access.

[EKLU02] provides an overview of IEEE 802.16. [KOFF02] and [JOHN04] cover the OFDM portion of 802.16a.

BOLC01 Bolcskei, H., et al. "Fixed Broadband Wireless Access: State of the Art, Challenges, and Future Directions." *IEEE Communications Magazine*, January 2001.

DALK96 Dalke, R.; Hufford, G.; and Ketchum, R. *Radio Propagation Considerations for Local Multipoint Distribution Systems.* National Telecommunications and Information Administration Publication PB97116511, August 1996.

EKLU02 Eklund, C., et al. "IEEE Standard 802.16: A Technical Overview of the WirelessMAN Air Interface for Broadband Wireless Access." *IEEE Communications Magazine*, June 2002.

FREE97 Freeman, R. *Radio System Design for Telecommunications*. New York: Wiley, 1997.

FUNG98 Fung, P. "A Primer on MMDS Technology." *Communication Systems Design*, April 1998. Available at www.commsdesign.com.

JOHN04 Johnston, D., and Yaghoobi, H. "Peering into the WiMAX Spec." Communications System Design, January 2004. Available at www.commsdesign.com.

KELL00 Keller, T., and H. "Adaptive Multicarrier Modulation: A Convenient Framework for Time-Frequency Processing in Wireless Communication." *Proceedings of the IEEE*, May 2000.

KOFF02 Koffman, I., and Roman, V. "Broadband Wireless Access Solutions Based on OFDM Access in IEEE 802.16." *IEEE Communications Magazine*, April 2002.

MORA04 Morais, D. *Fixed Broadband Wireless Communications: Principles and Practical Applications*. Upper Saddle River, NJ: Prentice Hall, 2004.

NORD00 Nordbotten, A. "LMDS Systems and Their Application." *IEEE Communications Magazine*, June 2000.

PHIL98 Phillips, J., and Namee, G. *Personal Wireless Communications with DECT and PWT.* Boston: Artech House, 1998.

WEBB00 Webb, W. *Introduction to Wireless Local Loop: Broadband and Narrowband Systems.* Boston: Artech House, 2000.

Recommended Web Sites:

- **Wireless Communications Association International:** Represents the fixed broadband wireless access industry worldwide. Good set of links.
- **The IEEE 802.16 Working Group on Broadband Wireless Access Standards:** Contains working group documents plus discussion archives.
- **WiMAX Forum:** An industry group promoting the interoperability of 802.16 products with each other.
- **NIST Radio Frequency Technology Division:** The U.S. National Institute of Standards and Technology. Good source of information on fixed wireless access and other topics.
- **OFDM Forum:** Industry consortium to promote OFDM.

11.5 KEY TERMS, REVIEW QUESTIONS, AND PROBLEMS

Key Terms

adaptive differential PCM (ADPCM)	fixed wireless access	multicarrier modulation
cordless	Fresnel zone	multichannel multipoint distribution service (MMDS)
differential quantization	linear predictive filter	orthogonal frequency division multiplexing (OFDM)
digital enhanced cordless telecommunications (DECT)	local multipoint distribution service (LMDS)	time division duplex (TDD)
fixed broadband wireless	logical link control (LLC)	wireless cable
	MAC frame	wireless local loop (WLL)
	medium access control (MAC)	

Review Questions

11.1 In what ways has traditional cordless telephony been extended by standardization?

11.2 What is the difference between TDD and TDM?

11.3 List and briefly define the DECT logical channels.

11.4 What are some key advantages of WLL over a wired subscriber loop?

11.5 What are the principal advantages of millimeter wave transmission compared to transmission at longer wavelengths?

11.6 What are the principal disadvantages of millimeter wave transmission compared to transmission at longer wavelengths?

11.7 What are the principal advantages of OFDM?
11.8 What are the relative advantages of MMDS compared to LMDS?
11.9 What are the key differences among IEEE 802.16, IEEE 802.16.2, and IEEE 802.16.3?

Problems

11.1 GSM, described in Chapter 10, makes use of a TDMA scheme in which there are a number of duplex channels, with each channel consisting of two dedicated frequency bands, one for transmission in each direction. Suppose that we wished to design a comparable system, using the same total amount of bandwidth, but using TDD. List the key parameters of a TDD-GSM system and compares these to the real GSM parameters.

11.2 A LOS microwave link 12 km long is planned for installation in Germany, which is in climate zone H (Table 11.7). The operational frequency is 38 GHz and the desired time availability is 99.99%. Local rain rate statistics are not available. The antenna polarization is horizontal.
a. What amount of attenuation is to be anticipated?
b. Repeat for 99.9% and 99% and comment on the practicality of the requirement for various availabilities.

APPENDIX 11A LINEAR PREDICTIVE FILTERS[10]

The linear predictive filter is based on using an approximation of the Taylor series. For a function $g(t)$ that has derivatives of all orders at t, the function can be represented by its Taylor series:

$$g(x) = \sum_{n=0}^{\infty} \frac{(x - t)^n}{n!} g^{(n)}(t) \tag{11.4}$$

where $g^{(n)}(t)$ is the nth derivative of $g(t)$. Now, suppose we are going to sample $g(t)$ with a sampling interval of T_s. Then, defining $T_s = x - t$, we can restate Equation (11.4) as

$$g(t + T_s) = \sum_{n=0}^{\infty} \frac{(T_s)^n}{n!} g^{(n)}(t) \tag{11.5}$$

Equation (11.5) shows that the value of the signal at time $t + T_s$ can be predicted from the value of its signal and its derivatives at time t. In fact, for small values of T_s (much less than one), we can produce a good approximation with just the first derivative:

$$g(t + T_s) \approx g(t) + T_s g'(t) \tag{11.6}$$

Let us denote the kth sample of $g(t)$ taken at time $t = kT_s$ as $m(k)$; then $m(k \pm 1) = g(kT_s \pm T_s)$. Further, we can approximate $g'(kT_s)$ by $[g(kT_s) - g(kT_s - T_s)]/T_s$. Therefore, from Equation (11.6), we have

$$\begin{aligned} m(k + 1) &\approx m(k) + T_s\left[\frac{m(k) - m(k - 1)}{T_s}\right] \\ &= 2m(k) - m(k - 1) \end{aligned}$$

[10]The development in this appendix is based on material in [LATH98].

Thus, we can compute an approximate predication of the sample at $(k + 1)$ from the preceding two samples. The approximation improves as we add more samples. If N samples are used, the approximation formula becomes:

$$m(k) \approx A_1 m(k-1) + A_2 m(k-2) + \cdots + A_N m(k-N) \qquad (11.7)$$

The right hand side of Equation (11.7) is $\hat{m}(k)$, the predicted value of $m(k)$. Thus,

$$\hat{m}(k) = A_1 m(k-1) + A_2 m(k-2) + \cdots + A_N m(k-N) \qquad (11.8)$$

This is the linear predictor illustrated in Figure 11.5. The prediction coefficients A_i are determined from the statistical properties of the samples.

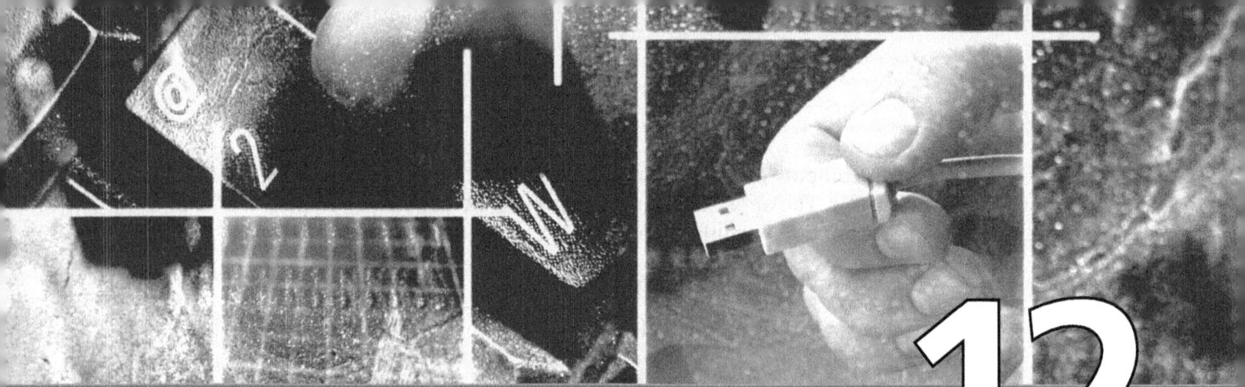

CHAPTER 12

Mobile IP and Wireless Application Protocol

In this chapter, we look at two standards that provide application-level support for wireless networking: Mobile IP and Wireless Application Protocol (WAP).

12.1 MOBILE IP

Mobile IP (or **IP mobility**) is an Internet Engineering Task Force (IETF) standard communications protocol that is designed to allow mobile device users to move from one network to another while maintaining a permanent IP address. Mobile IP for IPv4 is described in IETF RFC 3344, and updates are added in IETF RFC 4721. **Mobile IPv6**, the IP mobility implementation for the next generation of the Internet Protocol, IPv6, is described in RFC 3775.

As smartphones advanced and efficient connectivity solutions such as the iPhone and Droid, PDAs, and advanced devices such as the iPad become common in the marketplace, more advanced and effective connectivity solutions are necessary. Data connectivity solutions for this group of users is a very different requirement than it is for the fixed dialup user or the stationary wired LAN user. Cisco, for example, has integrated this new technology into their routing platforms to meet this need. Mobile IP is basically a tunneling-based solution which takes advantage of the Cisco-created GRE tunneling technology, as well as simpler IP-in-IP tunneling protocol. This tunneling enables a router on a user's home subnet to intercept and transparently forward IP packets to users while they roam beyond traditional network boundaries. This solution is a key enabler of wireless mobility, both in the wireless LAN arena, such as the 802.11 standard, and in the cellular environment for packet-based data offerings which offer connectivity to a user's home network and the Internet.

In response to the increasing popularity of palm-top and other mobile computers, Mobile IP was developed to enable computers to maintain Internet connectivity while moving from one Internet attachment point to another. Although Mobile IP can work with wired connections, in which a computer is unplugged from one physical attachment point and plugged into another, it is particularly suited to wireless connections.

The term *mobile* in this context implies that a user is connected to one or more applications across the Internet, that the user's point of attachment changes dynamically, and that all connections are automatically maintained despite the change. This is in contrast to a user, such as a business traveler, with a portable computer of some sort who arrives at a destination and uses the computer's notebook to dial into an ISP (Internet service provider). In this latter case, the user's Internet connection is terminated each time the user moves and a new connection is initiated when the user dials back in. Each time an Internet connection is established, software in the point of attachment (typically an ISP) is used to obtain a new, temporarily assigned IP address. This temporary IP address is used by the user's correspondent for each application-level connection (e.g., FTP, Web connection). A better term for this kind of use is *nomadic*.

We begin with a general overview of Mobile IP and then look at some of the details.

Operation of Mobile IP

As was described in Chapter 4, routers make use of the IP address in an IP datagram to perform routing. In particular, the **network portion** of an IP address (Figure 4.11) is used by routers to move a datagram from the source computer to the network to which the target computer is attached. Then the final router on the path, which is attached to the same network as the target computer, uses the **host portion** of the IP address to deliver the IP datagram to the destination. Further, this IP address is known to the next higher layer in the protocol architecture (Figure 4.1). In particular, most applications over the Internet are supported by TCP connections. When a TCP connection is set up, the TCP entity on each side of the connection knows the IP address of the correspondent host. When a TCP segment is handed down to the IP layer for delivery, TCP provides the IP address, and IP creates an IP datagram with that IP address in the IP header and sends the datagram out for routing and delivery. However, with a mobile host, the IP address may change while one or more TCP connections are active.

Figure 12.1 shows in general terms how Mobile IP deals with the problem of dynamic IP addresses. A mobile node is assigned to a particular network, known as its **home network**. Its IP address on that network, known as its **home address**, is static. When the mobile node moves its attachment point to another network, that network is considered a **foreign network** for this host. Once the mobile node is reattached, it makes its presence known by registering with a network node, typically a router, on the foreign network known as a **foreign**

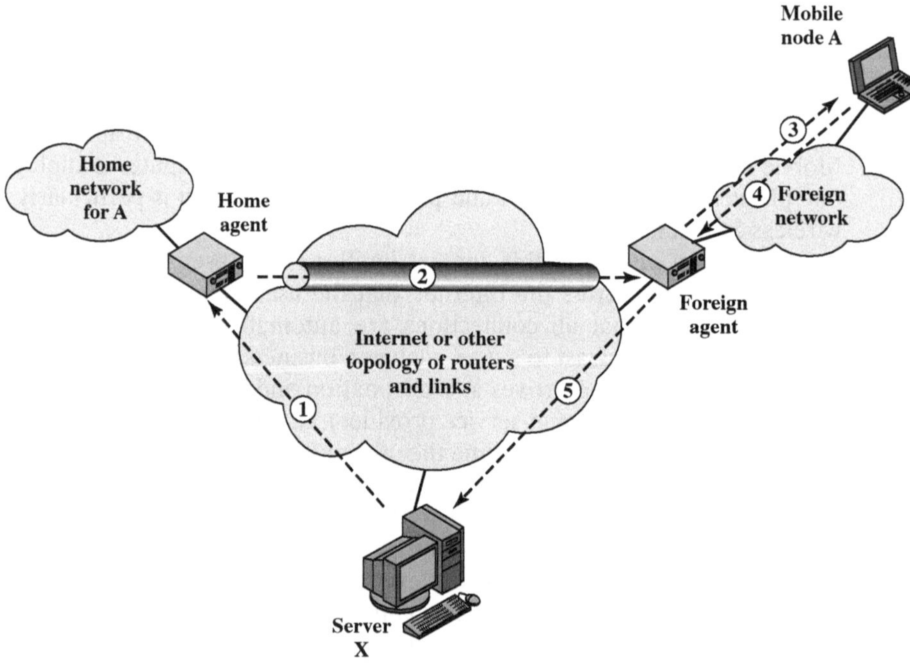

Figure 12.1 Mobile IP Scenario

agent. The mobile node then communicates with a similar agent on the user's home network, known as a **home agent**, giving the home agent the **care-of address** of the mobile node; the care-of address identifies the foreign agent's location. Typically, one or more routers on a network will implement the roles of both home and foreign agents.

When IP datagrams are exchanged over a connection between the mobile node and another host (a server in Figure 12.1), the following operations occur:

1. Server X transmits an IP datagram destined for mobile node A, with A's home address in the IP header. The IP datagram is routed to A's home network.
2. At the home network, the incoming IP datagram is intercepted by the home agent. The home agent encapsulates the entire datagram inside a new IP datagram that has the A's care-of address in the header, and retransmits the datagram. The use of an outer IP datagram with a different destination IP address is known as **tunneling**. This IP datagram is routed to the foreign agent.
3. The foreign agent strips off the outer IP header, encapsulates the original IP datagram in a network-level PDU (e.g., a LAN LLC frame), and delivers the original datagram to A across the foreign network.
4. When A sends IP traffic to X, it uses X's IP address. In our example, this is a fixed address; that is, X is not a mobile node. Each IP datagram is sent by A to a router on the foreign network for routing to X. Typically, this router is also the foreign agent.
5. The IP datagram from A to X travels directly across the Internet to X, using X's IP address.

To support the operations illustrated in Figure 12.1, Mobile IP includes three basic capabilities:

- **Discovery:** A mobile node uses a discovery procedure to identify prospective home agents and foreign agents.
- **Registration:** A mobile node uses an authenticated registration procedure to inform its home agent of its care-of address.
- **Tunneling:** Tunneling is used to forward IP datagrams from a home address to a care-of address.

Figure 12.2 indicates the underlying protocol support for the Mobile IP capability. The registration protocol communicates between an application on the mobile node and an application in the home agent and hence uses a transport-level protocol. Because registration is a simple request-response transaction, the overhead of the connection-oriented TCP is not required, and therefore UDP is used as the transport protocol. Discovery makes use of the existing ICMP (Internet Control Message Protocol) by adding the appropriate extensions to the ICMP header. ICMP, which is described in Appendix 12A, is a connectionless protocol well suited for the discovery operation. Finally, tunneling is performed at the IP level.

Mobile IP is specified in a number of RFCs. The basic defining document is RFC 2002. Table 12.1 lists some useful terminology from RFC 2002.

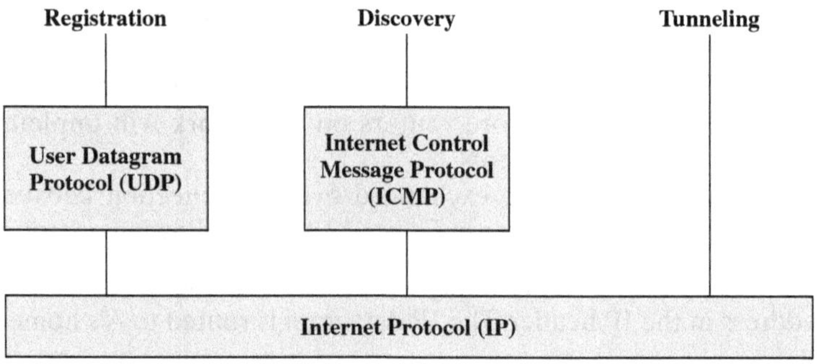

Figure 12.2 Protocol Support for Mobile IP

Table 12.1 Mobile IP Terminology (RFC 3220)

Mobile node	A host or router that changes its point of attachment from one network or subnetwork to another.A mobile node may change its location without changing itsIP address; it may continue to communicate withother Internet nodes at any location using its (constant) IPaddress, assuming link-layer connectivity to a pointof attachment is available
Home address	An IP address that is assigned for an extended period of time to a mobile node. It remains unchanged regardless of where the node is attached to the Internet.
Home agent	A router on a mobile node's home network which tunnels datagrams for delivery to the mobile node when it is away from home, and maintains current location information for the mobile node.
Home network	A network, possibly virtual, having a network prefix matching that of a mobile node's home address. Note that standard IP routing mechanisms will deliver datagrams destined to a mobile node's Home Address to the mobile node's Home Network.
Foreign agent	A router on a mobile node's visited network which provides routing services to the mobile node while registered. The foreign agent detunnels and delivers datagrams tothe mobile node that were tunneled by the mobile node's home agent. For datagrams sent by a mobile node, the foreign agent may serve as a default router for registered mobile nodes.
Foreign network	Any network other than the mobile node's Home Network.
Care-of address	The termination point of a tunnel toward a mobile node, for datagrams forwarded to the mobile node while it is away from home. The protocol can use two different types of care-of address: a "foreign agent care-of address" is an address of a foreign agent with which the mobile node is registered, and a "co-located care-of address" is an externally obtained local address which the mobile node has associated with one of its own network interfaces.
Correspondent node	A peer with which a mobile node is communicating. A correspondent node may be either mobile or stationary.
Link	A facility or medium over which nodes can communicate at the link layer. A link underlies the network layer.
Node	A host or a router.
Tunnel	The path followed by a datagram while it is encapsulated. The model is that, while it is encapsulated, a datagram is routed to a knowledgeable decapsulating agent, which decapsulates the datagram and then correctly delivers it to its ultimate destination.

Discovery

The discovery process in Mobile IP is very similar to the router advertisement process defined in ICMP (see Appendix 12A). Accordingly, agent discovery makes use of ICMP router advertisement messages, with one or more extensions specific to Mobile IP.

The mobile node is responsible for an ongoing discovery process. It must determine if it is attached to its home network, in which case IP datagrams may be received without forwarding, or if it is attached to a foreign network. Because handoff from one network to another occurs at the physical layer, a transition from the home network to a foreign network can occur at any time without notification to the network layer (i.e., the IP layer). Thus, discovery for a mobile node is a continuous process.

For the purpose of discovery, a router or other network node that can act as an agent periodically issues a router advertisement ICMP message (see Figure 12.20d in Appendix 12A) with an advertisement extension. The router advertisement portion of the message includes the IP address of the router. The advertisement extension includes additional information about the router's role as an agent, as discussed subsequently. A mobile node listens for these **agent advertisement messages**. Because a foreign agent could be on the mobile node's home network (set up to serve visiting mobile nodes), the arrival of an agent advertisement does not necessarily tell the mobile node that it is on a foreign network. The mobile node must compare the network portion of the router's IP address with the network portion of its own home address. If these network portions do not match, then the mobile node is on a foreign network.

The **agent advertisement extension** follows the ICMP router advertisement fields and consists of the following fields (Figure 12.3):

- **Type:** 16, indicates that this is an agent advertisement.
- **Length:** Number of bytes in the extension, excluding the Type and Length fields. The value is $(6 + 4N)$, where N is the number of care-of addresses advertised.
- **Sequence Number:** The count of agent advertisement messages sent since the agent was initialized.
- **Lifetime:** The longest lifetime, in seconds, that this agent is willing to accept a registration request from a mobile node.
- **R:** Registration with this foreign agent is required (or another foreign agent on this network). Even those mobile nodes that have already acquired a care-of address from this foreign agent must re-register.
- **B:** Busy. The foreign agent will not accept registrations from additional mobile nodes.
- **H:** This agent offers services as a home agent on this network.
- **F:** This agent offers services as a foreign agent on this network.
- **M:** This agent can receive tunneled IP datagrams that use minimal encapsulation, explained subsequently.

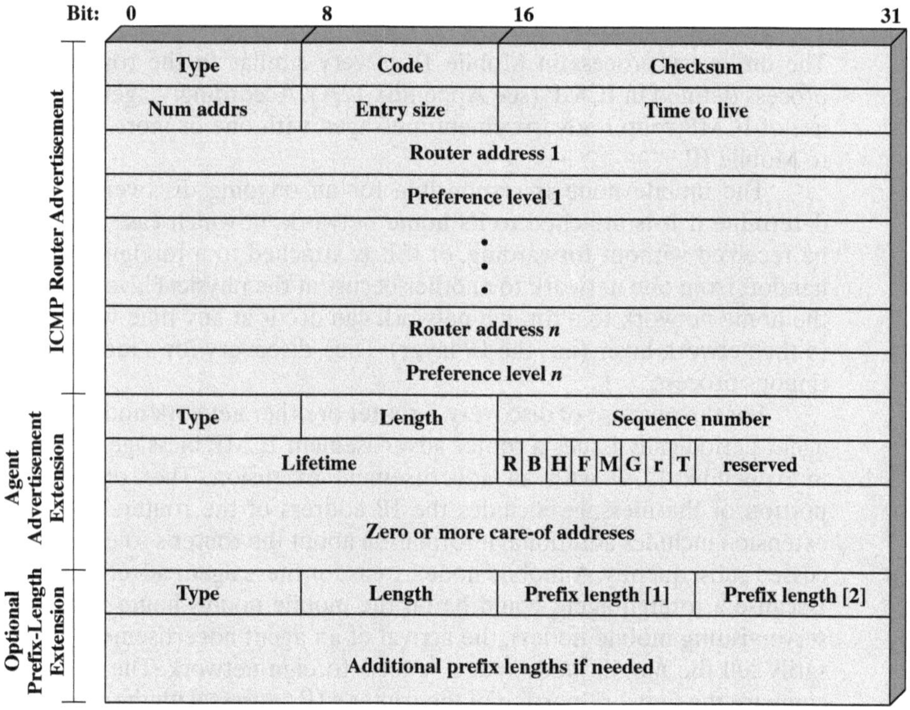

Figure 12.3 Mobile IP Agent Advertisement Message

- **G:** This agent can receive tunneled IP datagrams that use GRE encapsulation, explained subsequently.
- **r:** reserved.
- **T:** Foreign agent supports reverse tunneling.
- **Care-Of Address:** The care-of address or addresses supported by this agent on this network. There must be at least one such address if the F bit is set. There may be multiple addresses.

There may also be an optional **prefix-length extension** following the advertisement extension. This extension indicates the number of bits in the router's address that define the network number (Figure 4.11). The mobile node uses this information to compare the network portion of its own IP address with the network portion of the router. The fields are as follows:

- **Type:** 19, indicates that this is a prefix-length advertisement.
- **Length:** N, where N is the value of the Num Addrs field in the ICMP router advertisement portion of this ICMP message. In other words, this is the number of router addresses listed in this ICMP message.
- **Prefix Length:** The number of leading bits that define the network number of the corresponding router address listed in the ICMP router advertisement portion of this message. The number of Prefix Length fields matches the number of router address fields (N).

Agent Solicitation Foreign agents are expected to issue agent advertisement messages periodically. If a mobile node needs agent information immediately, it can issue an ICMP router solicitation message (see Figure 12.20e in Appendix 12A). Any agent receiving this message will then issue an agent advertisement.

Move Detection As was mentioned, a mobile node may move from one network to another due to some handoff mechanism, without the IP level being aware of it. The agent discovery process is intended to enable the agent to detect such a move. The agent may use one of two algorithms for this purpose:

- **Use of lifetime field:** When a mobile node receives an agent advertisement from a foreign agent that it is currently using or that it is now going to register with, it records the lifetime field as a timer. If the timer expires before the mobile node receives another agent advertisement from the agent, then the node assumes that it has lost contact with that agent. If, in the meantime, the mobile node has received an agent advertisement from another agent and that advertisement has not yet expired, the mobile node can register with this new agent. Otherwise, the mobile node should use agent solicitation to find an agent.
- **Use of network prefix:** The mobile node checks whether any newly received agent advertisement is on the same network as the node's current care-of address. If it is not, the mobile node assumes that it has moved and may register with the agent whose advertisement the mobile node has just received.

Co-Located Addresses The discussion so far has involved the use of a care-of address associated with a foreign agent; that is, the care-of address is an IP address for the foreign agent. This foreign agent will receive datagrams at this care-of address, intended for the mobile node, and then forward them across the foreign network to the mobile node. However, in some cases a mobile node may move to a network that has no foreign agents or on which all foreign agents are busy. As an alternative, the mobile node may act as its own foreign agent by using a co-located care-of address. A co-located care-of address is an IP address obtained by the mobile node that is associated with the mobile node's current interface to a network.

The means by which a mobile node acquires a co-located address is beyond the scope of Mobile IP. One means is to dynamically acquire a temporary IP address through an Internet service such as DHCP (Dynamic Host Configuration Protocol). Another alternative is that the co-located address may be owned by the mobile node as a long-term address for use only while visiting a given foreign network.

Registration

Once a mobile node has recognized that it is on a foreign network and has acquired a care-of address, it needs to alert a home agent on its home network and request that the home agent forward its IP traffic. The registration process involves four steps:

1. The mobile node requests the forwarding service by sending a registration request to the foreign agent that the mobile node wants to use.
2. The foreign agent relays this request to the mobile node's home agent.
3. The home agent either accepts or denies the request and sends a registration reply to the foreign agent.

4. The foreign agent relays this reply to the mobile node.

If the mobile node is using a co-located care-of address, then it registers directly with its home agent, rather than going through a foreign agent.

The registration operation uses two types of messages, carried in UDP segments (Figure 12.4). The **registration request message** consists of the following fields:

- **Type:** 1, indicates that this is a registration request.
- **S:** Simultaneous bindings. The mobile node is requesting that the home agent retain its prior mobility bindings. When simultaneous bindings are in effect, the home agent will forward multiple copies of the IP datagram, one to each care-of address currently registered for this mobile node. Multiple simultaneous bindings can be useful in wireless handoff situations, to improve reliability.
- **B:** Broadcast datagrams. Indicates that the mobile node would like to receive copies of broadcast datagrams that it would have received if it were attached to its home network.
- **D:** Decapsulation by mobile node. The mobile node is using a co-located care-of address and will decapsulate its own tunneled IP datagrams.

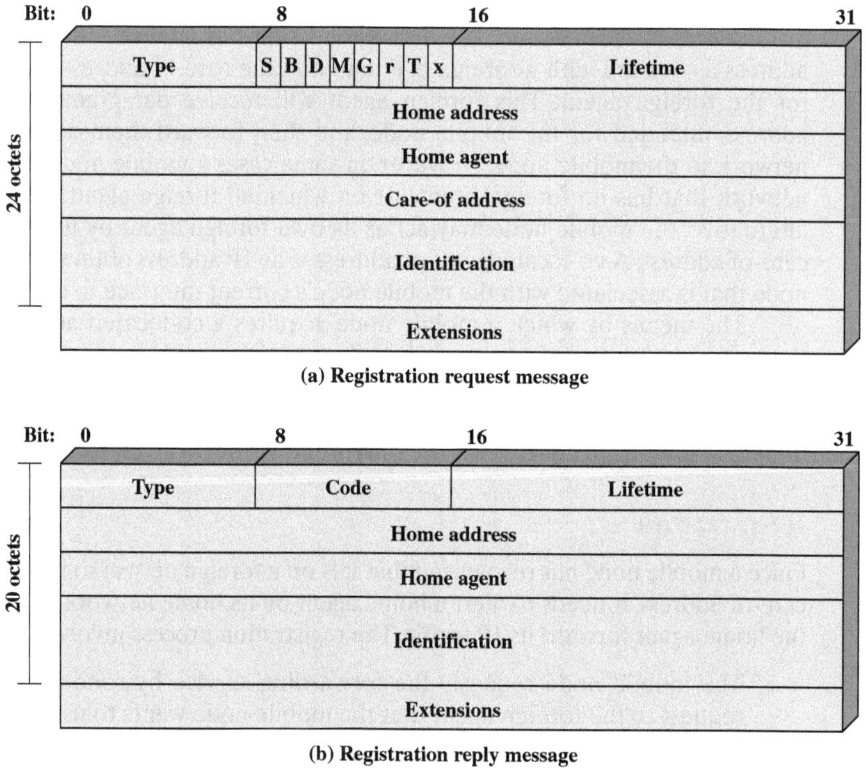

Figure 12.4 Mobile IP Registration Messages

- **M:** Indicates that the home agent should use minimal encapsulation, explained subsequently.
- **G:** Indicates that the home agent should use GRE encapsulation, explained subsequently.
- **r:** Reserved.
- **T:** Reverse tunneling requested.
- **x:** Reserved.
- **Lifetime:** The number of seconds before the registration is considered expired. A value of zero is a request for de-registration.
- **Home Address:** The home IP address of the mobile node. The home agent can expect to receive IP datagrams with this as a destination address, and must forward those to the care-of address.
- **Home Agent:** The IP address of the mobile node's home agent. This informs the foreign agent of the address to which this request should be relayed.
- **Care-Of Address:** The IP address at this end of the tunnel. The home agent should forward IP datagrams that it receives with mobile node's home address to this destination address.
- **Identification:** A 64-bit number generated by the mobile node, used for matching registration requests to registration replies and for security purposes, as explained subsequently.
- **Extensions:** The only extension so far defined is the authentication extension, explained subsequently.

The **registration reply message** consists of the following fields:

- **Type:** 3, indicates that this is a registration reply.
- **Code:** Indicates result of the registration request (Table 12.2).
- **Lifetime:** If the code field indicates that the registration was accepted, the number of seconds before the registration is considered expired. A value of zero indicates that the mobile node has been de-registered.
- **Home Address:** The home IP address of the mobile node.
- **Home Agent:** The IP address of the mobile node's home agent.
- **Identification:** A 64-bit number used for matching registration requests to registration replies.
- **Extensions:** The only extension so far defined is the authentication extension, explained subsequently.

Securing the Registration Procedure A key concern with the registration procedure is security. Mobile IP is designed to resist two types of attacks:

1. A node may pretend to be a foreign agent and send a registration request to a home agent so as to divert traffic intended for a mobile node to itself.
2. A malicious agent may replay old registration messages, effectively cutting the mobile node from the network.

Table 12.2 Code Values for a Mobile IP Registration Reply

Registration Successful	Registration Denied by the Foreign Agent
0 registration accepted	64 reason unspecified
1 registration accepted, but simultaneous mobility bindings unsupported	65 administratively prohibited
	66 insufficient resources
	67 mobile node failed authentication
Registration Denied by the Home Agent	68 home agent failed authentication
128 reason unspecified	69 requested Lifetime too long
129 administratively prohibited	70 poorly formed Request
130 insufficient resources	71 poorly formed Reply
131 mobile node failed authentication	72 requested encapsulation unavailable
132 foreign agent failed authentication	73 requested Van Jacobson compression unavailable
133 registration Identification mismatch	77 invalid care-of address
134 poorly formed Request	78 registration timeout
135 too many simultaneous mobility bindings	80 home network unreachable (ICMP error received)
136 unknown home agent address	81 home agent host unreachable (ICMP error received)
	82 home agent port unreachable (ICMP error received)
	88 home agent unreachable (other ICMP error received)

The technique that is used to protect against such attacks involves the use of message authentication and the proper use of the identification field of the registration request and reply messages (Figure 12.4).

For purposes of message authentication, each registration request and reply contains an **authentication extension** (Figure 12.5) with the following fields:

- **Type:** Used to designate the type of this authentication extension.
- **Length:** 4 plus the number of bytes in the authenticator.

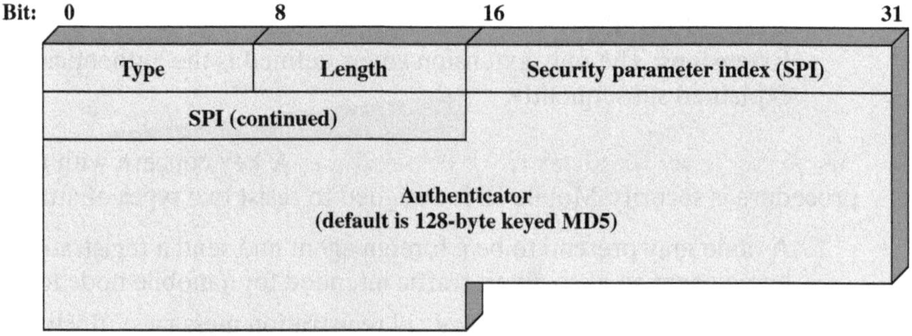

Figure 12.5 Mobile IP Authentication Extension

- **Security Parameter Index (SPI):** An index that identifies a security context between a pair of nodes. This security context is configured so that the two nodes share a secret key and parameters relevant to this association (e.g., authentication algorithm).
- **Authenticator:** A code used to authenticate the message. The sender inserts this code into the message using a shared secret key. The receiver uses the code to ensure that the message has not been altered or delayed. The authenticator protects the entire registration request or reply message, any extensions prior to this extension, and the type and length fields of this extension.

The default authentication algorithm is HMAC-MD5, defined in RFC 2104, which produces a 128-bit message digest. HMAC-MD4 is an example of what is known as a keyed hash code. Appendix 12B describes such codes. The digest is computed over a shared secret key, and the protected fields from the registration message.

Three types of authentication extensions are defined:

- **Mobile-home:** This extension must be present and provides for authentication of the registration messages between the mobile node and the home agent.
- **Mobile-foreign:** The extension may be present when a security association exists between the mobile node and the foreign agent. The foreign agent will strip this extension off before relaying a request message to the home agent and add this extension to a reply message coming from a home agent.
- **Foreign-home:** The extension may be present when a security association exists between the foreign agent and the home agent.

Note that the authenticator protects the identification field in the request and reply messages. As a result, the identification value can be used to thwart replay types of attacks. As was mentioned, the identification value enables the mobile node to match a reply to a request. Further, if the mobile node and the home agent maintain synchronization, so that the home agent can distinguish between a reasonable identification value from a suspicious one, then the home agent can reject suspicious messages. One way to do this is to use a timestamp value. As long as the mobile node and home agent have reasonably synchronized values of time, the timestamp will serve the purpose. Alternatively, the mobile node could generate values using a pseudorandom number generator. If the home agent knows the algorithm, then it knows what identification value to expect next.

Tunneling

Once a mobile node is registered with a home agent, the home agent must be able to intercept IP datagrams sent to the mobile node's home address so that these datagrams can be forwarded via tunneling. The standard does not mandate a specific technique for this purpose but references ARP (Address Resolution Protocol) as a possible mechanism. The home agent needs to inform other nodes on the same network (the home network) that IP datagrams with a destination address of the mobile node in question should be delivered (at the link level) to this agent. In effect, the home agent steals the identity of the mobile node in order to capture packets destined for that node that are transmitted across the home network.

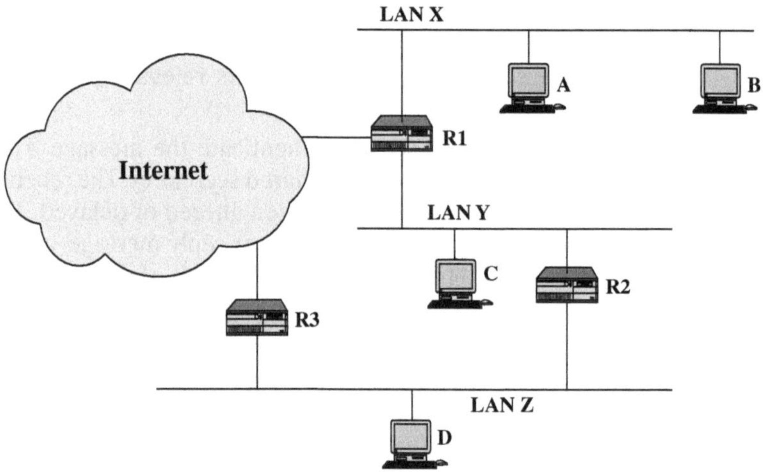

Figure 12.6 A Simple Internetworking Example

For example, suppose that R3 in Figure 12.6 is acting as the home agent for a mobile node that is attached to a foreign network elsewhere on the Internet. That is, there is a host H whose home network is LAN Z that is now attached to some foreign network. If host D has traffic for H, it will generate an IP datagram with H's home address in the IP destination address field. The IP module in D recognizes that this destination address is on LAN Z and so passes the datagram down to the link layer with instructions to deliver it to a particular MAC-level address on Z. Prior to this time, R3 has informed the IP layer at D that datagrams destined for that particular address should be sent to R3. Thus, D inserts the MAC address of R3 in the destination MAC address field of the outgoing MAC frame. Similarly, if an IP datagram with the mobile node's home address arrives at router R2, it recognizes that the destination address is on LAN Z and will attempt to deliver the datagram to a MAC-level address on Z. Again, R2 has previously been informed that the MAC-level address it needs corresponds to R3.

For traffic that is routed across the Internet and arrives at R3 from the Internet, R3 must simply recognize that for this destination address, the datagram is to be captured and forwarded.

To forward an IP datagram to a care-of address, the home agent puts the entire IP datagram into an outer IP datagram. This is a form of encapsulation, just as placing an IP header in front of a TCP segment encapsulates the TCP segment in an IP datagram. Three options for encapsulation are allowed for Mobile IP:

- **IP-within-IP encapsulation:** This is the simplest approach, defined in RFC 2003.
- **Minimal encapsulation:** This approach involves fewer fields, defined in RFC 2004.
- **Generic routing encapsulation (GRE):** This is a generic encapsulation procedure that was developed prior to the development of Mobile IP, defined in RFC 1701.

We review the first two of these methods.

IP-within-IP Encapsulation With this approach, the entire IP datagram becomes the payload in a new IP datagram (Figure 12.7a). The inner, original IP

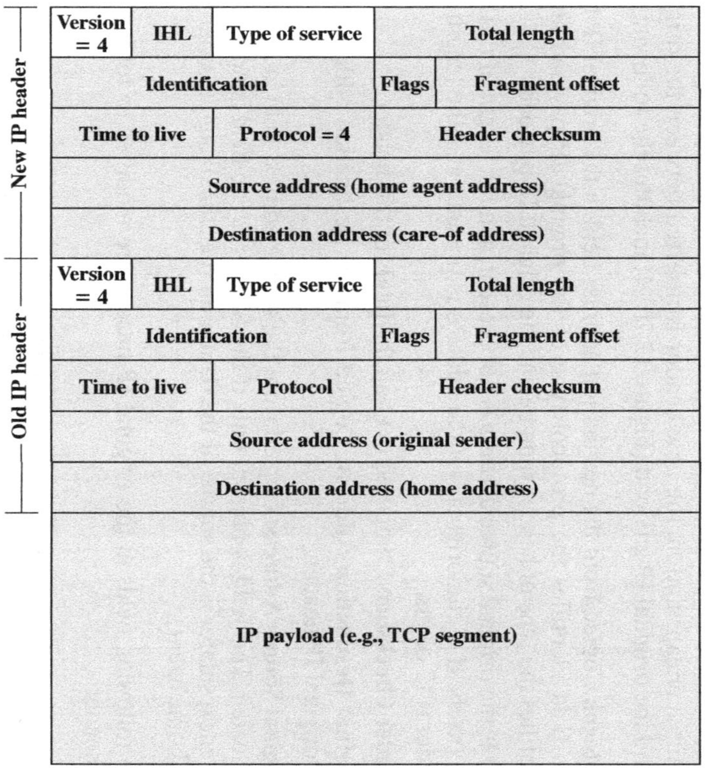

Unshaded fields are copied from the inner IP header to the outer IP header.

(a) IP-within-IP encapsulation

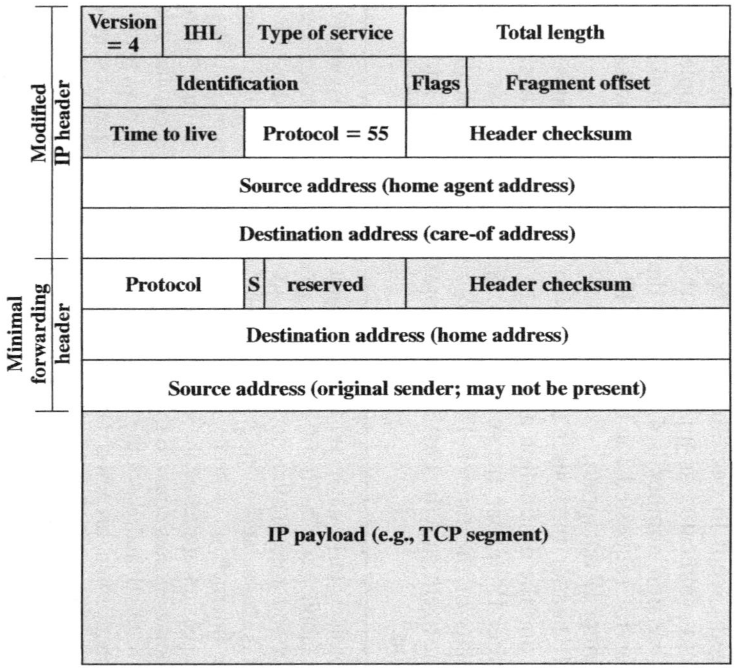

Unshaded fields in the inner IP header are copied from the original IP header.
Unshaded fields in the outer IP header are modified from the original IP header.

(b) Minimal encapsulation

Figure 12.7 Mobile IP Encapsulation

header is unchanged except to decrement TTL by 1. The outer header is a full IP header. Two fields (indicated as unshaded in the figure) are copied from the inner header: The version number is 4, which is the protocol identifier for IPv4, and the type of service requested for the outer IP datagram is the same as that requested for the inner IP datagram.

In the inner IP header, the source address refers to the host that is sending the original datagram, and the destination address is the home address of the intended recipient. In the outer IP header, the source and destination addresses refer to the entry and exit points of the tunnel. Thus, the source address typically is the IP address of the home agent, and the destination address is the care-of address for the intended destination.

Example 12.1 Consider an IP datagram that originates at server X in Figure 12.1 and that is intended for mobile node A. The original IP datagram has a source address equal to the IP address of X and a destination address equal to the IP home address of A. The network portion of A's home address refers to A's home network, and so the datagram is routed through the Internet to A's home network, where it is intercepted by the home agent. The home agent encapsulates the incoming datagram with an outer IP header, which includes a source address equal to the IP address of the home agent and a destination address equal to the IP address of the foreign agent on the foreign network to which A is currently attached. When this new datagram reaches the foreign agent, it strips off the outer IP header and delivers the original datagram to A.

Minimal Encapsulation Minimal encapsulation results in less overhead and can be used if the mobile node, home agent, and foreign agent all agree to do so. With minimal encapsulation, the new header is inserted between the original IP header and the original IP payload (Figure 12.7b). It includes the following fields:

- **Protocol:** Copied from the destination address field in the original IP header. This field identifies the protocol type of the original IP payload and thus identifies the type of header than begins the original IP payload.
- **S:** If 0, the original source address is not present, and the length of this header is 8 octets. If 1, the original source address is present, and the length of this header is 12 octets.
- **Header Checksum:** Computed over all the fields of this header.
- **Original Destination Address:** Copied from the destination address field in the original IP header.
- **Original Source Address:** Copied from the source address field in the original IP header. This field is present only if the S bit is 1. The field is not present if the encapsulator is the source of the datagram (i.e., the datagram originates at the home agent).

The following fields in the original IP header are modified to form the new outer IP header:

- **Total Length:** Incremented by the size of the minimal forwarding header (8 or 12).
- **Protocol:** 55; this is the protocol number assigned to minimal IP encapsulation.

- **Header Checksum:** Computed over all the fields of this header; because some of the fields have been modified, this value must be recomputed.
- **Source Address:** The IP address of the encapsulator, typically the home agent.
- **Destination Address:** The IP address of the exit point of the tunnel. This is the care-of address and may either be the IP address of the foreign agent or the IP address of the mobile node (in the case of a co-located care-of address).

The processing for minimal encapsulation is as follows. The encapsulator (home agent) prepares the encapsulated datagram with the format of Figure 12.7b. This datagram is now suitable for tunneling and is delivered across the Internet to the care-of address. At the care-of address, the fields in the minimal forwarding header are restored to the original IP header and the forwarding header is removed from the datagram. The total length field in the IP header is decremented by the size of the minimal forwarding header (8 or 12) and the header checksum field is recomputed.

12.2 WIRELESS APPLICATION PROTOCOL

The Wireless Application Protocol (WAP) is a universal, open standard developed by the WAP Forum to provide mobile users of wireless phones and other wireless terminals such as pagers and personal digital assistants (PDAs) access to telephony and information services, including the Internet and the Web. WAP is designed to work with all wireless network technologies (e.g., GSM, CDMA, and TDMA). WAP is based on existing Internet standards, such as IP, XML, HTML, and HTTP, as much as possible. It also includes security facilities. Ericsson, Motorola, Nokia, and Phone.com established the WAP Forum in 1997, which now has several hundred members. At the time of this writing, the current release of the WAP specification is version 2.0.

Strongly affecting the use of mobile phones and terminals for data services are the significant limitations of the devices and the networks that connect them. The devices have limited processors, memory, and battery life. The user interface is also limited, and the displays small. The wireless networks are characterized by relatively low bandwidth, high latency, and unpredictable availability and stability compared to wired connections. Moreover, all these features vary widely from terminal device to terminal device and from network to network. Finally, mobile, wireless users have different expectations and needs from other information systems users. For instance, mobile terminals must be extremely easy to use, much easier than workstations and personal computers. WAP is designed to deal with these challenges.

The WAP specification includes

- A programming model based on the WWW Programming Model
- A markup language, the Wireless Markup Language, adhering to XML
- A specification of a small browser suitable for a mobile, wireless terminal
- A lightweight communications protocol stack
- A framework for wireless telephony applications (WTAs)

The WAP specification consists of a number of different protocols and modules, whose relationship is depicted in Figure 12.8.

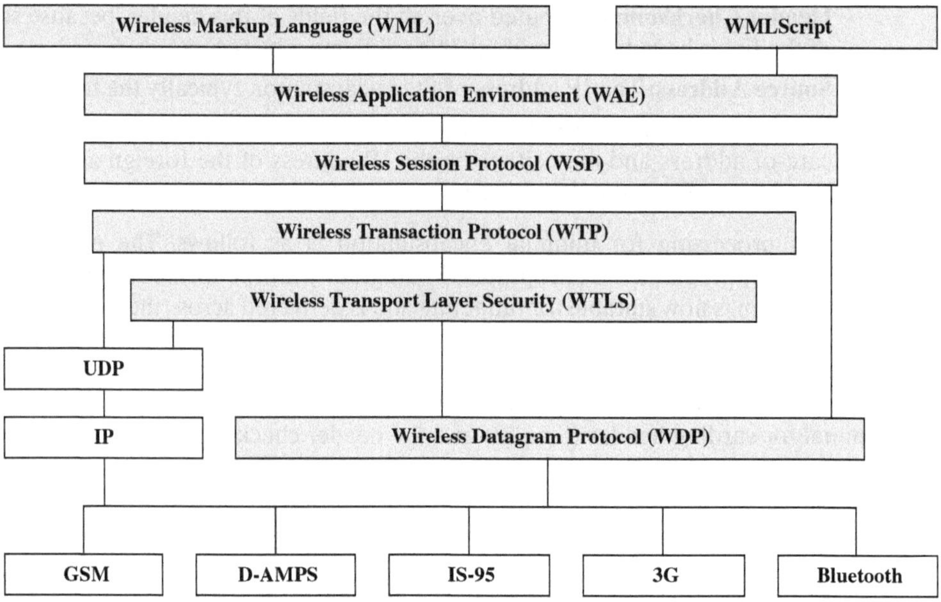

Figure 12.8 WAP Protocol Stack

Architectural Overview

The WAP Programming Model is based on three elements: the client, the gateway, and the original server (Figure 12.9). HTTP is used between the gateway and the original server to transfer content. The gateway acts as a proxy server for the wireless domain. Its processor(s) provide services that offload the limited capabilities of the hand-held, mobile, wireless terminals. For example, the gateway provides DNS services, converts between WAP protocol stack and the WWW stack (HTTP and TCP/IP), encodes information from the Web into a more compact form that minimizes wireless communication, and, in the other direction, decodes the compacted form into standard Web communication conventions. The gateway also caches frequently requested information.

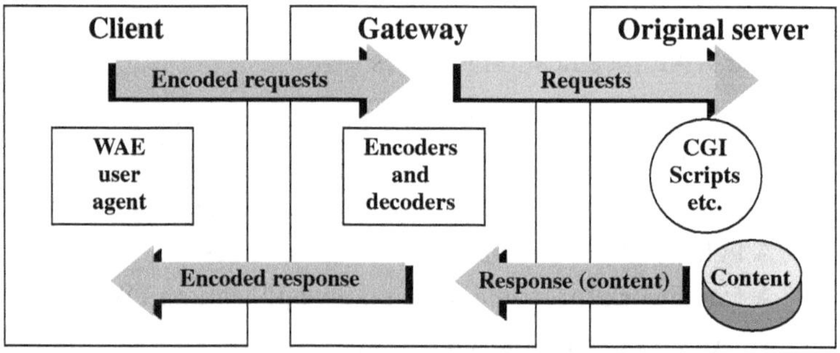

Figure 12.9 The WAP Programming Model

Figure 12.10 illustrates key components in a WAP environment. Using WAP, a mobile user can browse Web content on an ordinary Web server. The Web server provides content in the form of HTML-coded pages that are transmitted using the standard Web protocol stack (HTTP/TCP/IP). The HTML content must go through an HTML filter, which may either be colocated with the WAP proxy or in a separate physical module. The filter translates the HTML content into WML content. If the filter is separate from the proxy, HTTP/TCP/IP is used to deliver the WML to the proxy. The proxy converts the WML to a more compact form known as binary WML and delivers it to the mobile user over a wireless network using the WAP protocol stack.

If the Web server is capable of directly generating WML content, then the WML is delivered using HTTP/TCP/IP to the proxy, which converts the WML to binary WML and then delivers it to the mobile node using WAP protocols.

The WAP architecture is designed to cope with the two principal limitations of wireless Web access: the limitations of the mobile node (small screen size, limited

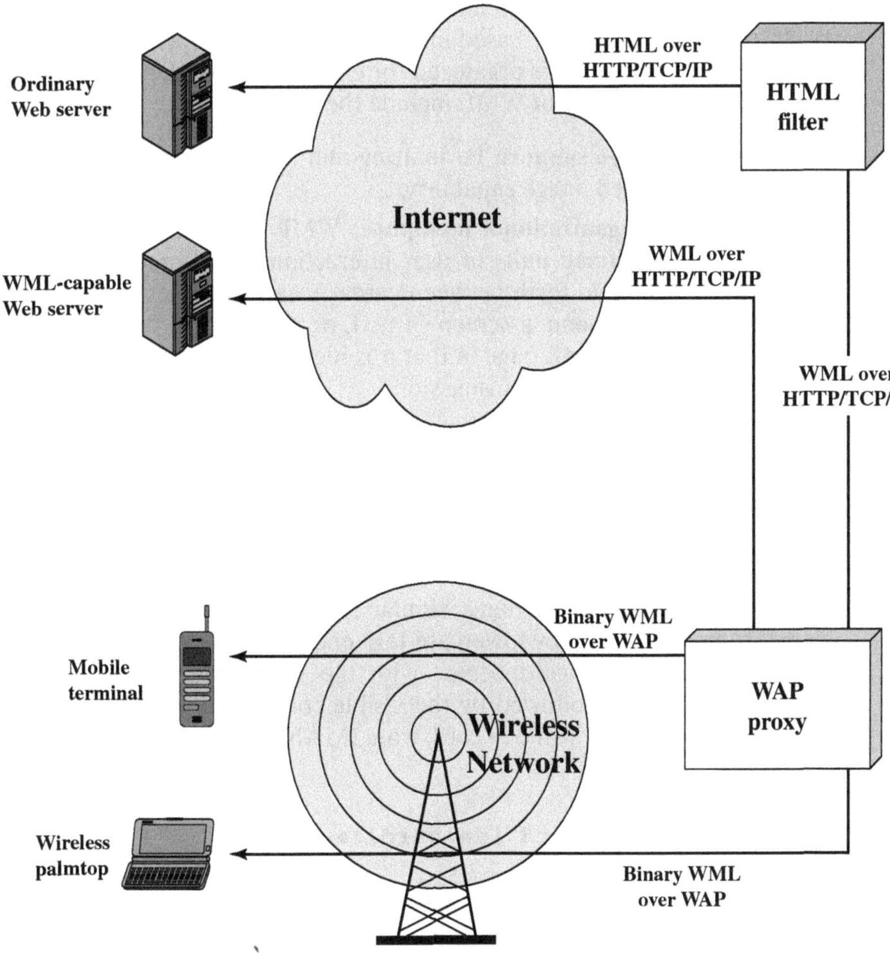

Figure 12.10 WAP Infrastructure

input capability) and the low data rates of wireless digital networks. Even with the introduction of 3G wireless networks, which will provide broadband data rates, the small hand-held mobile nodes will continue to have limited input and display capabilities. Thus WAP or a similar capability will be needed for the indefinite future.

Wireless Markup Language

WML was designed to describe content and format for presenting data on devices with limited bandwidth, limited screen size, and limited user input capability. It is designed to work with telephone keypads, styluses, and other input devices common to mobile, wireless communication. WML permits the scaling of displays for use on two-line screens found in some small devices, as well as the larger screens found on smart phones.

For an ordinary PC, a Web browser provides content in the form of Web pages coded with the Hypertext Markup Language (HTML). To translate an HTML-coded Web page into WML with content and format suitable for wireless devices, much of the information, especially graphics and animation, must be stripped away. WML presents mainly text-based information that attempts to capture the essence of the Web page and that is organized for easy access for users of mobile devices.

Important features of WML include the following:

- **Text and image support:** Formatting and layout commands are provided for text and limited image capability.
- **Deck/card organizational metaphor:** WML documents are subdivided into small, well-defined units of user interaction called cards. Users navigate by moving back and forth between cards. A card specifies one or more units of interaction (a menu, a screen of text, or a text-entry field). A WML deck is similar to an HTML page in that it is identified by a Web address (URL) and is the unit of content transmission.
- **Support for navigation among cards and decks:** WML includes provisions for event handling, which is used for navigation or executing scripts.

In an HTML-based Web browser, a user navigates by clicking on links. At a WML-capable mobile device, a user interacts with cards, moving forward and back through the deck.

WML is a tagged language, similar to HTML, in which individual language elements are delineated by lowercase tags enclosed in angle brackets. Typically, the WML definition of a card begins with the nonvisible portion, which contains executable elements, followed by the visible content. As an example, consider the following simple deck with one card, from [MANN99]:

```
<wml>
   <card id='card1'>
   <p>
      Hello WAP World.
   <p>
   </card>
</wml>
```

Table 12.3 WML Tags

Tag	Description
Deck Structure	
<access>	Access control
<card>	Card definition
<head>	Deck-level information (meta, access, template)
<meta>	Meta information
<template>	Deck-level event bindings
<wml>	Deck definition
Content	
<img>	Image
<p>	Paragraph, visible content
<table>	Table
<td>	Table data
<tr>	Table row
Formatting	
<b>	Bold
<big>	Large font
 	Line break
<em>	Emphasis
<i>	Italic
<small>	Small font
<strong>	Strong font
<u>	Underline
User Input	
<fieldset>	Data entry items grouping
<input>	Data entry
<optgroup>	Subset of a choice list
<option>	Single choice in a list
<select>	Choice list
Variables	
<postfield>	Set an http request variable
<setvar>	Set a variable in a task
Timers	
<Timer>	Set a timer
Tasks	
<go>	Go to a URL
<noop>	No action
<prev>	Go to previous card
<refresh>	Screen redraw
Task/Event Bindings	
<a>	Abbreviated anchor
<anchor>	Anchor
<do>	Response to user button press
<onevent>	Intrinsic event binding

The tags `<wml>`, `<card>`, and `<p>` enclose the deck, card, and paragraph, respectively. Like HMTL, most elements end with a terminating tag that is identical to the starting tag with the addition of the character `"\"`. When a wireless device receives this code, it will display the message "Hello WAP World" on the terminal's screen.

Table 12.3 lists the full set of WML tags, which are divided into eight functional groups.

WMLScript

WMLScript is a scripting language with similarities to JavaScript. It is designed for defining script-type programs in a user device with limited processing power and memory. Table 12.4 shows valid WMLScript statements. Important capabilities of WMLScript include the following:

- Check the validity of user input before it is sent to the content server.
- Access device facilities and peripherals.

Table 12.4 WMLScript Statements

Statement	Description
=	Assignment
break	Terminate the current loop
continue	Current loop iteration
for	Indexed loop
function	Function declaration
if..else	Conditional test
return	Exit the current function
var	Variable declaration
while	Boolean-controlled loop

- Interact with the user without introducing round trips to the origin server (e.g., display an error message).

Key WMLScript features include the following [WAPF98]:

- **JavaScript-based scripting language:** WMLScript is a subset of JavaScript, with some extensions.
- **Procedural logic:** WMLScript adds the power of procedural logic to the Wireless Application Environment (WAE), discussed subsequently.
- **Event based:** WMLScript may be invoked in response to certain user or environmental events.
- **Compiled implementation:** WMLScript can be compiled down to a more efficient byte code that is transported to the client.
- **Integrated into WAE:** WMLScript is fully integrated with the WML browser. This allows authors to construct their service using both WML and WMLScript.
- **Efficient extensible library support:** WMLScript can be used to expose and extend device functionality without changes to the device software.

Wireless Application Environment

The WAE specifies an application framework for wireless devices such as mobile telephones, pagers, and PDAs. In essence, the WAE consists of tools and formats that are intended to ease the task of developing applications and devices supported by WAP. The major elements of the WAE model are as follows (Figure 12.11):

- **WAE user agents:** Software that executes in the user's wireless device and that provides specific functionality (e.g., display content) to the end user.
- **Content generators:** Applications (or services) on origin servers (e.g., CGI scripts) that produce standard content formats in response to requests from user agents in the mobile terminal. WAE does not specify any standard content generators but expects that there will be a variety available running on typical HTTP origin servers commonly used in WWW today.

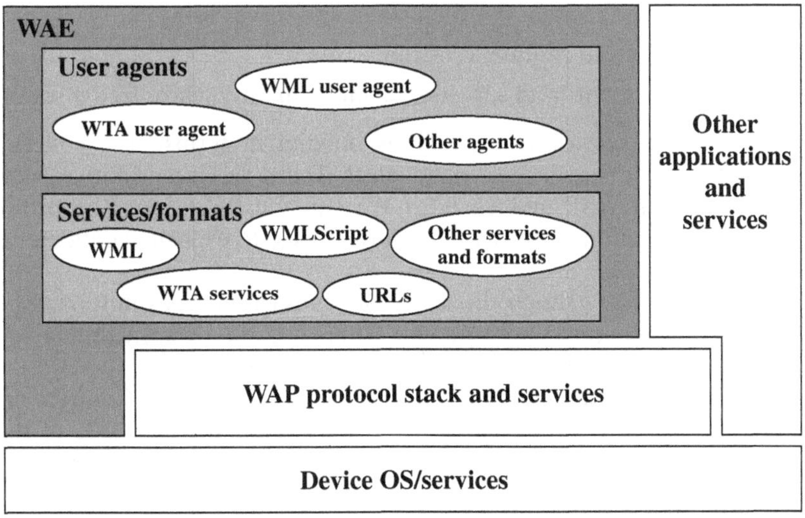

Figure 12.11 WAE Client Components [WAPF98]

- **Standard content encoding:** Defined to allow a WAE user agent (e.g., a browser) to conveniently navigate Web content.
- **Wireless telephony applications (WTA):** A collection of telephony-specific extensions for call and feature control mechanisms that provide authors advanced mobile network services. Using WTA, applications developers can use the microbrowser to originate telephone calls and to respond to events from the telephone network.

Wireless Session Protocol

WSP provides applications with an interface for two session services. The connection-oriented session service operates above the reliable transport protocol WTP, and the connectionless session service operates above the unreliable transport protocol WDP. In essence, WSP is based on HTTP with some additions and modifications to optimize its use over wireless channels. The principal limitations addressed are low data rate and susceptibility to loss of connection due to poor coverage or cell overloading.

WSP is a transaction-oriented protocol based on the concept of a request and a reply. Each WSP protocol data unit (PDU) consists of a body, which may contain WML, WMLScript, or images, and a header, which contains information about the data in the body and about the transaction. WSP also defines a server Push operation, in which the server sends unrequested content to a client device. This may be used for broadcast messages or for services, such as news headlines or stock quotes, that may be tailored to each client device.

WSP Service In general, a connection-mode WSP provides the following services:

- Establish a reliable session from client to server and release that session in an orderly manner.
- Agree on a common level of protocol functionality using capability negotiation.

- Exchange content between client and server using compact encoding.
- Suspend and resume a session.
- Push content from server to client in an unsynchronized manner.

At the service level, WSP is defined in terms of a collection of service primitives, with associated parameters. These service primitives define the interface between WSP and users of WSP in the WAE.[1] At the protocol level, the WSP specification defines a PDU format used to exchange data between peer WSP entities.

Figure 12.12 shows the key WSP transaction types in terms of the primitives and parameters that are exchanged. There are other transaction types, but these are sufficient to give a feel for the operation of WSP.

Session establishment involves the exchange of S-Connect primitives (Figure 12.12a). A WSP user acting as a client (mobile node side of the transaction) requests a session with a WSP user acting as a server (Web Server) on a remote system by issuing an S-Connect.req to WSP. Four parameters accompany the request:

- **Server address:** The peer with which the session is to be established.
- **Client address:** The originator of the session.
- **Client headers:** Contain attribute information that can be used for application-level parameters to be communicated to the peer. This information is passed without modification by WSP and is not processed by WSP.
- **Requested capabilities:** A set of capabilities for this session requested by the client; these are listed in Table 12.5.

The client's WSP then prepares a WSP PDU, containing these parameters, to convey the request to the peer WSP at the server. The server address, client address, and client headers are unchanged. However, the WSP service provider at the client or the WSP service provider at the server, or both, may modify the set of requested capabilities so that they do not imply a higher level of functionality than the provider can support. With this possible modification, an S-Connect.ind containing the same parameters as in the request is delivered to the WSP user at the server side. If the WSP user at the server accepts the session request, it responds by invoking WSP with an S-Connect.rsp containing server headers and negotiated capabilities. The negotiated capabilities parameter is optional. If it is absent, the WSP user agrees to the set of capabilities proposed in the S-Connect.ind. If it is present, it reflects the level of functionality that the WSP user will accept. Finally, an S-Connect.ind is delivered to the original requester, containing the server headers and the final set of negotiated capabilities.

The S-Disconnect primitive is used for **session termination**. Figure 12.12b shows the case in which the client WSP user initiates the termination. The request primitive includes the following parameters:

- **Reason code:** Cause of disconnection. If the cause is that the client is being redirected to contact a new server address, the next two parameters must be present.

---

[1]See Appendix 12C for a brief discussion of the concept of service primitives and parameters.

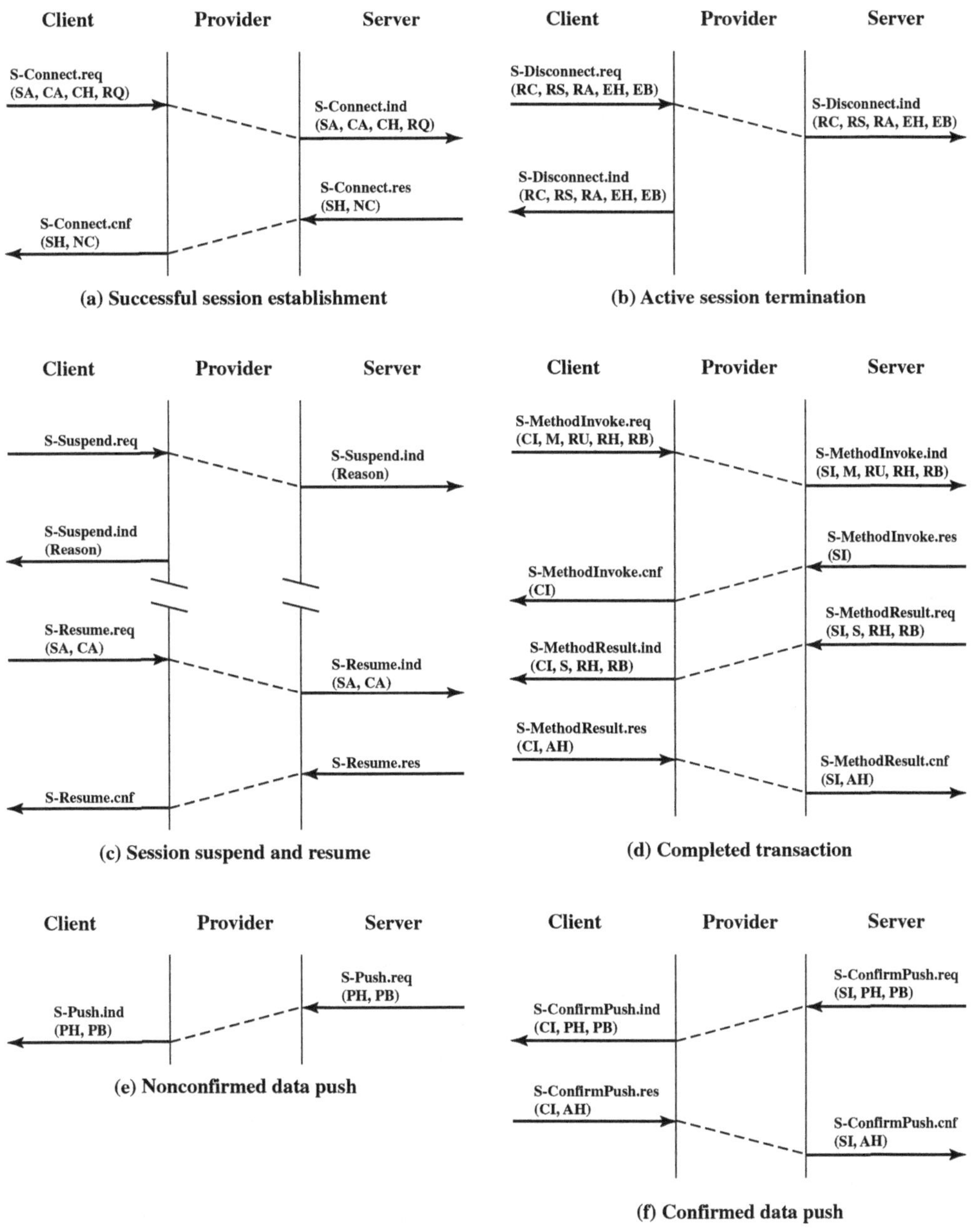

Figure 12.12 Wireless Session Protocol Primitives and Parameters

- **Redirect security:** Indicates whether or not the client may reuse the current secure session when redirecting.
- **Redirect addresses:** Alternate addresses to be used to establish a session.

Table 12.5 Wireless Session Protocol Capabilities

Name	Class	Type	Description
Aliases	I	List of addresses	Indicates which alternative addresses the peer may use to access this session service user. Can be used to facilitate a switch to a news bearer when a session is resumed.
Client SDU size	N	Positive integer	The size of the largest transaction service data unit that may be sent to the client during the session.
Extended methods	N	Set of method names	The set of extended methods (beyond and HTTP/1.1) that are supported by both client server peers.
Header code pages	N	Set of code page names	The set of extension header code pages that are supported by both client and server peers.
Maximum outstanding method requests	N	Positive integer	The maximum number of method invocations that can be active at the same time during the session.
Maximum outstanding push requests	N	Positive integer	The maximum number of confirmed push the invocations that can be active at the same time during the session.
Protocol options	N	Set of facilities and features	May include Push, Confirmed Push, Session Resume, and Acknowledgment Headers.
Server SDU size	N	Positive integer	The size of the largest transaction SDU that may be sent to the server during the session.

I = informational
N = negotiable

- **Error headers and error body:** If the termination is due to an error, these parameters may be included to provide information to the server WSP user about the error.

WSP acknowledges the receipt of the request by returning an S-Disconnect.ind to the client WSP user and conveying an S-Disconnect.ind to the server WSP user.

WSP supports **session suspend and resume**. An example of the use of this feature is when the client knows that it may be temporarily unavailable, due to roaming or disconnect and reconnect of the client device to the network. When a session is suspended, the state of the session is saved on both the client and server side and any in-transit data are lost. Figure 12.12c shows the sequence involved when the suspend and resume are initiated by the client. For suspension, the only parameter is a reason code in the S-Suspend.ind primitive. When a resume request is issued, the server address and client address are present in the request and indication primitives.

A **transaction** involves an exchange of data between a client and server using the S-MethodInvoke and S-MethodResult primitives (Figure 12.12d). S-MethodInvoke is used to request an operation to be executed by the server. The request contains the following parameters:

- **Client Transaction ID:** Used to distinguish between pending transactions
- **Method:** Identifies the requested operation

- **Request URI (uniform resource identifier):** Specifies the entity to which the operation applies
- **Request headers and body:** Attribute information and data associated with the request

The indication conveyed to the server includes the same parameters except that the client transaction ID is replaced by a server transaction ID. The response and confirm primitives are used to confirm that the request has been conveyed and contain transaction IDs.

S-MethodResult is used to return a response to an operation request. The request issued by the server includes the server transaction ID, the status associated with this response, and response headers and body containing attribute information and data associated with the response. The response and confirm primitives are used to confirm that the request has been conveyed and contain transaction IDs. These two primitives may also contain acknowledgment headers used to return some information to the server.

The **nonconfirmed data push** is used to send unsolicited information from the server to the client (Figure 12.12e). The only parameters associated with these primitives are push headers and a push body containing attributes and the information to be conveyed. With **confirmed data push**, the server receives a confirmation that the push data have been delivered to the client. In addition to push headers and a push body, the confirmed data push primitives include a push ID; the respond and confirm primitives may also include acknowledgment headers.

The connectionless session service provides a nonconfirmed capability for exchanging content entities between WSP users. Only the method invocation and push facilities are available.

WSP Protocol Data Units WSP conveys service requests and responses in WSP PDUs. Each PDU is passed down to the transport layer to be included as the body of a transport-level PDU. At the top level, the WSP PDU consists of three fields. The TID field is used to associated requests with replies in the connectionless WSP service and is not present in the connection-mode service. The Type field specifies the type and function of the PDU and basically corresponds to the type of service primitive that invoked WSP. Finally, the Type-Specific Contents contain all of the information to be conveyed as a result of a WSP service primitive.

Wireless Transaction Protocol

WTP manages transactions by conveying requests and responses between a user agent (such as a WAP browser) and an application server for such activities as browsing and e-commerce transactions. WTP provides a reliable transport service but dispenses with much of the overhead of TCP, resulting in a lightweight protocol that is suitable for implementation in "thin" clients (e.g., mobile nodes) and suitable for use over low-bandwidth wireless links. WTP includes the following features:

- Three classes of transaction service.
- Optional user-to-user reliability: WTP user triggers the confirmation of each received message.

- Optional out-of-band data on acknowledgments.
- PDU concatenation and delayed acknowledgment to reduce the number of messages sent.
- Asynchronous transactions.

WTP is transaction oriented rather than connection oriented. With WTP, there is no explicit connection setup or teardown but rather a reliable connectionless service.

WTP Transaction Classes WTP provides three transaction classes that may be invoked by WSP or another higher layer protocol:

- **Class 0:** Unreliable invoke message with no result message
- **Class 1:** Reliable invoke message with no result message
- **Class 2:** Unreliable invoke message with one reliable result message

Class 0 provides an unreliable datagram service, which can be used for an unreliable push operation. Data from a WTP user are encapsulated by WTP (the initiator, or client) in an Invoke PDU and transmitted to the target WTP (the responder, or server), with no acknowledgment. The responder WTP delivers the data to the target WTP user.

Class 1 provides a reliable datagram service, which can be used for a reliable push operation. Data from an initiator are encapsulated in an Invoke PDU and transmitted to the responder. The responder delivers the data to the target WTP user and acknowledges receipt of the data by sending back an ACK PDU to the WTP entity on the initiator side, which confirms the transaction to the source WTP user. The responder WTP maintains state information for some time after the ACK has been sent to handle possible retransmission of the ACK if it gets lost and/or the initiator retransmits the Invoke PDU.

Class 2 provides a request/response transaction service and supports the execution of multiple transactions during one WSP session. Data from an initiator are encapsulated in an Invoke PDU and transmitted to the responder, which delivers the data to the target WTP user. The target WTP user prepares response data, which are handed down to the local WTP entity. The responder WTP entity sends these data back in a result PDU. If there is a delay in generating the response data beyond a timer threshold, the responder may send an ACK PDU before sending the result PDU. This prevents the initiator from unnecessarily retransmitting the Invoke message.

Protocol Formats and Operation WTP makes use of six types of PDUs. Each PDU begins with a fixed header portion (Figure 12.13) and may be followed by a variable header portion that contains supplementary control information. The supplementary information is in the form of one or more transaction protocol items (TPIs).

The **Invoke PDU** is used to convey a request from an initiator to a responder; it is four bytes long and includes the following fixed header fields:

- **Continue Flag:** If this flag is set, there are one or more TPIs following the fixed header. In turn, each TPI begins with a continue flag bit to indicate whether there are more TPIs to follow or this is the last TPI.

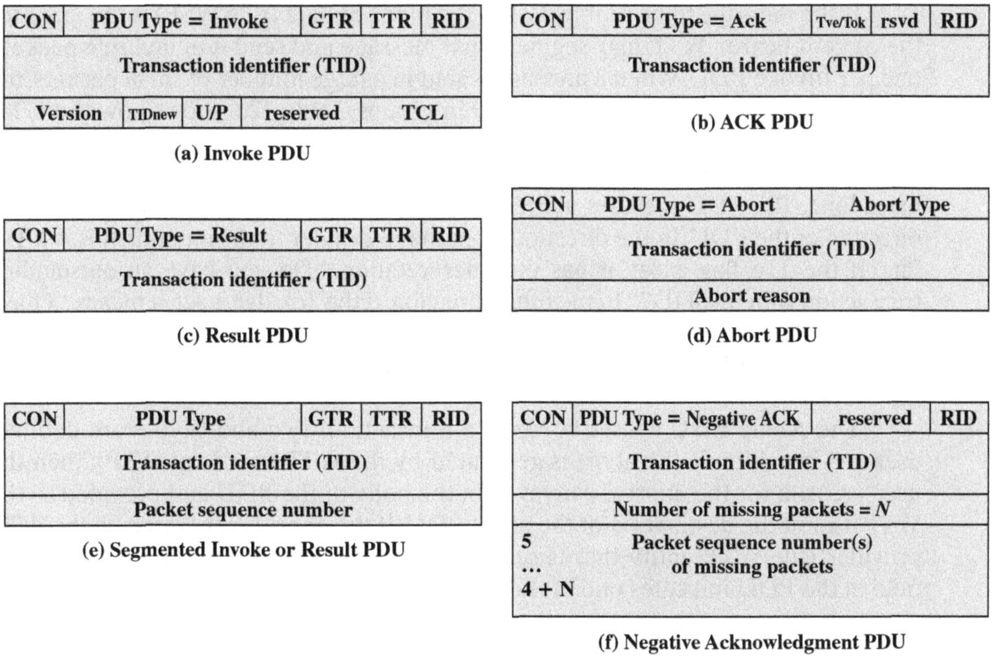

CON = continue flag
GTR = group trailer
TTR = transmission trailer
RID = retransmission indicator

TIDnew = TIDnew flag
U/P = user/provider acknowledgment flag
TCL = transaction class
Tve/Tok = TID verify/TID OK flag

Figure 12.13 WTP PDU Fixed Header Formats

- **PDU Type:** Indicates that this is an Invoke PDU.
- **Group Trailer Flag:** Used when segmentation and reassembly are employed, as explained subsequently.
- **Transmission Trailer Flag:** Also used with segmentation and reassembly.
- **Retransmission Indicator:** Indicates whether this is a retransmission. The initiator will retransmit an Invoke PDU if it does not receive an acknowledgment within a specified time.
- **Transaction Identifier:** Used to associate a PDU with a particular transaction.
- **Version:** Version of WTP.
- **TIDnew Flag:** Set when the initiator has "wrapped" the TID value; that is, the next TID will be lower then the previous one.
- **U/P Flag:** When set, it indicates that the initiator require a user acknowledgment from the server WTP user. This means the WTP user confirms every received message. When this flag is clear, the responding WTP entity may acknowledge an incoming PDU without a confirmation from its user.
- **Transaction Class:** Indicates the desired transaction class to be used in processing this Invoke PDU.

If the message to be sent by WTP (the block of data from WSP) is too large for the current bearer, WTP may segment that message and send it in multiple packets, one per Invoke PDU. When a message is sent in a large number of small packets, the packets may be sent and acknowledged in groups. Table 12.6 shows how the GTR and TTR flags are used to manage the process.

The **ACK PDU** is used to acknowledge an Invoke or Result PDU. It is three bytes long. The PDU includes a Tve/Tok flag, whose interpretation depends on the direction of the PDU. In the direction from the responder to the initiator, this is a Tve flag. If the Tve flag is set, it has the interpretation, "Do you have an outstanding transaction with this TID?" In the other direction, if the Tok flag is set, it means, "I have an outstanding transaction with this TID."

The **Result PDU** is a 3-byte PDU used to convey the response of the server to the client.

The **Abort PDU** is used to abort a transaction. Two abort types are defined: user and provider. If the abort is generated by the WTP user (e.g., WSP), then the user's reason for the abort is conveyed in the body of the PDU and provided to the WTP user at the destination of the abort PDU. If the abort is generated by the WTP provider (the WTP entity that is sending this abort PDU), then the abort reason field in the PDU indicates one of the following reasons:

- **Unknown:** Unexplained error.
- **Protocol error:** The received PDU could not be interpreted.
- **Invalid TID:** Used by the initiator as a negative result to the TID verification.
- **Not implemented Class 2:** The respondent does not support class 2, which was requested.
- **Not implemented SAR:** The respondent does not support segmentation and reassembly.
- **Not implemented user acknowledgment:** The responder does not support user acknowledgment.
- **WTP version 1:** The initiator requested a version of WTP that is not supported; current version is 1.
- **Capacity temporarily exceeded:** Due to an overload situation, transaction cannot be completed.

Table 12.6 Group Trailer (GTR) and Transmission Trailer (TTR) Combinations

GTR	TTR	Description
0	0	Not last packet
0	1	Last packet of message
1	0	Last packet of packet group
1	1	Segmentation and reassembly not supported

The **segmented invoke PDU** and the **segmented result PDU** may be used for segmentation and reassembly. When they are used, each packet is numbered sequentially. The **negative acknowledgment PDU** is used to indicate that one or more packets in a sequence did not arrive.

Figure 12.14 shows some basic examples of the time sequence of the use of WTP PDUs for the three classes of operation.

WTP Service The WTP service is defined by three primitives. TR-Invoke is used to initiate a new transaction. TR-Result is used to send back a result of a previously initiated transaction. And Tr-Abort is used to abort an existing transaction. Figure 12.15 shows the relationship between these primitives and a class 2 transaction with "hold on" acknowledgment. Compare with Figure 12.14d.

Figure 12.15 also shows how the WTP service supports the WSP service. The sequence of WSP service primitives provides for a completed transaction and is identical to the sequence shown in Figure 12.12d.

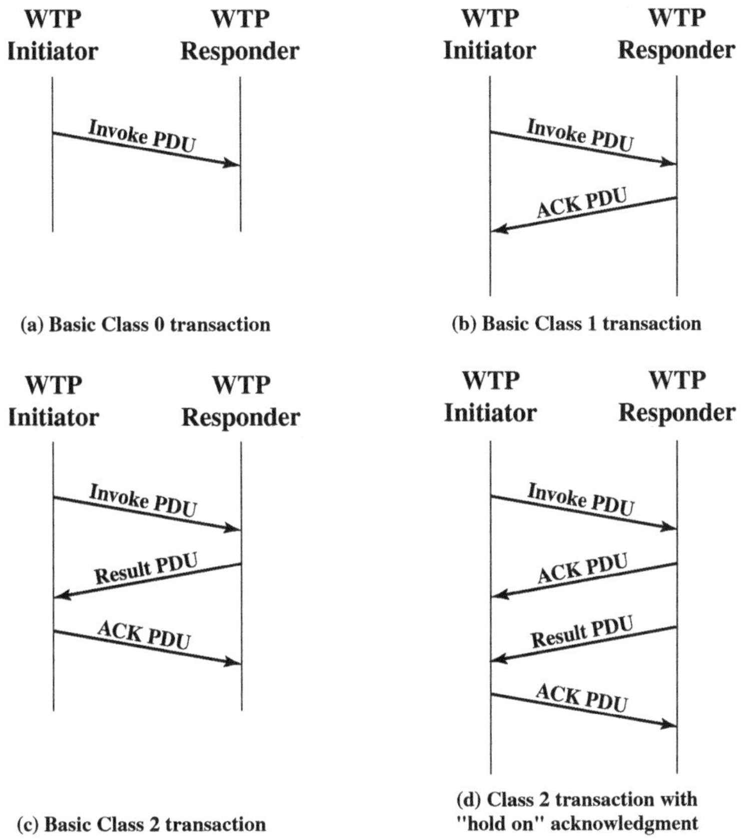

Figure 12.14 Examples of WTP Operation

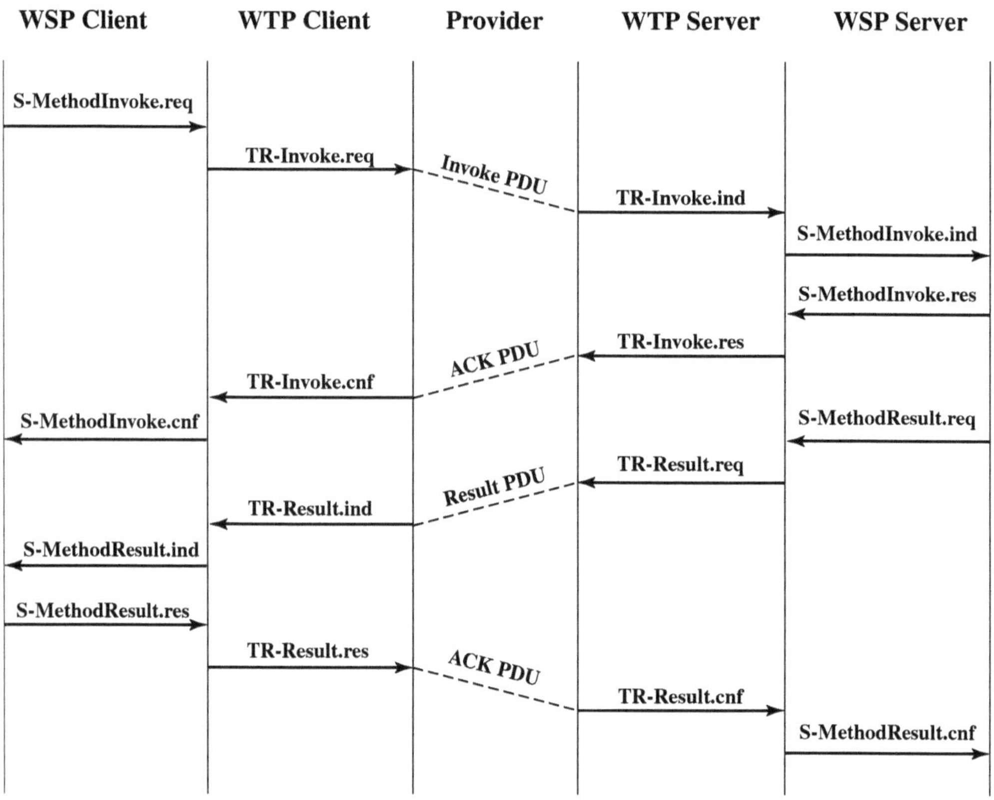

Figure 12.15 WSP-WTP Timing Diagram

Wireless Transport Layer Security

WTLS provides security services between the mobile device (client) and the WAP gateway. WTLS is based on the industry-standard Transport Layer Security (TLS) Protocol, which is a refinement of the secure sockets layer (SSL). TLS is the standard security protocol used between Web browsers and Web servers.[2] WTLS is more efficient that TLS, requiring fewer message exchanges. To provide end-to-end security, WTLS is used between the client and the gateway, and TLS is used between the gateway and the target server. WAP systems translate between WTLS and TLS within the WAP gateway. Thus, the gateway is a point of vulnerability and must be given a high level of security from external attacks.

WTLS provides the following features:

- **Data integrity:** Ensures that data sent between the client and the gateway are not modified, using message authentication

[2]For a detailed description of TLS, see [STAL03].

Figure 12.16 WTLS Protocol Stack

- **Privacy:** Ensures that the data cannot be read by a third party, using encryption
- **Authentication:** Establishes the authentication of the two parties, using digital certificates
- **Denial-of-service protection:** Detects and rejects messages that are replayed or not successfully verified

WTLS is not a single protocol but rather two layers of protocols, as illustrated in Figure 12.16. The WTLS Record Protocol provides basic security services to various higher-layer protocols. In particular, the Hypertext Transfer Protocol (HTTP), defined in RFC 2068 and which provides the transfer service for Web client/server interaction, can operate on top of WTLS. Three higher-layer protocols are defined as part of WTLS: the Handshake Protocol, The Change Cipher Spec Protocol, and the Alert Protocol.

WTLS Record Protocol The WTLS Record Protocol takes user data from the next higher layer (WTP, WTLS handshake protocol, WTLS alert protocol, WTLS change cipher spec protocol) and encapsulates these data in a PDU. The following steps occur (Figure 12.17):

1. The payload is compressed using a lossless compression algorithm.

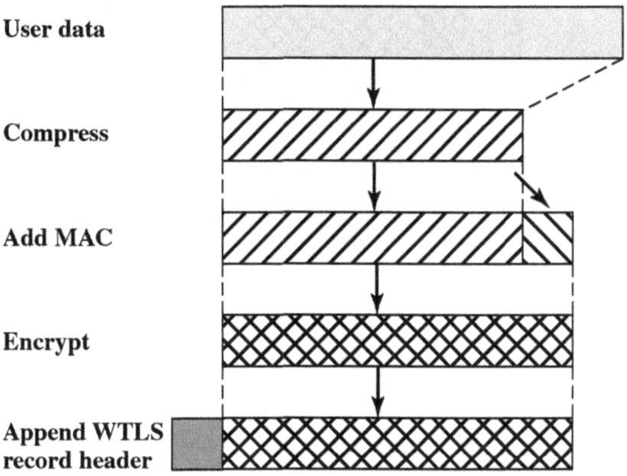

Figure 12.17 WTLS Record Protocol Operation

2. A message authentication code (MAC) is computed over the compressed data, using HMAC. HMAC is a keyed hash code similar to (but more complex than) the one described in Appendix 12B. One of several hash algorithms can be used with HMAC, including MD-5 and SHA-1. The length of the hash code is 0, 5, or 10 bytes. The MAC is added after the compressed data.
3. The compressed message plus the MAC code are encrypted using a symmetric encryption algorithm. The allowable encryption algorithms are DES, triple DES, RC5, and IDEA.
4. The Record Protocol prepends a header to the encrypted payload.

The Record Protocol header consists of the following fields (Figure 12.18):

- **Content Type (8 bits):** The higher-layer protocol above the WTLS Record Protocol.
- **Cipher Spec Indicator (1 bit):** If this bit is zero, it indicates that no compression, MAC protection, or encryption is used.
- **Sequence Number Field Indicator (1 bit):** Indicates whether a sequence number field is present.
- **Record Length Field Indicator (1 bit):** Indicates whether a record length field is present.
- **Sequence Number (16 bits):** A sequence number associated with this PDU. This provides reliability over an unreliable transport service.

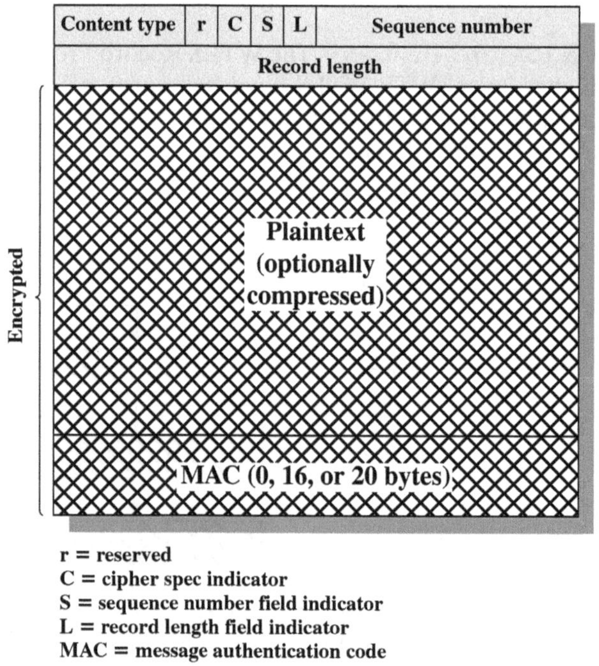

Figure 12.18 WTLS Record Format

- **Record Length (32 bits):** The length in bytes of the plaintext data (or compressed data if compression is used).

Change Cipher Spec Protocol Associated with the current transaction is a cipher spec, which specifies the encryption algorithm, the hash algorithm used as part of HMAC, and cryptographic attributes, such as MAC code size. There are actually a two states associated with each session. Once a session is established, there is a current operating state for both read and write (i.e., receive and send). In addition, during the Handshake Protocol, pending read and write states are created.

The Change Cipher Spec Protocol is one of the three WTLS-specific protocols that use the WTLS Record Protocol, and it is the simplest. This protocol consists of a single message, which consists of a single byte with the value 1. The sole purpose of this message is to cause the pending state to be copied into the current state, which updates the cipher suite to be used on this connection.

Alert Protocol The Alert Protocol is used to convey WTLS-related alerts to the peer entity. As with other applications that use WTLS, alert messages are compressed and encrypted, as specified by the current state.

Each message in this protocol consists of 2 bytes. The first byte takes the value warning(1), critical(2), or fatal(3) to convey the severity of the message. If the level is fatal, WTLS immediately terminates the connection. Other connections on the same session may continue, but no new connections on this session may be established. The second byte contains a code that indicates the specific alert. The following are examples of fatal alerts:

- **unexpected_message:** An inappropriate message was received.
- **bad_record_mac:** An incorrect MAC was received.
- **decompression_failure:** The decompression function received improper input (e.g., unable to decompress or decompress to greater than maximum allowable length).
- **handshake_failure:** Sender was unable to negotiate an acceptable set of security parameters given the options available.
- **illegal_parameter:** A field in a handshake message was out of range or inconsistent with other fields.

The following are examples of nonfatal alerts:

- **bad_certificate:** A received certificate was corrupt (e.g., contained a signature that did not verify).
- **unsupported_certificate:** The type of the received certificate is not supported.
- **certificate_revoked:** A certificate has been revoked by its signer.
- **certificate_expired:** A certificate has expired.
- **certificate_unknown:** Some other unspecified issue arose in processing the certificate, rendering it unacceptable.

Handshake Protocol The most complex part of WTLS is the Handshake Protocol. This protocol allows the server and client to authenticate each other and to negotiate an encryption and MAC algorithm and cryptographic keys to be used to protect data sent in a WTLS record. The Handshake Protocol is used before any application data are transmitted.

The Handshake Protocol consists of a series of messages exchanged by client and server. Figure 12.19 shows the initial exchange needed to establish a logical connection between client and server. The exchange can be viewed as having four phases.

The **first phase** is used to initiate a logical connection and to establish the security capabilities that will be associated with it. The exchange is initiated by the client.

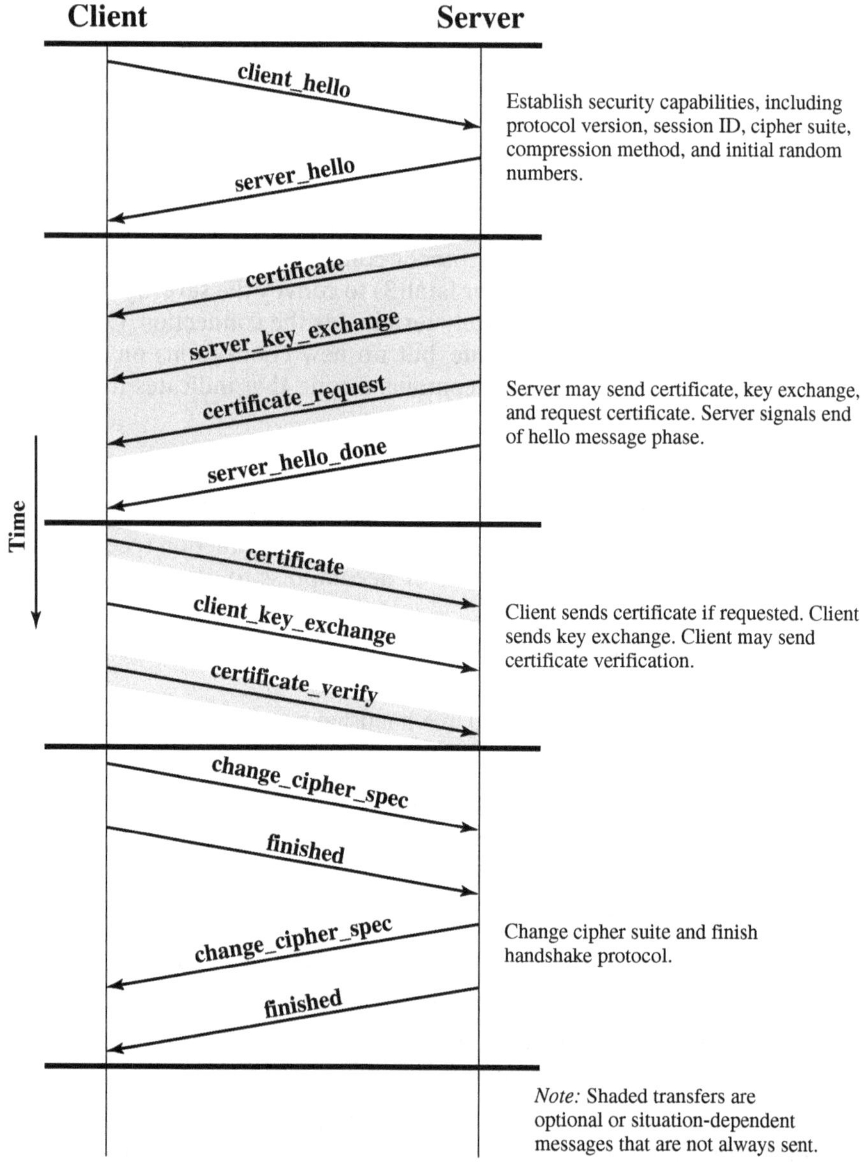

Figure 12.19 WTLS Handshake Protocol Action

The client sends a **client_hello** message that includes a session ID and a list of cryptographic and compression algorithms supported by the client (in decreasing order of preference for each algorithm type). After sending the **client_hello** message, the client waits for the **server_hello** message. This message indicates which cryptographic and compression algorithms will be used for the exchange.

The **second phase** is used for server authentication and key exchange. The server begins this phase by sending its public-key certificate, if it needs to be authenticated. Next, a **server_key_exchange** message may be sent if it is required. This message is needed for certain public-key algorithms used for symmetric key exchange. Next, the server can request a public key certificate from the client, using the **certificate_request** message. The final message in Phase 2, and one that is always required, is the **server_hello_done** message, which is sent by the server to indicate the end of the server hello and associated messages. After sending this message, the server will wait for a client response. This message has no parameters.

The **third phase** is used for client authentication and key exchange. Upon receipt of the **server_hello_done** message, the client should verify that the server provided a valid certificate if required and check that the **server_hello** parameters are acceptable. If all is satisfactory, the client sends one or more messages back to the server. If the server has requested a certificate, the client sends a certificate message. Next is the **client_key_exchange** message, which must be sent in this phase. The content of the message depends on the type of key exchange. Finally, in this phase, the client may send a **certificate_verify** message to provide explicit verification of a client certificate.

The **fourth phase** completes the setting up of a secure connection. The client sends a **change_cipher_spec** message and copies the pending CipherSpec into the current CipherSpec. Note that this message is not considered part of the Handshake Protocol but is sent using the Change Cipher Spec Protocol. The client then immediately sends the finished message under the new algorithms, keys, and secrets. The finished message verifies that the key exchange and authentication processes were successful. In response to these two messages, the server sends its own **change_cipher_spec** message, transfers the pending to the current CipherSpec, and sends its finished message. At this point the handshake is complete and the client and server may begin to exchange application layer data.

Wireless Datagram Protocol

WDP is used to adapt a higher-layer WAP protocol to the communication mechanism (called the bearer) used between the mobile node and the WAP gateway. Adaptation may include partitioning data into segments of appropriate size for the bearer and interfacing with the bearer network. WDP hides details of the various bearer networks from the other layers of WAP. In some instances, WAP is implemented on top of IP.

WDP Service The WDP service is defined by two service primitives. The T-DUnitdata primitive provides a nonconfirmed service with the following parameters:

- **Source address:** Address of the device making a request to the WDP layer
- **Source port:** Application address associated with the source address
- **Destination address:** Destination address for the data submitted to WDP
- **Destination port:** Application address associated with the destination address

- **User data:** User data from the next higher layer, submitted to WDP for transmission to the destination port

The T-Derror.ind primitive is used to alert a WDP user of a failure to deliver a WDP datagram. In addition to the source address, source port, destination address, and destination port parameters, T-Derror.ind includes an error code parameter with local significance.

WDP Protocol The following fields are necessary in a WDP PDU:

- Destination Port
- Source Port

If the underlying bearer does not provide segmentation and reassembly, the feature is implemented in WDP in a bearer-independent way.

For example, GSM (Global System for Mobile Communications) dictates a format for a user data header, in which the header consists of a sequence of information elements, and each element is defined by an identifier, a length, and one or more bytes of value. The WDH PDU for GSM has the following structure:

- **Header length (1 byte):** Length of header.
- **Port numbers identifier (1 byte):** The value 5 indicates that this information element consists of two port numbers.
- **Port numbers length (1 byte):** The value 4 indicates that the value portion of this information element is 4 bytes long.
- **Destination port (2 bytes)**
- **Source port (2 bytes)**
- **SAR identifier (1 byte):** The value 0 indicates that this information element consists of information for segmentation and reassembly.
- **SAR length (1 byte):** The value 3 indicates that the value portion of this information element is 3 bytes long.
- **Datagram reference number (1 bytes):** An identifier assigned to all of the segments that make up a block of user data.
- **Number of segments (1 byte):** The total number of segments that need to be reassembled.
- **Segment count:** A sequence number that identifies this segment within the sequence of all segments that need to be reassembled to form the block of user data.
- **User data (1 to n bytes)**

Wireless Control Message Protocol WCMP performs the same support function for WDP as ICMP does for IP (see Appendix 12A). WCMP is used in environments that do not provide an IP bearer and therefore do not lend themselves to the use of ICMP. WCMP is used by wireless nodes and WAP gateways to report errors encountered in processing WDP datagrams. WCMP can also be used for informational and diagnostic purposes.

Table 12.7 lists the WCMP messages and associated error codes.

Table 12.7 WCMP Messages

WCMP Message	WCMP Type	WCMP Code	WDP Node	WAP Gateway
Destination Unreachable	**51**			
• No route to destination		0	N/A	O
• Communication administratively prohibited		1	N/A	O
• Address unreachable		3	N/A	O
• Port unreachable		4	M	N/A
Parameter Problem	**54**			
• Erroneous header field		0	O	O
Message Too Big	**60**	0	M	N/A
Reassembly Failure	**61**			
• Reassembly time exceeded		1	O	N/A
• Buffer overflow		2	O	N/A
Echo Request	**178**	0	O	N/A
Echo Reply	**179**	0	M	N/A

M = mandatory
O = optional
N/A = not applicable

Today, WAP use has largely disappeared in Europe and the United States. There are several reasons for this. First, all modern handsets from the major vendors (Nokia, Motorola, Apple, etc.) support full HTML, and do not use any kind of WAP markup. The list of handsets supporting HTML is extensive, and includes all Android handsets, all Blackberry devices, all versions of the iPhone handset, all devices running Windows Phone, and many Nokia handsets. Second, the adoption of WAP in the hyperlink "/wiki/United_States_of_America" suffered because many cell phone providers required separate activation and additional fees for data support, and also because telecommunications companies have sought to limit data access to only approved data providers operating under license of the signal carrier.

In terms of speed, ease of use, appearance and interoperability, the reality fell far short of expectations when the first handsets became available in 1999. This led to the wide usage of derisive phrases such as "Worthless Application Protocol," "Wait And Pay," "What A Puke" and so on. WAP has not been the mainstream technology for web on mobile for a number of years.

Unlike in Europe, WAP has been a real success in Japan. All the major cellular operators in Japan, NTT DoCoMo, KDDI and SoftBank Mobile (previously Vodafone Japan) have all successfully deployed WAP technology.

12.3 RECOMMENDED READINGS AND WEB SITES

[PERK97] is a good survey article on Mobile IP; a somewhat less technical, more business-oriented description from the same author is [PERK98]. For greater detail, see [MOND03]. The August 2000 issue of *IEEE Personal Communications* contains a number of articles on enhancements to the current Mobile IP standard.

[MANN99] is an overview of WAP, while [PASS00] discusses building applications for wireless communications using WAP. [HEIJ00] provides detailed coverage of WAP.

HEIJ00 Heijden, M., and Taylor, M., eds. *Understanding WAP: Wireless Applications, Devices, and Services.* Boston: Artech House, 2000.

MANN99 Mann, S. "The Wireless Application Protocol." *Dr. Dobb's Journal*, October 1999.

MOND03 Mondal, A. *Mobile IP: Present State and Future.* New York: Kluwer Academic Publishers, 2003.

PASS00 Passani, L. "Creating WAP Services." *Dr. Dobb's Journal*, July 2000.

PERK97 Perkins, C. "Mobile IP." *IEEE Communications Magazine*, May 1997.

PERK98 Perkins, C. "Mobile Networking Through Mobile IP." *IEEE Internet Computing*, January–February 1998.

Recommended Web Sites:

- **IP Routing for Wireless/Mobile Hosts:** IETF Working Group on Mobile IP. Contains current RFCs and Internet drafts.
- **Open Mobile Alliance:** Consolidation of the WAP Forum and the Open Mobile Architecture Initiative. Provides WAP technical specifications and industry links.

12.4 KEY TERMS, REVIEW QUESTIONS, AND PROBLEMS

Key Terms

care-of address	Mobile IP	wireless transaction protocol (WTP)
encapsulation	tunneling	wireless transport layer security (WTLS)
foreign agent	wireless application environment (WAE)	wireless markup language (WML)
foreign network	wireless application protocol (WAP)	
hash function	wireless datagram protocol (WDP)	
home address	wireless session protocol (WSP)	
home agent		
home network		
internet control message protocol (ICMP)		

Review Questions

12.1 Explain the distinction between a mobile user and a nomadic user.

12.2 What is tunneling?

12.3 List and briefly define the capabilities provided by Mobile IP.

12.4 What is the relationship between Mobile IP discovery and ICMP?

12.5 What are the two different types of destination addresses that can be assigned to a mobile node while it is attached to a foreign network?

12.6 Under what circumstances would a mobile node choose to use each of the types of address referred to in Question 5?

12.7 What is the difference between an HTML filter and a WAP proxy?

12.8 What are the functional areas supported by WML?

12.9 What services are provided by WSP?

12.10 When would each of the three WTP transaction classes be used?

12.11 List and briefly define the security services provided by WTLS.

Problems

12.1 This problem refers to Figure 12.6. Suppose that LAN Z is the home network for host E and that D sends a block of data to E via IP.

a. Show the PDU structure, including the fields of the IP header and the lower-level headers (MAC, LLC) with the contents of address fields indicated for the case in which E is on its home network.

b. Repeat part a for the case in which E is on a foreign network reachable via the Internet through R3. Show formats for the MAC frame leaving D and the IP datagram leaving R3. Assume that IP-to-IP encapsulation is used.

c. Repeat part b for the IP datagram leaving R3, but now assume that minimal encapsulation is used.

12.2 Again referring to Figure 12.6, assume that A is a mobile node and that LAN X is a foreign network for A. Assume that an IP datagram arrives at R1 from the Internet to be delivered to A. Show the format of the IP datagram arriving at R1 and the MAC frame leaving R1 (include the IP header or headers) for the following cases:

a. IP-to-IP encapsulation is used and R1 is the care-of address.

b. Minimal encapsulation is used and R1 is the care-of address.

c. IP-to-IP encapsulation is used and A is the care-of address.

d. Minimal encapsulation is used and A is the care-of address.

12.3 In a typical Mobile IP implementation in a home agent, the agent maintains a mobility binding table to map a mobile node's home address to its care-of address for packet forwarding. What entries are essential for each row of the table?

12.4 In a typical Mobile IP implementation in a foreign agent, the agent maintains a visitor table that contains information about the mobile nodes currently visiting this network. What entries are essential for each row of the table?

12.5 In WTLS, why is there a separate Change Cipher Spec Protocol, rather than including a **change_cipher_spec** message in the Handshake Protocol?

APPENDIX 12A INTERNET CONTROL MESSAGE PROTOCOL

The IP standard specifies that a compliant implementation must also implement ICMP (RFC 792, RFC 950, RFC 1256). ICMP provides a means for transferring messages from routers and other hosts to a host. In essence, ICMP provides feedback about problems in the communication environment. Examples of its use are when a datagram cannot reach its destination, when the router does not have the buffering capacity to forward a datagram, and when the router can direct the station to send traffic on a shorter route. In most cases, an ICMP message is sent in response to a datagram, either by a router along the datagram's path or by the intended destination host.

ICMP is a user of IP. An ICMP message is constructed and then passed down to IP, which encapsulates the message with an IP header and then transmits the resulting datagram in the usual fashion. Because ICMP messages are transmitted in IP datagrams, their delivery is not guaranteed and their use cannot be considered reliable.

Figure 12.20 shows the format of the various ICMP message types. An ICMP message starts with a 64-bit header consisting of the following:

- **Type (8 bits):** Specifies the type of ICMP message.
- **Code (8 bits):** Used to specify parameters of the message that can be encoded in one or a few bits.
- **Checksum (16 bits):** Checksum of the entire ICMP message. This is the same checksum algorithm used for IP.
- **Parameters (32 bits):** Used to specify more lengthy parameters.

Type	Code	Checksum
Unused		
IP header + 64 bits of original datagram		

(a) Destination unreachable; time exceeded; source quench

Type	Code	Checksum
Pointer	Unused	
IP header + 64 bits of original datagram		

(b) Parameter problem

Type	Code	Checksum
Router IP address		
IP header + 64 bits of original datagram		

(c) Redirect

Type	Code	Checksum
Num addrs	Entry size	Lifetime
Router address 1		
Preference level 1		
• • •		
Router address *n*		
Preference level *n*		

(d) Router advertisement

Type	Code	Checksum
Unused		

(e) Router solicitation

Type	Code	Checksum
Identifer		Sequence number
Originate timestamp		

(f) Timestamp

Type	Code	Checksum
Identifer		Sequence number
Originate timestamp		
Receive timestamp		
Transmit timestamp		

(g) Timestamp reply

Type	Code	Checksum
Identifier		Sequence number
Optional data		

(h) Echo; echo reply

Type	Code	Checksum
Identifer		Sequence number

(i) Address mask request

Type	Code	Checksum
Identifer		Sequence number
Address mask		

(j) Address mask reply

Figure 12.20 ICMP Message Formats

For some message types, these fields are followed by additional information fields that further specify the content of the message.

In those cases in which the ICMP message refers to a prior datagram, the information field includes the entire IP header plus the first 64 bits of the data field of the original datagram. This enables the source host to match the incoming ICMP message with the prior datagram. The reason for including the first 64 bits of the data field is that this will enable the IP module in the host to determine which upper-level protocol or protocols were involved. In particular, the first 64 bits would include a portion of the TCP header or other transport-level header.

The **destination unreachable** message covers a number of contingencies. A router may return this message if it does not know how to reach the destination network. In some networks, an attached router may be able to determine if a particular host is unreachable and return the message. The destination host itself may return this message if the user protocol or some higher-level service access point is unreachable. This could happen if the corresponding field in the IP header was set incorrectly. If the datagram specifies a source route that is unusable, a message is returned. Finally, if a router must fragment a datagram but the Don't Fragment flag is set, the datagram is discarded and a message is returned.

A router will return a **time exceeded** message if the lifetime of the datagram expires. A host will send this message if it cannot complete reassembly within a time limit.

A syntactic or semantic error in an IP header will cause a **parameter problem** message to be returned by a router or host. For example, an incorrect argument may be provided with an option. The parameter field contains a pointer to the octet in the original header where the error was detected.

The **source quench** message provides a rudimentary form of flow control. Either a router or a destination host may send this message to a source host, requesting that it reduce the rate at which it is sending traffic to the internet destination. On receipt of a source quench message, the source host should cut back the rate at which it is sending traffic to the specified destination until it no longer receives source quench messages. The source quench message can be used by a router or host that must discard datagrams because of a full buffer. In that case, the router or host will issue a source quench message for every datagram that it discards. In addition, a system may anticipate congestion and issue source quench messages when its buffers approach capacity. In that case, the datagram referred to in the source quench message may well be delivered. Thus, receipt of a source quench message does not imply delivery or nondelivery of the corresponding datagram.

A router sends a **redirect** message to a host on a directly connected router to advise the host of a better route to a particular destination. The following is an example, using Figure 12.6. Router R1 receives a datagram intended for D from host C on network Y, to which R1 is attached. R1 checks its routing table and obtains the address for the next router, R2, on the route to the datagram's internet destination network, Z. Because R2 and the host identified by the internet source address of the datagram are on the same network, R1 sends a redirect message to C. The redirect message advises the host to send its traffic for network Z directly to router R2, because this is a shorter path to the destination. The router forwards the original datagram to its internet destination (via R2). The address of R2 is contained in the parameter field of the redirect message.

The **echo** and **echo reply** messages provide a mechanism for testing that communication is possible between entities. The recipient of an echo message is obligated to return the message in an echo reply message. An identifier and sequence number are associated with the echo message to be matched in the echo reply message. The identifier might be used like a service access point to identify a particular session, and the sequence number might be incremented on each echo request sent.

The **timestamp** and **timestamp reply** messages provide a mechanism for sampling the delay characteristics of the Internet. The sender of a timestamp message may include an identifier and sequence number in the parameters field and include the time that the message is sent (originate timestamp). The receiver records the time it received the message and the time that it transmits the reply message in the timestamp reply message. If the timestamp message is sent using strict source routing, then the delay characteristics of a particular route can be measured.

The **address mask request** and **address mask reply** messages are useful in an environment that includes subnets. The address mask request and reply messages allow a host to learn the address mask for the LAN to which it connects. The host broadcasts an address mask request message on the LAN. The router on the LAN responds with an address mask reply message that contains the address mask.

Router Discovery

A router discovery capability was added to ICMP with RFC 1256. The objective of the router discovery capability is to automate the process by which a host determines a router address. In order for a host to send an IP datagram beyond the network to which it is attached, the host must have the address of at least one router attached to that network. These router addresses can be preconfigured in the host, but this approach has limitations. In particular, for newly attached hosts, including mobile hosts, such configuration files may not be available. RFC 1256 provides a way by which hosts may discover router addresses. It is applicable on networks that provide a multicast and/or broadcast capability.[3]

RFC 1256 defines two new ICMP message types: router advertisement and router solicitation. Periodically, each router that conforms to RFC 1256 issues a **router advertisement** message. The message includes the following fields:

- **Num Addrs:** The number of router addresses advertised in this message.
- **Addr Entry Size:** The number of 32-bit words per each router address; the value must be 2.
- **Lifetime:** The maximum number of seconds that the router advertisement may be considered valid; the default value is 1800 (30 minutes).
- **Router Address i, for 1 ≤ *i* ≤ Num Addrs:** The sending router's IP address(es) on the interface from which the message was sent.
- **Preference Level i, for 1 ≤ *i* ≤ Num Addrs:** The preferability of each router address i as a default router address, relative to other router addresses on this network. This is a signed value in twos complement representation; a higher value indicates more preferable.

Typically, a router will have a single IP address on a network, but multiple IP addresses are allowed. There will be multiple IP addresses for a router if the router has multiple physical connections (interfaces) to the network. Multiple IP addresses may also be assigned to a single interface to serve multiple subnets; this latter use need not concern us here. The preference level is used by a host to determine a default router to use when the host does not have sufficient routing information to determine which router is best for a given destination address. For example, in Figure 12.6, an IP datagram from host D addressed to host C is best sent through router R2, whereas a datagram addressed to a remote host elsewhere in the network should be sent through R3. But initially, if D has no information about which router to use, it needs to send the datagram to a default router. In this example, if the network administrator determines that most internet traffic from LAN Z is local (to other LANs at this location), then R2 should be assigned a higher preference level; and if most of the traffic is remote, then R3 should be assigned a higher preference level.

As a default, routers should issue router advertisement messages once every 7 to 10 minutes. If all hosts on this network support the IP multicast feature, then the messages should be sent on the all-systems multicast address of 224.0.0.1. Otherwise the broadcast address of 255.255.255.255 must be used.

[3]A multicast address is an address that designates a group of entities within a domain (e.g., network, internet). A broadcast address is an address that designates all entities within a domain (e.g., network, internet). Multicast and broadcast are easily done on a local area network, because all stations share the same transmission medium. Multicast and broadcast are also available on a number of wireless and switched network technologies.

If a host is just becoming active on a network, it can solicit router advertisements from all attached routers by issues a **router solicitation** message. Note from Figure 12.20e that this message contains no information other than identifying the type of message. Its purpose is simply to stimulate all routers to issue advertisements; hence no additional information is needed. If all routers on this network support the IP multicast feature, then the messages should be sent on the all-routers multicast address of 224.0.0.2. Otherwise the broadcast address of 255.255.255.255 must be used.

APPENDIX 12B MESSAGE AUTHENTICATION

One of the requirements for the Mobile IP registration protocol is message authentication. This appendix provides a brief overview. For more detail, see [STAL03].

A message, file, document, or other collection of data is said to be authentic when it is genuine and came from its alleged source. Message authentication is a procedure that allows communicating parties to verify that received messages are authentic. The two important aspects are to verify that the contents of the message have not been altered and that the source is authentic. We may also wish to verify a message's timeliness (it has not been artificially delayed and replayed) and sequence relative to other messages flowing between two parties.

A common technique used for message authentication is based on a keyed one-way hash function.

One-Way Hash Function

A hash function maps a variable-length block of data into a smaller fixed-length block. The purpose of a hash function is to produce a "fingerprint" of a file, message, or other block of data. To be useful for message authentication, a hash function H must have the following properties:

1. H can be applied to a block of data of any size.
2. H produces a fixed-length output.
3. $H(x)$ is relatively easy to compute for any given x, making both hardware and software implementations practical.
4. For any given code h, it is computationally infeasible to find x such that $H(x) = h$.
5. For any given block x, it is computationally infeasible to find $y \neq x$ with $H(y) = H(x)$.
6. It is computationally infeasible to find any pair (x, y) such that $H(x) = H(y)$.

The first three properties are requirements for the practical application of a hash function to message authentication. The fourth property is the "one-way" property: It is easy to generate a code given a message but virtually impossible to generate a message given a code. This property is important if the authentication technique involves the use of a secret value, as described subsequently.

The fifth property guarantees that it is impossible to find an alternative message with the same hash value as a given message.

A hash function that satisfies the first five properties in the preceding list is referred to as a **weak hash function**. If the sixth property is also satisfied, then it is referred to as a **strong hash function**. The sixth property protects against a sophisticated class of attack known as the birthday attack.

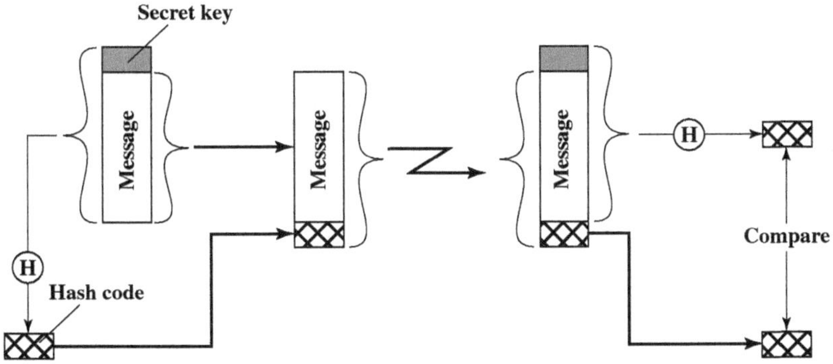

Figure 12.21 Message Authentication Using a One-Way Hash Function

In addition to providing authentication, a message digest also provides error detection. It performs the same function as an error detection code such as CRC: If any bits in the message are accidentally altered in transit, the message digest will be in error.

A widely used hash function is MD5, which produces a 128-bit message digest. MD5 is the default hash function for Mobile IP.

Keyed Hash Code

Figure 12.21 shows a technique that uses a hash function for message authentication. This technique assumes that two communicating parties, say A and B, share a common secret value S_{AB}. When A has a message to send to B, it calculates the hash function over the concatenation of the secret value and the message: $MD_M = H(S_{AB} \| M)$.[4] It then sends $[M \| MD_M]$ to B. Because B possesses S_{AB}, it can recompute $H(S_{AB} \| M)$ and verify MD_M. Because the secret value itself is not sent, it is not possible for an attacker to modify an intercepted message. As long as the secret value remains secret, it is also not possible for an attacker to generate a false message.

The keyed hash code approach depends on the hash function being one way. If the hash function is not one way, an attacker can easily discover the secret value: If the attacker can observe or intercept a transmission, the attacker obtains the message M and the hash code $MD_M = H(S_{AB} \| M)$. The attacker then inverts the hash function to obtain $S_{AB} \| M = H^{-1}(MD_M)$. Because the attacker now has both M and $S_{AB} \| M$, it is a trivial matter to recover S_{AB}.

APPENDIX 12C SERVICE PRIMITIVES AND PARAMETERS

In a communications architecture, such as the OSI model or the TCP/IP architecture (Figure 4.4), each layer is defined in two parts: the protocol between peer (at the same level) entities in different systems, and the services provided by one layer to the next higher layer in the same system.

The services between adjacent layers in a protocol architecture are expressed in terms of primitives and parameters. A primitive specifies the function to be performed, and the

[4] $\|$ denotes concatenation.

parameters are used to pass data and control information. The actual form of a primitive is implementation dependent. An example is a procedure call.

Four types of primitives are used in standards to define the interaction between adjacent layers in the architecture. These are defined in Table 12.8. The layout of Figure 12.22a suggests the time ordering of these events. For example, consider the transfer of a connection request from WSP user A to a peer entity B in another system. The following steps occur:

1. A invokes the services of WSP with an S-Connect.req primitive. Associated with the primitive are the parameters needed, such as the destination address.
2. The WSP entity in A's system prepares an WSP PDU to be sent to its peer WSP entity in B. This PDU is then sent encapsulated in a WTP PDU.
3. The destination WSP entity receives the WSP PDU and delivers the data to B via an S-Connect.ind, which includes the source address and other parameters.
4. B issues an S-Connect.res to its WSP entity.

Table 12.8 Service Primitive Types

Request	A primitive issued by a service user to invoke some service and to pass the parameters needed to specify fully the requested service.
Indication	A primitive issued by a service provider either to 1. indicate that a procedure has been invoked by the peer service user on the connection and to provide the associated parameters, or 2. notify the service user of a provider-initiated action.
Response	A primitive issued by a service user to acknowledge or complete some procedure previously invoked by an indication to that user.
Confirm	A primitive issued by a service provider to acknowledge or complete some procedure previously invoked by a request by the service user.

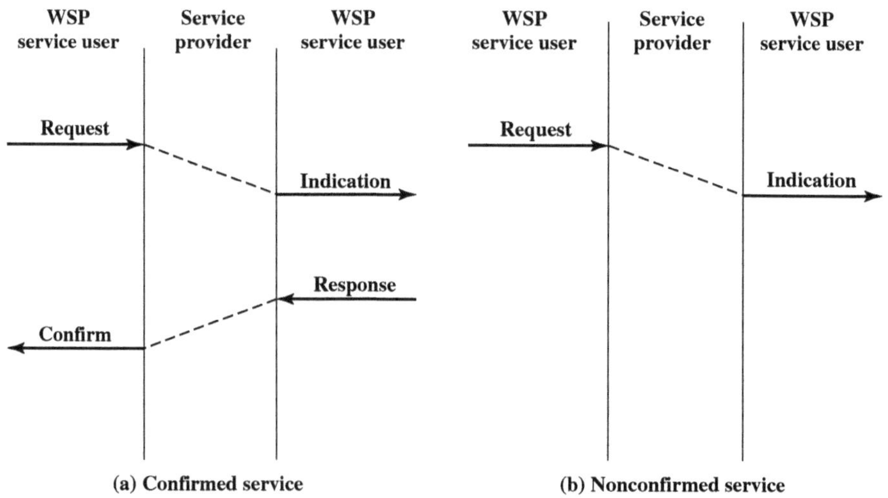

Figure 12.22 Times Sequence Diagrams for Service Primitives

5. B's WSP entity conveys the acknowledgment to A's WSP entity in a PDU.
6. The acknowledgment is delivered to A via an S-Connect.cnf.

This sequence of events is referred to as a **confirmed service**, as the initiator receives confirmation that the requested service has had the desired effect at the other end. If only request and indication primitives are involved (corresponding to steps 1 through 3), then the service dialogue is a **nonconfirmed service**; the initiator receives no confirmation that the requested action has taken place (Figure 12.22b).

PART FOUR

Wireless LANs

CHAPTER 13

WIRELESS LAN TECHNOLOGY

In just the past few years, wireless LANs have come to occupy a significant niche in the local area network market. Increasingly, organizations are finding that wireless LANs are an indispensable adjunct to traditional wired LANs, to satisfy requirements for mobility, relocation, ad hoc networking, and coverage of locations difficult to wire.

This chapter provides a survey of wireless LANs. We begin with an overview that looks at the motivations for using wireless LANs and summarizes the various approaches in current use. The next three sections examine in more detail the three principal types of wireless LANs, classified according to transmission technology: infrared, spread spectrum, and narrowband microwave.

13.1 OVERVIEW

As the name suggests, a wireless LAN is one that makes use of a wireless transmission medium. Until relatively recently, wireless LANs were little used. The reasons for this included high prices, low data rates, occupational safety concerns, and licensing requirements. As these problems have been addressed, the popularity of wireless LANs has grown rapidly.

In this section, we first look at the requirements for and advantages of wireless LANs and then preview the key approaches to wireless LAN implementation.

Wireless LAN Applications

[PAHL95] lists four application areas for wireless LANs: LAN extension, cross-building interconnect, nomadic access, and ad hoc networks. Let us consider each of these in turn.

LAN Extension Early wireless LAN products, introduced in the late 1980s, were marketed as substitutes for traditional wired LANs. A wireless LAN saves the cost of the installation of LAN cabling and eases the task of relocation and other modifications to network structure. However, this motivation for wireless LANs was overtaken by events. First, as awareness of the need for LANs became greater, architects designed new buildings to include extensive prewiring for data applications. Second, with advances in data transmission technology, there is an increasing reliance on twisted pair cabling for LANs and, in particular, Category 3 and Category 5 unshielded twisted pair. Most older buildings are already wired with an abundance of Category 3 cable, and many newer buildings are prewired with Category 5. Thus, the use of a wireless LAN to replace wired LANs has not happened to any great extent.

However, in a number of environments, there is a role for the wireless LAN as an alternative to a wired LAN. Examples include buildings with large open areas, such as manufacturing plants, stock exchange trading floors, and warehouses; historical buildings with insufficient twisted pair and where drilling holes for new wiring is prohibited; and small offices where installation and maintenance of wired LANs is not economical. In all of these cases, a wireless LAN provides an effective and more attractive alternative. In most of these cases, an organization will also have a wired LAN to support servers and some stationary workstations.

For example, a manufacturing facility typically has an office area that is separate from the factory floor but that must be linked to it for networking purposes. Therefore, typically, a wireless LAN will be linked into a wired LAN on the same premises. Thus, this application area is referred to as LAN extension.

Figure 13.1 indicates a simple wireless LAN configuration that is typical of many environments. There is a backbone wired LAN, such as Ethernet, that supports servers, workstations, and one or more bridges or routers to link with other networks. In addition, there is a control module (CM) that acts as an interface to a wireless LAN. The control module includes either bridge or router functionality to link the wireless LAN to the backbone. It includes some sort of access control logic, such as a polling or token-passing scheme, to regulate the access from the end systems. Note that some of the end systems are standalone devices, such as a workstation or a server. Hubs or other user modules (UMs) that control a number of stations off a wired LAN may also be part of the wireless LAN configuration.

The configuration of Figure 13.1 can be referred to as a single-cell wireless LAN; all of the wireless end systems are within range of a single control module. Another common configuration, suggested by Figure 13.2, is a multiple-cell wireless LAN. In this case, there are multiple control modules interconnected by a wired LAN. Each control module supports a number of wireless end systems within its transmission range. For example, with an infrared LAN, transmission is limited to a single room; therefore, one cell is needed for each room in an office building that requires wireless support.

Cross-Building Interconnect Another use of wireless LAN technology is to connect LANs in nearby buildings, be they wired or wireless LANs. In this case, a point-to-point wireless link is used between two buildings. The devices so connected are typically bridges or routers. This single point-to-point link is not a LAN per se, but it is usual to include this application under the heading of wireless LAN.

Nomadic Access Nomadic access provides a wireless link between a LAN hub and a mobile data terminal equipped with an antenna, such as a laptop computer or notepad computer. One example of the utility of such a connection is to enable an employee returning from a trip to transfer data from a personal portable computer to a server in the office. Nomadic access is also useful in an extended environment such as a campus or a business operating out of a cluster of buildings. In both of these cases, users may move around with their portable computers and may wish access to the servers on a wired LAN from various locations.

Ad Hoc Networking An ad hoc network is a peer-to-peer network (no centralized server) set up temporarily to meet some immediate need. For example, a group of employees, each with a laptop or palmtop computer, may convene in a conference room for a business or classroom meeting. The employees link their computers in a temporary network just for the duration of the meeting.

Figure 13.3 suggests the differences between a wireless LAN that supports LAN extension and nomadic access requirements and an ad hoc wireless LAN. In the former case, the wireless LAN forms a stationary infrastructure consisting of one or more cells with a control module for each cell. Within a cell, there may be a number of stationary end systems. Nomadic stations can move from one cell to

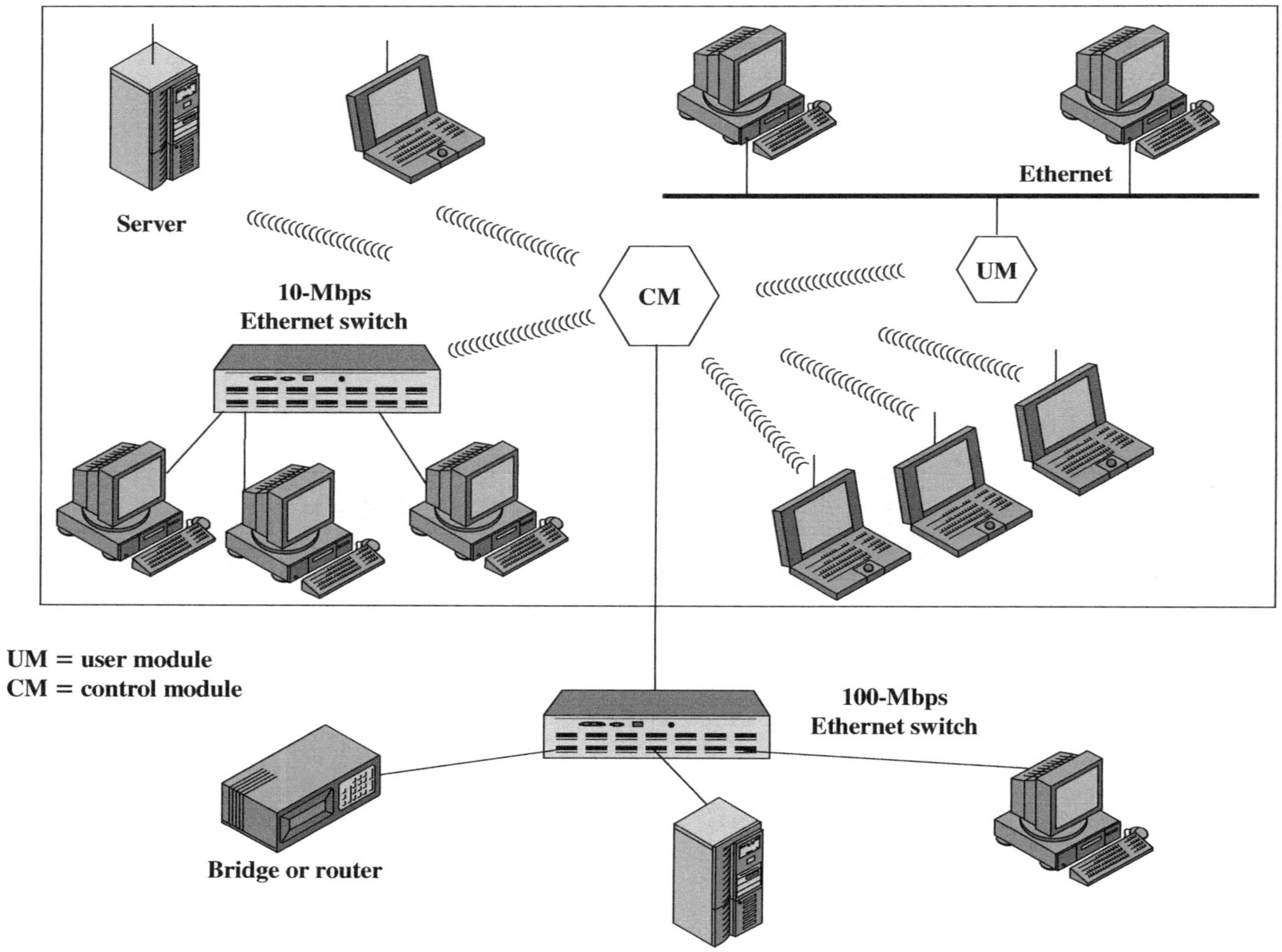

Figure 13.1 Example Single-Cell Wireless LAN Configuration

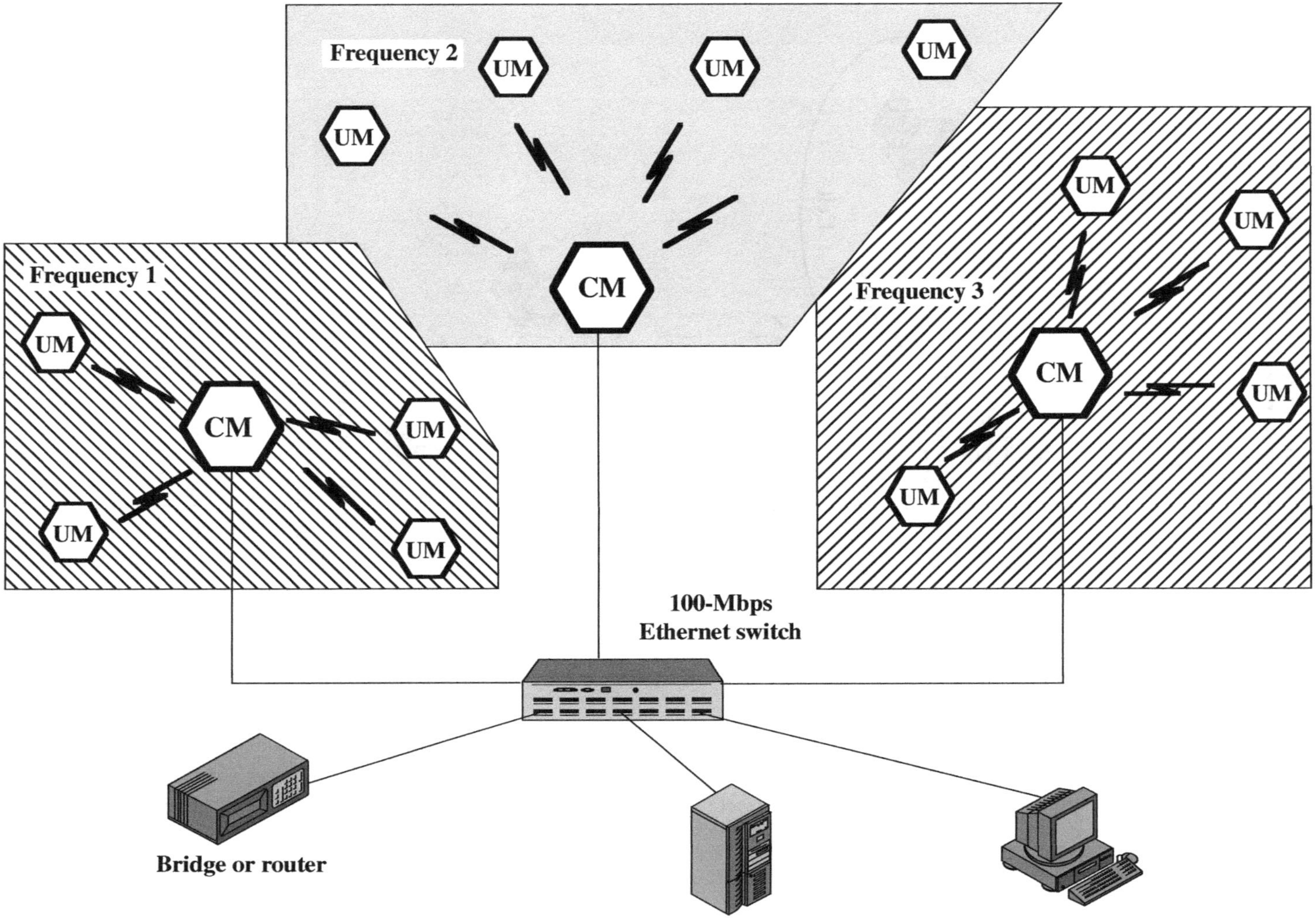

Figure 13.2 Example Multiple-Cell Wireless LAN Configuration

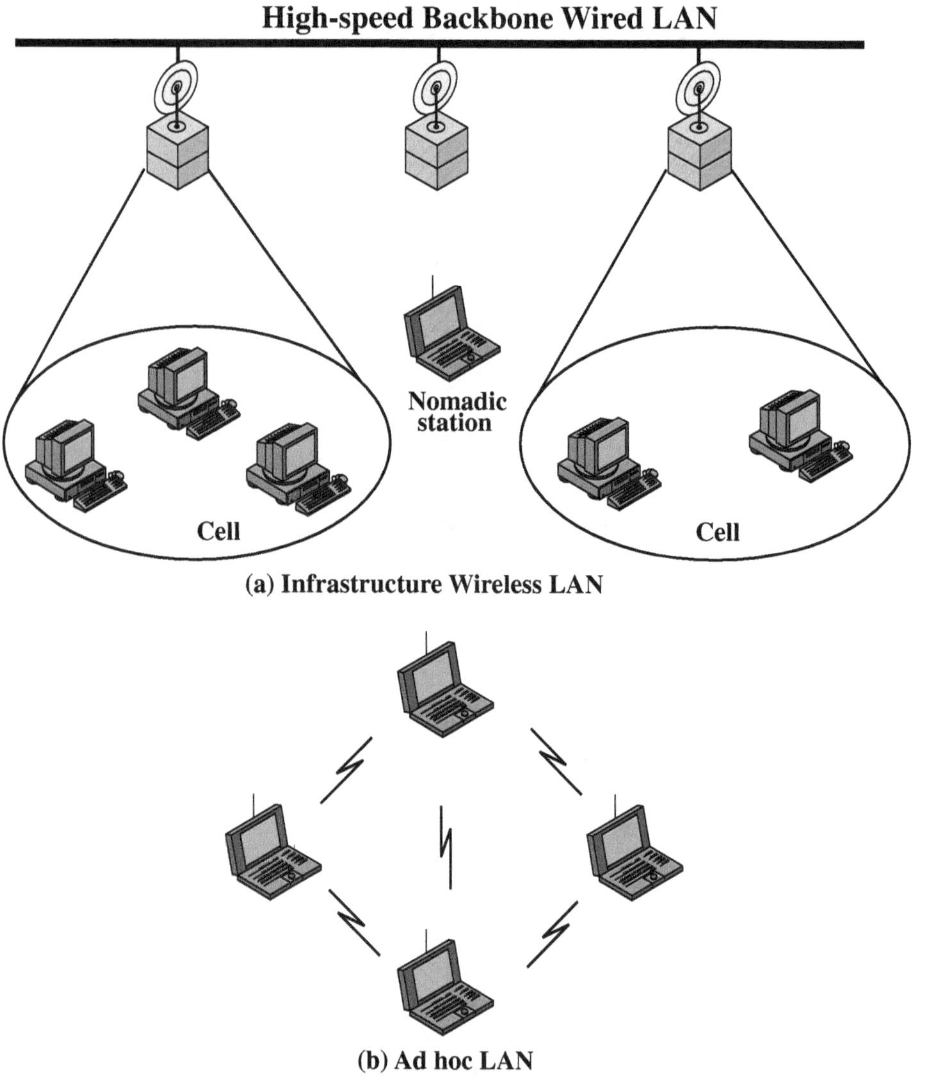

Figure 13.3 Wireless LAN Configurations

another. In contrast, there is no infrastructure for an ad hoc network. Rather, a peer collection of stations within range of each other may dynamically configure themselves into a temporary network.

Wireless LAN Requirements

A wireless LAN must meet the same sort of requirements typical of any LAN, including high capacity, ability to cover short distances, full connectivity among attached stations, and broadcast capability. In addition, there are a number of requirements specific to the wireless LAN environment. The following are among the most important requirements for wireless LANs:

- **Throughput:** The medium access control protocol should make as efficient use as possible of the wireless medium to maximize capacity.
- **Number of nodes:** Wireless LANs may need to support hundreds of nodes across multiple cells.
- **Connection to backbone LAN:** In most cases, interconnection with stations on a wired backbone LAN is required. For infrastructure wireless LANs, this is easily accomplished through the use of control modules that connect to both types of LANs. There may also need to be accommodation for mobile users and ad hoc wireless networks.
- **Service area:** A typical coverage area for a wireless LAN has a diameter of 100 to 300 m.
- **Battery power consumption:** Mobile workers use battery-powered workstations that need to have a long battery life when used with wireless adapters. This suggests that a MAC protocol that requires mobile nodes to monitor access points constantly or engage in frequent handshakes with a base station is inappropriate. Typical wireless LAN implementations have features to reduce power consumption while not using the network, such as a sleep mode.
- **Transmission robustness and security:** Unless properly designed, a wireless LAN may be interference prone and easily eavesdropped. The design of a wireless LAN must permit reliable transmission even in a noisy environment and should provide some level of security from eavesdropping.
- **Collocated network operation:** As wireless LANs become more popular, it is quite likely for two or more wireless LANs to operate in the same area or in some area where interference between the LANs is possible. Such interference may thwart the normal operation of a MAC algorithm and may allow unauthorized access to a particular LAN.
- **License-free operation:** Users would prefer to buy and operate wireless LAN products without having to secure a license for the frequency band used by the LAN.
- **Handoff/roaming:** The MAC protocol used in the wireless LAN should enable mobile stations to move from one cell to another.
- **Dynamic configuration:** The MAC addressing and network management aspects of the LAN should permit dynamic and automated addition, deletion, and relocation of end systems without disruption to other users.

It is instructive to compare wireless LANs to wired LANs and mobile data networks using Kiviat graphs,[1] as shown in Figure 13.4.

---

[1]A Kiviat graph provides a pictorial means of comparing systems along multiple variables. The variables are laid out at equal angular intervals. A given system is defined by one point on each variable; these points are connected to yield a shape that is characteristic of that system.

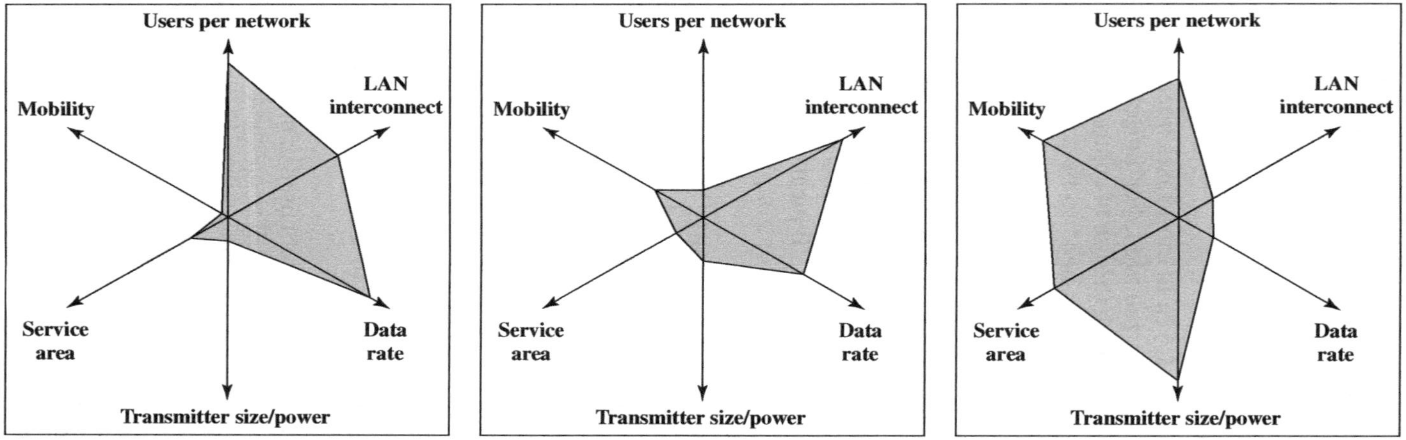

(a) Wired LANs (b) Wireless LANs (c) Mobile data networks

Figure 13.4 Kiviat Graphs for Data Networks

Wireless LAN Technology

Wireless LANs are generally categorized according to the transmission technique that is used. All current wireless LAN products fall into one of the following categories:

- **Infrared (IR) LANs:** An individual cell of an IR LAN is limited to a single room, because infrared light does not penetrate opaque walls.
- **Spread spectrum LANs:** This type of LAN makes use of spread spectrum transmission technology. In most cases, these LANs operate in the ISM (Industrial, Scientific, and Medical) bands so that no FCC licensing is required for their use in the United States.
- **Narrowband microwave:** These LANs operate at microwave frequencies but do not use spread spectrum. Some of these products operate at frequencies that require FCC licensing, while others use one of the unlicensed ISM bands.

Table 13.1 summarizes some of the key characteristics of these three technologies; the details are explored in the next three sections.

13.2 INFRARED LANS

Optical wireless communication in the infrared portion of the spectrum is commonplace in most homes, where it is used for a variety of remote control devices. More recently, attention has turned to the use of infrared technology to construct wireless LANs. In this section, we begin with a comparison of the characteristics of infrared LANs with those of radio LANs and then look at some of the details of infrared LANs.

Strengths and Weaknesses

The two competing transmission media for wireless LANs are microwave radio, using either spread spectrum or narrowband transmission, and infrared. Infrared offers a number of significant advantages over the microwave radio approaches. First, the spectrum for infrared is virtually unlimited, which presents the possibility of achieving extremely high data rates. The infrared spectrum is unregulated worldwide, which is not true of some portions of the microwave spectrum.

In addition, infrared shares some properties of visible light that make it attractive for certain types of LAN configurations. Infrared light is diffusely reflected by light-colored objects; thus it is possible to use ceiling reflection to achieve coverage of an entire room. Infrared light does not penetrate walls or other opaque objects. This has two advantages: First, infrared communications can be more easily secured against eavesdropping than microwave; and second, a separate infrared installation can be operated in every room in a building without interference, enabling the construction of very large infrared LANs.

Another strength of infrared is that the equipment is relatively inexpensive and simple. Infrared data transmission typically uses intensity modulation, so that IR receivers need to detect only the amplitude of optical signals, whereas most microwave receivers must detect frequency or phase.

Table 13.1 Comparison of Wireless LAN Technologies

	Infrared		Spread Spectrum		Radio
	Diffused Infrared	Directed Beam Infrared	Frequency Hopping	Direct Sequence	Narrowband Microwave
Data Rate (Mbps)	1 to 4	1 to 10	1 to 3	2 to 54	10 to 20
Mobility	Stationary/mobile	Stationary with LOS	Mobile	Stationary/mobile	
Range (m)	15 to 60	25	30 to 100	30 to 250	10 to 40
Detectability	Negligible		Little		Some
Wavelength/ frequency	λ: 800 to 900 nm		902 to 928 MHz 2.4 to 2.4835 GHz 5.725 to 5.85 GHz		902 to 928 MHz 5.2 to 5.775 GHz 18.825 to 19.205 GHz
Modulation technique	ASK		FSK	QPSK	FS/QPSK
Radiated power	—		<1 W		25 mW
Access method	CSMA	Token Ring, CSMA	CSMA		Reservation ALOHA, CSMA
License required	No		No		Yes unless ISM

The infrared medium also exhibits some drawbacks. Many indoor environments experience rather intense infrared background radiation, from sunlight and indoor lighting. This ambient radiation appears as noise in an infrared receiver, requiring the use of transmitters of higher power than would otherwise be required and also limiting the range. However, increases in transmitter power are limited by concerns of eye safety and excessive power consumption.

Transmission Techniques

There are three alternative transmission techniques commonly used for IR data transmission: the transmitted signal can be focused and aimed (as in a remote TV control); it can be radiated omnidirectionally; or it can be reflected from a light-colored ceiling.

Directed Beam Infrared Directed beam IR can be used to create point-to-point links. In this mode, the range depends on the emitted power and on the degree of focusing. A focused IR data link can have a range of kilometers. Such ranges are not needed for constructing indoor wireless LANs. However, an IR link can be used for cross-building interconnect between bridges or routers located in buildings within a line of sight of each other.

One indoor use of point-to-point IR links is to set up a token ring LAN (Figure 13.5). A set of IR transceivers can be positioned so that data circulate around them in a ring configuration. Each transceiver supports a workstation or a hub of stations, with the hub providing a bridging function.

Ominidirectional An omnidirectional configuration involves a single base station that is within line of sight of all other stations on the LAN. Typically, this station is mounted on the ceiling (Figure 13.6a). The base station acts as a multiport

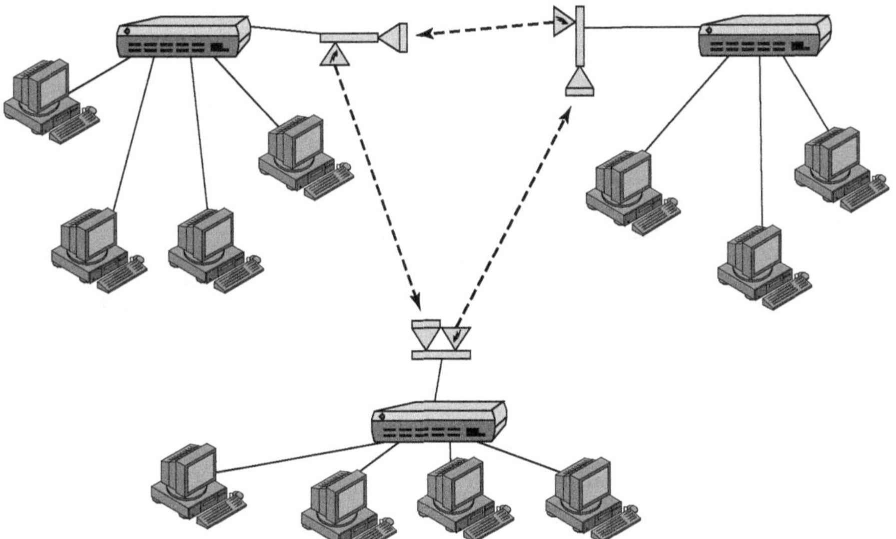

Figure 13.5 Token Ring LAN Using Point-to-Point Infrared Links

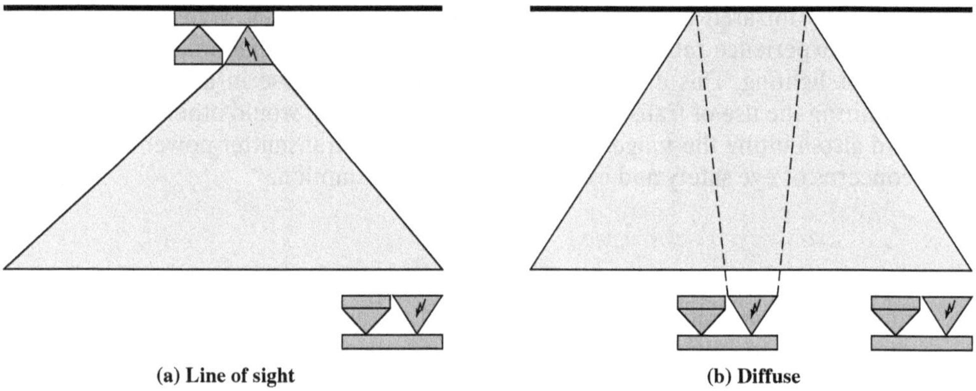

Figure 13.6 Configuration for Omnidirectional Infrared LANs

repeater. The ceiling transmitter broadcasts an omnidirectional signal that can be received by all of the other IR transceivers in the area. These other transceivers transmit a directional beam aimed at the ceiling base unit.

Diffused In this configuration, all of the IR transmitters are focused and aimed at a point on a diffusely reflecting ceiling (Figure 13.6b). IR radiation striking the ceiling is reradiated omnidirectionally and picked up by all of the receivers in the area.

Figure 13.7 shows a typical configuration for a wireless IR LAN installation. There are a number of ceiling-mounted base stations, one to a room. Each station

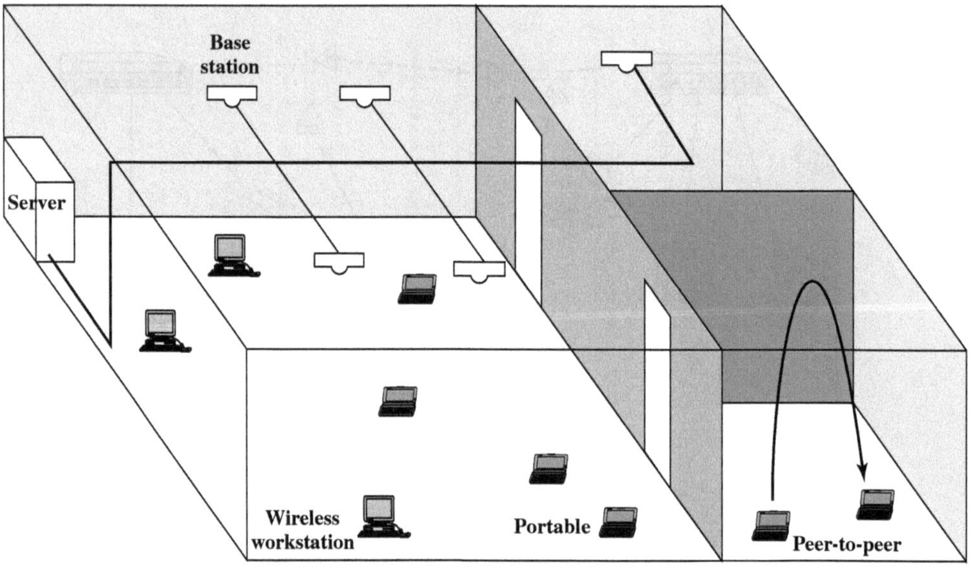

Figure 13.7 Network of Portable and Stationary Wireless Stations Using Infrared

provides connectivity for a number of stationary and mobile workstations in its area. Using ceiling wiring, the base stations are all connected back to a server that can act as an access point to a wired LAN or a WAN. In addition, there may be conference rooms without a base station where ad hoc networks may be set up.

13.3 SPREAD SPECTRUM LANS

The most popular type of wireless LAN uses spread spectrum techniques.

Configuration

Except for quite small offices, a spread spectrum wireless LAN makes use of a multiple-cell arrangement, as was illustrated in Figure 13.2. Adjacent cells make use of different center frequencies within the same band to avoid interference.

Within a given cell, the topology can be either hub or peer to peer. The hub topology is indicated in Figure 13.2. In a hub topology, the hub is typically mounted on the ceiling and connected to a backbone wired LAN to provide connectivity to stations attached to the wired LAN and to stations that are part of wireless LANs in other cells. The hub may also control access, as in the IEEE 802.11 point coordination function. The hub may also control access by acting as a multiport repeater with similar functionality to the multiport repeaters of 10-Mbps and 100-Mbps Ethernet. In this case, all stations in the cell transmit only to the hub and receive only from the hub. Alternatively, and regardless of access control mechanism, each station may broadcast using an omnidirectional antenna so that all other stations in the cell may receive; this corresponds to a logical bus configuration.

One other potential function of a hub is automatic handoff of mobile stations. At any time, a number of stations are dynamically assigned to a given hub based on proximity. When the hub senses a weakening signal, it can automatically hand off to the nearest adjacent hub.

A peer-to-peer topology is one in which there is no hub. A MAC algorithm such as CSMA is used to control access. This topology is appropriate for ad hoc LANs.

Transmission Issues

A desirable, though not necessary, characteristic of a wireless LAN is that it be usable without having to go through a licensing procedure. The licensing regulations differ from one country to another, which complicates this objective. Within the United States, the Federal Communications Commission (FCC) has authorized two unlicensed applications within the ISM band: spread spectrum systems, which can operate at up to 1 watt, and very low power systems, which can operate at up to 0.5 watts. Since the FCC opened up this band, its use for spread spectrum wireless LANs has become popular.

In the United States, three microwave bands have been set aside for unlicensed spread spectrum use: 902–928 MHz (915 MHz band), 2.4–2.4835 GHz

(2.4 GHz band), and 5.725–5.825 GHz (5.8 GHz band). Of these, the 2.4 GHz is also used in this manner in Europe and Japan. The higher the frequency, the higher the potential bandwidth, so the three bands are of increasing order of attractiveness from a capacity point of view. In addition, the potential for interference must be considered. There are a number of devices that operate at around 900 MHz, including cordless telephones, wireless microphones, and amateur radio. There are fewer devices operating at 2.4 GHz; one notable example is the microwave oven, which tends to have greater leakage of radiation with increasing age. At present there is little competition at the 5.8 GHz band; however, the higher the frequency band, in general the more expensive the equipment.

Until recently, typical spread spectrum wireless LANs were limited to just 1 to 3 Mbps. As is discussed in Chapter 14, newer standards options provide for up to 54 Mbps.

13.4 NARROWBAND MICROWAVE LANS

The term narrowband microwave refers to the use of a microwave radio frequency band for signal transmission, with a relatively narrow bandwidth—just wide enough to accommodate the signal. Until recently, all narrowband microwave LAN products have used a licensed microwave band. More recently, at least one vendor has produced a LAN product in the ISM band.

Infrared LANs are rapidly being phased out, because they only operate at speeds less than 10 Mbps due to the limitation of infrared. Infrared requires line-of-sight or it will travel only short distances. Have you ever pointed your TV remote away from but close to your set? It still activated your television; however, the distance limitation of infrared is severe.

13.5 RECOMMENDED READINGS AND WEB SITES

[PAHL95] and [BANT94] are detailed survey articles on wireless LANs. [KAHN97] provides good coverage of infrared LANs. The April 2003 issue of IEEE Communications Magazine covers infrared LANs in depth.

BANT94 Bantz, D., and Bauchot, F. "Wireless LAN Design Alternatives." IEEE Network, March/April, 1994.

KAHN97 Kahn, J., and Barry, J. "Wireless Infrared Communications." Proceedings of the IEEE, February 1997.

PAHL95 Pahlavan, K.; Probert, T.; and Chase, M. "Trends in Local Wireless Networks." IEEE Communications Magazine, March 1995.

Recommended Web Sites:

- **Wireless LAN Association:** Gives an introduction to the technology, including a discussion of implementation considerations and case studies from users. Links to related sites.

13.6 KEY TERMS, REVIEW QUESTIONS, AND PROBLEMS

Key Terms

ad hoc networking	Kiviat graph	nomadic access
infrared	LAN extension	wireless LAN

Review Questions

13.1 List and briefly define four application areas for wireless LANs.
13.2 List and briefly define key requirements for wireless LANs.
13.3 What is the difference between a single-cell and a multiple-cell wireless LAN?
13.4 What is a Kiviat graph?
13.5 What are some key advantages of infrared LANs?
13.6 What are some key disadvantages of infrared LANs?
13.7 List and briefly define three transmission techniques for infrared LANs.

Problems

13.1 How much do you know about your wireless network?
 a. What is the SSID (service set ID, which identifies a particular wireless LAN)?
 b. Who is the equipment vendor?
 c. What standard are you using?
 d. What is the size of the network?

13.2 Using what you know about wired and wireless networks, draw the topology of your network.

13.3 There are many free tools and applications available for helping decipher wireless networks. One of the most popular is Netstumbler. Obtain the software at www.netstumbler.com and follow the links for downloads. The site has a list of supported wireless cards. Using the Netstumbler software, determine the following:
 a. How many access points in your network have the same SSID?
 b. What is your signal strength to your access point?
 c. How many other wireless networks and access points can you find?

13.4 Most wireless cards come with a small set of applications that can perform tasks similar to Netstumbler. Using your own client software, determine the same items you did with Netstumbler. Do they agree?

13.5 Try this experiment: How far can you go and still be connected to your network? This will depend to a large extent on your environment.

13.6 Compare and contrast wired and wireless LANs. What unique concerns must be addressed by the designer of a wireless LAN network?

13.7 Two documents related to safety concerns associated with wireless media are the FCC OET-65 Bulletin and the ANSI/IEEE C95.1-1999. Briefly describe the purpose of these documents and briefly outline the safety concerns associated with wireless LAN technology.

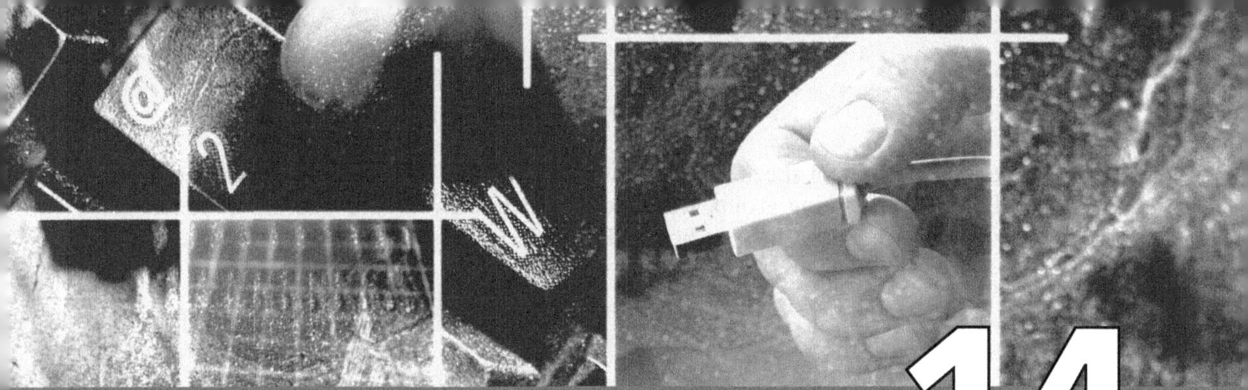

CHAPTER 14

Wi-Fi and the IEEE 802.11 Wireless LAN Standard

14.1 **IEEE 802 Architecture**

14.2 **IEEE 802.11 Architecture and Services**

14.3 **IEEE 802.11 Medium Access Control**

14.4 **IEEE 802.11 Physical Layer**

14.5 **Other IEEE 802.11 Standards**

14.6 **Wi-Fi Protected Access**

14.7 **Recommended Readings and Web Sites**

14.8 **Key Terms, Review Questions, and Problems**

Appendix 14A Scrambling

The most prominent specification for wireless LANs (WLANs) was developed by the IEEE 802.11 working group. We look first at the overall architecture of IEEE 802 standards and then at the specifics of IEEE 802.11.

14.1 IEEE 802 ARCHITECTURE

The architecture of a LAN is best described in terms of a layering of protocols that organize the basic functions of a LAN. This section opens with a description of the standardized protocol architecture for LANs, which encompasses physical, medium access control, and logical link control layers. We then look in more detail at medium access control and logical link control.

Protocol Architecture

Protocols defined specifically for LAN and MAN (metropolitan area network) transmission address issues relating to the transmission of blocks of data over the network. In OSI terms, higher-layer protocols (layer 3 or 4 and above) are independent of network architecture and are applicable to LANs, MANs, and WANs. Thus, a discussion of LAN protocols is concerned principally with lower layers of the OSI model.

Figure 14.1 relates the LAN protocols to the OSI architecture (Figure 4.3). This architecture was developed by the IEEE 802 committee and has been adopted by all organizations working on the specification of LAN standards. It is generally referred to as the IEEE 802 reference model.[1]

Working from the bottom up, the lowest layer of the IEEE 802 reference model corresponds to the **physical layer** of the OSI model and includes such functions as

- Encoding/decoding of signals (e.g., PSK, QAM, etc.)
- Preamble generation/removal (for synchronization)
- Bit transmission/reception

In addition, the physical layer of the 802 model includes a specification of the transmission medium and the topology. Generally, this is considered "below" the lowest layer of the OSI model. However, the choice of transmission medium and topology is critical in LAN design, and so a specification of the medium is included. For some of the IEEE 802 standards, the physical layer is further subdivided into sublayers. In the case of IEEE 802.11, two sublayers are defined:

- **Physical layer convergence procedure (PLCP):** Defines a method of mapping 802.11 MAC layer protocol data units (MPDUs) into a framing format suitable for sending and receiving user data and management information between two or more stations using the associated PMD sublayer
- **Physical medium dependent sublayer (PMD):** Defines the characteristics of, and method of transmitting and receiving, user data through a wireless medium between two or more stations

[1]A supporting document at this book's Web site provides an overview of the key organizations involved in developing communication and protocol standards, including the IEEE 802 Standards Committee.

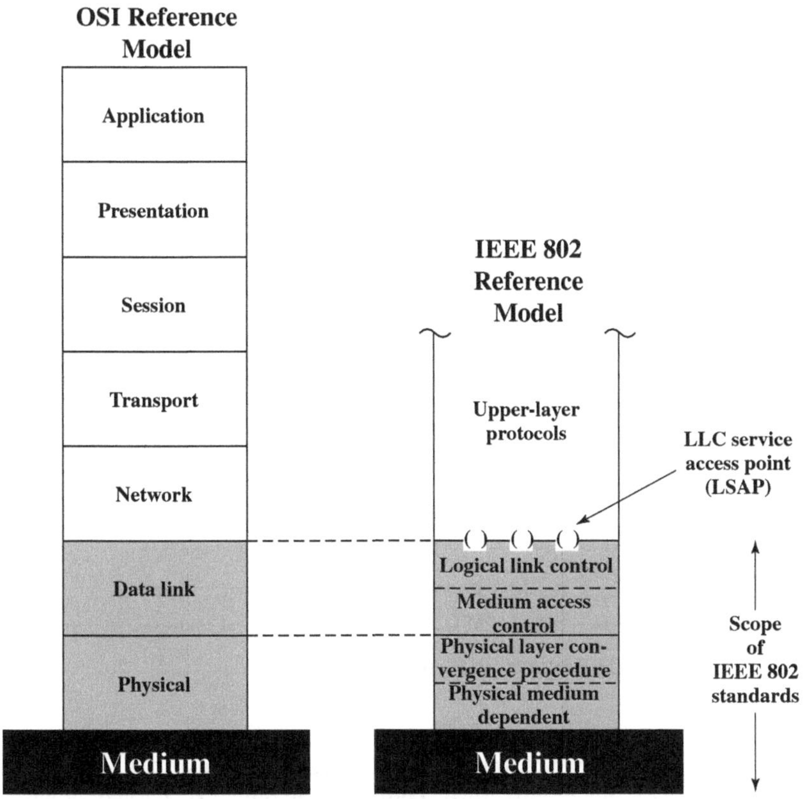

Figure 14.1 IEEE 802 Protocol Layers Compared to OSI Model

Above the physical layer are the functions associated with providing service to LAN users. These include

- On transmission, assemble data into a frame with address and error detection fields.
- On reception, disassemble frame, and perform address recognition and error detection.
- Govern access to the LAN transmission medium.
- Provide an interface to higher layers and perform flow and error control.

These are functions typically associated with OSI layer 2. The set of functions in the last bullet item is grouped into a **logical link control (LLC)** layer. The functions in the first three bullet items are treated as a separate layer, called **medium access control (MAC)**. The separation is done for the following reasons:

- The logic required to manage access to a shared-access medium is not found in traditional layer 2 data link control.
- For the same LLC, several MAC options may be provided.

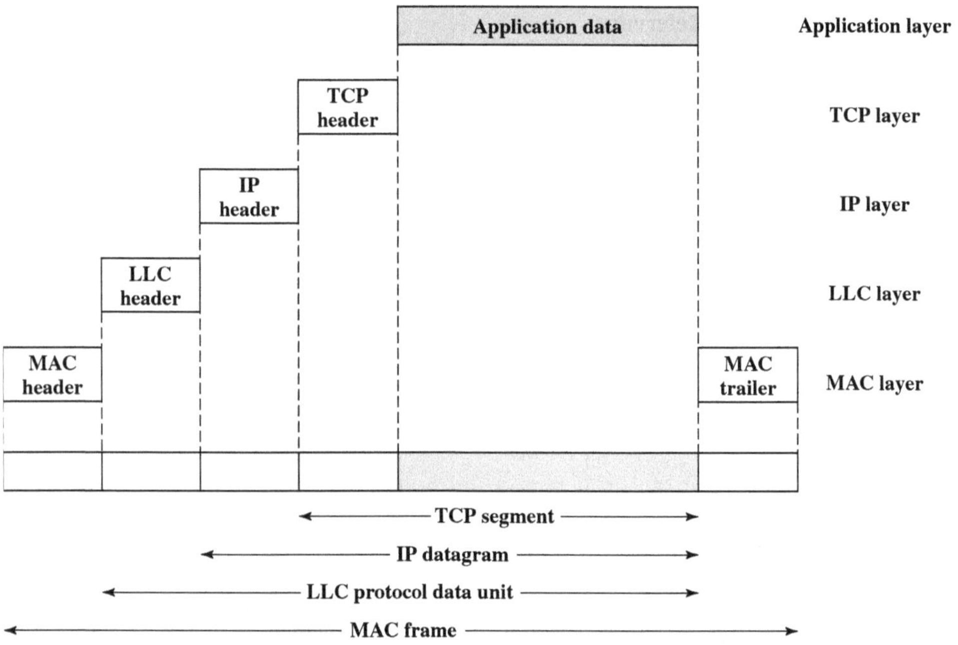

Figure 14.2 IEEE 802 Protocols in Context

Figure 14.2, which reproduces Figure 11.14, illustrates the relationship between the levels of the architecture. Higher-level data are passed down to LLC, which appends control information as a header, creating an **LLC protocol data unit (PDU)**. This control information is used in the operation of the LLC protocol. The entire LLC PDU is then passed down to the MAC layer, which appends control information at the front and back of the packet, forming a **MAC frame**. Again, the control information in the frame is needed for the operation of the MAC protocol. For context, the figure also shows the use of TCP/IP and an application layer above the LAN protocols.

MAC Frame Format

The MAC layer receives a block of data from the LLC layer and is responsible for performing functions related to medium access and for transmitting the data. As with other protocol layers, MAC implements these functions making use of a protocol data unit at its layer. In this case, the PDU is referred to as a MAC frame.

The exact format of the MAC frame differs somewhat for the various MAC protocols in use. In general, all of the MAC frames have a format similar to that of Figure 14.3. The fields of this frame are as follows:

- **MAC Control:** This field contains any protocol control information needed for the functioning of the MAC protocol. For example, a priority level could be indicated here.
- **Destination MAC Address:** The destination physical attachment point on the LAN for this frame.

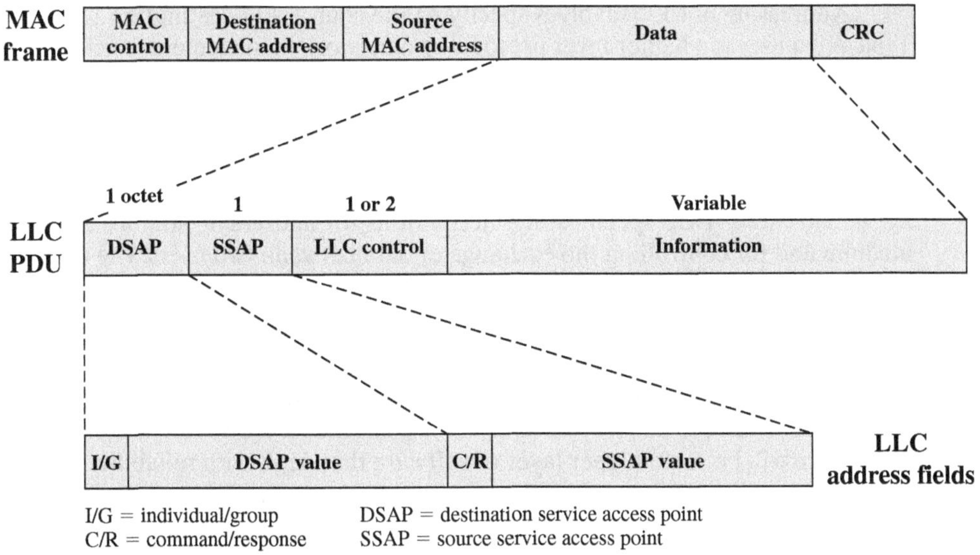

Figure 14.3 LLC PDU in a Generic MAC Frame Format

- **Source MAC Address:** The source physical attachment point on the LAN for this frame.
- **Data:** The body of the MAC frame. This may be LLC data from the next higher layer or control information relevant to the operation of the MAC protocol.
- **CRC:** The cyclic redundancy check field (also known as the frame check sequence, FCS, field). This is an error-detecting code, as described in Section 8.1. The CRC is used in virtually all data link protocols, such as HDLC (Appendix C).

In most data link control protocols, the data link protocol entity is responsible not only for detecting errors using the CRC but for recovering from those errors by retransmitting damaged frames. In the LAN protocol architecture, these two functions are split between the MAC and LLC layers. The MAC layer is responsible for detecting errors and discarding any frames that are in error. The LLC layer optionally keeps track of which frames have been successfully received and retransmits unsuccessful frames.

Logical Link Control

The LLC layer for LANs is similar in many respects to other link layers in common use. Like all link layers, LLC is concerned with the transmission of a link-level PDU between two stations, without the necessity of an intermediate switching node. LLC has two characteristics not shared by most other link control protocols:

1. It must support the multiaccess, shared-medium nature of the link (this differs from a multidrop line in that there is no primary node).
2. It is relieved of some details of link access by the MAC layer.

Addressing in LLC involves specifying the source and destination LLC users. Typically, a user is a higher-layer protocol or a network management function in the station. These LLC user addresses are referred to as service access points (SAPs), in keeping with OSI terminology for the user of a protocol layer.

We look first at the services that LLC provides to a higher-level user, and then at the LLC protocol.

LLC Services LLC specifies the mechanisms for addressing stations across the medium and for controlling the exchange of data between two users. The operation and format of this standard is based on HDLC. LLC provides three alternative services for attached devices:

- **Unacknowledged connectionless service:** This is a datagram-style service. It is a very simple service that does not involve any flow- and error-control mechanisms. Thus, the delivery of data is not guaranteed. However, in most devices, there will be some higher layer of software that deals with reliability issues.
- **Connection-mode service:** This service is similar to that offered by HDLC. A logical connection is set up between two users exchanging data, and flow control and error control are provided.
- **Acknowledged connectionless service:** This is a cross between the previous two services. It provides that datagrams are to be acknowledged, but no prior logical connection is set up.

Typically, a vendor will provide these services as options that the customer can select when purchasing the equipment. Alternatively, the customer can purchase equipment that provides two or all three services and select a specific service based on application.

The **unacknowledged connectionless service** requires minimum logic and is useful in two contexts. First, it will often be the case that higher layers of software will provide the necessary reliability and flow-control mechanism, and it is efficient to avoid duplicating them. For example, TCP could provide the mechanisms needed to ensure that data are delivered reliably. Second, there are instances in which the overhead of connection establishment and maintenance is unjustified or even counterproductive (for example, data collection activities that involve the periodic sampling of data sources, such as sensors and automatic self-test reports from security equipment or network components). In a monitoring application, the loss of an occasional data unit would not cause distress, as the next report should arrive shortly. Thus, in most cases, the unacknowledged connectionless service is the preferred option.

The **connection-mode service** could be used in very simple devices, such as remote sensors, that have little software operating above this level. In these cases, it would provide the flow control and reliability mechanisms normally implemented at higher layers of the communications software.

The **acknowledged connectionless service** is useful in several contexts. With the connection-mode service, the logical link control software must maintain some sort of table for each active connection, to keep track of the status of that connection. If the user needs guaranteed delivery but there is a large number of destinations for data, then the connection-mode service may be impractical because of the large number of tables required. An example is a process control or automated factory environment where a central site may need to communicate with a large number of processors and programmable controllers. Another use of this is the handling of important and time-critical alarm or emergency control signals in a factory. Because of their importance, an acknowledgment is needed so that the sender can be assured that the signal got through. Because of the urgency of the signal, the user might not want to take the time first to establish a logical connection and then send the data.

LLC Protocol The basic LLC protocol is modeled after HDLC and has similar functions and formats. The differences between the two protocols can be summarized as follows:

- LLC makes use of the asynchronous balanced mode of operation of HDLC, to support connection-mode LLC service; this is referred to as type 2 operation. The other HDLC modes are not employed.
- LLC supports an unacknowledged connectionless service using the unnumbered information PDU; this is known as type 1 operation.
- LLC supports an acknowledged connectionless service by using two new unnumbered PDUs; this is known as type 3 operation.
- LLC permits multiplexing by the use of LLC service access points (LSAPs).

All three LLC protocols employ the same PDU format (Figure 14.3), which consists of four fields. The DSAP and SSAP fields each contain a 7-bit address, which specify the destination and source users of LLC, respectively. One bit of the DSAP indicates whether the DSAP is an individual or group address. One bit of the SSAP indicates whether the PDU is a command or response PDU. The format of the LLC control field is identical to that of HDLC (Figure C.1, Appendix C), using extended (7-bit) sequence numbers.

For **type 1 operation**, which supports the unacknowledged connectionless service, the unnumbered information (UI) PDU is used to transfer user data. There is no acknowledgment, flow control, or error control. However, there is error detection and discard at the MAC level.

Two other PDU types, XID and TEST, are used to support management functions associated with all three types of operation. Both PDU types are used in the following fashion. An LLC entity may issue a command (C/R bit = 0) XID or TEST. The receiving LLC entity issues a corresponding XID or TEST in response. The XID PDU is used to exchange two types of information: types of operation supported and window size. The TEST PDU is used to conduct a loopback test of the transmission path between two LLC entities. Upon receipt of a TEST command PDU, the addressed LLC entity issues a TEST response PDU as soon as possible.

With **type 2 operation**, a data link connection is established between two LLC SAPs prior to data exchange. Connection establishment is attempted by the type 2 protocol in response to a request from a user. The LLC entity issues a SABME PDU[2] to request a logical connection with the other LLC entity. If the connection

[2]This stands for *set asynchronous balanced mode extended*. It is used in HDLC to choose ABM and to select extended sequence numbers of 7 bits. Both ABM and 7-bit sequence numbers are mandatory in type 2 operation.

is accepted by the LLC user designated by the DSAP, then the destination LLC entity returns an unnumbered acknowledgment (UA) PDU. The connection is henceforth uniquely identified by the pair of user SAPs. If the destination LLC user rejects the connection request, its LLC entity returns a disconnected mode (DM) PDU.

Once the connection is established, data are exchanged using information PDUs, as in HDLC. Information PDUs include send and receive sequence numbers, for sequencing and flow control. The supervisory PDUs are used, as in HDLC, for flow control and error control. Either LLC entity can terminate a logical LLC connection by issuing a disconnect (DISC) PDU.

With **type 3 operation**, each transmitted PDU is acknowledged. A new (not found in HDLC) unnumbered PDU, the acknowledged connectionless (AC) information PDU, is defined. User data are sent in AC command PDUs and must be acknowledged using an AC response PDU. To guard against lost PDUs, a 1-bit sequence number is used. The sender alternates the use of 0 and 1 in its AC command PDU, and the receiver responds with an AC PDU with the opposite number of the corresponding command. Only one PDU in each direction may be outstanding at any time.

14.2 IEEE 802.11 ARCHITECTURE AND SERVICES

In 1990, the IEEE 802 Committee formed a new working group, IEEE 802.11, specifically devoted to wireless LANs, with a charter to develop a MAC protocol and physical medium specification. The initial interest was in developing a wireless LAN operating in the ISM (industrial, scientific, and medical) band. Since that time, the demand for WLANs, at different frequencies and data rates, has exploded. Keeping pace with this demand, the IEEE 802.11 working group has issued an ever-expanding list of standards (Table 14.1). Table 14.2 briefly defines key terms used in the IEEE 802.11 standard.

It should be noted that the speeds referenced in Table 14.1 and elsewhere in this text are rarely achieved in normal operating mode due to propagation factors such as noise, attenuation, etc.

For example, *802.11n* networks support approximately 300 *Mbps* of rated (theoretical) bandwidth under the best conditions. Unfortunately, an 802.11n network will many times operate at much lower speeds (130 Mbps and below).

For an 802.11n network to run at its maximum speed, Wireless *routers network adapters* must be linked and running in a *channel bonding* mode.

802.11n and Channel Bonding[3]

In 802.11n, bonding utilizes two adjacent *Wi-Fi* channels simultaneously to double the bandwidth of the wireless link compared to 802.11b/g. The 802.11n standard specifies 300 Mbps theoretical bandwidth is available when using channel bonding. Without it, about 50% of this bandwidth is lost (actually slightly more due to

---

[3]Source: http://compnetworking.about.com/od/wireless/f/80211n-300-mbps.htm

Table 14.1 IEEE 802.11 Standards

Standard	Date	Scope
IEEE 802.11	1997	Medium access control (MAC): One common MAC for WLAN applications
		Physical layer: Infrared at 1 and 2 Mbps
		Physical layer: 2.4-GHz FHSS at 1 and 2 Mbps
		Physical layer: 2.4-GHz DSSS at 1 and 2 Mbps
IEEE 802.11a	1999	Physical layer: 5-GHz OFDM at rates from 6 to 54 Mbps
IEEE 802.11b	1999	Physical layer: 2.4-GHz DSSS at 5.5 and 11 Mbps
IEEE 802.11c	2003	Bridge operation at 802.11 MAC layer
IEEE 802.11d	2001	Physical layer: Extend operation of 802.11 WLANs to new regulatory domains (countries)
IEEE 802.11e	Ongoing	MAC: Enhance to improve quality of service and enhance security mechanisms
IEEE 802.11f	Ongoing	Recommended practices for multivendor access point interoperability
IEEE 802.11g	2003	Physical layer: Extend 802.11b to data rates >20 Mbps
IEEE 802.11h	Ongoing	Physical/MAC: Enhance IEEE 802.11a to add indoor and outdoor channel selection and to improve spectrum and transmit power management
IEEE 802.11i	Ongoing	MAC: Enhance security and authentication mechanisms
IEEE 802.11j	Ongoing	Physical: Enhance IEEE 802.11a to conform to Japanese requirements
IEEE 802.11k	Ongoing	Radio resource measurement enhancements to provide interface to higher layers for radio and network measurements
IEEE 802.11m	Ongoing	Maintenance of IEEE 802.11-1999 standard with technical and editorial corrections
IEEE 802.11n	Ongoing	Physical/MAC: Enhancements to enable higher throughput

Table 14.2 IEEE 802.11 Terminology

Access point (AP)	Any entity that has station functionality and provides access to the distribution system via the wireless medium for associated stations
Basic service set (BSS)	A set of stations controlled by a single coordination function
Coordination function	The logical function that determines when a station operating within a BSS is permitted to transmit and may be able to receive PDUs
Distribution system (DS)	A system used to interconnect a set of BSSs and integrated LANs to create an ESS
Extended service set (ESS)	A set of one or more interconnected BSSs and integrated LANs that appear as a single BSS to the LLC layer at any station associated with one of these BSSs
MAC protocol data unit (MPDU)	The unit of data exchanged between two peer MAC entities using the services of the physical layer
MAC service data unit (MSDU)	Information that is delivered as a unit between MAC users
Station	Any device that contains an IEEE 802.11 conformant MAC and physical layer

protocol overhead considerations), and 802.11n equipment will generally report connections in the 130–150 Mbps rated range in those cases.

Channel bonding substantially increases the risk of interfering with nearby Wi-Fi networks due to the increased spectrum and power it consumes.

Setting Up 802.11n Channel Bonding

802.11n products normally do not enable this mode by default but instead run in traditional single channel mode to keep the risk of interference low. Both the Wireless N router and network adapters must be configured to run in a channel bonding mode together to achieve any performance benefit. The steps to configure channel bonding vary depending on the product.

Software will sometimes refer to single channel mode as *20 MHz* operation (20 MHz being the width of a Wi-Fi channel) and channel bonding mode as *40 MHz* operation.

Limitations of 802.11n Channel Bonding

802.11n equipment can ultimately fail to run in the maximum (300 Mbps) performance range for these reasons:

- Some 802.11n gear cannot support channel bonding. For example, this mode of wireless signaling is government regulated in certain countries, such as the UK.
- If the 802.11n network includes any 802.11b/g clients, performance of the entire network may be negatively affected, depending on the router's capabilities. Because 802.11b/g clients do not support channel bonding, these must be set up properly with a *mixed mode* Wireless N router to minimize performance impact.
- Interference from other 802.11n networks nearby can prevent a Wireless N router from sustaining channel bonded connections. In fact, some Wireless N routers automatically fall back to single channel operation when they detect wireless interference on the channels.

As with other networking standards, applications running on an 802.11n network will typically see substantially less actual bandwidth than the rated maximums imply even with channel bonding in place. A 300 Mbps rated 802.11n connection will often yield 200 Mbps or less of user data throughput.

The Wi-Fi Alliance

The first 802.11 standard to gain broad industry acceptance was 802.11b. Although 802.11b products are all based on the same standard, there is always a concern whether products from different vendors will successfully interoperate. To meet this concern, the Wireless Ethernet Compatibility Alliance (WECA), an industry consortium, was formed in 1999. This organization, subsequently renamed the Wi-Fi (Wireless Fidelity) Alliance, created a test suite to certify interoperability for 802.11b products. As of 2011, products from over 1,000 vendors have been certified.

The term used for certified 802.11b products is *Wi-Fi*. Wi-Fi certification has been extended to 802.11n products, and over 200 vendors have so far been qualified. The Wi-Fi Alliance has also developed a certification process for 802.11a products, called *Wi-Fi5*. So far, 32 vendors have qualified for Wi-Fi5 certification.

Testing Programs—Core Technology & Security

There are four generations of Wi-Fi technology currently available—802.11n is the newest. All devices that undergo Wi-Fi CERTIFIED testing are tested according to their capabilities. An overview of these generations is below:

Wi-Fi Technology Frequency Band Bandwidth or Maximum Data Rate

802.11a 5 GHz 54 Mbps

802.11b 2.4 GHz 11 Mbps

802.11g 2.4 GHz 54 Mbps

802.11n 2.4 GHz, 5 GHz, 2.4 or 5 GHz (selectable), or 2.4 and 5 GHz (concurrent) 450 Mbps

Additionally, all Wi-Fi CERTIFIED devices are tested to ensure that they support robust security capabilities. WPA2 (Wi-Fi Protected Access 2) certification indicates that a device can operate with both strong security and privacy.

The Wi-Fi Alliance is concerned with a range of market areas for WLANs, including enterprise, home, and hot spots.

IEEE 802.11 Architecture

Figure 14.4 illustrates the model developed by the 802.11 working group. The smallest building block of a wireless LAN is a **basic service set (BSS)**, which consists of some number of stations executing the same MAC protocol and competing for access to the same shared wireless medium. A BSS may be isolated or it may connect to a backbone **distribution system (DS)** through an **access point (AP)**. The AP functions as a bridge and a relay point. In a BSS, client stations do not communicate directly with one another. Rather, if one station in the BSS wants to communicate with another station in the same BSS, the MAC frame is first sent from the originating station to the AP, and then from the AP to the destination station. Similarly, a MAC frame from a station in the BSS to a remote station is sent from the local station to the AP and then relayed by the AP over the DS on its way to the destination station. The BSS generally corresponds to what is referred to as a cell in the literature. The DS can be a switch, a wired network, or a wireless network.

When all the stations in the BSS are mobile stations, with no connection to other BSSs, the BSS is called an **independent BSS (IBSS)**. An IBSS is typically an ad hoc network. In an IBSS, the stations all communicate directly, and no AP is involved.

A simple configuration is shown in Figure 14.4, in which each station belongs to a single BSS; that is, each station is within wireless range only of other stations within the same BSS. It is also possible for two BSSs to overlap geographically, so that a single station could participate in more than one BSS. Further, the association

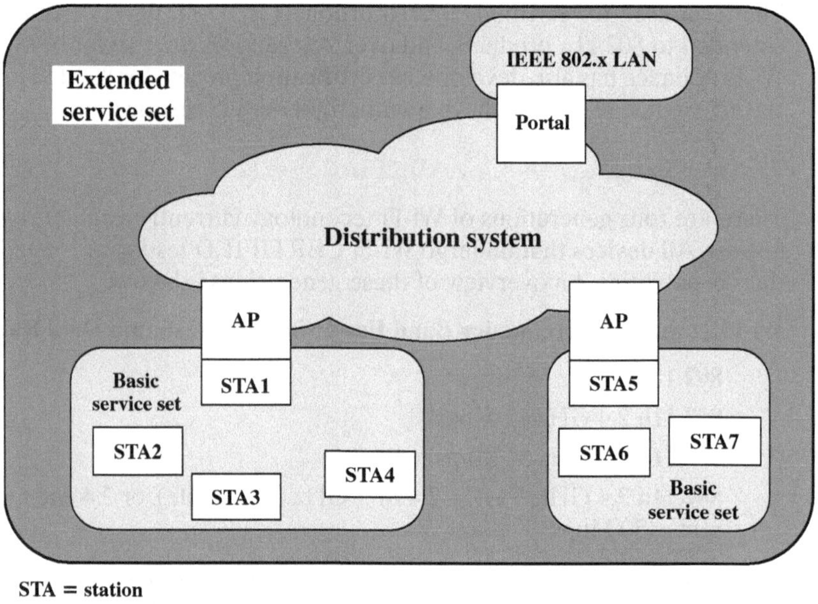

Figure 14.4 IEEE 802.11 Architecture

between a station and a BSS is dynamic. Stations may turn off, come within range, and go out of range.

An **extended service set (ESS)** consists of two or more basic service sets interconnected by a distribution system. Typically, the distribution system is a wired backbone LAN but can be any communications network. The extended service set appears as a single logical LAN to the logical link control (LLC) level.

Figure 14.4 indicates that an access point (AP) is implemented as part of a station; the AP is the logic within a station that provides access to the DS by providing DS services in addition to acting as a station. To integrate the IEEE 802.11 architecture with a traditional wired LAN, a **portal** is used. The portal logic is implemented in a device, such as a bridge or router, that is part of the wired LAN and that is attached to the DS.

IEEE 802.11 Services

IEEE 802.11 defines nine services that need to be provided by the wireless LAN to provide functionality equivalent to that which is inherent to wired LANs. Table 14.3 lists the services and indicates two ways of categorizing them.

1. The service provider can be either the station or the distribution system (DS). Station services are implemented in every 802.11 station, including access point (AP) stations. Distribution services are provided between basic service sets (BSSs); these services may be implemented in an AP or in another special-purpose device attached to the distribution system.
2. Three of the services are used to control IEEE 802.11 LAN access and confidentiality. Six of the services are used to support delivery of MAC service data

Table 14.3 IEEE 802.11 Services

Service	Provider	Used to Support
Association	Distribution system	MSDU delivery
Authentication	Station	LAN access and security
Deauthentication	Station	LAN access and security
Disassociation	Distribution system	MSDU delivery
Distribution	Distribution system	MSDU delivery
Integration	Distribution system	MSDU delivery
MSDU delivery	Station	MSDU delivery
Privacy	Station	LAN access and security
Reassocation	Distribution system	MSDU delivery

units (MSDUs) between stations. The MSDU is the block of data passed down from the MAC user to the MAC layer; typically this is a LLC PDU. If the MSDU is too large to be transmitted in a single MAC frame, it may be fragmented and transmitted in a series of MAC frames. Fragmentation is discussed in Section 14.3.

Following the IEEE 802.11 document, we next discuss the services in an order designed to clarify the operation of an IEEE 802.11 ESS network. **MSDU delivery**, which is the basic service, has already been mentioned.

Distribution of Messages within a DS The two services involved with the distribution of messages within a DS are distribution and integration. **Distribution** is the primary service used by stations to exchange MAC frames when the frame must traverse the DS to get from a station in one BSS to a station in another BSS. For example, suppose a frame is to be sent from station 2 (STA 2) to STA 7 in Figure 14.4. The frame is sent from STA 2 to STA 1, which is the AP for this BSS. The AP gives the frame to the DS, which has the job of directing the frame to the AP associated with STA 5 in the target BSS. STA 5 receives the frame and forwards it to STA 7. How the message is transported through the DS is beyond the scope of the IEEE 802.11 standard.

If the two stations that are communicating are within the same BSS, then the distribution service logically goes through the single AP of that BSS.

The **integration** service enables transfer of data between a station on an IEEE 802.11 LAN and a station on an integrated IEEE 802.x LAN. The term *integrated* refers to a wired LAN that is physically connected to the DS and whose stations may be logically connected to an IEEE 802.11 LAN via the integration service. The integration service takes care of any address translation and media conversion logic required for the exchange of data.

Association-Related Services The primary purpose of the MAC layer is to transfer MSDUs between MAC entities; this purpose is fulfilled by the distribution service. For that service to function, it requires information about stations within the ESS, which is provided by the association-related services. Before the distribution service can deliver data to or accept data from a station, that station must be *associated*. Before looking at the concept of association, we need to describe the concept of mobility. The standard defines three transition types based on mobility:

- **No transition:** A station of this type is either stationary or moves only within the direct communication range of the communicating stations of a single BSS.
- **BSS transition:** This is defined as a station movement from one BSS to another BSS within the same ESS. In this case, delivery of data to the station requires that the addressing capability be able to recognize the new location of the station.
- **ESS transition:** This is defined as a station movement from a BSS in one ESS to a BSS within another ESS. This case is supported only in the sense that the station can move. Maintenance of upper-layer connections supported by 802.11 cannot be guaranteed. In fact, disruption of service is likely to occur.

To deliver a message within a DS, the distribution service needs to know where the destination station is located. Specifically, the DS needs to know the identity of the AP to which the message should be delivered in order for that message to reach the destination station. To meet this requirement, a station must maintain an association with the AP within its current BSS. Three services relate to this requirement:

- **Association:** Establishes an initial association between a station and an AP. Before a station can transmit or receive frames on a wireless LAN, its identity and address must be known. For this purpose, a station must establish an association with an AP within a particular BSS. The AP can then communicate this information to other APs within the ESS to facilitate routing and delivery of addressed frames.
- **Reassociation:** Enables an established association to be transferred from one AP to another, allowing a mobile station to move from one BSS to another.
- **Disassociation:** A notification from either a station or an AP that an existing association is terminated. A station should give this notification before leaving an ESS or shutting down. However, the MAC management facility protects itself against stations that disappear without notification.

Access and Privacy Services There are two characteristics of a wired LAN that are not inherent in a wireless LAN.

1. In order to transmit over a wired LAN, a station must be physically connected to the LAN. On the other hand, with a wireless LAN, any station within radio range of the other devices on the LAN can transmit. In a sense, there is a form of authentication with a wired LAN, in that it requires some positive and presumably observable action to connect a station to a wired LAN.
2. Similarly, in order to receive a transmission from a station that is part of a wired LAN, the receiving station must also be attached to the wired LAN. On the other hand, with a wireless LAN, any station within radio range can receive. Thus, a wired LAN provides a degree of privacy, limiting reception of data to stations connected to the LAN.

IEEE 802.11 defines three services that provide a wireless LAN with these two features:

- **Authentication:** Used to establish the identity of stations to each other. In a wired LAN, it is generally assumed that access to a physical connection conveys authority to connect to the LAN. This is not a valid assumption for a wireless LAN, in which connectivity is achieved simply by having an attached antenna that is properly tuned. The authentication service is used by stations to establish their identity with stations they wish to communicate with. IEEE 802.11 supports several authentication schemes and allows for expansion of the functionality of these schemes. The standard does not mandate any particular authentication scheme, which could range from relatively unsecure handshaking to public key encryption schemes. However, IEEE 802.11 requires mutually acceptable, successful authentication before a station can establish an association with an AP.
- **Deauthentication:** This service is invoked whenever an existing authentication is to be terminated.
- **Privacy:** Used to prevent the contents of messages from being read by other than the intended recipient. The standard provides for the optional use of encryption to assure privacy.

Section 14.6 discusses authentication and privacy features of 802.11.

14.3 IEEE 802.11 MEDIUM ACCESS CONTROL

The IEEE 802.11 MAC layer covers three functional areas: reliable data delivery, medium access control, and security. This section covers the first two topics.

Reliable Data Delivery

As with any wireless network, a wireless LAN using the IEEE 802.11 physical and MAC layers is subject to considerable unreliability. Noise, interference, and other propagation effects result in the loss of a significant number of frames. Even with error-correction codes, a number of MAC frames may not successfully be received. This situation can be dealt with by reliability mechanisms at a higher layer, such as TCP. However, timers used for retransmission at higher layers are typically on the order of seconds. It is therefore more efficient to deal with errors at the MAC level. For this purpose, IEEE 802.11 includes a frame exchange protocol. When a station receives a data frame from another station, it returns an acknowledgment (ACK) frame to the source station. This exchange is treated as an atomic unit, not to be interrupted by a transmission from any other station. If the source does not receive an ACK within a short period of time, either because its data frame was damaged or because the returning ACK was damaged, the source retransmits the frame.

Thus, the basic data transfer mechanism in IEEE 802.11 involves an exchange of two frames. To further enhance reliability, a four-frame exchange may be used. In this scheme, a source first issues a request to send (RTS) frame to the destination.

The destination then responds with a clear to send (CTS). After receiving the CTS, the source transmits the data frame, and the destination responds with an ACK. The RTS alerts all stations that are within reception range of the source that an exchange is under way; these stations refrain from transmission in order to avoid a collision between two frames transmitted at the same time. Similarly, the CTS alerts all stations that are within reception range of the destination that an exchange is under way. The RTS/CTS portion of the exchange is a required function of the MAC but may be disabled.

Medium Access Control

The 802.11 working group considered two types of proposals for a MAC algorithm: distributed access protocols, which, like Ethernet, distribute the decision to transmit over all the nodes using a carrier-sense mechanism; and centralized access protocols, which involve regulation of transmission by a centralized decision maker. A distributed access protocol makes sense for an ad hoc network of peer workstations (typically an IBSS) and may also be attractive in other wireless LAN configurations that consist primarily of bursty traffic. A centralized access protocol is natural for configurations in which a number of wireless stations are interconnected with each other and some sort of base station that attaches to a backbone wired LAN; it is especially useful if some of the data is time sensitive or high priority.

The end result for 802.11 is a MAC algorithm called DFWMAC (distributed foundation wireless MAC) that provides a distributed access control mechanism with an optional centralized control built on top of that. Figure 14.5 illustrates the

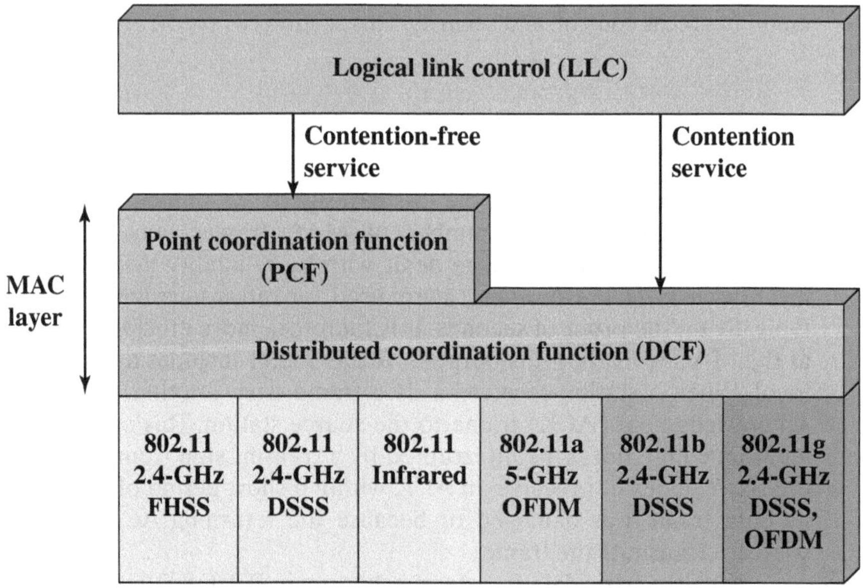

Figure 14.5 IEEE 802.11 Protocol Architecture

architecture. The lower sublayer of the MAC layer is the distributed coordination function (DCF). DCF uses a contention algorithm to provide access to all traffic. Ordinary asynchronous traffic directly uses DCF. The point coordination function (PCF) is a centralized MAC algorithm used to provide contention-free service. PCF is built on top of DCF and exploits features of DCF to assure access for its users. Let us consider these two sublayers in turn.

Distributed Coordination Function The DCF sublayer makes use of a simple CSMA (carrier sense multiple access) algorithm, which functions as follows. If a station has a MAC frame to transmit, it listens to the medium. If the medium is idle, the station may transmit; otherwise the station must wait until the current transmission is complete before transmitting. The DCF does not include a collision detection function (i.e., CSMA/CD) because collision detection is not practical on a wireless network. The dynamic range of the signals on the medium is very large, so that a transmitting station cannot effectively distinguish incoming weak signals from noise and the effects of its own transmission.

To ensure the smooth and fair functioning of this algorithm, DCF includes a set of delays that amounts to a priority scheme. Let us start by considering a single delay known as an interframe space (IFS). In fact, there are three different IFS values, but the algorithm is best explained by initially ignoring this detail. Using an IFS, the rules for CSMA access are as follows (Figure 14.6):

1. A station with a frame to transmit senses the medium. If the medium is idle, it waits to see if the medium remains idle for a time equal to IFS. If so, the station may transmit immediately.
2. If the medium is busy (either because the station initially finds the medium busy or because the medium becomes busy during the IFS idle time), the station defers transmission and continues to monitor the medium until the current transmission is over.
3. Once the current transmission is over, the station delays another IFS. If the medium remains idle for this period, then the station backs off a random amount of time and again senses the medium. If the medium is still idle, the station may transmit. During the backoff time, if the medium becomes busy, the backoff timer is halted and resumes when the medium becomes idle.
4. If the transmission is unsuccessful, which is determined by the absence of an acknowledgement, then it is assumed that a collision has occurred.

To ensure that backoff maintains stability, a technique known as **binary exponential backoff** is used. A station will attempt to transmit repeatedly in the face of repeated collisions, but after each collision, the mean value of the random delay is doubled up to some maximum value. The binary exponential backoff provides a means of handling a heavy load. Repeated failed attempts to transmit result in longer and longer backoff times, which helps to smooth out the load. Without such a backoff, the following situation could occur. Two or more stations attempt to transmit at the same time, causing a collision. These stations then immediately attempt to retransmit, causing a new collision.

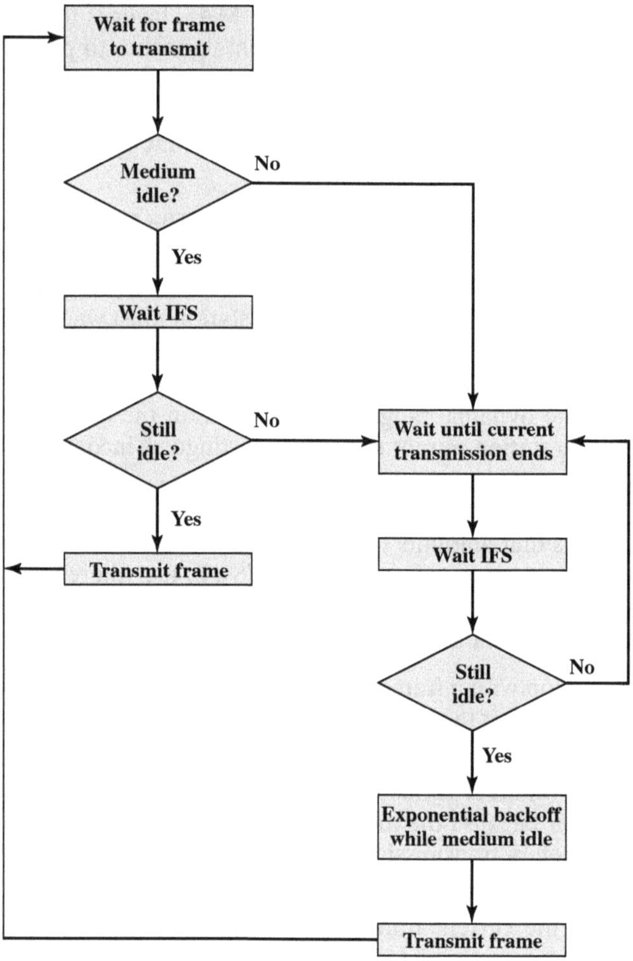

Figure 14.6 IEEE 802.11 Medium Access Control Logic

The preceding scheme is refined for DCF to provide priority-based access by the simple expedient of using three values for IFS:

- **SIFS (short IFS):** The shortest IFS, used for all immediate response actions, as explained in the following discussion
- **PIFS (point coordination function IFS):** A midlength IFS, used by the centralized controller in the PCF scheme when issuing polls
- **DIFS (distributed coordination function IFS):** The longest IFS, used as a minimum delay for asynchronous frames contending for access

Figure 14.7a illustrates the use of these time values. Consider first the SIFS. Any station using SIFS to determine transmission opportunity has, in effect, the highest

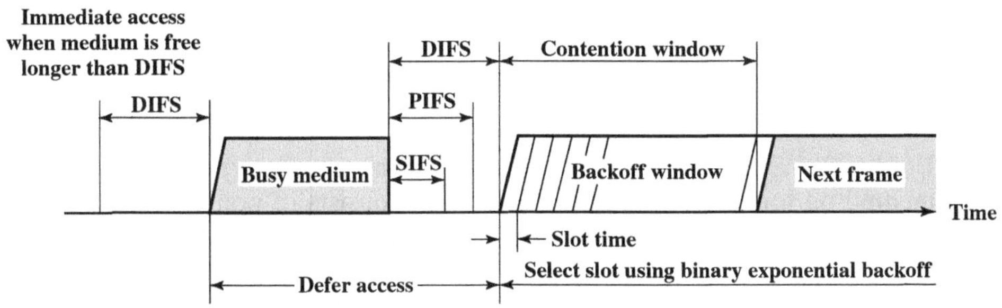

(a) Basic access method

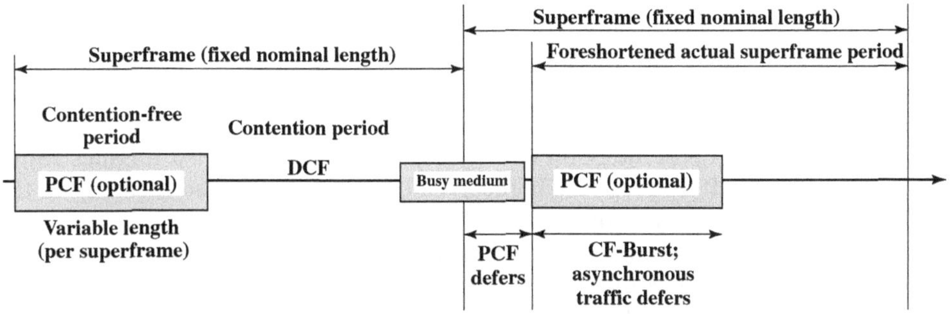

(b) PCF superframe construction

Figure 14.7 IEEE 802.11 MAC Timing

priority, because it will always gain access in preference to a station waiting an amount of time equal to PIFS or DIFS. The SIFS is used in the following circumstances:

- **Acknowledgment (ACK):** When a station receives a frame addressed only to itself (not multicast or broadcast) it responds with an ACK frame after waiting only for an SIFS gap. This has two desirable effects. First, because collision detection is not used, the likelihood of collisions is greater than with CSMA/CD, and the MAC-level ACK provides for efficient collision recovery. Second, the SIFS can be used to provide efficient delivery of an LLC protocol data unit (PDU) that requires multiple MAC frames. In this case, the following scenario occurs. A station with a multiframe LLC PDU to transmit sends out the MAC frames one at a time. Each frame is acknowledged after SIFS by the recipient. When the source receives an ACK, it immediately (after SIFS) sends the next frame in the sequence. The result is that once a station has contended for the channel, it will maintain control of the channel until it has sent all of the fragments of an LLC PDU.
- **Clear to Send (CTS):** A station can ensure that its data frame will get through by first issuing a small Request to Send (RTS) frame. The station to which this frame is addressed should immediately respond with a CTS frame if it is ready to receive. All other stations receive the RTS and defer using the medium.
- **Poll response:** This is explained in the following discussion of PCF.

The next longest IFS interval is the PIFS. This is used by the centralized controller in issuing polls and takes precedence over normal contention traffic. However, those frames transmitted using SIFS have precedence over a PCF poll.

Finally, the DIFS interval is used for all ordinary asynchronous traffic.

Point Coordination Function PCF is an alternative access method implemented on top of the DCF. The operation consists of polling by the centralized polling master (point coordinator). The point coordinator makes use of PIFS when issuing polls. Because PIFS is smaller than DIFS, the point coordinator can seize the medium and lock out all asynchronous traffic while it issues polls and receives responses.

As an extreme, consider the following possible scenario. A wireless network is configured so that a number of stations with time-sensitive traffic are controlled by the point coordinator while remaining traffic contends for access using CSMA. The point coordinator could issue polls in a round-robin fashion to all stations configured for polling. When a poll is issued, the polled station may respond using SIFS. If the point coordinator receives a response, it issues another poll using PIFS. If no response is received during the expected turnaround time, the coordinator issues a poll.

If the discipline of the preceding paragraph were implemented, the point coordinator would lock out all asynchronous traffic by repeatedly issuing polls. To prevent this, an interval known as the superframe is defined. During the first part of this interval, the point coordinator issues polls in a round-robin fashion to all stations configured for polling. The point coordinator then idles for the remainder of the superframe, allowing a contention period for asynchronous access.

Figure 14.7b illustrates the use of the superframe. At the beginning of a superframe, the point coordinator may optionally seize control and issues polls for a give period of time. This interval varies because of the variable frame size issued by responding stations. The remainder of the superframe is available for contention-based access. At the end of the superframe interval, the point coordinator contends for access to the medium using PIFS. If the medium is idle, the point coordinator gains immediate access and a full superframe period follows. However, the medium may be busy at the end of a superframe. In this case, the point coordinator must wait until the medium is idle to gain access; this results in a foreshortened superframe period for the next cycle.

MAC Frame

Figure 14.8a shows the 802.11 frame format when no security features are used. This general format is used for all data and control frames, but not all fields are used in all contexts. The fields are as follows:

- **Frame Control:** Indicates the type of frame and provides control information, as explained presently.
- **Duration/Connection ID:** If used as a duration field, indicates the time (in microseconds) the channel will be allocated for successful transmission of a MAC frame. In some control frames, this field contains an association, or connection, identifier.

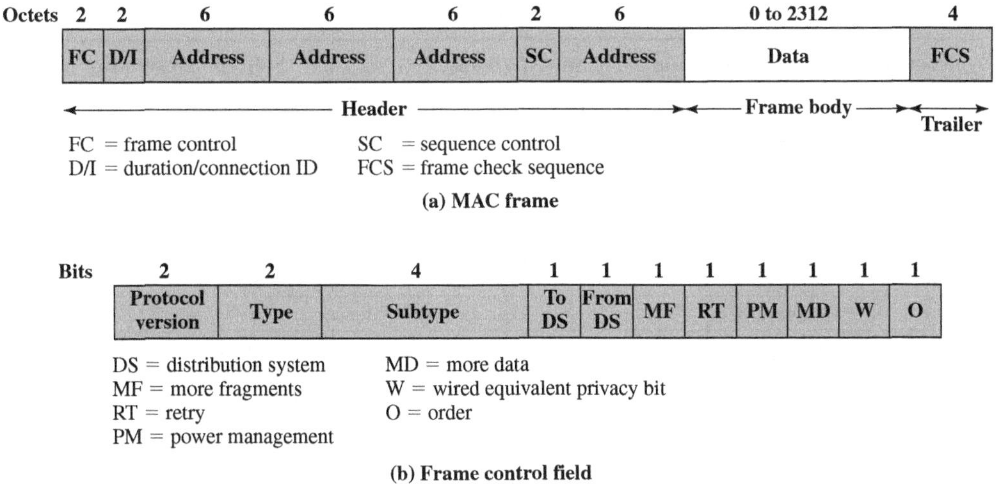

Figure 14.8 IEEE 802.11 MAC Frame Format

- **Addresses:** The number and meaning of the 48-bit address fields depend on context. The **transmitter address** and **receiver address** are the MAC addresses of stations joined to the BSS that are transmitting and receiving frames over the wireless LAN. The **service set ID** (SSID) identifies the wireless LAN over which a frame is transmitted. For an IBSS, the SSID is a random number generated at the time the network is formed. For a wireless LAN that is part of a larger configuration the SSID identifies the BSS over which the frame is transmitted; specifically, the SSID is the MAC-level address of the AP for this BSS (Figure 14.4). Finally the **source address** and **destination address** are the MAC addresses of stations, wireless or otherwise, that are the ultimate source and destination of this frame. The source address may be identical to the transmitter address and the destination address may be identical to the receiver address.
- **Sequence Control:** Contains a 4-bit fragment number subfield used for fragmentation and reassembly, and a 12-bit sequence number used to number frames sent between a given transmitter and receiver.
- **Frame Body:** Contains an MSDU or a fragment of an MSDU. The MSDU is a LLC protocol data unit or MAC control information.
- **Frame Check Sequence:** A 32-bit cyclic redundancy check.

The frame control field, shown in Figure 14.8b, consists of the following fields:

- **Protocol Version:** 802.11 version, currently version 0.
- **Type:** Identifies the frame as control, management, or data.
- **Subtype:** Further identifies the function of frame. Table 14.4 defines the valid combinations of type and subtype.
- **To DS:** The MAC coordination sets this bit to 1 in a frame destined to the distribution system.

Table 14.4 Valid Type and Subtype Combinations

Type Value	Type Description	Subtype Value	Subtype Description
00	Management	0000	Association request
00	Management	0001	Association response
00	Management	0010	Reassociation request
00	Management	0011	Reassociation response
00	Management	0100	Probe request
00	Management	0101	Probe response
00	Management	1000	Beacon
00	Management	1001	Announcement traffic indication message
00	Management	1010	Dissociation
00	Management	1011	Authentication
00	Management	1100	Deauthentication
01	Control	1010	Power save-poll
01	Control	1011	Request to send
01	Control	1100	Clear to send
01	Control	1101	Acknowledgment
01	Control	1110	Contention-Free (CF)-End
01	Control	1111	CF-End + CF-Ack
10	Data	0000	Data
10	Data	0001	Data + CF-Ack
10	Data	0010	Data + CF-Poll
10	Data	0011	Data + CF-Ack+CF-Poll
10	Data	0100	Null function (no data)
10	Data	0101	CF-Ack (no data)
10	Data	0110	CF-Poll (no data)
10	Data	0111	CF-Ack + CF-Poll (no data)

- **From DS:** The MAC coordination sets this bit to 1 in a frame leaving the distribution system.
- **More Fragments:** Set to 1 if more fragments follow this one.
- **Retry:** Set to 1 if this is a retransmission of a previous frame.
- **Power Management:** Set to 1 if the transmitting station is in a sleep mode.
- **More Data:** Indicates that a station has additional data to send. Each block of data may be sent as one frame or a group of fragments in multiple frames.
- **WEP:** Set to 1 if the optional wired equivalent protocol is implemented. WEP is used in the exchange of encryption keys for secure data exchange. This bit also is set if the newer WPA security mechanism is employed, as described in Section 14.6.
- **Order:** Set to 1 in any data frame sent using the Strictly Ordered service, which tells the receiving station that frames must be processed in order.

We now look at the various MAC frame types.

Control Frames Control frames assist in the reliable delivery of data frames. There are six control frame subtypes:

- **Power Save-Poll (PS-Poll):** This frame is sent by any station to the station that includes the AP (access point). Its purpose is to request that the AP transmit a frame that has been buffered for this station while the station was in power-saving mode.
- **Request to Send (RTS):** This is the first frame in the four-way frame exchange discussed under the subsection on reliable data delivery at the beginning of Section 14.3. The station sending this message is alerting a potential destination, and all other stations within reception range, that it intends to send a data frame to that destination.
- **Clear to Send (CTS):** This is the second frame in the four-way exchange. It is sent by the destination station to the source station to grant permission to send a data frame.
- **Acknowledgment:** Provides an acknowledgment from the destination to the source that the immediately preceding data, management, or PS-Poll frame was received correctly.
- **Contention-Free (CF)-End:** Announces the end of a contention-free period that is part of the point coordination function.
- **CF-End + CF-Ack:** Acknowledges the CF-end. This frame ends the contention-free period and releases stations from the restrictions associated with that period.

Data Frames There are eight data frame subtypes, organized into two groups. The first four subtypes define frames that carry upper-level data from the source station to the destination station. The four data-carrying frames are as follows:

- **Data:** This is the simplest data frame. It may be used in both a contention period and a contention-free period.
- **Data + CF-Ack:** May only be sent during a contention-free period. In addition to carrying data, this frame acknowledges previously received data.
- **Data + CF-Poll:** Used by a point coordinator to deliver data to a mobile station and also to request that the mobile station send a data frame that it may have buffered.
- **Data + CF-Ack + CF-Poll:** Combines the functions of the Data + CF-Ack and Data + CF-Poll into a single frame.

The remaining four subtypes of data frames do not in fact carry any user data. The Null Function data frame carries no data, polls, or acknowledgments. It is used only to carry the power management bit in the frame control field to the AP, to indicate that the station is changing to a low-power operating state. The remaining three frames (CF-Ack, CF-Poll, CF-Ack + CF-Poll) have the same functionality as the corresponding data frame subtypes in the preceding list (Data + CF-Ack, Data + CF-Poll, Data + CF-Ack + CF-Poll) but without the data.

Management Frames Management frames are used to manage communications between stations and APs. The following subtypes are included:

- **Association Request:** Sent by a station to an AP to request an association with this BSS. This frame includes capability information, such as whether encryption is to be used and whether this station is pollable.
- **Association Response:** Returned by the AP to the station to indicate whether it is accepting this association request.
- **Reassociation Request:** Sent by a station when it moves from one BSS to another and needs to make an association with the AP in the new BSS. The station uses reassociation rather than simply association so that the new AP knows to negotiate with the old AP for the forwarding of data frames.
- **Reassociation Response:** Returned by the AP to the station to indicate whether it is accepting this reassociation request.
- **Probe Request:** Used by a station to obtain information from another station or AP. This frame is used to locate an IEEE 802.11 BSS.
- **Probe Response:** Response to a probe request.
- **Beacon:** Transmitted periodically to allow mobile stations to locate and identify a BSS.
- **Announcement Traffic Indication Message:** Sent by a mobile station to alert other mobile stations that may have been in low power mode that this station has frames buffered and waiting to be delivered to the station addressed in this frame.
- **Dissociation:** Used by a station to terminate an association.
- **Authentication:** Multiple authentication frames are used in an exchange to authenticate one station to another.
- **Deauthentication:** Sent by a station to another station or AP to indicate that it is terminating secure communications.

14.4 IEEE 802.11 PHYSICAL LAYER

The physical layer for IEEE 802.11 has been issued in four stages. The first part, simply called IEEE 802.11, includes the MAC layer and three physical layer specifications, two in the 2.4-GHz band (ISM) and one in the infrared, all operating at 1 and 2 Mbps. IEEE 802.11a operates in the 5-GHz band at data rates up to 54 Mbps. IEEE 802.11b operates in the 2.4-GHz band at 5.5 and 11 Mbps. IEEE 802.11g also operates in the 2.4-GHz band, at data rates up to 54 Mbps. Figure 14.9 shows the relationship among the various standards developed for the physical layer, and Table 14.5 provides some details. We look at each of these in turn.

Original IEEE 802.11 Physical Layer

Three physical media are defined in the original 802.11 standard:

- **Direct sequence spread spectrum (DSSS)** operating in the 2.4-GHz ISM band, at data rates of 1 Mbps and 2 Mbps. In the United States, the FCC (Federal Communications Commission) requires no licensing for the use of this band.

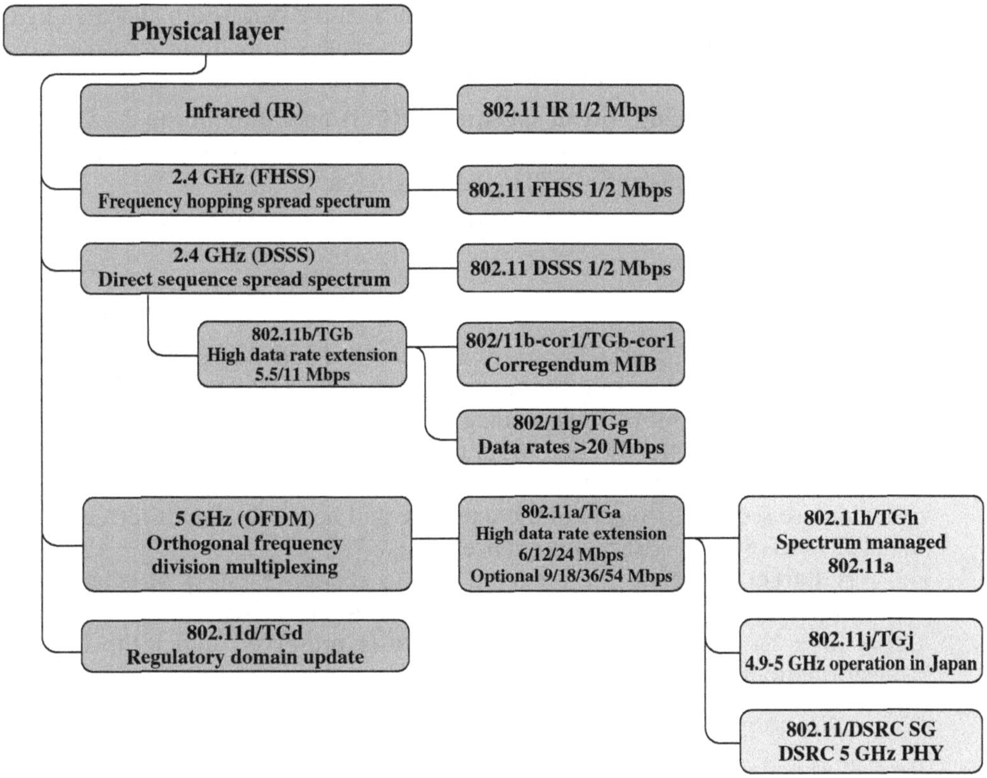

Figure 14.9 IEEE 802.11 Activities—Physical Layer

Table 14.5 IEEE 802.11 Physical Layer Standards

	802.11	802.11a	802.11b	802.11g
Available bandwidth	83.5 MHz	300 MHz	83.5 MHz	83.5 MHz
Unlicensed frequency of operation	2.4–2.4835 GHz DSSS, FHSS	5.15–5.35 GHz OFDM 5.725–5.825 GHz OFDM	2.4–2.4835 GHz DSSS	2.4–2.4835 GHz DSSS, OFDM
Number of nonoverlapping channels	3 (indoor/outdoor)	4 indoor 4 (indoor/outdoor) 4 outdoor	3 (indoor/outdoor)	3 (indoor/outdoor)
Data rate per channel	1, 2 Mbps	6, 9, 12, 18, 24, 36, 48, 54 Mbps	1, 2, 5.5, 11 Mbps	1, 2, 5.5, 6, 9, 11, 12, 18, 24, 36, 48, 54 Mbps
Compatibility	802.11	Wi-Fi5	Wi-Fi	Wi-Fi at 11 Mbps and below

The number of channels available depends on the bandwidth allocated by the various national regulatory agencies. This ranges from 13 in most European countries to just one available channel in Japan.

- **Frequency-hopping spread spectrum (FHSS)** operating in the 2.4-GHz ISM band, at data rates of 1 Mbps and 2 Mbps. The number of channels available ranges from 23 in Japan to 70 in the United States.
- **Infrared** at 1 Mbps and 2 Mbps operating at a wavelength between 850 and 950 nm

Table 14.6 summarizes key details.

Direct Sequence Spread Spectrum Up to three non overlapping channels, each with a data rate of 1 Mbps or 2 Mbps, can be used in the DSSS scheme. Each channel has a bandwidth of 5 MHz. The encoding scheme that is used is DBPSK (differential binary phase shift keying) for the 1 Mbps rate and DQPSK for the 2 Mbps rate.

Recall from Chapter 7 that a DSSS system makes use of a chipping code, or pseudonoise sequence, to spread the data rate and hence the bandwidth of the signal. For IEEE 802.11, a Barker sequence is used.

A **Barker sequence** is a binary $\{-1, +1\}$ sequence $\{s(t)\}$ of length n with the property that its autocorrelation values $R(\tau)$ satisfy $|R(\tau)| \leq 1$ for all $|\tau| \leq (n - 1)$. Further, the Barker property is preserved under the following transformations.

$$s(t) \rightarrow -s(t) \qquad s(t) \rightarrow (-1)^t s(t) \qquad \text{and} \qquad s(t) \rightarrow -s(n - 1 - t)$$

as well as under compositions of these transformations. Only the following Barker sequences are known:

$$\begin{array}{ll} n = 2 & ++ \\ n = 3 & ++- \\ n = 4 & +++- \\ n = 5 & +++-+ \\ n = 7 & +++--+- \\ n = 11 & +--+-+++--- \\ n = 13 & +++++--++-+-+ \end{array}$$

IEEE 802.11 DSSS uses the 11-chip Barker sequence. Each data binary 1 is mapped into the sequence $\{+--+-+++---\}$, and each binary 0 is mapped into the sequence $\{-++-+---+++\}$.

Important characteristic of Barker sequences are their robustness against interference and their insensitivity to multipath propagation.

Frequency-Hopping Spread Spectrum Recall from Chapter 7 that a FHSS system makes use of a multiple channels, with the signal hopping from one channel to another based on a pseudonoise sequence. In the case of the IEEE 802.11 scheme, 1-MHz channels are used.

The details of the hopping scheme are adjustable. For example, the minimum hop rate for the United States is 2.5 hops per second. The minimum hop

Table 14.6 IEEE 802.11 Physical Layer Specifications

(a) Direct sequence spread spectrum (802.11, 802.11b)

Data Rate	Chipping Code Length	Modulation	Symbol Rate	Bits/Symbol
1 Mbps	11 (Barker sequence)	DBPSK	1 Msps	1
2 Mbps	11 (Barker sequence)	DQPSK	1 Msps	2
5.5 Mbps	8 (CCK)	DQPSK	1.375 Msps	4
11 Mbps	8 (CCK)	DQPSK	1.375 Msps	8

(b) Frequency hopping spread spectrum (802.11)

Data Rate	Modulation	Symbol Rate	Bits/Symbol
1 Mbps	Two-level GFSK	1 Msps	1
2 Mbps	Four-level GFSK	1 Msps	2

(c) Infrared (802.11)

Data Rate	Modulation	Symbol Rate	Bits/Symbol
1 Mbps	16-PPM	4 Msps	0.25
2 Mbps	4-PPM	4 Msps	0.5

(d) Orthogonal FDM (802.11a)

Data rate	Modulation	Coding Rate	Coded Bits per Subcarrier	Code Bits per OFDM Symbol	Data Bits per OFDM Symbol
6 Mbps	BPSK	1/2	1	48	24
9 Mbps	BPSK	3/4	1	48	36
12 Mbps	QPSK	1/2	2	96	48
18 Mbps	QPSK	3/4	2	96	72
24 Mbps	16-QAM	1/2	4	192	96
36 Mbps	16-QAM	3/4	4	192	144
48 Mbps	64-QAM	2/3	6	288	192
54 Mbps	64-QAM	3/4	6	288	216

distance in frequency is 6 MHz in North America and most of Europe and 5 MHz in Japan.

For modulation, the FHSS scheme uses two-level Gaussian FSK for the 1-Mbps system. The bits zero and one are encoded as deviations from the current carrier frequency. For 2 Mbps, a four-level GFSK scheme is used, in which four different deviations from the center frequency define the four 2-bit combinations.

Infrared The IEEE 802.11 infrared scheme is omnidirectional (Figure 13.6) rather than point to point. A range of up to 20 m is possible. The modulation scheme for the

1-Mbps data rate is known as 16-PPM (pulse position modulation). In pulse position modulation (PPM), the input value determines the position of a narrow pulse relative to the clocking time. The advantage of PPM is that it reduces the output power required of the infrared source. For 16-PPM, each group of 4 data bits is mapped into one of the 16-PPM symbols; each symbol is a string of 16 bits. Each 16-bit string consists of fifteen 0s and one binary 1. For the 2-Mbps data rate, each group of 2 data bits is mapped into one of four 4-bit sequences. Each sequence consists of three 0s and one binary 1. The actual transmission uses an intensity modulation scheme, in which the presence of a signal corresponds to a binary 1 and the absence of a signal corresponds to binary 0.

IEEE 802.11a

Channel Structure IEEE 802.11a makes use of the frequency band called the Universal Networking Information Infrastructure (UNNI), which is divided into three parts. The UNNI-1 band (5.15 to 5.25 GHz) is intended for indoor use; the UNNI-2 band (5.25 to 5.35 GHz) can be used either indoor or outdoor, and the UNNI-3 band (5.725 to 5.825 GHz) is for outdoor use.

IEEE 80211.a has several advantages over IEEE 802.11b/g:

- IEEE 802.11a utilizes more available bandwidth than 802.11b/g. Each UNNI band provides four nonoverlapping channels for a total of 12 across the allocated spectrum.
- IEEE 802.11a provides much higher data rates than 802.11b and the same maximum data rate as 802.11g.
- IEEE 802.11a uses a different, relatively uncluttered frequency spectrum (5 GHz).

Figure 14.10 shows the channel structure used by 802.11a. The first part of the figure indicates a transmit spectrum mask, which is defined in 802.11b as follows:[4] The transmitted spectrum mask shall have a 0 dBr (dB relative to the maximum spectral density of the signal) bandwidth not exceeding 18 MHz, −20 dBr at 11 MHz frequency offset, −28 dBr at 20 MHz frequency offset and −40 dBr at 30 MHz frequency offset and above. The transmitted spectral density of the transmitted signal shall fall within the spectral mask. The purpose of the spectrum mask is to constrain the spectral properties of the transmitted signal such that signals in adjacent channels do not interfere with one another. Figures 14.10b and 14.10c show the 12 channels available for use in 802.11b.

Coding and Modulation Unlike the 2.4-GHz specifications, IEEE 802.11 does not use a spread spectrum scheme but rather uses orthogonal frequency division multiplexing (OFDM). Recall from Section 11.2 that OFDM, also called multicarrier modulation, uses multiple carrier signals at different frequencies, sending some of the bits on each channel. This is similar to FDM. However, in the case of OFDM, all of the subchannels are dedicated to a single data source.

To complement OFDM, the specification supports the use of a variety of modulation and coding alternatives. The system uses up to 48 subcarriers that are modulated

---

[4]See Appendix B.2 for a discussion of power spectral density.

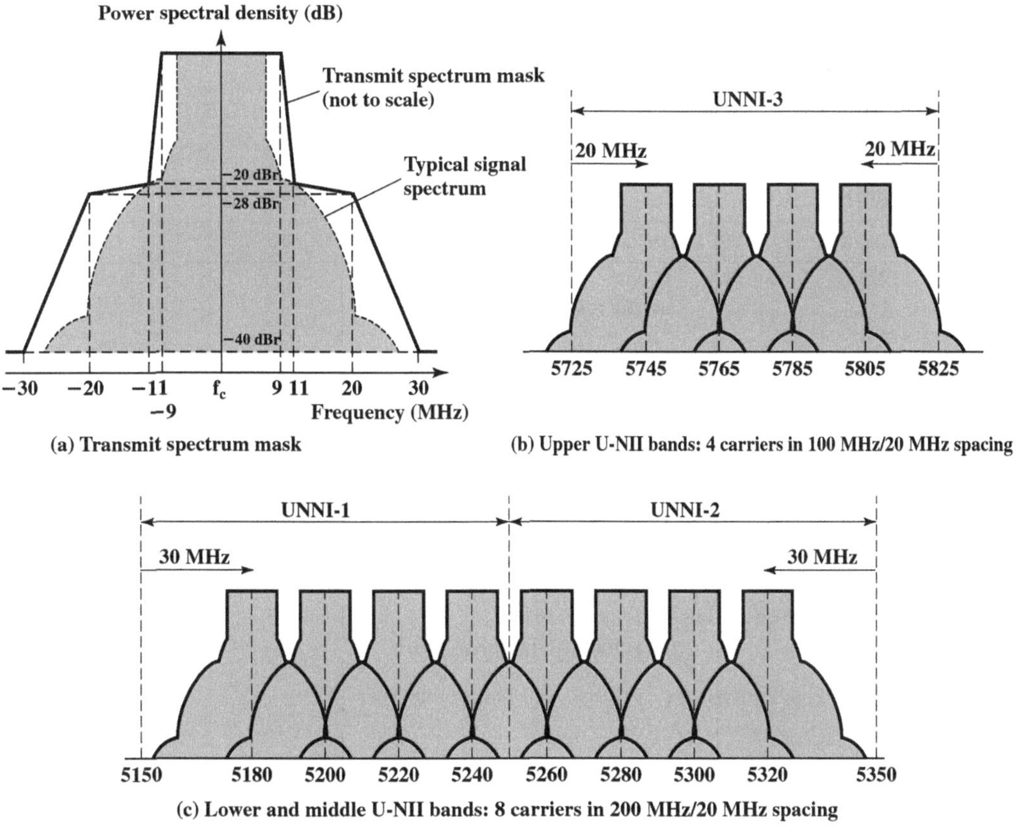

Figure 14.10 IEEE 802.11a Channel Scheme

using BPSK, QPSK, 16-QAM, or 64-QAM. Subcarrier frequency spacing is 0.3125 MHz. A convolutional code at a rate of 1/2, 2/3, or 3/4 provides forward error correction. The combination of modulation technique and coding rate determines the data rate.

Table 14.6d summarizes key parameters for 802.11a.

Physical-Layer Frame Structure The primary purpose of the physical layer is to transmit medium access control (MAC) protocol data units (MPDUs) as directed by the 802.11 MAC layer. The PLCP sublayer provides the framing and signaling bits needed for the OFDM transmission and the PDM sublayer performs the actual encoding and transmission operation.

Figure 14.11a illustrates the physical layer frame format. The **PLCP Preamble** field enables the receiver to acquire an incoming OFDM signal and synchronize the demodulator. Next is the **Signal** field, which consists of 24 bits encoded as a single OFDM symbol. The Preamble and Signal fields are transmitted at 6 Mbps using BPSK. The signal field consists of the following subfields:

- **Rate:** Specifies the data rate at which the data field portion of the frame is transmitted

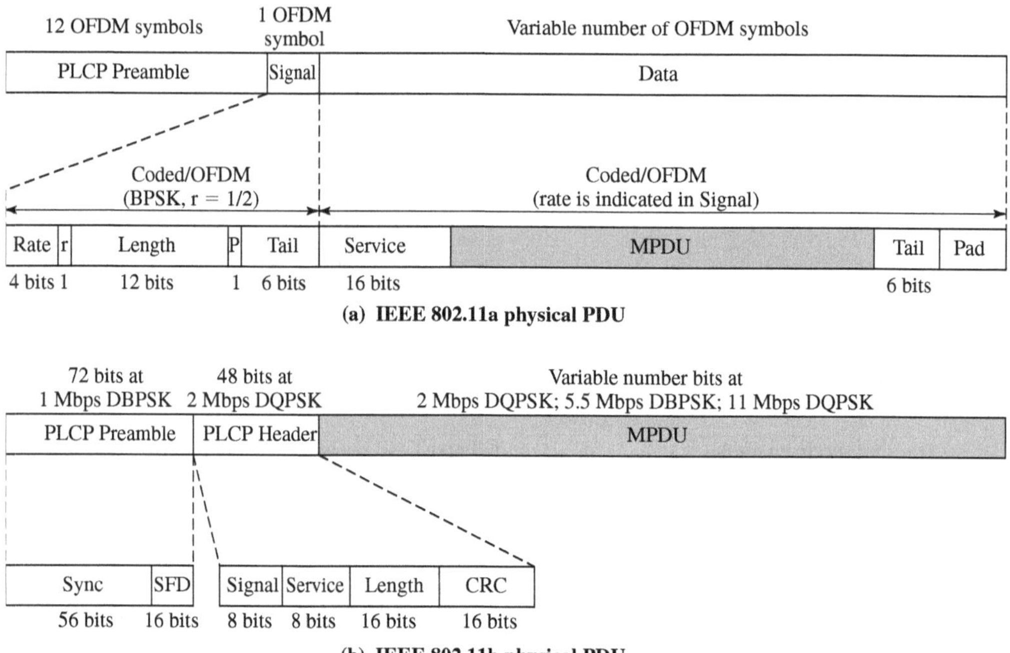

(a) IEEE 802.11a physical PDU

(b) IEEE 802.11b physical PDU

Figure 14.11 IEEE 802 Physical Level Protocol Data Units

- **r:** Reserved for future use
- **Length:** Number of octets in the MAC PDU
- **P:** An even parity bit for the 17 bits in the Rate, r, and Length subfields.
- **Tail:** Consists of 6 zero bits appended to the symbol to bring the convolutional encoder to zero state

The **Data** field consists of a variable number of OFDM symbols transmitted at the data rate specified in the Rate subfield. Prior to transmission, all of the bits of the Data field are scrambled (see Appendix 14A for a discussion of scrambling). The Data field consists of four subfields:

- **Service:** Consists of 16 bits, with the first 6 bits set to zeros to synchronize the descrambler in the receiver, and the remaining 9 bits (all zeros) reserved for future use.
- **MAC PDU:** Handed down from the MAC layer. The format is shown in Figure 14.8.
- **Tail:** Produced by replacing the six scrambled bits following the MPDU end with 6 bits of all zeros; used to re-initialize the convolutional encoder.
- **Pad:** The number of bits required to make the Data field a multiple of the number of bits in an OFDM symbol (48, 96, 192, or 288).

IEEE 802.11b

IEEE 802.11b is an extension of the IEEE 802.11 DSSS scheme, providing data rates of 5.5 and 11 Mbps in the ISM band. The chipping rate is 11 MHz, which is the same as the original DSSS scheme, thus providing the same occupied bandwidth. To achieve a higher data rate in the same bandwidth at the same chipping rate, a modulation scheme known as complementary code keying (CCK) is used.

The CCK modulation scheme is quite complex and is not examined in detail here. Figure 14.12 provides an overview of the scheme for the 11-Mbps rate. Input data are treated in blocks of 8 bits at a rate of 1.375 MHz (8 bits/symbol $\times$ 1.375 MHz = 11 Mbps). Six of these bits are mapped into one of 64 codes sequences based on the use of the 8 $\times$ 8 Walsh matrix (Figure 7.17). The output of the mapping, plus the two additional bits, forms the input to a QPSK modulator.

An optional alternative to CCK is known as packet binary convolutional coding (PBCC). PBCC provides for potentially more efficient transmission at the cost of increased computation at the receiver. PBCC was incorporated into 802.11b in anticipation of its need for higher data rates for future enhancements to the standard.

Physical-Layer Frame Structure IEEE 802.11b defines two physical-layer frame formats, which differ only in the length of the preamble. The long preamble of 144 bits is the same as used in the original 802.11 DSSS scheme and allows interoperability with other legacy systems. The short preamble of 72 bits provides improved throughput efficiency. Figure 14.11b illustrates the physical layer frame format with the short preamble. The **PLCP Preamble** field enables the receiver to acquire an incoming signal and synchronize the demodulator. It consists of two subfields: a 56-bit **Sync** field for synchronization, and a 16-bit start-of-frame delimiter (**SFD**). The preamble is transmitted at 1 Mbps using differential BPSK and Barker code spreading.

Following the preamble is the **PLCP Header**, which is transmitted at 2 Mbps using DQPSK. It consists of the following subfields:

- **Signal:** Specifies the data rate at which the MPDU portion of the frame is transmitted.
- **Service:** Only 3 bits of this 8-bit field are used in 802.11b. One bit indicates whether the transmit frequency and symbol clocks use the same local oscillator.

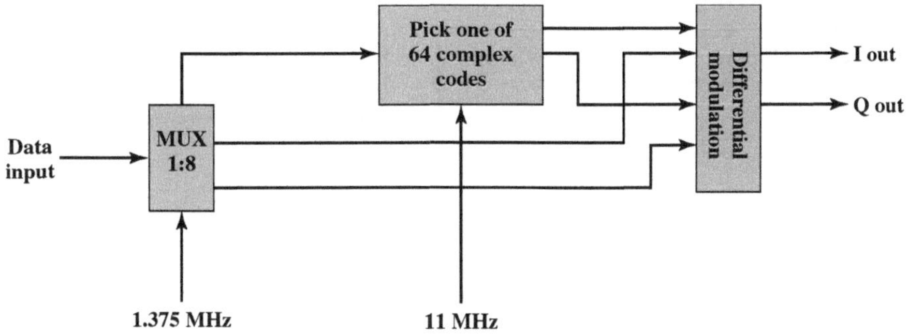

Figure 14.12 11-Mbps CCK Modulation Scheme

Another bit indicates whether CCK or PBCC encoding is used. A third bit acts as an extension to the Length subfield.

- **Length:** Indicates the length of the MPDU field by specifying the number of microseconds necessary to transmit the MPDU. Given the data rate, the length of the MPDU in octets can be calculated. For any data rate over 8 Mbps, the length extension bit from the Service field is needed to resolve a rounding ambiguity.
- **CRC:** A 16-bit error-detection code used to protect the Signal, Service, and Length fields.

The **MPDU** field consists of a variable number of bits transmitted at the data rate specified in the Signal subfield. Prior to transmission, all of the bits of the physical layer PDU are scrambled (see Appendix 14A for a discussion of scrambling).

IEEE 802.11g

IEEE 802.11g extends 802.11b to data rates above 20 Mbps, up to 54 Mbps. Like 802.11b, 802.11g operates in the 2.4-GHz range and thus the two are compatible. The standard is designed so that 802.11b devices will work connecting to an 802.11g AP, and 802.11g devices will work connecting to and 802.11b AP, in both cases using the lower 802.11b data rate.

IEEE 802.11g offers a wider array of data rate and modulation scheme options, as shown in Table 14.7. IEEE 802.11g provides compatibility with 802.11 and 802.11b by specifying the same modulation and framing schemes as these standards for 1, 2, 5.5, and 11 Mbps. At data rates of 6, 9, 12, 18, 24, 36, 48, and 54 Mbps, 802.11g adopts the 802.11a OFDM scheme, adapted for the 2.4 GHz rate; this is referred to as ERP-OFDM, with ERP standing for extended rate physical layer. In addition, and ERP-PBCC scheme is used to provide data rates of 22 and 33 Mbps.

The IEEE 802.11 standards do not include a specification of speed versus distance objectives. Different vendors will give different values, depending on environment. Table 14.8, based on [LAYL04] gives estimated values for a typical office environment.

Table 14.7 IEEE 802.11g Physical Layer Options

Data Rate (Mbps)	Modulation Scheme	Data Rate (Mbps)	Modulation Scheme
1	DSSS	18	ERP-OFDM
2	DSSS	22	ERP-PBCC
5.5	CCK or PBCC	24	ERP-OFDM
6	ERP-OFDM	33	ERP-PBCC
9	ERP-OFDM	36	ERP-OFDM
11	CCK or PBCC	48	ERP-OFDM
12	ERP-OFDM	54	ERP-OFDM

Table 14.8 Estimated Distance (m) versus Data Rate

Data Rate (Mbps)	802.11b	802.11a	802.11g
1	90+	—	90+
2	75	—	75
5.5(b)/6(a/g)	60	60+	65
9	—	50	55
11(b)/12(a/g)	50	45	50
18	—	40	50
24	—	30	45
36	—	25	35
48	—	15	25
54	—	10	20

Read about how Douglas County School District successfully uses 802.11n wireless LANs: http://c541678.r78.cf2.rackcdn.com/case-studies/cs-dcsd.pdf.

14.5 OTHER IEEE 802.11 STANDARDS

In addition to the standards so far discussed, which provide specific physical layer functionality, a number of other 802.11 standards have been issued or are in the works.

IEEE 802.11c is concerned with bridge operation. A bridge is a device that links two LANs that have a similar or identical MAC protocol. It performs functions similar to those of an IP-level router, but at the MAC layer. Typically, a bridge is simpler and more efficient than an IP router. The 802.11c task group completed its work on this standard in 2003, and it was folded into the IEEE 802.1D standard for LAN bridges.

IEEE 802.11d is referred to as a regulatory domain update. It deals with issues related to regulatory differences in various countries.

IEEE 802.11e makes revisions to the MAC layer to improve quality of service and address some security issues. It accommodates time-scheduled and polled communication during null periods when no other data is being sent. In addition, it offers improvements to the efficiency of polling and enhancements to channel robustness. These enhancements should provide the quality required for such services as IP telephony and video streaming. Any station implementing 802.11e is referred to as a QoS station, or QSTA. In a QSTA, the DCF and PCF (Figure 14.5) modules are replaced with a hybrid coordination function (HCF), which in turn consists of enhanced distributed channel access (EDCA) and HCF controlled channel access (HCCA). EDCA is an extension of the legacy DCF mechanism to include priorities. As with the PCF, HCCA centrally manages medium access, but does so in a more efficient and flexible manner.

IEEE 802.11f addresses the issue of interoperability among access points (APs) from multiple vendors. In addition to providing communication among WLAN stations in its area, an AP can function as a bridge that connects two 802.11 LANs across another type of network, such as a wired LAN (e.g., Ethernet) or a wide area network. This standard facilitates the roaming of a device from one AP to another while insuring continuity of transmission.

IEEE 802.11h deals with spectrum and power management issues. The objective is to make 802.11a products compliant with European regulatory requirements. In the EU, part of the 5-GHz band is used by the military for satellite communications. The standard includes a dynamic channel selection mechanism to ensure that the restricted portion of the frequency band is not selected. The standard also includes transmit power control features to adjust power to EU requirements.

IEEE 802.11i defines security and authentication mechanisms at the MAC layer. This standard is designed to address security deficiencies in the wire equivalent privacy (WEP) mechanism originally designed for the MAC layer of 802.11. The 802.11i scheme uses stronger encryption and other enhancements to improve security and is discussed in Section 14.6.

IEEE 802.11k defines Radio Resource Measurement enhancements to provide mechanisms to higher layers for radio and network measurements. The standard defines what information should be made available to facilitate the management and maintenance of a wireless and mobile LANs. Among the data provided are the following:

- To improve roaming decisions, an AP can provide a site report to a station when it determines that the station is moving away from it. The site report is an ordered list of APs, from best to worst service, that a station can use in changing over to another AP.
- An AP can collect channel information from each station on the WLAN. Each station provides a noise histogram that displays all non-802.11 energy on that channel as perceived by the station. The AP also collects statistics on how long a channel is used during a given time. These data enable the AP to regulate access to a given channel.
- APs can query stations to collect statistics, such as retries, packets transmitted, and packets received. This gives the AP a more complete view of network performance.
- 802.11k extends the transmit power control procedures defined in 802.11h to other regulatory domains and frequency bands, to reduce interference and power consumption and to provide range control.

IEEE 802.11m is an ongoing task group activity to correct editorial and technical issues in the standard. The task group reviews documents generated by the other task groups to locate and correct inconsistencies and errors in the 802.11 standard and its approved amendments.

IEEE 802.11n has been released since 2009. It allows for speeds up to 450 Mbps. It can be found at www.ieee.org.

14.6 WI-FI PROTECTED ACCESS

The original 802.11 specification included a set of security features for privacy and authentication which, unfortunately, were quite weak. For **privacy**, 802.11 defined the Wired Equivalent Privacy (WEP) algorithm. WEP makes use of the RC4 encryption algorithm using a 40-bit key.[5] A later revision enables the use of a 104-bit key. For **authentication**, 802.11 requires that the two parties share a secret key not shared by any other party and defines a protocol by which this key can be used for mutual authentication.

The privacy portion of the 802.11 standard contained major weaknesses. The 40-bit key is woefully inadequate. Even the 104-bit key proved to be vulnerable, due to a variety of weaknesses both internal and external to the protocol supporting WEP. These vulnerabilities include the heavy reuse of keys, the ease of data access in a wireless network, and the lack of any key management within the protocol. Similarly, there are a number of problems with the shared-key authentication scheme.

The 802.11i task group has developed a set of capabilities to address the WLAN security issues. In order to accelerate the introduction of strong security into WLANs, the Wi-Fi Alliance promulgated **Wi-Fi Protected Access (WPA)** as a Wi-Fi standard. WPA is a set of security mechanisms that eliminates most 802.11 security issues and was based on the current state of the 802.11i standard. As 802.11i evolves, WPA will evolve to maintain compatibility.

IEEE 802.11i addresses three main security areas: authentication, key management, and data transfer privacy. To improve authentication, 802.11i requires the use of an authentication server (AS) and defines a more robust authentication protocol. The AS also plays a role in key distribution. For privacy, 802.11i provides three different encryption schemes. The scheme that provides a long-term solution makes use of the Advanced Encryption Standard (AES) with 128-bit keys. However, because the use of AES would require expensive upgrades to existing equipment, alternative schemes based on 104-bit RC4 are also defined.

Figure 14.13 gives a general overview of 802.11i operation. First, an exchange between a station and an AP enables the two to agree on a set of security capabilities to be used. Then an exchange involving the AS and the station provides for secure authentication. The AS is responsible for key distribution to the AP, which in turn manages and distributes keys to stations. Finally, strong encryption is used to protect data transfer between the station and the AP.

---

[5]RC4 is described in a document at this book's Web site.

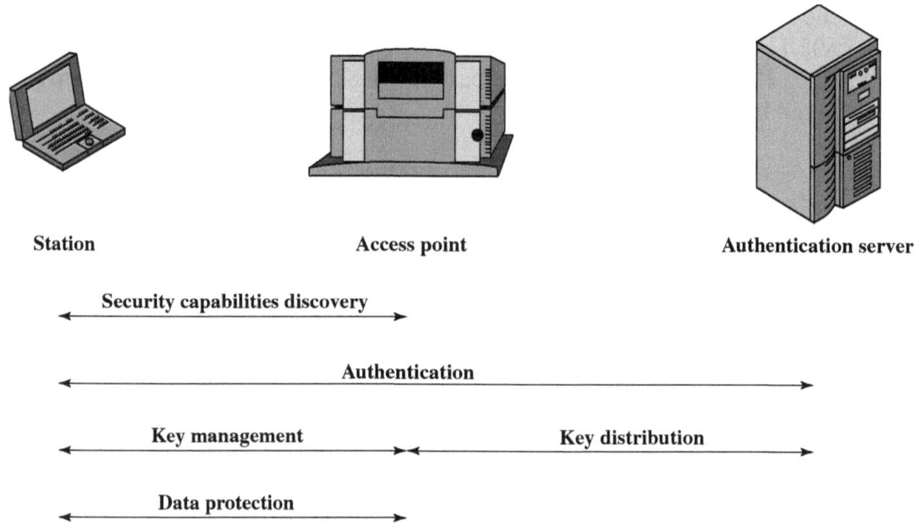

Figure 14.13 802.11i Operational Phases

The 802.11i architecture consists of three main ingredients:

- **Authentication:** A protocol is used to define an exchange between a user and an AS that provides mutual authentication and generates temporary keys to be used between the client and the AP over the wireless link.
- **Access control:** This function enforces the use of the authentication function, routes the messages properly, and facilitates key exchange. It can work with a variety of authentication protocols.
- **Privacy with message integrity:** MAC-level data (e.g., an LLC PDU) are encrypted, along with a message integrity code that ensures that the data have not been altered.

Authentication operates at a level above the LLC and MAC protocols and is considered beyond the scope of 802.11. There are a number of popular authentication protocols in use, including the Extensible Authentication Protocol (EAP) and the Remote Authentication Dial-In User Service (RADIUS). These are not covered in this book. The remainder of this section examines access control and privacy with message integrity.

Access Control[6]

IEEE 802.11i makes use of another standard that was designed to provide access control functions for LANs. The standard is IEEE 802.1X, Port-Based Network

---

[6]In this subsection, we are discussing access control as a security function. This is a different function than medium access control (MAC) as described in Section 14.3. Unfortunately, the literature and the standards use the term *access control* in both contexts.

Access Control. IEEE 802.1X uses the terms *supplicant, authenticator*, and *authentication server* (AS). In the context of an 802.11 WLAN, the first two terms correspond to the wireless station and the AP. The AS is typically a separate device on the wired side of the network (i.e., accessible over the DS) but could also reside directly on the authenticator.

Before a supplicant is authenticated by the AS, using an authentication protocol, the authenticator only passes control or authentication messages between the supplicant and the AS; the 802.1X control channel is unblocked but the 802.11 data channel is blocked. Once a supplicant is authenticated and keys are provided, the authenticator can forward data from the supplicant, subject to predefined access control limitations for the supplicant to the network. Under these circumstances, the data channel is unblocked.

As indicated in Figure 14.14, 802.1X uses the concepts of controlled and uncontrolled ports. Ports are logical entities defined within the authenticator and refer to physical network connections. For a WLAN, the authenticator (the AP) may have only two physical ports, one connecting to the DS and one for wireless communication within its BSS. Each logical port is mapped to one of these two physical ports. An uncontrolled port allows the exchange of PDUs between the supplicant and other the AS regardless of the authentication state of the supplicant. A controlled port allows the exchange of PDUs between a supplicant and other systems on the LAN only if the current state of the supplicant authorizes such an exchange.

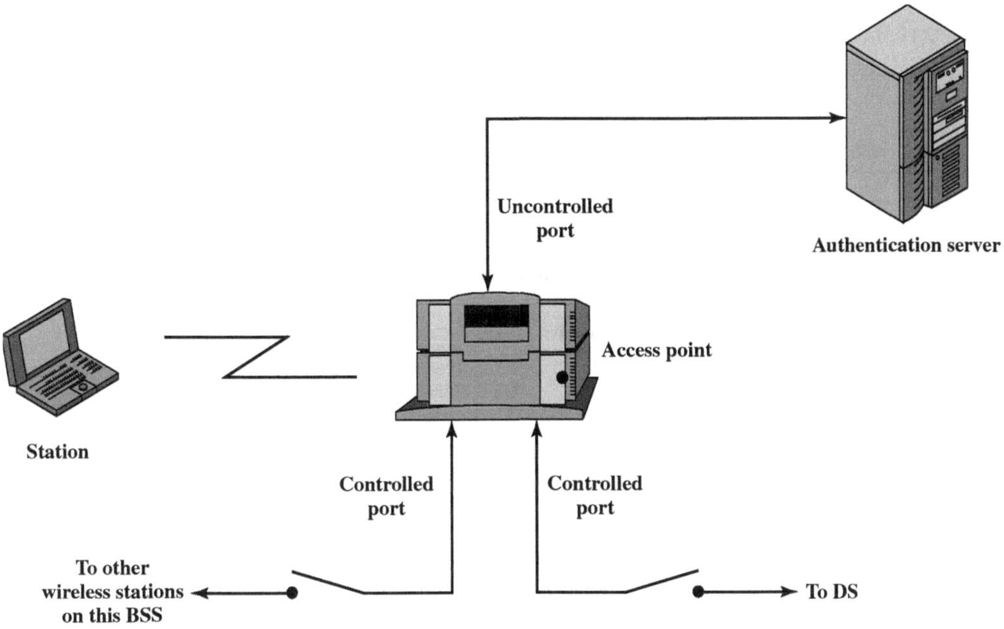

Figure 14.14 802.11i Access Control

The 802.1X framework, with an upper-layer authentication protocol, fits nicely with a BSS architecture that includes a number of wireless stations and an AP. However, for an IBSS, there is no AP. For an IBSS, 802.11i provides a more complex solution that, in essence, involves pairwise authentication between stations on the IBSS.

Privacy with Message Integrity

IEEE 802.11i defines two schemes for protecting data transmitted in 802.11 MAC PDUs. The first scheme is known as the Temporal Key Integrity Protocol (TKIP) or WPA-1. TKIP is designed to require only software changes to devices that are implemented with WEP and uses the same RC4 encryption algorithm as WEP. The second scheme is known as Counter Mode-CBC MAC Protocol (CCMP) or WPA-2. CCMP makes use of the Advanced Encryption Standard (AES) encryption protocol.[7] We begin with an overview of TKIP.

TKIP To understand TKIP, it is useful to start by examining the MAC frame, shown in Figure 14.15a. TKIP begins with an unsecured MAC frame (Figure 14.8) and adds four fields: an initialization vector (IV), an extended IV (EIV), a message integrity check (MIC), and an integrity check value (ICV).

The **initialization vector** is a value that was introduced for use with WEP RC4 encryption algorithm. RC4 is known as a stream encryption algorithm and

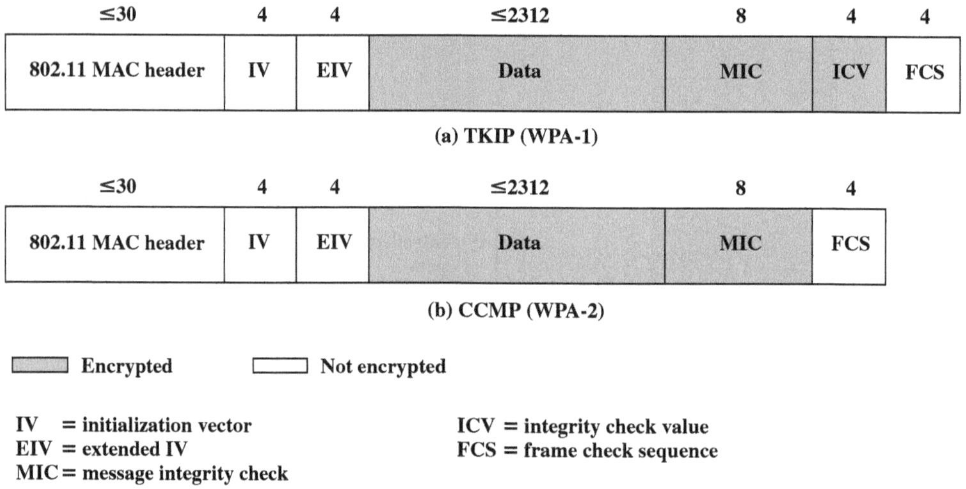

Figure 14.15 Encrypted 802.11i MAC Frames

[7]The AES algorithm is described in detail in [STAL03] and [STAL02].

works in the following manner. The initial 104-bit RC4 key acts as the starting point for an algorithm that generates a key stream, which is simply an unlimited number of bits whose value is determined by the starting key. Encryption is achieved by a bit-by-bit XOR of the key stream with the stream of bits to be encrypted. If the same key stream starting point is used on each MAC frame, it is easier to attack the system. To counter this threat, a 24-bit IV is concatenated with the RC4 key before the key stream is generated. In effect, a 128-bit key is used. If a different IV is used for each frame, then the key stream will be different for each frame. The IV is transmitted in the clear (unencrypted) so that the receiver can combine the IV with the shared secret RC4 key for decryption. In the frame format, 4 bytes are reserved for the IV, but only the first 3 bytes contain the 24-bit value.

The 24-bit IV is too short to provide adequate security. To deal with this problem, TKIP incorporates an **extended IV**. The EIV serves two purposes. First, a 48-bit IV is extracted from the combination of the IV and EIV fields. This IV is combined with the 104-bit RC4 key to produce the encryption key. However, rather than just appending the IV to the RC4 key, the 48-bit IV, the RC4 key, and the transmitter MAC address serve as inputs to a mixing function that produces a 128-bit RC4 encryption key. This produces a stronger key. In addition, bytes from the IV and EIV also function as a sequence counter, which is incremented by one for each new frame transmitted. The sequence counter is designed to counter a replay attack, in which a third party captures a MAC frame and later retransmits it to produce an unintended effect. Because the receiving entity discards any frame that is out of sequence, the replay attack is thwarted.

The **integrity check value** was also introduced for use with WEP. The ICV is a cyclic redundancy check (CRC) calculated on all the fields of the frame. This field is then encrypted, along with the data field, using the same RC4 key. Although both the ICV and FCS fields use a CRC calculation, they serve different purposes. The FCS field is used to detect bit errors in transmission, as was explained in Section 8.1. The ICV field is used for message authentication, a concept that is described in Appendix 12B. When a WEP MAC frame arrives and is decrypted, the receiver recalculates the ICV and compares the calculated value to the received value. If the two differ, it is assumed that the Data field has been altered in transit. The theory behind the ICV is that if an attacker alters an encrypted data message, the ICV will show this. Because the ICV is also encrypted, it is difficult for an attacker to modify the ICV so as to match the modifications to the encrypted data field.

It can be shown that the ICV is easily defeated [EDNE04]. To deal with this problem, TKIP adds a new **message integrity code**. For backward compatibility, the ICV field is retained. The MIC is a new algorithm, called Michael, that computes a 64-bit value calculated using the source and destination MAC address values and the Data field. This value is then encrypted using a separate RC4 key from that used for encrypting the Data and ICV fields. The use of a more complex algorithm, a separate encryption key, and a 64-bit length all make the MIC and substantially stronger message authentication feature than the ICV.

CCMP Figure 14.15b shows the format of a MAC frame using CCMP. The only format difference is that CCMP does not include the legacy ICV field. The most significant difference is that AES is used as the encryption algorithm.

14.7 RECOMMENDED READINGS AND WEB SITES

[ROSH04] provides a good up-to-date technical treatment of IEEE 802.11. Another useful book is [BING02]. [OHAR99] is an excellent technical treatment of IEEE 802.11 but does not cover many recent developments. [CROW97] is a good survey article on the 802.11 standards but does not cover IEEE 802.11a and IEEE 802.11b. A brief but useful survey of 802.11 is [MCFA03]. [GEIE01] has a good discussion of IEEE 802.11a. [PETR00] summarizes IEEE 802.11b. [SHOE02] provides an overview of IEEE 802.11g. [XIAO04] discusses 802.11e.

Two useful but brief overviews of 802.11i and WPA are [CHEU04] and [EAT02]. For a thorough treatment, the book to read is [ENDE04].

BING02 Bing, B. *Wireless Local Area Networks.* New York: Wiley, 2002.

CHEU04 Cheung, D. "WLAN Security & Wi-Fi Protected Access." *Dr. Dobb's Journal,* June 2004.

CROW97 Crow, B., et al. "IEEE 802.11 Wireless Local Area Networks." *IEEE Communications Magazine,* September 1997.

EATO02 Eaton, D. "Diving into the IEEE 802.11i Spec: A Tutorial." *Communications System Design,* November 2002. www.commsdesign.com

EDNE04 Edney, J., and Arbaugh, W. *Real 802.11 Security: Wi-Fi Protected Access and 802.11i.* Reading, MA: Addison-Wesley, 2004.

GEIE01 Geier, J. "Enabling Fast Wireless Networks with OFDM." *Communications System Design,* February 2001. www.commsdesign.com

MCFA03 McFarland, B., and Wong, M. "The Family Dynamics of 802.11" *ACM Queue,* May 2003.

OHAR99 Ohara, B., and Petrick, A. *IEEE 802.11 Handbook: A Designer's Companion.* New York: IEEE Press, 1999.

PETR00 Petrick, A. "IEEE 802.11b—Wireless Ethernet." *Communications System Design,* June 2000. www.commsdesign.com

ROSH04 Roshan, P., and Leary, J. *802.11 Wireless LAN Fundamentals.* Indianapolis: Cisco Press, 2004.

SHOE02 Shoemake, M. "IEEE 802.11g Jells as Applications Mount." *Communications System Design,* April 2002. www.commsdesign.com.

XIAO04 Xiao, Y. "IEEE 802.11e: QoS Provisioning at the MAC Layer." *IEEE Communications Magazine,* June 2004.

Recommended Web Sites:

- **The IEEE 802.11 Wireless LAN Working Group:** Contains working group documents plus discussion archives
- **Wi-Fi Alliance:** An industry group promoting the interoperability of 802.11 products with each other

14.8 KEY TERMS, REVIEW QUESTIONS, AND PROBLEMS

Key Terms

access point (AP)	medium access control (MAC)	point coordination function (PCF)
authentication server (AS)	distribution system (DS)	service set identifier (SSID)
Barker sequence	extended service set (ESS)	shared key authentication
basic service set (BSS)	independent basic service set (IBSS)	Temporal Key Integrity Protocol (TKIP)
binary exponential backoff	logical link control (LLC)	wired equivalent privacy (WEP)
complementary code keying (CCK)	MAC protocol data unit (MPDU)	Wi-Fi
coordination function	MAC service data unit (MSDU)	Wi-Fi protected access (WPA)
Counter Mode-CBC MAC Protocol (CCMP)	open system authentication	
distributed coordination function (DCF)		

Review Questions

14.1 List and briefly define the IEEE 802 protocol layers.

14.2 What is the difference between a MAC address and an LLC address?

14.3 List and briefly define LLC services.

14.4 What is the difference between an access point and a portal?

14.5 Is a distribution system a wireless network?

14.6 List and briefly define IEEE 802.11 services.

14.7 How is the concept of an association related to that of mobility?

14.8 What characteristics of a wireless LAN present unique security challenges not found in wired LANs?

14.9 Which form of authentication is more secure and why: open system authentication or shared key authentication?

Problems

14.1 Consider the sequence of actions within a BSS depicted in Figure 14.16. Draw a timeline, beginning with a period during which the medium is busy and ending with a period in which the CF-End is broadcast from the AP. Show the transmission periods and the gaps.

14.2 Using Equation (7.10), find the autocorrelation for the 11-bit Barker sequence as a function of τ.

14.3 a. For the 16-PPM scheme used for the 1-Mbps IEEE 802.11 infrared standard,
 a1. What is the period of transmission (time between bits)?
 For the corresponding infrared pulse transmission,
 a2. What is the average time between pulses (1 values) and the corresponding average rate of pulse transmission?
 a3. What is the minimum time between adjacent pulses?
 a4. What is the maximum time between pulses?
 b. Repeat (a) for the 4-PPM scheme used for the 2-Mbps infrared standard.

14.4 For IEEE 802.11a, show how the modulation technique and coding rate determine the data rate.

14.5 For the 802.11 scrambler and descrambler,
 a. Show the expression with exclusive-or operators that corresponds to the polynomial definition.
 b. Draw a figure similar to Figure 14.17.

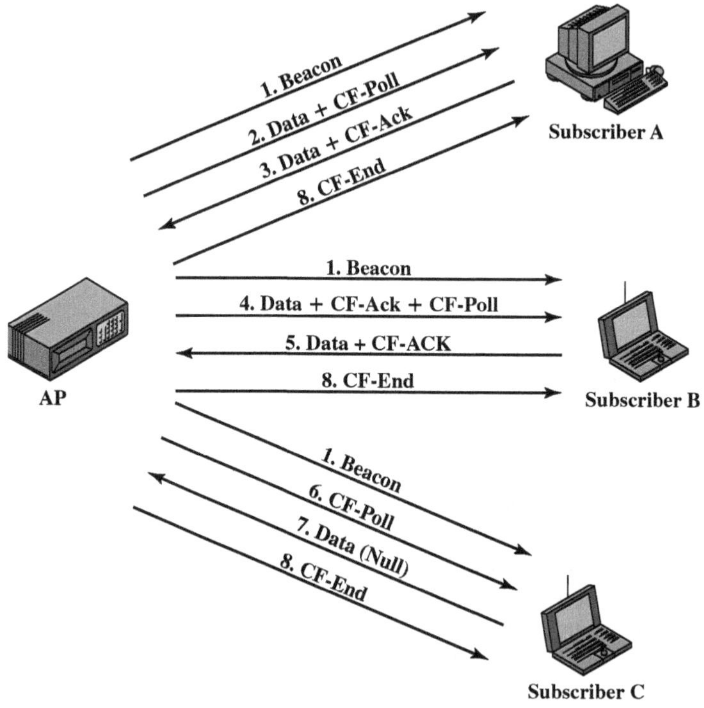

Figure 14.16 Configuration for Problem 14.1

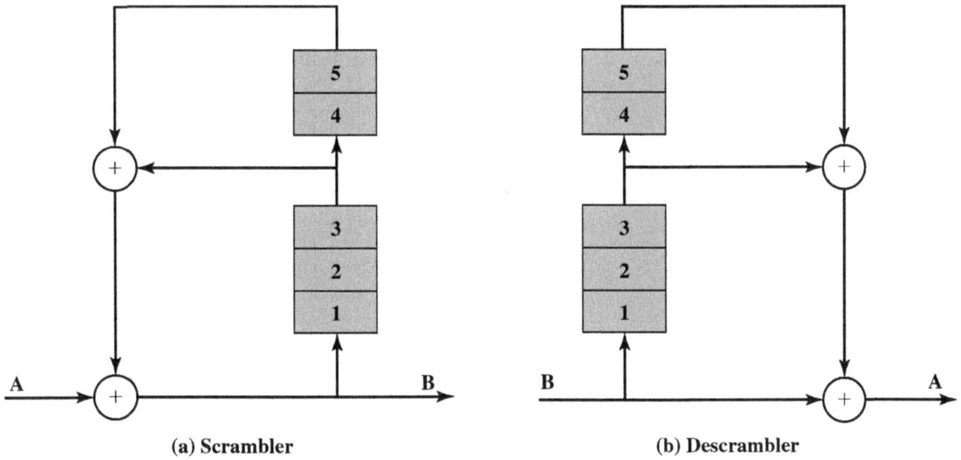

Figure 14.17 Scrambler and Descrambler

APPENDIX 14A SCRAMBLING

For some digital data encoding techniques, a long string of binary zeros or ones in a transmission can degrade system performance. Also, other transmission properties, such as spectral properties, are enhanced if the data are more nearly of a random nature rather than constant or repetitive. A technique commonly used to improve signal quality is scrambling and descrambling. The scrambling process tends to make the data appear more random.

The scrambling process consists of a feedback shift register, and the matching descrambler consists of a feedforward shift register. An example is shown in Figure 14.17. In this example, the scrambled data sequence may be expressed as follows:

$$B_m = A_m \oplus B_{m-3} \oplus B_{m-5}$$

where $\oplus$ indicates the exclusive-or operation. The descrambled sequence is

$$\begin{aligned} C_m &= B_m \oplus B_{m-3} \oplus B_{m-5} \\ &= (A_m \oplus B_{m-3} \oplus B_{m-5}) \oplus B_{m-3} \oplus B_{m-5} \\ &= A_m(\oplus B_{m-3} \oplus B_{m-3}) \oplus (B_{m-5} \oplus B_{m-5}) \\ &= A_m \end{aligned}$$

As can be seen, the descrambled output is the original sequence.

We can represent this process with the use of polynomials. Thus, for this example, the polynomial is $P(X) = 1+X^3+X^5$. The input is divided by this polynomial to produce the scrambled sequence. At the receiver the received scrambled signal is multiplied by the same polynomial to reproduce the original input. Figure 14.18 is an example using the polynomial $P(X)$ and an input of 101010100000111. The scrambled transmission, produced by dividing by $P(X)$ (100101), is 101110001101001. When this number is multiplied by $P(X)$, we get the

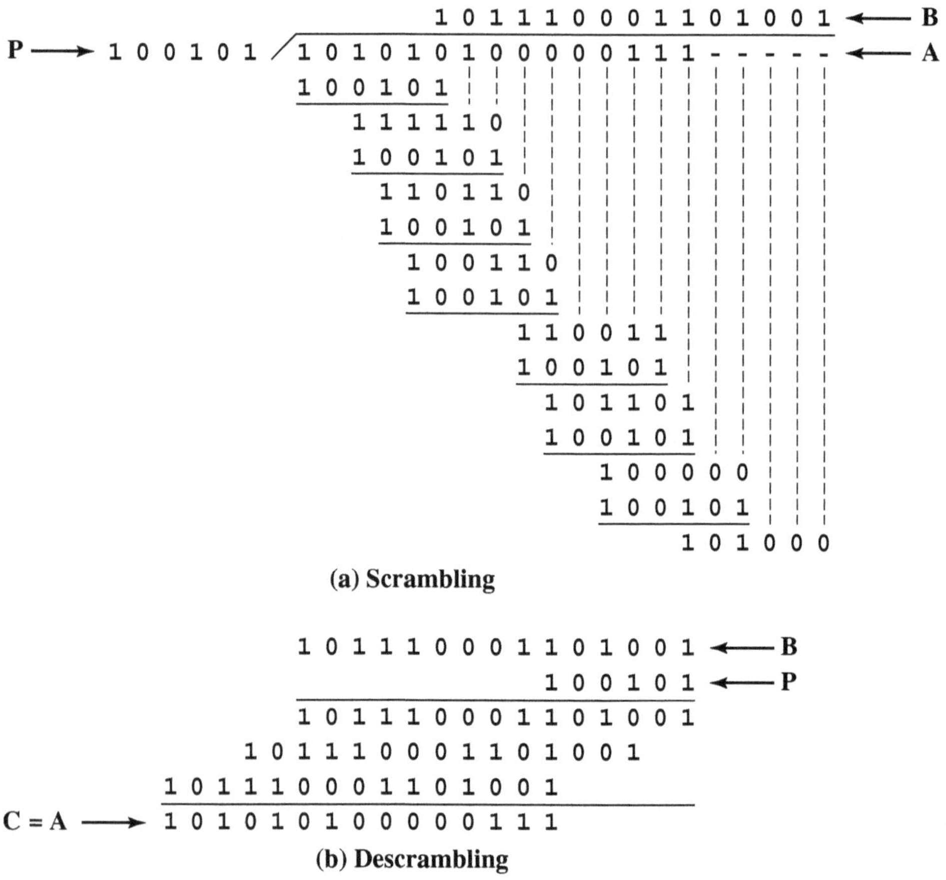

Figure 14.18 Example of Scrambling with $P(X) = 1+X^{-3}+X^{-5}$

original input. Note that the input sequence contains the periodic sequence 10101010 as well as a long string of zeros. The scrambler effectively removes both patterns.

For 802.11, the scrambling equation is

$$P(X) = 1+X^4+X^7$$

In this case the shift register consists of seven elements, used in the same manner as the five-element register in Figure 14.17.

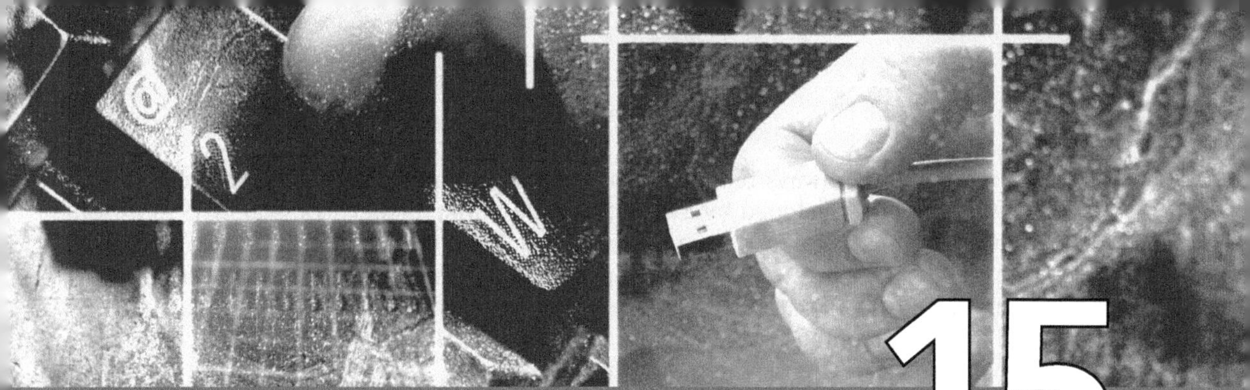

CHAPTER 15

BLUETOOTH AND IEEE 802.15

Bluetooth[1] is an always-on, short-range radio hookup that resides on a microchip. It was initially developed by Swedish mobile-phone maker Ericsson in 1994 as a way to let laptop computers make calls over a mobile phone. Since then, several thousand companies have signed on to make Bluetooth the low-power short-range wireless standard for a wide range of devices. The Bluetooth standards are published by an industry consortium known as the Bluetooth SIG (special interest group). This chapter provides an overview.

Following the discussion of Bluetooth, the chapter covers IEEE 802.15, which is concerned with personal area networks (PANs). PANs are local networks in which all of the devices are controlled by a single user or a family. IEEE 802.15 covers Bluetooth plus two other PAN standards, known as IEEE 802.15.3 and IEEE 802.15.4.

15.1 OVERVIEW

The concept behind Bluetooth is to provide a universal short-range wireless capability. Using the 2.4-GHz band, available globally for unlicensed low-power uses, two Bluetooth devices within 10 m of each other can share up to 720 kbps of capacity. Bluetooth is intended to support an open-ended list of applications, including data (e.g., schedules and telephone numbers), audio, graphics, and even video. For example, audio devices can include headsets, cordless and standard phones, home stereos, and digital MP3 players. The following are examples of some of the capability Bluetooth can provide consumers:

- Make calls from a wireless headset connected remotely to a cell phone.
- Eliminate cables linking computers to printers, keyboards, and the mouse.
- Hook up MP3 players wirelessly to other machines to download music.
- Set up home networks so that a couch potato can remotely monitor air conditioning, the oven, and childrens' Internet surfing.
- Call home from a remote location to turn appliances on and off, set the alarm, and monitor activity.

Bluetooth Applications

Bluetooth is designed to operate in an environment of many users. Up to eight devices can communicate in a small network called a **piconet.** Ten of these piconets can coexist in the same coverage range of the Bluetooth radio. To provide security, each link is encoded and protected against eavesdropping and interference.

[1]The name comes from King Harald Blaatand (Bluetooth) of Denmark, who lived in the tenth century A.D. Unlike his Viking counterparts, King Harald had dark hair (thus the name Bluetooth, meaning a dark complexion) and is credited with bringing Christianity to Scandiavia along with uniting Denmark and Norway. The blue logo that identifies Bluetooth-enabled devices is derived from the runes of his initials.

Bluetooth provides support for three general application areas using short-range wireless connectivity:

- **Data and voice access points:** Bluetooth facilitates real-time voice and data transmissions by providing effortless wireless connection of portable and stationary communications devices.
- **Cable replacement:** Bluetooth eliminates the need for numerous, often proprietary, cable attachments for connection of practically any kind of communication device. Connections are instant and are maintained even when devices are not within line of sight. The range of each radio is approximately 10 m but can be extended to 100 m with an optional amplifier.
- **Ad hoc networking:** A device equipped with a Bluetooth radio can establish instant connection to another Bluetooth radio as soon as it comes into range.

Table 15.1 gives some examples of Bluetooth uses.

Table 15.1 Bluetooth User Scenarios [HAAR98]

Three-in-one phone When you are in the office, your phone functions as an intercom (no telephony charge). At home, it functions as a cordless phone (fixed-line charge). When you are on the move, it functions as a mobile phone (cellular charge).	**Briefcase e-mail** Access e-mail while your portable PC is still in the briefcase. When your PC receives an e-mail message, you are notified by your mobile phone. You can also use the phone to browse incoming e-mail and read messages.
Internet bridge Use your portable PC to surf the Internet anywhere, whether you are connected wirelessly through a mobile phone (cellular) or through a wired connection (PSTN, ISDN, LAN, xDSL).	**Delayed messages** Compose e-mail on your PC while you are on an airplane. When you land and are allowed to switch on your mobile phone, the messages are sent immediately.
Interactive conference In meetings and at conferences, you can share information instantly with other participants. You can also operate a projector remotely without wire connectors.	**Automatic synchronization** Automatically synchronize your desktop computer, portable PC, notebook, and mobile phone. As soon as you enter the office, the address list and calendar in your notebook automatically updates the files on your desktop computer or vice versa.
The ultimate headset Connect a headset to your mobile PC or to any wired connection and free your hands for more important tasks at the office or in your car.	**Instant digital postcard** Connect a camera cordlessly to your mobile phone or to any wire-bound connection. Add comments from you mobile phone, a notebook, or portable PC and send them instantly.
Portable PC speakerphone Connect cordless headsets to your portable PC, and use it as a speaker phone regardless of whether you are in the office, your car, or at home.	**Cordless desktop** Connect your desktop/laptop computer cordlessly to printers, scanner, keyboard, mouse, and the LAN.

Bluetooth Standards Documents

The Bluetooth standards present a formidable bulk—well over 1500 pages, divided into two groups: core and profile. The **core specifications** describe the details of the various layers of the Bluetooth protocol architecture, from the radio interface to link control. Related topics are covered, such as interoperability with related technologies, testing requirements, and a definition of various Bluetooth timers and their associated values.

The **profile specifications** are concerned with the use of Bluetooth technology to support various applications. Each profile specification discusses the use of the technology defined in the core specifications to implement a particular usage model. The profile specification includes a description of which aspects of the core specifications are mandatory, optional, and not applicable. The purpose of a profile specification is to define a standard of interoperability so that products from different vendors that claim to support a given usage model will work together. In general terms, profile specifications fall into one of two categories: cable replacement or wireless audio. The cable replacement profiles provide a convenient means for logically connecting devices in proximity to one another and for exchanging data. For example, when two devices first come within range of one another, they can automatically query each other for a common profile. This might then cause the end users of the device to be alerted, or cause some automatic data exchange to take place. The wireless audio profiles are concerned with establishing short-range voice connections.

Protocol Architecture

Bluetooth is defined as a layered protocol architecture (Figure 15.1) consisting of core protocols, cable replacement and telephony control protocols, and adopted protocols.

The **core protocols** form a five-layer stack consisting of the following elements:

- **Radio:** Specifies details of the air interface, including frequency, the use of frequency hopping, modulation scheme, and transmit power.
- **Baseband:** Concerned with connection establishment within a piconet, addressing, packet format, timing, and power control.
- **Link manager protocol (LMP):** Responsible for link setup between Bluetooth devices and ongoing link management. This includes security aspects such as authentication and encryption, plus the control and negotiation of baseband packet sizes.
- **Logical link control and adaptation protocol (L2CAP):** Adapts upper-layer protocols to the baseband layer. L2CAP provides both connectionless and connection-oriented services.
- **Service discovery protocol (SDP):** Device information, services, and the characteristics of the services can be queried to enable the establishment of a connection between two or more Bluetooth devices.

RFCOMM is the **cable replacement protocol** included in the Bluetooth specification. RFCOMM presents a virtual serial port that is designed to make replacement

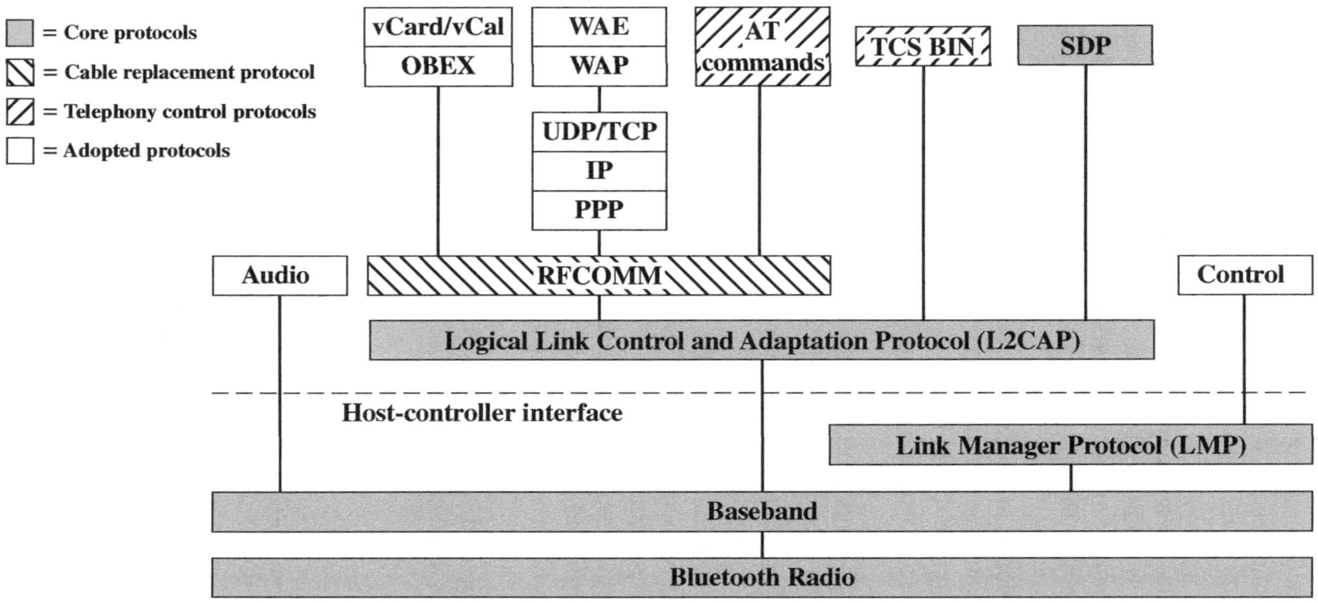

AT	= attention sequence (modem prefix)	TCS BIN	= telephony control specification—binary
IP	= Internet Protocol	UDP	= User Datagram Protocol
OBEX	= Object Exchange Protocol	vCal	= virtual calendar
PPP	= Point-to-Point Protocol	vCard	= virtual card
RFCOMM	= radio frequency communications	WAE	= wireless application environment
SDP	= Service Discovery Protocol	WAP	= Wireless Application Protocol
TCP	= Transmission Control Protocol		

Figure 15.1 Bluetooth Protocol Stack

of cable technologies as transparent as possible. Serial ports are one of the most common types of communications interfaces used with computing and communications devices. Hence, RFCOMM enables the replacement of serial port cables with the minimum of modification of existing devices. RFCOMM provides for binary data transport and emulates EIA-232 control signals over the Bluetooth baseband layer. EIA-232 (formerly known as RS-232) is a widely used serial port interface standard.

Bluetooth specifies a **telephony control protocol.** TCS BIN (telephony control specification—binary) is a bit-oriented protocol that defines the call control signaling for the establishment of speech and data calls between Bluetooth devices. In addition, it defines mobility management procedures for handling groups of Bluetooth TCS devices.

The **adopted protocols** are defined in specifications issued by other standards-making organizations and incorporated into the overall Bluetooth architecture. The Bluetooth strategy is to invent only necessary protocols and use existing standards whenever possible. The adopted protocols include the following:

- **PPP:** The point-to-point protocol is an Internet standard protocol for transporting IP datagrams over a point-to-point link.
- **TCP/UDP/IP:** These are the foundation protocols of the TCP/IP protocol suite (described in Chapter 4).
- **OBEX:** The object exchange protocol is a session-level protocol developed by the Infrared Data Association (IrDA) for the exchange of objects. OBEX provides functionality similar to that of HTTP, but in a simpler fashion. It also provides a model for representing objects and operations. Examples of content formats transferred by OBEX are vCard and vCalendar, which provide the format of an electronic business card and personal calendar entries and scheduling information, respectively.
- **WAE/WAP:** Bluetooth incorporates the wireless application environment and the wireless application protocol into its architecture (described in Chapter 12).

Usage Models

A number of usage models are defined in Bluetooth profile documents. In essence, a usage model is set of protocols that implement a particular Bluetooth-based application. Each profile defines the protocols and protocol features supporting a particular usage model. Figure 15.2, taken from [METT99], illustrates the highest-priority usage models:

- **File transfer:** The file transfer usage model supports the transfer of directories, files, documents, images, and streaming media formats. This usage model also includes the capability to browse folders on a remote device.
- **Internet bridge:** With this usage model, a PC is wirelessly connected to a mobile phone or cordless modem to provide dial-up networking and fax capabilities. For dial-up networking, AT commands are used to control the mobile

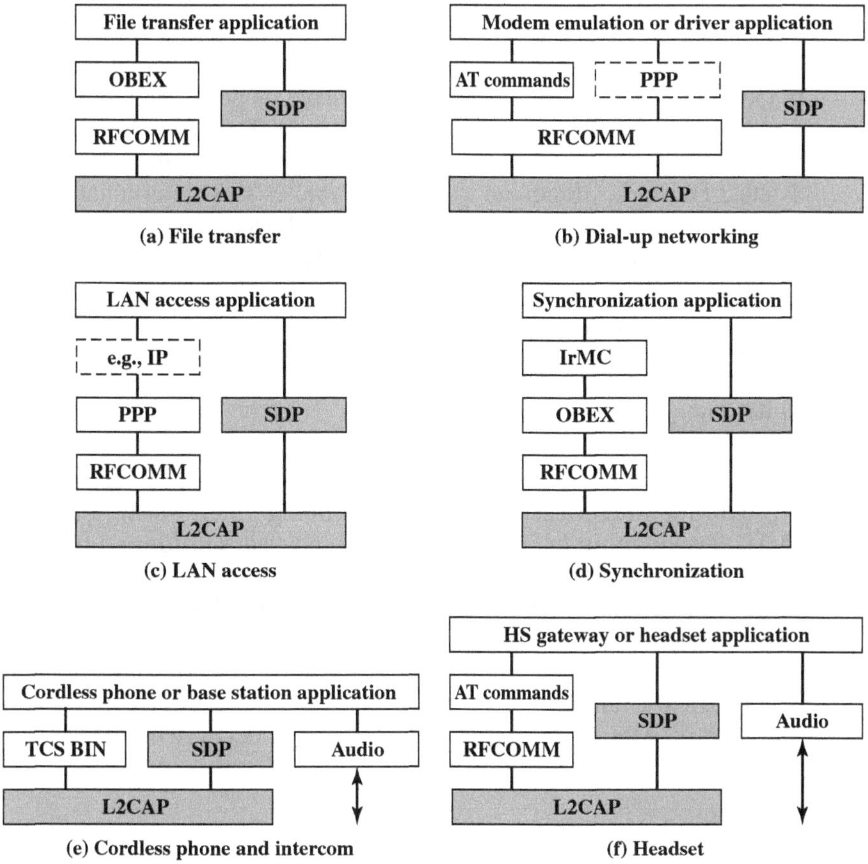

Figure 15.2 Bluetooth Usage Models

phone or modem, and another protocol stack (e.g., PPP over RFCOMM) is used for data transfer. For fax transfer, the fax software operates directly over RFCOMM.

- **LAN access:** This usage model enables devices on a piconet to access a LAN. Once connected, a device functions as if it were directly connected (wired) to the LAN.
- **Synchronization:** This model provides a device-to-device synchronization of PIM (personal information management) information, such as phone book, calendar, message, and note information. IrMC (Ir mobile communications) is an IrDA protocol that provides a client/server capability for transferring updated PIM information from one device to another.
- **Three-in-one phone:** Telephone handsets that implement this usage model may act as a cordless phone connecting to a voice base station, as an intercom device for connecting to other telephones, and as a cellular phone.
- **Headset:** The headset can act as a remote device's audio input and output interface.

Piconets and Scatternets

As was mentioned, the basic unit of networking in Bluetooth is a **piconet**, consisting of a master and from one to seven active slave devices. The radio designated as the master makes the determination of the channel (frequency-hopping sequence) and phase (timing offset, i.e., when to transmit) that shall be used by all devices on this piconet. The radio designated as master makes this determination using its own device address as a parameter, while the slave devices must tune to the same channel and phase. A slave may only communicate with the master and may only communicate when granted permission by the master. A device in one piconet may also exist as part of another piconet and may function as either a slave or master in each piconet (Figure 15.3). This form of overlapping is called a **scatternet**. Figure 15.4, based on one in [HAAR00a], contrasts the piconet/scatternet architecture with other forms of wireless networks.

The advantage of the piconet/scatternet scheme is that it allows many devices to share the same physical area and make efficient use of the bandwidth. A Bluetooth system uses a frequency-hopping scheme with a carrier spacing of 1 MHz. Typically, up to 80 different frequencies are used for a total bandwidth of 80 MHz. If frequency hopping were not used, then a single channel would correspond to a single 1-MHz band. With frequency hopping a logical channel is defined by the frequency-hopping sequence. At any given time, the bandwidth available is 1 MHz, with a maximum of eight devices sharing the bandwidth. Different logical channels (different hopping sequences) can simultaneously share the same 80-MHz bandwidth. Collisions will occur when devices in different

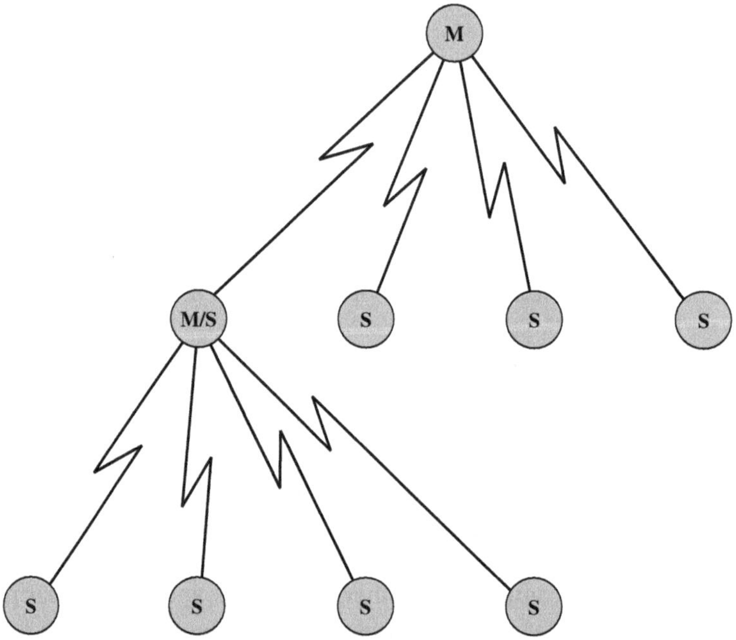

Figure 15.3 Master/Slave Relationships

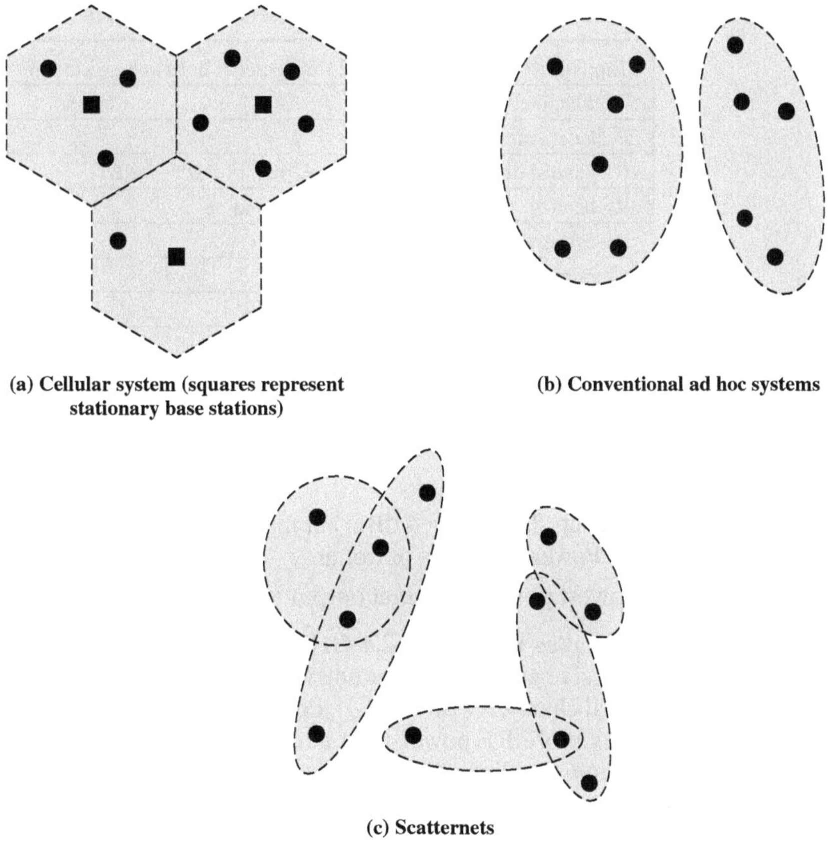

Figure 15.4 Wireless Network Configurations

piconets, on different logical channels, happen to use the same hop frequency at the same time. As the number of piconets in an area increases, the number of collisions increases, and performance degrades. In summary, the physical area and total bandwidth are shared by the scatternet. The logical channel and data transfer are shared by a piconet.

15.2 RADIO SPECIFICATION

The Bluetooth radio specification is a short document that gives the basic details of radio transmission for Bluetooth devices. Some of the key parameters are summarized in Table 15.2.

One aspect of the radio specification is a definition of three classes of transmitters based on output power:

- **Class 1:** Outputs 100 mW (+20 dBm) for maximum range, with a minimum of 1 mW (0 dBm). In this class, power control is mandatory, ranging from 4 to 20 dBm. This mode provides the greatest distance.

Table 15.2 Bluetooth Radio and Baseband Parameters

Topology	Up to 7 simultaneous links in a logical star
Modulation	GFSK
Peak data rate	1 Mbps
RF bandwidth	220 kHz (−3dB), 1 MHz (−20dB)
RF band	2.4 GHz, ISM band
RF carriers	23/79
Carrier spacing	1 MHz
Transmit power	0.1 W
Piconet access	FH-TDD-TDMA
Frequency hop rate	1600 hops/s
Scatternet access	FH-CDMA

- **Class 2:** Outputs 2.4 mW (+4 dBm) at maximum, with a minimum of 0.25 mW (−6 dBm). Power control is optional.
- **Class 3:** Lowest power. Nominal output is 1 mW.

Bluetooth makes use of the 2.4-GHz band within the ISM (industrial, scientific, and medical) band. In most countries, the bandwidth is sufficient to define 79 1-MHz physical channels (Table 15.3). Power control is used to keep the devices from emitting any more RF power than necessary. The power control algorithm is implemented using the link management protocol between a master and the slaves in a piconet.

Modulation for Bluetooth is Gaussian FSK, with a binary one represented by a positive frequency deviation and a binary zero represented by a negative frequency deviation from the center frequency. The minimum deviation is 115 kHz.

15.3 BASEBAND SPECIFICATION

One of the most complex of the Bluetooth documents is the baseband specification. In this section we provide an overview of the key elements.

Table 15.3 International Bluetooth Frequency Allocations

Area	Regulatory Range	RF Channels
U.S., most of Europe, and most other countries	2.4 to 2.4835 GHz	$f = 2.402 + n$ MHz, $n = 0, \ldots, 78$
Japan	2.471 to 2.497 GHz	$f = 2.473 + n$ MHz, $n = 0, \ldots, 22$
Spain	2.445 to 2.475 GHz	$f = 2.449 + n$ MHz, $n = 0, \ldots, 22$
France	2.4465 to 2.4835 GHz	$f = 2.454 + n$ MHz, $n = 0, \ldots, 22$

Frequency Hopping

Frequency hopping (FH) in Bluetooth serves two purposes:

1. It provides resistance to interference and multipath effects.
2. It provides a form of multiple access among co-located devices in different piconets.

The FH scheme works as follows. The total bandwidth is divided into 79 (in almost all countries) **physical channels**, each of bandwidth 1 MHz. FH occurs by jumping from one physical channel to another in a pseudorandom sequence. The same hopping sequence is shared by all of the devices on a single piconet; we will refer to this as an **FH channel**.[2] The hop rate is 1600 hops per second, so that each physical channel is occupied for a duration of 0.625 ms. Each 0.625-ms time period is referred to as a slot, and these are numbered sequentially.

Bluetooth radios communicate using a time division duplex (TDD) discipline. Recall from Chapter 11 that TDD is a link transmission technique in which data are transmitted in one direction at a time, with transmission alternating between the two directions. Because more than two devices share the piconet medium, the access technique is TDMA. Thus piconet access can be characterized as FH-TDD-TDMA. Figure 15.5 illustrates the technique.[3] In the figure, k denotes the slot number, and $f(k)$ is the physical channel selected during slot period k.

Transmission of a packet starts at the beginning of a slot. Packet lengths requiring 1, 3, or 5 slots are allowed. For multislot packets, the radio remains at the same frequency until the entire packet has been sent (Figure 15.6). In the next slot after the multislot packet, the radio returns to the frequency required for its hopping sequence, so that during transmission, two or four hop frequencies have been skipped.

Using TDD prevents crosstalk between transmit and receive operations in the radio transceiver, which is essential if a one-chip implementation is desired. Note that because transmission and reception take place at different time slots, different frequencies are used.

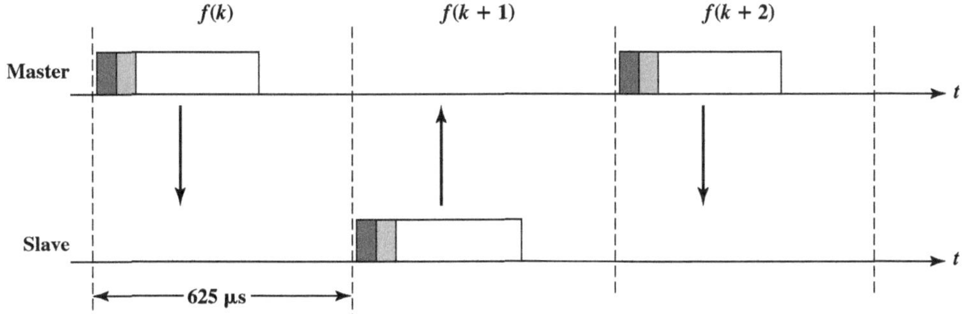

Figure 15.5 Frequency-Hop Time Division Duplex

[2]The term *FH channel* is not used in the Bluetooth documents but is introduced here for clarity.

[3]The three regions indicated in each packet (dark gray, light gray, white) depict the three major subdivisions of each packet (access code, header, payload), as explained subsequently.

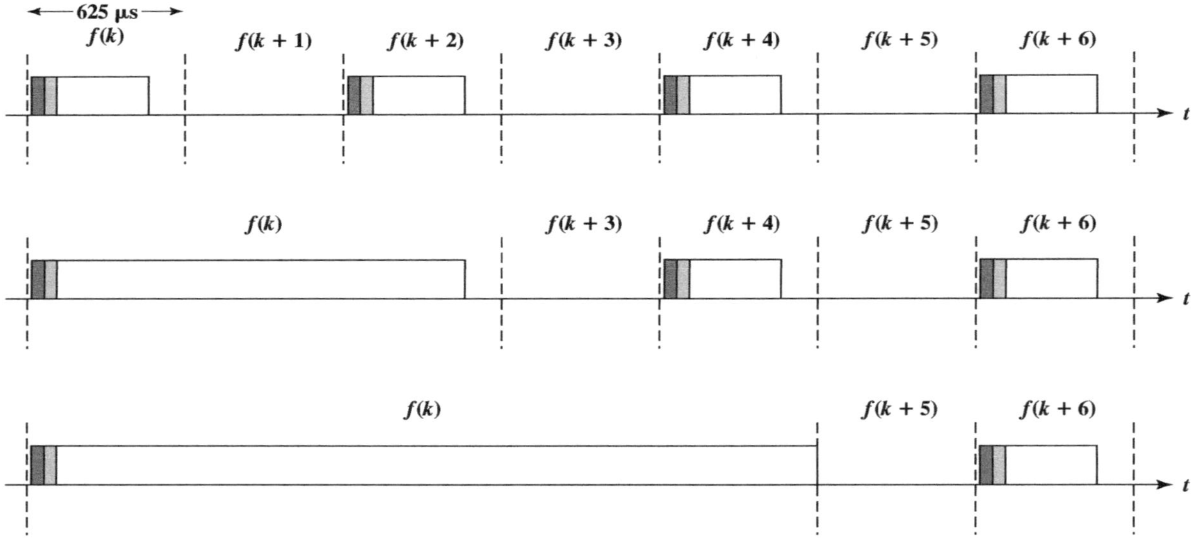

Figure 15.6 Examples of Multislot Packets

The FH sequence is determined by the master in a piconet and is a function of the master's Bluetooth address. A rather complex mathematical operation involving permutations and exclusive-OR (XOR) operations is used to generate a pseudorandom hop sequence.

Because different piconets in the same area will have different masters, they will use different hop sequences. Thus, most of the time, transmissions on two devices on different piconets in the same area will be on different physical channels. Occasionally, two piconets will use the same physical channel during the same time slot, causing a collision and lost data. However, because this will happen infrequently, it is readily accommodated with forward error correction and error detection/ARQ techniques. Thus, a form of code division multiple access (CDMA) is achieved between devices on different piconets in the same scatternet; this is referred to as FH-CDMA.

Physical Links

Two types of links can be established between a master and a slave:

- **Synchronous connection oriented (SCO):** Allocates a fixed bandwidth between a point-to-point connection involving the master and a single slave. The master maintains the SCO link by using reserved slots at regular intervals. The basic unit of reservation is two consecutive slots (one in each transmission direction). The master can support up to three simultaneous SCO links while a slave can support two or three SCO links. SCO packets are never retransmitted.
- **Asynchronous connectionless (ACL):** A point-to-multipoint link between the master and all the slaves in the piconet. In slots not reserved for SCO links, the master can exchange packets with any slave on a per-slot basis, including a slave already engaged in an SCO link. Only a single ACL link can exist. For most ACL packets, packet retransmission is applied.

SCO links are used primarily to exchange time-bounded data requiring guaranteed data rate but without guaranteed delivery. One example, used in a number of Bluetooth profiles, is digitally encoded audio data with built-in tolerance to lost data. The guaranteed data rate is achieved through the reservation of a particular number of slots.

ACL links provide a packet-switched style of connection. No bandwidth reservation is possible and delivery may be guaranteed through error detection and retransmission. A slave is permitted to return an ACL packet in the slave-to-master slot if and only if it has been addressed in the preceding master-to-slave slot. For ACL links, 1-slot, 3-slot, and 5-slot packets have been defined. Data can be sent either unprotected (although ARQ can be used at a higher layer) or protected with a 2/3 forward error correction code. The maximum data rate that can be achieved is with a 5-slot unprotected packet with asymmetric capacity allocation, resulting in 721 kbps in the forward direction and 57.6 kbps in the reverse direction. Table 15.4 summarizes all of the possibilities.

Table 15.4 Achievable Data Rates on the ACL Link

Type	Symmetric (kbps)	Asymmetric (kbps)	
DM1	108.8	108.8	108.8
DH1	172.8	172.8	172.8
DM3	256.0	384.0	54.4
DH3	384.0	576.0	86.4
DM5	286.7	477.8	36.3
DH5	432.6	721.0	57.6

DMx = x-slot FEC-encoded

DHx = x-slot unprotected

Packets

The packet format for all Bluetooth packets is shown in Figure 15.7. It consists of three fields:

- **Access code:** Used for timing synchronization, offset compensation, paging, and inquiry
- **Header:** Used to identify packet type and to carry protocol control information
- **Payload:** If present, contains user voice or data and, in most cases, a payload header

Access Code

There are three types of access codes:

- **Channel access code (CAC):** Identifies a piconet (unique for a piconet)
- **Device access code (DAC):** Used for paging and its subsequent responses
- **Inquiry access code (IAC):** Used for inquiry purposes

An access code consists of a preamble, a sync word, and a trailer. The **preamble** is used for DC compensation. It consists of the pattern 0101 if the least significant (leftmost) bit in the sync word is 0 and the pattern 1010 if the least significant bit in the sync word is 1. Similarly, the **trailer** is 0101 if the most significant bit (rightmost) of the sync word is 1 and 1010 if the most significant bit is 0.

The 64-bit **sync word** consists of three components (Figure 15.8) and is worth examining in some detail. Each Bluetooth device is assigned a globally unique 48-bit address. The 24 least significant bits are referred to as the lower address part (LAP) and are used in forming the sync word. For a CAC, the LAP of the master is used; for a DAC, the LAP of the paged unit. There are two different IACs. The general IAC (GIAC) is a general inquiry message used to discover which Bluetooth devices are in range, and for this a special reserved value of LAP is available. A dedicated IAC (DIAC) is common for a dedicated group of Bluetooth units that share a common characteristic, and a previously defined LAP corresponding to that characteristic is used.

Using the appropriate LAP, the sync word is formed as follows:

1. To the 24-bit LAP, append the 6 bits 001101 if the most significant bit (MSB) of the LAP is 0, and append 110010 if the MSB is 1. This forms a 7-bit Barker

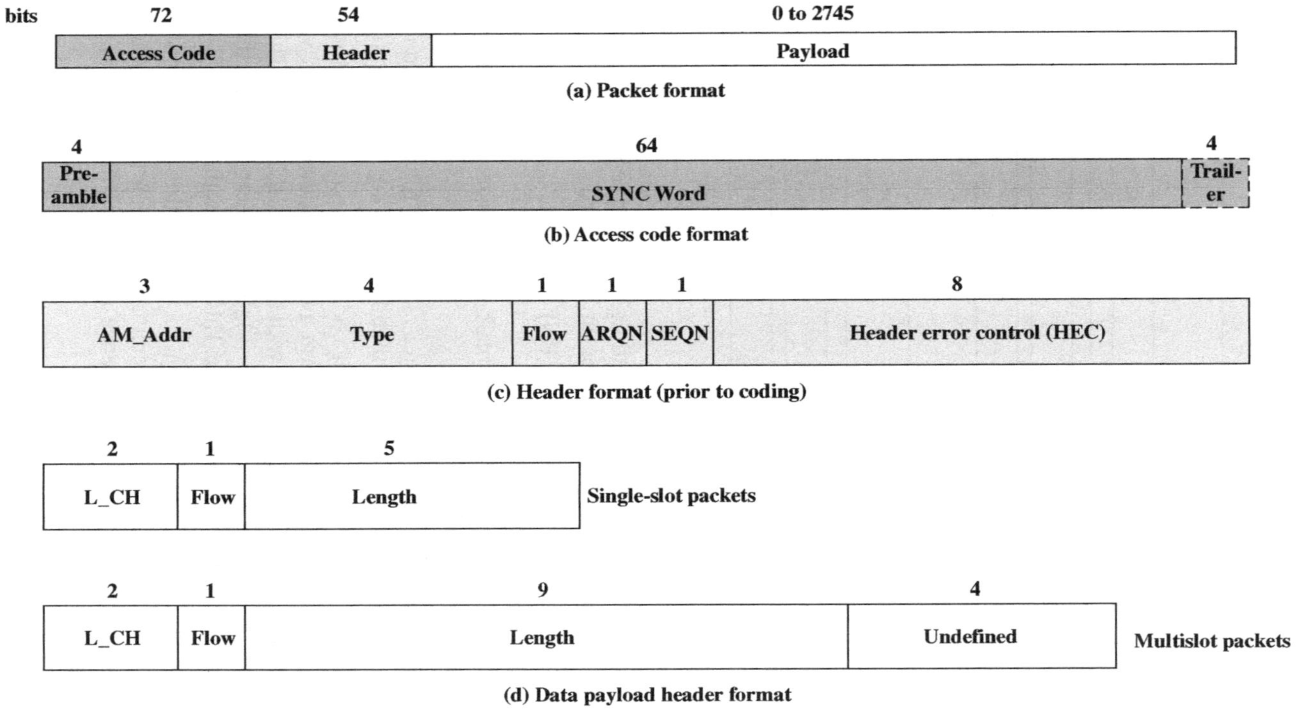

Figure 15.7 Bluetooth Baseband Formats

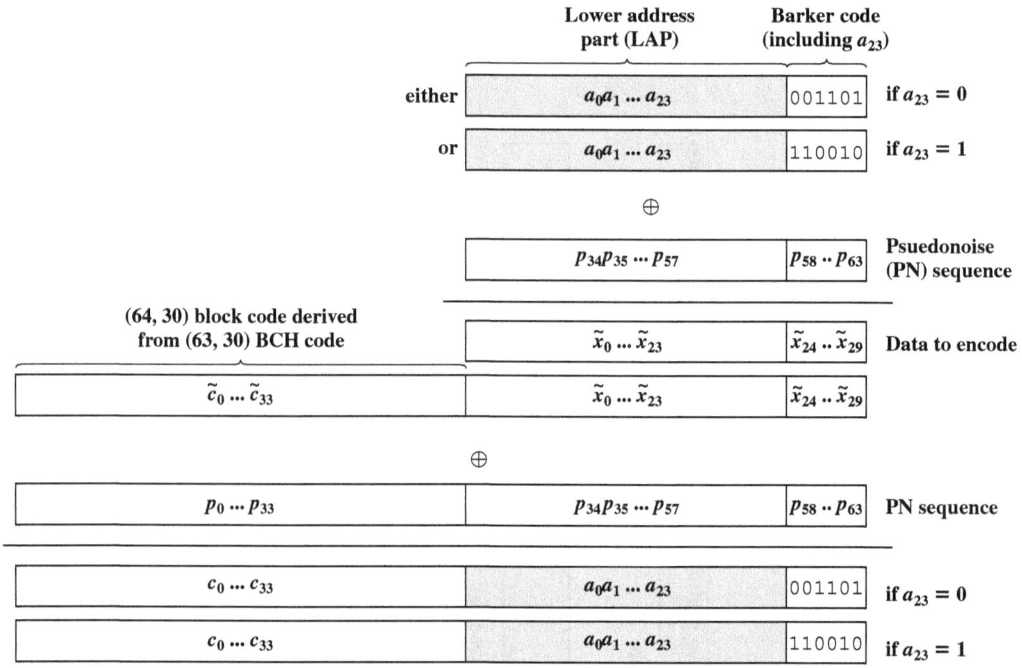

Figure 15.8 Construction of Sync Word

sequence.[4] The purpose of including a Barker sequence is to further improve the autocorrelation properties of the sync word.

2. Generate a 64-bit pseudonoise (PN) sequence, $p_0, p_1, \ldots, p_{63}$. The sequence is defined by the equation $P(X) = 1 + X^2 + X^3 + X^5 + X^6$ and can be implemented with a 6-bit linear feedback shift register. The seed value for the PN sequence is 100000.[5]
3. Take the bitwise XOR of $p_{34}, p_{35}, \ldots, p_{63}$ and the 30-bit sequence produced in step 1. This "scrambles" the information, removing unwanted regularities.
4. Generate a 34-bit error-correcting code for the scrambled information block and place this at the beginning to form a 64-bit codeword. Thus, we have a (64, 30) code. To generate this code, start with a (63, 30) BCH code.[6] Then define the generator polynomial $g(X) = (1 + X)g'(X)$, where $g'(X)$ is the generator polynomial for the (63, 30) BCH code. This produces the desired 34-bit code.
5. Take the bitwise XOR of $p_0, p_a, \ldots, p_{63}$ and the 64-bit sequence produced in step 4. This step descrambles the information part of the codeword so that the original LAP and Barker sequence are transmitted. The step also scrambles the block code.

[4]See Section 14.4 for a discussion of Barker sequences.

[5]See Section 7.5 for a discussion of PN sequence generation and generating equations [e.g., Equation (7.9)].

[6]See Section 8.2 for a discussion of BCH codes.

The scrambling of the information part of the codeword in step 3 is designed to strengthen the error-correcting properties of the block code. The subsequent descrambling enables the receiver to recover the LAP easily. In the words of the specification, the scrambling of the 34-bit error code removes the cyclic properties of the underlying code. This might give better transmission spectral qualities and also improve autocorrelation properties.

Packet Header The header format for all Bluetooth packets is shown in Figure 15.7c. It consists of six fields:

- **AM_ADDR:** Recall that a piconet includes at most seven active slaves. The 3-bit AM_Addr contains the "active mode" address (temporary address assigned to this slave in this piconet) of one of the slaves. A transmission from the master to a slave contains that slave's address; a transmission from a slave contains its address. The 0 value is reserved for a broadcast from the master to all slaves in the piconet.
- **Type:** Identifies the type of packet (Table 15.5). Four type codes are reserved for control packets common to both SCO and ACL links. The remaining packet types are used to convey user information. For SCO links, the HV1, HV2, HV3 packets each carry 64-kbps voice. The difference is the amount of error protection provided, which dictates how frequently a packet must be sent to maintain the 64-kbps data rate. The DV packet carries both voice and data. For ACL links, 6 different packets are defined. These, together with the DM1 packet, carry user data with different amounts of error protection and different data rates (Table 15.4). There is another packet type common to both physical links; it consists of only the access code, with a fixed length of 68 bits (does not include trailer). This is referred to as the ID packet and is used in the inquiry and access procedures.
- **Flow:** Provides a 1-bit flow control mechanism for ACL traffic only. When a packet with Flow = 0 is received, the station receiving the packet must temporarily halt the transmission of ACL packets on this link. When a packet with Flow = 1 is received, transmission may resume.
- **ARQN:** Provides a 1-bit acknowledgment mechanism for ACL traffic protected by a CRC (Table 15.5). If the reception was successful, an ACK (ARQN = 1) is returned; otherwise a NAK (ARQN = 0) is returned. When no return message regarding acknowledge is received, a NAK is assumed implicitly. If a NAK is received, the relevant packet is retransmitted.
- **SEQN:** Provides a 1-bit sequential numbering schemes. Transmitted packets are alternately labeled with a 1 or 0. This is required to filter out retransmissions at the destination; if a retransmission occurs due to a failing ACK, the destination receives the same packet twice.
- **Header error control (HEC):** An 8-bit error detection code used to protect the packet header.

Payload Format For some packet types, the baseband specification defines a format for the payload field. For voice payloads, no header is defined. For all of the

Table 15.5 Bluetooth Packet Types

Type Code	Physical Link	Name	Number of Slots	Description
0000	Common	NULL	1	Has no payload. Used to return link information to the source regarding the success of the previous transmission (ARQN), or the status of the RX buffer (FLOW). Not acknowledged.
0001	Common	POLL	1	Has no payload. Used by master to poll a slave. Acknowledged.
0010	Common	FHS	1	Special control packet for revealing device address and the clock of the sender. Used in page master response, inquiry response, and frequency hop synchronization. 2/3 FEC encoded.
0011	Common	DM1	1	Supports control messages and can also carry user data. 16-bit CRC. 2/3 FEC encoded.
0101	SCO	HV1	1	Carries 10 information bytes; typically used for 64-kbps voice. 1/3 FEC encoded.
0110	SCO	HV2	1	Carries 20 information bytes; typically used for 64-kbps voice. 2/3 FEC encoded.
0111	SCO	HV3	1	Carries 30 information bytes; typically used for 64-kbps voice. Not FEC encoded.
1000	SCO	DV	1	Combined data (150 bits) and voice (50 bits) packet. Data field 2/3 FEC encoded.
0100	ACL	DH1	1	Carries 28 information bytes plus 16-bit CRC. Not FEC encoded. Typically used for high-speed data.
1001	ACL	AUX1	1	Carries 30 information bytes with no CRC or FEC. Typically used for high-speed data.
1010	ACL	DM3	3	Carries 123 information bytes plus 16-bit CRC. 2/3 FEC encoded.
1011	ACL	DH3	3	Carries 185 information bytes plus 16-bit CRC. Not FEC encoded.
1110	ACL	DM5	5	Carries 226 information bytes plus 16-bit CRC. 2/3 FEC encoded.
1111	ACL	DH5	5	Carries 341 information bytes plus 16-bit CRC. Not FEC encoded.

ACL packets and for the data portion of the SCO DV packet, a header is defined. For data payloads, the payload format consists of three fields:

- **Payload header:** An 8-bit header is defined for single-slot packets, and a 16-bit header is defined for multislot packets.
- **Payload body:** Contains user information.
- **CRC:** A 16-bit CRC code is used on all data payloads except the AUX1 packet.

The payload header, when present, consists of three fields (Figure 15.7d):

- **L_CH:** Identifies the logical channel (described subsequently). The options are LMP message (11); an unfragmented L2CAP message or the start of a fragmented L2CAP message (10); the continuation of a fragmented L2CAP message (01); or other (00).
- **Flow:** Used to control flow at the L2CAP level. This is the same on/off mechanism provided by the Flow field in the packet header for ACL traffic.
- **Length:** The number of bytes of data in the payload, excluding the payload header and CRC.

Error Correction

At the baseband level, Bluetooth makes use of three error correction schemes:

- 1/3 rate FEC (forward error correction)
- 2/3 rate FEC
- ARQ (automatic repeat request)

These error correction schemes are designed to satisfy competing requirements. The error correction scheme must be adequate to cope with the inherently unreliable wireless link but must also be streamlined and efficient.

The **1/3 rate FEC** is used on the 18-bit packet header and also for the voice field in an HV1 packet. The scheme simply involves sending three copies of each bit. A majority logic is used: Each received triple of bits is mapped into whichever bit is in the majority.

The **2/3 rate FEC** is used in all DM packets, in the data field of the DV packet, in the FHS packet, and in the HV2 packet. The encoder is a form of Hamming code with parameters (15, 10). This code can correct all single errors and detect all double errors in each codeword.

The **ARQ scheme** is used with DM and DH packets and the data field of DV packets. The scheme is similar to ARQ schemes used in data link control protocols (Section 8.4). Recall that ARQ schemes have the following elements:

- **Error detection:** The destination detects errors and discards packets that are in error. Error detection is achieved with a CRC error-detecting code supplemented with the FEC code.
- **Positive acknowledgment:** The destination returns a positive acknowledgment to successfully received, error-free packets.

- **Retransmission after timeout:** The source retransmits a packet that has not been acknowledged after a predetermined amount of time.
- **Negative acknowledgment and retransmission:** The destination returns a negative acknowledgment to packets in which an error is detected. The source retransmits such packets.

Bluetooth uses what is referred to as a *fast ARQ* scheme, which takes advantage of the fact that a master and slave communicate in alternate time slots. Figure 15.9 illustrates the technique. When a station receives a packet, it determines if an error has occurred using a 16-bit CRC. If so, the ARQN bit in the header set to 0 (NAK); if no error is detected, then ARQN is set to 1 (ACK). When a station receives a NAK, it retransmits the same packet as it sent in the preceding slot, using the same 1-bit SEQN in the packet header. With this technique, a sender is notified in the next time slot if a transmission has failed and, if so, can retransmit. The use of 1-bit sequence numbers and immediate packet retransmission minimizes overhead and maximizes responsiveness.

Figure 15.10 shows the ARQ mechanism in more detail. On reception of a packet (Figure 15.10a), the device first checks that the header is valid, using the HEC; if not the packet is rejected and ARQN is set to NAK in the next time slot. Then the device does an address match and checks whether this is the type of packet that uses the ARQ mechanisms. Having passed these tests, the device next checks whether this is a new sequence number (SEQN) or the same as the last SEQN. If the SEQNs are the same, then this is a retransmission, which is ignored. If the SEQN is new, then the device checks the CRC. If no error is detected, the next outgoing packet has ARQN = ACK, and if an error is detected, the next outgoing packet has ARQN = NAK.

On the transmit side (Figure 15.10b), the next DM, DH, or DV packet to be transmitted is determined by the value of the immediately preceding incoming ARQN. So long as ACKs are received, the device sends out new payload, alternating SEQN values between 0 and 1. If a NAK or no acknowledgment at all is received, the device will retransmit the old payload repeatedly until an ACK is received or until some threshold is reached, at which time the old payload is flushed from the transmit buffer and a new payload is transmitted.

Logical Channels

Bluetooth defines five types of logical data channels designated to carry different types of payload traffic.

- **Link control (LC):** Used to manage the flow of packets over the link interface. The LC channel is mapped onto the packet header. This channel carries low-level link control information like ARQ, flow control, and payload characterization. The LC channel is carried in every packet except in the ID packet, which has no packet header.
- **Link manager (LM):** Transports link management information between participating stations. This logical channel supports LMP traffic and can be carried over either an SCO or ACL link.
- **User asynchronous (UA):** Carries asynchronous user data. This channel is normally carried over the ACL link but may be carried in a DV packet on the SCO link.

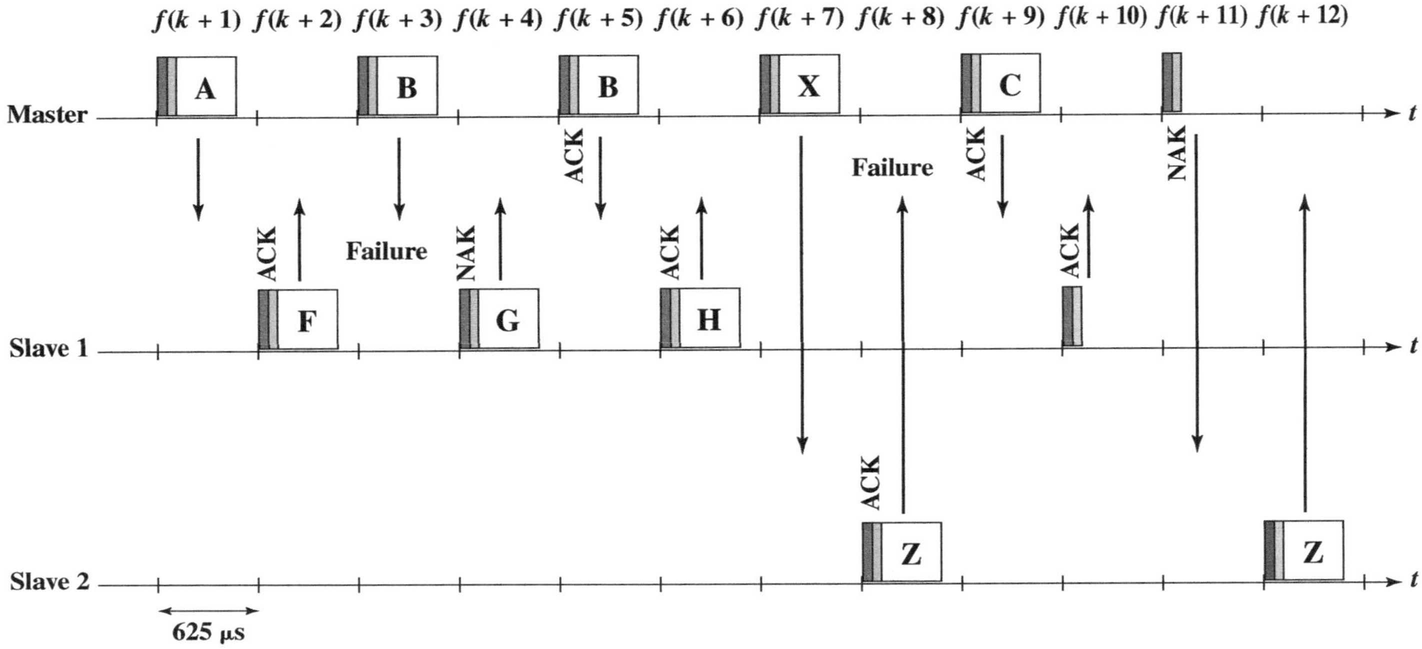

Figure 15.9 An Example of Retransmission Operation

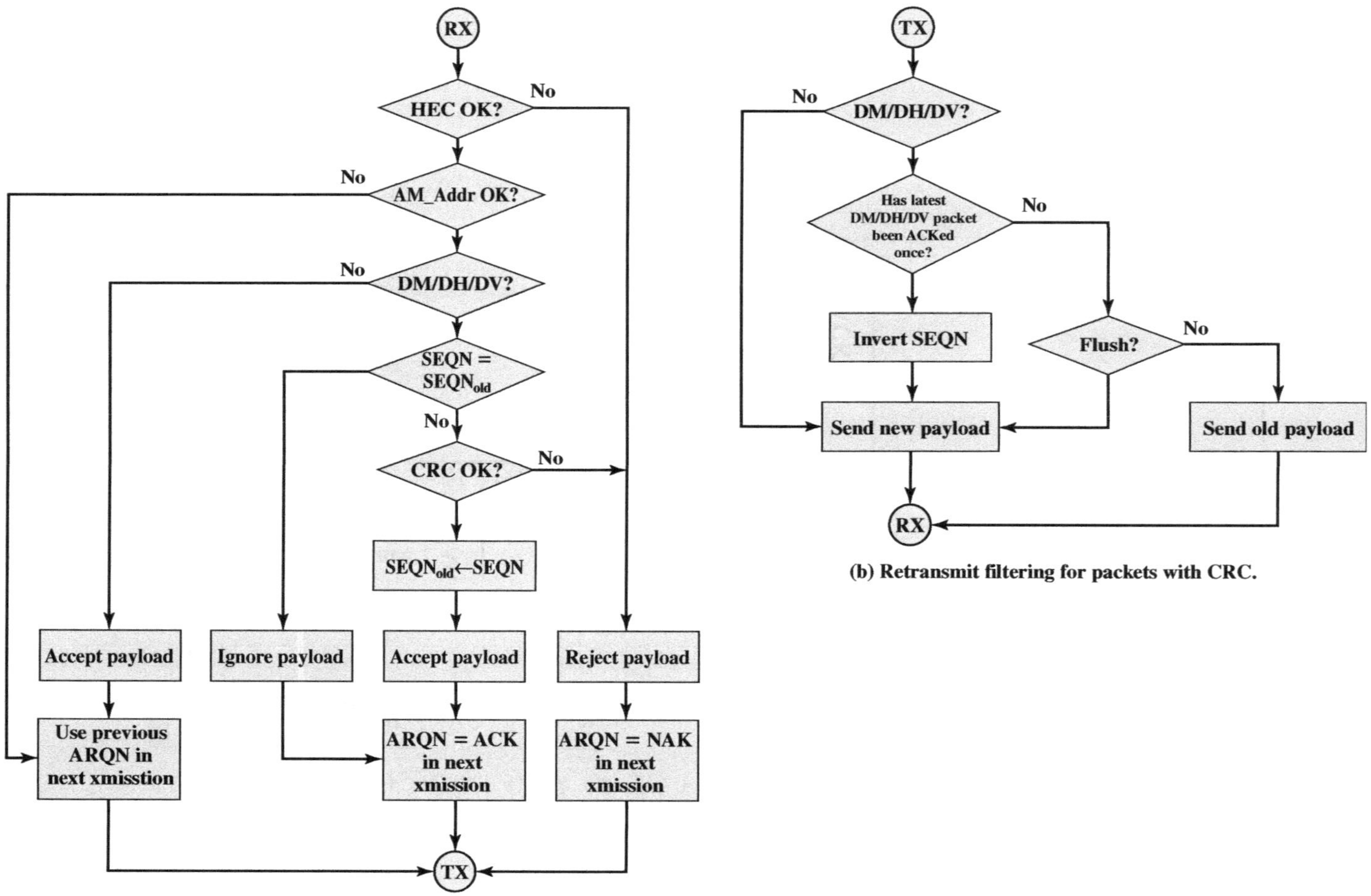

(a) Receive protocol for determining the ARQN bit.

(b) Retransmit filtering for packets with CRC.

Figure 15.10 Bluetooth ARQ Scheme

- **User isochronous (UI):** Carries isochronous user data.[7] This channel is normally carried over the ACL link but may be carried in a DV packet on the SCO link. At the baseband level, the UI channel is treated the same way as a UA channel. Timing to provide isochronous properties is provided at a higher layer.
- **User synchronous (US):** Carries synchronous user data. This channel is carried over the SCO link.

Channel Control

The operation of a piconet can be understood in terms of the states of operation during link establishment and maintenance (Figure 15.11). There are two major states:

- **Standby:** The default state. This is a low-power state in which only the native clock is running.
- **Connection:** The device is connected to a piconet as a master or a slave.

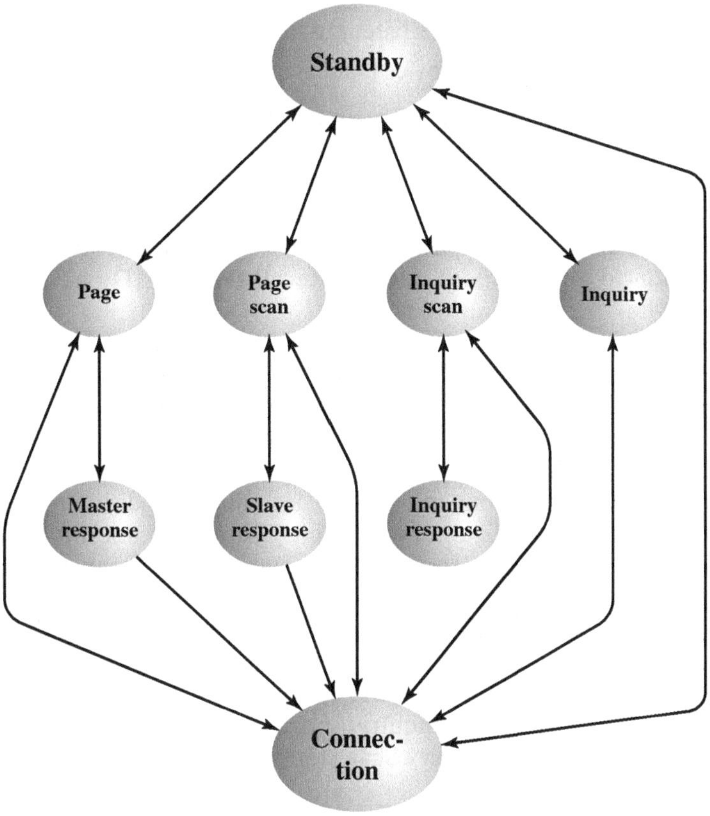

Figure 15.11 Bluetooth State Transition Diagram

---

[7]The term *isochronous* refers to blocks of data that recur with known periodic timing.

In addition, there are seven interim substates that are used to add new slaves to a piconet. To move from one state to the other, either commands from the Bluetooth link manager are used or internal signals in the link controller are used. The substates are as follows:

- **Page:** Device has issued a page. Used by the master to activate and connect to a slave. Master sends page message by transmitting slave's device access code (DAC) in different hop channels.
- **Page scan:** Device is listening for a page with its own DAC.
- **Master response:** A device acting as a master receives a page response from a slave. The device can now enter the connection state or return to the page state to page for other slaves.
- **Slave response:** A device acting as a slave responds to a page from a master. If connection setup succeeds, the device enters the connection state; otherwise it returns to the page scan state.
- **Inquiry:** Device has issued an inquiry, to find the identity of the devices within range.
- **Inquiry scan:** Device is listening for an inquiry.
- **Inquiry response:** A device that has issued an inquiry receives an inquiry response.

Inquiry Procedure The first step in establishing a piconet is for a potential master to identify devices in range that wish to participate in the piconet. A device begins an inquiry procedure for this purpose under the impetus of a user or application on the device. The inquiry procedure begins when the potential master transmits an ID packet with an inquiry access code (IAC), which is a code common to all Bluetooth devices. Recall that the ID packet has no header and no payload.

Of the 79 radio carriers, 32 are considered wake-up carriers. The master broadcasts the IAC over each of the 32 wake-up carriers in turn. This occurs in the Inquiry state (Figure 15.11). Meanwhile, devices in the Standby state periodically enter the Inquiry Scan state to search for IAC messages on the wake-up carriers. When a device receives the inquiry, it enters the Inquiry Response state and returns an FHS packet (Table 15.5) containing its device address and timing information required by the master to initiate a connection. The master does not respond to the FHS packet and may remain in the Inquiry state until it is satisfied that all radios have been found.

Once a device has responded to an Inquiry, it moves to the page scan state to await a page from the master in order to establish a connection. However, if a collision occurred in the Inquiry Response phase (two or more devices simultaneously respond to an inquiry), no page will be received and the device may need to return to the Inquiry Scan state to attempt another inquiry and response.[8]

---

[8]The state diagram of Figure 15.12 is taken from the baseband specification and does not show a transition from Inquiry Response to Page Scan but does show a transition from Inquiry Response to Inquiry Scan. However, the accompanying text in the specification corresponds to the explanation we give.

Page Procedure Once the master has found devices within its range, it is able to establish a connection to each device, setting up a piconet. For each device to be paged, the master uses that device's address (BD_ADDR) to calculate a page frequency-hopping sequence, the aim of which is to contact the device during paging. The master pages by using an ID packet, this time with a device access code (DAC) of the specific slave. Recall that the DAC is the lower address part of the slave's device address. The slave responds by returning the same DAC ID packet to the master in the same hopping sequence (known as the page-mode-hopping sequence) that was used by the master. The master responds to this in the next master-to-slave slot with its own FHS packet, containing its device address and its real-time Bluetooth clock value. Once again, the slave sends a response DAC ID packet to the master to confirm the receipt of the master's FHS packet. The slave at this point transitions from the Slave Response state to the Connection state and begins to use the connection hopping sequence defined in the master's FHS packet. Meanwhile, the master may continue to page until it has connected to all the desired slaves; the master then enters the Connection state.

Connection State For each slave, the Connection state starts with a Poll packet sent from the master to verify that the slave has switched to the master's timing and channel frequency hopping. The slave can respond with any type of packet.

Once the slave is in the Connection state, it can be in one of four modes of operation:

- **Active:** The slave actively participates in the piconet by listening, transmitting, and receiving packets. The master periodically transmits to the slaves to maintain synchronization.
- **Sniff:** The slave does not listen on every receive slot (every other slot) but only on specified slots for its messages. The slave can operate in a reduced-power status the rest of the time. For sniff mode to operate, the master designates a reduced number of time slots for transmission to a specific slave.
- **Hold:** The device in this mode does not support ACL packets and goes to reduced power status. The slave may still participate in SCO exchanges. During periods of no activity, the slave is free to idle in a reduced power status or possibly participate in another piconet.
- **Park:** When a slave does not need to participate on the piconet but still is to be retained as part of the piconet, it can enter the park mode, which is a low-power mode with very little activity. The device is given a parking member address (PM_ADDR) and loses its active member (AM_ADDR) address. With the use of the park mode, a piconet may have more than seven slaves.

Bluetooth Audio

The baseband specification indicates that either of two voice encoding schemes can be used: pulse code modulation (PCM) or continuously variable slope delta (CVSD) modulation. The choice is made by the link managers of the two communicating devices, which negotiate the most appropriate scheme for the application.

PCM was discussed in Section 6.4. CVSD is a form of delta modulation (DM), also discussed in Section 6.4. Recall that with delta modulation, an analog input is approximated by a staircase function that moves up or down by one quantization level (δ) at each sampling interval (T_s). Thus, the output of the delta modulation process can be represented as a single binary digit for each sample. In essence, a bit stream is produced by approximating the derivative of an analog signal rather than its amplitude: A 1 is generated if the staircase function is to go up during the next interval; a 0 is generated otherwise.

As was discussed, there are two forms of error in a DM scheme: quantizing noise, which occurs when the waveform is changing very slowly, and slope overload noise, when the waveform is changing rapidly (Figure 6.18). CVSD is designed to minimize both these types of error by using a variable quantization level, one that is small when the waveform is changing slowly and large when the waveform is changing rapidly (Figure 15.12; based on one in [HAAR98]). The slope is monitored by considering the K most recent output bits. The resulting scheme is more resistant to bit errors than PCM and more resistant to quantizing and slope overload errors than DM.

Figure 15.13 illustrates the CVSD encoding and decoding (Compare Figure 6.19). As with DM, a binary output is converted into a staircase function that tracks the original waveform as closely as possible. For encoding, the following occurs: The input to the encoder is 64-kbps PCM. At each sampling time, the PCM input $x(k)$ is compared to the most recent value of the approximating staircase function, expressed as $\hat{x}(k-1)$. The output of the comparator $b(k)$ is defined as

$$b(k) = \begin{cases} 1 & x(k) - \hat{x}(k-1) \geq 0 \\ -1 & x(k) - \hat{x}(k-1) < 0 \end{cases}$$

For transmission, these numbers are represented by the sign bit (negative numbers are mapped to binary 1; positive numbers are mapped to 0). The output $b(k)$ is used as to produce the magnitude of the next step in the staircase, $\delta(k)$, as follows:

$$\delta(k) = \begin{cases} \min[\delta_{\min} + \delta(k-1), \delta_{\max}] & \text{if at least } J \text{ of the last } K \text{ output bits } b(\cdot) \text{ are the same} \\ \max[\beta \times \delta(k-1), \delta_{\min}] & \text{otherwise} \end{cases}$$

Table 15.6 shows the default parameter values. The effect of the preceding definition is that if the waveform is changing rapidly (at least J of the last K steps have been in the same direction), then the magnitude of the step change, $\delta(k)$, increases in a linear fashion by a constant amount $\delta_{\min}$, up to some maximum magnitude $\delta_{\max}$. On the other hand, if the waveform is not changing rapidly, then the magnitude of the step change gradually decays by a *decay factor* β, down to a minimum value of $\delta_{\min}$. The sign of the step change is determined by the sign of the output $b(t)$.

The step change is then added to the most recent value of the staircase function to produce $\hat{y}(k)$.

$$\hat{y}(k) = \hat{x}(k-1) + b(k)\delta(k)$$

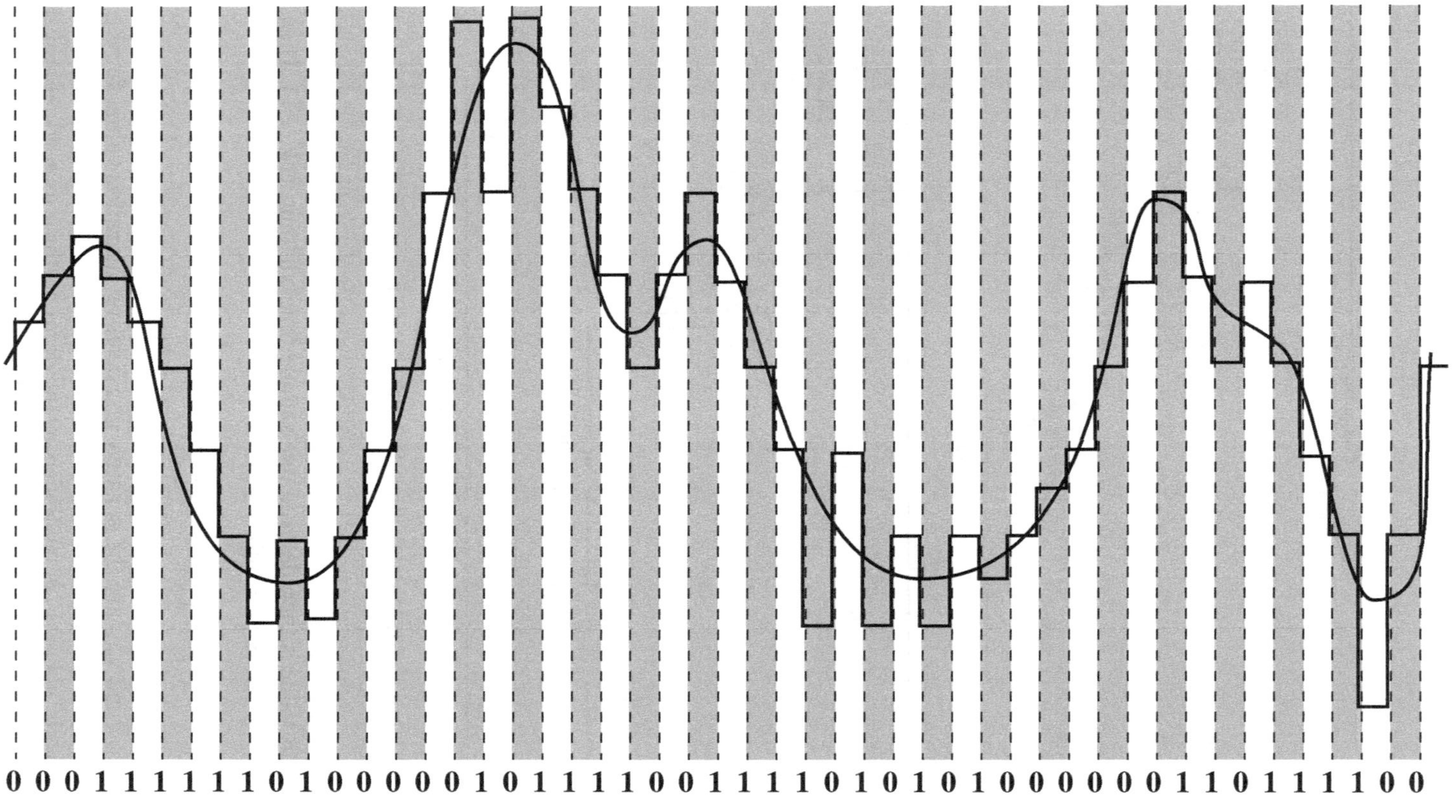

Figure 15.12 Example of Continuously Variable Slope Delta Modulation

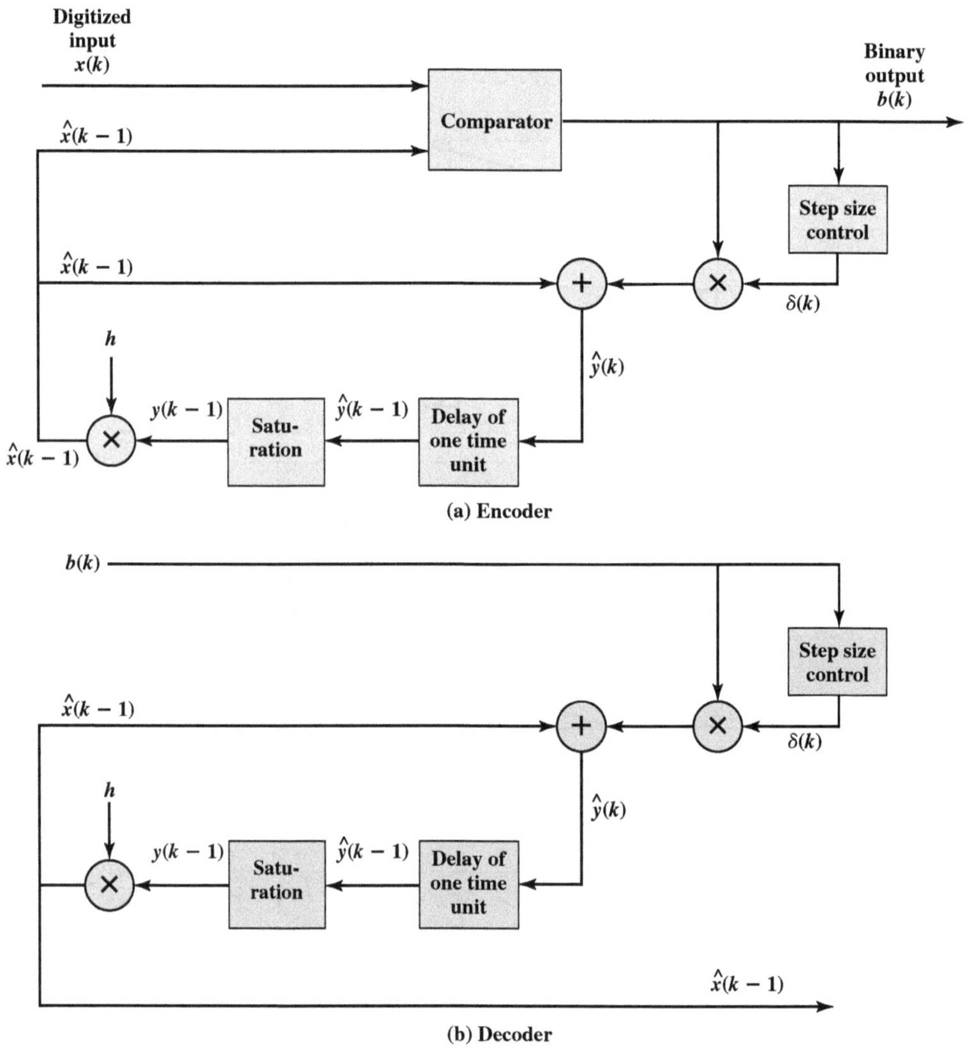

Figure 15.13 Continuously Variable Slope Delta Modulation

This value is then delayed one sample time, yielding $\hat{y}(k-1)$. Then a *saturation function* is applied, defined as

$$y(k-1) = \begin{cases} \min[\hat{y}(k-1), y_{\max}] & \hat{y}(k-1) \geq 0 \\ \max[\hat{y}(k-1), y_{\min}] & \hat{y}(k-1) < 0 \end{cases}$$

where $y_{\min}$ and $y_{\max}$ are the negative and positive saturation values for the encoder, limiting the total range of the staircase function.

Finally, $y(k-1)$ is multiplied by the decay factor h to yield the waveform estimate $\hat{x}(k-1)$. The decay factor determines how quickly the output of the CVSD decoder returns to zero in the absence of a strongly changing input.

Table 15.6 CVSD Parameter Values

Parameter	Value
h	$1 - \frac{1}{32} = 0.96875$
β	$1 - \frac{1}{1024} \approx 0.999$
J	4
K	4
δ_{min}	10
δ_{max}	1280
y_{min}	-2^{15} or $-2^{15} + 1$
y_{max}	$2^{15} - 1$

15.4 LINK MANAGER SPECIFICATION

LMP manages various aspects of the radio link between a master and a slave. The protocol involves the exchange of messages in the form of LMP PDUs (protocol data units) between the LMP entities in the master and slave. Messages are always sent as single slot packets with a 1-byte payload header that identifies the message type and a payload body that contains additional information pertinent to this message.

The procedures defined for LMP are grouped into 24 functional areas, each of which involves the exchange of one or more messages. Table 15.7 lists these areas, together with the PDUs involved in each area.[9] We briefly look at each area in turn.

The two **general response** messages are used to reply to other PDUs in a number of different procedures. The accepted PDU includes the opcode of the message that is accepted. The not_accepted PDU includes the opcode of the message that is not accepted and the reason why it is not accepted.

LMP supports various security services with mechanisms for managing authentication, encryption, and key distribution. These services include

- **Authentication:** Authentication is defined in the baseband specification but involves the exchange of two LMP PDUs, one containing the random number and one containing the signed response (Figure 15.14).
- **Pairing:** This service allows mutually authenticated users to automatically establish a link encryption key. As a first step, an initialization key is generated by both sides and used in the authentication procedure to authenticate that the two sides have the same key. The initialization key is generated from a common personal identification number (PIN) entered in both devices. The two sides then exchange messages to determine if the link key to be used for

[9]In the LMP specification, each PDU name begins with LMP_. For example, the first PDU listed in Table 15.7 has the name LMP_ accepted. For brevity, we omit the LMP_ prefix.

Table 15.7 LMP PDUs

Function	PDUs
General response	accepted, not_accepted
Security Service	
Authentication	au_rand, sres
Pairing	in_rand, au_rand, sres, comb_key, unit_key
Change link key	comb_key
Change current link key	temp_rand, temp_key, use_semi_permanent_key
Encryption	encryption_mode_req, encryption_key_size_req, start_encryption_req, stop_encryption_req
Time/Synchronization	
Clock offset request	clkoffset_req, clkoffset_res
Slot offset information	Slot_offset
Timing accuracy information request	timing_accuracy_req, timing_accuracy_res
Station Capability	
LMP version	version_req, version_res
Supported features	features_req, features_res
Mode Control	
Switch master/slave role	Switch_req
Name request	name_req, name_res
Detach	detach
Hold mode	hold, hold_req
Sniff mode	sniff, sniff_req, unsniff_req
Park mode	park_req, park, set_broadcast_window, modify_beacon, unpark_PM_ADDR_req, unpark_BD_ADDR_req
Power control	incr_power_req, decr_power_req, max_power, min_power
Channel quality-driven change between DM and DH	auto_rate, preferred_rate
Quality of service	quality_of_service, quality_of_service_req
SCO links	SCO_link_req, remove_SCO_link_req
Control of multislot packets	max_slot, max_slot_req
Paging scheme	page_mode_req, page_scan_mode_req
Link supervision	supervision_timeout

future encryptions will be a secret key already configured or a combination key that is calculated based on the master's link key.

- **Change link key:** If two devices are paired and use a combination key, then that key can be changed. One side generates a new key and sends it to the other side XORed with the old link key. The other side accepts or rejects the key.

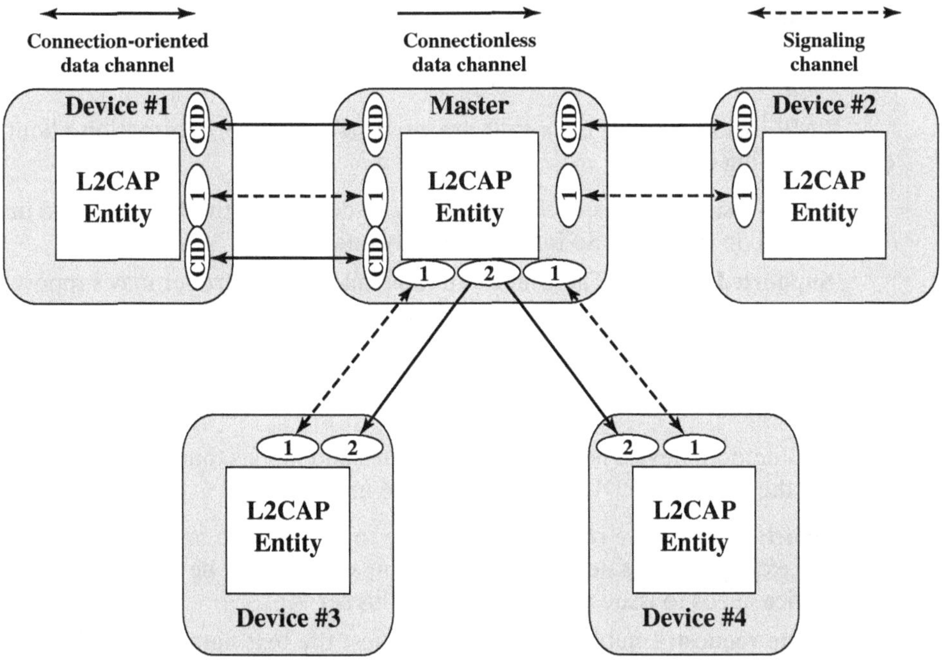

Figure 15.14 L2CAP Channels

- **Change current link key:** The current link key can be changed temporarily. The exchange involves the use of random numbers and XOR calculations to generate the temporary key, which is used for a single session.
- **Encryption:** LMP is not directly involved in link **encryption** but provides services to manage the encryption process. A number of parameters may be negotiated, including the operating encryption mode (no encryption, point-to-point only, point-to-point and broadcast), the size of the key, and the random seed key use to start a new encryption session. LMP is also used to begin and end the use of encryption.

LMP provides mechanisms for synchronizing the clocks in the various piconet participants:

- **Clock offset request:** When a slave receives the FHS packet, the difference is computed between its own clock and the master's clock value included in the payload of the FHS packet. The clock offset is also updated each time a packet is received from the master. The master can request this clock offset anytime during the connection. By saving this clock offset the master knows on what RF channel the slave wakes up to PAGE SCAN after it has left the piconet. This can be used to speed up the paging time the next time the same device is paged.
- **Slot offset information:** An initiating device can transmit a message that describes timing differences (time difference between slot boundaries) between two adjacent piconets.

- **Timing accuracy information request:** Used by a device to retrieve the accuracy parameters of another device's timing subsystem. Parameters include long-term clock drift and clock jitter.

LMP includes two PDUs that are used to exchange information about the communicating devices:

- **LMP version:** Allows each LMP entity to determine the LMP version implemented in the other. So far, there is only one version.
- **Supported features:** The Bluetooth radio and link controller may support only a subset of the packet types and features described in Baseband Specification and Radio Specification. The PDU LMP_features_req and LMP_features_res are used to exchange this information. Table 15.8 lists the features that may be exchanged.

A Bluetooth device has a number of states and modes that it can occupy. LMP provides the following PDUs to manage these modes.

- **Switch master/slave role:** Allows a slave to become the master of the piconet. For example, this is needed when a paging device must be the master. If a new device needs to issue a page, it can use this service.
- **Name request:** Enables a device to request the text name of another device.
- **Detach:** Enables a device to remove itself from a connection. This can be issued by either master or slave.

Table 15.8 LMP Supported Feature List

3-slot packets
5-slot packets
Encryption
Slot offset
Timing accuracy
Switch
Hold mode
Sniff mode
Park mode
RSSI
Channel quality-driven data rate
SCO link
HV2 packets
HV3 packets
μ-law log
A-law log
CVSD
Paging scheme
Power control

- **Hold mode:** Places the link between a master and slave in hold mode for a specified time.
- **Sniff mode:** To enter sniff mode, master and slave negotiate a sniff interval T sniff and a sniff offset, D sniff, which specifies the timing of the sniff slots. The offset determines the time of the first sniff slot; after that the sniff slots follows periodically with the sniff interval T sniff.
- **Park mode:** Places a slave in park mode.
- **Power control:** Used by a device to direct another device to increase or decrease the second device's transmit power.
- **Channel quality-driven change between DM and DH:** A device is configured to use DM packets always or to use DH packets always or to adjust its packet type automatically according to the quality of the channel. This service allows an explicit change among these three alternatives. The difference between DM and DH is that the payload in a DM packet is protected with a 2/3 FEC code, whereas the payload of a DH is not protected with any FEC.
- **Quality of service:** Two parameters define Bluetooth QoS. The *poll interval*, which is the maximum time between transmissions from a master to a particular slave, is used for capacity allocation and latency control. The *number of repetitions for broadcast packets* (NBC). Broadcast packets are not acknowledged and so the automatic retransmission of all broadcast packets improves reliability.
- **SCO links:** Used to establish an SCO link.
- **Control of multislot packets:** Arbitrates the maximum number of time slots a packet can cover. The default value is one. This mechanism can be used to select 3 or 5.
- **Paging scheme:** Controls the type of paging scheme to be used between devices on the piconet. There is a default scheme that is mandatory for implementation. Additional optional schemes may be defined.
- **Link supervision:** Controls the maximum time a device should wait before declaring the failure of a link.

15.5 LOGICAL LINK CONTROL AND ADAPTATION PROTOCOL

Like Logical Link Control (LLC) in the IEEE 802 specification, L2CAP provides a link-layer protocol between entities across a shared-medium network. As with LLC, L2CAP provides a number of services and relies on a lower layer (in this case, the baseband layer) for flow and error control.

L2CAP makes use of ACL links; it does not provide support for SCO links. Using ACL links, L2CAP provides two alternative services to upper-layer protocols:

- **Connectionless service:** This is a reliable datagram style of service.
- **Connection-mode service:** This service is similar to that offered by HDLC. A logical connection is set up between two users exchanging data, and flow control and error control are provided.

L2CAP Channels

L2CAP provides three types of logical channels:

- **Connectionless:** Supports the connectionless service. Each channel is unidirectional. This channel type is typically used for broadcast from the master to multiple slaves.
- **Connection oriented:** Supports the connection-oriented service. Each channel is bidirectional (full duplex). A quality of service (QoS) flow specification is assigned in each direction.
- **Signaling:** Provides for the exchange of signaling messages between L2CAP entities.

Figure 15.14 provides an example of the use of L2CAP logical channels. Associated with each logical channel is a channel identifier (CID). For connection-oriented channels, a unique CID is assigned at each end of the channel to identify this connection and associate it with an L2CAP user on each end. Connectionless channels are identified by a CID value of 2, and signaling channels are identified by a CID value of 1. Thus, between the master and any slave, there is only one connectionless channel and one signaling channel, but there may be multiple connection-oriented channels.

L2CAP Packets

Figure 15.15 shows the format of L2CAP packets. For the connectionless service, the packet format consists of the following fields:

- **Length:** Length of the information payload plus PSM fields, in bytes.
- **Channel ID:** A value of 2, indicating the connectionless channel.
- **Protocol/service multiplexer (PSM):** Identifies the higher-layer recipient for the payload in this packet.
- **Information payload:** Higher-layer user data. This field may be up to 65533 ($2^{16} - 3$) bytes in length.

Connection-oriented packets have the same format as connectionless packets, but without the PSM field. The PSM field is not needed because the CID identifies the upper-layer recipient of the data. The information payload field may be up to 65535 ($2^{16} - 1$) bytes in length.

Signaling command packets have the same header format as the connection-oriented packets. In this case, the CID value is 1, indicating the signaling channel. The payload of a signaling packet consists of one or more L2CAP commands, each of which consists of four fields:

- **Code:** Identifies the type of command.
- **Identifier:** Used to match a request with its reply. The requesting device sets this field and the responding device uses the same value in its response. A different identifier must be used for each original command.
- **Length:** Length of the data field for this command, in bytes.
- **Data:** Additional data, if necessary, relating to this command.

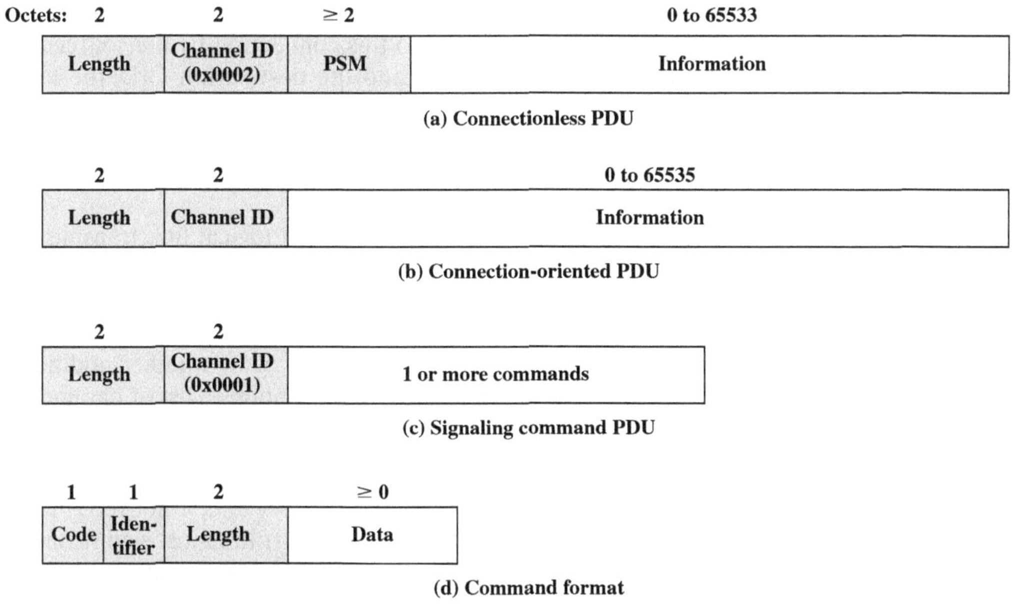

Figure 15.15 L2CAP Formats

Signaling Commands

There are eleven commands in five categories (Table 15.9). The **command reject command** can be sent in response to any command to reject it. Reasons for rejection include invalid CID or length exceeded.

Connection commands are used to establish a new logical connection. The request command includes a PSM value indicating the L2CAP user for this connection. Three values are so far defined, for the service discovery protocol, RFCOMM, and the telephony control protocol. Other PSM values are assigned

Table 15.9 L2CAP Signaling Command Codes

Code	Description	Parameters
0x01	Command reject	Reason
0x02	Connection request	PSM, Source CID
0x03	Connection response	Destination CID, Source CID, Result, Status
0x04	Configure request	Destination CID, Flags, Options
0x05	Configure response	Source CID, Flags, Result, Options
0x06	Disconnection request	Destination CID, Source CID
0x07	Disconnection response	Destination CID, Source CID
0x08	Echo request	Data (optional)
0x09	Echo response	Data (optional)
0x0A	Information request	InfoType
0x0B	Information response	InfoType, Result, Data (optional)

dynamically and are implementation dependent. The request command also includes the CID value that will be assigned to this connection by the source. The response command includes the source CID and the destination CID, the latter assigned to this channel by the respondent. The result parameter indicates the outcome (successful, pending, rejected) and, if the result is pending, the status field indicates the current status that makes this a pending connection (e.g., authentication pending, authorization pending).

Configure commands are sent to establish an initial logical link transmission contract between two L2CAP entities and to renegotiate this contract whenever appropriate. Each configuration parameter in a configuration request is related exclusively to either the outgoing or the incoming data traffic. The request command includes a flags field; currently the only flag is an indicator of whether additional configuration commands will be sent. The options field contains a list of parameters and their values to be negotiated. Each parameter is defined by three fields:

- **Type (1 byte):** The 7 least significant bits of this byte identify the option. If the most significant bit is set to 0, the option is mandatory and, if not recognized, the recipient must refuse the configuration request. If the most significant bit is set to 1, the option is optional and may be ignored by the recipient.
- **Length (1 byte):** The length of the option payload. A length of 0 indicates no payload.
- **Option payload:** Further information about this option.

The following parameters may be negotiated:

- **Maximum transmission unit (MTU):** The largest L2CAP packet payload, in bytes, that the originator of the request can accept for that channel. The MTU is asymmetric and the sender of the request shall specify the MTU it can receive on this channel if it differs from the default value. L2CAP implementations must support a minimum MTU size of 48 bytes. The default value is 672 bytes. This is not a negotiated value but simply informs the recipient of the size of MTU that the sender of this request can accept.
- **Flush timeout option:** Recall in our discussion of the baseband specification that as part of the ARQ mechanism, a payload will be flushed after failure on repeated attempts to retransmit. The flush timeout is the amount of time the originator will attempt to transmit an L2CAP packet successfully before giving up and flushing the packet.
- **Quality of service (QoS):** Identifies the traffic flow specification for the local device's traffic (outgoing traffic) over this channel. This parameter is described in the following subsection.

In the latter two cases, a negotiation takes place, in which the recipient can accept the flush timeout and QoS parameters or request an adjustment. The initial sender can then accept or reject the adjustment.

The configure response command also includes a Flags field with the same meaning as in the configuration request command. The Result field in the response command indicates whether the preceding request is accepted or rejected. The Options field contains the same list of parameters as from the corresponding request command.

For a successful result, these parameters contain the return values for any wild card parameters (see discussion of QoS, subsequently). For an unsuccessful result, rejected parameters should be sent in the response with the values that would have been accepted if sent in the original request.

The **disconnection commands** are used to terminate a logical channel.

The **echo commands** are used to solicit a response from a remote L2CAP entity. These commands are typically used for testing the link or passing vendor-specific information using the optional data field.

The **information commands** are used to solicit implementation-specific information from a remote L2CAP entity.

Quality of Service

The QoS parameter in L2CAP defines a traffic flow specification based on RFC 1363.[10] In essence, a **flow specification** is a set of parameters that indicate a performance level that the transmitter will attempt to achieve.

When included in a Configuration Request, this option describes the outgoing traffic flow from the device sending the request to the device receiving it. When included in a positive Configuration Response, this option describes the incoming traffic flow agreement as seen from the device sending the response. When included in a negative Configuration Response, this option describes the preferred incoming traffic flow from the perspective of the device sending the response.

The flow specification consists of the following parameters:

- Service type
- Token rate (bytes/second)
- Token bucket size (bytes)
- Peak bandwidth (bytes/second)
- Latency (microseconds)
- Delay variation (microseconds)

The **service type** parameter indicates the level of service for this flow. A value of 0 indicates that no traffic will be transmitted on this channel. A value of 1 indicates a best effort service; the device will transmit data as quickly as possible but with no guarantees about performance. A value of 2 indicates a guaranteed service; the sender will transmit data that conform to the remaining QoS parameters.

The **token rate** and **token bucket size** parameters define a token bucket scheme that is often used in QoS specifications. The advantage of this scheme is that it provides a concise description of the peak and average traffic load the recipient can expect and it also provides a convenient mechanism by which the sender can implement the traffic flow policy.

A token bucket traffic specification consists of two parameters: a token replenishment rate R and a bucket size B. The token rate R specifies the continually sustainable data rate; that is, over a relatively long period of time, the average data rate to be supported for this flow is R. The bucket size B specifies the

[10] *A Proposed Flow Specification*, RFC 1363, September 1992.

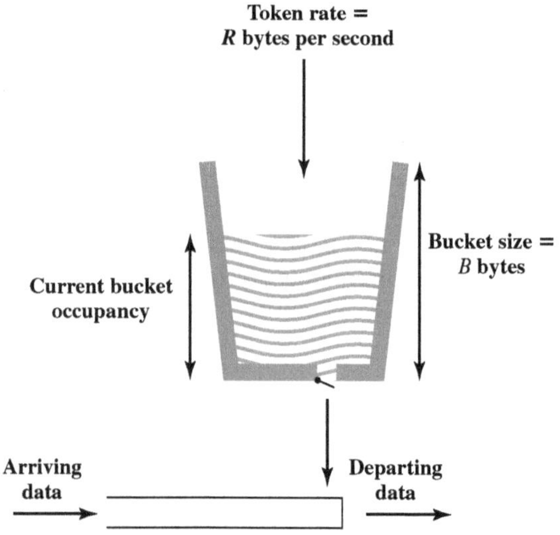

Figure 15.16 Token Bucket Scheme

amount by which the data rate can exceed R for short periods of time. The exact condition is as follows: During any time period T, the amount of data sent cannot exceed $RT + B$.

Figure 15.16 illustrates this scheme and explains the use of the term *bucket*. The bucket represents a counter that indicates the allowable number of bytes of data that can be sent at any time. The bucket fills with *byte tokens* at the rate of R (i.e., the counter is incremented R times per second), up to the bucket capacity (up to the maximum counter value). Data arrive from the L2CAP user and are assembled into packets, which are queued for transmission. A packet may be transmitted if there are sufficient byte tokens to match the packet size. If so, the packet is transmitted and the bucket is drained of the corresponding number of tokens. If there are insufficient tokens available, then the packet exceeds the specification for this flow. The treatment for such packets is not specified in the document; typically, the packet will simply be queued for transmission until sufficient tokens are available.

Over the long run, the rate of data allowed by the token bucket is R. However, if there is an idle or relatively slow period, the bucket capacity builds up, so that at most an additional B bytes above the stated rate can be accepted. Thus, B is a measure of the degree of burstiness of the data flow that is allowed.

For L2CAP, a value of zero for the two parameters implies that the token scheme is not needed for this application and will not be used. A value of all 1s is the wild card value. For best effort service, the wild card indicates that the requestor wants as large a token or as large a token bucket size, respectively, as the responder will grant. For guaranteed service, the wild card indicates that the maximum data rate or bucket size, respectively, is available at the time of the request.

The **peak bandwidth**, expressed in bytes per second, limits how fast packets may be sent back-to-back from applications. Some intermediate systems can take advantage of this information, resulting in more efficient resource allocation. Consider that if the token bucket is full, it is possible for the flow to send a series of back-to-back packets equal to the size of the token bucket. If the token bucket size is large, this back-to-back run may be long enough to exceed the recipient's capacity. To limit this effect, the maximum transmission rate bounds how fast successive packets may be placed on the network.

The **latency** is the maximum acceptable delay between transmission of a bit by the sender and its initial transmission over the air, expressed in microseconds.

The **delay variation** is the difference, in microseconds, between the maximum and minimum possible delay that a packet will experience. This value is used by applications to determine the amount of buffer space needed at the receiving side in order to restore the original data transmission pattern. If a receiving application requires data to be delivered in the same pattern that the data were transmitted, it may be necessary for the receiving host briefly to buffer data as they are received so that the receiver can restore the old transmission pattern. An example of this is a case where an application wishes to send and transmit data such as voice samples, which are generated and played at regular intervals. The amount of buffer space that the receiving host is willing to provide determines the amount of variation in delay permitted for individual packets within a given flow.

15.6 IEEE 802.15

The IEEE 802.15 Working Group for Wireless Personal Area Networks (PANs) was formed to develop standards for short range wireless PANs (WPANs). A PAN is communications network within a small area in which all of the devices on the network are typically owned by one person or perhaps a family. Devices on a PAN may include portable and mobile devices, such as PCs, Personal Digital Assistants (PDAs), peripherals, cell phones, pagers, and consumer electronic devices. The first effort by the working group was to develop 802.15.1, with the goal of creating a formal standard of the Bluetooth specification; this standard was approved in 2002.

Because most or all of the planned 802.15 standards would operate in the same frequency bands as used by 802.11 devices, both the 802.11 and 802.15 working groups were concerned about the ability of these various devices to successfully coexist. The 802.15.2 Task Group was formed to develop recommended practices for coexistence. This work resulted in a recommended practices document in 2003.

Following the 802.15.1 standard, the 802.15 work went in two directions. The 802.15.3 task group is interested in developing standards for devices that are low cost and low power compared to 802.11 devices, but with significantly higher data rates than 802.15.1. An initial standard for 802.15.3 was issued in 2003 and, as of this writing, work continues on 802.15.3a, which will provide higher data rates than 802.15.3, using the same MAC layer. Meanwhile, the 802.15.4 task group developed a standard for very low cost, very low power devices at data rates lower than 802.15.1, with a standard issued in 2003.

Figure 15.17 shows the current status of the 802.15 work. Each of the three wireless PAN standards has not only different physical layer specifications but different requirements for the MAC layer. Accordingly, each has a unique MAC specification. Figure 15.18, based on one in [ZHEN04], gives an indication of the relative scope of application of the wireless LAN and PAN standards. As can be seen,

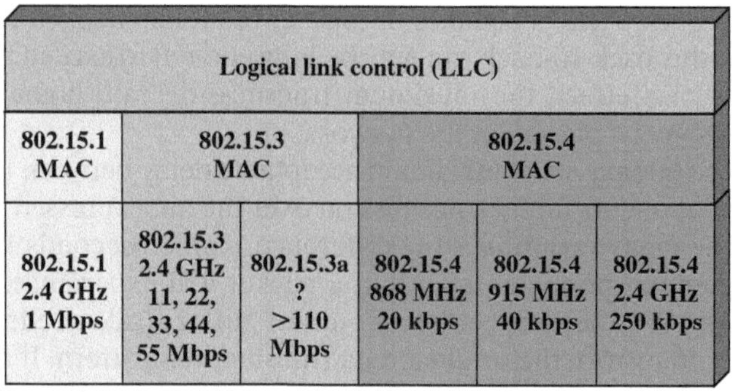

Figure 15.17 IEEE 802.15 Protocol Architecture

the 802.15 wireless PAN standards are intended for very short range, up to about 10 m, which enables the use of low power, low cost devices.

This section provides an overview of 802.15.3 and 802.15.4.

IEEE 802.15.3

The 802.15.3 task group is concerned with the development of high data rate WPANs. Examples of applications that would fit a WPAN profile but would also require a relatively high data rate include [GILB04]

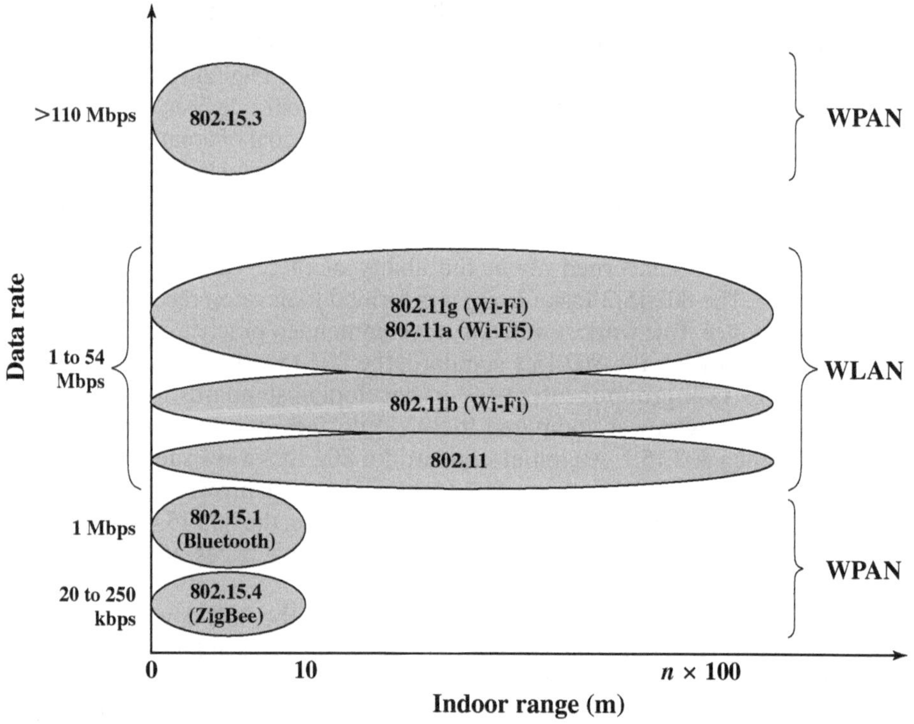

Figure 15.18 Wireless Local Networks

- Connecting digital still cameras to printers or kiosks
- Laptop to projector connection
- Connecting a personal digital assistant (PDA) to a camera or PDA to a printer
- Speakers in a 5:1 surround-sound system connecting to the receiver
- Video distribution from a set-top box or cable modem
- Sending music from a CD or MP3 player to headphones or speakers
- Video camera display on television
- Remote view finders for video or digital still cameras

These applications are mainly in the consumer electronics area and generate the following requirements:

- **Short range:** On the order of 10 m.
- **High throughput:** Greater than 20 Mbps to support video and/or multichannel audio.
- **Low power usage:** To be useful in battery-powered portable devices.
- **Low cost:** To be reasonable for inexpensive consumer electronic devices.
- **QoS (quality of service) capable:** To provide guaranteed data rate and other QoS features for applications sensitive to throughput or latency.
- **Dynamic environment:** Refers to a piconet architecture in which mobile, portable, and stationary devices enter and leave the piconet often. For mobile device, a speed of less than 7 kilometers per hour is addressed.
- **Simple connectivity:** To make networking easy and eliminate the need for a technically sophisticated user.
- **Privacy:** To assure the user that only the intended recipients can understand what is being transmitted.

These requirements are not readily met with an IEEE 802.11 network, which was not designed with this set of applications and requirements in mind.

Medium Access Control An 802.15.3 network consists of a collection of devices (DEVs). One of the DEVs also acts as a piconet coordinator (PNC). The PNC assigns time for connections between devices; all commands are between the PNC and DEVs. Note the contrast between a PNC and an 802.11 access point (AP). The AP provides a link to other networks and acts as a relay point for all MAC frames. The PNC is used to control access to the time resources of the piconet and is not involved in the exchange of data frames between DEVs.

The QoS feature of the 802.15.3 MAC layer is based on the use of a TDMA (time division multiple access) architecture with the provision of guaranteed time slots (GTSs).

Physical Layer The 802.15.3 physical layer operates in the 2.4-GHz band, using five modulation formats with an 11 Mbaud symbol rate to achieve data rates from 11 to 55 Mbps. Table 15.10 summarizes the key parameters. The most significant aspect of the scheme is the use of **trellis-coded modulation** (TCM). TCM is an old

Table 15.10 IEEE 802.15.3 Physical Layer Characteristics

Modulation	Coding	Data Rate
QPSK	8-state TCM	11 Mbps
DQPSK	None	22 Mbps
16-QAM	8-state TCM	33 Mbps
32-QAM	8-state TCM	44 Mbps
64-QAM	8-state TCM	55 Mbps

QPSK = quadrature phase-shift keying
DQPSK = differential QPSK
QAM = quadrature amplitude modulation
TCM = trellis-coded modulation

technique, used in voice-grade telephone network modems. In the remainder of this subsection, we provide an overview of TCM.

Before proceeding, we briefly review some definitions from Chapter 6 (Table 6.1). A **bit** is the fundamental unit that takes on the values 0 or 1. A **signal element**, or **symbol**, is that part of a signal that occupies the shortest interval of a signaling code; typically, it is a pulse of constant frequency, phase, and amplitude and may represent one or more bits. The **signaling rate** is measured in signaling elements per second, or baud.

In all of the approaches to transmission that we have seen so far in this book, signal encoding, or modulation, is performed separately from encoding for forward error correction. Furthermore, error control is achieved by adding additional bits to the data bits, which has the effect of lower the data transmission rate per channel bandwidth. When faced with a combination of a channel of limited bandwidth and a high data rate requirement, an effective approach is to combine modulation and coding and treat them as a single entity. This approach is referred to as TCM and has three basic features:

1. The number of different signal elements used is larger than what is required for the given modulation scheme and data rate. The additional signal elements allow redundancy for forward error correction without sacrificing data rate.
2. Convolutional coding is used to introduce dependency between successive signal elements, such that only certain sequences of signal elements are allowed.
3. Decoding is done by modeling the coder as a trellis and using a Viterbi-type decoding algorithm to perform error correction.

The concepts mentioned in points (2) and (3) are discussed in Section 8.3. Recall that the convolutional code gives rise to a state transition diagram that can be laid out in a trellis pattern. Also, decoding involves use of a Viterbi algorithm, typically with a metric based on Hamming distance. In the case of TCM, the metric used is Euclidean distance. We next explain these concepts using a simple example based on a QPSK modulation scheme. Keep in mind that TCM can be used with more complex modulation schemes, such as QAM.

Any analog modulation scheme based on phase and/or amplitude, such as PSK or QAM, can be defined by a two-dimensional layout that indicates the phase and amplitude of each signal element. Recall from Chapter 6 that QPSK, uses phase shifts separated by multiples of $\pi/2$ (90°) to define signal elements:

$$\textbf{QPSK} \quad s(t) = \begin{cases} A\cos\left(2\pi f_c t + \frac{\pi}{4}\right) & 11 \\ A\cos\left(2\pi f_c t + \frac{3\pi}{4}\right) & 01 \\ A\cos\left(2\pi f_c t - \frac{3\pi}{4}\right) & 00 \\ A\cos\left(2\pi f_c t - \frac{\pi}{4}\right) & 10 \end{cases}$$

Each signal element represents two bits rather than one. Figure 15.19a shows this scheme on a graph, where each signal element is represent by a point at unit distance from the origin, representing amplitude, and at an angle from the horizontal, representing phase. The minimum Euclidean distance between signal elements on the graph is a measure of the difficulty of decoding the signal. Of course, in the case of a pure PSK scheme, such as QPSK, the minimum phase angle between signal elements is an equivalent measure. However, in more complex schemes, such as QAM, signal elements will differ both by phase and amplitude, and so the more general measure of Euclidean distance is used.

For TCM, we expand the number of signal points to eight (Figure 15.19b), separated by a minimum of 45°. This would seem to make the decoding problem worse, because now the decoder must be able to distinguish a phase shift of 45° rather than a phase shift of 90°. However, the TCM code can be defined in such a way as to prohibit phase shifts of less than 90°. Thus we have not lost any discrimination power. Furthermore, the use of an additional bit adds redundancy which, if coded properly, allows for forward error correction so as to reduce errors.

Figure 15.19c shows the way in which convolutional encoding is used. Input is taken two bits at a time to produce a signal element. One of the bits, designated $a_1(n)$ for the nth pair of input bits, bypasses the convolutional encoder. The other bit of the pair, $a_0(n)$, passes through a (2, 1, 3) encoder (compare Figure 8.9a). The two encoder output bits are combined with the passed-through bit to produce a 3-bit output that designates one of the eight signal elements. Figure 15.19d shows the allowable state transitions using a trellis diagram (compare Figure 8.10). The four possible states are defined by the two preceding input bits. Thus, state 10 corresponds to $a_0(n-1) = 1$ and $a_0(n-2) = 0$. The transition from a state is determined by the two input bits and each transition produces three output bits and a move to a new state. For example, one of the transitions from state 00 to state 10 is labeled 01/010 (90°). The first part of the label refers to the two input bits: $a_1(n) = 0$ and $a_0(n) = 1$. The second part of the label refers to the three output bits: $b_2(n) = 0,\ b_1(n) = 1,\ b_0(n) = 0$. The final part of the label indicates the phase shift corresponding to the three output bits. For states 01 and 11, the first part of the label is not included but left as an exercise for the reader. Note that successive state transitions are constrained to produce a minimum phase shift of 90°.

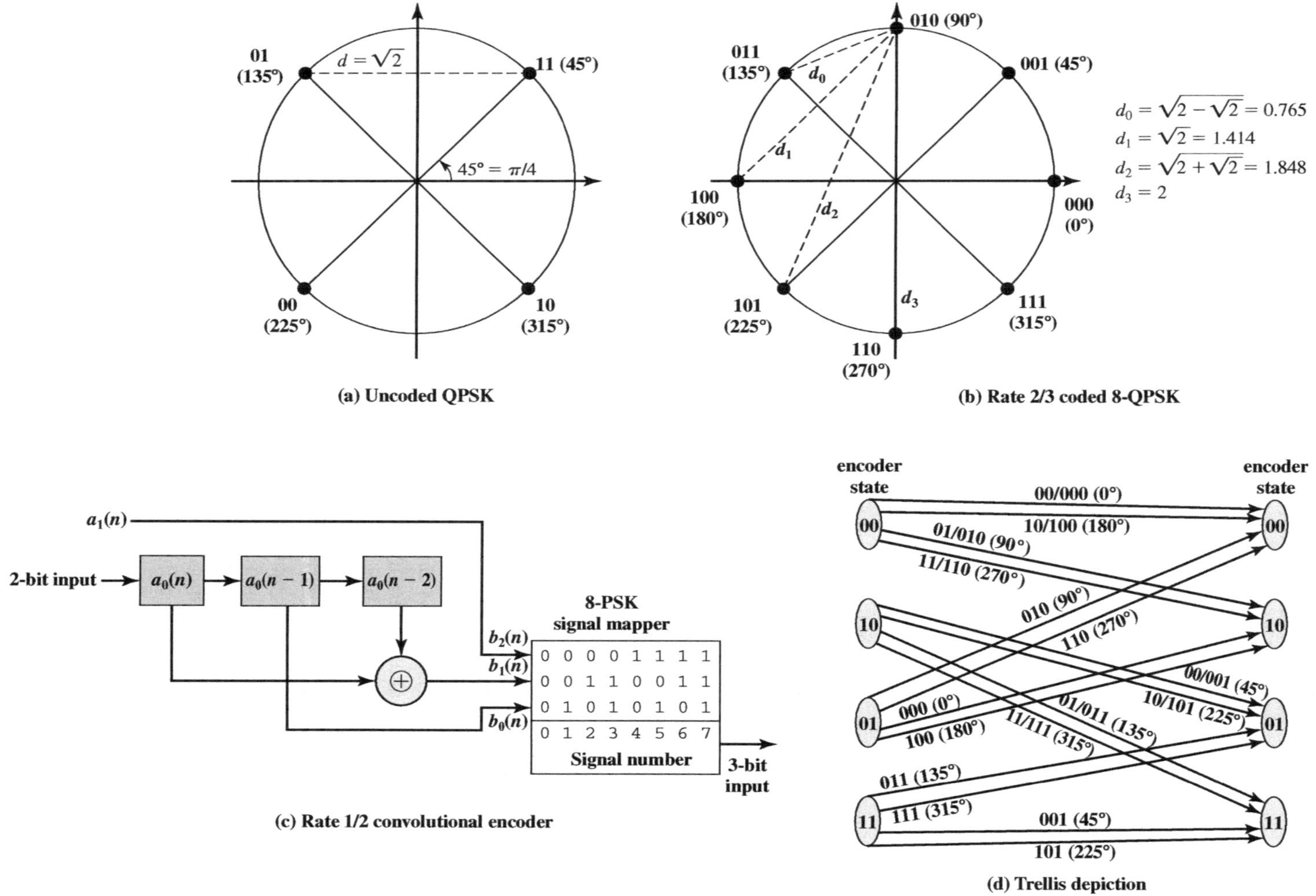

Figure 15.19 Example of Trellis-Coded Modulation

Table 15.11 Sequence and Error Determination for Example 15.1

States	Signals	Symbol Errors (°)	Total Error (°)
10-01-10-01	1-4-1	2.5, 62.5, 12.5	77.5
10-01-10-11	1-4-3	2.5, 62.5, 102.5	167.5
10-01-00-00	1-6-0	2.5, 27.5, 32.5	62.5
10-01-00-10	1-6-2	2.5, 27.5, 57.5	87.5
10-11-11-11	3-5-1	92.5, 17.5, 12.5	122.5
10-11-11-01	3-5-3	92.5, 17.5, 102.5	212.5
10-11-01-10	3-7-0	92.5, 72.5, 32.5	197.5
10-11-01-00	3-7-2	92.5, 72.5, 57.5	222.5

Example 15.1[11] For the TCM system of Figure 15.19, a receiver detects a phase sequence of 42.5°, 242.5°, and 32.5°. The receiver must determine the allowable sequence of three signal elements with the closest distance to the received sequence. Assume a starting state of 10. The closest point to each received signal element is 45°, 225°, and 45°, respectively. However, this corresponds to an output sequence of 1-5-1 (001-101-001), which is not possible starting from state 10. An output of 001 would transition to state 01, and from that state, there is no output of 101. From state 10, there are 8 possible state sequences of length 3. These are listed in Table 15.11. For each state transition, the most likely signal element of each pair of signal elements that can produce the transition is indicated. The next two columns show the amount of phase error in each transition followed by the total sequence error. The result is that the most likely state sequence (minimum error) is 01-00-00 with a signal sequence of 1-6-0. Note that there are two other sequences that are fairly close in terms of error (1-4-1 and 1-6-2). These three sequences have different end states. Thus, subsequent received signal elements will provide more information that may cause a revision of the estimated output.

IEEE 802.15.3a

The WPAN Higher Rate Alternate PHY Task Group (TG3a) is chartered to draft and publish a new standard that will provide a higher speed (110 Mbps or greater) PHY amendment to the draft P802.15.3 standard. This will address streaming video and other multimedia applications. The new PHY will use the P802.15.3 MAC with limited modification. As of the time of writing, this work is still in progress.

IEEE 802.15.4

The WPAN Low Rate Task Group (TG4) is chartered to investigate a low data rate solution with multimonth to multiyear battery life and very low complexity. This standard specifies two physical layers: an 868-MHz/915-MHz direct sequence spread spectrum PHY and a 2.4-GHz direct sequence spread spectrum PHY. The 2.4-GHz PHY supports an over air data rate of 250 kb/s and the 868-MHz/915-MHz

[11]This example is based on one in [BELL00].

PHY supports over the air data rates of 20 kbps and 40 kbps. The physical layer chosen depends on local regulations and user preference. Potential applications are sensors, interactive toys, smart badges, remote controls, and home automation.

Low-data-rate wireless applications have been largely ignored until recently because of the lack of standards and appropriate technology to develop transmitters and receivers of very low cost, very low power consumption, and very small size. At the physical and MAC layers, IEEE 802.15.4 is designed to address the need for such devices. Above the LLC layer, the ZigBee Alliance is producing specifications to operate over 802.15.4 implementations. The ZigBee specification addresses the network, security, and application interface layers.

15.7 RECOMMENDED READINGS AND WEB SITES

[HAAR00a], [HAAR00b], and [SAIR02] provide good overviews of Bluetooth. Two other surveys, both multipart, are also of interest: [WILS00] and [RODB00]. There are two good book-length technical treatments: [BRAY01] and [MILL01]; the former provides somewhat more technical detail than the latter.

[GILB04] is a thorough treatment of 802.15.3. Three good sources for TCM are [UNGE87], [VITE89], and [FORN84].

[GUTI03] thoroughly covers 802.15.4. The following papers provide useful though short treatments of 802.15.4: [GUTI01], [CALL02], and [ZHEN04].

BRAY01 Bray, J., and Sturman, C. *Bluetooth: Connect Without Cables*. Upper Saddle River, NJ: Prentice Hall, 2001.

CALL02 Callaway, E., et al. "Home Networking with IEEE 802.15.4: A Developing Standard for Low-Rate Wireless Personal Area Networks." *IEEE Communications Magazine*, August 2002.

FORN84 Forney, G., et al. "Efficient Modulation for Band-Limited Channels." *IEEE Journal on Selected Areas in Communications*, September 1984.

GILB04 Gilb, J. *Wireless Multimedia: A Guide to the IEEE 802.15.3 Standard.* New York: IEEE Press, 2004.

GUTI01 Gutierrez, J., et al. "IEEE 802.15.4: A Developing Standard for Low-Power Low-Cost Wireless Personal Area Networks." *IEEE Network*, September/October 2001.

GUTI03 Gutierrez, J.; Callaway, E.; and Barrett, R. *Low-Rate Wireless Personal Area Networks: Enabling Wireless Sensors with IEEE 802.15.4.* New York: IEEE Press, 2003.

HAAR00a Haartsen, J. "The Bluetooth Radio System." *IEEE Personal Communications*, February 2000.

HAAR00b Haartsen, J., and Mattisson, S. "Bluetooth—A New Low-Power Radio Interface Providing Short-Range Connectivity." *Proceedings of the IEEE*, October 2000.

MILL01 Miller, B., and Bisdikian, C. *Bluetooth Revealed.* Upper Saddle River, NJ: Prentice Hall, 2001.

RODB00 Rodbell, M. "Bluetooth: Wireless Local Access, Baseband and RF Interfaces, and Link Management." *Communications System Design*, March, April, May 2000. (www.csdmag.com)

SAIR02 Sairam, K.; Gunasekaran, N.; and Reddy, S. "Bluetooth in Wireless Communication." *IEEE Communications Magazine*, June 2002.

UNGE87 Ungerboeck, G. "Trellis-Coded Modulation with Redundant Signal Sets, Part 1: Introduction." *IEEE Communications Magazine*, February 1987.

VITE89 Viterbi, A., et al. "A Pragmatic Approach to Trellis-Coded Modulation." *IEEE Communications Magazine*, July 1989.

WILS00 Wilson, J., and Kronz, J. "Inside Bluetooth: Part I and Part II." *Dr. Dobb's Journal*, March, April 2000.

ZHEN04 Zhent, J., and Lee, M. "Will IEEE 802.15.4 Make Ubiquitous Networking a Reality?: A Discussion on a Potential Low Power, Low Bit Rate Standard." *IEEE Communications Magazine*, June 2004.

Recommended Web Sites:

- **Bluetooth SIG:** Contains all the standards, numerous other documents, and news and information on Bluetooth companies and products
- **Infotooth:** An excellent supplementary source of information on Bluetooth
- **The IEEE 802.15 Working Group on Personal Area Networks:** Contains working group documents plus discussion archives
- **ZigBee Alliance:** White papers, documents, and vendor information concerning ZigBee and IEEE 802.15.4

15.8 KEY TERMS, REVIEW QUESTIONS, AND PROBLEMS

Key Terms

Bluetooth	logical link control and adaptation protocol (L2CAP)	RFCOMM
cable replacement protocol	personal area network (PAN)	scatternet
core specification	piconet	service discovery protocol
flow specification	profile specification	trellis-coded modulation (TCM)
link manager (LM)		usage model

Review Questions

15.1 In general terms, what application areas are supported by Bluetooth?

15.2 What is the difference between a core specification and a profile specification?

15.3 What is a usage model?

15.4 What is the relationship between master and slave in a piconet?

15.5 How is it possible to combine frequency hopping and time division duplex?

15.6 How does FH-CDMA differ from DS-CDMA?

15.7 List and briefly define the types of links that can be established between a master and a slave.

15.8 What error correction schemes are used in Bluetooth baseband?
15.9 List and briefly define Bluetooth baseband logical channels.
15.10 What security services are provided by Bluetooth?
15.11 List and briefly define L2CAP logical channels.
15.12 What is a flow specification?

Problems

15.1 Describe, step by step, the activity in each of the 12 time slots of Figure 15.9.

15.2 Using Equation (7.10), find the autocorrelation for the 7-bit Barker sequence as a function of τ.

15.3 Section 15.3 describes the use of a 64-bit PN sequence in constructing the sync word in the packet format, defined by the equation $P(X) = 1 + X^2 + X^3 + X^5 + X^6$.
   a. Show the linear feedback shift register implementation of this equation.
   b. Show the first 8 bits of the sequence. The seed value for the PN sequence is 000001. Using the notation of Figure 7.12, $B_0 = 1$ and B_1 through B_5 are all set to 0.

15.4 The CVSD scheme is described in the Bluetooth audio subsection of Section 15.3. Assume that the current value of $x(k)$ is 1000, the current value of $\hat{x}(k - 1)$ is 990, and the current value of $\delta(k - 1)$ is 30.
   a. Assume that the last 4 output bits are the same. Calculate the next value of $\hat{x}(k - 1)$.
   b. Repeat part (a) when the last 4 outputs are not the same.

15.5 The token bucket scheme places a limit on the length of time at which traffic can depart at the maximum data rate. Let the token bucket be defined by a bucket size B octets and a token arrival rate of R octets/second, and let the maximum output data rate be M octets/s.
   a. Derive a formula for S, which is the length of the maximum-rate burst. That is, for how long can a flow transmit at the maximum output rate when governed by a token bucket?
   b. What is the value of S for $b = 250$ KB, $r = 2$ MB/s, and $M = 25$ MB/s?
   Hint: The formula for S is not so simple as it might appear, because more tokens arrive while the burst is being output.

15.6 For the TCM example of Figure 15.19:
   a. Express the three b_i variables as a function of the two a_i variables.
   b. The trellis diagram of Figure 15.19d can also be expressed as a state transition matrix in the following format:

$a_0(n-2)$	$a_0(n-1)$	$a_0(n)$	$a_1(n)$	$b_2(n)$	$b_1(n)$	$b_0(n)$
0	0	0	0	0	0	0

   Fill in the remaining rows of the matrix.
   c. In Figure 15.19d, fill in the missing portions of the labels on the state transitions.

APPENDIX A

TRAFFIC ANALYSIS

Section 10.1 introduced the concept of traffic analysis. This appendix provides more detail.[1]

A.1 BASIC TRAFFIC CONCEPTS

Traffic engineering concepts were developed in the design of telephone switches and circuit-switching telephone networks, but the concepts equally apply to cellular networks. Consider a cell able to handle N simultaneous users (capacity of N channels) that has L potential subscribers (L mobile units). If $L < N$, the system is referred to as *nonblocking*; all calls can be handled all the time. If $L > N$, the system is *blocking*; a subscriber may attempt a call and find the capacity fully in use and therefore be blocked. For a blocking system, the fundamental performance questions we wish to answer are as follows:

1. What is the degree of blocking; that is, what is the probability that a call request will be blocked? Alternatively, what capacity (N) is needed to achieve a certain upper bound on the probability of blocking?
2. If blocked calls are queued for service, what is the average delay? Alternatively, what capacity is needed to achieve a certain average delay?

Two parameters determine the amount of load presented to a system:

- λ: the mean rate of calls (connection requests) attempted per unit time
- h: the mean holding time per successful call

The basic measure of traffic is the traffic intensity, expressed in a dimensionless unit, the Erlang:

$$A = \lambda h$$

The parameter A, as a measure of busy-hour traffic (discussed in Section 10.1), serves as input to a traffic model. The model is then used to answer questions such as those posed in the beginning of this subsection. There are two key factors that determine the nature of the model:

- The manner in which blocked calls are handled
- The number of traffic sources

Blocked calls may be handled in one of two ways. First, blocked calls can be put in a queue awaiting a free channel; this is referred to as **lost calls delayed** (LCD), although in fact the call is not lost, merely delayed. Second, a blocked call can be rejected and dropped. This in turn leads to two assumptions about the action of the user. If the user hangs up and waits some random time interval before another call attempt, this is known as **lost calls cleared** (LCC). If the user repeatedly attempts calling, it is known as **lost calls held** (LCH). For each of these blocking options, formulas have been developed that characterize the performance of the system. For cellular systems, the LCC model is generally used and is generally the most accurate.

[1]This appendix makes use of concepts from queuing analysis. A basic refresher on queuing analysis can be found at the Computer Science Student Resource Site at WilliamStallings.com/StudentSupport.html.

The second key element of a traffic model is whether the number of users is assumed to be finite or infinite. Figure A.1 illustrates this difference. For an **infinite source** model, there is assumed to be a fixed mean arrival rate. For the **finite source** case, the arrival rate will depend on the number of sources already engaged. In particular, if the total pool of users is L, each of which generates calls at an average rate of λ/L, then, when the cell is totally idle, the arrival rate is λ. However, if there are K users occupied at time t, then the instantaneous arrival rate at that time is $\lambda(L - K)/L$. Infinite source models are analytically easier to deal with. The infinite source assumption is reasonable when the number of sources is at least 5 to 10 times the capacity of the system.

A.2 MULTISERVER MODELS

We are now ready to turn to the use of the various traffic models for system sizing. For each of the four models of Figure A.1, formulas have been derived for the quantities of interest. The most important relationships are summarized in Table A.1. These formulas are based on the following assumptions:

- Poisson arrivals
- Exponential holding time (not needed for infinite sources, LCC)
- Equal traffic intensity per source
- Calls served in order of arrival (for delay calculations)

Even with these assumptions, it can be seen that the formulas involve lengthy summations. In earlier days, much of the work of traffic theorist lay in simplifying assumptions to the point that the equations could be calculated at all. The results were and are published in tables (e.g., [MART94]). Unfortunately, the tendency would be to try to use the available tables in situations whose assumptions did not fit any of the tables. The problem is now alleviated with the use of the computer. Nevertheless, the tabular results are still useful for quick and rough sizing.

Several parameters in Table A.1 warrant comment. For LCC systems, P is the probability that a call request will be cleared, or lost. This is the ratio of calls unable to obtain service to the total call requests; in telephone traffic, it is also called **grade of service**. For LCD systems, an arriving call will be delayed rather than cleared. In this case, $P(>0)$ is the probability that a call request will find the system fully utilized and hence be delayed. $P(>t)$ is the probability that any call request is delayed by an amount greater than t, whereas $P_2(>t)$ is the probability that a call that is delayed will be delayed by an amount greater than t.

Infinite Sources, Lost Calls Cleared

This case is discussed in Section 10.1. As was mentioned, the equation of Table A.1a is referred to as *Erlang B*. Table 10.3 provides an extract of an Erlang B table. Figure A.2 plots the probability of loss as a function of offered load with the number of servers as a parameter.

Finite Sources, Lost Calls Cleared

In reality, the number of sources is not infinite, and Table A.1c applies. This is a more complicated formula and, because of the extra parameter L, the tables are

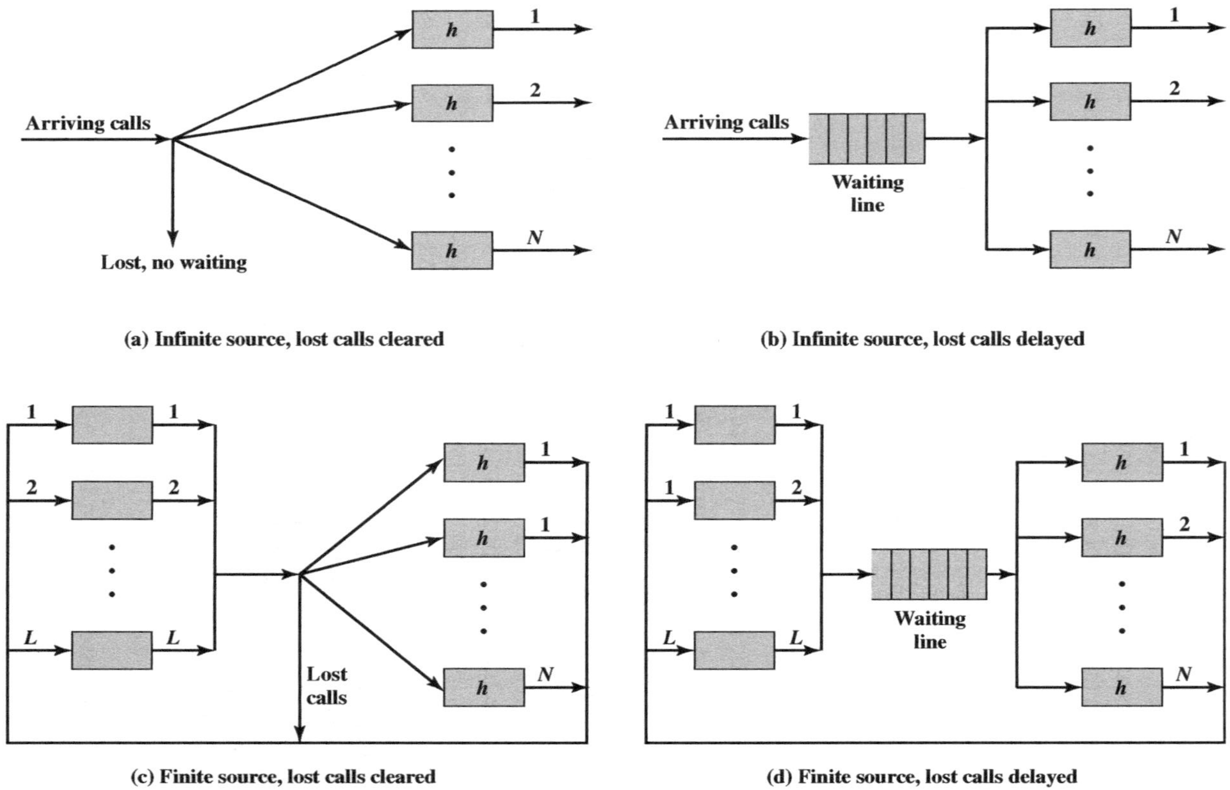

Figure A.1 Multiserver Queuing Models

Table A.1 Traffic Formulas

(a) Infinite sources, lost calls cleared

$$P = \frac{\dfrac{A^N}{N!}}{\displaystyle\sum_{x=0}^{N} \frac{A^x}{x!}}$$

(b) Infinite sources, lost calls delayed

$$P(>0) = \frac{\dfrac{A^N}{N!}\dfrac{N}{N-A}}{\displaystyle\sum_{x=0}^{N-1} \frac{A_x}{x!} + \frac{A^N}{N!}\frac{N}{N-A}}$$

$$P(>t) = P(>0)e^{-(N-A)t/h}$$

$$D_1 = P(>0)\frac{h}{N-A}$$

$$D_2 = \frac{h}{N-A}$$

$$P_2(>t) = e^{-(N-A)t/h}$$

(c) Finite sources, lost calls cleared

$$P = \frac{\binom{L-1}{N}M^N}{\displaystyle\sum_{x=0}^{N}\binom{L-1}{x}M^x}$$

where

$$\binom{L-1}{x} = \frac{(L-1)!}{x!(L-1-x)!}$$

$$M = \frac{A}{L - A(1-P)}$$

(d) Finite sources, lost calls delayed

$$P(>0) = \frac{\displaystyle\sum_{x=N}^{L} \frac{L!}{N!}\frac{M^x}{(L-x)!N^{x-N}}}{\displaystyle\sum_{x=0}^{N-1}\binom{L}{x}M^x + \sum_{x=N}^{L}\frac{L!}{N!}\frac{M^x}{(L-x)!N^{x-N}}}$$

where

$$M = \frac{A}{L+1-A(1-P)} \approx \frac{A}{L+1-A}$$

A = offered traffic, Erlangs
N = number of servers
L = number of sources
h = mean holding time
P = probability of loss (blocking, delay)
$P(>0)$ = Probability of delay greater than 0
$P(>t)$ = Probability of delay greater than t
$P_2(>t)$ = Probability of delay greater than t on calls delayed
D_1 = mean delay, all calls
D_2 = mean delay, delayed calls

more unwieldy than for Erlang B. In many cases, the infinite source assumption will suffice.

To get a handle on the relative size of the difference between finite and infinite source assumptions, let us compare two systems One is infinite source with a calling rate of λ; the other is a finite source with a calling rate per source of λ/L. We then have:

$$\begin{aligned} A_\infty &= \lambda h \\ A_L &= \frac{\lambda}{L}(L-K)h \\ &= \lambda h\left(1 - \frac{K}{L}\right) \geq \lambda h\left(1 - \frac{N}{L}\right) \end{aligned}$$

where

A_∞ = offered traffic, infinite source case
A_L = offered traffic, L sources
K = number of sources currently engaged in a call

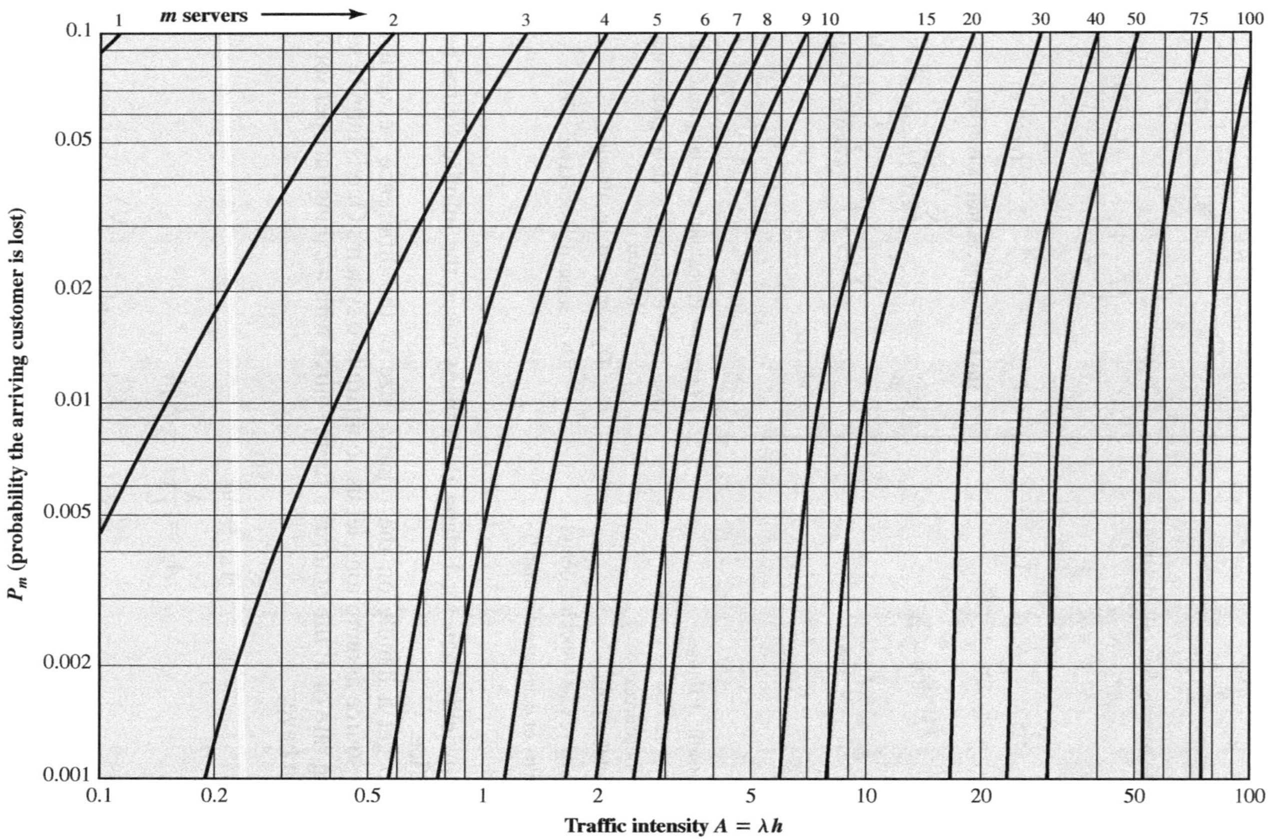

Figure A.2 Probability of Loss for Infinite Sources, LCC Systems

Table A.2 Lost Calls Cleared, Finite and Infinite Sources (number of servers = 10)

	Offered load (Erlangs)		
Number of sources	$p = 0.005$	$p = 0.01$	$p = 0.05$
∞	2.8	4.46	6.22
50	4.16	4.64	6.4
25	4.6	5.1	6.81
20	4.81	5.32	7.06
15	5.27	5.78	7.41
12	5.97	6.47	8.02
10	10	10	10

The inequality results from the fact that the number of sources engaged cannot exceed the total capacity N of the system.

We have

$$A_\infty > A_L \geq A_\infty\left(1 - \frac{N}{L}\right)$$

We can see that for L much larger than N, A_∞ is a good approximation of A_L.

This conclusion is confirmed by Table A.2, which shows that as the number of sources gets large compared to capacity, the effective capacity approaches the value of the infinite source case. Note that as the probability of loss decreases, the approximation becomes relatively less accurate. You should also be able to deduce from Table A.2 that the probability of loss is always less for a finite system than for a similar system with an infinite source. Thus, the infinite source model gives conservative estimates for sizing.

Lost Calls Delayed

When queuing is allowed, the designer may be more interested in the delay characteristics than the blocking characteristics of the switch. Table A.1b shows several formulas for the infinite source, LCD case. The designer might be interested in the probability of any delay (Erlang C formula), the probability of delay greater than a given amount, or the mean value of delay.

The probability of delay, the probability of delay greater than a given amount, and the average delay on all offered calls are complex functions of A and N and can be solved only with the aid of a computer or the appropriate tables. Fortunately, the average delay and the probability of delay greater than a given amount, for calls that are delayed, are easily calculated and are of some interest.

Example A.1 What is the load that can be offered to a switch of capacity 1500 with a mean holding time of 1000 s if the fraction of delayed calls waiting longer then 1 minute is not to exceed 10%? We have $N = 1500$, $h = 1000$, $t = 60$, and $P_2(>60) = 0.1$. Substituting, we have

$$\ln(0.1) = -(1500 - A) \times (0.06)$$

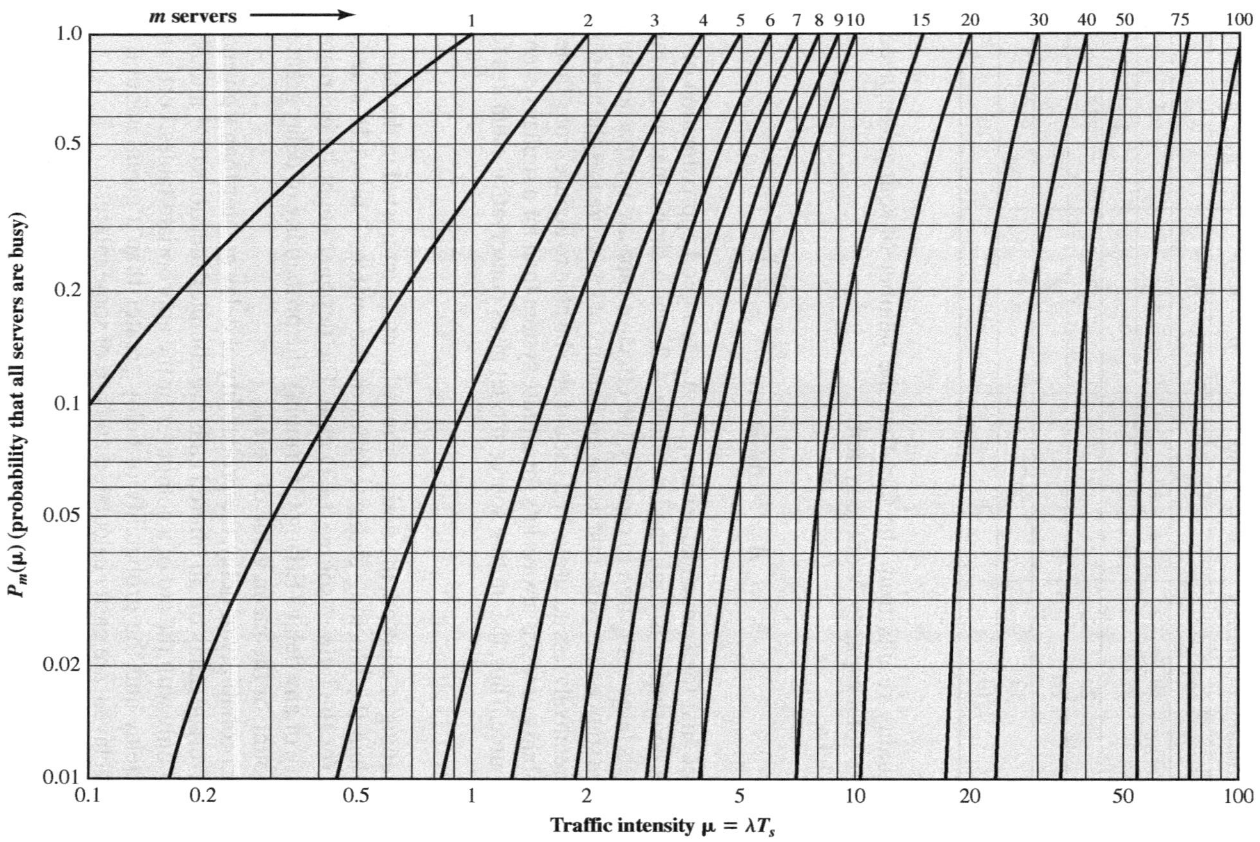

Figure A.3 Probability of Delay for Infinite Sources, LCD Systems

Solving for A yields $A = 1462$. Therefore, for these requirements, the load on the system may be very near to the total capacity.

Example A.2 This example makes use of Figure A.3, which shows the probability of delay for infinite sources, LCD. Consider a switch with capacity 20 that experiences an average call holding time of 5 minutes. If the load on the system is 16 Erlangs, what is the fraction of all calls that will be delayed greater than 2.5 minutes? First, we need the fraction of calls that will be delayed at all. From Figure A.3, with $A = 16$ and $N = 20$, we have that $P(>0)$ is approximately 0.25. Then

$$\begin{aligned} P(>150) &= P(>0) \times e^{-(N-A)t/h} \\ &= 0.25 \times e^{-(20-16)(150/300)} \\ &= 0.03 \end{aligned}$$

The average delay on calls delayed is $h/(N - A) = 75$ s. The average delay for all calls is $P(>0) \times 75 = 18.75$ s.

Table A.1d shows the formula for finite source, LCD. This is the most complicated analytically, and the infinite source case should be used for a first approximation.

Summary

Using either tables or computer programs, the equations of Table A.1 can be used in a variety of ways. For infinite sources, LCC, there are three variables: P, N, and A (which can be determined from x and h). Given any two variables, one can solve for the third. Example questions are as follows:

- Given a measured value of P for a particular N, how much must N be increased to reduce P to a given level?
- Given x, h, and a desired value for P, what capacity (N) is required?

For infinite source, LCD, there is the additional parameter of the delay. As before, among the variables $P(>0)$, N, and A, given any two the third can be found. To determine D, h must be known.

The same considerations apply for the finite source cases (LCC and LCD). For finite sources, a fixed L is used and then the same types of questions can be addressed.

A.3 RECOMMENDED READING

A good practical reference to the queuing theory underlying the concepts of this appendix is [GUNT00].

GUNT00 Gunther, N. *The Practical Performance Analyst.* Lincoln, NE: *Authors Choice Press*, 2000.

APPENDIX B

FOURIER ANALYSIS

In this appendix, we provide an overview of key concepts in Fourier analysis.

B.1 FOURIER SERIES REPRESENTATION OF PERIODIC SIGNALS

With the aid of a good table of integrals, it is a remarkably simple task to determine the frequency domain nature of many signals. We begin with periodic signals. Any periodic signal can be represented as a sum of sinusoids, known as a Fourier series:[1]

$$x(t) = \frac{A_0}{2} + \sum_{n=1}^{\infty}[A_n \cos(2\pi n f_0 t) + B_n \sin(2\pi n f_0 t)]$$

where f_0 is the reciprocal of the period of the signal ($f_0 = 1/T$) The frequency f_0 is referred to as the **fundamental frequency** or **fundamental harmonic**; integer multiples of f_0 are referred to as **harmonics**. Thus a periodic signal with period T consists of the fundamental frequency $f_0 = 1/T$ plus integer multiples of that frequency. If $A_0 \neq 0$, then $x(t)$ has a **dc component**.

The values of the coefficients are calculated as follows:

$$A_0 = \frac{2}{T}\int_0^T x(t)\,dt$$

$$A_n = \frac{2}{T}\int_0^T x(t)\cos(2\pi n f_0 t)\,dt$$

$$B_n = \frac{2}{T}\int_0^T x(t)\sin(2\pi n f_0 t)\,dt$$

This form of representation, known as the sine-cosine representation, is the easiest form to compute but suffers from the fact that there are two components at each frequency. A more meaningful representation, the amplitude-phase representation, takes the form

$$x(t) = \frac{C_0}{2} + \sum_{n=1}^{\infty} C_n \cos(2\pi n f_0 t + \theta_n)$$

This relates to the earlier representation as follows:

$$C_0 = A_0$$

$$C_n = \sqrt{A_n^2 + B_n^2}$$

$$\theta_n = \tan^{-1}\left(\frac{-B_n}{A_n}\right)$$

Examples of the Fourier series for periodic signals are shown in Figure B.1.

---

[1]Mathematicians typically write Fourier series and transform expressions using the variable w_0, which has a dimension of radians per second and where $w_0 = 2\pi f_0$. For physics and engineering, the f_0 formulation is preferred; it makes for simpler expressions, and is it intuitively more satisfying to have frequency expressed in Hz rather than radians per second.

Signal	Fourier Series
Square wave 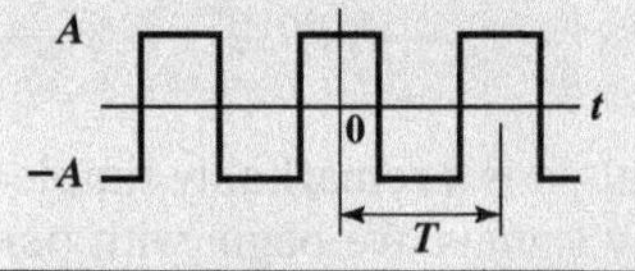	$(4A/\pi) \times [\cos(2\pi f_1 t) - (1/3)\cos(2\pi(3f_1)t) + (1/5)\cos(2\pi(5f_1)t) - (1/7)\cos(2\pi(7f_1)t) + \ldots]$
Triangular wave 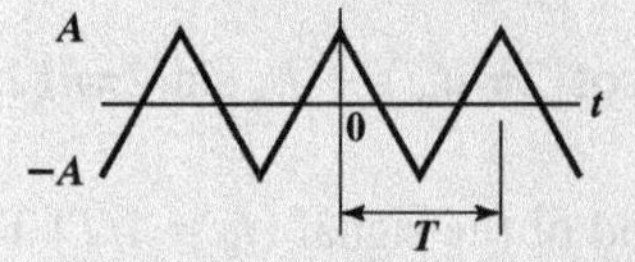	$C_0 = 0$ $C_n = 0$ for n even $C_n = 8A/(n\pi)^2$ for n odd
Sawtooth wave 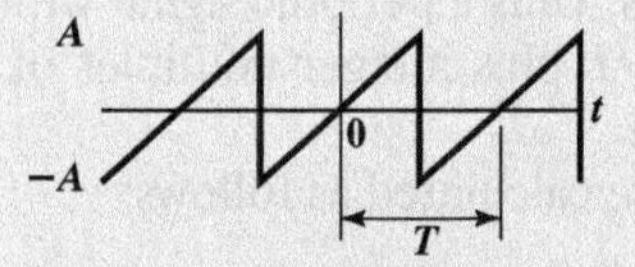	$A_0 = 0$ $A_n = 0$ for n even $B_n = -(-1)^{(n)} \times (2A/\pi n)$
Half-wave rectified cosine 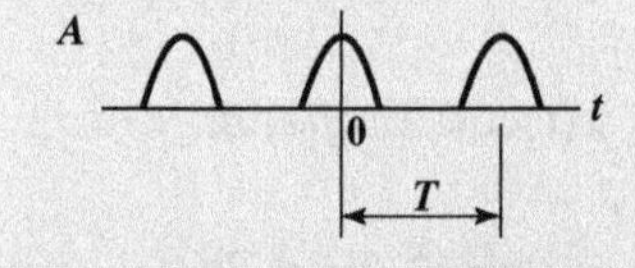	$C_0 = 2A/\pi$ $C_n = 0$ for n odd $C_n = (2A/\pi) \times (-1)^{(1+n/2)} \times (2/(n^2 - 1))$ for n even
Full-wave rectified cosine 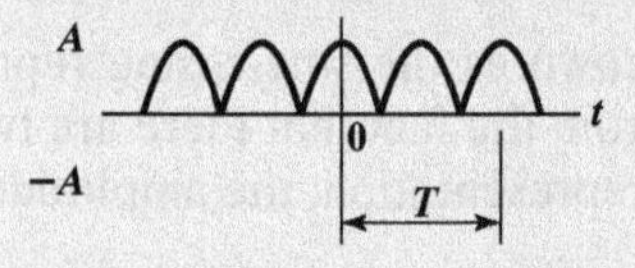	$C_0 = 4A/\pi$ $C_n = (4A/\pi) \times (-1)^n \times (1/(4n^2 - 1))$
Pulse train 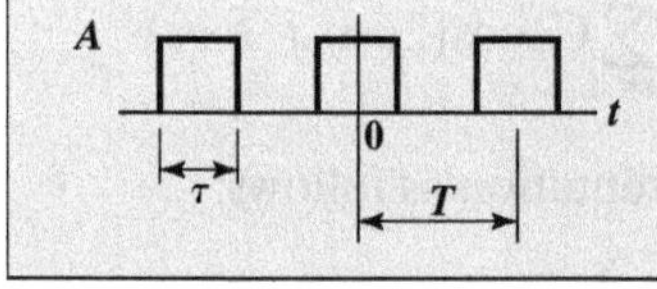	$C_n = (2A\tau/T) \times (\sin(n\pi\tau/T)/(n\pi\tau/T))$

Figure B.1 Some Common Periodic Signals and Their Fourier Series

B.2 FOURIER TRANSFORM REPRESENTATION OF APERIODIC SIGNALS

For a periodic signal, we have seen that its spectrum consists of discrete frequency components, at the fundamental frequency and its harmonics. For an aperiodic signal, the spectrum consists of a continuum of frequencies. This spectrum can be defined by the Fourier transform. For a signal $x(t)$ with a spectrum $X(f)$, the following relationships hold:

$$x(t) = \int_{-\infty}^{\infty} X(f)\, e^{j2\pi ft}\, df$$

$$X(f) = \int_{-\infty}^{\infty} x(t)\, e^{-j2\pi ft}\, dt$$

where $j = \sqrt{-1}$. The presence of an imaginary number in the equations is a matter of convenience. The imaginary component has a physical interpretation having to do with the phase of a waveform, and a discussion of this topic is beyond the scope of this book.

Figure B.2 presents some examples of Fourier transform pairs.

Signal $x(t)$	Fourier Transform $X(f)$
Rectangular pulse 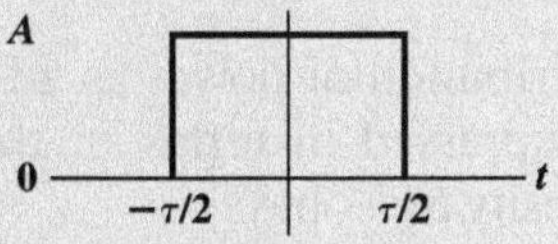	$A\tau \frac{\sin(\pi f\tau)}{\pi f\tau}$
Triangular pulse 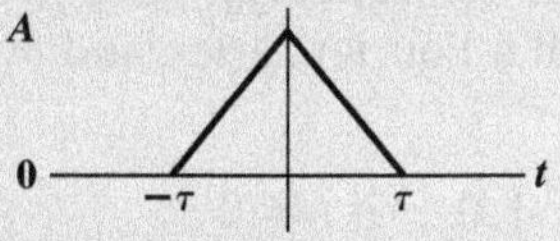	$A\tau \left(\frac{\sin(\pi f\tau)}{\pi f\tau}\right)^2$
Sawtooth pulse 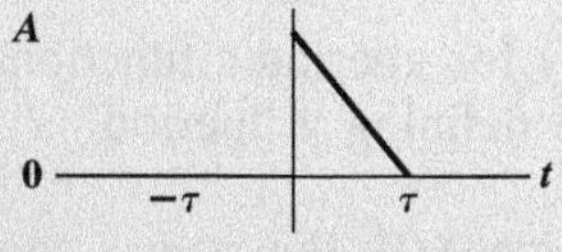	$(jA/2\pi f) \times \{[(\sin(\pi f\tau)/\pi f\tau)]\exp(-j\pi f\tau) - 1\}$
Cosine pulse 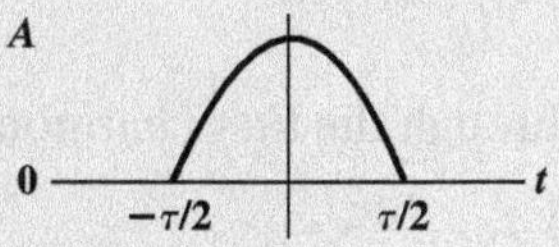	$\frac{2A\tau}{\pi} \times \frac{\cos(\pi f\tau)}{1-(2f\tau)^2}$

Figure B.2 Some Common Aperiodic Signals and Their Fourier Transforms

Power Spectral Density and Bandwidth

The absolute bandwidth of any time-limited signal is infinite. In practical terms, however, most of the power in a signal is concentrated in some finite band, and the effective bandwidth consists of that portion of the spectrum that contains most of the power. To make this concept precise, we need to define the power spectral density (PSD). In essence, the PSD describes the power content of a signal as a function of frequency, so that it shows how much power is present over various frequency bands.

First, we observe the power in the time domain. A function $x(t)$ usually specifies a signal in terms of either voltage or current. In either case, the instantaneous power in the signal is proportional to $|x(t)|^2$. We define the average power of a time-limited signal as

$$P = \frac{1}{t_1 - t_2} \int_{t_1}^{t_2} |x(t)|^2 \, dt$$

For a periodic signal the average power in one period is

$$P = \frac{1}{T} \int_0^T |x(t)|^2 \, dt$$

We would like to know the distribution of power as a function of frequency. For periodic signals, this is easily expressed in terms of the coefficients of the Fourier series. The power spectral density $S(f)$ obeys

$$S(f) = \sum_{n=-\infty}^{\infty} |C_n|^2 \delta(f - nf_0)$$

where f_0 is the inverse of the period of the signal ($f_0 = 1/T$), C_n is the coefficient in the amplitude-phase representation of a Fourier series, and $\delta(t)$ is the unit impulse, or delta, function, defined as:

$$\delta(t) = \begin{cases} 0 & \text{if } t \neq 0 \\ \infty & \text{if } t = 0 \end{cases}$$

$$\int_{-\infty}^{\infty} \delta(t) \, dt = 1$$

The power spectral density $S(f)$ for aperiodic functions is more difficult to define. In essence, it is obtained by defining a "period" T_0 and allowing T_0 to increase without limit.

For a continuous valued function $S(f)$, the power contained in a band of frequencies, $f_1 < f < f_2$, is

$$P = 2 \int_{f_1}^{f_2} S(f) \, df$$

For a periodic waveform, the power through the first j harmonics is

$$P = \frac{1}{4} C_0^2 + \frac{1}{2} \sum_{n=1}^{j} C_n^2$$

With these concepts, we can now define the half-power bandwidth, which is perhaps the most common bandwidth definition. The half-power bandwidth is the interval between frequencies at which *S(f)* has dropped to half of its maximum value of power, or 3 dB below the peak value.

B.3 RECOMMENDED READINGS

A very accessible treatment of Fourier series and Fourier transforms is [JAME01]. For a thorough understanding of Fourier series and transforms, the book to read is [KAMM00].

JAME01 James, J. *A Student's Guide to Fourier Transforms*. Cambridge, England: Cambridge University Press, 2001.

KAMM00 Kammler, D. *A First Course in Fourier Analysis*. Upper Saddle River, NJ: Prentice Hall, 2000.

APPENDIX C

DATA LINK CONTROL PROTOCOLS

Throughout this book, a number of references have been made to the use of data link control protocols as part of a protocol architecture. A key mechanism that is part of most data link control protocols is error control using automatic repeat request (ARQ), which is discussed in Section 8.4. This appendix looks at HDLC, which is representative of data link control protocols and indeed is the base from which most such protocols have been derived.

C.1 HIGH-LEVEL DATA LINK CONTROL

The most important data link control protocol is HDLC (ISO 3009, ISO 4335). Not only is HDLC widely used, but also it is the basis for many other important data link control protocols, which use the same or similar formats and the same mechanisms as employed in HDLC.

HDLC Frame Structure

Perhaps the best way to begin an explanation of HDLC is to look at the frame structure. The operation of HDLC involves the exchange of two sorts of information between the two connected stations. First, HDLC accepts user data from some higher layer of software and delivers that user data across the link to the other side. On the other side, HDLC accepts the user data and delivers it to a higher layer of software on that side. Second, the two HDLC modules must exchange control information, to provide for flow control, error control, and other control functions. The method by which this is done is to format the information that is exchanged into a **frame**. A frame is a predefined structure that provides a specific location for various kinds of control information and for user data.

Figure C.1 depicts the format of the HDLC frame. The frame has the following fields:

- **Flag:** Used for synchronization. It appears at the beginning and end of the frame and always contains the pattern 01111110.
- **Address:** Indicates the secondary station for this transmission. It is needed in the case of a multidrop line, where a primary may send data to one of a number of secondaries, and one of a number of secondaries may send data to the primary. This field is usually 8 bits long but can be extended (Figure C.1b).
- **Control:** Identifies the purpose and functions of the frame. It is described later in this subsection.
- **Information:** Contains the user data to be transmitted.
- **Frame Check Sequence:** Contains a 16- or 32-bit cyclic redundancy check, used for error detection.

HDLC defines three types of frames, each with a different control field format. Information frames (I frames) carry the user data to be transmitted for the station. Additionally, the information frames contain control information for flow control and error control. Supervisory frames (S frames) provide another means of

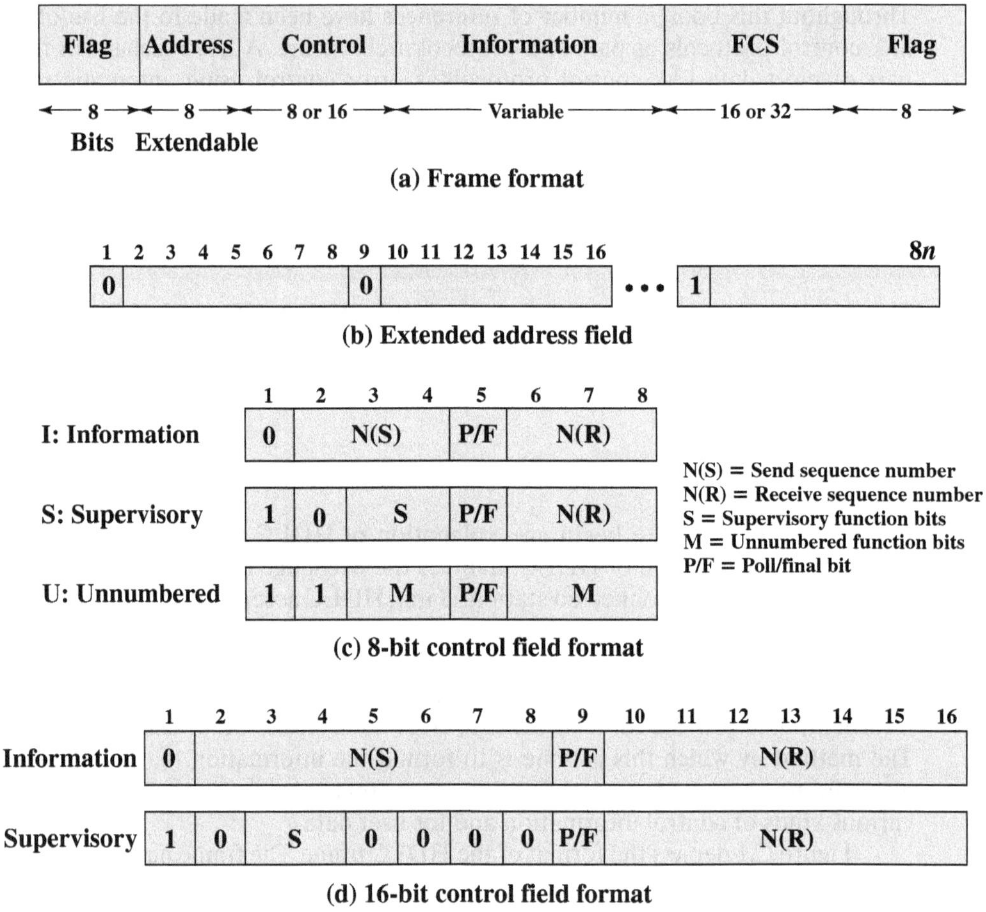

Figure C.1 HDLC Frame Structure

exercising flow control and error control. Unnumbered frames (U frames) provide supplemental link control functions.

The first one or two bits of the control field serve to identify the frame type. The remaining bit positions are organized into subfields, as indicated in Figures C.1c and C.1d. Their use is explained in the discussion of HDLC operation, which follows. Note that the basic control field for S and I frames uses 3-bit sequence numbers. With the appropriate set-mode commands, an extended control field can be used that employs 7-bit sequence numbers.

All of the control field formats contain the poll/final (P/F) bit. Its use depends on context. Typically, in command frames, it is referred to as the P bit and is set to 1 to solicit (poll) a response frame from the peer HDLC entity. In response frames, it is referred to as the F bit and is set to 1 to indicate the response frame transmitted as a result of a soliciting command.

Table C.1 HDLC Commands and Responses

Name	Command/ Response	Description
Information (I)	C/R	Exchange user data
Supervisory (S)		
Receive ready (RR)	C/R	Positive acknowledgment; ready to receive I frame
Receive not ready (RNR)	C/R	Positive acknowledgment; not ready to receive
Reject (REJ)	C/R	Negative acknowledgment; go back N
Selective reject (SREJ)	C/R	Negative acknowledgment; selective reject
Unnumbered (U)		
Set normal response/extended mode (SNRM/SNRME)	C	Set mode; extended = 7-bit sequence numbers
Set asynchronous response/extended mode (SARM/SARME)	C	Set mode; extended = 7-bit sequence numbers
Set asynchronous balanced/extended mode (SABM, SABME)	C	Set mode; extended = 7-bit sequence numbers
Set initialization mode (SIM)	C	Initialize link control functions in addressed station
Disconnect (DISC)	C	Terminate logical link connection
Unnumbered Acknowledgment (UA)	R	Acknowledge acceptance of one of the set-mode commands
Disconnected mode (DM)	R	Responder is in disconnected mode
Request disconnect (RD)	R	Request for DISC command
Request initialization mode (RIM)	R	Initialization needed; request for SIM command
Unnumbered information (UI)	C/R	Used to exchange control information
Unnumbered poll (UP)	C	Used to solicit control information
Reset (RSET)	C	Used for recovery; resets N(R), N(S)
Exchange identification (XID)	C/R	Used to request/report status
Test (TEST)	C/R	Exchange identical information fields for testing
Frame reject (FRMR)	R	Report receipt of unacceptable frame

HDLC Operation

HDLC operation consists of the exchange of I frames, S frames, and U frames between two stations. The various commands and responses defined for these frame types are listed in Table C.1. In describing HDLC operation, we will discuss these three types of frames.

The operation of HDLC involves three phases. First, one side or another initializes the data link so that frames may be exchanged in an orderly fashion. During this phase, the options that are to be used are agreed upon. After initialization, the two sides exchange user data and the control information to exercise flow and error control. Finally, one of the two sides signals the termination of the operation.

Initialization Either side may request initialization by issuing one of the six set-mode commands. This command serves three purposes:

1. It signals the other side that initialization is requested.
2. It specifies which of the three modes is requested; these modes have to do with whether one side acts as a primary and controls the exchange or whether the two sides are peers and cooperate in the exchange.
3. It specifies whether 3- or 7-bit sequence numbers are to be used.

If the other side accepts this request, then the HDLC module on that end transmits an Unnumbered Acknowledged (UA) frame back to the initiating side. If the request is rejected, then a Disconnected Mode (DM) frame is sent.

Data Transfer When initialization has been requested and accepted, a logical connection is established. Both sides may begin to send user data in I frames, starting with sequence number 0. The N(S) and N(R) fields of the I frame are sequence numbers that support flow control and error control. An HDLC module sending a sequence of I frames will number them sequentially, modulo 8 or 128, depending on whether 3- or 7-bit sequence numbers are used, and place the sequence number in N(S). N(R) is the acknowledgment for I frames received; it enables the HDLC module to indicate which number I frame it expects to receive next.

S frames are also used for flow control and error control. The Receive Ready (RR) frame is used to acknowledge the last I frame received by indicating the next I frame expected. The RR is used when there is no reverse user data traffic (I frames) to carry an acknowledgment. Receive Not Ready (RNR) acknowledges an I frame, as with RR, but also asks the peer entity to suspend transmission of I frames. When the entity that issued RNR is again ready, it sends an RR. REJ initiates the go-back-N ARQ. It indicates that the last I frame received has been rejected and that retransmission of all I frames beginning with number N(R) is required. Selective reject (SREJ) is used to request retransmission of just a single frame.

Disconnect Either HDLC module can initiate a disconnect, either on its own initiative if there is some sort of fault or at the request of its higher-layer user. HDLC issues a disconnect by sending a Disconnect (DISC) frame. The other side must accept the disconnect by replying with a UA.

Examples of Operation To better understand HDLC operation, several examples are presented in Figure C.2. In the example diagrams, each arrow includes a legend that specifies the frame name, the setting of the P/F bit, and, where appropriate, the values of N(R) and N(S). The setting of the P or F bit is 1 if the designation is present and 0 if absent.

Figure C.2a shows the frames involved in link setup and disconnect. The HDLC entity for one side issues an SABM command[1] to the other side and starts a timer. The other side, upon receiving the SABM, returns a UA response and sets local variables and counters to their initial values. The initiating entity receives the UA response, sets its variables and counters, and stops the timer. The logical

[1]This stands for set asynchronous mode balanced. The SABM command is a request to start an exchange. The ABM part of the acronym refers to the mode of transfer, a detail that need not concern us here.

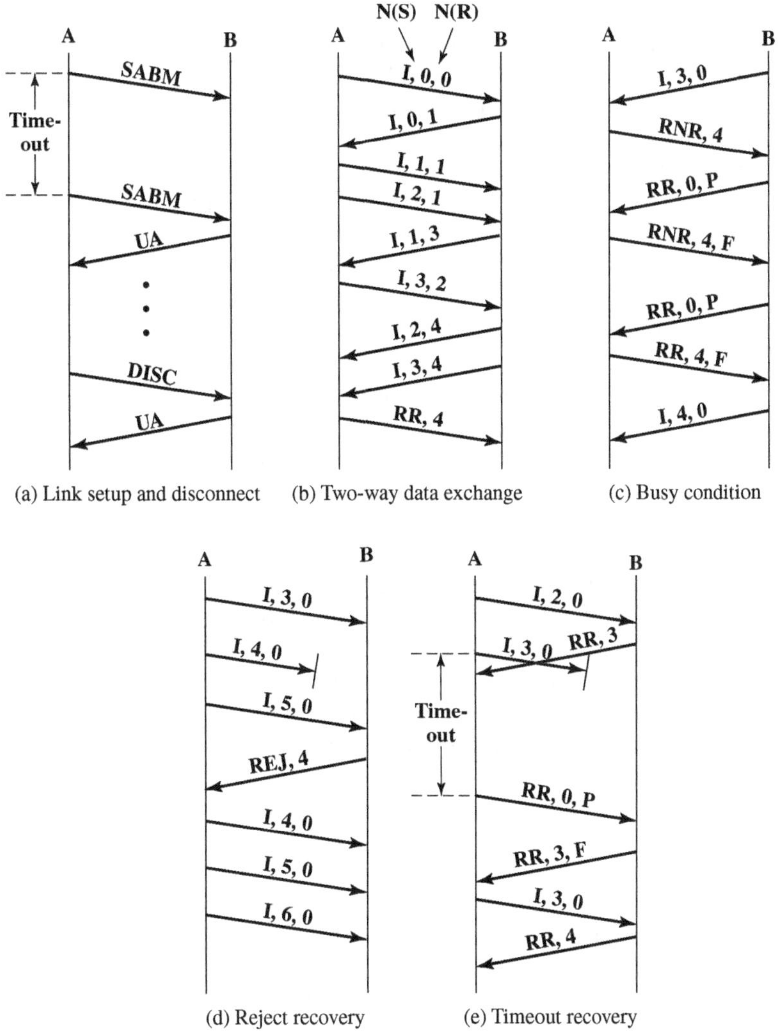

Figure C.2 Examples of HDLC Operation

connection is now active, and both sides may begin transmitting frames. Should the timer expire without a response, the originator will repeat the SABM, as illustrated. This would be repeated until a UA or DM is received or until, after a given number of tries, the entity attempting initiation gives up and reports failure to a management entity. In such a case, higher-layer intervention is necessary. The same figure (Figure C.2a) shows the disconnect procedure. One side issues a DISC command, and the other responds with a UA response.

Figure C.2b illustrates the full-duplex exchange of I frames. When an entity sends a number of I frames in a row with no incoming data, then the receive sequence number, N(R), is simply repeated (e.g., I,1,1; I,2,1 in the A-to-B direction). When an entity receives a number of I frames in a row with no outgoing frames, then the receive sequence number in the next outgoing frame must reflect the cumulative activity (e.g., I,1,3 in the B-to-A direction). Note that, in addition to I frames, data exchange may involve supervisory frames.

Figure C.2c shows an operation involving a busy condition. Such a condition may arise because an HDLC entity is not able to process I frames as fast as they are arriving, or the intended user is not able to accept data as fast as they arrive in I frames. In either case, the entity's receive buffer fills up and it must halt the incoming flow of I frames, using an RNR command. In this example, station A issues an RNR, which requires the other side to halt transmission of I frames. The station receiving the RNR will usually poll the busy station at some periodic interval by sending an RR with the P bit set. This requires the other side to respond with either an RR or an RNR. When the busy condition has cleared, A returns an RR, and I frame transmission from B can resume.

An example of error recovery using the REJ command is shown in Figure C.2d. In this example, A transmits I frames numbered 3, 4, and 5. Frame 4 suffers an error. B detects the error and discards the frame. When B receives I frame 5, it discards this frame because it is out of order and sends an REJ with an N(R) of 4. This causes A to initiate retransmission of all I frames sent, beginning with frame 4. It may continue to send additional frames after the retransmitted frames.

An example of error recovery using a timeout is shown in Figure C.2e. In this example, A transmits I frame number 3 as the last in a sequence of I frames. The frame suffers an error. B detects the error and discards it. However, B cannot send an REJ. This is because there is no way to know if this was an I frame. If an error is detected in a frame, all of the bits of that frame are suspect, and the receiver has no way to act upon it. A, however, started a timer as the frame was transmitted. This timer has a duration long enough to span the expected response time. When the timer expires, A initiates recovery action. This is usually done by polling the other side with an RR command with the P bit set, to determine the status of the other side. Because the poll demands a response, the entity will receive a frame containing an N(R) field and be able to proceed. In this case, the response indicates that frame 3 was lost, which A retransmits.

These examples are not exhaustive. However, they should give the reader a good feel for the behavior of HDLC.

GLOSSARY

amplitude modulation A form of modulation in which the amplitude of a carrier wave is varied in accordance with some characteristic of the modulating signal.

amplitude-shift keying Modulation in which the two binary values are represented by two different amplitudes of the carrier frequency.

analog data Data represented by a physical quantity that is considered to be continuously variable and whose magnitude is made directly proportional to the data or to a suitable function of the data.

analog signal A continuously varying electromagnetic wave that may be propagated over a variety of media.

analog transmission The transmission of analog signals without regard to content. The signal may be amplified, but there is no intermediate attempt to recover the data from the signal.

angle modulation Modulation in which the angle of a sine wave carrier is varied. Phase and frequency modulation are particular forms of angle modulation.

antenna That part of a transmitting or receiving system that is designed to radiate or to receive electromagnetic waves.

attenuation The reduction of strength of a signal as a function of distance traveled.

aperiodic A function or signal that is not periodic.

application layer Layer 7 of the OSI model. This layer determines the interface of the system with the user.

asynchronous transfer mode (ATM) A form of packet transmission using fixed-size packets, called cells.

atmospheric absorption The loss of energy in transmission of radio waves, due to dissipation in the atmosphere.

automatic repeat request A feature that automatically initiates a request for retransmission when an error in transmission is detected.

bandwidth The difference in Hertz between the limiting (upper and lower) frequencies of a spectrum.

bit error rate The probability that a transmitted bit is received in error.

block error correction code A technique in which a k-bit block of data is mapped into an n-bit block ($n > k$) called a **codeword**, using an FEC (forward error correction) encoder.

broadband In data communications generally refers to systems that provide user data rates of greater than 2 Mbps, up to 100s of Mbps.

burst error A burst error of length B is a contiguous sequence of B bits in which the first and last bits and any number of intermediate bits are received in error.

carrier frequency A continuous frequency capable of being modulated or impressed with a second (information-carrying) signal.

cell relay The packet-switching mechanism used for the fixed-size packets called cells. ATM is based on cell relay technology.

cellular network A wireless communications network in which fixed antennas are arranged in a hexagonal pattern and mobile stations communicate through nearby fixed antennas.

channel A single path for transmitting electric signals. *Note*: The word *path* is to be interpreted in a broad sense to include separation by frequency division or time division. The term *channel* may signify either a one-way or a two-way path.

channel capacity The maximum possible information rate through a channel subject to the constraints of that channel.

checksum An error-detecting code based on a summation operation performed on the bits to be checked.

circuit switching A method of communicating in which a dedicated communications path is established between two devices through one or more intermediate switching nodes. Unlike packet switching, digital data are sent as a continuous stream of bits. Bandwidth is guaranteed, and delay is essentially limited to propagation time. The telephone system uses circuit switching.

code division multiple access A multiplexing technique used with spread spectrum.

crosstalk Undesired energy appearing in one signal path as a result of coupling from other signal paths.

cyclic redundancy check An error detecting code in which the code is the remainder resulting from dividing the bits to be checked by a predetermined binary number.

datagram In packet switching, a packet, independent of other packets, that carries information sufficient for routing from the originating data terminal equipment (DTE) to the destination DTE without the necessity of establishing a connection between the DTEs and the network.

decibel A measure of the relative strength of two signals. The number of decibels is 10 times the log of the ratio of the power of two signals, or 20 times the log of the ratio of the voltage of two signals.

diffraction Deviation of part of a beam, determined by the wave nature of radiation, and occurring when the radiation passes the edge of an opaque obstacle.

digital data Data consisting of a sequence of discrete elements.

digital signal A discrete or discontinuous signal, such as voltage pulses.

digital transmission The transmission of digital data, using either an analog or digital signal, in which the digital data are recovered and repeated at intermediate points to reduce the effects of noise.

dipole antenna Any one of a class of antennas producing a radiation pattern approximating that of an elementary electric dipole.

direct sequence spread spectrum A form of spread spectrum in which each bit in the original signal is represented by multiple bits in the transmitted signal, using a spreading code.

Doppler shift The effective change of frequency of a received signal due to the relative velocity of a transmitter with respect to the receiver.

downlink The communications link from satellite to earth station.

downstream Refers to the direction of transmission from a base station to a subscriber in a cellular or wireless local loop system.

electric dipole An elementary radiator consisting of a pair of equal and opposite oscillating electric charges an infinitesimal distance apart.

encapsulation The addition of control information by a protocol entity to data obtained from a protocol user.

error correction code A code in which each expression conforms to specific rules of construction, so that departures from this construction can be automatically detected, and permits the automatic correction of some or all of the errors.

error-detecting code A code in which each expression conforms to specific rules of construction, so that if certain errors occur in an expression, the resulting expression will not conform to the rules of construction and thus the presence of the errors is detected.

fading The time variation of received signal power caused by changes in the transmission medium or path(s).

flat fading That type of fading in which all frequency components of the received signal fluctuate in the same proportions simultaneously.

flow control The function performed by a receiving entity to limit the amount or rate of data that is sent by a transmitting entity.

forward channel In a cellular or cordless network, the communications link from the base station to the mobile unit.

forward error correction Procedures whereby a receiver, using only information contained in the incoming digital transmission, a receiver corrects bit errors in the data.

frame check sequence An error-detecting code inserted as a field in a block of data to be transmitted. The code serves to check for errors upon reception of the data.

free space loss Loss in signal energy caused by the dispersion of the signal over distance.

frequency Rate of signal oscillation in hertz.

frequency division multiplexing (FDM) The division of a transmission facility into two or more channels by splitting the frequency band transmitted by the facility into narrower bands, each of which is used to constitute a distinct channel.

frequency domain A characterization of a function or signal in terms of its component frequencies.

frequency-hopping spread spectrum A form of spread spectrum in which the signal is broadcast over a seemingly random series of radio frequencies, hopping from frequency to frequency at fixed intervals.

frequency modulation Modulation in which the frequency of an alternating current is the characteristic varied.

frequency-shift keying Modulation in which the two binary values are represented by two different frequencies near the carrier frequency.

fundamental frequency The lowest frequency component in the Fourier representation of a periodic quantity.

gain (of an antenna) The ratio of the radiation intensity, in a given direction, to the radiation intensity that would be obtained if the power accepted by the antenna were radiated isotropically.

geostationary Refers to a geosynchronous satellite angle with zero inclination so the satellite appears to hover over one spot on the earth's equator.

geosynchronous The Clarke circular orbit above the equator. For a planet the size and mass of the earth, this point is 35,863 miles above the surface.

ground wave A radio wave propagated over the earth and is ordinarily affected by the presence of the ground and troposphere. Notes: (1) The ground wave include all components of a radio wave over the earth except ionospheric and tropospheric waves. (2) The ground wave is refracted because of variations in the dielectric constant of the troposphere.

guided medium A transmission medium in which the waves are guided along a solid medium, such as copper twisted pair, copper coaxial cable, or optical fiber.

half-wave dipole A wire antenna consisting of two straight collinear conductors of equal length, separated by a small feeding gap, with each conductor approximately a quarter-wavelength long.

Hamming distance The number of digit positions in which two binary numbers of the same length are different.

hash function A function that maps a variable length data block or message into a fixed-length value called a hash code. The function is designed in such a way that, when protected, it provides an authenticator to the data or message. Also referred to as a message digest.

header System-defined control information that precedes user data.

impulse noise A high-amplitude, short-duration noise pulse.

infrared Electromagnetic waves whose frequency range is above that of microwave and below the visible spectrum: 3×10^{11} to 4×10^{14} Hz.

intermodulation noise Noise due to the nonlinear combination of signals of different frequencies.

internet A collection of packet-switched networks connected via routers.

Internet Protocol An internetworking protocol that provides connectionless service across multiple packet-switching networks.

ionosphere That part of the earth's outer atmosphere where ionization caused by incoming solar radiation affects the transmission of radio waves. It generally extends from a height of about 50 km to about 400 km above the earth's surface.

isochronous The time characteristic of an event or signal recurring at known, periodic time intervals.

local area network (LAN) A communications network that encompasses a small area, typically a single building or cluster of buildings, used to connect various data processing devices, including PCs, workstations, and servers.

local loop Transmission path, generally twisted pair, between the individual subscriber and the nearest switching center of the public telecommunications network.

medium access control For broadcast networks, the method of determining which device has access to the transmission medium at any time.

microwave Electromagnetic waves in the frequency range 1 to 40 GHz.

millimeter wave An imprecise term. Generally, millimeter wave systems operate in a region between 10 GHz (wavelength = 30 mm) and 300 GHz (wavelength = 1 mm).

modulation A process whereby certain characteristics of a wave, called a carrier, are varied or selected in accordance with a modulating function.

multipath The propagation phenomenon that results in signals reaching the receiving antenna by two or more paths.

multiplexing In data transmission, a function that permits two or more data sources to share a common transmission medium such that each data source has its own channel.

network layer Layer 3 of the OSI model. Responsible for routing data through a communication network.

noise Unwanted signals that combine with and hence distort the signal intended for transmission and reception.

packet A group of bits that includes data plus source and destination addresses. Generally refers to a network layer (layer 3) protocol.

packet switching A method of transmitting messages through a communications network, in which long messages are subdivided into short packets. The packets are then transmitted as in message switching. Usually, packet switching is more efficient and rapid than message switching.

parity bit A binary digit appended to an array of binary digits to make the sum of all the binary digits, including the parity bit, always odd (odd parity) or always even (even parity).

peak amplitude The maximum value or strength of a signal over time; typically, this value is measured in volts.

period The absolute value of the minimum interval after which the same characteristics of a periodic waveform recur.

periodic waveform A waveform $f(t)$ that satisfies $f(t) = f(t + nk)$ for all integers n, with k being a constant.

personal area network (PAN) A communications network within a small area in which all of the devices attached to the network are typically owned by one person or perhaps a family. Devices on a PAN may include portable and mobile devices, such as PCs, personal digital assistants (PDAs), peripherals, cell phones, pagers, and consumer electronic devices.

phase For a periodic signal $f(t)$, the fractional part t/P of the period P through which t has advanced relative to an arbitrary origin. The origin is usually taken at the last previous passage through zero from the negative to the positive direction.

phase modulation Modulation in which the phase angle of a carrier is the characteristic varied.

phase-shift keying Modulation in which the phase of the carrier signal is shifted to represent digital data.

physical layer Layer 1 of the OSI model. Concerned with the electrical, mechanical, and timing aspects of signal transmission over a medium.

presentation layer Layer 6 of the OSI model. Provides for the selection of a common syntax for representing data and for transformation of application data into and from the common syntax.

protocol A set of rules governing the exchange of data between two entities.

protocol data unit A set of data specified in a protocol of a given layer and consisting of protocol control information of that layer, and possibly user data of that layer.

pseudonoise A sequence of numbers that are apparently statistically random.

pulse code modulation A process in which a signal is sampled, and the magnitude of each sample with respect to a fixed reference is quantized and converted by coding to a digital signal.

radiation pattern A graphical representation of the radiation properties of an antenna as a function of space coordinates. Typically, the distance from the antenna to each point on the radiation pattern is proportional to the power radiated from the antenna in that direction.

reflection Occurs when an electromagnetic signal encounters a surface that is large relative to the wavelength of the signal; the angle of incidence equals the angle of reflection.

refraction The bending of a beam in transmission through an interface between two dissimilar media or in a medium whose refractive index is a continuous function of position.

reverse channel In a cellular or cordless network, the communications link from the mobile unit to the base station.

router A device used to link two or more networks. The router makes use of an internet protocol, which is a connectionless protocol operating at layer 3 of the OSI model.

scattering The production of waves of changed direction, frequency, or polarization when radio waves encounter matter.

selective fading Fading that affects unequally the different spectral components of a radio signal.

service access point A means of identifying a user of the services of a protocol entity. A protocol entity provides one or more SAPs for use by higher-level entities.

session layer Layer 5 of the OSI model. Manages a logical connection (session) between two communicating processes or applications.

sky wave A radio wave propagated obliquely toward, and returned from, the ionosphere.

spectrum Refers to an absolute range of frequencies. For example, the spectrum of infrared is 3×10^{11} to 4×10^{14} Hz.

spread spectrum A technique in which the information in a signal is spread over a wider bandwidth using a spreading code.

spreading code A sequence of digits used to spread bandwidth in a spread spectrum system. Also called a spreading sequence or a chipping code.

subscriber loop Synonymous with local loop.

synchronous time division multiplexing A method of TDM in which time slots on a shared transmission line are assigned to I/O channels on a fixed, predetermined basis.

thermal noise Statistically uniform noise due to the temperature of the transmission medium.

time division duplex A link transmission technique in which data are transmitted in one direction at a time, with transmission alternating between the two directions.

time division multiplexing (TDM) The division of a transmission facility into two or more channels by allotting the facility to several different information channels, one at a time.

time domain A characterization of a function or signal in terms of value as a function of time.

transmission medium The physical path between transmitters and receivers in a communications system.

transport layer Layer 4 of the OSI model. Provides reliable, transparent transfer of data between endpoints.

troposphere That portion of the earth's atmosphere in which temperature generally decreases with altitude, clouds form, and convection is active. The troposphere occupies the space from the earth's surface up to a height ranging from about 6 km at the poles to about 18 km at the equator.

unguided medium A transmission medium, such as air, vacuum, or water, in which an antenna is employed for transmission and reception.

uplink The communications link from earth station to satellite.

upstream Refers to the direction of transmission from a subscriber to a base station in a cellular or wireless local loop system.

virtual circuit A packet-switching service in which a connection (virtual circuit) is established between two stations at the start of transmission. All packets follow the same route, need not carry a complete address, and arrive in sequence.

wavelength The distance between two points in a periodic wave that have the same phase.

wireless Refers to electromagnetic transmission through air, vacuum, or water by means of an antenna.

REFERENCES

ABBREVIATIONS

ACM Association for Computing Machinery
IEEE Institute of Electrical and Electronics Engineers

ADAM91 Adamek, J. *Foundations of Coding.* New York: Wiley, 1991.

ANDE95 Anderson, J.; Rappaport, T.; and Yoshida, S. "Propagation Measurements and Models for Wireless Communications Channels." *IEEE Communications Magazine*, January 1995.

ASH90 Ash, R. *Information Theory.* New York: Dover, 1990.

BANT94 Bantz, D., and Bauchot, F. "Wireless LAN Design Alternatives." *IEEE Network*, March/April, 1994.

BELL00 Bellamy, J. *Digital Telephony.* New York: Wiley, 2000.

BEND00 Bender. P., et al. "CDMA/HDR: A Bandwidth-Efficient High-Speed Wireless Data Service for Nomadic Users." *IEEE Communications Magazine*, July 2000.

BERE02 Berezdivin, R.; Breinig, R.; and Topp, R. "Next-Generation Wireless Communications Concepts and Technologies." *IEEE Communications Magazine*, March 2002.

BERL80 Berlekamp, E. "The Technology of Error-Correcting Codes." *Proceedings of the IEEE*, May 1980.

BERL87 Berlekamp, E.; Peile, R.; and Pope, S. "The Application of Error Control to Communications." *IEEE Communications Magazine*, April 1987.

BERR96 Berrou, C., and Glavieux, A. "Near Optimum Error Correcting Codes and Decoding: Turbo Codes." *IEEE Transactions on Communications*, October 1996.

BERT92 Bertsekas, D., and Gallager, R. *Data Networks.* Englewood Cliffs, NJ: Prentice Hall, 1992.

BERT94 Bertoni, H.; Honcharenko, W.; Maciel, L.; and Xia, H. "UHF Propagation Prediction for Wireless Personal Communications." *Proceedings of the IEEE*, September 1994.

BERT00 Bertoni, H. *Radio Propagation for Modern Wireless Systems.* Upper Saddle River, NJ: Prentice Hall, 2000.

BHAR83 Bhargava, V. "Forward Error Correction Schemes for Digital Communications." *IEEE Communications Magazine*, January 1983.

BING02 Bing, B. *Wireless Local Area Networks.* New York: Wiley, 2002.

BI03 Bi, Q., et al. " Performance of 1xEV-DO Third-Generation Wireless High-Speed Data Systems." *Bell Labs Technical Journal*, Vol. 7, No. 3 2003.

BLAC99a Black, U. *Second-generation Mobile and Wireless Networks.* Upper Saddle River, NJ: Prentice Hall, 1999.

BLAC99b Black, U. *ATM Volume I: Foundation for Broadband Networks.* Upper Saddle River, NJ: Prentice Hall, 1992.

BOLC01 Bolcskei, H., et al. "Fixed Broadband Wireless Access: State of the Art, Challenges, and Future Directions." *IEEE Communications Magazine*, January 2001.

BRAY01 Bray, J., and Sturman, C. *Bluetooth: Connect Without Cables.* Upper Saddle River, NJ: Prentice Hall, 2001.

CALL02 Callaway, E., et al. "Home Networking with IEEE 802.15.4: A Developing Standard for Low-Rate Wireless Personal Area Networks." *IEEE Communications Magazine*, August 2002.

CARN99 Carne, E. *Telecommunications Primer: Data, Voice, and Video Communications.* Upper Saddle River, NJ: Prentice Hall, 1999.

CHEU04 Cheung, D. "WLAN Security & Wi-Fi Protected Access." *Dr. Dobb's Journal*, June 2004.

CISC00 Cisco Systems, Inc. *Overcoming Multipath in Non-Line-of-Sight High-Speed Microwave Communication Links.* White Paper, 2000. (www.cisco.com)

COTT00 Cottrell, R.; Langhammer, M.; and Mauer, V. "Turbo Decoding for Comm Apps." *Communication Systems Design*, August 2000.

COUC01 Couch, L. *Digital and Analog Communication Systems.* Upper Saddle River, NJ: Prentice Hall, 2001.

CROW97 Crow, B., et al. "IEEE 802.11 Wireless Local Area Networks." *IEEE Communications Magazine*, September 1997.

DALK96 Dalke, R.; Hufford, G.; and Ketchum, R. *Radio Propagation Considerations for Local Multipoint Distribution Systems.* National Telecommunications and Information Administration Publication PB97116511, August 1996.

DAUM82 Daumer, W. "Subjective Evaluation of Several Efficient Speech Coders." *IEEE Transactions on Communications*, April 1982.

DINA98 Dinan, E., and Jabbari, B. "Spreading Codes for Direct Sequence CDMA and Wideband CDMA Cellular Networks." *IEEE Communications Magazine*, September 1998.

DIXO94 Dixon, R. *Spread Spectrum Systems with Commercial Applications.* New York: Wiley, 1994.

EATO02 Eaton, D. "Diving into the IEEE 802.11i Spec: A Tutorial." *Communications System Design*, November 2002. www.commsdesign.com

ECON99 "The World in Your Pocket." *The Economist*, October 1999.

EDEL82 Edelson, B.; Marsten, R.; and Morgan, W. "Greater Message Capacity for Satellites.' *IEEE Spectrum*, March 1982.

EDNE04 Edney, J., and Arbaugh, W. *Real 802.11 Security: Wi-Fi Protected Access and 802.11i.* Reading, MA: Addison-Wesley, 2004.

EKLU02 Eklund, C., et al. "IEEE Standard 802.16: A Technical Overview of the WirelessMAN Air Interface for Broadband Wireless Access." *IEEE Communications Magazine*, June 2002.

ELBE99 Elbert, B. *Introduction to Satellite Communication.* Boston: Artech House, 1999.

ENGE00 Engelmann, R. "The Origins of Radio." *IEEE Potentials*, October/November 2000.

EVAN98 Evans, J. "New Satellites for Personal Communications." *Scientific American*, April 1998.

EVER94 Everitt, D. "Traffic Engineering of the Radio Interface for Cellular Mobile Networks." *Proceedings of the IEEE*, September 1994.

EYUB02 Eyuboglu, V. "CDAM2000 1xEV-DO Delivers 3G Wireless." *Network World*, February 25, 2002.

FORN84 Forney, G., et al. "Efficient Modulation for Band-Limited Channels." *IEEE Journal on Selected Areas in Communications*, September 1984.

FREE97 Freeman, R. *Radio System Design for Telecommunications.* New York: Wiley, 1997.

FREE98a Freeman, R. *Telecommunication Transmission Handbook.* New York: Wiley, 1998.

FREE98b Freeman, R. "Bits, Symbols, Baud, and Bandwidth." *IEEE Communications Magazine*, April 1998.

FREE99 Freeman, R. *Fundamentals of Telecommunications.* New York: Wiley, 1999.

FREE04 Freeman, R. *Telecommunication System Engineering.* New York: Wiley, 2004.

FROD01 Frodigh, M., et al. "Future Generation Wireless Networks." *IEEE Personal Communications*, October 2001.

FUNG98 Fung, P. "A Primer on MMDS Technology." *Communication Systems Design*, April 1998. Available at csdmag.com.

GARG99 Garg, V., and Wilkes, J. *Principles and Applications of GSM.* Upper Saddle River, NJ: Prentice Hall, 1999.

GEIE01 Geier, J. "Enabling Fast Wireless Networks with OFDM." *Communications System Design*, February 2001. www.commsdesign.com

GIBS93 Gibson, J. *Principles of Digital and Analog Communications.* New York: Macmillan, 1993.

GILB04 Gilb, J. *Wireless Multimedia: A Guide to the IEEE 802.15.3 Standard.* New York: IEEE Press, 2004.

GUNT00 Gunther, N. *The Practical Performance Analyst.* Lincoln, NE: *Authors Choice Press*, 2000.

GUTI01 Gutierrez, J., et al. "IEEE 802.15.4: A Developing Standard for Low-Power Low-Cost Wireless Personal Area Networks." *IEEE Network*, September/October 2001.

GUTI03 Gutierrez, J.; Callaway, E.; and Barrett, R. *Low-Rate Wireless Personal Area Networks: Enabling Wireless Sensors with IEEE 802.15.4.* New York: IEEE Press, 2003.

HAAR98 Harrtsen, J. "Bluetooth: The Universal Radio Interface for ad hoc, Wireless Connectivity." *Ericsson Review*, No. 3, 1998. (www.ericsson.se)

HAAR00a Haartsen, J. "The Bluetooth Radio System." *IEEE Personal Communications*, February 2000.

HAAR00b Haartsen, J., and Mattisson, S. "Bluetooth—A New Low-Power Radio Interface Providing Short-Range Connectivity." *Proceedings of the IEEE*, October 2000.

HAAS00 Haas, Z. "Wireless and Mobile Networks." In [TERP00].

HATA80 Hata, M. "Empirical Formula for Propagation Loss in Land Mobile Radio Services." *IEEE Transactions on Vehicular Technology*, March 1980.

HEIJ00 Heijden, M., and Taylor, M., eds. *Understanding WAP: Wireless Applications, Devices, and Services.* Boston: Artech House, 2000.

INGL97 Inglis, A., and Luther, A. *Satellite Technology: An Introduction.* Boston: Focal Press, 1997.

ITU02 International Telecommunications Union. *Handbook on Satellite Communications.* New York: Wiley, 2002.

JAIN90 Jain, Y. "Convolutional Codes Improve Bit-Error Rate in Digital Systems." *EDN*, August 20, 1990.

JAME01 James, J. *A Student's Guide to Fourier Transforms.* Cambridge, England: Cambridge University Press, 2001.

JAYA84 Jayant, N., and Noll, P. *Digital Coding of Waveforms.* Englewood Cliffs, NJ: Prentice Hall, 1984.

JOHN04 Johnston, D., and Yaghoobi, H. "Peering into the WiMAX Spec." Communications System Design, January 2004. Available at www.commsdesign.com.

JONE93 Jones, E. *Digital Transmission.* New York: McGraw-Hill, 1993.

KAHN97 Kahn, J., and Barry, J. "Wireless Infrared Communications." *Proceedings of the IEEE*, February 1997.

KAMM00 Kammler, D. *A First Course in Fourier Analysis.* Upper Saddle River, NJ: Prentice Hall, 2000.

KELL00 Keller, T., and Hanzo, L. "Adaptive Multicarrier Modulation: A Convenient Framework for Time-Frequency Processing in Wireless Communication." *Proceedings of the IEEE*, May 2000.

KNUT98 Knuth, D. *The Art of Computer Programming, Volume 2: Seminumerical Algorithms.* Reading, MA: Addison-Wesley, 1998.

KOFF02 Koffman, I., and Roman, V. "Broadband Wireless Access Solutions Based on OFDM Access in IEEE 802.16." *IEEE Communications Magazine*, April 2002.

KROO86 Kroon, P, and Deprettere, E. "Regular Pulse Excitation—A Novel Approach to Effective Multipulse Coding of Speech." *IEEE Transactions on Acoustics, Speech, and Signal Processing*, No. 5, 1986.

LATH98 Lathi, B. *Modern Digital and Analog Communication Systems.* New York: Oxford University Press, 1998.

LAYL04 Layland, R. "Understanding Wi-Fi Performance." *Business Communications Review*, March 2004.

LEBO98 Lebow, I. *Understanding Digital Transmission and Recording.* New York: IEEE Press, 1998.

MACW76 Macwilliams, F., and Sloane, N. "Pseudo-Random Sequences and Arrays." *Proceedings of the IEEE*, December 1976. Reprinted in [TANT98].

MANN99 Mann, S. "The Wireless Application Protocol." *Dr. Dobb's Journal*, October 1999.

MARK99 Marks, R. "The IEEE 802.16 Working Group on Broadband Wireless." *IEEE Network*, March/April 1999.

MART94 Martine, R. *Basic Traffic Analysis.* Upper Saddle River, NJ: Prentice Hall, 1994.

MCDY99 McDysan, D., and Spohn, D. *ATM: Theory and Application.* New York: McGraw-Hill, 1999.

MCFA03 McFarland, B., and Wong, M. "The Family Dynamics of 802.11" *ACM Queue*, May 2003.

METT99 Mettala, R., et al. *Bluetooth Protocol Architecture Version 1.0.* Bluetooth Whitepaper 1.C.120/1.0, 25 August 1999. (www.bluetooth.com)

MILL01 Miller, B., and Bisdikian, C. *Bluetooth Revealed.* Upper Saddle River, NJ: Prentice Hall, 2001.

MOND03 Mondal, A. *Mobile IP: Present State and Future.* New York: Kluwer Academic Publishers, 2003.

MORA04 Morais, D. Fixed Broadband Wireless Communications: Principles and Practical Applications. Upper Saddle River, NJ: Prentice Hall, 2004.

NORD00 Nordbotten, A. "LMDS Systems and Their Application." *IEEE Communications Magazine*, June 2000.

OHAR99 Ohara, B., and Petrick, A. *IEEE 802.11 Handbook: A Designer's Companion.* New York: IEEE Press, 1999.

OJAN98 Ojanpera, T., and Prasad, G. "An Overview of Air Interface Multiple Access for IMT-2000/UMTS." *IEEE Communications Magazine*, September 1998.

OKUM68 Okumura, T., et. al., "Field Strength and Its Variability in VHF and UHF Land Mobile Radio Service." *Rev. Elec. Communication Lab.* 1968.

ORLI98 Orlik, P., and Rappaport, S. "Traffic Performance and Mobility Modeling of Cellular Communications with Mixed Platforms and Highly Variable Mobilities." *Proceedings of the IEEE*, July 1998.

ORTI00 Ortiz, S. "Broadband Fixed Wireless Travels the Last Mile." *Computer*, July 2000.

PAHL95 Pahlavan, K.; Probert, T.; and Chase, M. "Trends in Local Wireless Networks." *IEEE Communications Magazine*, March 1995.

PAPA97 Papazian, P.; Hufford, G.; Aschatz, R.; and Hoffman, R. "Study of the Local Multipoint Distribution Service Radio Channel." *IEEE Transactions on Broadcasting*, June 1997.

PARK88 Park, S., and Miller, K. "Random Number Generators: Good Ones are Hard to Find." *Communications of the ACM*, October 1988.

PASS00 Passani, L. "Creating WAP Services." *Dr. Dobb's Journal*, July 2000.

PASU79 Pasupathy, S. "Minimum Shift Keying: A Spectrally Efficient Modulation." *IEEE Communications Magazine*, July 1979.

PEAR92 Pearson, J. *Basic Communication Theory.* Englewood Cliffs, NJ: Prentice Hall, 1992.

PERK97 Perkins, C. "Mobile IP." *IEEE Communications Magazine*, May 1997.

PERK98 Perkins, C. "Mobile Networking Through Mobile IP." *IEEE Internet Computing*, January-February 1998.

PETE61 Peterson, W., and Brown, D. "Cyclic Codes for Error Detection." *Proceedings of the IEEE*, January 1961.

PETE95 Peterson, R.; Ziemer, R.; and Borth, D. *Introduction to Spread Spectrum Communications.* Englewood Cliffs, NJ: Prentice Hall, 1995.

Peterson, W. W. and Brown, D. T. (January 1961). "Cyclic Codes for Error Detection." *Proceedings of the IRE.*

PETR00 Petrick, A. "IEEE 802.11b—Wireless Ethernet." *Communications System Design*, June 2000. www.commsdesign.com

PHIL98 Phillips, J., and Namee, G. *Personal Wireless Communications with DECT and PWT.* Boston: Artech House, 1998.

PICK82 Pickholtz, R.; Schilling, D.; and Milstein, L. "Theory of Spread Spectrum Communications—A Tutorial." *IEEE Transactions on Communications*, May 1982. Reprinted in [TANT98].

POLL96 Pollini, G. "Trends in Handover Design." *IEEE Communications Magazine*, March 1996.

POOL98 Polle, I. *Your Guide to Propagation.* Potters Bar, Herts., U.K.: Radio Society of Great Britain, 1998.

PRAS98 Prasad, R., and Ojanpera, T. "An Overview of CDMA Evolution: Toward Wideband CDMA." *IEEE Communications Surveys*, Fourth Quarter 1998. Available at www.comsoc.org.

PRAS00 Prasad, R.; Mohr, W.; and Konhauser, W., eds. *Third-generation Mobile Communication Systems.* Boston: Artech House, 2000.

PRAT03 Pratt, T.; Bostian, C.; and Allnutt, J. *Satellite Communications.* New York: Wiley, 2003.

PROA01 Proakis, J. *Digital Communications.* New York: McGraw-Hill, 2001.

PROA02 Proakis, J. *Communication Systems Engineering.* Upper Saddle River, NJ: Prentice Hall, 2002.

RABI95 Rabiner, L. "Toward Vision 2001: Voice and Audio Processing Considerations." *AT&T Technical Journal*, March/April 1995.

RAMA88 Ramabadran, T., and Gaitonde, S. "A Tutorial on CRC Computations." *IEEE Micro*, August 1988.

RAPP02 Rappaport, T. *Wireless Communications: Principles and Practice.* Upper Saddle River, NJ: Prentice Hall, 2002.

RODB00 Rodbell, M. "Bluetooth: Wireless Local Access, Baseband and RF Interfaces, and Link Management." *Communications System Design*, March, April, May 2000. (www.csdmag.com)

RODR02 Rodriguez, A., et al. *TCP/IP Tutorial and Technical Overview.* Upper Saddle River: NJ: Prentice Hall, 2002.

RAHN93 Rahnema, M. "Overview of the GSM System and Protocol Architecture." *IEEE Communications Magazine*, April 1993.

ROSH04 Roshan, P., and Leary, J. *802.11 Wireless LAN Fundamentals*. Indianapolis: Cisco Press, , 2004.

SAIR02 Sairam, K.; Gunasekaran, N.; and Reddy, S. "Bluetooth in Wireless Communication." *IEEE Communications Magazine*, June 2002.

SCHI00 Schiller, J. *Mobile Communications.* Reading, MA: Addison-Wesley, 2000.

SHOE02 Shoemake, M. "IEEE 802.11g Jells as Applications Mount." *Communications System Design*, April 2002. www.commsdesign.com.

SKLA93 Sklar, B. "Defining, Designing, and Evaluating Digital Communication Systems." *IEEE Communications Magazine*, November 1993.

SKLA97a Sklar, B. "Rayleigh Fading Channels in Mobile Digital Communication Systems." *IEEE Communications Magazine*, July 1997.

SKLA97b Sklar, B. "A Primer on Turbo Code Concepts." *IEEE Communications Magazine*, December 1997.

SKLA01 Sklar, B. *Digital Communications: Fundamentals and Applications.* Upper Saddle River, NJ: Prentice Hall, 2001.

SPOH02 Spohn, D. *Data Network Design.* New York: McGraw-Hill, 2002.

STAL02 Stallings, W. "The Advanced Encryption Standard." *Cryptologia*, July 2002.

STAL03 Stallings, W. *Cryptography and Network Security: Principles and Practice, Third Edition.* Upper Saddle River, NJ: Prentice Hall, 2003.

STAL04a Stallings, W. *Data and Computer Communications, Seventh Edition.* Upper Saddle River: NJ: Prentice Hall, 2004.

STAL04b Stallings, W. *Computer Networking with Internet Protocols and Technology.* Upper Saddle River, NJ: Prentice Hall, 2004.

TANT98 Tantaratana, S, and Ahmed, K., eds. *Wireless Applications of Spread Spectrum Systems: Selected Readings.* Piscataway, NJ: IEEE Press, 1998.

TERP00 Terplan, K., and Morreale, P. eds. *The Telecommunications Handbook.* Boca Raton, FL: CRC Press, 2000.

THUR00 Thurwachter, C. *Data and Telecommunications: Systems and Applications.* Upper Saddle River, NJ: Prentice Hall, 2000.

UNGE87 Ungerboeck, G. "Trellis-Coded Modulation with Redundant Signal Sets, Part 1: Introduction." *IEEE Communications Magazine*, February 1987.

VITE89 Viterbi, A., et al. "A Pragmatic Approach to Trellis-Coded Modulation." *IEEE Communications Magazine*, July 1989.

VUCE00 Vucetic, B., and Yuan, J. *Turbo Codes: Principles and Applications.* Boston: Kluwer Academic Publishers, 2000.

WAPF98 WAP Forum. *Wireless Application Environment Overview.* WAP Forum document, April 1998.

WEBB00 Webb, W. *Introduction to Wireless Local Loop: Broadband and Narrowband Systems.* Boston: Artech House, 2000.

WILS00 Wilson, J., and Kronz, J. "Inside Bluetooth: Part I and Part II." *Dr. Dobb's Journal*, March, April 2000.

XIAO04 Xiao, Y. "IEEE 802.11e: QoS Provisioning at the MAC Layer." *IEEE Communications Magazine*, June 2004.

XION94 Xiong, F. "Modem Techniques in Satellite Communications." *IEEE Communications Magazine*, August 1994.

XION00 Xiong, F. *Digital Modulation Techniques.* Boston: Artech House, 2000.

ZENG00 Zeng, M.; Annamalai, A.; and Bhargava, V. "Harmonization of Global Third-generation Mobile Systems. *IEEE Communications Magazine*, December 2000.

ZHEN04 Zhent, J., and Lee, M. "Will IEEE 802.15.4 Make Ubiquitous Networking a Reality?: A Discussion on a Potential Low Power, Low Bit Rate Standard." *IEEE Communications Magazine*, June 2004.

HYPERLINK http://academic.research.microsoft.com/Author/322223/sergio-benedetto *Sergio Benedetto*

HYPERLINK http://academic.research.microsoft.com/Author/2959664/colin-f-n-cowan *Colin F. N. Cowan*

HYPERLINK http://academic.research.microsoft.com/Author/439660/guido-montorsi *Guido Montorsi*

HYPERLINK http://academic.research.microsoft.com/Author/2216417/juriaan-simonis *Juriaan Simonis*

HYPERLINK http://academic.research.microsoft.com/Author/667026/jinsong-wu *Jinsong Wu*

HYPERLINK http://academic.research.microsoft.com/Author/2299062/pei-xiao *Pei Xiao*

Journal: HYPERLINK ../../Journal/433/tit-ieee-transactions-on-information-theory *IEEE Transactions on Information Theory - TIT*, vol. 46, no. 4, pp. 1544-1545, 2000.

Journal: HYPERLINK ../../Journal/855/twc-ieee-transactions-on-wireless-communications *IEEE Transactions on Wireless Communications - TWC*, vol. 59, no. 1, pp. 26-32, 2011.

Index

A

B

C

D

E

F

G

H

I

J

K

L

M

N

O

P

Q

R

S

T

U

V

W

T

U

V

W

X

Z